With Mercy and with Juagement

With Mercy and with Judgement: Strict Baptists and the First World War

With mercy and with judgement
My web of time he wove,
And aye the dews of sorrow
Were lustered with his love;
I'll bless the hand that guided,
I'll bless the heart that planned
When throned where glory dwelleth
In Immanuel's land.

Samuel Rutherford (1600-1661) in verse, by A. R. Cousin

… Dear Parents, may God bless you both. I long to see you all again, but *I have proved France to be Immanuel's land,* and if it had not been for his holy appearance, at times I should have sunk, but 'such a prop can hold the world and all things up' …

Sapper Alfred M. Dye, in a letter written from the front

By Matthew J. Hyde

Gospel Standard Trust Publications
2016

ISBN: 978 1 897837 56 6

Gospel Standard Trust Publications, 12(b) Roundwood Lane, Harpenden, Hertfordshire, AL5 3BZ
www.gospelstandard.org.uk

Pictures: Many of the photographs and a number of the accounts reproduced in this book have been kindly provided by the families of the men and women concerned. Out of respect to them, we would ask anybody wishing to reproduce images or text from this book to seek the families' permission to do so, by contacting the publishers in the first instance. We have endeavoured to trace all original copyright owners for consent to use their images. If we have failed to identify any copyrights on images, we apologise. Please contact us so that this can be immediately corrected in any future printings.

matthew.hyde02@imperial.ac.uk

For Kennedy

and all who, without living witnesses to the events described in this book, have to rely on records
such as those preserved in this book for a testimony to God's mercy and judgement during the First World War

Contents

Illustrations

Acknowledgements

Many people have helped me in producing this book, and the final product would not have been achievable without any one of them. Thanks are due to: Mr and Mrs J. F. Ashby, Mr and Mrs M. G. Bailey, Mrs E. Beadle, Mrs J. Broome, Miss G. Buggs, Mr and Mrs J. Burrows, Mr G. D. Buss, Mr D. J. Christian, Mr P. Clark, Miss A. Collins, Mr G. S. Collins, Mrs M. Cook, Mrs E. Dawson, Miss R. Delves, Mrs A. Durbidge, Mr T. Evans, Mr R. D. G. Field, Mr D. Field, Mr J. Flitton, Miss N. Grace, Mr P. Green, Mrs S. Haddow, Mr and Mrs G. E. Hadley, Mr P. Hanks, Mr J. B. Hart, Mr D. Holman, Mr B. Honeysett, Mr P. Hopkins, Mrs J. Hugo, Mr and Mrs P. L. Hyde, Mr S. A. Hyde, Mr J. R. Ince, Mr and Mrs B. E. Izzard, Miss M. Julyan, Mr G. Main, Mr J. E. North, Mr J. Pack, Mr M. Pack, Mr P. Page, Mr and Mrs E. Palmer, Mrs M. Palmer, Mr C. A. Pearce, Mrs M. Pearce, Miss E. Pickles, Mr and Mrs H. M. Pickles, Mr S. Piggott, Mr D. Piggott, Mrs R. Pocock, the late Mr D. R. Pollington, Mrs M. R. Pont, Mr T. W. S. Pont, Mr A. Rayner, Mr M. R. Ridout, Mr A. Robinson, Mr J. Roe, Mr T. J. Rosier, Mr J. Ruse, Mr J. E. Rutt, Mr S. Salkeld, Mr H. Sant, Mr J. Sayers, Stanley Delves Trust, Mr P. Topping, Trinitarian Bible Society, Mr S. Tyler, Mrs P. Watts, West Sussex County Times, Mr and Mrs C. Woodhouse.

More particularly, I owe a debt of gratitude to Mr T. Abbott who has commented on numerous drafts of this book, and produced the excellent maps (these have drawn heavily on: Banks, Arthur (2013) *A Military Atlas of the First World War*. Pen and Sword Military). Mr J. A. Kingham helped enormously with preparation of the illustrations. Again, my aunt, Miss M. G. Hyde and her fellow librarians at the Gospel Standard Library have provided much material, allowed extended loans of a number of books, and looked up endless references for me. The Birmingham City Archives kindly allowed access to the material relating to J. W. Tiptaft. Mr B. A. Ramsbottom, Mr P. Ramsbottom, Mr G. D. Buss, Miss E. Pickles, Mr T. W. S. Pont and Mr H. Sant have all gone beyond the call of duty in reading, commenting on the drafts, and providing material and information. Mrs M. R. Pont kindly checked the index to the Muster Rolls against the original magazines for accuracy. Mr J Roe and Mr P. Skelton have both provided excellent editorial and proof reading assistance.

The book could not have been produced without the support of the Gospel Standard Trust, and may never have seen the light of day had not Christian Values in Education asked me to speak on the subject, which spurred me to put an idea into action and undertake the research which has come together in this volume.

Finally, to my wife, who is a most patient editor and friendly critic, the book owes any polished appearance that it possesses. She has also allowed me many hours given over to this book, and that I can never repay.

Abbreviations used in this book

CP	*The Christian's Pathway*
FC	*The Friendly Companion*
GH	*Gadsby's Selection of Hymns*
GS	*The Gospel Standard*
LG	*The Little Gleaner*
ZW	*Zion's Witness*

Introduction

What pen will be able to describe the extent, the depth of the woe created by the war in which we are parties? Lands drenched with blood of men; rivers reddened with human gore and choked with corpses; cities and villages heaps of blackened stones and charred timber; the seas turned into graves for ships that floated as so many cities; widows and fatherless children numberless, whose hearts are throbbing with helpless, hopeless anguish; the financial world full of confusion, ruin, and misery, the world's wealth wasted in the combatants' fierce attempts to annihilate each other. Oh woe! enough to make the sun blush that ever he shone on men so vile as to make the fair creation groan in desolation! For a few miles of territory, for a day's power over men, a man will plunge the whole world into a black night of sorrow.

J. K. Popham[1]

The people described in this book, called to serve their country, witnessed in the war itself, in their comrades and in their own lives and souls' experience, both the mercies and the judgements of God. That it was a painful and yet in its way a blessed experience comes across clearly in the memories that they recorded in later life, and with more immediacy in the diaries and letters they wrote home from the battlefield, which are collected together in this volume. The aim of this book is to preserve these records of God's mercies and judgements manifested to Strict Baptists during the First World War. This is not so much for the glory of those whose testimonies and letters are published here, as for the glory of the God who sustained them under every load.

In the first part I have endeavoured to give a brief background to the war and Strict Baptist involvement in it. In the second part of the book I have let those who were involved in the First World War speak for themselves. It is hoped that the introduction will serve to set their writings in context and to draw together some points and common themes for the reader to bear in mind as they progress through the book.

The material published here is both spiritual and natural. Although it may seem that there is less soul profit in what is not purely spiritual, I have taken the view that the preserving mercies of the Lord in keeping the souls of his people are set in their fullest glory against the contrast of those who lived the war in a careless, unregenerate state. It has been a surprise to me just how few men could tell of the experiences of war being blessed to the awakening of their soul, and a seeking of a Saviour. The accounts testify to the truth of the fact that:

> Law and terrors do but harden,
> All the while they work alone.[2]

They also confirm that, ordinarily, it is the means of his Word that the Lord uses in calling sinners to himself. Furthermore, unless the Holy Spirit blesses and sanctifies people's providential circumstances to their souls, it is solemnly true that:

> Judgements nor mercies ne'er can sway
> Their roving feet to wisdom's way.[3]

Some may feel that the focus of this book is too narrow. Strict Baptists were certainly not the only people to see the mercies and judgements of God in the war. However, from the volume and quality of material available from solely Strict Baptist sources, it became pragmatic to limit the scope of the book to the experience of Strict Baptists alone. It is hoped that this will not prejudice readers from other denominational backgrounds from reading the book and finding profit in it. No doubt similar records could be drawn together from many other church backgrounds. It would be a source of pleasure and thankfulness to the publishers if this book were to act as a stimulus to any other denomination to research and publish records of the Lord's goodness to them during the Great War, in a similar manner.

Conversely, some may be inclined to think that the definition of Strict Baptist used in this book has been too broad. Indeed, several of the men, ministers and churches mentioned did not remain associated with the 'Gospel Standard' group of Strict Baptist churches in the years after the First World War. It is right to acknowledge up front that this book has not been confined to providing an account of men associated only with churches currently adhering to *The Gospel Standard*. However, the material has largely been confined to what could be gleaned from four magazines circulating within the homes of Strict Baptists attending 'Gospel Standard' churches at the time – *The Gospel Standard*, *The Friendly Companion*, *The Christian's Pathway* and *The Sower*.

Although the search for material was originally confined to these four magazines, a number of friends, hearing of the project, have very kindly provided unpublished material for possible inclusion. This material has added greatly to the value of this book, and the generosity of those who have given it freely for this purpose is much appreciated. However, the amount of material has been overwhelming. It was initially the intention to publish all available material, but, given the size of the final manuscript, some of the letters and accounts have had to be edited. Material has been selected for inclusion on two grounds: firstly and primarily its spiritual content, and secondly its value as a historical source. Indeed, this book contains important eyewitness accounts of the war, including the first use of tanks and of lethal gas, and of service in some of the lesser known arenas of war, such as North Russia during the Russian Civil War of 1918-19, and Ireland in the aftermath of the 1916 Easter Rising.

In producing the book I have become increasingly aware that, despite the extensive amount of material available to draw on, what has been left on record to be gathered together represents only a small portion of the Strict Baptists who served in the war, or who lost loved ones in the war. Most of the men who served in the war have already passed forgotten into the mists of time, or what is known of them is fragmentary at best. My maternal grandfather, James Field, lost two uncles to the war.[4] Both were brought up to attend the Strict Baptist Chapel at Blackboys, East Sussex. I have visited their graves in France, but with the exception of a few photographs that exist within family collections, we know little about them and they are virtually forgotten. This is the case with the vast majority of young men who went to fight in the war, and Strict Baptists are no exception. The reader should bear this in mind when moving through this book; it is by no means a comprehensive record of the impact the war had on Strict Baptists.

David Field (left) & Edward O'Kill Dadswell (right), uncles of the author's grandfather, both killed in the war

However small or imperfect a record, I nevertheless hope that the primary end of this book might be the glory of God, who was, in Isaac Watts' timeless words, 'our help in ages past,' and must be 'our hope for years to come.'[5] Therefore, above whatsoever natural interest in the war may be aroused through reading this book, it is my desire that the Lord might bless its contents to the spiritual good of souls, and that readers might be enabled to join wholeheartedly with the sentiment expressed by Joseph Hart:

Thy mercy, Lord, we praise;
Of judgement too we sing;
For all the riches of thy grace
Our grateful tribute bring.

Thy mercies bid us trust;
Thy judgements strike with awe;
We fear the last, we bless the first,
And love thy righteous law.

Who can thy acts express,
Or trace thy wondrous ways?
How glorious is thy holiness;
How terrible thy praise!

Thy judgements are too deep
For reason's line to sound.
Thy tender mercies to thy sheep
No bottom know, nor bound.[6]

A detachment from the Middlesex Regiment.
Arthur W. Pither, who attended Providence Chapel, Ponsard Road, London, is second from the left (see p. 68)

Services at Brockham Green Chapel, Surrey, shortly before the outbreak of the First World War. The four men in the centre of the photo are (from left to right), Richard Shillingford (Guildford, chairman for many years of the Gospel Standard Societies), James Dickens (pastor at Rotherfield), Henry Haddow (pastor at Brockham Green and secretary of the Gospel Standard Societies), and Peter Wadey (Horley, supply minister)

Overview

Overview

When the year 1914 opened on Europe, political storm clouds had been gathering thickly for some time. The nations of Europe, driven by rampant imperialism, had been building their military might, and the peace which existed had a definite air of fragility. Britain, while not foremost in the arms race, had not been idle in this contest.

Among Strict Baptist churches the year started uneventfully. William *Gadsby's Selection of Hymns*, the hymn book used among most Strict Baptist congregations, marked the 100th anniversary of its first publication in the summer of the year. The churches continued as they had for many a year, meeting week by week for worship, and uniting together for mutual benefit around monthly spiritual magazines and charitable funds for the relief of the poor. But by the end of the year Europe and her subjects, Strict Baptists among them, had been plunged into a war which changed the face of Europe dramatically.

Mr Walter Croft, the pastor of West Street Chapel, Croydon, described the events which led to the war in the following piece, published in *The Friendly Companion* in 1921.

> ✍ In June, 1914, there occurred an event on the Continent of Europe serious indeed, but not serious enough in itself to produce a world-wide catastrophe. The state of the nations of Europe, however, at that particular time, was one of formidable armaments on every hand, and only a spark was needed to set Europe ablaze. The assassination of the Austrian Crown Prince and his wife at Sarajevo was the spark which fired the powder magazines of Europe. Austria charged Serbia with plotting the murder of the Archduke and his wife, and demanded reparation for the crime, together with many internal reforms of government within a short time limit, under the threat of war if she failed to comply. Serbia replied that she was prepared to hand over for trial any Serbian subject, without regard to his situation or rank, of whose complicity in the crime of Sarajevo proofs were forthcoming; also she offered to comply with practically all the requirements of Austria. Austria declared that Serbia had not answered in a satisfactory manner her note of July 23rd, 1914, and immediately declared war.
>
> At the critical moment, when the question of peace or war between Austria and Serbia was hanging in the balance, everything depended on the attitude of Germany. Germany assured Austria of her whole-hearted support in any action she proposed to take against Serbia, and at the same time declined to take any part in the proposed conference in London to try and settle the matters in dispute between Austria and Serbia.
>
> Russia declared that if, in spite of all her efforts to avoid bloodshed, Serbia was not successful in doing so, she would lend Serbia what support she could. Whereupon Germany addressed a note to Belgium stating that the German Government would be compelled to carry out by force of arms measures considered indispensable to her safety. The King of the Belgians instantly appealed to the King of

England to help him in defending his kingdom against invasion, and the British Government sent a strong note to Germany asking her to refrain from violating a treaty to which she herself had subscribed. As no satisfactory answer was returned to this appeal, England, France and Russia, under Treaty obligations, declared war on Germany, and on August 4th, 1914, German troops entered Belgian territory, and summoned the town of Liège to surrender.[7]

Walter Croft

It is our intention in the following pages to gather together what we know about Strict Baptists during the four years of war which followed, in order to set the scene for the diaries, letters and poems written by Strict Baptist men and women during the war, which together comprise the larger part of this book.

The Strict Baptist response to war

When Britain declared war on Germany on 4th August, 1914, there was little active protest from Strict Baptists against the war. The almost universal view amongst Strict Baptists appears to have been that this was a just war, that it was according to the sovereign purposes of God, that it was a judgement on the nation for her backsliding, and that the root cause of the war was sin.[8]

One personal Strict Baptist expression of this is found in the obituary of Henry Wiles, brother of Joseph P. Wiles,[9] and a Strict Baptist minister.[10] It records: "With the clear and unsophisticated vision of faith, he [*Henry*] found that the patent facts of human life corroborated only too clearly the Scripture record of the fall of man, and the Great War was to him but one more clear evidence of the sinful man's dire need of a Saviour." It continues:

> ✎ He perceived great spiritual forces in the unseen world behind the death-dealing inventions of the Great War, 1914-1918. At the same time, he accepted with clear common sense the teaching of the Apostle in the Letter to the Romans in regard to 'the sword' and 'the powers that be,' holding the defence of the realm to be a clear bounden duty, and repudiating the reasoning of the conscientious objector in general, though he admired the sincerity and courage of some individuals in their ranks.[11]

Although in 1914 there were various religious denominations who *en masse* conscientiously objected to warfare, the Strict Baptists, as a denomination, were not among them. Nevertheless, the question of the justice of the war did of course arise, and there are a few reports of Strict Baptists taking the part of conscientious objectors and refusing to join up, or refusing to bear arms.

The Strict Baptist arguments against the war can be summarised into three themes. *Firstly*, the war was said to be the fruit of a haughty imperialism, of which Britain was as guilty as Germany, and for which there was no Scriptural basis, particularly in the New Testament. *Secondly*, Britain's opponents were felt to be our kith and kin, Britain being a nation of Germanic descent. *Thirdly*, the Germans were a Protestant nation, and Protestant Britain was thought to share more religious interests with Lutheran Germany than with Romanist France and Orthodox Russia, the nations with whom Britain united against Germany.[12]

With the benefit of hindsight, we may well feel that the majority of Strict Baptists may have been swept along by the prevailing sentiments of the day and did not properly consider these objections. Certainly, Britain's opponents in the First World War never posed the same threat to her liberties as did Hitler, Nazism, and her other opponents in the Second World War. It would, however, be unwise to sit in judgement, either on those who willingly joined up to fight, or on those who conscientiously objected. Thoughtful and exercised Christians took both lines, and neither the decision to sign up, nor to conscientiously object, could have been easy, or taken lightly.

Certainly, objections to the war gained little hearing in the country at large. After all, at the time tremendous social stigma was placed on conscientious objectors, there was a strong and carefully choreographed propaganda machine which was designed to encourage enlistment, and conscription eventually made signing up compulsory.[13] Yet, despite these pressures, some of the objectors held their position very passionately. One young Strict Baptist who appeared before the courts for refusing to sign up, exclaimed in court, "I'd rather be shot, sir, than shoot another man."[14]

Four young Strict Baptist brothers from the Birkenhead congregation refused to fight.[15] According to the newspaper report, "Applicants believed that war was contrary to the teaching of Christ, and they would have nothing to do with either saving life or taking life in connection with war." They went so far as to refuse the proposal that they should serve on fishing trawlers in order to provide for the food needs of the country, because they regarded that as aiding and abetting the cause of war. In the arguments they put, they even said that they would not rescue men who had fought in the war from a sinking ship. While these arguments might appear extreme, they were responses given to the provoking questions asked at these tribunals, which often asked the objectors if they would kill anybody attempting to kill their parents, or violate their sister. The men lost their case before the magistrates, and it is assumed they were compelled to sign up or imprisoned.

Not all objectors to the war among Strict Baptists objected on religious grounds – one man objected because he was a piano tuner by occupation, and refused to fight on the grounds that shell and gun fire might damage his hearing, resulting in loss of livelihood. His appeal stood, and he was excused from combative duties, although he was required to join the Royal Army Medical Corps.[16]

Some, while deciding they would rather not personally bear arms, actively chose to join the stretcher parties of the Royal Army Medical Corps, offering humanitarian support to the forces. Of course, serving in the Medical Corps was in no sense the coward's choice. Lance Corporal John Parsons, a stretcher-bearer from the congregation at South Chard, wrote home to his parents from Gallipoli:

> ✍ … In the early morning, a party of forty of them [*the 32nd Field Ambulance*] advanced too far with their stretchers, and got cut off by the Turks. At least five of them were killed and five wounded, and about ten are missing … The Lord has once more been very, very merciful to me and been indeed a shield to guard me from danger … I saw my poor comrades shot dead beside me; another was dying for hours beside me as I lay all that day behind a stone, not daring to move, for the Turks were only 100 yards away. I was in the rear of our line as we advanced along the ridge, and, with another man, dressed a poor comrade whose leg was shattered, while another dashed off for a stretcher. He did not return, so the two of us made a dash to get one, and my comrade was shot through the lungs, dying seven hours later. I got a bullet through the fleshy part of the upper part of my left arm, and managed to crawl back to safety fifteen hours later.[17]

Many men expressed gratitude to the brave stretcher-bearers from the Royal Army Medical Corps. One example is Private A. G. Ord, from the Hartlepool congregation. He wrote of his wartime experience:

> ✍ It was about six o'clock on Sunday night, July 25th, 1915. I was sitting in the trench talking to my mates about a German airman that had just been brought down, when suddenly there was a thud and I saw a shell lying at my feet; I could not get up and run. Then there was a bang, and I felt myself lifted off my feet and up, up in the air, wondering when I was coming down again, and I called as I have never called upon the Lord before to help me, a sinner. 'Lord, have mercy on my soul! Lord, have mercy on me! Lord, help me!' and I cannot thank him enough, for he heard my cries and brought me safely through. For as I stopped shouting, somebody got hold of me and said, 'Let's have you out of this,' but I could not move, my legs were doubled up under me and peppered with bits of shell. Then began the journey out to headquarters, and I will never forget it. It is only those that have to go through it that know what it is; but God bless those brave chaps that are never heard of in the papers, 'the stretcher-bearers.'[18]

A. G. Ord

Mr John H. Gosden, who would later become pastor at Maidstone and editor of *The Gospel Standard* magazine, refused to bear arms, serving instead in the Royal Army Medical Corps as a stretcher-bearer, ministering to wounded soldiers. It is known that Mr Gosden disagreed with his pastor, Mr J. K. Popham, as to whether the war was just.[19] Despite finding himself in the position of being compelled to serve in a war which he could not conscientiously support, Mr Gosden speaks of blessings in this time in his life: "I shall never forget, I hope, when walking across a parade ground in the north of England, on the eve of proceeding to France, during the First World War, feeling an inkling of that word in the midst of chaos and trouble: 'Therefore being justified by faith, we have peace with God through our Lord Jesus Christ.'" For his bravery on the battlefield, when, under heavy fire, he went alone to tend to a young wounded soldier, and was himself wounded in the act, Mr Gosden was awarded the Military Medal.[20] Mr S. F. Paul, his biographer, says that during Mr Gosden's war service, "There is no doubt, he used every opportunity of speaking to the wounded and dying soldiers." Ultimately, it was in that war service, that the Lord opened the door to Mr Gosden to the work of the ministry.[21]

Whether the war was just or not was not the only consideration that weighed with the Strict Baptists. Whatever the view held as to the rightness of the war, the Strict Baptists universally believed that the war was according to the sovereign purposes of God. As Mr Popham wrote in *The Gospel Standard*:

> ✍ 'Without cause' God was moved against Job, and permitted a fourfold evil to befall him. And to Job there were no Sabeans, no fire, no Chaldeans, no wind, but only God. Shall not we, against whom God has many things, acknowledge him the author of this present calamity?[22]

They also universally agreed that the root cause of war was sin, as Mr Popham also stated in *The Gospel Standard*:

> ✍ We must begin with that which is the cause of all trouble and suffering, and punishment – SIN. It is against God's nature and revealed will. No sin, no divine displeasure, no outpourings of wrath. So no sin, no wars. 'God is angry with the wicked every day.' As with individuals, so with nations that forget God. 'Upon the wicked he shall rain snares, fire and brimstone, and an horrible tempest: this shall be the portion of their cup' (Psalm 11: 6). Man was made for God, but he disbelieved, disobeyed, and revolted. For their sins he said of Israel, 'Shall not my soul be avenged on such a nation as this' (Jeremiah 5: 9). This is a universal rule.[23]

Cornelius Midmer and his wife

Preaching at Ebenezer Chapel, Clapham, less than a month after the declaration of war, the pastor, Mr

Cornelius Midmer said:

> ✍ Then we look at ourselves under these terribly sad and solemn circumstances, and what do we see here at home? Nothing very cheering, much to make us sad, especially the apathy of so many around us; what multitudes still pursuing their foolish, carnal pleasures, totally indifferent as to whether it be peace or war, with no fear of God before their eyes. Thus the voice is not heard, the chastening and judgement upon us are not regarded. We see the hardening effects of sin, and when the Lord's hand is lifted up, when he comes out of his place to punish the nations for their iniquity, they will not see.[24]

In a previous generation, at the height of the Crimean War, J. C. Philpot (1802-1869) had written at length on the topic of war in *The Gospel Standard*.[25] He concluded with the following practical points for consideration:

> ✍ Suffer us, Christian readers, to add a word of *instruction,* and to point out how these events should be viewed in harmony with the revealed will of God and the spirit of faith in a believer's heart, as well as what is the becoming path of those who fear the Lord at this eventful crisis.
>
> 1. The first grand point is to view them as *all working out God's decreed purposes* and bringing about the plans and designs of the Most High. Whilst the unbelieving world sees nothing in these events beyond the hand of man, let the Christian see behind the cloud the directing, controlling, overruling hand of God. This will enable us to look at them with a degree of calmness not otherwise attainable, and preserve us from being elated or depressed by every gust of prosperous or adverse tidings. 'The LORD reigneth' is or should be sufficient to still every fear and remove every doubt as to the eventual issue. That issue, beyond all doubt, must be the glory of God and the good of those who fear his great name.
>
> … We may be sure that the events now on the wheels are full of importance both to the church and the world. Their ultimate effect none can foresee, but few can doubt that the intervening period will be marked with suffering and blood. The latter we may not be called upon to spill or witness; the former we may have, in some measure, to endure. So great a calamity as war cannot occur without seriously affecting all classes of society. Heavy taxes, commercial embarrassments, serious losses in trade and business, and general rise of prices, may press deeply on those of our readers who have a little measure of this world's goods; and dear provisions, failing employment, and scanty wages may sorely try those who have to live by the skill of their fingers or labour of their hands. But let us only believe that the Lord holds the reins of government, and must reign until he hath put all enemies under his feet, and it will be like oil on the troubled sea, stilling every wave into a calm.
>
> 2. Now what we would desire to feel in ourselves and to see in our Christian friends, is what will certainly flow from such a believing view as we have just spoken of, *a patient submission* to what we may be called upon to endure. We cannot alter matters. The war may be a great evil, and we may be ready, under the pressure it may bring, to murmur against our rulers for plunging the nation into it. But there it is; and all our murmurings and frettings against heavy taxes and dear provisions will not put an end to it.

The load, however, which cannot be shaken off, may be made lighter by submission under it.

3. The last point to which we would direct the mind of our readers is the desirableness of *bringing these matters before the throne of grace,* especially in the assembling of ourselves together. We have of late felt ourselves reproved in conscience as guilty of having too much neglected the apostolic injunction (1 Timothy 2: 1, 2). Afraid of formality, and chiefly pleading for spiritual blessings, we have most commonly closed our public petitions without dropping a word of supplication for our Queen and 'for all that are in authority; that we may lead a quiet and peaceable life in all godliness and honesty.' In so doing we have neglected that which the Holy Spirit declares is 'good and acceptable in the sight of God our Saviour.' Without falling, then, into that dry and formal round of praying for everything and everybody which characterises the congregations of the dead, we would press on those who are mouth for the people, whether ministers or private Christians, in our public assemblies, that they would put up a word for our beloved country, and for those who sit at the helm of government. And why should not a word be dropped for our poor soldiers, among whom there may be some who fear God? To this and every other thing really needed in providence and grace, the good word of God fully encourages us; for if we are invited 'in *every thing* by prayer and supplication with thanksgiving let your requests be made known unto God,' we have a full warrant to ask of him who alone can make 'peace in our borders,' to put a stop to this horrid bloodshed, and grant us a secure, lasting, and honourable peace.

J. C. Philpot

The fact that Strict Baptists were directed back to this article written by Mr Philpot, and particularly so by Mr Kirby in the pages of *The Christian's Pathway,*[26] suggests that the sentiments of Strict Baptists during the First World War were in accord with it.

Reasons given for joining up

Despite occasional instances of opposition to the war, the evidence suggests that most Strict Baptists of the time willingly joined up, placing themselves at the disposal of the country in fighting against Germany and its allies. From 1915 to 1919, *The Christian's Pathway* ran a feature called 'The Muster Roll.' For a small fee, people could send in photos of those serving in the war, along with a few personal details. Although some accused it of being a gallery for boasting, it served a useful purpose at the front, providing those serving in the forces with details of peers whom they might meet during their service (with a photo to aid recognition).[27] Over 600 pictures and accounts were published, hinting that a considerable number of Strict Baptist signed up, although it is impossible to give a precise number as to how many actually did. Of the churches contributing to 'The Muster Roll,' we know their submissions did not include every man who signed up from their congregations. There are records of many from Strict Baptist chapels who served in the war, and who do not appear on 'The Muster Roll.' Only 87 churches are represented on 'The Muster Roll,' from an estimated 550 Strict Baptist congregations at the time.[28]

Some men, of course, had less than noble reasons for joining up. Andrew Woodford, who in later life was a church member at Downton, Wiltshire, wrote:

> ✍ I decided to join the army and get to France where I might have a 'good time.' What grief this caused my wife and dear mother! But the Lord's hand was in it all. I had to be shown and made to bow at the feet of a mighty God, and cry for mercy and pardon for past and present sins. I could see that I was to face death, and after death the judgement; which made me cry for mercy, knowing and feeling myself to be a hell-deserving sinner. What I thought would be a time of enjoyment in worldly pleasures, turned out to be three years of prayer. I can truly say that I was brought as Paul says to 'pray without ceasing.'[29]

Similarly, William Swan, who would later become a minister of the gospel, and pastor at Haywards Heath, joined the army in 1917, "intending to have a good time."[30]

William Swan

Thankfully, however, this was not the case with all. Before conscription was introduced, it was, of course, a matter of choice whether or not to volunteer for the armed forces. The strong feeling of duty to king and country shines through in numerous accounts.

There are records of many who joined up during this period only after a great deal of consideration and prayer. For instance, Reuben Paul of Brighton searched the Scriptures and prayed for guidance. He was killed in France in 1918, aged 25. His parents wrote in his obituary:

> ✍ We trust that this our great loss is our dear

boy's eternal gain … We believe the Word of God was his guide in every difficulty, and he searched it to find direction and guidance. His nervous temperament naturally shrank from joining the army, and in this the latter part of Numbers 32: 6: 'Shall your brethren go to war, and shall ye sit here?' helped him to decide; also 1 Peter 2: 17: 'Fear God. Honour the king.'

In 1912 he obtained a situation in London, and from that time frequently wrote home expressing his anxious desires that he might find Divine guidance in every step … He was much affected by witnessing a bad air raid in London in September, 1915,[31] and in October wrote, 'I suppose you have seen the King's letter this morning; I think that should appeal to everyone; it made me think of the scripture, "Fear God. Honour the king."' This led him to volunteer, and on November 20th, 1915, he entered the 18th King's Royal Rifle Corps.[32]

Another young man who volunteered was John Woodfield. He is an instance of someone who, faced with the enormity of the decision to volunteer, was driven to prayer in making this decision, even though in his case this prayerfulness was unexpected by his parents. John Woodfield's father recorded:

✍ One morning, after talking with his mother about the matter, he came to me and said: 'Dad, what do you think about me joining up?' I said, 'Well, I do not know what to advise for the best; but do not be in a hurry, consider it well first.' But although never before anxious to enlist, his mind seemed set upon it, so that I did not dissuade him further. When leaving home, he said, 'Mother, you know I am not doing this without prayer,' which surprised her, as he had never before said anything as to prayerful exercise of mind.[33]

During the first 18 months of the war, voluntary enlistment to the army provided sufficient manpower. However, with the death toll rising, and as voluntary enlistment dropped off, the Military Service Act was passed in January, 1916, to introduce conscription for all single men aged 18-41 years. A few months later, in May, 1916, this was also extended to married men. Once conscription was introduced, men found themselves without any choice in whether they joined the forces or not. This providence could be very hard to understand, yet unusual submission often seems to have been given. This was so in the case of Joseph Brooks of Bexley:

Joseph Brooks

✍ In another letter, speaking of the trial in having to join the army and leaving home and friends, he says, 'I know not the reason now, but am content to stand and look on like Manoah and his wife while the angel of the Lord works wondrously.' Again, writing from France he says, 'I am now in a position I did not want to be in, but still it is only my duty, and by God's help I will endeavour to do it; I feel I can say, with the poet,

Where is death's sting? where, grave, thy victory?
I triumph still, if thou abide with me.'[34]

Life in the forces

In the early part of the First World War, those signing up had some liberty to choose which service they joined, whether army, navy, or air force. However, as the war wore on, there was less choice, and those signing up were placed wherever they were needed.

Strict Baptists appear to have been represented in each of the forces, perhaps predominantly in the army, although this is unsurprising, as the army was numerically the largest of the services. There are letters and reports of Strict Baptists serving all over the world, including in France, Belgium, Ireland, Italy, Greece, Turkey, Egypt, Palestine, and India.

We will briefly survey the forces in turn, giving a few biographical extracts from men serving in each of them.

The Army

The vast majority of Strict Baptists serving in the army joined the ranks as privates.[35] A few of these earned promotion through the ranks of corporal, sergeant, and a couple even held the rank of sergeant major (the highest non-commissioned rank). There were a few who entered the army as commissioned officers, generally because of their position in society, or their education. Of these, perhaps the most notable Strict Baptists were Lieutenant Grey Hazlerigg and Captain Thomas Maynard Hazlerigg, the two sons of Grey Hazlerigg, the pastor at Leicester, and for a time editor of *The Gospel Standard* magazine.[36] Before joining the Strict Baptists and becoming a minister, their father, Grey Hazlerigg, had himself held office in the army, joining the 48th Regiment of Foot in 1837.[37] His brother was the 12th Baronet Hesilrige, and his great nephew, Arthur Grey Hazlerigg, became the 13th Baronet in 1890. Captain Thomas Maynard Hazlerigg had a distinguished military career in the Royal Army Service Corps, being awarded the Military Cross for bravery on the battlefields of France, and later serving with the British forces in the Russian Civil War in North Russia and the Black Sea area. After the war he was appointed Crown Solicitor in Hong Kong, and in recognition of this service he was made a Commander of the Order of the British Empire.[38] Sadly, it does not appear that either of Grey Hazlerigg's sons followed their father with regards to the things of grace.

Lieut. G. Hazlerigg (left) & Capt. T. M. Hazlerigg (right)

Rank, however, did not protect the men serving in the army from the worst of the war. The sights these men saw and experienced are difficult for us to relate to today.

Not long after he was sent to France, Samuel Saunderson, from the congregation at Southill Chapel, had a comrade die in his arms. As the weeks passed and conditions deteriorated, he wrote to his mother to tell her that he did not expect to survive, and that consequently she must consider the money he had saved prior to being called up as her own.

Shortly after writing that letter, the verse by Joseph Hart came powerfully to him:

> But they that in the Lord confide,
> And shelter in his wounded side,
> Shall see the danger overpast,
> Stand every storm, and live at last.[39]

Very soon after, he was shot in the knee and returned to hospital at Poole, in England. Mercifully, healing was granted, and he was restored to health.[40]

Samuel Saunderson

Henry Julyan served in the Royal Engineers. He could recall an occasion when he was sent to the front with a dispatch, and set off amidst heavy shelling. He came to a point where he feared to go on because of the shelling, but, in answer to prayer, the shelling stopped, and he went on. After delivering the message he returned, and when he came to the same place where he had been when the shelling stopped on the outward journey, the enemy shelling recommenced, but he was enabled to return to the camp in safety.[41]

In the face of these terrible conditions, men showed remarkable bravery, and this was acknowledged with the award of medals, or mention in officers' dispatches. A number of Strict Baptists were decorated for their bravery. One example of this is Lance Corporal William Wylde, a member of the congregation at Bolton, who served with the 2nd Battalion, Loyal North Lancashire Regiment in East Africa. He was awarded the Distinguished Conduct Medal for "conspicuous bravery and coolness under very heavy fire in the action at Tanga, German East Africa, and on several occasions rallying together parties of men, and thereby checking the enemy's fierce counter-attacks."[42] To our knowledge, the most decorated Strict Baptist was Reuben S. Paul, of Brighton, who received the Distinguished Conduct Medal, the Military Medal, and, posthumously, the French Croix de Guerre.[43]

William Wylde

Some spent only an extremely brief time in the trenches. Private John Luther Walton, West Yorkshire

Regiment, who was a member of the congregation at Zion Chapel, Siddal, was sent out to the front in April, 1916. He served just two days in the trenches before being killed on 19th May, 1916, aged 25 years.[44] He is buried in Tranchée de Mecknes Cemetery, France.

John Luther Walton

For some, the Lord used their war experiences as the means to call them by grace. Albert Wilson, later deacon at Ebenezer Chapel, Luton, wrote,

> ✍ I became morally corrupted, and when I joined the army at seventeen years and four months, I tried to throw all religion off, though I used to pray at times. At the Battle of Messines in 1917, the Lord touched my heart and made me happy though in danger. In July, 1917, I was deeply convicted under hymn 1050:

Albert Wilson

> Then may I sin forsake,
> The world for thee resign;
> Gracious Redeemer, take, O take,
> And seal me ever thine!
>
> From then on I was a seeker, hanging on the Word to see if there was any hope for me. In 1919, when I was demobbed, I came to Luton. One Sunday morning Mr Kemp preached from: 'The fruit of the Spirit is faith,' and I trembled how it would be with me, but instead of condemnation I had consolation, and the closing hymn of the service was on repentance:
>
> Nor is it such a dismal thing
> As 'tis by some men named;
> A sinner may repent and sing,
> Rejoice and be ashamed.[45]
>
> I walked then for a short time in gospel liberty, and I remember the Scripture flowing into my mind when viewing the beauties of nature, 'And all the trees of the field shall clap their hands.'[46]

Of the many accounts of men serving in the army, nearly all of them make reference to the blessing, help and encouragement they found in the couplet from John Ryland's hymn (Gadsby's Hymns, number 64):

> Not a single shaft can hit,
> Till the God of love sees fit.

One such example is as follows:

> ✍ Charles Hubbard joined the army, beginning of September, 1914. He first joined the Warwicks, but the company being too rough for him, he exchanged into the 2nd Wiltshires, and was made corporal. He was sent to the front last spring. Fearing, however, the responsibility of a corporal, he gave up his stripe.[47] He was in the dreadful battle of Neuve Chapelle. When he and six of his company were advancing quite near the

Charles Hubbard

German trenches, they were all cut down and killed but Charles, who, while bullets were whistling all around, got back a distance into a hole made by a 'Jack Johnson.'[48] After he crouched down in this hole the firing ceased, the Germans apparently thinking they had killed him. Then he found he was lying by the side of a dead man, but there he kept until darkness came on, when he succeeded in creeping back to the British lines unhurt, thinking much upon the two lines of Dr Ryland's hymn, which I quoted in one of my letters to him (so he wrote and told us):

> Not a single shaft can hit,
> Till the God of love sees fit.[49]

Another example is that of Private Henry Job Stubbs, Leicestershire Regiment, who attended Providence Chapel, Oakham. In his diary for 1st and 2nd July, 1916, he wrote that what he saw of the dead and wounded unnerved him; but while thinking over his narrow escape from death, the words came to mind,

Henry Job Stubbs

> Not a single shaft can hit,
> Till the God of love sees fit.

Just two days later, on 4th July, the 'shaft' was to hit him, and he passed away in a casualty clearing station the next day, aged 25 years.[50] He is buried in Warlincourt Halte British Cemetery, France.

For some, when the 'shaft' hit, they plainly saw God's love in it. This was the case with George Relf, who had been baptised at Biddenden Chapel just before joining the army, and would later be sent into the ministry.

✍ Joining the army at the close of 1915, he saw active service in France, and experienced many remarkable deliverances. For 16 months he faced death every day; there were many errands to the throne of grace. Wounded in 1918, he was sent back

George Relf and his wife

to England, never to return to the fighting line. This remarkable deliverance proved to him the truth of the lines:

> Plagues and deaths around me fly,
> Till he bids I cannot die;
> Not a single shaft can hit,
> Till the God of love sees fit.[51]

For the battle was very fierce just after, many of his fellow soldiers being killed, so that the wounding was a blessing in disguise.[52]

The comfort men drew from the hymn was not that they were to be untouched by the fighting, but rather, that if and when they were hit, it was in the loving purposes of a sovereign God. This comes across in a letter written by Corporal Percy Cornwell, from Jireh Chapel, Brixton, to a friend: "I am glad to be able to know that he who has preserved me thus far in this war can keep me under his care *until he sees fit* …" When the Lord did see fit to take Percy Cornwell home he died from a single wound, on 24th May, 1917, aged 34 years.[53] He is buried in Warlincourt Halte British Cemetery, France.

Percy Cornwell

Other hymns were made a particular blessing too. The widow of Joseph Obbard, of Tunbridge Wells, wrote in his obituary:

Joseph Obbard

> ✍ His last letters were chiefly upon better things. He seemed to fully realise his solemn position, and he spoke of that verse being so sweet to him only two days before his death:
>
> His love in time past forbids me to think
> He'll leave me at last in trouble to sink;
> Each sweet Ebenezer I have in review
> Confirms his good pleasure to help me quite
> [through.[54]
>
> He hoped he should be spared to come home to his loved ones and his little business, but the Lord willed it otherwise.[55]

He was killed instantaneously by a shell bursting over his dugout on 19th September, 1917. He has no known grave and is commemorated on the Tyne Cot Memorial, Belgium.

Several of the men also speak about the impression made on them by the promise in Psalm 91: 7, '… a thousand shall fall at thy side, and ten thousand at thy right hand; but it shall not come nigh thee.' Some soldiers had remarkable experiences of the fulfilment of this. The father of Trumpeter George Holmes, of the Strict Baptist congregation at Brantford, Ontario, Canada, who served in the Royal Canadian Dragoons during the war, sent the following account of his son to *The Friendly Companion*:

> ✍ He had been sent with 49 other soldiers to perform some special duty.

George Holmes

We assume the duty had been accomplished and he saw one of his comrades lying before him. He spoke to him and, not receiving any answer, put out his hand and touched him, he found him to have been shot dead, and then he found that all the 49 others were dead in a like manner, and he alone had been spared, having only a bad flesh wound, which healed in due time and he returned again to the front.[56]

Thomas Burfoot and his wife

It is recorded of Thomas Burfoot, later a deacon at Hope Chapel, Blackboys, Sussex: "When in the trenches on the front line, Psalm 91: 1-7 was made very appropriate when many of his fellow-soldiers around were mown down by gunfire while he was spared. He was also favoured at times under these circumstances to feel peace in his soul and communion with the Lord."[57] In later life, Mr Burfoot was approached by a young girl doing a school project on the war, who asked about his army experiences. As soon as the trenches were mentioned his eyes filled with tears and all he could say was, "Ah, sweet times they were! Yes, sweet times, they were sweet times." He just kept repeating these same words and seemed unable to say anything else. There was no mention of the deprivations, the dead and the dying, and all the other things the young girl expected to hear. The Lord had clearly been very near and dear to him in the terrible experiences of the war.[58]

Fred Smith

The words of Psalm 91: 7 could also have been applied to Private Fred Smith, who served in the 1st Battalion, 6th Lancashire Fusiliers. While in Gallipoli, Turkey, he survived three bayonet charges, out of which only 17 of his regiment escaped unharmed (he being one of them). The remainder were either killed or wounded.[59] Six Victoria Crosses were awarded to the battalion for their bravery on the opening day of the Gallipoli campaign, on 25th April, 1915.

Today, when we think of the First World War, we generally think of the Western Front, and the terrible scenes on the Somme and at Passchendaele. However, it was not called a 'world war' without reason. The conflict spread from the countries immediately bordering Germany, throughout South East Europe, and on to the Asian and African continents. Much of this spread of conflict was driven by the nature of the war – a war of empires. The nations of Europe, which were at the centre of the war, had empires which circled the globe. Additionally, the Turkish (or Ottoman) Empire sided with Germany, formally entering the war in November, 1914, bringing the conflict to the Middle East as well. Strict Baptists were represented in the army serving in all these various arenas of war. The men fighting in these far off places, no less than the men serving on the Western Front, saw the Lord's preserving mercies in striking ways. A. V. Dougan served in Palestine during the war. He wrote of a deliverance afforded from a sandstorm:

> ✍ In the early months of 1917, as a unit of the British Army which captured Palestine, after marching over the Sinai desert, we lay encamped at Khan Tunis, a village on the Palestine border. As orders came for an attack on Gaza, a town famous in Old Testament history (you will remember Samson carried away its gates), the writer, along with another soldier, was detailed to proceed to the ration dump ten miles distant to bring back our supply of food, and forage for our animals. Mounted on Bedouin racing camels and armed in case of danger, we set out accompanied by twelve luggage camels and two

The Camel Corps

native camel drivers. All went well for six miles or so of the way, when suddenly grains of sand began to sting our faces, and the camels became restless. Looking towards the south east, we saw approaching us the spiral columns of sand whirling and dancing like the dervishes of the Sudan, and in their train what appeared to be a solid wall of sand. It was the dreaded sand storm. To turn and flee before it with our swift racing camels might have enabled us to reach a place of safety, but with the slow moving baggage animals in our charge, it was impossible. Nothing could be done but to make the camels kneel down and for us to take shelter behind them, hoping that the storm might alter its course. The camels, as though knowing the danger, without their usual grumbling at the command to *barakh* (Arabic: kneel down), at once went down on their fore-knees, and gathering their hind legs under their bellies, squatted on the sand, a living wall, four deep. Seating ourselves with the natives in the shelter of the camels' bodies, we awaited the coming storm. With a noise like an angry sea it it reached us, and with the falling sand the light of the sun was hidden from us. After what seemed like hours, the camels began to move about, and after a heave or two, as if throwing off a heavy weight, arose to their feet, and in the clearance made by them we were able to free ourselves from the sand which from the chest downward held us captive, and rise to our feet also. The sand was clinging to our faces and clothes, but our lives were spared. The camels, in the providence of God, proved to be our safety, our 'hidingplace from the tempest.'[60]

For some serving in Palestine, the war also provided an opportunity to see some of the sites associated with Biblical history, especially those associated with the life of the Lord Jesus. It is recorded of Mr Frank Hare, who was the deacon at Stotfold for 42 years until his death in 1975:

Feeling it to be his duty to serve his nation, in 1915 he enrolled in the army and saw active service in Palestine. This land of the Bible provided him with much profitable interest in his off-duty hours as he searched the Scriptures. On one particular occasion, he felt a measure of the blessing in Luke 24: 50-51 [*And he led them out as far as to Bethany, and he lifted up his hands, and blessed them. And it came to pass, while he blessed them, he was parted from the, and carried up into heaven*] in his own soul, as he sat by the roadside on the Mount of Olives near to Bethany reading that portion.[61]

Frank Hare

Perhaps one of the more unexpected spheres of service during the war was Ireland. The war produced serious discontent in Ireland, especially when there appeared to be a threat of conscription of Irish men to join the British armed forces. In response to this, the Irish Nationalists, who were seeking independence for Ireland, rose up against the British rule, taking the opportunity of the distraction to the British Government offered by the First World War. The resulting Easter Rising of 1916, led, among others, by Padraig Pearse, a member of the Irish Republican Brotherhood, was quickly overpowered and put down by the British Army. Mr Reginald Morris, who would later become pastor at Clifton Chapel, Bedfordshire, was sent to Dublin on 27th April, 1916, to help quell the Irish rebellion. He then spent six months stationed in The Curragh, till his regiment was called back to England in January, 1917, to head for the Somme a month later.[62] Mr Morris sent back a number of postcards to his family showing the damage done by the Easter Rising, and some of these are reproduced in this book.

Reginald Morris

John Pack

During this period, the situation in Ireland became quite dangerous for the British troops stationed there. John Pack, the son of Seth Pack, and brother to J. Oliver Pack, both successively pastors at Irthlingborough, kept a diary, detailing his stay in Ireland while in military training. He records some interesting eyewitness accounts of the effect of the discontent on the British Army:

Postcard sent home by Mr Morris showing the damage caused from the Easter Rising

✍ Since the outbreak of the Sinn Fein rebellion we had been confined to barracks [*in Ballincollig*], as in the region around Bandon and all this southern part of Ireland, the sympathies of many of the people were with the 'Sinn Feiners.' I had been receiving letters from Bandon; there was a little battle there between some and they used the [*Presbyterian*] Manse as a first aid post for the wounded … During this time we heard of the landing at Dingle Bay of a man from a German submarine (I have forgotten his name). He was to lead the rebellion, but was captured, and I believe later executed for treason … Early in the spring of 1916 I got a pass for home leave … We went to Cork, then got the first train we could to Dublin where we arrived in the evening. We found out it was several hours before our boat sailed, so three of us took a walk down Sackville Street to see the damage, as the fighting there had been so severe.[63]

SINN FEIN REBELLION
B.C. SACKVILLE STREET, DUBLIN.
BEFORE AND AFTER

Another of Mr Morris's postcards showing the ruins in Dublin

Of course, in order to get to Ireland, or any part of the front line, all had to cross the sea. This had its own dangers, often comparable to fighting at the front. German submarines attacked the ships regularly, and the journey could be terrifying. Private John Parish, the superintendent of the Sabbath School at Rochdale Road Chapel, Manchester, sent the following letter recalling his journey from home to fight at the Dardanelles, in Turkey:

> ✍ No doubt you will have read in the papers of the terrible disaster which befell our ship the *Royal Edward* on Friday last. I hasten to let you know that I was among the rescued, and now am safe at Alexandria … I was in my cabin at the time the submarine attacked us and fired the torpedo which struck us amidships, so that the ship sunk in less than five minutes … and just had time to fasten on my lifebelt and walk to the side down to the next deck lower; and seeing the water rising rapidly I plunged into the sea and swam away from the ship out to a lifeboat, which had got well away. This boat contained about 28 men, and was so full of water that it was entirely submerged, but did not sink … After four hours in this boat we were picked up by a French minesweeper.[64]

The precise death toll of the sinking of the *Royal Edward* is unknown, although it is generally given as being about 1,000 men.

One mother wrote describing a remarkable account of preservation granted from a submarine attack:

> ✍ I thought you would like to know and rejoice with me at the Lord's goodness and preserving mercy to our dear Ernest up till the 21st of last month. It seems they were going to A— when they saw a

submarine coming toward them. The captain told them nothing but a fog could save them; when, to their surprise, a dense fog came over them in three-and-a-half minutes, which lasted three-and-a-half hours, which hid and shielded them from the sight of the enemy. When the fog passed away and they saw they were safe, the captain called them together on deck, and held a thanksgiving service for their deliverance.[65]

The Royal Navy

For the navy, of course, the threat from submarines, mines, and torpedoes was constant, and many men lost their lives at sea.

Albert Murray, Officer's Steward on board *H.M.S. Arabis*, was drowned with the sinking of his ship during the Battle of Dogger Bank on 11th February, 1916. He was a member of the congregation at Ebenezer Chapel, Legh Street, Warrington. His father served during the war in the navy too, aboard *H.M.S. Highflyer*.[66]

Albert Murray

John Victor Bear, a member of the congregation at Mount Zion Chapel, Ramsgate, had joined the Royal Navy before the war, in September, 1910, and served as

Troops embarking for France

chief telegraphist on *H.M.S. Hampshire*. From 1915, *H.M.S. Hampshire* had been stationed with the Grand Fleet in Scapa Flow, in the Orkney Islands. On 30th May, 1916, she sailed for the Battle of Jutland, returning safely to Scapa Flow on the 3rd June. On the evening of 5th June, Lord Kitchener, Field Marshall of the British Army, joined the ship. Lord Kitchener (famous for the recruiting posters, which showed him pointing at the reader, with the slogan "your country needs you") was to sail to Russia for diplomatic talks with the Tsar. However, shortly after leaving Scapa Flow, *H.M.S. Hampshire* struck a minefield laid by a German submarine. The explosion ripped the ship apart. A Force 9 gale was blowing at the time, and the ship sank within 15 minutes. Just 12 men survived the wrecking, and, demonstrating that the ravages of war have no regard to rank or eminence, both Lord Kitchener and John Bear were lost. John Bear was aged 22 at the time. John's younger brother, Harold Owen Alfred Bear, also served in the Royal Navy, as leading signalman on *H.M. Submarine G12*. He was accidently drowned on 6th May, 1918. The bodies of both brothers were never reclaimed from the sea, and they are remembered today on the Naval Memorial at Chatham.

John V. Bear (left) & Harold O. A. Bear (right)

Just as in all the forces, for some men serving in the navy exposure to the death of their comrades was sometimes the means used by the Holy Spirit, either to commence or to advance the work of grace in their souls. It is recorded of Edgar Hargreaves, deacon at Zoar Chapel, Bradford, that: "During the 1914-1918 War, he served in the Royal Navy and passed through many hardships. The washing overboard of one of the ship's company while he was on watch, created a deep impression on his mind as to his standing and condition had he been in his mate's place. Although oft in perils on the sea, his life was preserved." [67]

Edgar Hargreaves

For others, gentler means in their path of duty were used for the good of their souls. Mr Percy Lodge, who for many years was the deacon at Gravesend, and served on the committee of the Gospel Standard Societies and as chairman of the Gospel Standard Trust, entered the navy on 1st April, 1917. There is no record of his service, except this comment in his obituary: "While stationed at Portsmouth, he attended the chapel there, where the dear Lord used an old sailor, who hobbled about with a wooden leg, to deepen the work of grace in his heart by his simple prayers at the prayer meetings." [68]

Service in the navy also had the disadvantage that men were enclosed in a small space with worldly company, with less opportunity than on land to find quiet places apart. Mr Gilbert Collier served on a minesweeper during the war. He wrote of his time in service:

> ✍ I was thrown into company where there was no fear of God. My state was wretched. I crept into secluded parts of the ship and cried to the Lord for hours. At length I felt a sweet peace, the mind was calmed. Such preciousness was felt towards the dear Redeemer, and a persuasion that I should come through the outward dangers for the purpose of telling of his goodness and grace; and though it seemed a remote and impossible thing, there was a persuasion I should be brought to a realization of it.[69]

The persuasion Mr Collier received while serving at sea was in time fulfilled. Spared during the war, he later became pastor of the Strict Baptist Chapel at Linslade.

Naval vessels in action

Gilbert Collier

A number of Strict Baptists also served in the Royal Naval Air Service, operating early flying boats. One example of this was Mechanic Percy W. H. Jobson, who attended Jireh Chapel, Meadvale, Reigate. While serving in the Royal Naval Air Service he was stationed at Dundee. Other men were in the Royal Naval Division, which consisted of battalions which fought on the land (these were formed by Winston Churchill in August 1914, from men enlisted in the Royal Navy, but who were surplus to requirements to crew the naval fleet). One Strict Baptist who saw service in the Royal Naval Division was Ordinary Seaman Benjamin Upton, who served in Nelson Battalion, and died on 6th May, 1915, from wounds received fighting in the Dardanelles (Gallipoli). He was buried at sea.[70] A few Strict Baptists are reported as having served in the Royal Marines too, among them Charles Walker[71] of Blackheath, a nephew of Mr George Rose, the then pastor at Providence Chapel, Cranbrook.

Percy W. H. Jobson

Benjamin Upton (left) & Charles Walker (right)

The Air Forces

In contrast to the army and navy, accounts of Strict Baptist men serving in the air forces are more limited. Of course, the air forces were the newest of the services, following on the heels of the Wright brothers' invention of a functional aeroplane, in December 1903. The Royal Flying Corps (part of the army) had been formed in 1912, and the Royal Naval Air Service in July, 1914. The Royal Air Force was not formed until 1st

April, 1918, by the amalgamation of the Royal Flying Corps and the Royal Naval Air Service. Flying in the early twentieth century was dangerous in itself, without the additional hazards of combat, as aviation was still a new technology and the planes were often unreliable. This is borne out by the account of Lieutenant Rupert E. Neve of the Royal Flying Corps, who was killed on 26th January, 1918:

> ✍ He had about six months' active service in France. In March of last year, when making an attack with his machine, he was severely wounded, but was able to land in the English lines. His injuries were such as to necessitate his remaining in hospital for some time, but he made a complete recovery, and resumed flying at an aeroplane centre where he was Commanding Officer of one of the flights, and also acted as an instructor. He was testing a new machine, which had been flown by a Major the day previously. He had not ascended to a great height when it was observed that he was experiencing engine trouble, as the engine was heard to stop, and no doubt he tried to rectify matters, but owing possibly to the vibration, the machine collapsed and fell to the earth. He was killed instantaneously. The funeral took place at the Maidenhead Cemetery. His dear mother writing to us says, 'It is a comfort to me that he did not suffer; as for himself, he always asked for God's protection when he entered the machine, and thanked him when he got out. I can only say, "He was not, for God took him," but for us, the heartache is hard to bear.' When he was hourly in danger last year in France, just before he was wounded in March, he wrote, 'For whether we live, we live unto the Lord; and whether we die, we die unto the Lord: whether we live therefore, or die, we are the Lord's' (Romans 14: 8). He was one of England's noble sons. He was up for promotion and was expecting every day to be gazetted Captain.[72]

Rupert E. Neve

Another Strict Baptist who served in the air forces was William Hatton, the grandson of Joseph Hatton, who had been editor of *The Gospel Standard* magazine between 1881 and 1884.[73] Two of his letters are included in this book.[74]

A First World War biplane

A final example is Edgar P. Coleman, an Australian Strict Baptist. While he served in the air forces during the First World War, an exercise commenced in his soul concerning the work of the ministry. After the war, he returned to Australia, and became pastor of the Strict Baptist Chapel in Smithfield, New South Wales, for a number of years. This is recorded in his obituary as follows:

🙞 In 1916 he enlisted and was trained to be a pilot in the air force. He left Australia for England and joined the Royal Navy Air Force in England and was there till hostilities ceased. While there he became very ill with pneumonia, the aftermath of which affected him for the rest of his life. He was sent to 'Pebbles' hospital[75] in Scotland and while there had a very vivid dream, in which he saw the sky light up and then saw a beautiful crown, followed by a voice which spoke to him; 'Be thou faithful unto death and I will give thee a crown of life.' This impression entered deeply into his heart and remained till his deathbed, and was found to be very true of him in his church and personal life, in walk and doctrine. So, being faithful in that which was least, he manifested the courage of his convictions. He visited and ministered to many aged pilgrims for many years, and was blessed in his work amongst them, as also the Lord blessed him in the end of his life. Psalm 41: 1-3 was fulfilled: 'Blessed is he that considereth the poor: the LORD will deliver him in time of trouble,' and the fulfilling of verse three was very pronounced: 'The LORD will strengthen him upon the bed of languishing: thou wilt make all his bed in his sickness.'[76]

Prisoners of war

Some servicemen, although their life was spared, found themselves prisoners of war in enemy hands. Perhaps the best known example of this among the Strict Baptists is Mr Harry Salkeld, who tells of his experience in his book *The Vital Year.*[77] Although most prisoners of war appear to have been put to hard manual labour, the conditions they were kept in were generally good, at least until towards the end of the war, as Germany itself entered a period of extreme privation (arising from the naval blockade preventing supplies reaching Germany), when conditions did deteriorate considerably.

Edgar P. Coleman in the pilot's seat

Two Strict Baptists are known to have died while prisoners of war in Germany. The first was Clifford G. B. Platt, a member of the congregation at Ebenezer Chapel, Harwich. He was called up at the age of 18, and arrived in France at just about the time the Germans made their final push in the first half of 1918. He was taken prisoner, and sent to a camp in Worms, Germany. It is recorded that in his last letter, sent on 3rd November, 1918, he expressed the hope that "if it were God's will, the war would soon be over." He died on

6th November, just five days before the Armistice was signed. His father wrote, "We leave him with a 'who can tell?' knowing that our God is a prayer-answering God, and that he is too wise to err, too good to be unkind, and so we leave our dear boy with the One who knoweth best."[78]

Frank Booth

The second example was Frank Booth, the youngest son of John Booth, the pastor at Zoar Chapel, Bradford. Frank had been reported missing, and was believed to be a prisoner of war in Germany. On the first Lord's Day of January, 1919, Mr John Booth received a letter from an ex-prisoner of war, who had been repatriated in poor condition from Germany to a hospital in Edinburgh. The letter described how Mr Booth's son, Frank, had died of starvation while being transported into Belgium by his German captors. Mr Booth's *Memoir* describes that Lord's Day morning, as follows:

> ✍ He arrived in the vestry, but so overwhelmed was he with grief, the deacons persuaded him to stay there, and we proceeded to hold a prayer meeting. At

John Booth and Bradford Chapel

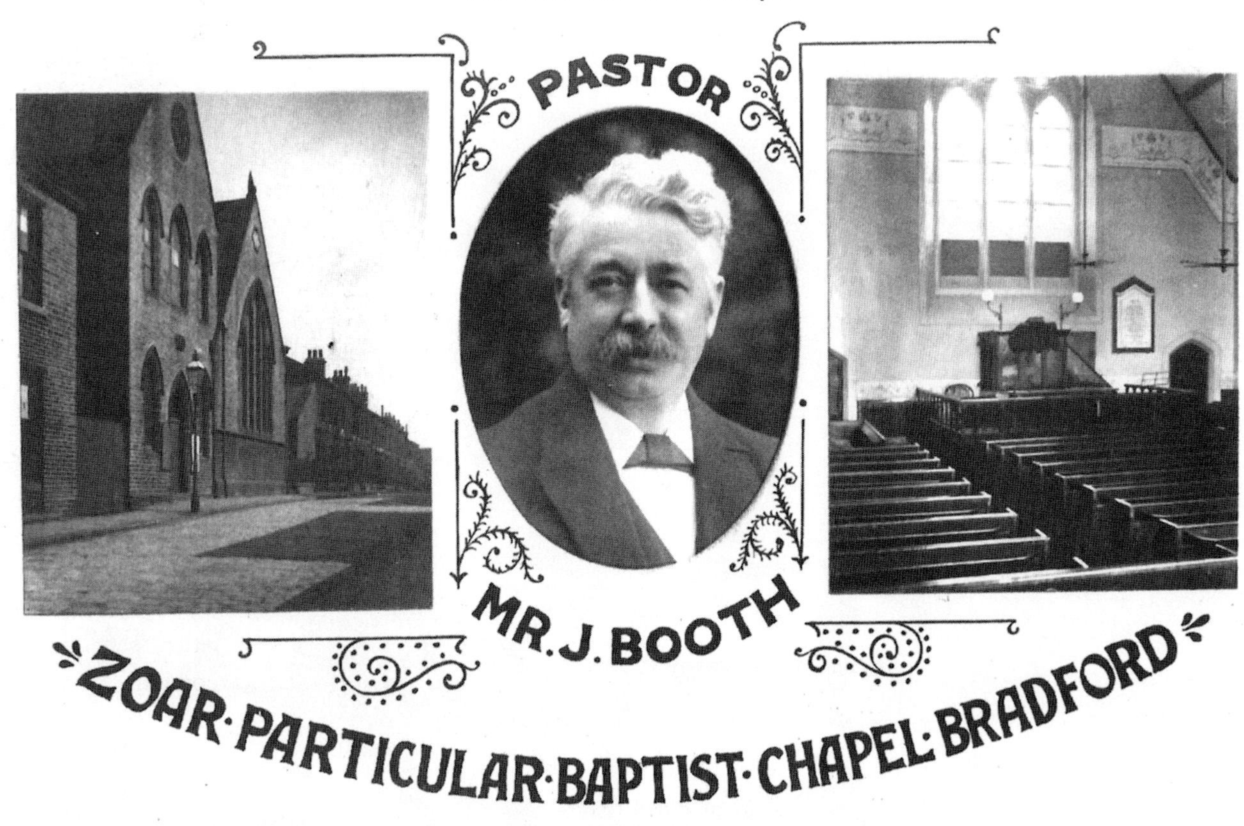

PASTOR
MR. J. BOOTH
ZOAR·PARTICULAR·BAPTIST·CHAPEL·BRADFORD

11 o'clock, when he usually commenced to preach, he ascended the pulpit. Hearts were softened and tears flowed in loving sympathy, as he declared he felt he could not preach, but must try to speak on the word given him: 'Shall we receive good at the hand of God, and shall we not receive evil?' We had now a visible manifestation of his strength being made perfect in the weakness of his servant, who was enabled to speak forth through his tears, his faith strengthened moment by moment until the climax: 'Though he slay me, yet will I trust in him.' It was a day to be remembered in our midst, and was sanctified to the souls of not a few. He continued through the services of the day, and was much helped, and made a help to others.[79]

Confusion about the situation of those who had gone missing in combat was common, with families being left uncertain as to whether their loved ones had been killed or taken prisoner. The family of Ebenezer Burgess of Bounds Cross Chapel, Biddenden, had an especially trying time.

Preparing to return to France after home leave, a prayer-meeting was held at his home; his wife, father and brother being present, and it was decided that should he be granted a safe return in peace, another such meeting should be held for prayer and thanksgiving. Shortly after returning to France he was reported wounded and missing, seven months passing without news of him. There came a day when his wife received official notification of his presumed

British prisoners of war being marched between German guards in France

death, but the same day also a card arrived from him saying he was well and a prisoner of war in Germany. Soon after the war ended he was released, and the meeting for thanksgiving was held, father and sons praying, in turn.[80]

At the end of the war, the prisoners held by Germany were quickly repatriated, with the first of them reaching England on 15th November, 1918, just four days after the Armistice.

Worldly influences in service

It was not just principalities and powers that the Lord's people in military service had to fight against, but spiritual wickedness in their own heart, and in the lives of the ungodly they were surrounded with in service. Four things seem to stand out in the accounts as being issues which the young men from the churches particularly struggled with.

Firstly, bad language. Constant swearing and blasphemy were a sad part of life in the forces. But some were given particular grace, not only to keep their tongue, but to speak out against blasphemy. Mr George Crowter left the following account in his writings:

> ✍ One Sunday when we were back at rest, I was in a hut crowded with troops, trying to read a sermon my dear father had sent me, when a warrant officer senior to me entered and called aloud the most dreadful blasphemy concerning the birth of the Lord Jesus Christ. I could not be silent, and reproved him openly. He said, 'Who are you talking to?' I replied, 'To you, for if that name means nothing to you, it does to some of us. I cannot stand your remarks.'[81]

Secondly, Sabbath desecration and lack of access to public worship. It was a burden to the Lord's people serving at the front that each day was much the same as the next, with little to mark the Lord's Day apart as being holy. The men were, of course, under orders, and, at the front, to have refused to undertake tasks on the Lord's Day would have meant risking danger from the enemy and discipline from their commanding officers and we would not judge those who found themselves in such an invidious situation. Worship was of course held behind the lines, overseen by the large number of chaplains who served the troops, and, especially in the earlier parts of the war, there seems to have been generally good attendance at these field services.

Some mention should be made of the endeavours of the Young Men's Christian Association (YMCA). During the war the YMCA rendered invaluable service, by setting up shops along the front line where soldiers could purchase stamps, stationery, and food and drink. They also provided a form of chaplaincy service to the men. Mr Francis Kirby recorded some appreciation of this service in *The Christian's Pathway*: "On Saturday last I received a letter from one of our Rochdale young men to the effect that he enjoys Sunday morning service in the YMCA hut, but is pained by the low class songs and ragtime ditties which float around him on Sunday afternoons."[82]

For some the YMCA services proved a real blessing. Mr Samuel Pollington, later the deacon at Rotherfield, wrote of a service the YMCA organised which he attended while serving in Italy:

> ✍ Once, attending a service at a YMCA hut I received a lift up, as it were. A subject was brought before us from these words: 'Seek ye first the kingdom of God, and his righteousness; and all these

things shall be added unto you.' I saw such a necessity of being made right, and whatever else was needful, that this would be given.[83]

Samuel Pollington

While some of the young Strict Baptist men appear to have been favoured with a good ministry from their serving chaplains, there is always a note of wistfulness in their letters home about not being able to attend the chapels they had left behind. It also seems that, as the war wore on, there was a dropping off in the attendance of servicemen at worship, and later reports of the war suggest that most preferred singing and playing games above worship.

Thirdly, the difficulty of keeping up daily Bible reading and prayer. It must have taken a lot of courage to have knelt down in a barrack room, morning and evening, knowing that you were surrounded, not only by people who would not understand you, but some who were openly antagonistic to religion. Mr Herbert Banfield, the deacon at Galeed Chapel, Brighton, wrote the following:

✍ The First World War soon after broke out, and I, with my two elder brothers,[84] volunteered for service. I little thought of the sacrifice my parents made to let us go, but father stressed on us when we left home, 'Them that honour me I will honour,' and this rested on my mind. We lodged in huge huts which held about 250 men in each. This was a fresh experience for us, when we were brought into close contact with mankind with all restraint cast aside, each one vying with the next to appear the most vile. We were given little truckle beds, and I wondered what I should do when kneeling for prayer at the close of the day, as I had been wont to do. However, the exhortation father had spoken to us helped me to make a venture, and the Lord restrained voice and hand, and no one endeavoured to molest. The orderly sergeant for the day came round as I was so engaged, and made some general comment, but a big fellow, well known as a boxer, immediately spoke up on my behalf, and expressed in a very forcible way that if anyone ventured to touch me, he would knock his head off; and no one ever did interfere with me.[85]

There are records, though, of times when the reading of the Word of God was especially blessed to the souls of the young men at the front. Thomas Fenner, who would later become deacon at Rotherfield Chapel, provides one example of this:

✍ The First World War came and I was called up in October 1917. In January 1918, I was sent to France. In April I had influenza and was in hospital in Calais, afterwards going to a convalescent camp at Boulogne. For some weeks the words, 'Ye worship ye know not what,' had tried me. I felt I did not know the Lord. When I left Calais, I was too ill to pack my kitbag, and my Bible was left behind. I asked the chaplain of the camp for one, and he gave me the Gospel according to John. I went outside the camp and leaned over a bar-way,[86] feeling to be at the ends of the earth. I opened the little book at the 14th chapter: 'Let not your heart be troubled: ye believe in God, believe also in me.' As I read these words, joy and peace filled my heart. On reading the 6th verse [*Jesus saith unto him, I am the way, the truth, and the life: no man cometh unto the Father, but by me*], it was revealed to me that Jesus Christ was the only way of approach unto God the Father. From that time I have felt at times sweet access at the throne of grace.[87]

Finally, the lack of the Lord's people with whom they could enjoy fellowship. Despite the large numbers serving together in the war, young Strict Baptist men often wrote in their letters about a feeling of isolation. One wrote, "Can you realise my position. Since last leaving home I have never to my knowledge seen, and certainly have not spoken to one of my own faith (with the exception of the friends at Surrey Tabernacle)."[88] Nevertheless, some did find unexpected companions. Mr Reginald Honeysett, later the pastor at Providence Chapel, Cranbrook, records:

✍ The Sergeant in charge picked out four men, myself among them, and dismissed the rest. Two were sent to the 'wet' canteen, and two to the 'dry' canteen, to scrub tables and floors, etc … While the other lad and I were absolute strangers, we soon found we had something in common: a respect for the Sabbath day and the Word of God. A friendship began, which was only broken by his death in France at the end of that year.[89]

This meeting was to provide more than just a friendship, for in time, Mr Honeysett would become acquainted with this young man's sister, who in turn became his wife.

Of course, these were not only problems for those serving abroad. Many young men found themselves forced to leave home to serve, not in the forces, but in reserved occupations, or 'home service' as it was known. Mr Sydney Garnham, who later held pastorates among the Strict Baptists at Derby Road Chapel, Croydon, and Abingdon in Oxfordshire, was one such case. His obituary stated:

✍ In 1917 he was called up for the army, but a weak heart confined him to 'home service.' This period he would have liked to pass over, being painful to record. He describes in much detail how rapidly he was drawn into many evils, a willing slave, when he felt he was nearer actual hell than ever before or since, although since then knowing something of the 'believer's hell' in experience. Looking back on this time, he writes: 'The lines of the hymn fully describe my case:

Why was I made to hear thy voice,
And enter while there's room?[90]

and this fills my heart with wonder, love and praise.' [91]

The war on the home front

The witnessing of God's mercies and judgements was not confined to those serving on the front line. As with any warfare, fighting does not have to be local to have a devastating impact on the civilian population. The First World War was, however, the first 'total war' – it involved everyone. Bombing raids brought fighting behind the front lines, to target civilians directly. Not only was there universal conscription for eligible men later in the war, but women were also expected to work, providing support for the war effort and substituting for the many men engaged in combat. Nobody escaped the effects of the war.

While there was no fighting on home soil, the Western Front was not far away. Benjamin D. Wileman wrote of walking through the Sussex countryside, through the leafy lanes and wild flowers:

> ✍ All still and peaceful … yet as I walked I became aware of a vague undercurrent of sound, hardly to be described as sound at all, yet distinctly heard. It was like a murmur or a crowding of the air, a faint trembling of the atmosphere … It was like a continuous roll of distant thunder, with now and then the sound of a distant explosion. It was the sound of English guns in France. The sea was eleven miles south of me, and the wind blew from the South-East. The atmospheric conditions were favourable for carrying the sound from France to Sussex, a distance of about 150 miles. It seemed difficult to realise that I was enjoying so lovely a prospect of beauty and peace within hearing of the signs of death and destruction. The sharp contrast produced a feeling of awe and of sadness, as I thought of our brave men facing death, and of many of them being cut down in the prime of manhood in the defence of their homeland and their loved ones.[92]

Yet the peace of Britain was broken in a far more painful way than this, for the many families who suddenly found their husbands, fathers, sons and brothers called away to fight. It was not always easy to be submissive in such situations.

Anxiety for servicemen's families

The pain began for many when their loved one left home to join up. Emma Littleton,[93] the widow of John Littleton,[94] pastor at Sydney, Australia (brother of Ebenezer Littleton, pastor at Crowborough), records the following:

> ✍ I may tell you I have 26 children and grand-children; last week my youngest and dearest son John left for France in the Royal Army Medical Corps. He is 40 years of age, and in very deed my youngest and dearest.[95] It was hard, but the fact, 'He that spared not his own Son,' prevailed, and then it had to be 'freely, *freely*,' nothing less.[96]

Once men had gone abroad to the front, many anxious hours were spent at home waiting for news of them, and in many cases, coping with bereavement.[97]

One of the sons of Mr Edward Carr, pastor at Bath, was missing for several months. Mr Carr wrote, "The suspense seems to be wearing out our hearts and our lives." Another of his sons had already been lost in battle, leaving a widow and fatherless children.[98] Like Mr Carr, a number of other ministers had sons called up for active service, and a number were bereaved.

Joseph Field,[99] the founder and pastor of Pick Hill

Chapel, Horam, East Sussex, lost his son David Field during the war. David, who served in the Machine Gun Corps, died on 26th April, 1917, and is buried in Béthune Town Cemetery, France (see p.15). As with many who lost sons in the war, there is no record of the impact this had on Joseph Field, his family, or his ministry. There are, though, exceptions to this, where a more detailed record is preserved.

Joseph Field

Mr Samuel Curtis, pastor at Southill, had three sons called up to fight. His wife has left quite an extensive account of this period. It commences: "Many anxious days and nights we passed through; and many were our cries to the Lord that he would keep and preserve them and bring them home to us again." One of their sons, Benjamin John Curtis, had volunteered in 1915, and saw action at Arras, Ypres, Cambrai, and the Somme. After he had been on the front line for three months, he was wounded, and sent home. After four months at home, and against his parents' hopes that he would not have to return, he was sent to the front again. His mother wrote, "Poor boy! I shall never forget our feelings at that time. He felt he would never return to us, and we also had our fears." After about five months back in France, he was wounded at Péronne, and died

Samuel Curtis

of his wounds on 21st March, 1918, aged 20. He has no known grave, but is commemorated on the Pozières Memorial, France. At the time, his parents were not without hope of him. His mother could say that they had seen a difference in him during the last year of his life, and his letters gave them hope that the Lord was working in his soul. On 22nd March, 1918, before his parents knew he had been wounded and died, his father had a vision in which he saw his daughter Ruth, who had died in 1912, aged 29, and his son Benjamin meet and embrace, before soaring away. He described them as being "clothed in beautiful white garments, and their countenances shone with a brightness inexpressible." Mr Curtis was persuaded that the Lord had taken his son home to glory. At the same time, Mrs Curtis was especially comforted by the word, 'They shall walk with me in white.' She writes: "The remarkable thing was that I neither knew his thoughts, nor he mine, until we spoke of them afterwards together. These things comforted us both. My dear husband (though he never believed much in visionary things) was never shaken from the hope that it was well with our son."[100]

In *The Gospel Standard* for 1918 there is an account of Adelaide Downing, who was a member at Spring Meadow Chapel, Old Hill. Her husband, Mark S. Downing, was an itinerant minister among the Midland churches.[101] Her pastor, Mr Paul H. Robbins, wrote:

> ✍ She was for many years a quiet, unobtrusive, consistent member of our church, well laden with trials without and within, often fearing, but sometimes helped to hope on in the Lord's Word. Two of her sons had joined the army, causing many cries to the Lord. Sometimes she appeared crushed, but when helped a little, her face would show that her strength was within. On the Monday previous to her death she was, as was her wont, at the prayer meeting. On Thursday afternoon she was taken to Birmingham Hospital for an operation, but passed away the same night. About the same time one of her sons was killed,[102] the other badly wounded.[103]

Paul H. Robbins

Alfred Levell, who served in the King's Royal Rifle Corps, was killed in action just before the end of the war. His son, also Alfred, served as Chairman of the Trinitarian Bible Society, as well as being secretary of the Gospel Standard Trust, and a member of the committees of the Gospel Standard Societies and Bethesda Fund. Alfred wrote concerning his father:

> ✍ In 1917, writing to a sister-in-law and referring to the painfulness of a parting from his loved ones, he says: 'My dear wife comforted me by saying when I left her: "If it is his will to take you, he can take care and provide for me and the boy"' (and indeed the

writer [*Alfred Levell Jr.*] can say how this trust has been fulfilled over the last 50 years). On his last leave, in 1918, my father appears to have had some premonition that he would not come home any more. Having left his loved ones and gone down the road, he returned for a few minutes to tell my mother this – that he felt he would never see her again. He was killed in action a few weeks later on 18th October, 1918, aged 32, and buried at Le Cateau.[104] Some months afterwards my mother discovered that hymn 591 in the hymn book [*Gadsby's Selection*] he had used abroad was side-marked, against the last verse being written, 'Very sweet to me,' and giving a date a short time before his death:

The time is now fixed, and soon it will come,
When Christ will his messenger send,
To fetch him from Meshech and carry him home;
And then all his sorrows will end.

Thus was the righteous 'taken away from the evil to come' (Isaiah 57: 1). His death was a great blow to my mother, but she was supported and brought to that place where she could feelingly say it was 'not in anger, but from his dear covenant love.'[105]

Alfred Levell (Jr.)

It is recorded in the obituary of Mr Levell's son, Alfred, that, "his father had told his mother how many times he had prayed for his son while on sentry duty, and this son was to prove the truth contained in Psalm 68: 5, and in Hosea 14: 3, 'For in thee the fatherless findeth mercy.'"[106]

Many children were bereft of their fathers during the war, and, with the loss of the bread winner forcing their mothers to work, were brought up by grandparents, or with the help of aunts and uncles. Mr Frank Ayers, for many years the deacon at Swavesey, lost his father in the war, and was brought up by his grandparents.[107]

Some children never knew their fathers, who had died for the liberties they were to later enjoy. This was true of the late Naomi (always known as Nancy) Brooks of Brabourne, who was successively matron of nearly all of the Gospel Standard Bethesda Homes. Her father, George Brooks (Sr.), volunteered towards the end of the war, even though he was in a reserved occupation. The last time he was at chapel before going to fight, he was especially blessed through

Naomi Brooks

George Brooks (Sr.) and his wife, Ruth

the singing of the hymn, 'Be still, my heart! these anxious cares,'[108] especially the verse,

> Did ever trouble yet befall,
> And he refuse to hear thy call?
> And has he not his promise passed,
> That thou shalt overcome at last?

He was killed a matter of weeks later, at the front in France, leaving two little children, and the third, Naomi, at that point unborn. He was buried at the Highland British Cemetery, Le Cateau, France. He is remembered on the war memorial at Brabourne Chapel.[109] The hard times the family had are hinted at in the obituary of Naomi's brother, George Brooks (Jr.), who died in 2012:

> ✎ His father was killed in the First World War when George was only four years of age, and so his mother had a very hard time bringing him and his two sisters up. The Lord wonderfully helped them through these difficult times. George did all that he could to help his dear mother, and as soon as he was old enough, he went out to work [*as a gardener*] to help provide for the family. He had to pray his way along from those very early days, both in the things of providence and for his own soul's safety.[110]

In *The Christian's Pathway*, 1917, the following notice appeared:

> ✎ Private P. Newington was killed in action on February 27th, 1917. His parents received some letters from him which encourage them to believe that with him it is well. A week later his dear wife (Eva) passed away, leaving two little girls, respectively aged 4 years and 2 years. The will of the Lord be done.[111]

P. Newington

While many children were left fatherless by the war, accounts of children being left orphans, like the Newington children, are thankfully rarer. Private Newington is buried in Faubourg d'Amiens Cemetery, France.

When a family member was killed at the front, the information often reached home through a personal letter from a friend of the fallen serviceman. The friends of those killed were often the first to communicate the news of the death to the family, even before the official notification. It cannot have been an easy task for anyone, who, having been bereaved of a comrade, had to write and convey that to the parents. One such letter, sent to a Strict Baptist family, read as follows:

> ✍ Dear Mr and Mrs Buggs,
> It is with deepest regret that I write to tell you of the death of your son Frank. The one consolation I can give you is, that his death was instantaneous, and really painless. I was quite close to him at the time, but fortunately escaped. I need hardly say how I feel it, as Frank and myself were always the best of pals. His death occurred on the 7th September, in the morning. In conclusion, I ask you to accept my sincere sympathy in your great loss. Yours respectfully,
> Rifleman J. H. Chapman.
> September 8th, 1916.[112]

Whenever possible, following the news of their bereavement, the families eventually had to take receipt of their loved one's possessions, which often carried testament to his death. The Buggs family received the possessions of their son Frank on 9th December, 1916. These included his books, letters, watch and chain, and things he carried in his pocket. His sister wrote in her diary for that day, "How sad it seemed to look at the things the dear laddie had carried about with him! The bloodstained Bible and hymn book, and a match case with a little piece of shell still lodged in it. I was glad to have the little Bible again I had given him, and he had carried for the ten months of his soldier life."[113]

Frank Buggs

For some, the loss was softened greatly by the evidences that their loved one killed in the war was 'with Christ, which is far better.' George Smith, Strict Baptist minister at Colchester, lost his son, George, who died at Thiepval in France leaving a young widow. He wrote:

> ✍ The pain to nature is often still great, but the abundant grace and mercy of God to him, and us in so teaching him, far exceed the downcastings of bereavement. In his letters to us he wrote much of the Lord's presence with him, and I am often filled with wonder and amazement, and humbled under the mighty hand of God, that he should so graciously distinguish one so vile and unworthy of the least of all his mercies as I feel myself to be. Our only son is now in Palestine, having been with the Egyptian force over two years … So that God has taken one, and, so far, left us one – one we believe is with him in glory, and one with us at the throne of grace.[114]

As one might expect, parents and spouses caught hold of the smallest shred of evidence that it might be well with their loved one. No doubt, in such a situation it would have been an encouragement even to notice that a son, who had perhaps previously dragged his feet in attending the means of grace, appeared to sing the hymns heartily on the last occasion he was home on leave. Others reported words of Scripture being given to them, and even dreams, as the basis for their hope. Thankfully, there were many who left much clearer evidence that it was indeed well with the departed.

In some cases, it was not until after they had been killed that the evidence became known. Henry John Piggott, the deacon at Hope Chapel, Horsham, and his wife lost a son, Joseph, who had never said anything to them regarding his spiritual state so that, although they had not been without hope of their son's eternal standing, they had no certainty. After his death, however, a young girl, whom he had been writing to, gave them the letters he had written to her. These letters provided clear evidence that their son was one of the Lord's people. An illustrative extract from one of these letters follows:

> ✍ Even in England I have often felt that God was taking control of my affairs, but I still went on in my sinful path. My constant dread now is that my thoughts on eternity are only remembrances of youthful teaching revived by the nearness of death; and what is the use of these without being born again? It is mere hypocrisy, and I dread that more than a state of open sin. I hope I sometimes feel a longing to be made right, to be 'born again' as remarked above. I often fear that, being brought up under the sound of the Gospel, I may only get the teaching without the power … How true that … verse … is to me out here:
>
> My God, I would not long to see
> My fate with curious eyes;
> What gloomy lines are writ for me,
> Or what bright scenes may rise.[115]
>
> And I hope my prayer will always be the last verse, 'In thy fair book of life and grace,' etc. You are the only one I have written to like this, as I want to feel that I can honestly say I am a real Christian before saying anything in my letters home.[116]

Women's role in the war

For women, the war brought a call-up too, to serve as nurses, to work the land and to undertake many jobs which in pre-war society had been traditionally the preserve of men. Although this is sometimes seen now as being the start of the shift in society towards feminism, and what has been seen by many as an outworking of feminism in society, this is difficult to establish. Due to the number of men sent abroad to fight (nearly a quarter of the male population joined the armed services), the country was obliged to call on women to work in order to keep going. There was still quite clear gender segregation in the roles fulfilled by men and women. Women were not called to fight, but to hold crucial support roles.

One young Strict Baptist woman who found herself in this position was Lydia Durling.[117] Lydia had just turned 17 when the war broke out. As a result of this, she was sent to work on 11th March, 1916, at the Vickers factory at Crayford. The factory made the famous 'Vickers' machine gun, and some early aircraft too. Lydia's elder sister also worked there, and in due course, their father, Albert, a village carpenter and joiner, was to join them in the aeroplane shop on 22nd January, 1917, obviously using his woodworking skills on the early wood and canvas structured aeroplanes. The war had an immense impact on the Durling family. Lydia lost a brother, Maurice, who was killed at the Somme on 14th August, 1916. Maurice has no known grave and is remembered on the Villers-Bretonneux Memorial, France. Other brothers served in the forces, and at least one received significant wounds during the conflict. The changing employment and circumstances caused by the war resulted in the family relocating from Meopham to Gravesend. This move was the cause of Lydia meeting her future husband, Percy Lodge, who had been brought up at the chapel there, and would later hold the office of deacon in the church.[118]

Women working in a munitions factory

Lydia and Percy were married in August, 1923. Lydia joined the church at Gravesend and was a faithful member there until her death in 1977. Although the details are sketchy, this is one example of how the war affected a young Strict Baptist lady and illustrates the pressures on family life during these years.

Another Strict Baptist lady who found herself working in a munitions factory was Martha Palmer, the eldest daughter of Eli Ashdown, the pastor of Zoar Chapel, Great Alie Street, London. Her husband, Archdale S. Palmer, was a deacon at Galeed Chapel, Brighton, and the son of Lady Biddulph.[119] Martha records:

> ✍ We both worked on munitions, but the sedentary life gave me terrible headache, and the constant sitting brought on sciatica. I had reluctantly to give up work, and at the same time my husband was unable to continue; we were full of trouble, our income was very much reduced, and we had to give up keeping servants.
>
> I inwardly groaned for strength, as I was suffering a good deal from sciatica. When lying down a little later my mother was reading to me, and though I was scarcely able to listen, when she came to the word, 'I will strengthen thee, yea, I will help thee, yea, I will uphold thee,' it was God's voice and put strength in me.[120]

There was some encouragement from within the churches for women to take up these working roles. Mr Francis Kirby wrote at the outbreak of hostilities: "There are many ways in which our sisters can render valuable help – by qualifying for nurses, by learning how to render first aid, by making garments, and by preparing requisites for nursing; and for these purposes our schoolrooms and vestries can easily be utilized."[121]

Accounts of the experiences of Strict Baptist women who took up nursing, or served in the forces, have not been located, but that does not mean women ignored the call to serve. The women of Rochdale Road Chapel, Manchester, were very wholehearted in their attempts to render assistance to the war effort. In 1915, they reported the following:

> ✍ A Society was organized and put into form at the beginning of the war (August 17th, 1914) by the

> deacons' wives, along with members of the church and congregation. Permission and full sympathy in the work were obtained from our minister, Mr Gruber, and all the deacons, and the use of a dining-room attached to the chapel was granted us for our work. Our minister's wife, Mrs Gruber, and the deacons' wives, formed themselves into a committee, and added other names thereto, so forming a committee of 18 ladies … We have sent many parcels through the Red Cross Society, and a great many have been sent to the front, to Egypt, and to soldiers returning from India to the front. Individual outfits have been sent to our young men from Sunday school and chapel that have joined the army (18 have already gone and others are expecting to join); also other individual outfits to cases that have been recommended to us. The outfit consists of two warm shirts, two pairs of socks, one each of body-belt, muffler, pair of mittens, pocket-handkerchief, Testament and letter.[122] We have received many letters of true thankfulness and appreciation, especially from those at the Front. The work has been done and the money given from our own people connected with us here. *All the shirts* have been made by our friends here that have lost some of their employment through the war, and the committee have paid them for making them. In this way we have been able to help them.[123]

Rochdale Road Chapel, Manchester

The report showed that, during the first year of the war, the women of Rochdale Road Chapel raised £130 12s. 6d. This work continued throughout the duration of the conflict.

There are also records of individual women doing what they could in their situations and according to their means. Miss Rhoda Brooker, of Hastings, published a poem, titled *A Prayer for the Nation*.[124] She sold these for one penny, and raised a total of £13 15s. 6d. after expenses. This she spent on:

> ✍ Various woollen winter comforts for soldiers and sailors, £9 10s.; Bibles and Franco-British Books, 19s. 6d.; 3 X'mas Funds, 21s.; Belgian Refugee Fund, 10s.; Streatham Hospital, 10s.; Boy Scouts' Clothing, Sandbags, Red Cross (5s. each), 15s.; Institute for Blind, 3s.; Lint and Cotton Wool, 2s.; Chocolates, etc., 5s.

This was described by the editor of *The Friendly Companion* as "a laudable work." [125]

At Providence Chapel, Cranbrook, Mr George Rose, the pastor, is known to have encouraged the women in the congregation to write regularly to the men who had gone to fight, so that contact would be maintained with the praying congregation at home. In one of these cases, the letter writing even progressed to romance after the war.[126]

Providence Chapel, Cranbrook (Interior)

For some women, the war meant they had to enter the family business to take on the work of their brothers who had been called to fight. May Hooper, of Forest Hill, London, was one example of a young girl in this situation. For her, it was a time of considerable tribulation, but also one of blessing:

> ✍ The war still being on, I had to go to a city warehouse, when there was the first daylight air raid, and as the bombs were falling close to me, I with many others was sent down into the cellar. I cannot describe my feelings but felt again all was lost, and I should soon be in hell. When we were told to go home, I did so as quickly as I could, but my body was trembling, and so was my soul. I boarded a bus, and I shall never forget the words that were spoken into my heart in my frightened state. The verse came:
>
> But they that in the Lord confide,
> And shelter in his wounded side,
> Shall see the danger overpast,
> Stand every storm, and live at last.[127]
>
> Never shall I forget how all fear was gone.[128]

George Ruse

Apart from these endeavours to help, the war certainly did not leave women untouched. One poignant relic of the war which has been shared with me is a photo of George Ruse, who, at the time of being sent to France in July, 1916, was engaged to be married to Violet Brooks. On the back of the photo is written: "To Violet, from dear George on his departure for France, July, 1916." When he left, he told his family, "I don't think I will return." He was killed on 18th September, 1918, aged 32, and is buried in the Péronne Communal Cemetery Extension, France. His parents, Herbert John and Mary Ruse, had a good hope that it was well with him. His fiancée, Violet, would later marry his brother Mark Ruse, who had also served in the army during the war, but mercifully was spared to return home.[129]

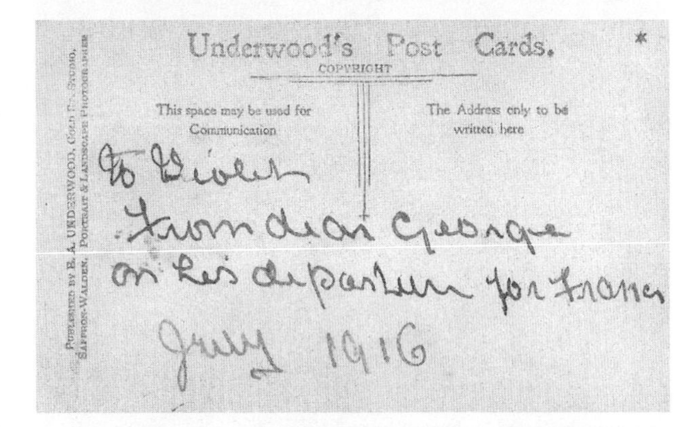

George Ruse's message on the back of his photo

Many women had anxious days as their husband, sons, brothers, or father, were away fighting. For some the day came when they realised they would never see their husband alive again; and where there were children, these women were faced with having to bring up and provide for their children alone. In some cases, the Lord was particularly gracious and granted wonderful submission to his solemn dispensations. Ruth Stevens, who was a sister to Mr John and Mr Frank Gosden,[130] wrote of the blessing she received during the war, and how it sanctified the adverse providence she was passing through, in such a way that she felt resigned to everything:

> ✍ Next I remember, when 22 years old, during the 1914-18 War, I was married and my husband had to go to the war as an infantryman. I usually heard regularly from him, but there came a long silence, and I knew he was in the midst of fighting. As the days went by, the suspense brought me very low, and one Sunday I was too poorly to go to chapel. But as I lay in bed, the Lord visited my soul and lifted my heart and affections so to him that, though my trouble was still so great, it was entirely removed. Had I then

Ruth Stevens

> received news that he had been killed, what I was enjoying outweighed it all. I had peace in my soul. May I not hope this was the Lord's doing? My husband was brought home in a few days right to Brighton, though badly wounded.[131]

Similarly, it is recorded of Mrs Elizabeth Caton, wife of Henry Caton, the pastor at Liverpool:

> ✍ During the 1914-18 War, being in a very low place, four brothers in the war,[132] and mother on her deathbed, in very frosty weather her hands were cracked and sore. She was bemoaning her hard lot, when (she said), 'two pierced hands appeared before my mind's eye. Ah yes, I saw the nail marks in those blessed hands. No words came, but, O, the feeling was, "I bore this for thee." What was my trouble then? It fled. It was nothing compared to what he bore.'[133]

For some women, the change of situation the war brought was an opportunity to escape chapel attendance, and to take up the pleasures of the world. Mary Harrison was an example of this. Leaving home during the war to live with a widowed sister, she took the opportunity to please herself. The Lord permitted her to do so for a time, but in mercy he caused her to feel her need of a Saviour and to return. In later life, she was a member at Rochdale Road Chapel, Manchester. Sadly, a number who turned away from the means of grace at this time probably never returned.

Others found some of the worldly influences the war provided to be a painful snare. May Hooper wrote:

> ✍ During the First World War my elder brother was gassed and sent home to a London hospital. It was Christmas time, and my brother's wife and myself were invited to a tea at the hospital. After tea there were games and amusements. When we left, I felt such guilt not having courage to leave when I should. What distress I felt before the Lord, and as the next Sunday was the ordinance service, I felt, how could I go to the Lord's table? I had several sleepless nights, and then the last night all I could say was, 'Lord, have mercy on me, a sinner.'[134]

In such a place, the Lord came and revealed himself to her:

> ✍ The words came sweetly to me: 'Clinging to Christ.' All my sins had gone, and I felt Christ had done all for me and would take me to heaven when I died. I fully realise that if the Lord did not take me *all* the way to heaven, I should never get there.[135]

Henry Caton

The impact within the home

It is difficult to separate the impact of the war on women from the effect the war had on family life in general. Family life was particularly disrupted by the practice of billeting troops in private homes. When men signed up, they spent many weeks training at home, before they went abroad. During this time they had to be boarded and fed, and one of the ways the government achieved this was by compulsorily billeting troops with members of the general public. Anyone with a house with spare rooms, within suitable distance of a service base, was liable to have their rooms requisitioned by the army. Mrs Elsie Dawson (then Miss Elsie Aldworth) leaves a detailed account of this happening in her home in St Albans.[136] The Aldworth family had two soldiers billeted with them, and, as they were shopkeepers, they were also required to open their shop longer hours in order to serve the army population.[137] She describes it as a time of considerable trial and tension. In part this was added to by the bad language used by some of the servicemen, which the family found vexing. It quickly became known, however, that bad language was not tolerated in the Aldworths' shop, and on the whole the men respected this. Elsie's mother used to make piles of rock buns and homemade lemonade which they served to the soldiers when they finished parade each day. She and her family obviously greatly pitied the men, and attempted to do all they could to help them. On the Lord's Day, her father, Joseph Aldworth, would distribute religious material among the men (mainly old magazines). When the men departed for the front, the Aldworths found it a time of sadness.

Joseph Aldworth (centre) with his two sons-in-law, William Hope (pastor at Abingdon; left) and Herbert Dawson (pastor at Bethersden; right)

Mrs Dawson describes one of these occasions:

During the time I was at home, after the war started, we saw at least two battalions leave at midnight to embark on the train that took them to the seaport from where they went to France. On those occasions, public houses were out of bounds for many hours, so that the men should be sober, and well aware of what they were expected to do. We were asked (or rather told) to keep our shop open, and to serve the men with anything they required before starting. The few whom we knew to be professed Christians (although not belonging to our denomination) came in and warmly shook hands with us,

Elsie Dawson (née Aldworth) with her first child, in 1917

and asked us to think about them. Many who had regularly bought things from us, came in and thanked us for the kindness we had shown to them. It was very evident, however, that all of them were feeling the strain and the solemnity of their position. Oh, how we wished that they knew, too, the comfort that only true religion could impart in such an hour. When they moved away along the street, lined by the people with whom they had been billeted, and others who had tried to be friendly to them, there was no martial sound of music. We watched them march out of sight, but, on the night air, the tramp of hundreds of them, down the long road to the station, could be heard. There was a peculiarly poignant and sad element in the sound. It made me think of death very clearly, and when the sound of tramping feet died away, and all the people went into their homes, scarcely anyone uttered a word. Many of those young men never returned. In less than a fortnight after their departure, one of the two who were billeted in our home was shot down, when carrying a message from one officer to another in the trenches. Many others were quickly gone.[138]

Leonard Broome

There were also many children in the homes where soldiers were billeted, and this sometimes meant that an ungodly influence suddenly entered their home. Mr Leonard Broome, later the pastor at Southampton, writes of this in his autobiography. Although he lost two uncles in the war, and his grandparents had no hope of their two boys, at the time it was not sanctified to his soul. Instead, he immersed himself in the world:

> ✍ The declaration of the 1914-18 War brought solemn changes all round. It meant a complete change in a little place like Farnborough Street, which was situated halfway between the main station to London, and the smaller South Eastern and Chatham Railway (to Reading one way and Aldershot the other). Soldiers were everywhere, and so were horses, mules, and troops on the march, with bands at regular intervals. Soldiers were billeted on us at a moment's notice, and the cavalry were marshalled in the large goods sidings. I earned more than one shilling holding the horses for the officers. That was a lot of money in those days. When the troops were cooking up in their large cauldrons we often had a good taste of the stew. But, alas, I also got a good taste for something else, and that was their bad language. Here I learnt to swear, and other evil things besides: it was my first introduction, I fear, to the world.[139]

Although many men, women and children came under worldly influences during the war, and never broke away from it afterwards, in the Lord's mercy this was not the case with Mr Broome, and after he was called by grace, he served the churches as a minister.

It is indeed possible that there were children for whom the Lord used the events of the war to bring them into spiritual concern. In a copy of John Gadsby's *Larger Sunday School Hymnal*, given as a Sabbath school prize, the inscription expressed the desire that the Lord would cause even the children to pray for deliverance:

> ✍ Presented to Anna Ashby in commemoration of this terrible war we are now passing through as a nation. May the Lord help one and all to pray to him for deliverance. Zoar Chapel Sunday School, Dicker, July, 1915.[140]

Even when bereavement did not directly affect a child, it would have been impossible to escape seeing in the streets the injured returned from the front. In 1916 *The Little Gleaner* carried a piece for children on the subject of wounded soldiers:

> ✍ All over our country are poor wounded soldiers back from the war. You children must often see them when you are out walking – young, strong men with only one arm, or one leg, or their arms in slings; some with strappings on their faces, or their hands bandaged … Do you ever think about these poor wounded men, and remember that they have suffered and risked their lives for us, that they have fought our enemies and been wounded, that we who live at home on these islands might have peace, and comfort, and food and clothes, and our homes to live in? … We cannot do enough for our brave soldiers. You children can ask God to bless them and help them every day. Perhaps some of you live near War Supplies Depots, and would be able to take them some good things. Fruit and flowers, vegetables and cakes and jam are all accepted. Remember, 'God loveth a cheerful giver,' and he accepts the smallest gift given with a good motive.[141]

In ways like these, although the war was not fought on British soil, nobody at home, not even the children, remained untouched by war and its effects.

Bombing raids

Although there is a tendency to associate the bombing of Britain with the Blitz of the Second World

War, it was also the case that during the First World War Britain suffered from aerial bombardment. The first Zeppelin (airship) raids started in 1915-16, and took Britain by surprise. These massive German airships concentrated on London and the southern and eastern regions, but they also reached into the north of the country. Then towards the end of the war the Germans began bombing the country with squadrons of 'Gotha' bomber aeroplanes. While the damage was nowhere near the scale of the Blitz, it was nevertheless significant.

Arthur Wilcockson

Several Strict Baptist families suffered bomb damage to their homes, and at least one Baptist chapel (in Hartlepool) was damaged by enemy action. *The Christian's Pathway* records two soldiers whose homes were ruined in the bombings of London on the 13th October, 1915.[142] The editor of *Zion's Witness*, a magazine received by many Strict Baptist homes, Arthur Wilcockson, died during a Zeppelin raid on Hull, during the night of 8th August, 1916. It is reported that "he was in bed when he heard the crash of a bomb. He arose, walked to the window and lifted up the sash, when another bomb fell close by. The shock caused him to fall, and he died on the floor."[143] He was 86 years old, and had been editor for 58 years.[144]

William Sutherden Cooper, the pastor at Lakenheath, wrote of the bombing which occurred in the village in March, 1916:

> ✍ We had 21 bombs dropped near our village, which shook it from end to end; but all fell in the fen land. Surely the hand of the Lord was in it to preserve us! Many pale faces, and some mothers with children ran out in their night attire. We are in perilous times, and few think so.[145]

Mr Alfred Dye, the pastor at Rowley Regis, wrote of a Zeppelin raid in 1916:

> ✍ You are of course aware, through the press, that we had a visit of the German Zeppelins. On January 31st we were holding our usual Monday night prayer meeting, when, about 8 o'clock, as one of our friends was engaging [*in prayer*], there was a heavy thud, then another, and another; indeed *many*. Our female friends soon began to show great nervousness, and of course I had to close the meeting ... we did not at once realise the fact of falling bombs. Many bombs

> fell not very far from us; and flashlights also were seen, and the fire engine signals were given.[146]

William Sutherden Cooper

Mr Seth Pack, then the pastor at Irthlingborough (later at Hanover Chapel, Tunbridge Wells), records the downing of a Zeppelin airship in London on one of his preaching visits to Zoar, Whitechapel. He was woken by the noise of bombs falling, and anti-aircraft fire:

> ❧ I did as my friends had advised me, got out of bed and dressed the best way I could in the dark … Mr Jay and I first went into the garden at the rear of the house, when we found that four or five of our searchlights had located the intruding monster. Our hearts were up to the Lord for mercy and protection. O how we trembled inwardly! The Zeppelin was not immediately over us, but a little to the north, and still moving in that direction. As it moved, we went through the house to the street, and were standing together on the edge of the pavement, when suddenly all our guns ceased firing. This led us to fear our defenders were unable to do anything effectively with our foes. Thus our hopes sank and our fears ran high for a few moments, when all of a sudden a flame was seen in the direction of the Zeppelin; in a few moments more the flame had increased to the appearance of a huge furnace. The flaming monster turned to earth and came down a burning mass. The streets being filled with people, I never before heard such clapping of hands and shouts of joy. I neither clapped nor shouted, but I did rejoice to see that destroyed which would have destroyed us. But I also thought of, and felt for, the poor men therein, whose position was so dreadful as the news next day proved, for they were all burned to death or killed by jumping from the burning Zeppelin. This happened between 2 and 3 o'clock that Lord's Day morning. Mrs Jay made me a cup of tea, which we took with a morsel of food; then, after thanking the Lord for his preserving mercies, we again retired to our beds. Still I had scarcely any sleep for I could hear our guns firing far away as other Zeppelins came that night.[147]

According to the wrapper of *The Gospel Standard*, the dates Mr Pack is recorded as preaching at Philip's Hall during the war were 9th January, 6th and 13th February, 20th April, 3rd September, 5th and 26th November, and 14th December, 1916. So it is likely that this is an eyewitness account of the shooting down of the first German airship on English soil, on 3rd September, 1916. The airship was the 'Schütte-Lanz SL11' (not actually a Zeppelin, although it was described as such in the English press), and was shot down by an aeroplane piloted by 2nd Lieutenant William Leefe Robinson, who was later awarded the Victoria Cross for this unprecedented act. The airship came to ground at Cuffley, Hertfordshire, and it is reported that the burning wreck could be seen up to 50 miles away.

Seth Pack

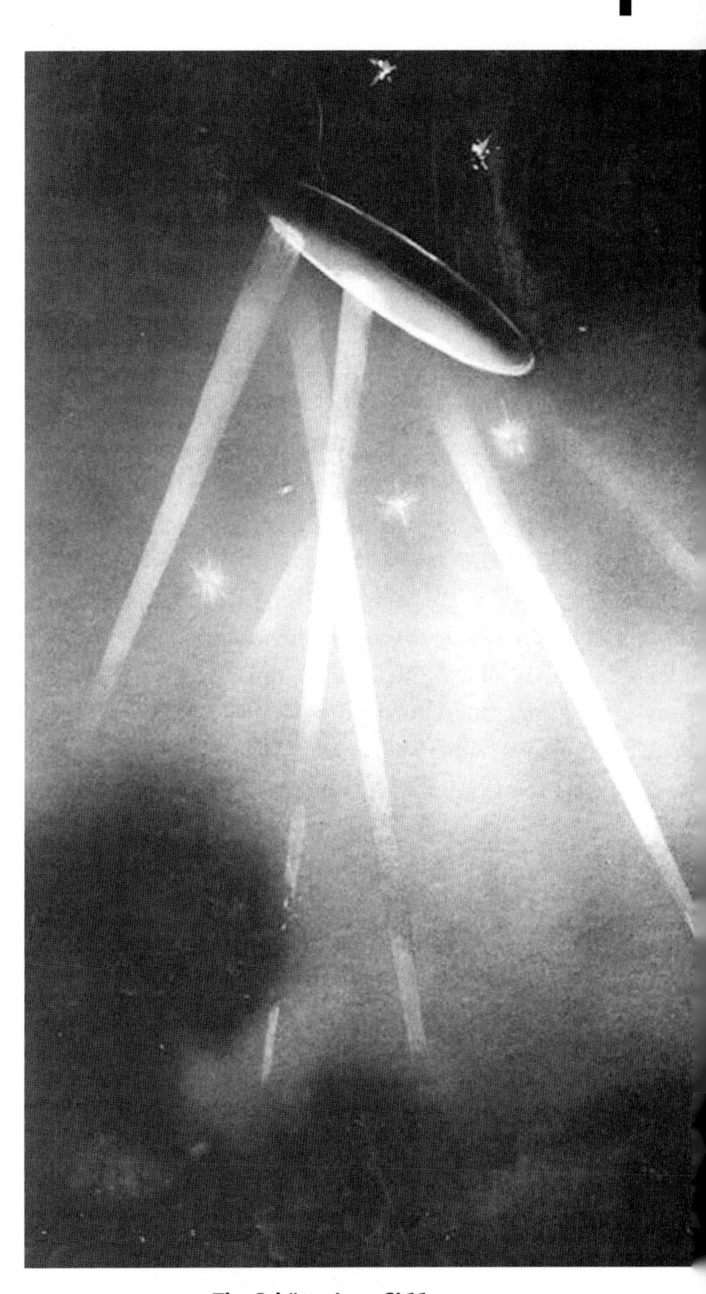

The Schütte-Lanz SL11, photographed just before it was shot down

These events did strike fear into the hearts of many, but the Lord was gracious to his people, and there are frequent accounts of the blessing attending the reminders to them that the Lord Jesus Christ was a safe refuge in the day of trouble. One example of this is found in an entry in the diary of Mr Fred Windridge, the pastor at Providence Chapel, Ponsard Road, London:

> ✍ March 25th, 1917: Heard this day disturbing reports of a raid and invasion. After returning from chapel in the evening, these words came quietly into my mind and afforded a little relief: 'He shall not be afraid of evil tidings: his heart is fixed, trusting in the Lord' (Psalm 112: 7). Lord, give me a grateful heart for such a precious word. And, Oh, do raise me from self, bondage, guilt, and wretchedness. Show me that thou art mine – my Jesus and my all.[148]

In the case of one of Mr Windridge's congregation, Arthur W. Pither, a bombing raid in 1918 was the means the Lord used to bring him into concern about the eternal welfare of his soul. He worked in the coal trade, a reserved occupation, so, while he joined up as a reserve and served in the Middlesex Regiment, he never saw 'active service' during the war. He recorded the following in his writings about an evening with his family:

> ✍ We were sitting together quietly and comfortably when a heavy bomb fell some distance away, shaking our house ... The thought struck me: 'If that bomb had fallen on our house, what would have become of my soul?' This made me shake and set me seeking for mercy, for I felt hell would have been my portion. I needed more than formal prayers and chapel-going to save me.[149]

Fred Windridge with his first wife, Hannah

Of course, with aerial bombing came the necessity for blackouts, in order to hide lights at night, and conceal buildings and potential targets from the overhead bombers. While this blackout was not universal, and the rules and regulations concerning it were local, it was still legally enforceable, and many fell foul of the rules. At Jireh Chapel, St Michael's (a suburb of Tenterden, Kent), it was reported in the local paper that the pastor, Mr Reuben Weeks, was fined for failure to observe the blackout:

> ✍ PETTY SESSIONS – Wednesday, before the Mayor (Councillor Harry Judge), Messrs J. Checksfield, J. Ellis Mace and E. G. Bennett. Reuben Weeks, of Ashford Road, was charged with permitting lights that were not sufficiently obscured at Jireh Chapel, St. Michael's. Defendant pleaded guilty. Sergeant Buss said that at 7.30 p.m. on the 5th of April, he saw three bright lights showing from the chapel. All the windows had buff-coloured blinds, but the light shone through; and in front there were two windows with no blinds drawn … Fined 8s. 6d.[150]

Reuben Weeks

Another highly significant event on the 'home front', both in terms of loss of life and also German audacity, was the bombardment of Scarborough, Hartlepool, and Whitby on 16th December, 1914. Warships from the German Navy drew up off the coast and opened fire on the towns from the sea. Shells poured in on the towns, with many casualties – 137 people were killed, and a further 592 were injured, mainly civilians.

An eyewitness, Mr Spaldon, wrote to Mr Gruber, the pastor at Rochdale Road Chapel, Manchester, to describe the event:

> ✍ I commenced my business with my men at eight o'clock, only a few minutes after the guns commenced firing. We, thinking it might be our naval men practising, continued work until the shells were flying on all sides of us. I exclaimed, 'Men, the Germans are here!' and that we soon found out to be true, so we took shelter behind a big stack of deals;[151] the shells were coming over our heads five or six at a time … I said, 'Lord, we are all in thy care,' and I felt whatever happened it was he who permitted it … One shell struck a stack of deals very near us; I wish you could have heard the crack. We jumped off our feet, but the pieces were prevented coming to us by striking another stack, and only a few pieces fell at our feet. We could see the gas works ablaze, also the broken tram wires; we do not know the number killed, but there were so many that they were burying them all day Sunday.[152]

Such an audacious attack drew outrage from the British public, although the uproar was not just focussed on the German Navy for targeting civilians, but also at the Royal Navy for failing to stop the attack.

Hugo Gruber

There were, in fact, other naval bombardments, but these attacks were thankfully rare during the First World War. In total, combining the number of those killed by attacks from airships, bomber aeroplanes, and the naval bombardments, 1,570 civilians were killed (4,050 injured) by enemy action on British soil, compared with over 67,000 killed in the Second World War.[153]

In addition to the deaths caused by direct enemy action, official records show that on the 'home front' 109,000 deaths were attributable to wartime privations, and this was followed by 183,000 deaths in the Spanish 'flu pandemic of 1918-1920.[154] Inflation pushed food prices up, driving many into a state of poverty, while the naval blockade, and the sinking of mercantile shipping by the German Navy, led to food and fuel shortages, and rationing was introduced in the last stages of the war. During the last year or so of the war *The Gospel Standard* wrapper carried large adverts asking its readers to eat less bread.[155]

Advert in *The Gospel Standard* asking people to reduce their bread intake

Mrs Elsie Dawson describes how panic buying at the start of the war quickly led to frustration as supplies became very low. For her parents, Mr and Mrs Joseph Aldworth, in their shop at St Albans, it was a relief when rationing was introduced, and they no longer had to feel personal responsibility for attempting to share out food fairly, as it was mandated by the government. Mrs Dawson wrote:

> ✍ It was difficult to get supplies to the shop, and difficult to ration them out fairly and justly when they did come. When, at last, rationing was introduced, it took the onus of the lack of supplies off the shopkeeper's shoulders, and people could then see that we could not do what they had previously thought we would not do.[156]

Support for the war effort

At home there was, of course, widespread public sympathy for those fighting for their country, and also for those affected by their loved one's call up. Some churches were especially active in supporting the war effort.

At Rehoboth Chapel, Coventry, there were regular reports in the local papers of generous collections being taken at the chapel on behalf of the Prince of Wales' National Relief Fund, and this was no doubt replicated in many other chapels.[157] This fund was established to help those suffering from 'industrial distress', a rather quaint way of referring to those reduced to poverty because the main wage earner had joined the forces. Established in the early days of the war, the fund raised one million pounds within a week of its formation.

The Friendly Companion regularly carried reports of the efforts of the congregation at Rochdale Road, Manchester, to supply the needs of those serving in the forces. The Particular Baptist War Work Society, Manchester, was able to report the following at the end of the war:

Rehoboth Chapel, Coventry

> ✍ They have obtained from August 17th, 1914, to March 1st, 1919, by donations, collections, etc., £876 18s. 11d. This has been used to send the following comforts, etc.: 591 pillows and cushions, 121 body belts, 129 washers, 302 pairs of mittens, 702 testaments and books, 818 handkerchiefs, 790 parcels food comforts, 1,270 shirts, 1,639 pairs socks, 58 bed jackets, 398 woollen mufflers, 200 woollen helmets and caps, 58 surgical slippers, 3 merlin chairs[158] (£5 each, sent to home for permanently injured and incurable cases), 11 woollen jackets; soap, stationery, sundries and magazines; also gifts to Serbian refugees, £2 19s. 6d. In addition to the above, £44 0s. 4d. was raised by a Young Ladies' Effort, October, 1918, by which parcels were sent to 'The Boys,' and £4 paid to Soldiers' Dependents.[159]

For some Strict Baptists such endeavours were regarded as tending towards legalistic works. Mr

Popham may have been reproving such thoughts when he placed the following quote below the report in *The Friendly Companion*: "We do not become righteous by doing what is righteous, but having become righteous we do what is righteous. *Luther*."

Letters from 'The Lads' survive, showing their appreciation of this work. One soldier wrote from Egypt:

> ✍ I received your most welcome parcel safe and sound, for which I thank you very much. I am still in the best of condition. I have seen ——, he was camped next to us, but we have moved again; I do not think he is far away, because we all moved together. He is looking well … The weather here is terribly hot, but we can stand it, for we are getting properly acclimatised to Egyptian weather … Kindly remember me at Sunday School. I thank you once more for your kindly thoughtfulness, and I hope that God will watch over us, and in the hour of battle give us courage to fight for the right, and when all is over return us safe and sound to dear old England.[160]

A similar work was carried out, knitting and sewing items of clothing for the troops, by the Young Women's Improvement Class at Hope Chapel, Rochdale, while the Young Men's Improvement Class sent packages of chocolates and other treats to the men serving abroad. The congregation at Rochdale also collected £21 for the Prince of Wales' National Relief Fund.[161]

Reading material for the front

Alongside the practical needs, the thirst for reading material on the front was immense. Many of the letters home ask for more sermons or magazines to be sent out, and there are many allusions to the blessing these were made to the men serving. Mr Salkeld writes of a time when he was a prisoner of war, with very little to do. His fellow prisoners almost fought over Bibles and other reading material in order to while away the hours.[162] Many sermons, particularly the monthly sermons published by Mr J. K. Popham and Mr Joseph Jarvis, were sent out to the men in the trenches.

The denominational magazines set up free distribution funds, which ensured that there was a plentiful supply of this literature to those serving in the forces, and many wrote from the front to thank the editors for the magazines:

> ✍ Dear Sir,
>
> I am enclosing 10 lire[163] for *The Friendly Companion* Free Distribution Fund. I think you will be a little encouraged to know that *The Friendly Companion* has found its way to Italy. We need such magazines, as there is very little opportunity to hear the gospel in the army; anything else but the truth. I think it a shame such books should be cut down, while Sunday newspapers should be allowed to increase their numbers into millions and boast about it. The other 10 lire is for *The Gospel Standard* Free Distribution Fund, if you will send it on, and oblige,
>
> T. Atkins,
>
> Italy,
>
> March, 1918.[164]

Another example:

> ✍ Dear Sir,
>
> Will you please accept £5 remittance for *The Friendly Companion* Free Distribution Fund ... I receive *The Friendly Companion* regularly and many a time have

Joseph Jarvis

> been helped and comforted when reading them. May God's blessing rest upon your work. I pray that more such literature may be spread about and be food for hungry souls, and be the means used to bring sinners to Christ...
>
> From a soldier.
>
> 7th May, 1918.[165]

One little paper produced for the troops during the war was *The Anzac Gospel Echo*, subtitled, "A Message from Home for the Men at the Front, for the Camp, the Deck and the Trenches." It was published by Benjamin D. Wileman, the son of the minister William Wileman, and brother to Clement Wileman, the editor of *The Gospel Echo*. The first number, published in September, 1916, consisted of four double column pages of general religious material. One piece signed "W" (possibly William Wileman, who was a prodigious writer of gospel tracts and pamphlets), and entitled "K. of K." was on Lord Kitchener of Khartoum, accompanying the front cover illustration of Kitchener. Why it took the name 'Anzac' – which stands for Australian and New Zealand Army Corps – is unknown, and whether more than one issue was ever published, remains unclear.

William Wileman

Unfortunately, one of the effects of the war was a severe shortage of paper, which had a direct impact on the publishing of the denominational magazines, sermons,[166] and other helpful literature.[167] First the quality of the paper had to be reduced, and then, as the war progressed, the magazines had to be shortened to have fewer and fewer pages each month, although despite this, the price of the magazines continued to rise. The last wartime issue of *The Gospel Standard* carried a notice stating that the magazine had not only had to be further reduced to just 24 pages, but that the printers would not be able to print enough copies for all subscribers to receive a copy, and that those they could print would be distributed as evenly as possible between the churches.[168]

James Walter Tiptaft

Strict Baptist businesses and the war

Some passing reference has already been made to the impact of the war on family owned businesses. Where the young men running the businesses were called up, it fell to the women in the family to take up the roles of the men and keep things going. For those who were shopkeepers, there were the additional burdens created by rationing, while almost every business was hit by a short supply of materials and rising costs.[169]

A cap badge made by J. W. Tiptaft and Son Ltd.

For one Strict Baptist business the war provided a different type of opportunity. In 1885, James Walter Tiptaft[170] started a jewellery business in Birmingham. James was a great-nephew of William Tiptaft, the well-known seceder from the Church of England, founder and pastor of the Strict Baptist church at Abingdon. At his great-uncle's funeral it is recorded that James prayed

Next page: Facsimile of the first issue of *The Anzac Gospel Echo*

No. 1 September, 1916

The Anzac Gospel Echo:

A MESSAGE FROM HOME FOR THE MEN AT THE FRONT.

For the Camp, the Deck, and the Trenches.

The Thunder of the Guns.

THERE are some lovely bits of countryside, "somewhere in Sussex," that suggest prosperity, content, and peace. I walked yesterday through meadows gay with flowers, through fields of corn just changing colour, and among the wild flowers, that bloom so richly by the margins of the lovely leafy lanes. It was all still and peaceful, though full of life; it was a haunt of ancient peace.

Yet as I walked, I became aware of a vague undercurrent of sound, hardly to be described as sound at all, yet distinctly heard. It was like a murmur or a crowding of the air, a faint trembling of the atmosphere. It was perhaps as much *felt* as heard, for at times it was as if the earth trembled in response to the vibration of the air. It was like a continuous roll of distant thunder, with now and then the sound of a distinct explosion.

It was the sound of our English guns in France. The sea was eleven miles to the south of me, and the wind blew from the south-east. The atmospheric conditions were favourable for carrying the sound from France to Sussex, a distance of about a hundred-and-fifty miles.

It seemed difficult to realise that I was enjoying so lovely a prospect of beauty and peace within hearing of the signs of death and destruction. The sharp contrast produced a feeling of awe and of sadness, as I thought of our brave men facing death, and of many of them being cut down in the prime of manhood in the defence of their homeland and their loved ones.

And even if the end is yet delayed, there can be no question as to the issue. Fraud and violence shall never win the final victory. That is reserved for liberty and justice, in whose name and cause the guns of Britain are thundering to-day.

LORD KITCHENER OF KHARTOUM

"K. of K."

These well-known initials have for some years been used to indicate the late Lord Kitchener, the hero of Khartoum, from which city and event he took his title. We cannot but admire his straightforward honesty of purpose, his quiet devotion to duty, and his uprightness of life. Nor can we overlook his value as a wise administra- in the service of the State. The great qualities of those who are placed in power at the present time must be viewed as gifts of God for the benefit of the nation. And it would be good for the nation if those in power would more acknowledge God in their counsels, and seek His guidance and help in the national crisis. Human power and wisdom can only be successful as they are guided by Him.

While looking at these initials a day or two ago, they seemed to suggest that they were familiar in another connection; and at once I remembered that they were to be found in my Bible. The Lord Jesus Christ is "*The King of Kings.*" He rules and reigns and overrules in the kingdoms of the earth, and has all power in heaven and in earth. He is not yet manifestly and openly the King of all the earth, for "we see not yet all things put under Him." But the day is coming when "He shall have put down all rule, and all authority, and power," and take His rightful place as universal King. Then "the kingdoms of this world shall become the kingdoms of our God and of His Christ, and He shall reign for ever and ever."

That will be a joyful era. There will then be an end of war, and there shall be an abundance of peace. His throne shall be established in righteousness, and all nations shall be His subjects.

W.

What Was the Reason?

A Bible on the continent once had a remarkable experience. The poor woman who owned it prized it very highly, and the priest wanted to have it destroyed. One day, as she was kneading her dough, she saw the priest coming, and at once placed her precious treasure inside a lump of dough, which in due time was sent to the oven. The Bible escaped, and the priest was disappointed.

Why did the woman want to keep her Bible? What was the reason?

There is now in England a Bible that has gone through some strange adventures. When H. M. Stanley started to cross the continent of Africa on his memorable journey, he had seventy-three books in three packs, weighing one hundred and eighty pounds. After he had gone three hundred miles he was obliged to throw away some of the books, on account of the fatigue of those carrying his baggage. As he continued on his journey, his library gradually diminished, until he had only one book left. We can imagine what that last one was. It was his Bible! He read that Book through three times during the journey. The Bible thus accompanies us through the changing and trying journey we are pursuing.

Why did not Stanley throw away his Bible? What was the reason?

"Cover my Defenceless Head."

A party of tourists formed part of a large company, gathered on the deck of an excursion steamer that was moving slowly down the Potomac river, one beautiful evening in the summer of 1881. A gentleman, who has since gained a national reputation as an evangelist, had been delighting the party with his happy rendering of many familiar hymns, the last being the sweet petition, so dear to every Christian heart, "Jesus, Lover of my soul."

The singer gave the first two verses with much feeling, and a peculiar emphasis upon the concluding lines that thrilled every heart. A hush had fallen upon the listeners, that was not broken for some seconds after the musical notes had died away. Then a gentleman made his way from the outskirts of the crowd to the side of the singer, and accosted him with, "Beg your pardon, stranger, but were you actively engaged in the late war?"

"Yes, sir," the man of song answered courteously, I fought under General Grant."

"Well," the first speaker continued, with something like a sigh, "I did my fighting on the other side, and think—indeed, am quite sure—I was very near you one bright night eighteen months ago this very month. It was much such a night as this. I am not mistaken—you were on guard duty. We of the South had sharp business on hand, and you were one of the enemy. I crept near your post of duty, my murderous weapon in my hand; the shadows hid me. Your beat led you into the clear light. As you paced back and forth, you were humming the tune of the hymn you have just sung. I raised my gun and aimed at your heart, and I had been selected by our commander for the work, for I was a sure shot. Then out upon the night rang the words:—

> 'Cover my defenceless head
> With the shadow of Thy wing.'

Your prayer was answered. I could'nt fire after *that.* And there was no attack made upon your camp that night. I felt sure, when I heard you sing this evening, that you were the man whose life I was spared from taking."

The singer grasped the hand of the Southerner, and said with much emotion, "I remember the night very well, and distinctly the feeling of depression and loneliness with which I went forth to my duty. I knew my post was one of great danger, and I was more dejected than I remember to have been at any other time during the service. I paced my lonely beat, thinking of home and friends, and all that life holds dear. The thought of God's care for all that He has created came to me with peculiar force. If He so cares for the sparrow, how much more for man created after His own image! and I sang the prayer of my heart, and ceased to feel alone. *How* the prayer was answered I never knew until this evening. My Heavenly Father thought best to keep the knowledge from me for eighteen years. How much of his goodness to us we shall be ignorant of until it is revealed to us by the light of eternity! 'Jesus, Lover of my soul,' has been a favourite hymn; now it will be inexpressibly dear."

The incident related in the above sketch is a true one, and was related to the writer by a lady who was one of the party on the steamer.

A Story of Lord Kitchener.

The Rev. G. E. Darlaston, of Crouch End, had the following authentic story of Lord Kitchener told him by a chaplain. "It was in India," said Mr. Darlaston in a sermon on the late War Secretary, which now appears in the Park Chapel magazine, "and this chaplain was much concerned with the amount of drinking in the Indian Army. He wrote to Lord Kitchener asking if he might have a few minutes to put certain plans before him and some of his staff. The meeting was arranged. 'Hope you have got it all cut-and-dried,' said one of the officers; 'K. can't stand palaver.' At the appointed time the General came in; as he took his seat he said, 'Well, what's the business, chaplain?' 'It is the King's business,' said the chaplain, 'and I think, your lordship, we ought to ask the King's guidance on what we shall do.' Kitchener looked into his eyes and said, 'You mean prayer?' 'Yes,' said the man, wondering at his own daring. 'Right you are!' said Kitchener, and he and all present knelt down. The chaplain poured out his soul, and prayed for men he knew and plans he had elaborated.

That night Kitchener sat for two hours over those plans, entered into every detail, exact and critical, and yet fruitful in suggestion, and when the business was done he gave his sanction that the scheme should be carried through. When it was over, the officer who had spoken before said, 'Well done; you are made for life.' And as a matter of fact, that chaplain is to-day one of the Superintendent-chaplains at the front. "Kitchener believed in a man who believed in his faith, who took his orders from his King, and who went right on at all risks to carry them out."

His Wife Worth Gold.

At a khaki wedding at Stevenage recently, the bridegroom produced a gold coin to pay the fees. Gold has become so rare that the parson asked him how he had possessed himself of the coin. The answer came pat: "I kept it for the occasion; I thought my wife was worth gold." As the gallant soldier was formerly a labourer the compliment was not merely a "pretty phrase." He deserves a good wife, and doubtless the bride is proud of her "boy."

A Little "Great" Man.

There lived a little man who has sometimes been called Napoleon "the Great," who tried to subdue the whole of Europe to his iron will. We have read of his schemes, his battles, and of his final downfall. He said in 1812, on his march to Moscow: "My five hundred thousand bayonets will accomplish more than the Prayers of Russia." But the prayers of Russia prevailed; and Napoleon brought back to France very few either bayonets or men.

There was a praying man on board a ship on one of the American lakes. His name was John Rutledge. The ice gathered around the ship, and destruction seemed inevitable, for the immense masses were gradually closing in, and the captain told them that no human effort could save them. He knelt down and prayed, and, as he prayed, the wind, which had been against them, changed, and blew behind, and opened a way through the ice, pushing it back from the ship and widening a passage, so that she was saved.

And when they came to the captain and said, "Shall we put on more canvas?" his reply was, "No! don't touch her! *Someone else is managing this ship.*"

It would be a grand thing for England to day if there were more prayer to God for help. He knows better how to "manage the ship" than the wisest of our statesmen, our admirals, and our generals. Victory is more likely to come to us by prayer than by anything we can do.

Three Facts that Cannot be Denied.

The *first* fact that cannot be denied is that any nation giving itself up to pleasure is on the high road to ruin. The *second* fact that cannot be denied is that the pages of history record the downfall of every nation that has thus tried to shut God out of its mind. And the *third* fact that cannot be denied is that England to-day is madly going after sinful pleasure even in the face of the sore judgment of God. Let the nation pause in its downward career of folly. It is still true of nations, as of individuals, that "whatsoever they sow, that shall they also reap."

Here are three instances, still fresh in the memory of writer and reader:—

1.—Martinique.

In 1902, the terrible volcanic eruption of Mont Pelee, which destroyed Martinique, and buried 40,000 of its inhabitants under the burning lava, was preceded by a long period of the most appalling wickedness and moral degradation on the part of the people, who, it is said, blasphemously crucified a pig on the Good Friday before the disaster. So that the special correspondent of the *Times* (March 29th, 1910), writing on the subject eight years after the event, said: "There are legends now of blasphemous rites which were in progress when the fire from the Lord out of heaven was rained down. There seems to have been good ground for describing Martinique as the wickedest spot in the West Indies."

2.—San Francisco.

And when on the morning of April 18th, 1916, earthquake and fire suddenly wiped out San Francisco, we are told by those well acquainted with the facts, that in "that gorgeous city of the West"—"that Californian Sodom"—"that refined sink of the most positive iniquity"—not only had "fair, dignified and educated women" acquired the opium habit, but the aristocracy generally were given over to lust and vice. This is quoted from *Blackwood*, June, 1906. And thus, having boasted of vile iniquity for nearly sixty years, God at length saw fit to pour down His wrath upon that city of the plain, worse than even Sodom.

3.—Messina.

Nor was there any exception in the case of the appalling disaster which befell Messina and Reggio; for at the close of 1908, only a few hours before that devastating earthquake, which laid Messina and the surrounding district in ruins, the unspeakably wicked and irreligious condition of some of the inhabitants was expressed in a series of violent resolutions which were passed *against all religious principles.* While the Journal "Il Telefono," printed in Messina, actually published in its Christmas number an abominable parody daring the Almighty to make Himself known by *sending an earthquake!* And in three days the earthquake came!

My Substitute.

By the late Sir James Young Simpson, the celebrated physician of Edinburgh.

When I was a boy at school, I saw a sight I never can forget—a man tied to a cart and dragged, before the people's eyes, through the streets of my native town, his back torn and bleeding from the lash. It was a shameful punishment. For *many* offences? No; for *one* offence. Did any of the townsmen offer to divide the lashes with him? No; he who committed the offence bore the penalty all alone. It was the penalty of a changing human law; for it was the last instance of its infliction.

I saw another sight—it matters not when—myself a sinner standing on the brink of ruin, deserving nothing but hell. For *one* sin? No; for many, many sins committed against the unchanging laws of God. But again I looked, and saw Jesus, my Substitute, scourged in my stead, and dying on the cross for me. I looked and cried, and was forgiven. And it seemed to me to be my duty to come here to tell you of that Saviour.

Printed for and Published by B. D. Wileman, 49, Imperial Buildings, Ludgate Circus, E.C.
2s. 6d. per 100, postage 6d.; 25s. per 1,000 carriage paid.

that William Tiptaft's mantle might fall on him; the extent to which that request was fulfilled cannot be readily ascertained, but he was later sent out to preach, and for over 40 years served as an itinerant minister until his death in 1923. In 1909, his son Norman[171] entered his father's jewellery business and during the First World War the expanding firm was required to produce items for the War Office and the Admiralty, including large numbers of cap badges and accoutrements for the uniform of both the British and Commonwealth armed forces. Many examples of the military badges from the period carry their stamp – J. W. Tiptaft and Son. The firm was also forced to diversify to become a munitions factory, and, alongside the medals and the cap badges, parts of armaments also rolled off the production lines.[172]

John Player

Another Strict Baptist business whose products most certainly reached the front in large quantities was John Player and Sons, the tobacconist. The company was founded in Nottingham, during 1877, by John Player, the son of John Dane Player, the Strict Baptist pastor at Saffron Waldon.[173] John Player sat under Mr Alfred Coughtry's ministry at Nottingham.[174] Mr Coughtry was, for a few years, editor of *The Gospel Standard*. After John Player died, his two sons, John Dane Player Jr., and William Goodacre Player, took the business on. Both were brought up at Nottingham Chapel. Smoking was endemic at the front during the First World War, with many of the men chain-smoking to calm their nerves. It is from this sort of behaviour that the expression, 'smoking like a trooper' had originated. It was not until 1929 that the first tentative evidence was published suggesting a link between smoking and lung cancer. As this evidence grew society's perception of smoking slowly changed, but during the war it would not have been unusual for Strict Baptist men to have smoked.

The war and the churches

As a specific part of studying the effect of the war on the home front, we also need to consider the effect of the war on the Strict Baptist churches.

Loss to the churches

The obvious and immediate effect of the war on the churches was the loss of young men, who would have been expected to be useful in the Lord's cause if they

A gathering of Strict Baptist ministers and deacons at Bexley, taken around the end of the war

Front row (left to right): Mr Durbridge (deacon), J. H. Gosden (Maidstone), A. H. Pounds (Bexley), J. Jarvis (Greenwich), C. Warren (Bexley), F. J. Prickett (Dartford and Tonbridge). Back row: G. Brooks (Foots Cray), Mr Fountain (deacon), H. L. Whitney (St Mary Cray), A. Brooks (Foots Cray), F. C. Mills (Bexley), J. C. Burt (Bexley)

had lived. Often there had been hope of a church member, a Sabbath school teacher, or an office-bearer in the church, but, when these young men were suddenly cut down, that hope was lost, and the Lord's people would have mourned, both for the loss of a loved one, and for the loss to the church on earth.

The onset of the war was keenly felt in the Sabbath schools, where classes for older students lost many of their boys. Sabbath school teachers were suddenly lost too. Mr F. C. Mills (see photo above), of Bexley, recorded in the obituary of one young man from the congregation, Rifleman Charles Pollard:

> ✍ The subject of this memoir was for many years the esteemed secretary of the Sunday School, and it was a great blow to many of the friends when he decided to close his business and join the army, saying, 'it was his duty to go.'

Charles Pollard

Yet, despite Mr Mills' evident sorrow at the decision, he shared the general desire of the Lord's people to see the Lord's hand in the matter and submission was given on both sides. With this in mind, he continues the obituary:

> ✍ In this, as in other things, he gave manifest evidence of the grace granted to commit his way unto the Lord, and through the subsequent course of training, and during the time in France, in letters to friends he abundantly testified to the power of that grace in the hour of need. Writing from France to a friend, he said, 'I prove more and more that his grace sustains, restrains and constrains.' [175]

Later on, many Sabbath Schools had to report at their annual prize givings the loss of students killed in fighting during the year. At the sixth Annual Meeting of the Sabbath School at Matfield, in 1917, the following was recorded:

> ✍ Mention was made of four young men who have lost their lives on the battlefield during the year. The first was Frank Buggs,[176] a scholar from the first, who was killed instantaneously on the morning of September 7th, aged 20 years, after being in the army only 10 months. Of him, there was reason to 'sorrow not, even as others which have no hope,' and as it might be of interest to some who were present, and to the praise and glory of God, an extract from a letter written by his mother was given …[177]
>
> The next to be killed was Percy Feaver, who also attended the Sunday School for a little while; then Stanley Standing and George Playford, who had been to the chapel as members of the congregation. What a mercy if any of us should meet,
>
> Where congregations ne'er break up,
> And Sabbaths have no end![178]

Ebenezer Chapel, Matfield (old chapel)

Another example comes from the Annual Gathering of the Sabbath School at Ebenezer Chapel, Clapham, on 13th March, 1918, where a public record of two deaths was made:

> ✍ Private Reginald Parris of the Royal Flying Corps[179] was taken ill with spotted fever and died at

Aldershot; this is a keen bereavement to his dear parents, he being their only child. The family left Clapham to reside in Croydon, and there the dear boy became deeply attached to the friends at Tamworth Road, where he became very useful in the Sabbath School. We have evidence that the work of grace was begun in his soul many months previous to joining the army. He was laid to rest by Mr Medhurst of Croydon, 'in sure and certain hope of a glorious resurrection!'

Private Willie Appleton of the Queen's Royal West Surrey Regiment was killed in action by a shell during the heavy fighting of last September in France. He was a scholar in this school for many years; letters have been received by various friends intimating that the Word of God was his chief delight and comfort, even in the trenches. He had been in several engagements before the final one in which he met his death. He was much strengthened and helped to endure the roughness, exposure and privations of a soldier's life by the words, 'My times are in thy hand' (Psalm 31: 15), being applied with power to his soul. To a friend he wrote, a few weeks before the end came,

Willie Appleton

'I soon may be actively engaged in all the horrors of war, as my regiment is now in the front-line trenches, and we may receive orders at any moment to go over the top. Those words, "My times are in thy hand" are still sweet to me, and I feel it a great favour to know that I have so many praying friends at home, for "the effectual fervent prayer of a righteous man availeth much." I have to continually ask God to prepare me for whatsoever his sovereign will has ordained for me in the future.'

Our dear young friend has now been slain upon the battlefield, and we esteem it a great favour that we have not to sorrow as those without hope, and are comforted in believing that with him, 'It is well.' [180]

While the war undoubtedly brought loss to the churches in some cases, it was also the means used in the Lord's strange providence to make provision for the churches. Clement Drury, the deacon at Enford Chapel, not only met his wife in the war, but was also moved from Ticehurst, in Kent, to Wiltshire, where it was the Lord's will that he should serve as a deacon for the remainder of his life. His obituary reads:

✍ He joined the army in 1914, during which time he saw active service in France, and in 1916 was posted to Larkhill on Salisbury plain when, whilst attending Netheravon Chapel, he met his wife. This was the means of him eventually coming to Enford Chapel, where the aged deacon sought his help in the services. He was baptised by Mr Caleb Sawyer, pastor at Mayfield, in January, 1939, and appointed deacon in 1943. A good many of our friends who were engaged in the 1939-45 War, and who were posted to the plain, will remember the warmth of the welcome they had at Enford.[181]

The felt need of prayer

Another effect of the war on the churches was to bring people to pray. At the very beginning of the war, Mr Popham called for a week of prayer among the 'Gospel Standard' churches.[182] In fact, the nation at large turned to prayer. For some, these prayer meetings were among their earliest memories. Mildred Steere, the wife of David Steere, the pastor at Shoreham, was just two years old when war was declared. She wrote of her childhood memories of the wartime prayer meetings: "During the First World War, after the services at chapel, we all met in the Old School, Knockholt, for prayer meetings. I can remember how burdened the old men were in prayer for our men at the front." [183]

David Steere

From January, 1916, the Archbishop of Canterbury, Randall Davidson, set aside the first Lord's Day in the year for prayer, and similarly 4th August, the anniversary of the outbreak of the war in 1914. While these days of prayer were primarily observed by the Church of England, other churches were encouraged to follow their lead. Onc example, reported in the local newspaper, was a meeting for prayer at the Strict Baptist Chapel in Tenterden:

> ✎ SPECIAL INTERCESSIONAL SERVICES were held in all the churches and chapels on Sunday. At Jireh Chapel reference was made to the state of the country and the war. Prayer was offered by the pastor, Mr Weeks; a special prayer meeting was held, at which a large number were present. Reference was made to the special need of prayer and supplication, with confession of sins to God, on behalf of our nation.[184]

Jireh Chapel, Tenterden, prior to the renovations of the 1980s

However, Archbishop Davidson resolutely refused to call for a day for national humiliation and prayer, believing that the term "humiliation" would be interpreted as a sign of weakness in enemy propaganda, and would therefore hinder the war effort. His mistake in this was, of course, not to accept that humiliation in this context would have referred to an attitude before God, in the light of the war being an effect of human sin and of divine judgement, and an acknowledgement of the nation's dependence on the help of God, rather than any inclination to yield before the enemy. Eventually, however, in the face of a number of petitions and public campaigns, a day of national humiliation and prayer was called by King George V on the first Lord's Day of 1918, 6th January.[185]

On that day appointed for national humiliation and

Tadworth Strict Baptist Chapel

prayer, the Prime Minister, David Lloyd George, famously attended a service at the Strict Baptist Chapel at Tadworth, Surrey. Someone who was present at the service wrote:

> ✍ Doubtless you will be interested to know that Mr Lloyd George and his secretary were at chapel tonight. They did not come in till about 6.45 p.m., but doubtless he thought the service commenced at 6.30 p.m. instead of 6 o'clock. I was very surprised and very pleased to see him there, considering it was a very dark and wet night, and his house is a mile and a quarter away from the chapel. It being the first Lord's Day in the month, it was ordinance Sunday, and the Prime Minister and his secretary stopped to witness it. After the service he spoke to several of the people, and seemed loath to go, for he seemed quite at home. He congratulated Mr Adams (the minister) for his admirable sermon, and apologised for being late. He gave Mr I— his donation and his secretary did the same. Mr Adams is a very patriotic man, and prayed for the king and nation very nicely. The king's proclamation was read twice, and really the services were most applicable for the occasion. The morning text was Haggai 2, last clause of 19th verse; and the evening one was Deuteronomy 9, the first four words of 7th verse.[186]

However, the national movement for prayer was not without its problems. A friend writing to Mr Popham enquired whether it was right for ministers and members of 'Gospel Standard' churches to mix with other denominations for the purpose of public meetings in which various churches in a locality came together for 'intercessory prayer' on behalf of the land and nation. Mr Popham replied in the negative in the wrapper of *The Gospel Standard*:

> ✍ We have our own chapels in which to meet and unite in prayer for our king, country, army and navy, and for the kingdom of God to come. How can people, whose views of God, of sin, of salvation, are diametrically opposed, agree in worship, confession, and hope? 'Can two walk together except they be agreed?' We much dislike the word 'intercessory' in this connection. It should be remembered by our people that it is used by the sacerdotalist, who loves to magnify his priestly position. Why should we follow him in his Romeward movement? All his ritual is doctrine in his meaning. Philpot said true religion

might be described by one word: 'Separation, separation, separation.'[187]

While there was appreciation that the king had called for national prayer, there was some concern as to whether it was right to set aside the Lord's Day for this purpose, rather than continuing to devote the Lord's Day wholly to the worship of the Lord. Mr Windridge, the pastor at Providence Chapel, Ponsard Road, London, expressed this concern in his diary:

> ✍ It may be remembered that the king issued a proclamation setting apart the first Lord's Day in 1918, as a day of national prayer in our time of distress. I could not feel that this was right, as the Lord's Day is already set apart by the King of kings for the worship of himself. The church therefore passed the following resolution: 'While exceedingly glad to see that the king has called upon us as a nation to seek unto God in our national distress, we feel that a week-day would be more appropriately set apart for this purpose than a Lord's Day; and we accordingly appoint the two hours from 10 a.m. to 12 p.m. on December 26th, for our own church and congregation to meet for humiliation on account of national calamities, confession of national sins, and prayer for national deliverance.' I was afterwards accused of being disloyal to the king; but there was nothing new in such a charge: Ezra 4: 15; Nehemiah 6: 6-7; Esther 3: 8; Luke 23: 2; Acts 16: 20-21.[188]

The mixture of distress at the fact the Church of England still seemed to reject the need of a national day for prayer; joy that despite this the king had appointed a day for prayer; and yet concern that the day appointed was the Lord's Day, was aptly summed up in poetry by Charles Jefferies in *The Friendly Companion*:

Charles Jefferies

> Well; though our rulers do not seem
> To honour God; nor to esteem
> His name or power of any worth,
> Our king, God save him, issues forth
> A proclamation that one day
> Be used to supplicate and pray
> The Majesty of heaven to heed
> Our nation's hour of direst need.
> He passes powers and prelates by
> To raise to heaven an ardent cry;
> While church and state the need reject –

> The king, as head, does prayer elect.
> And with him let *our* voices join,
> And supplicate heaven's throne divine;
> Casting our sloth and pride aside
> And beg the Lord will with us bide.
> And though we'd choose a different day
> To weep and mourn, and beg and pray;
> Yet let us seize the day that's given,
> And importune the God of heaven.
> On the first Sabbath of the year
> Let all before the Lord appear;
> And pray the Lord of earth and heaven
> Successes to our hosts be given.[189]

Mr Walter Croft, writing in *The Friendly Companion,* reported on the national day of prayer called for Lord's Day, 4th August, 1918. His report also states, however, that the Strict Baptists held a meeting for prayer on the Monday, presumably because of their concern over using the Lord's Day for national prayer:

> ✍ It was announced that Lord's Day, August 4th, 1918, had been set apart by the king to be observed as a national day of prayer for Divine help and deliverance. On that memorable day the king and queen, prime minister, cabinet ministers, judges, magistrates and other responsible men attended Divine service, and unitedly implored God's help in our national extremity. In nearly all the churches and chapels throughout the land, special prayers for the nation were offered up on that day.
>
> On the following day, Monday, August 5th, a large open air prayer meeting was held at Bexley, Kent, under the presidency of Pastor A. H. Pounds, Strict Baptist Chapel, Bexley. We sang together that grand old hymn, 'O God, our help in ages past,' and several brethren, including Messrs Booth, Jarvis and Pounds, interceded with our Triune God to appear for us as a nation. Many of us then thought that deliverance was certain to follow these Scriptural proceedings, and the events that followed confirmed our hopes.[190]

A. H. Pounds

Mr Croft backs up his final assertion by quoting an assessment of the progress of the war in the days immediately following the national day of prayer, by the historian, Major General Sir Archibald Montgomery:

> ✍ So far as one can judge, no surprise has ever been more complete than was that of the Germans on August 8th, 1918. It is astonishing that this should have been so, for between July 30th and August 8th, the Cavalry Corps of three divisions, 14 divisions of infantry, over 2,000 guns, and some 450 tanks were concentrated east of Amiens on a front of about ten miles, within striking distance of the unsuspecting Von der Marwitz, who commanded the opposing German Army. The actual attack … went without a hitch. The cavalry, after its many disappointments in previous offensives, at last found its opportunity. The Germans were swept off their feet, and never really recovered from the overwhelming nature of the disaster.[191]

Surely an example of answered prayer!

Witness against Sabbath desecration

The war also elicited a witness on the part of the churches against the particular evil of desecrating the Lord's Day. While there was understanding that at the front line the Lord's Day may not be observed in the same manner as at home in peaceful conditions, yet this certainly did not constitute grounds for failure to observe the Lord's Day away from the front line. During the harvest of 1917, for example, Sabbath farm labour received direct sanction from the Archbishop of Canterbury. Meetings were arranged in protest against this, including a meeting at Providence Chapel, Cranbrook, on 30th April, 1917, where the pastor, Mr George Rose, moved the resolution: "That this meeting of Cranbrook inhabitants deplore the Archbishop of Canterbury in violating the express commands of the Bible in relation to Sunday work, and respectfully call upon parliament to discourage all work that tends to the secularization of the Lord's Day." [192]

Mr H. J. Piggott, the deacon at Hope Chapel, Horsham, wrote to his local paper:

> ✍ Dear Sir,
>
> I beg to offer my sincere protest to the suggestion of Mr J. E. Barnard that the rifle range be opened on Sundays. Most emphatically do I say, 'Better not know how to shoot at all than desecrate the Lord's Day by practising then.' I presume that none but an infidel will deny but that victory and defeat are in the hands of the Lord. How then can we expect his blessing upon what would be a direct breach of the 4th commandment? …[193]

Personal stands also had to be made against Sabbath desecration. Mr William Savory, of Coventry,[194] was

George Rose and Providence Chapel, Cranbrook

requested by his manager to go in to work at the Humber car factory on the Lord's Day, to light the furnaces, so that production of military equipment could be increased. He conscientiously refused, saying that he would not come in to work before midnight on the Lord's Day evening. His manager told him the furnaces would never be hot enough for work first thing Monday morning, if he lit them so late. Eventually, under pressure, the manager reluctantly agreed to allow Mr Savory to attempt lighting them in the early hours of Monday morning. The first Monday morning, Mr Savory rose at midnight and went in to light the furnace, and when the men arrived on the factory floor the heat in the furnace was hotter than had ever been known before. After that, the furnaces at the Humber factory were never lit before Monday morning, and production was increased according to requirements.[195]

William Savory and his wife, Mary Ann

Continuing despite the circumstances

Generally, however, whatever was happening in the congregation, the ministry of the churches continued as it always had. Church business did not stop for the war, and we find ministers continuing to be called to take up pastorates, and men being sent out to preach. At Folkestone, Kent, the settlement of Mr T. H. B. Hayler as pastor was reported as follows in the local newspaper:

> On Sunday last Mr H. [*sic*] Hayler commenced his ministry at the Zion Strict Baptist Chapel, St Michael's Street, Folkestone. This old established place of worship has been without a pastor for 39 years. The newly appointed minister comes from Brighton. A special service for humiliation, confession, supplication, and thanksgiving was held on Sunday.[196]

Thomas H. B. Hayler

A number of well-known ministers were also taken to their eternal rest during the war. Mr John Newton, the beloved pastor at Hanover, Tunbridge Wells, died on 15th November, 1914. An account of him was subsequently published in *The Friendly Companion.* Letters written by some of the young soldiers in this book suggest that this account was made a special blessing to some of those facing the pressures of army life away from home and church.[197]

Meanwhile, Mr Edwin Picknell, the pastor at Station Road Chapel, Redhill, and the chairman of the Gospel Standard Societies, passed away suddenly on Monday morning, 22nd April, 1918. Both of these deaths were reported in the daily newspapers of the time.

Newspapers also provide other evidence that, for the home churches, life during the war continued pretty much as it had before. One example of this is the report of the annual winter Sabbath School treat at Ebenezer

John Newton

Strict Baptist Chapel, Broad Oak, Heathfield. The report records that the children met in the schoolroom at 1.30 p.m. for a short service and address by the pastor, Mr William W. West, who "gave some sound advice to the young people, and impressed upon them the importance of honesty and obedience when they grow up into business life, as by the exercise of such qualities, success and prosperity were within the reach of all."[198] After tea, between 30 and 40 children gave recitations, and the pastor presented prizes for attendance and good conduct.

Edwin Picknell

Also in connection with Ebenezer Chapel, Broad Oak, is the report of a burial in the chapel graveyard accompanied with full military honours. The deceased, Ebenezer John Miles, had died suddenly while carrying out his shoe making business in Heathfield town centre, and was attended by an off duty medic from the Royal

Army Medical Corps. Mr West took the funeral, and the local paper reports that "while the mourners stood bareheaded in the sunshine, round the remains of their loved one, the Last Post was sounded by Bugler Reeves, of the 3rd (London) Royal Army Medical Corps, Sergeant Major James, Staff Sergeant Fairman, and six men of the Royal Army Medical Corps standing at attention by the graveside."[199]

William W. West

It is evident that the soldiers returning on leave from the front, and those in training in various parts of the country, found the services of the Lord's house to be a great comfort to them. In the midst of massive change in their lives, and the loss of many things they held dear, there was some comfort to be had that the worship of God continued, without change or abatement. To some extent, it mirrored the unchangeable nature of the God they worshipped, and would have directed them to words of comfort, such as: "I am the LORD, I change not; therefore ye sons of Jacob are not consumed" (Malachi 3: 6).

Ebenezer Sayers

This was true for Ebenezer Sayers, whose appreciation of being able to attend Mr John Kemp Jr's ministry at Ebenezer Chapel, Luton, is evident in the obituary his wife wrote after his early death, at the age of 27, in 1925:

> ✍ He joined the army, and went to Luton to train, where he met many kind friends. Mr Kemp's ministry was very helpful to him, and he said he felt unable to thank the Lord sufficiently for placing him where he could hear the Word so faithfully set forth. After a time, he went to France, and although in the midst of danger, he was preserved, and brought safely through. Very many times I felt he would never return, and his letters made me feel he was being prepared for another world, as his one thought was eternity. But God's watchful eye was upon him, and towards the last part of the terrible war, he was sent back as instructor at a school several miles behind the line. Oh what terrible times they were, and how merciful the Lord was in sparing him, while thousands were cut down without hope! He never had to go in the line again, and came home at the Armistice being signed. He went to work in London, where he remained until his death.[200]

Another Strict Baptist soldier, from the chapel in Brantford, Canada, wrote most appreciatively of the opportunities he had of worshipping at the Strict Baptist chapels in England. He said:

> ✍ It was a great comfort for me to get away from the camp and to get amongst the people of God. If these lines come before any God-fearing man who served in the army, he will understand what I mean. While at Bramshott Camp, I went on leave into Yorkshire and spent the Sabbath day amongst the dear people at Thurlstone, where I felt myself one of them in Christian fellowship. I also visited Slaithwaite Particular Baptist Church during my leave. I had about two months amongst the friends at Hastings, and enjoyed sitting under the Gospel as preached by Mr Brooker, and I made many friends there. Also I remember the friends at Shoreham-on-Sea, Haslemere, Fernhurst, Ripe and Maidstone.[201]

Hymns for time of war

A number of hymns were written for use in worship during the war. It was obviously a concern during the war that *Gadsby's Selection of Hymns* (as it then stood, without the supplement of Occasional Hymns) was somewhat deficient in hymns related to topics associated with the war – including repentance for national sins. Some of the hymns written during the war were undoubtedly composed in an attempt to fill that gap. To our knowledge, none of these are still in use, so we reproduce one written by the Strict Baptist minister, Mr Benjamin A. Warburton, pastor at Preston and later at The Tabernacle, Brighton:

> O God of hosts, arise!
> Hear our united cries,
> Make war to cease:
> Its desolating hand
> Doth press upon our land
> O do thou take command;
> Lord, send us peace.
>
> We own thy sovereign right
> Our country thus to smite,
> For sins increase.
> Thy Word, with wisdom stored,
> Is mocked – thy day ignored,
> Yet do have mercy, Lord;
> O send us peace!

Those who on sea and land
For our defence do stand,
In mercy bless.
Teach them to look to thee,
Thou their protector be,
Grant speedy victory;
Lord, send us peace.

Those who now wounded lie,
In quivering agony,
Deign thou to ease;
Close thou the glazing eyes,
And hear the suppliant's cries;
O God of mercy, rise!
Send, send us peace![202]

In 1916, B. A. Warburton gathered together six of the hymns he had composed during the war and published a small booklet entitled *Hymns for Time of War*.[203] Given Mr Warburton's poetic abilities, it is likely that these hymns were all original compositions. It has not proved possible to locate a copy of this booklet, though there is extant a larger booklet of 29 hymns by B. A. Warburton, also entitled *Hymns for Time of War*. Although it is undated, it contains references to tunes in *The Companion Tune Book*, showing that it must post-date 1927, when the tune book was compiled. This suggests that it was probably published during the Second World War.

Later in the war, a pamphlet of ten hymns was published by Farncombe and Sons, entitled *Hymns for Times of National Distress*. It is reputed to have been published by the Gospel Standard Societies, and contained hymns by Isaac Watts, Samuel Medley, John Newton, and Anne Steele.[204] It was first advertised in the wrapper of *The Gospel Standard* in May, 1918.

NOW READY.

THE STRICT BAPTIST
ACTIVE SERVICE HYMNBOOK,
Containing 50 Hymns from
GADSBY'S SELECTION.
In stiff paper covers.

Price 3d. each (postage ½d.), 12 copies 3s. (postage 3d.), 50 cop
12s. 6d. (post free).

Can be localised, with name of Chapel, etc.
Terms on application.
London: C. J. Farncombe & Sons, Ltd., 30 Imperial Buildings, Ludgate Circus, E.

Advert for the *Active Service Hymnbook* that appeared in *The Gospel Standard*

Because of its physical size, *Gadsby's* hymn book was difficult for soldiers to carry, along with a Bible, in their packs. In response to this problem, in 1918 Mr John Raven, the pastor at Smallfield and Shaw's Corner Chapel, Redhill, published a selection of 50 hymns taken from *Gadsby's* in a little 32 page booklet, entitled *The Strict Baptist Active Service Hymnbook*.[205] Although produced late in the war,[206] the little hymn book appears to have been well received by the servicemen.

The war also gave rise to some hymn tunes. One of these is the six line, 7s metre tune, Harold, which is published in *The Companion Tune Book*. It was composed by John Grace, the deacon at Thornhill Chapel, Yorkshire, and father of Er Grace, later pastor at Ossett. The tune was named after John Grace's son, Private Harold Grace, who served in the Durham Light Infantry. Sent to France on 30th January, 1918, Harold was killed on 21st March, during the Battle of St. Quentin, the opening engagement of the Second Battle of the Somme. He was 19 years old and had seen just seven weeks of active service. His body was never located, and he has no known burial place; his name is commemorated on the Arras Memorial.

Harold Grace

It is understood that the common metre tune, Passchendale, attributed to Ethel Allan in *The CompanionTune Book*, also has its origins in the war, although the story associated with it now appears to be lost in the mists of time.[207]

Right: John Grace and his wife

Below: Opening lines of the tune 'Harold'

The war and ministers

As the war rolled on, problems started to arise among the churches with regard to the ministry. On a practical level, travel became very expensive, and, with many churches reliant on an itinerant ministry, this placed a severe financial burden on them. A campaign by *The Christian's Pathway* magazine to get reduced rail fares for ministers was unsuccessful, despite letters to the Board of Trade, the Railway Executive Committee, and the railway companies.[208] The editor, Francis J. Kirby, therefore gave the advice: "It remains for the churches to pay the increased cost of travel, not the minister, unless exceptional circumstances exist, and then only by mutual agreement." [209]

Several sermons were published in the magazines of the period on the subject of war and its effects. One example of these is entitled "The Soldier's Vocation", on the text, 'Fight the good fight of faith, lay hold on eternal life, whereunto thou art also called, and hast professed a good profession before many witnesses' (1 Timothy 6:12). It was a memorial sermon preached at Union Chapel, Bethersden, by Mr Herbert Dawson, after the death of Private James Pearson, a member of the congregation, on the battlefield in France.[210]

James Pearson

Despite the trying circumstances, there are many records of the blessing the ministry was made. Grace

Herbert Dawson

Lilian Paul, of Brighton, wrote in her diary about the time of the death of her brother Reuben in the war:

> ✍ Heard Mr [*Caleb*] Sawyer very well indeed. It was the first time he preached at Galeed [*Chapel, Brighton*] and he knew nothing at all of our sorrow and loss, and his remarks were most fitting when he spoke of rejoicing in Christ as a Brother born for adversity, and said it might be in some heavy blow, just as if he had known our case.[211]

On another occasion Grace wrote:

> ✍ Our pastor [*Mr J. K. Popham*] spoke from John 11: 15: 'I am glad for your sakes that I was not there' etc. It was a remarkable discourse on Christ delaying answers for our good and his glory. He said: 'Could not the Lord have prevented this trouble, this death? Yes, but it is better that he should not, better for you, and glory will come to him.'[212]

Ministers and conscription

With the introduction of conscription, many ministers found themselves obliged to sign up. While ministers associated with any formally registered church body were exempted from military service, the 'Gospel Standard' churches were independent and unregistered, so the ministers of these churches were not automatically exempted.[213] In most cases, those ministers holding the office of pastor were recognised as 'regular ministers of a religious denomination', and thus exempted from service, but for itinerant ministers the situation was quite different. Generally, the courts did not recognise itinerant ministers as being 'regular ministers' and forced them to sign up.[214] In some cases, the committee of the Gospel Standard Societies had to make representations on behalf of ministers,[215] and it must have been an anxious time for many churches. It is recorded of Walter Croft, who later became the pastor at West Street Chapel, Croydon:

> ✍ During the First World War (1914-18), Mr Croft, who was far from being robust and suffered from poor eyesight, feared he might be called upon to serve in the army. This caused many a prayer to ascend to the throne of grace, and in due time he received an exemption from active service, but was required to join the local volunteers instead.[216]

Some ministers who had to sign up were, in God's kind providence, given posts which meant they could continue preaching. One example of this was Mr J. S. Partridge, of Wellingborough. Mr Partridge signed up under the Red Cross and St John's Ambulance, and spent the war nursing wounded soldiers at Burghley House, near Stamford.[217]

J. S. Partridge

Other ministers who were called up were sent to the front, and exercised the ministry where possible. The following is recorded of Mr Reginald Morris, later the pastor at Clifton, Bedfordshire:

> ✍ Reginald Morris enlisted as a sergeant and was appointed as a clerk in the Royal Engineers section of the 59th North Midland Divisional Headquarters [*The Staffordshire Regiment*] on 24th February, 1915. That day he noted the appointment in his diary and wrote 'The LORD shall be thy confidence, and shall keep thy foot from being taken.' Two days later on 26th February he noted in his diary: 'But I am jealous of my heart lest it should once from thee depart.' An elderly friend at Bethel Chapel, Luton remembered that when she was about seven or eight years old, he preached at Bethel in his army uniform, and addressed the Sunday School during the afternoon, speaking on the subject of the twelve wells of water at Elim in Exodus 15: 27.[218]

Reginald Morris

Throughout his life, Mr Morris, like the vast majority of his generation, remained very reticent to talk about his wartime experiences. He saw front line service on the Western Front, and was mentioned in dispatches for bravery on 7th April, 1918, at Passchendaele, during the Fourth Battle of Ypres.[219] He was also awarded the Meritorious Service Medal for bravery.[220]

Mr Samuel G. May had been sent out to preach in 1904, but at the commencement of the war in 1914, he signed up, and joined the army. Throughout the war he was stationed in Calais, where he was put in charge of the army bakery. At the end of the war he returned to the ministry, and was always counted a most acceptable minister.[221]

Samuel May

Some men entered the ministry during the war, and were then immediately faced with the issue of conscription. Richard Nock of Windmill Lane Chapel, Smethwick, was sent out to preach in February, 1916, just after compulsory conscription. The authorities refused to recognise his appointment as a minister, and took him to court for failing to join up. The magistrates formed the opinion that "the appellant was not a regular minister, that he was elected only by a body of persons, who were not named or defined and had no identity, and that he was practically self-elected and not actually responsible to any congergation, church, committee, or other body. They therefore held that he was not exempted from military service."[222] Richard Nock had to enlist in the army, and served in the Devonshire Regiment. However, as *The Christian's Pathway* reported in May, 1918: "As he has been moved from one locality to another, so opportunities have arisen for him to preach the gospel, and, from all we hear, not without results."[223] This seems, therefore, to have been one of the instances where, despite appearances, the things which happened had 'fallen out rather unto the furtherance of the gospel.'

Richard Nock

Another minister sent out to preach during the war was Mr Thomas W. R. Walter:

> ✍ He became exercised about the work of the ministry, but kept his exercises to himself for years; fearing all arose from pride, he attempted to put them aside. It seems, however, that God's constraint was upon him, and the words followed him: 'Cry aloud, spare not, lift up thy voice like a trumpet, and shew my people their transgression, and the house of Jacob their sins' (Isaiah 58:1). He still shrank back, feeling his unworthiness and unfitness. He said: 'How can I go who am such a sinner, so full of imperfections? Surely the people will say, "Physician, heal thyself."' During these exercises he became eligible for military service, and he made a vow to the Lord that if exempted from this he would enter the Lord's service upon the first opening. To the surprise of many and the extreme annoyance of the official, he was exempted so long as he remained in the employment he then had. After he had been preaching a short while, the urgent need of men resulted in his being called up for service, but he was posted to the Pay Corps and stationed near to his home thus enabled to fulfil his engagements. In this he saw the Lord's overruling power.[224]

Other ministers who were not granted exemption included Mr John Stone,[225] the pastor at West Hartlepool,[226] and Mr William P. Belcher of Southport,[227] both of whose appeals against conscription were thrown out by the courts, and they were compelled to enlist. Mr Ebenezer S. Hickmott, of Hawkhurst was also forced to join up in spite of the intervention of Mr Francis J. Kirby, who spoke for him at the West Kent Appeals Tribunal, explaining that, as the appellant's congregation was poor, he had to make ends meet by taking on boot mending work, but that he was engaged to preach every Lord's Day, and for the purposes of the law was a minister of religion.[228]

John Stone

Ebenezer Hickmott

Matthew Mercer

For Mr Matthew Mercer, of Cranbrook, the pathway was quite different. The Lord preserved him from conscription so that he could preach. While he was under exercise concerning the work of the ministry, he felt he had a higher calling than going to fight. He watched in dismay as many men of his age voluntarily signed up, and then seemingly mocked him for not being willing to go, telling him he was fighting against God's will in not going. Then, after conscription was introduced, the way to the ministry seemed closed against him, and it looked as if he would have to join up. But in this situation, it somehow came about that he was not required to sign up. Although he does not record details, he regarded this as the appearing of the Lord to deliver him from conscription. He wrote, "When the Lord makes a way it matters not who may be against him. He is of one mind and none can turn him, and he stands by those who feel most helpless and needy." Eventually, in December, 1917, the door opened for him to commence preaching.[229]

Because the 'Gospel Standard' churches were unregistered, they did not send any chaplains to preach to those serving on the front, although several other denominations did, including the Free Presbyterian Church of Scotland.[230] One of Mr J. K. Popham's sons, Rev. Alfred E. Popham, served as a padre in the Church of England during the war, and was decorated twice for his bravery – he was gazetted for the Military Cross on 23rd June, 1915, and awarded a bar to the Military Cross on 31st July, 1917. He later became the vicar of Boxgrove Priory, West Sussex.

New openings for ministry

For some Strict Baptist ministers, the war provided new openings for their ministry.

Mr Joseph Reed[231] had been called to the pastorate at Trinity Chapel, Aldershot, in 1912 (he would later hold a brief pastorate at Mount Zion Chapel, Leatherhead). During the war his congregation was suddenly swelled with a large number of servicemen stationed in the nearby Aldershot Barracks. These young men caused him considerable concern, both for their spiritual and their natural welfare. He wrote to *The Christian's Pathway* soon after the beginning of the war, "If there are any friends connected with the Strict Baptists to whom we in Aldershot could be of any service – I am thinking especially of our soldiers – the friends would esteem the rendering of that service a

Joseph Reed and his family

great pleasure and privilege."[232] In this endeavour he was greatly assisted by Mr and Mrs Drake, members of his congregation. Mr Drake had served in the 9th Lancers during the Boer War, and was able to give helpful advice to the young men stationed at Aldershot and attending Trinity Chapel. Mrs Drake sent up details of several of the men stationed with them to 'The Muster Roll' in *The Christian's Pathway*, including details of Mr Frank L. Gosden, who would later hold pastorates at Heathfield and Brighton.[233]

Mr Joseph P. Wiles was the pastor at Devizes. His son, Harold Wiles, was severely injured at the battle of Loos on 25th September, 1915, and Mr Wiles was given the information that Harold was not expected to live.

Mr Wiles therefore made the journey to France, in order to see his son in the military hospital. While he was in France, Mr Wiles was invited to preach on Lord's Day evening, 3rd October, 1915, at a local Reformed church, in Boulogne-sur-Mer, which he did, in French. Bilingual notes of the sermon were published in *The Little Gleaner*, alongside an account of how he came to preach there.[234] In the event, Harold Wiles survived. He held high office in the civil service, and was knighted for his services to the country.[235]

The war and the call to the ministry

As the war would have been a formative influence in the experience of all the men who returned, in the Lord's providence it also played a part in the experience of those who later became ministers. Several Strict Baptist ministers first received intimation that they were to preach the gospel, while serving on the battlefield. Mr James Burgess, who later became pastor at Bournemouth, began to have thoughts of the ministry during a period of hospitalisation in England, following severe injury while fighting:

> ✍ … it was about this time of his suffering that he was exercised about the ministry, which exercise was confirmed by the word, 'I shall not die, but live, and declare the works of the LORD.' Although so weak, he was gradually strengthened and eventually received the consent of his church at home to speak in the Lord's Name, whilst still serving in the army.[236]

The obituary of Mr George Humberstone records:

> ✍ It was during the First World War in 1917 that I received, I believe, my first real impressions concerning the ministry … In the summer of 1917, I was on the Somme Front, and we were out of the front line for a short rest, in a village just behind the field artillery, when the enemy began to literally rain shells at the village. It was a dreadful time, and I was filled with solemn feelings and many fears, when the last verse in hymn 64 [*Gadsby's Selection*] was spoken to me powerfully:
>
> Plagues and deaths around me fly;
> Till he bids, I cannot die;
> Not a single shaft can hit,
> Till the God of love sees fit.
>
> Faith rose in a moment, but this followed just as powerfully: 'I shall not die, but live, and declare the works of the LORD,' and I felt a solemn persuasion that I should be brought through, return home, and one day preach the gospel. I was brought through some of the worst scenes in the war, had very many narrow escapes, without an injury. Many years of exercise followed concerning the ministry. When favoured and Christ was precious, it was desired and longed for; when darkness, trial and temptation were mine, which they often were, then I felt the biggest fool for ever thinking about it. Yet the exercise was more or less kept alive in my heart, and oftentimes the last verse in hymn 144 [*Gadsby's Selection*] would be very precious,
>
> Then will I tell to sinners round,
> What a dear Saviour I have found;
> I'll point to thy redeeming blood,
> And say, 'Behold the way to God.'[237]

Mr Frank L. Gosden says:

> ✍ In October 1916, when, through exposure, my health began to fail, before I was invalided home, in reading Psalm 91 I felt the lovingkindness of the Lord, and a desire to be brought back to meet again among his people. And I made a vow that if the Lord brought me back safely, I would, as he might so enable me, walk in the ordinances of his house. At that same time the thought of preaching entered into my mind. That was the beginning. I want you to take particular notice of this, the *thought* of preaching entered into my mind. Do not set any more value upon that than is due, because under those peculiar circumstances (when the Lord had, as I believe, pitied me even as a father pitieth his children), under such circumstances it is quite likely that many might have had such thoughts come into their mind; the *thought* of preaching. I will not call it the commencement of *exercise* with respect to the ministry, but the *thought* began there.[238]

Benjamin Walshaw (left) & William B. G. Vaughan (right)

Two men who would later serve as pastor at Bradford, both saw war service. Mr Benjamin Walshaw signed up in 1915 when just 16 years old.[239] Mr William B. G. Vaughan, pastor at Bradford prior to Mr Walshaw, was called up in 1916, was wounded the following year, and, after many months in hospital, was discharged in 1918. While in hospital he was greatly blessed. Writing in 1932 of this time, he said:

> ✍ I had such a sense of the love of God and the presence of the Lord Jesus Christ, as I have never had before nor since. Also these words: 'They that wait upon the LORD shall renew their strength.' Oh, what hope was revived! He had weakened my strength in the way. Surely before honour is humility. Humbled under a sense of his love and mercy, I indeed wept for joy![240]

Colin Turton (left) & William Wolstenholme (right)

A number of other men, who would later serve as ministers among the northern Strict Baptist churches, can also be found in 'The Muster Roll' of *The Christian's Pathway*. These include Mr Colin Turton,[241] Mr Thomas Catterall,[242] Mr Henry Jackson,[243] and Mr William Wolstenholme.[244]

Some men who would later enter the ministry spent the war in unregeneracy. The obituary of Mr Frederick

Sewell, who later was a faithful supply minister for 41 years, records that:

> ✍ In his own words, he 'lived until 33 years of age in total ignorance of either my state as a fallen sinner, God's purity and holiness, or the plan of salvation as revealed in the Word of God.' He had checks of conscience, and made resolves which proved as the morning mist. When in danger during the 1914-18 War, he would pray to be spared; then, when the danger was over, so too were his prayers, and he would go on in his sinful course. Looking back later, he could but wonder at the Lord's mercy in watching over him – rescued from a burning ship, uninjured in a 'smash' in France, captured by the enemy, and later escaping to Sweden.[245]

Frederick Sewell

After the war, in 1919, he joined the Metropolitan Police. It was another ten years before the Lord called him by grace, in the autumn of 1929.

Similarly, for Enos Hadley, later the pastor at Attleborough, Birmingham, and Lakenheath, the war appears to have had no effect. He wrote, "I was taken up, and had been for years, with various kinds of sport – especially football, as a player – until I was severely wounded the third time during the 1914-1918 War; and then afterwards, an ardent follower of the sport, which became more to me than anything else in this world." But the time came, in 1923, when the Lord began a work in his soul, and convinced him of sin. He wrote:

Enos Hadley

> ✍ I can best describe the experience that morning in the following words. I had been severely wounded three times (yet mercifully preserved), but I had never received such a wound as when the Holy Ghost sent that word into my heart, 'Ye cannot serve God and mammon,' a wound which no earthly physician could heal, and I was lost. O, the indescribable agony that followed! I did cry for mercy; and for months, the 938th hymn [*Gadsby's Selection*, 'When thou, my righteous Judge, shalt come'] continued with me, apart from the last verse, which I felt I could not enter into. But after much law work, pulling down, stripping, and being so humbled before God, I was made to realise:
>
> If ever my poor soul be saved,
> 'Tis Christ must be the way.[246]

Alfred G. Charman

In God's sovereign purposes, for another minister, Mr Alfred Charman, later pastor at Brockham Green Chapel, it would appear that the Lord used his wartime experience in calling him by grace: "The Lord met with Alfred on the battlefield in the First War. He was the only one that was spared when the hut they were in was bombed." He himself wrote of his experience, "In my own case I have been, as a soldier, facing death continually for months on end, and if anything will make you pray, that will, knowing that when it came it would be sudden. How I promised the Lord then that, if he spared me, and brought me back to my dear ones, I would live a right life! Have I kept my promise since? No, I have not."[247]

Mr B. A. Ramsbottom, speaking at the 50th Northern Meetings of the Gospel Standard Societies, said of this generation of ministers, that they were:

> ✍ Men of varying ability; men of different gifts, each one having his own line. But they were men of God, they were men of stature, they knew what they believed, they knew why they believed it, they had a testimony to bear, and the truth had been burnt home in their souls. Many of them had known what it was to serve in the trenches in the First World War. Many of them had known the severe depression after the First World War. These things had been sanctified to them.[248]

A typical First World War military camp, in this case on the Curragh, Ireland, where Mr Reginald Morris was stationed for a time

The end of the war

Fighting ended at 11 o'clock, on 11th November, 1918, and, although what was actually declared was only an armistice, or effectively a treaty agreeing to a cease fire for just six weeks, it was evident from the beginning that the peace was more than just a temporary halt in hostilities. Negotiations continued, and lasting peace was eventually declared in 1919. Charles Jefferies, writing in *The Friendly Companion* in December, 1918, recorded how the Armistice was accompanied by joy mingled with sorrow for nearly every town, village, extended family, and probably almost every Strict Baptist chapel, in England:

> ✍ How much the nation has at length been, in many varying and earnest ways, divided and united in celebrating its thanksgivings on account of the, we trust, lasting humiliation and defeat of Germany. As yet it is but the Armistice by which the agreed cessation of war has its effect for six weeks; but it is in such a form and manner as to leave little ground for fear as to its permanency. May the Lord's name be praised for the prospect. There will, nevertheless, be a very gloomy and sorrowful lining of grief to the silver cloud. Many lives have been lost, and many futures blighted; so that our weeping and rejoicing are much divided. Perhaps the most telling way of celebration will be the reverent singing of the grand doxology.[249]

Sadly, many men were killed in the weeks and days that led up to the Armistice, and the fighting continued even as the leaders were in peace talks. These deaths, so close to peace, must have been especially hard for the families of the men involved.

One example was Arthur Cornelius Morley, from Nottingham. He had joined the army in 1917, on reaching the age of 18, and served in the Northumberland Fusiliers. He had seen action at the front from April, 1918, and was brought through several heavy engagements in safety. But then, while resting at a camp several miles from the firing line, he was wounded by a high explosive shell on 2nd November, 1918, and died within two hours. He is buried in the Forest Communal Cemetery, France. The words on his gravestone read: "Redeemed – 'Not a single shaft can hit, till the God of love sees fit.'" It is recorded of him:

Arthur Cornelius Morley

> ✍ In a letter to his parents, he wrote: 'One day last week shells were bursting overhead and all around, and death seemed very near, when these words came to my mind:
>
> Not a single shaft can hit,
> Till the God of love sees fit.[250]
>
> After that I felt quite resigned to whatever might happen, and I was never so calm under fire.' When his parents heard he was wounded these words came to both of them at the same time: 'He's gone in endless bliss to dwell,' and, 'I shall go to him, but he shall not return to me,' so that his mother was sure he was killed. His letters home and the above words were

indeed made a means of consolation to them in their heavy loss.[251]

Mr Salkeld records how he heard the joyous news of the Armistice while a prisoner of war in Germany:

> ✍ The day began, as far as we were concerned, just as other days, and we carried on as usual with our allotted tasks among the timber and sawdust … however, during the late afternoon a young woman, who worked at the sawmill, came running towards us, nearly out of breath, and very excitedly called out to us in German. We heard her say: '*Mein vater hat gesagt* …' and then we lost the rest until she came to the word, '*Stillstand*.' The gist of her message was this: 'My father has just said the war is over, and an armistice (*Stillstand*) was signed at 11 a.m., in France, on this, the 11th day of November.' We looked at each other for a moment or two, as if unable to take it in, and then we broke out into a cheer, as we shook hands one with another warmly, and with deep feeling.[252]

Francis J. Kirby

Services of thanksgiving were held in many Strict Baptist chapels on Lord's Day, 17th November, to mark the cessation of hostilities. At Ramsgate, Mr Francis J. Kirby preached from 'The LORD gave them rest round about' (2 Chronicles 15: 15).[253] The sermon preached by Mr Joseph P. Wiles at the Old Baptist Chapel, Devizes, from 'But thanks be to God which giveth us the victory through our Lord Jesus Christ' (1 Corinthians 15: 57), was published as a pamphlet, entitled *Victory and Thanksgiving*.

Mount Zion Chapel, Ramsgate (Mr Francis Kirby, inset)

In the pages of *The Gospel Standard*, Mr Popham exhorted the churches to thanksgiving:

> ✍ By the mercy of God the terrible war has come to an end. We can never be sufficiently thankful for this. I hope that all of our congregations have met to offer praise for his marvellous intervention for us … Soon the survivors of the noble band of dear young men, who went from us to fight for our hearths, will be with us again. To them, and to us, may their preservation be deeply sanctified; also the sorrows of the many, whose husbands and sons are no more.[254]

Mr Popham himself preached at Galeed Chapel, Brighton, from Ephesians 2: 14: "For he is our peace, who hath made both one, and hath broken down the middle wall of partition between us," on the morning of 17th November.[255]

Of course, although peace had come in the form of armistice, the soldiers could not simply leave their guns and make their way home there and then. Until lasting peace was signed, there was always the possibility that Germany and her allies would break the armistice, and recommence hostilities. For many, there were weeks and months of occupation of former German territory ahead of them, before they could finally return to their families. Conscription did not actually end until the middle of 1919, and so men were still joining the forces during this period, although the active conflict was over.

One Strict Baptist, Stephen Clark, from Newick, Sussex, wrote of his experience of the end of the war, and occupying Germany:

> ✍ I now come to the last day of the war, November 11th, 1918 … I had been spared. It was a great relief to know I had been preserved thus far; yet we felt the need of being spared in other ways. We had to travel the road the enemy had gone, and many dangers were still to be faced. No one knew if any mines had been laid in the roads or bridges. It was my lot with many others to march into Germany. We were told to pack up, our destination being Frechen, a village near Cologne, marching by day and taking our rest by night. What a happy change – trenches were exchanged for nice warm beds. We could sleep soundly, after committing soul and body into the hands of him who neither slumbers nor sleeps. We were allotted comfortable quarters for the night in villages on our way. It took three days to complete our journey. What a strange experience! We arrived at the German village of Frechen, where we made a stay of nearly four months. The line, or the towns that our troops occupied, was about six miles in front of our battery. These positions were taken up just as if we were still at war, but only as a safeguard … Like in all towns and villages, there was much agitation as to who caused the World War. Just think of enemy forces pouring through the towns and villages. This was a bitter experience for some of the inhabitants; but on the whole, we were welcomed …[256]

Peace with Germany was signed in a more lasting way with the Treaty of Versailles, on 28th June, 1919. Following the signing of this treaty, most of the soldiers still abroad began the journey home. Legally, the wider war did not actually finish until the signing of the Treaty of Lausanne, on 24th July, 1923, which officially ended hostilities with Turkey. Mr Kirby wrote in *The Christian's Pathway*:

✍ Saturday, June 28th, 1919, was a memorable day – the day of the signing of the great peace. Towards this day the nations looked with longing hearts. The Psalmist David, rapt in the spirit of prophecy, said, 'He [*God*] maketh wars to cease unto the end of the earth.' 'Surely the wrath of man shall praise thee: the remainder of wrath shalt thou restrain.' To this same Almighty One may we render praise and thanksgiving, blending with the praise the prayer, 'Thy kingdom come. Thy will be done in earth, as it is in heaven.'[257]

Mr Popham wrote to the young readers of *The Friendly Companion*:

✍ My dear young Friends,

Doubtless all of you, in common with the whole Empire and our allies, are rejoicing that peace is signed. Every loyal Englishman must feel a spirit of deep gladness for the victory which God has given us. From what he has saved us in crushing the diabolical German we cannot realise, though we have reason to believe that terms of the most merciless kind would have been imposed on us, if the long premeditated and carefully prepared war against the world had been successful. But God had ordered matters otherwise than the common foe of humanity designed. And we rejoice in a God-given victory.

Before these few words reach you, personal, national, empire, and world rejoicings will have found long and loud expression, in which every English boy and girl will have joined. But with many, deeper feelings will have been uttered in tears; silent thanks, mingled with sobs for absent ones, uttered in secret before the Lord God of Hosts. Among these many of my young friends will have been. Let us not forget who has given us the great victory, nor forget to thank him; and with the thanks, may many prayers be mingled, that peace will come to our nation and the world.

God bless you all!

So prays, your affectionate friend,

J. K. Popham

Brighton, July 4th, 1919.[258]

Just as they had been at the Armistice, thanksgiving services were held in Strict Baptist chapels to mark the signing of peace at Versailles. Some held thanksgiving services the next day, on 29th July. This was the case at Ramsgate, where Mr Francis J. Kirby is recorded as preaching from "Now the Lord of peace himself give you peace always by all means" (2 Thessalonians 3: 16).[259] The king appointed the following Lord's Day, 6th July, as a day for national thanksgiving. Miss Esther Harmer, who after the war married Mr Stanley Delves, the pastor at Crowborough, Sussex, wrote of these services at Rehoboth Chapel, Tunbridge Wells:

✍ On the first Sunday of July the signing of peace was observed through the country in all the churches and chapels. We had a grand service of praise and thanksgiving at chapel in the morning. Mr Evans[260] made some appropriate remarks and read several portions; he also read the king's proclamation and an ancient collect, very suitable for the occasion. We finished up with the national anthem. In the afternoon we had another thanksgiving service (Sunday School) held in the chapel. Mr B. Wilmshurst (demobilised) read and prayed and spoke to the children, also my dear Stan gave quite a nice address. We went to Rehoboth in the evening. Mr Evans was very nice indeed and the ordinance afterwards was much enjoyed. It seemed nice to see Stanley sitting down among us again after two years of absence.[261]

Amidst the thanksgiving there were solemn reflections about the ongoing Russian Revolution and the murder of Tsar Nicholas II – some of the aftermaths of war. Mr Francis Kirby wrote:

> Amidst legitimate rejoicings, and we desire no other, may we remember that there are forces working today which logically make for disintegration and civil war, from which in his great mercy may the Lord spare us. Civil strife inflicts a wound upon the heart of the country; it destroys tranquillity, roots out confidence which is essential to national life, exposes all things to the mercy of a ruthless mob, renders property, life and liberty insecure, retards trade, checks agriculture, and, as a consequence, plunges the people into starvation and ruin. Whatever changes take place in this country, we may well pray that they may be constitutionally effected.[262]

Mr Popham, writing in *The Gospel Standard,* directed the reader to look beyond the outward events, however great and remarkable they appeared to be, and to see the ultimate end of these matters:

> There are also many external events of the first importance, events so wonderful, so sudden, so unexpected by the majority of men, that they might be called miracles. God has risen to shake terribly the earth. Empires have broken up. Emperors have lost their autocratic thrones. The river Euphrates is dried up – the infamous Turk has lost the power he so cruelly, so vilely exercised for over four centuries. Thus has God avenged himself on some of his enemies, and it becomes his people to worship him in this his so awful work. 'Who can stand before his indignation? and who can abide in the fierceness of his anger? his fury is poured out like fire, and the rocks are thrown down by him' (Nahum 1: 6).
>
> But none of these events, however important, and occupying most properly so large a place in men's thoughts, affecting most deeply the future of the world, appear to us so important as the wondrous end towards which they are tending – each contributing its share to the great whole – the glory of God in the church by Christ Jesus.[263]

The needs of the returning men

Esther Delves (née Harmer)

Once peace had been signed in a lasting way, it was time for the soldiers to return home to their families. It was a joyous reunion for many. Miss Esther Harmer (later Mrs Stanley Delves) wrote on 15th July, 1919, concerning Mr Delves' arrival home: "Three weeks ago today our dear old Stan turned up. He arrived in Scotland a week before and called here on his way to Hailsham. He looks and seems much older, but is still the same dear old boy." [264]

However, coming home was not as easy as it might sound. Many of the men had been absent from their families for so long that children who were hardly walking and talking when they left home, were now attending school. In the churches there would undoubtedly have been empty pews, which had been occupied when they left. In some cases, their pastor had died or moved on, and in others new pastors had taken up office while they had been away. The jobs they had held at the start of the war, in many cases, no longer existed. Many of the men were also suffering from 'shell shock', and other mental health issues, caused by the conditions and inhumane events they had been exposed to.[265] Strict Baptists were not unaware of these problems. As early as November, 1916, Mr Kirby reviewed a book in *The Christian's Pathway* titled: *When the men come home*. He wrote, "What are we [*Strict Baptists*] proposing to do when the men come home? Their return will present problems well worthy of the careful and prayerful consideration of every Christian man." He welcomed suggestions from the readers.[266] While it is unclear what, if anything, arose from this request, the men returning to Strict Baptist congregations undoubtedly found prayerful and loving support in the difficult transitions they had to make.

At Nottingham, the pastor, Mr Henry T. Stonelake, addressed the returning men warmly and plainly, at a thanksgiving service held at Chaucer Street Chapel, Nottingham, on Thursday evening, January 1st, 1920.

> ✍ Let me remind you that during the time you have been away, you have not been forgotten by the friends here. Many petitions have been presented at the throne of grace in this chapel for you. No doubt most of you in times of danger and distress have cried to the Lord for his help and his protection, but let me ask again, how many of you have been troubled and distressed about your sins, and have cried unto the Lord for the salvation of your never-dying souls?
>
> 'The Angel which redeemed me from all evil, bless the lads.' God has already blessed you in bringing you back to us in safety. May he bless you each with the comforts of home life. May he bless you all with good health, with natural strength, with much mental energy. May he bless you all with wisdom and ability in your employment, or in the business in which you are engaged day by day.
>
> Great changes have occurred during the war, and changes in various directions are still taking place, and will continue to do so. Some of you had situations waiting for you when you returned. Others were not so favoured. The Lord go before and direct you as to your future steps. Some of you have recently started in business on your own account. May God bless you with wisdom and direction, and prosper the work of your hands. I trust in all your business dealings you will ever act honourably to all men. Be truthful, be honest, at all times. Some people, who are determined to make money, do not care how they get it, whether honestly or dishonestly. God keep us from their spirit! Be straightforward in what you undertake. The Lord bless you all, if it is his will, with such a measure of worldly prosperity as will enable you to live in comfort. I will not say in luxury and idleness, for these are great evils, and to be avoided by all those who fear God.
>
> But these blessings I have mentioned, excellent as they are, are only temporal, and in a few years many of us will need them no longer. May God bless you with his grace and fear, for godliness is profitable for the life that now is, and for that which is to come. This is the blessing that maketh rich. Without this blessing, all is vain.
>
> Remember, 'Ye must be born again,' or you

cannot see the kingdom of God. Without this blessing we are spiritually dead; and can never, while in that state, know anything of the life of God. Let me mention some of the blessings of the new birth. There is true conviction of sin; godly sorrow for sin; repentance unto salvation; the tender fear of God, and hope in the mercy of God. Hope is an anchor which keeps the trembling sinner from sinking into despair. Then there is faith and love felt by such in the wisdom and power of God, who is 'a rewarder of them that diligently seek him.' Also, love to the Lord Jesus Christ, to his people, to his ways, and to his truth and cause. If sin troubles you, seek for a manifestation of his pardoning love and mercy. The Lord bless you with these divine favours, if it can please him; and such of you as have had any sweet hope in his grace, may he give you more grace, for he has promised to give more grace unto the humble.

It is a great pleasure for us to see you among us again. As you know, one of your number has died in France.[267] The Lord support and comfort his parents. There is another of our young friends, who, owing to great weakness, is quite unable to be with us tonight. We desire his restoration, if the Lord will grant this favour. All the others who joined the army, I believe, are now well.

One more word: I do hope that every one of you will endeavour to attend the services of God's house regularly on the Sabbath, and, as far as possible, meet with us in the week likewise. May none of you ever forget the greatness of God's goodness and mercy to you during those terrible years, and may his goodness and mercy humble you and lead you to repentance.[268]

Sadly, many men had found their religion shaken by the war. After the war, many denominations discovered that the empty pews were not just a result of young men being killed in the war, but that also some of the returning men had lost the religion of their youth on the battlefield. An outward religion, without the root of faith in the heart, will never stand the fire. Trials and tribulations show up what sort of faith we have, and the trial of war was no exception. Mr J. H. Gosden wrote later of a very solemn case of this, which he came across while serving in the army:

> ✍ In the last war [*the First World War*] I met with an awful case of reprobation. A young non-commissioned officer said to me: 'I was once a Strict Baptist. But God would not give me grace; now he can keep it.' I hardly like to print the blasphemy, which at the time made me tremble. That young man the next day started out with a ration party and was never heard of, or seen again. O dear young people, God preserve you from trifling with the truth and Word of God! May we ever revere his holy name and truth.[269]

It is difficult to gauge to what extent this attrition in attendance was also seen in Strict Baptist chapels.

A different response to the difficult questions raised by their wartime experiences was seen in a small group of young men from Croydon. J. Bridges, A. Bridges, V. Cockram, R. Smith, H. Smith, C. G. Stevens, A. Wadey, and N. Wood had come into close contact with people of other denominations and beliefs, while fighting, and now that they had returned from the war, these young men sought further instruction in the Scriptures and the distinctive beliefs of the Strict

V. Cockram (left) & N. Wood (right)

Baptists. With the encouragement and guidance of Mr Walter Brooke, pastor of West Street Chapel, Croydon, these eight young men established the Strict Baptist Education Society, with the aim of "mutual edification and study of the Word of God by regular public meetings." A committee was formed, and Mr Brooke was appointed the first president. An invitation was sent

Walter Brooke

to the congregation at Tamworth Road Chapel, Croydon, to join the society. The first meeting was held on 8th October, 1920, at West Street Chapel, with an address being given by Mr F. J. Farncombe. The meetings still continue to be held today, almost 100 years later.

Spanish 'flu

Closely associated with the end of the First World War was the outbreak of so called 'Spanish' influenza, a particularly virulent 'flu pandemic, which spread across the world between January 1918 and December 1920.

At least one Strict Baptist minister died of the 'flu during this period. Mr William Smith, of Brighton, preached on Lord's Day, 2nd February, 1919, but was then taken ill with 'flu, which was complicated with pneumonia, and died on 11th February, aged 64. His wife survived him by just three days, before also succumbing to the 'flu. They were buried together in the Brighton and Preston Cemetery, by Mr S. Anscombe.[270]

The 'flu did not just affect the aged and the weak, but the young and the strong too. Miss Alice Baughan, of Southport, was at work on Wednesday, fell ill on Thursday, took to her bed on the Lord's Day, and died on the Tuesday. She was 27 years old. Her father wrote:

> ✍ We wrestled much with God in prayer to spare her life and raise her up again, but if it was not his will to do so, would he have mercy on her and give us some word or words, as a foundation upon which we might rest and feel assured that it would be well with her. We believe the Lord answered our prayer, for a few hours before she died she quite gave up all hopes

Alice Baughan

of getting better and asked me to pray for her, and said she had loved to hear good sermons and had no desire for other places, but was like the Psalmist when he said: 'I have loved the habitation of thy house, and the place where thine honour dwelleth.' She sent her love to several of her friends, hoping to meet them in that happy land and to see us all in heaven. The various words she spoke gave us a good hope that it would be well with her, as they clearly indicated that her mind was set upon heaven and divine things; and does not Jesus say, 'Where your treasure is, there will your heart be also.' We feel our loss greatly, but cannot sorrow as others may, who have no hope.[271]

Coming in the wake of the losses of the war, we can only feel that the mass deaths, attributed to the outbreak of influenza, must have been very hard for those families bereaved by it.

Burying and remembering the dead

During the war, attempts had been made to honour the fallen by giving them decent burials. The Imperial War Graves Commission was established by Royal Charter in 1917, and commenced the cataloguing of war graves. With the Armistice, attempts began in earnest to gather together the bodies of the fallen into suitable cemeteries. In many cases this involved exhuming

The British Cemetery at Haringhe, as it appeared immediately after the war

the bodies and reinterring them in new plots. In the newly laid out cemeteries, the graves were first marked with a wooden cross, and then, as time went on, a headstone made of Portland stone was provided for each grave, with a standard wording inscribed. There was also the option for the next of kin to pay to have additional words on the graves of their loved ones. In visiting the war cemeteries today, the eye is readily drawn to the graves on which Scripture texts appear, or notes which hint that the body that reposes there is one for which there is a good hope of a glorious resurrection. Of course, there were a large number of bodies which could not be identified. These were treated with the same dignity, each having the same white Portland headstone, but were inscribed simply: "A Soldier of the Great War – Known unto God." The names of those soldiers, whose remains were never found or identified, were gathered together, and inscribed on stone plinths mounted on massive memorials, such as those at Thiepval on the Somme, and the Menin Gate, and at Tyne Cot cemetery in the Ypres Salient.

For many families, a visit to the graves of their loved ones was an important part in the natural process of grieving. An account of one such visit is left by Esther Wild, whose brother, Frank Buggs, was buried in the Dantzig Alley British Cemetery, France:

> ✍ In due course we were informed of the whereabouts of Frank's grave, and my father and elder brother were the first to visit it, in the beginning of August, 1921. I went with a sister in July, 1925. We stayed in the still battle-scarred town of Albert, and were driven to a cemetery in the Danzie Valley [*sic*], and found the dear boy's grave; and strolled about the country roads near, probably looking upon the same scenes which Frank had looked upon and told us about, and saw some church or churches with the iron memorials, etc., and still unfilled shell holes in some of the graves; and by the wayside were reminders of soldiers and horses, in remnants of their trappings lying about. But life went on; the fields growing corn; the French men and women going about their duties.[272]

When the Cenotaph was unveiled, and the Unknown Warrior was buried amid much ceremony in Westminster Abbey, *The Friendly Companion* covered it at some length in its pages.[273] Some Strict Baptist chapels erected their own war memorials, the chapels at Brabourne and Bexley, in Kent, being examples. At Bexley, the memorial was most practical, taking the form of almshouses built in memory of the 11 men from the congregation who lost their lives during the war.[274] *The Christian's Pathway* commented, "How much better than a wayside shrine, or an idol, or a crucifix. For within these walls some weary ones may find peace and a quiet resting place."[275]

At Lakenheath, it is reported that the aged pastor, William Sutherden Cooper, used to take the Sabbath School scholars down to observe the remembrance service at the war memorial, in the years following its unveiling, although the practice came to an abrupt halt when the remembrance service started to incorporate prayers for the dead.[276]

The war memorial at Brabourne Strict Baptist Chapel

Strict Baptists have always freely purchased poppies from the annual British Legion fundraising campaign, and often sing Isaac Watts' hymn, "O God, our help in ages past,"[277] which has become inseparably connected with Armistice Day, the 11th November, and Remembrance Sunday, the Lord's Day closest to the 11th November, each year. However, in general, Strict Baptists have avoided remembrance services, wreath laying, or the other forms of remembrance practised more generally in the nation. This reserve undoubtedly sprang from the concern that the emphasis of these occasions turned more to the glorifying and honouring of the dead, rather than a remembrance of God's goodness to the nation during the war. Mr Frank L. Gosden left a record of his own experience in this regard:

> ✍ In 1919, it was proposed to erect at Ticehurst a cross in memory of those who fell in the war, and Mr Cooper asked me if I would collect for that purpose, which I immediately consented to do. On my way home there came upon my spirit an exceedingly solemn consideration with respect to the cross of Christ. It had an effect which I shall never forget; so much so that I felt it impossible to collect for such a thing which was to be erected for the glory of men who fell in the war.[278]

In addition, the 1920s saw the rise of a school of theological thought which conflated the deaths of the young men in the war, fighting on behalf of loved ones at home, with the vicarious, sin-atoning death of the Lord Jesus Christ on behalf of his people. Despite the blasphemy involved in such thinking, it became a widespread teaching, which infiltrated many of the yearly acts of remembrance, and undoubtedly caused many God-fearing people to draw back from involvement in these proceedings.

The Cenotaph, Whitehall, London

Conclusion

In this first part of the book we have attempted to survey and record the experiences of Strict Baptists during the First World War. It has not been our intention to glorify the Strict Baptists, or the men who fought so admirably for the nation during this conflict. Rather, our desire would be to glorify God, who, in the midst of the judgements of the war, granted much mercy to his people, and the nation at large.

When David, King of Israel, sinned and came under the subsequent judgement of God, he confessed that even in judgement God's mercy is still very great (1 Chronicles 21: 13). So the Lord's people learned by experience during the First World War that, even in the midst of God's judgements on the country, the Lord's mercy was still abundant.

Today, we should still be thankful, both for the mercies shown to the nation during the First World War, and the mercies the nation has experienced since. Although we deserve judgements as much as our forefathers did in 1914, yet the Lord still lengthens out his mercies to us. Many readers of this book will have lived through more than 70 years of peace on home soil, since the close of the Second World War. Despite the recent recession, we still have relative prosperity, the benefits of stable government, and a healthcare system and welfare state which are the envy of many nations. Over and above our many temporal blessings, we also have spiritual privileges to be thankful for. The gospel is still faithfully preached in this country, and there are still evidences of blessing following the preaching of the Word. These manifestations of God's mercy are still evident among Strict Baptists, and we should be abundantly thankful for them. The accounts of God's mercies, in life and death, which are gathered together in this book, should encourage us all to still trust in his name, and leave all our cares in his hand. 'Let Israel hope in the LORD: for with the LORD there is mercy, and with him is plenteous redemption' (Psalm 130: 7).

Aeroplanes over the front in France

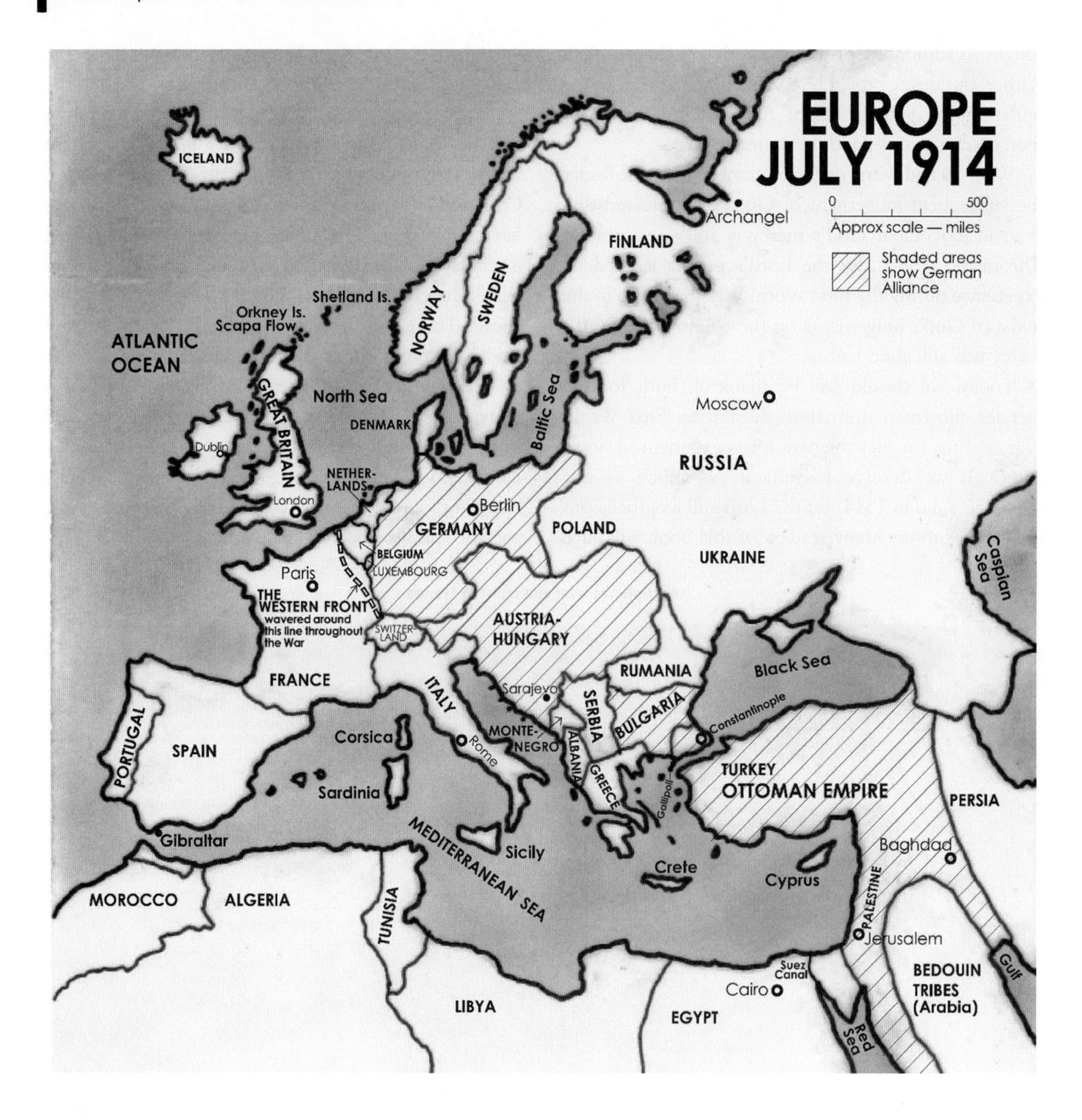
EUROPE
JULY 1914
0
500
Approx scale — miles
Shaded areas show German Alliance
ICELAND
ATLANTIC OCEAN
Shetland Is.
Orkney Is.
Scapa Flow
North Sea
NORWAY
SWEDEN
FINLAND
Archangel
Baltic Sea
Moscow
RUSSIA
DENMARK
GREAT BRITAIN
Dublin
London
NETHER-LANDS
Berlin
GERMANY
POLAND
UKRAINE
BELGIUM
LUXEMBOURG
Paris
THE WESTERN FRONT
wavered around this line throughout the War
SWITZER-LAND
AUSTRIA-HUNGARY
FRANCE
RUMANIA
Black Sea
Caspian Sea
ITALY
Sarajevo
SERBIA
BULGARIA
Constantinople
PORTUGAL
SPAIN
Corsica
Rome
MONTE-NEGRO
ALBANIA
GREECE
Gallipoli
TURKEY
OTTOMAN EMPIRE
PERSIA
Sardinia
Gibraltar
MEDITERRANEAN SEA
Sicily
Crete
Cyprus
Baghdad
PALESTINE
Jerusalem
MOROCCO
ALGERIA
TUNISIA
Gulf
Suez Canal
Cairo
BEDOUIN TRIBES (Arabia)
LIBYA
EGYPT
Red Sea

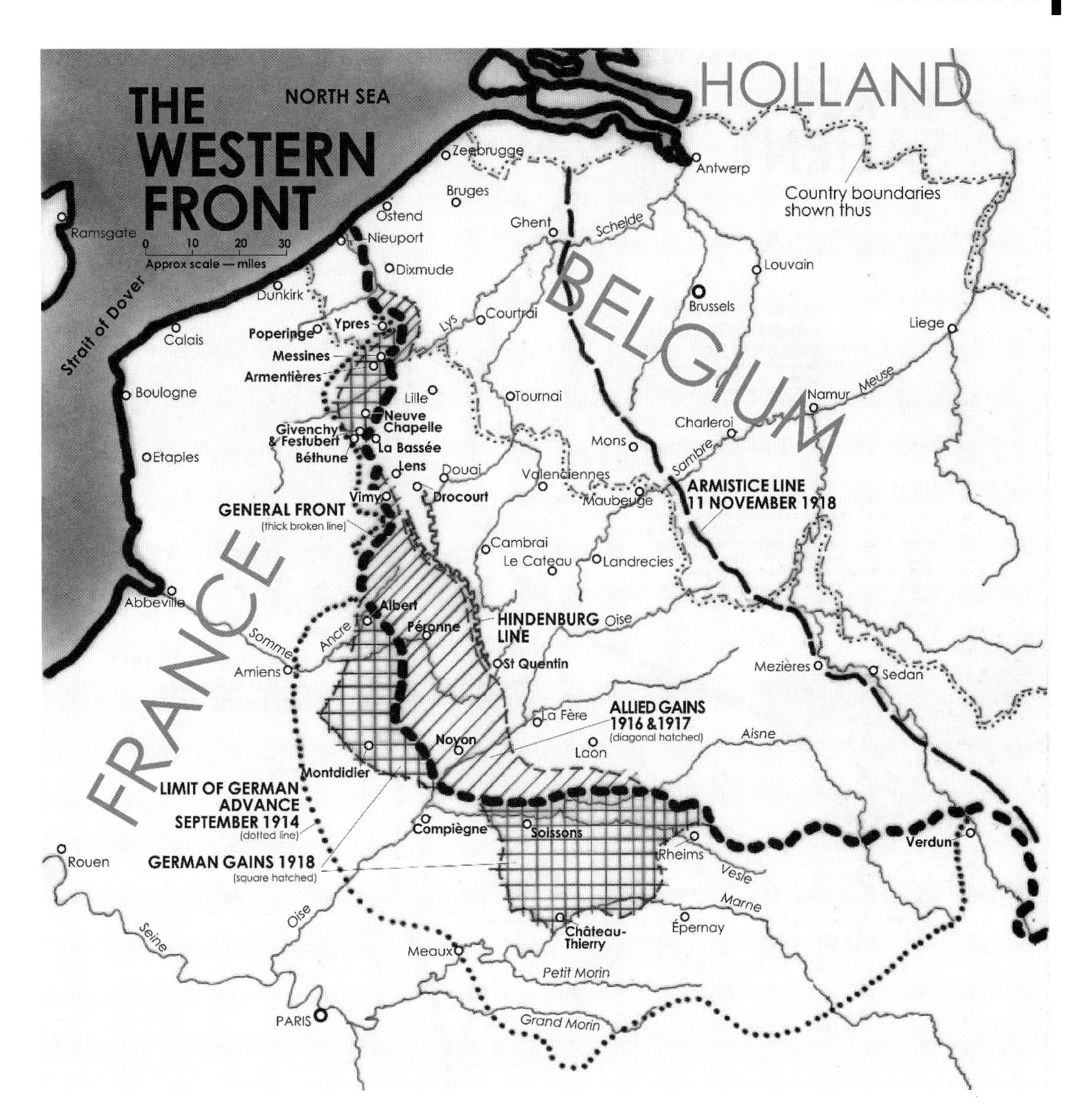
THE WESTERN FRONT
NORTH SEA
HOLLAND
BELGIUM
FRANCE
Strait of Dover
0 10 20 30
Approx scale — miles
Country boundaries shown thus
Ramsgate
Zeebrugge
Antwerp
Bruges
Ostend
Nieuport
Ghent
Scheldt
Louvain
Dixmude
Dunkirk
Brussels
Courtrai
Lys
Poperinge
Ypres
Calais
Messines
Armentières
Liege
Boulogne
Lille
Tournai
Namur
Meuse
Neuve Chapelle
Givenchy & Festubert
La Bassée
Béthune
Charleroi
Mons
Sambre
Etaples
Lens
Douai
Valenciennes
Drocourt
Vimy
Maubeuge
ARMISTICE LINE 11 NOVEMBER 1918
GENERAL FRONT
(thick broken line)
Cambrai
Le Cateau
Landrecies
Abbeville
Albert
Ancre
Péronne
HINDENBURG LINE
Oise
Somme
Amiens
St Quentin
Mezières
Sedan
La Fère
ALLIED GAINS 1916 &1917
(diagonal hatched)
Aisne
Noyon
Laon
Montdidier
LIMIT OF GERMAN ADVANCE SEPTEMBER 1914
(dotted line)
Compiègne
Soissons
Verdun
Rouen
GERMAN GAINS 1918
(square hatched)
Rheims
Vesle
Marne
Oise
Seine
Château-Thierry
Épernay
Meaux
Petit Morin
PARIS
Grand Morin

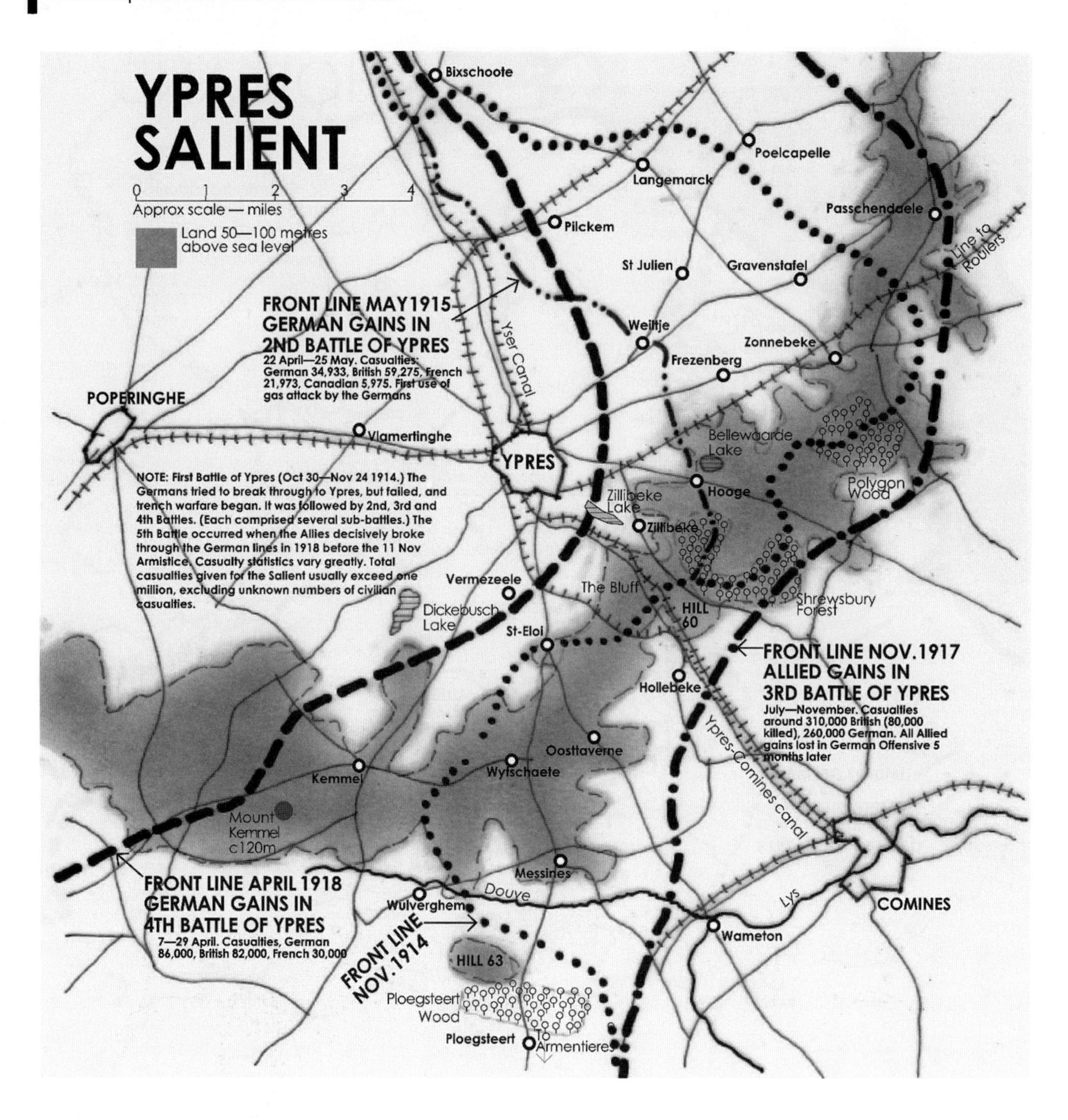
YPRES SALIENT
0 1 2 3 4
Approx scale — miles
Land 50—100 metres above sea level
Bixschoote
Poelcapelle
Langemarck
Passchendaele
Pilckem
Line to Roulers
St Julien
Gravenstafel
FRONT LINE MAY1915 GERMAN GAINS IN 2ND BATTLE OF YPRES
22 April—25 May. Casualties: German 34,933, British 59,275, French 21,973, Canadian 5,975. First use of gas attack by the Germans
Yser Canal
Weiltje
Zonnebeke
Frezenberg
POPERINGHE
Vlamertinghe
Bellewaarde Lake
YPRES
NOTE: First Battle of Ypres (Oct 30—Nov 24 1914.) The Germans tried to break through to Ypres, but failed, and trench warfare began. It was followed by 2nd, 3rd and 4th Battles. (Each comprised several sub-battles.) The 5th Battle occurred when the Allies decisively broke through the German lines in 1918 before the 11 Nov Armistice. Casualty statistics vary greatly. Total casualties given for the Salient usually exceed one million, excluding unknown numbers of civilian casualties.
Polygon Wood
Zillibeke Lake
Hooge
Zillibeke
Vermezeele
The Bluff
Shrewsbury Forest
Dickebusch Lake
HILL 60
St-Eloi
FRONT LINE NOV.1917 ALLIED GAINS IN 3RD BATTLE OF YPRES
July—November. Casualties around 310,000 British (80,000 killed), 260,000 German. All Allied gains lost in German Offensive 5 months later
Hollebeke
Ypres-Comines canal
Oosttaverne
Kemmel
Wytschaete
Mount Kemmel c120m
Messines
FRONT LINE APRIL 1918 GERMAN GAINS IN 4TH BATTLE OF YPRES
7—29 April. Casualties, German 86,000, British 82,000, French 30,000
Douve
Wulverghem
Lys
COMINES
FRONT LINE NOV.1914
Wameton
HILL 63
Ploegsteert Wood
Ploegsteert
To Armentieres

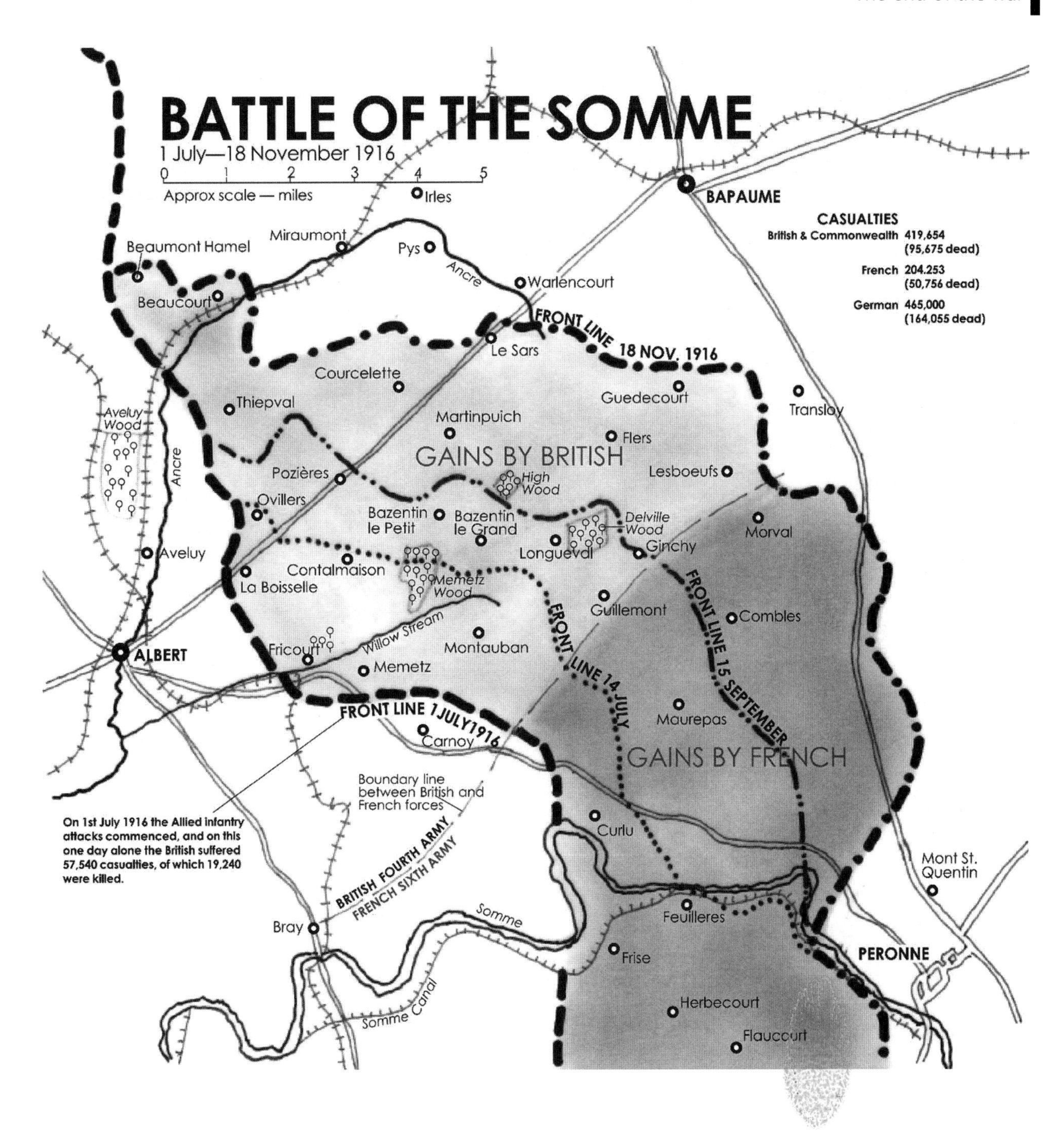
BATTLE OF THE SOMME
1 July—18 November 1916
0 1 2 3 4 5
Approx scale — miles
Irles
BAPAUME
CASUALTIES
British & Commonwealth 419,654 (95,675 dead)
French 204.253 (50,756 dead)
German 465,000 (164,055 dead)
Miraumont
Pys
Beaumont Hamel
Beaucourt
Ancre
Warlencourt
FRONT LINE 18 NOV. 1916
Le Sars
Courcelette
Guedecourt
Transloy
Thiepval
Aveluy Wood
Martinpuich
Flers
GAINS BY BRITISH
Lesboeufs
Pozières
High Wood
Ovillers
Bazentin le Petit
Bazentin le Grand
Delville Wood
Morval
Longueval
Ginchy
Aveluy
Contalmaison
La Boisselle
Memetz Wood
FRONT LINE 15 SEPTEMBER
Guillemont
Combles
Willow Stream
Fricourt
Montauban
ALBERT
Memetz
FRONT LINE 14 JULY
Maurepas
FRONT LINE 1 JULY 1916
Carnoy
GAINS BY FRENCH
Boundary line between British and French forces
On 1st July 1916 the Allied infantry attacks commenced, and on this one day alone the British suffered 57,540 casualties, of which 19,240 were killed.
Curlu
BRITISH FOURTH ARMY
FRENCH SIXTH ARMY
Mont St. Quentin
Feuilleres
Somme
Bray
Frise
PERONNE
Herbecourt
Somme Canal
Flaucourt

Contelmaison Wood
Contelmaison Villa
Lower Wood
Pearl Wood
Mash Valley
Bailiff Wood
Contalmaison
Memetz Wood
La Boisselle
Peake Wood
Acid Drop Copse
FRONT LINE AT DAWN 1 JULY 1916
Sausage Valley
Birch Tree Wood
GERMAN TRENCH NETWORKS
The Quadrangle
GERMAN BARBED WIRE ENTANGLEMENTS
Shelter Wood
Bottom Wood
Willow Stream
Lozenge Wood
Becourt
Fricourt Farm
Fricourt Wood
Becourt Wood
0 500 1000
Approx scale — yards
FRICOURT
MAMETZ
Willow Stream
FRICOURT SALIENT
GERMAN LINES
through which the Allies fought July 1916 — a typical section of the Battle of Somme

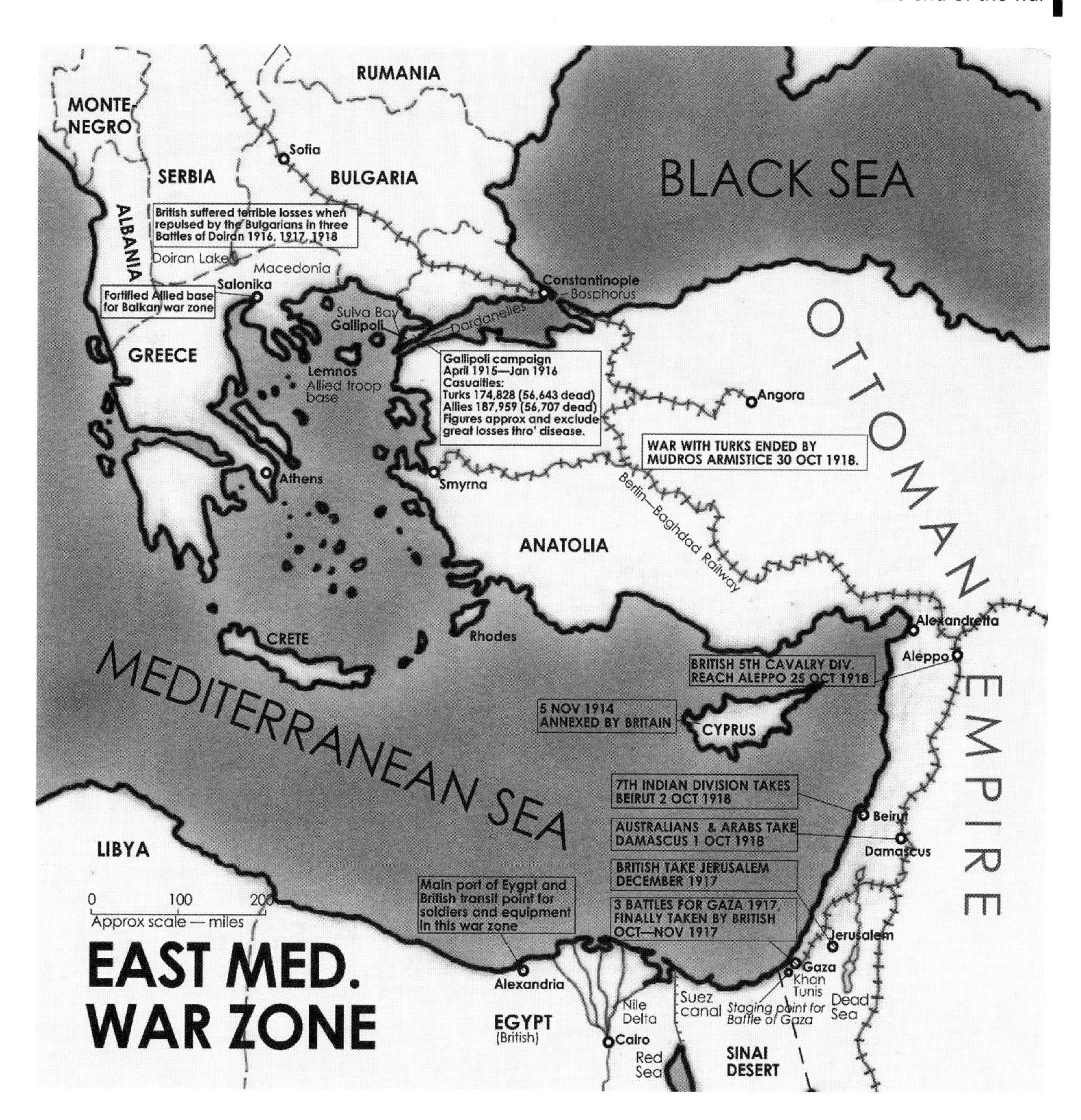
RUMANIA
MONTE-NEGRO
Sofia
SERBIA
BULGARIA
BLACK SEA
ALBANIA
British suffered terrible losses when repulsed by the Bulgarians in three Battles of Doiran 1916, 1917, 1918
Doiran Lake
Macedonia
Salonika
Fortified Allied base for Balkan war zone
Constantinople
Bosphorus
Sulva Bay
Gallipoli
Dardanelles
GREECE
Lemnos
Allied troop base
Gallipoli campaign
April 1915—Jan 1916
Casualties:
Turks 174,828 (56,643 dead)
Allies 187,959 (56,707 dead)
Figures approx and exclude great losses thro' disease.
Angora
OTTOMAN EMPIRE
WAR WITH TURKS ENDED BY MUDROS ARMISTICE 30 OCT 1918.
Athens
Smyrna
Berlin—Baghdad Railway
ANATOLIA
CRETE
Rhodes
Alexandretta
Aleppo
BRITISH 5TH CAVALRY DIV. REACH ALEPPO 25 OCT 1918
MEDITERRANEAN SEA
5 NOV 1914 ANNEXED BY BRITAIN
CYPRUS
7TH INDIAN DIVISION TAKES BEIRUT 2 OCT 1918
Beirut
AUSTRALIANS & ARABS TAKE DAMASCUS 1 OCT 1918
Damascus
LIBYA
BRITISH TAKE JERUSALEM DECEMBER 1917
0 100 200
Approx scale — miles
Main port of Eygpt and British transit point for soldiers and equipment in this war zone
3 BATTLES FOR GAZA 1917, FINALLY TAKEN BY BRITISH OCT—NOV 1917
Jerusalem
EAST MED. WAR ZONE
Alexandria
Gaza
Khan Tunis
Nile Delta
Suez canal
Staging point for Battle of Gaza
Dead Sea
EGYPT
(British)
Cairo
Red Sea
SINAI DESERT

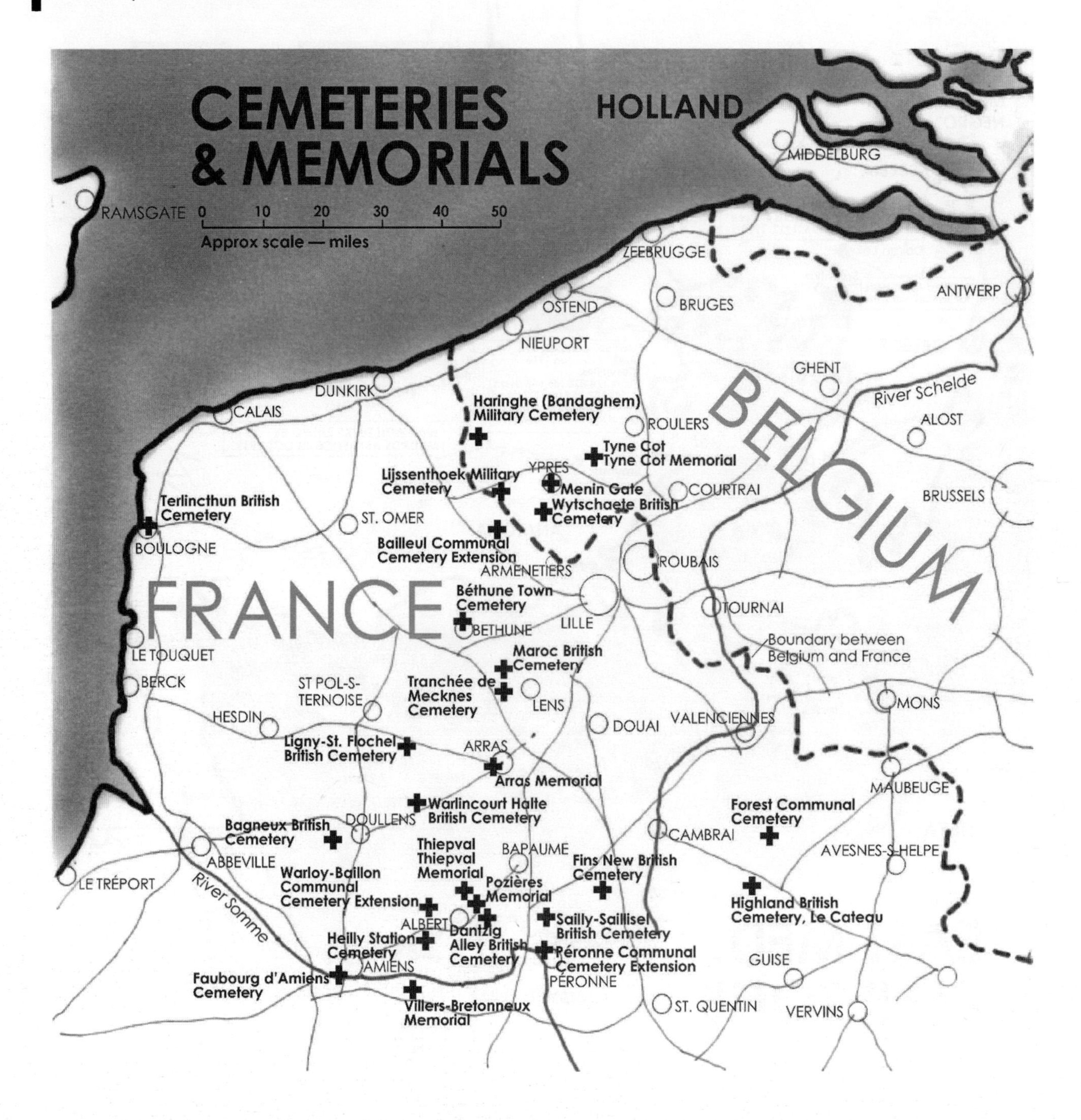
CEMETERIES & MEMORIALS
HOLLAND
MIDDELBURG
RAMSGATE
0 10 20 30 40 50
Approx scale — miles
ZEEBRUGGE
ANTWERP
OSTEND
BRUGES
NIEUPORT
GHENT
River Schelde
DUNKIRK
CALAIS
Haringhe (Bandaghem) Military Cemetery
ROULERS
BELGIUM
ALOST
Tyne Cot
Tyne Cot Memorial
YPRES
Lijssenthoek Military Cemetery
Menin Gate
Wytschaete British Cemetery
COURTRAI
BRUSSELS
Terlincthun British Cemetery
ST. OMER
BOULOGNE
Bailleul Communal Cemetery Extension
ARMENETIERS
ROUBAIS
FRANCE
Béthune Town Cemetery
LILLE
TOURNAI
BETHUNE
LE TOUQUET
Maroc British Cemetery
Boundary between Belgium and France
BERCK
ST POL-S-TERNOISE
Tranchée de Meckness Cemetery
LENS
MONS
HESDIN
DOUAI
VALENCIENNES
Ligny-St. Flochel British Cemetery
ARRAS
Arras Memorial
MAUBEUGE
Warlincourt Halte British Cemetery
Forest Communal Cemetery
Bagneux British Cemetery
DOULLENS
CAMBRAI
Thiepval
Thiepval Memorial
BAPAUME
ABBEVILLE
AVESNES-S-HELPE
Warloy-Baillon Communal Cemetery Extension
Fins New British Cemetery
LE TRÉPORT
River Somme
Pozières Memorial
Highland British Cemetery, Le Cateau
ALBERT
Dantzig Alley British Cemetery
Sailly-Saillisel British Cemetery
Heilly Station Cemetery
Péronne Communal Cemetery Extension
GUISE
AMIENS
Faubourg d'Amiens Cemetery
PÉRONNE
Villers-Bretonneux Memorial
ST. QUENTIN
VERVINS

No Man's Land, somewhere in Flanders, during the war

Diaries and Memories

Diaries and Memories

The First World War left life-long scars for those that fought in it. I remember being told by a man whose father had fought in the trenches that he could never get his father to talk about his trench experiences, and when he pressed him particularly on one occasion with the question, "Did you ever shoot anybody during the war?" his father only sat in silence while tears rolled down his cheeks. Many refused to talk about their involvement and left little record that they had even witnessed the fighting, let alone, in some cases, been decorated for considerable bravery.

Nevertheless, we do have lengthy testimonies from some servicemen. From the records they have left of God's preserving care, and of special blessings received even in the midst of the battlefield, their aim can be seen to be the glory of God.

Clement Kay Baldwin

Clement Kay Baldwin was for 28 years a deacon at Ebenezer Chapel, Worthing, then latterly a member at Galeed Chapel, Brighton. He died on 8th January, 1993, aged 96. The following is extracted from his writings:

✍ In July 1916, after initial training, I was drafted to join the 12th Battalion Royal Sussex Regiment in France, and went straight into the firing line. My eyes were up unto the Lord – there was my safety and comfort. My dear one sent me the monthly periodicals, and in a *Gospel Standard* there was a piece about prayer by Mr J. K. Popham.[279] O it was such a help and comfort to me as we moved to the Somme. There we were under almost constant shell fire and I truly felt:

> Plagues and deaths around me fly;
> Till he bids, I cannot die;
> Not a single shaft can hit,
> Till the God of love sees fit.[280]

Many were killed around me, two being buried alive in the end of the trench where I was. In another fierce bombardment, with shells falling all around, I was at the Lewis gun[281] when a little bird like a sparrow came and settled on the sandbag breastwork, and immediately this word dropped with power upon my spirit, concerning the sparrows: 'One of them shall not fall on the ground without your Father ... ye are of more value than many sparrows.' That was in June 1917 and I often think of it now when I see a sparrow; I love the sparrows. In one counter-attack in Belgium, we were ordered to advance over an open field with the enemy shelling very heavily, when these verses came to mind:

> Had I a glance of thee, my God,
> Kingdoms and men would vanish soon;
> Vanish as though I saw them not,
> As a dim candle dies at noon.
>
> Then they might fight, and rage, and rave,
> I should perceive the noise no more
> Than we can hear a shaking leaf,
> While rattling thunders round us roar.[282]

I felt a peace come over me, and the attack was called off, the commanders fearing too many casualties.

On April 26th, 1918, we were surrounded during a German attack and taken prisoner. During the next four months we had little to eat, and some starved and died. I became ill with bronchitis and was sent to a hospital in Westphalia. There I had a dream that I was embarking on a ship, and I felt that deliverance was near. I was too ill to be moved immediately after the Armistice was signed, but left Germany on December 18th, and on the 20th embarked at Rotterdam exactly as I had seen it in my dream some twelve weeks before.

After my safe return, I was put into Brighton Eye Hospital for two months, and was able to attend the services at Galeed and hear Mr J. K. Popham. I was eventually demobilized in August 1919.[283]

Herbert Pitt Banfield

Herbert Banfield attended Galeed Chapel, Brighton, throughout his life. He was baptised there by Mr J. K. Popham in 1934, and at the time of his death, in 1992, was the last surviving member of Mr Popham's church. He was a deacon at Galeed Chapel for nearly 57 years. During the war he served in the Signal Corps. Three other brothers, Marcus (whose diary follows this account), Arthur and Legh, also served in the war. A letter written to the Banfield brothers by Mr Popham, when they joined up, can be found on page 436. The following is the account Herbert wrote of his own war service. It is taken from his obituary in *The Gospel Standard*:

✍ The First World War soon after broke out, and I, with my two elder brothers, volunteered for service.

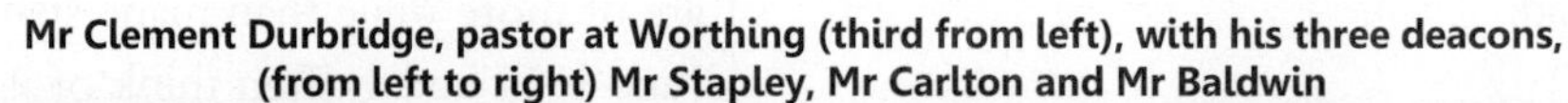
Mr Clement Durbridge, pastor at Worthing (third from left), with his three deacons, (from left to right) Mr Stapley, Mr Carlton and Mr Baldwin

Herbert (left) and Arthur Banfield (right)

I little thought of the sacrifice my parents made to let us go, but father stressed on us when we left home, 'Them that honour me I will honour,' and this rested on my mind. We lodged in huge huts which held about 250 men in each. This was a fresh experience for us, when we were brought into close contact with mankind with all restraint cast aside, each one vying with the next to appear the most vile. We were given little truckle beds, and I wondered what I should do when kneeling for prayer at the close of the day as I had been wont to do. However, the exhortation father had spoken to us helped me to make a venture, and the Lord restrained voice and hand, and no one endeavoured to molest. The orderly sergeant for the day came round as I was so engaged and made some general comment, but a big fellow, well known as a boxer, immediately spoke up on my behalf and expressed in a very forcible way that if anyone ventured to touch me, he would knock his head off; and no one ever did interfere with me.

On another occasion we had an outbreak of spotted fever in our hut, and we were all isolated and swabs taken from each one's throat, and anticipation was rife regarding a serious and fatal outbreak. The Lord was pleased to speak home to me the 91st Psalm, and the 6th and 7th verses were a strength, and I felt persuaded that I should escape. When eventually the roll was called of all those that were found free from infection, my name was the first given out, which encouraged my faith in God exceedingly.

Eventually we went overseas, and I was over two years in France and Belgium, often preserved in danger, but being a signaller on battalion headquarters, spared some of the worst of trench warfare. Twice, when the battalion went 'over the top,' I was kept behind to help form a reserve of specialists in case of the worst, and on each occasion headquarters suffered serious casualties. However, in March 1918, I was wounded and withdrawn, and, after a week in Rouen, sent back to England, where in the providence of God I was kept until the war ended. I finished my soldiering days at Newhaven, and could often get home, and the Lord made my heart tender (there had been a gradual hardening effect), and I received many distinct answers to my poor prayers whilst there, the memory of which still abide. The Lord also caused me to read Ezekiel chapter 36, verses 21 to 32, and this portion has ever been a comfort and strength to me when brought fresh to the mind.[284]

Marcus Ebenezer Banfield

Marcus Banfield was an older brother of Herbert Banfield, whose account precedes this. Marcus was brought up at Galeed Chapel, Brighton. He joined up in 1915, with his brother Herbert (Bert), and served in the Royal Sussex Regiment. He died in Belgium, 26th April, 1918, aged 24, as a result of wounds received in enemy action. He is buried in Haringhe (Bandaghem) Military Cemetery, Belgium, grave number V. B. 42. Engraved on his gravestone are the following words, "Them also which sleep in Jesus will God bring with him." The diary Marcus kept during the war was serialised after his death in *The Friendly Companion* between June 1919 and April 1920. The diary is reproduced here as it appeared in that magazine.

✍ *1915* – We left home about 9 a.m. (January 12th) having to get to the recruiting office in the Church Road pretty early. Here we were told to wait.

A youth from Steyning, who regrets very forcibly ever joining, was the first to arrive of those who were to form the party for Bexhill. A little later a disreputable man came in, with a terribly torn coat, whose name we learnt was Swann. We still waited for a third party, but as the minutes went by and he did not turn up, we were told to get ready to leave to catch the 11 o'clock train. A sergeant turned up, and we were for the first time in our lives escorted through the streets by an officer of the army. For some reason or other I felt a bit ashamed – probably being in the company of the man with the torn coat had something to do with it. We halted at the office of the Southdowns at North Street Quadrant for more recruits, but on finding there were none we marched on to the station. Arriving there, the sergeant got our tickets and delivered them, for safe custody, if I remember aright, to the disreputable Swann. He shook our hands, and said some nice things to us, which I am sorry not to remember. He was a decent chap; if they were all like him, the army would not be bad.

The train started with one 1st Battalion man in one corner of the carriage; he looked very fat, and slept most of the time. Just before getting to London Road Station, I saw my aunts waving a cloth of some kind out of the window of their house, in the hope of our seeing it. I saw it, but dare not stir from my seat for obvious reasons.

The journey was slow, the train going into Eastbourne and out again, and on to Bexhill. On arriving at Bexhill, we looked out for some man who was to meet us and conduct us to the orderly room. One of my first impressions of this man was the overwhelming desire on his part for an easy time of it. It evidently required a great deal of energy for him to come and meet us. He led us to the Bexe[285], and we then were told to wait in the hall. I was expecting a major or someone to come, but instead there turned

Marcus E. Banfield

up a corporal, who (I believe for the first and last time) smilingly told us he was sorry to keep us waiting. He then took our names, ages, etc. Then we were told to go to the police station to get our billets.

We were still in the company of Swann and the Steyning youth, and together we marched along to the police station. Here we were taken to the charge room where we were confronted by a jovial sergeant and a constable. The sergeant seemed to take particular notice of the unhappy Swann, and asked where he had seen him before. Swann denied all previous acquaintance, however! After a little confabulation with the constable, he said we should be quite all right at the Manor Cottage. Swann and the Steyning youth were given a billet in the Victoria Road. Just as we were going out, the sergeant called me back and said he did not like the look of Swann. I felt, though I did not say so, that the feeling was mutual, but at the same time I did not think him a bad character. Further, the sergeant told us that directly he saw us he had it in his mind to put us[286] together; he said he never liked to separate brothers. He was an exceedingly decent chap.

We were then escorted to our billets by the constable. As we went along we saw some of the 3rd Southdowns. The first thing we saw at our billet was a woman at the washing tub, which, however, she left to show us our bedrooms. We soon found that we should be fairly comfortable, and much better than we expected. We were too late for dinner, so we had to go out and buy some, after which we strolled on to the front. It was not long before I was thoroughly miserable. I looked out over the sea and wished I was wounded and being sent over to England; this, I expect, was homesickness. We then went back to the billet to tea. The landlady gave us her best room and made us very comfortable. She had a family of two boys and two girls, her husband being the gardener at the Manor House.

The next morning we went on to the front, where the battalion paraded, and reported ourselves at the Bexe Hotel, and then were told to join No. 4 Company.

This we found, and together with a little group of recruits like ourselves, formed up in something like order, but were speedily sent to a little shelter, where our names were taken by a tall Grenadier Guardsman, who proved to be our company sergeant major. He seemed to be a very decent sort of man, but was very blunt. We then formed up and marched to the Hotel Metropole, where the battalion had its quartermaster's stores. Here we had to wait a good while for our kit, and had the first taste of the quality of the men we had to mix with. The language was the most awful we had ever heard, each one seeming to see who could be the worst.

We got on better with our drills than we anticipated. Every afternoon we went for a route march, arriving back about 4 p.m. On Sundays we paraded on the sea front for church parade. This was held at —. The service was conducted by the vicar, the hymns being led by our band. The man preached very empty sermons, though the church was not 'high.'[287] After service, which lasted about half an hour, we had a short march until dinnertime. On one occasion we were marched round Cooden Camp, which was the first time we had seen it closely. The huts looked very large, and we wondered whenever we should get used to such a place. Up to this time, in fact till we left billets in March, we were hardly on speaking terms with the other men. After a route march, our band always played us on to the parade ground with our fine march, 'Sussex by the Sea.'

In early March we left our comfortable billets for Cooden Camp. I do not think I shall easily forget those first few days. It was the first time we had really been thrown into such close contact with those around us. Though there was, and is, much in them that we would pray to be kept from, yet I will say that they are the most kind-hearted men I have ever met with. This may be because of their number, but I am speaking generally and from what I have experienced of them.

We had in the section one or two 'characters.' 'Uncle' R—, a dirty chap in appearance, who would attach himself to me.[288] Though I used to tease him till he was in the most furious rage, the next minute he would be as friendly as ever. Another man, W—, used to make us laugh, especially at meals. One remark of his about an aged bloater I shall not easily forget. Looking at the offending article, he sternly said: 'I think I've told you about this before – don't let me see you again.' He then resignedly placed it aside. The huts at Cooden were very large, holding a company each. Down each side were spaces for sleeping accommodation; in the centre, the space for meals. They were very comfortable, and in the camp itself we had every convenience. The camp was situated fairly high, looking over the Pevensey marshes to Eastbourne, with the South Downs behind. The nearest village was Little Common, where we could buy anything not obtainable in the canteens. Bexhill was only two miles away, and most of us went over there.

The usual parades were physical drill before breakfast, the ordinary drills morning and evening. I forgot to say that before leaving Bexhill my brother and I were picked out for signallers. I do not know whether this has been for the best. The men, or boys, are extremely childish and foolish, their language being vile beyond description. Most of them are chums of the sergeant instructor, living in the same place as he did at home. I did not know anything of this when joining the class, or most probably it would have prevented me from joining. I sometimes think that One above knew about this even from the beginning, and he also knows the end. I would that I knew he might make all things work for my eternal good. He knows the temptation and my weakness. I read hymn 1072 (*Gadsby's Selection*); may it be true of me.

We soon found out what sort of a man our sergeant was: wholly unconscientious, and about the laziest man I ever knew. How we ever learnt is a marvel. I have never had anything in common with any of the men, and now, after six months, I do not desire it any more. If it were not that I found the signalling interesting, I should have done my best to leave them; as it was, once or twice I did make up my mind to do so, but father said we should not, so we stayed on.

Life went on its usual way week after week. Every third week we had a weekend at home, and who can say, except those who live away, what a weekend at home is.

After a stay of about three months at Cooden, we left about the end of June for Detling, near

Maidstone. Here we were trenching for one of the lines of defence for London. We were not sorry, on the whole, to leave Cooden, as we were quite ready for a change. We entrained there, so had our first experience of a troop train. There were some touching farewells at the station, but it was soon over.

We left Bexhill at 10 a.m., reaching Maidstone about 1.30. After detraining, we marched to Detling, about three miles off. Detling village is pretty and old-fashioned, the camp lying about half-a-mile off, at the foot of the North Downs. The country is very pretty, but for some reason I soon wished I was back at Cooden; but this soon passed off, and we began to settle down.

On the Monday we had our first taste of trenching, which we soon found hard enough work. We signallers had to do it for the first week, but afterwards carried on as usual. Things were naturally rougher under canvas than in huts. We slept on the ground, with three blankets and a waterproof sheet; this we very soon got used to. The food was very rough, especially the meat, owing to the difficulty of cooking. While trenching, we had to cook our own dinner. This I found a sickening process, especially when out signalling, as sometimes in the middle of receiving a message the pot would boil over and nearly put the fire out. Sundays were the best days we spent in the army; either Mrs Weeks or Mr Marsh would have us to dinner or tea, so we felt very comfortable there. Mrs Weeks especially was very kind. In the evenings we went to the Priory Chapel, where we heard various ministers – Messrs Thomas,[289] Boorman,[290] Picknell,[291] Little[292] and Hazelton.[293] On Saturdays we often went into Maidstone to have baths and tea, and then for short walks. One Saturday we went over to Staplehurst, where we spent a very nice time with Mrs Pounds. Altogether we spent a good time at Detling, staying there till the end of September.

The last day and night there we shall not soon forget. The rain came down in misty sheets at intervals in the night. I thought the tent would come down because of the violence of the wind; it, however, stood the shock, and did not let much water through until the morning, when it dripped in several places. In the morning it was just as bad, so we did what we could as regards rolling our blankets, etc. We packed our rations for twenty-four hours in our haversacks, and got ready to march off. As it was raining, we had to do this in our overcoats, which made it rather hard work. The band accompanied us, but minus the big drum, which sounded rather strange. We reached Maidstone, but as it was wet and rather early, there were not many people about. We saw Fred Marsh looking out for us. We then entrained for Aldershot, via Redhill and Guildford. We got out at Farnborough, and marched to North Comp, where we were stationed in the Marlborough Lines – Malplaquet Barracks. We were very comfortable here; nevertheless I did not approve of it, the place being too military for my liking. The barracks are brick and certainly comfortable, with washing house attached to each block, which is a great convenience. Baths were quite handy, also a canteen and a YMCA[294] hut. One hardly sees a civilian about. Aldershot town is the most abominable place I know of; plenty of public houses, fried fish shops, and the inevitable cinemas. There seems to be a sort of curse over the place, and

I shall be quite content never to see it again. The country around is flat and uninteresting, except to the south. One hardly had the spirit to go far at Aldershot. To my great relief we only stayed there a fortnight. Just before leaving we had an inspection by our divisional commander, Major General Barnardiston. He is an exceedingly nice man, and spoke to several of the men, especially to those who had any ribbons.[295]

On leaving Aldershot (personally without a pang), we marched to a camp near Witley. One of my feet gave a bit of trouble, but I managed to stick it. We came through Elstead and Milford way, passing over the Hog's Back and Crooksbury Hill. The country looked very beautiful. Witley Camp is situated in a beautiful spot, surrounded by pine trees and heather. The huts are of wood, are fairly watertight, and quite comfortable. For the first time we have a separate mess room, which is rather nice.

While at Aldershot we signallers had our field telephones, and we are now busy practising with them.

Sundays are very miserable here; no satisfactory churches or chapels near.

About now we had an officer placed over us for the first time. This was disagreeable at first to a great many, for obvious reasons. He had a great many new ideas, and we had to unlearn a good deal. I find he has a great partiality for the old 'E' Company lads, but I think he will find out his mistake soon. We now put in a good deal of time practising on the telephones, and can sometimes read pretty efficiently on them. I had to take a new class of signallers and teach them semaphore and Morse codes on flags. This was quite

Aldershot Strict Baptist Chapel

new work to me, and for a time I liked it, but it got rather stale at times. About this time I received a stripe.[296] I naturally wanted it, but now I have it, I am not so sure it is all so nice as it looks. As the signallers are practically without discipline, it is a bit difficult to manage them at times. One day we had to run a new cable from our commanding officer's house to the orderly room; this we did, and had the satisfaction of having it work properly.

About December 1st we were hurriedly sent home on Christmas leave. We did not exactly approve of the short notice, but had to go. We were told it was the last War Office leave. The weather was bad while at home, but we had a good time. We went down to the shop and said goodbye. I did not like leaving home much. Father came to the station with us and saw us off. On the way down he spoke to us of the throne of grace, and said that the best of it was, it was for sinners.

After this, things went on pretty quietly, we still practising signalling, etc. We did not have any early morning parades, but generally had one in the evening for lamp reading.

Christmas Day came on. We had nearly four days' holiday, but the weather was unfortunately bad, so we could not go out much. Christmas morning we had a voluntary church parade, which was well attended. The food was not bad considering everything, but the attendant festivities I could have very well done without. We had dinner in No. 10 Platoon hut, which was decked with holly, etc. Captain Humble-Crofts, Lieutenants Elliott and Elphick, and the Adjutant had dinner with us, and I hope they enjoyed it. I was very glad when it was all over. The young fellow (B——), who slept next to me, came in drunk for the first time in his life, and I think he was quite ashamed of himself. The three following days were wet, so we had to keep indoors, and altogether I was very glad to be on parade again.

About this time we were very busy on musketry, as we were shortly going on our musketry course. About a fortnight after Christmas we marched off to Aldershot for the purpose. We were put in Tournai Barracks – wretched prison-like places. Every morning we had to get up at five o'clock for breakfast, and then to march off to Ash Ranges, where we did our firing. The range, where we were, ran up to 600 yards, and that was the farthest we had to shoot in this course. We were allowed a practice first to get used to our rifles, and I soon found that the much exaggerated kick of the rifle was nothing. I got on much better than I expected, getting well over the first class mark, though not reaching to 'marksman.' The weather was very fine while firing, though rather cold. There was a lot of waiting about for one's turn – in fact, we generally only fired about ten rounds each per day, this only taking ten minutes. Aldershot I found as bad as ever. While there, Bert and I went over to Camberley.

At Camberley we saw Arthur,[297] who was in hospital there. We found him up and better, expecting shortly to be out. Camberley is pretty much like Aldershot, only more high class; everyone caters for the military. What must the countries be like where they have conscription? Still, it looks as if we are to have a mild sort of it here! I hope it will never be really so after the war. I was very glad to be packing up again to get back to Witley. It is rather dull and depressing here sometimes, but there is the country to go to, and on a fine day it is glorious to get right out and away from everything military. Once I had a very decent stroll with Bert across country to Tilford. We kept right off the main roads, and enjoyed ourselves alright. Another stroll to Haslemere, which was very fine. There is a beautiful view from the main Portsmouth road, about two miles from the top of Hindhead, looking east, also another from an old tree stump, looking over the same ground, only lower down, Hindhead towering up to the west. I think the view stretches right away to Sussex.

Soon after leaving Aldershot, the Brigade started granting weekend leave, which was very decent. We managed to get one in, but at the present moment we are rather afraid they are all over. We keep hearing reports that we shall soon be at the front; in fact, they must be true, as they come from the men who know. We are now on the lookout to see whether last leave of 48 hours will be given.

March 7th, 1916 – We left Witley Camp on Sunday, about 9.30 a.m., travelling by train to Southampton Docks. This was the first time I had been there, and I was very interested in the docks and the shipping. Our boat was the *Australind*, a very slow goer. The train ran right up to the quay. We got out into a large shed, where there was a canteen where we could obtain hot coffee, etc. We arrived about 1 p.m., and as we did not have to embark until 5.30, we were at liberty to walk about the docks. There were two or three large Union Castle liners in the dock, converted into Red Cross ships, having large red crosses painted on the sides and funnels. We also saw an armed merchantman with several big guns. The tugs plying about the harbour seemed very powerful, though only small in size. We could see Netley Hospital on the other side of the water. The cranes looked very powerful, and it was most interesting to watch the transport carts, etc., being swung aboard. About 5.30 p.m. we marched on board, and were taken down into the hold, which was low-pitched, having fixed tables and forms. I did not stay there long – it seemed rather stuffy, so I went on deck and had my last look at England. It was rather misty in the dusk, and I naturally wondered when and under what conditions I should see it again. The boat did not leave until 8.30. I stood at the bulwarks for nearly an hour, and did not feel very sad about leaving, as the novelty and excitement took it off a bit. As the boat moved off, I quite made up my mind to be sick. I stayed on deck nearly an hour, and then went below to try to get a sleep. To my surprise I could hardly feel the boat moving, and soon dozed off. I was rather anxious about submarines, especially as Germany had just started her second submarine policy.[298] We picked up, however, a respectable escort of destroyers, which attended us across the Channel. We were each issued out with a lifebelt, which we had to tie round our bodies. I would feel grateful to the Lord for bringing us safely over, and thus delivering us from one great danger. We sighted the French coast about seven o'clock the next morning. I came on deck about 6 a.m., and felt rather unsteady for a few moments, but soon got over it. There was a fresh wind on, and the sea was swelling a good deal. Soon after we dropped anchor just outside the harbour of Le Havre. Here we saw vessels of several nationalities, Norway, Denmark, etc., being the most prominent. They had their respective flags painted on their sides, so that the Hun 'subs' should have no excuse. Inside the harbour we saw a boat sunk, with only her funnels and mast above water.

Later we learned she had been torpedoed just

outside the harbour, just missing the transport with the 11th and 12th Battalions by a few hours. We had to wait in the harbour nearly two hours before disembarking, so we were very glad when the order came.

About the first thing we saw was a party of German prisoners marching to their work, escorted by French soldiers with fixed bayonets. They looked very rough and indifferent, though I noticed one who seemed rather proud and supercilious, and who walked with his head in the air. Somehow I felt rather sorry for them. We stayed for the night at a rest camp just outside the town, under canvas. As the ground was covered with snow, this was far from nice. I had a warm night, however, which was better than I expected. At 3.30 the next morning we were up, marched to Le Havre station, and were entrained in some cattle trucks. This seemed a very rough way of travelling, but we all accepted it cheerfully. We were fortunately able to get some hot tea and French cakes before starting.

The journey, which took us nineteen hours, was very interesting, but we were only able to look out occasionally. We passed through Rouen, and I was just able to see the cathedral. The country is generally very flat and not very interesting round this part. As we got farther east it was rather prettier.

We at length reached our destination, Steinbach. It was snowing pitilessly when we arrived, and it was an unpleasant journey up to the camp, a distance of two miles. At 4 a.m. we again found ourselves under canvas, which did not mend matters. We all lay down and tried to sleep, in no very genial frame of mind. In the morning we were allotted our tents, and quickly settled down. We soon found we were in a very interesting part of the country, in places only twelve to fourteen miles from the front. We could distinctly hear the guns at times. About the camp we could see the graves of officers and men who had fallen in battles round here. The French people had put up a lot of wooden crosses over them. The houses near all showed marks of the fighting.

We stayed in this camp two or three days, and then moved off to the firing line. The march took us two days, arriving the first night at Estaires, or rather just outside. We were billeted in a barn, which seemed rather rough, but it was a good thing to have a roof over us. The next morning we arose at 4 a.m., had breakfast, and then I, in company with the sergeant and three others, went on our cycles to secure billets for the battalion. It was an awful ride, which I shall not easily forget. After three or four hours of it, we arrived at the place, having gone several miles out of the way. For the first time since leaving England we are in something like a comfortable place, though within range of the German guns. One shell *did* drop near 'A' Company's billet. We have a very snug little place for our signalling office, and I hope we shall find it comfortable.

March 12th – Today I saw the first German aeroplane – our anti-aircraft guns firing at it. They fortunately brought it down. It was a very thrilling sight, and I was naturally glad to see the foe defeated. Last night I heard machine guns in action for the first time. I am now on duty at headquarters until 8 p.m. I hope to keep the diary daily if at all possible.

In a few hours I shall have been in France a week, and have been through hardships, etc., such as I have never experienced before, but am thankful to say strength has been given me. I am now about to start on the most serious part of it, in fact, *am* in it, as we are so near the firing line.

March 13th – Not a very busy day. Had an interesting time watching the Royal Garrison Artillery firing some of their 4.7 inch guns. Several anti-aircraft guns in action today, but no results on either side. Germans shelled Fleurbaix this afternoon, causing some casualties in the 11th Battalion, but particulars not yet to hand. These are most serious times. Oh, to know for certain that the Lord is watching over us both! The hymns, 1113 (*Gadsby's Selection*; 'How watchful is the loving Lord') and 'Abide with me,' seem so nice. I think sometimes if it shall ever be true of me I must be the happiest person alive. I think the hymn 'Abide with me' very suitable for soldiers. It was Gordon's favourite hymn.[299]

I am now on duty, but come off at eleven o'clock. Another round of our 4.7s[300] has just gone off, and has shaken our billet to the foundations. Today all the battalion signallers, except Bert and me and two others who were away, went up to the trenches for instruction. I am rather wondering if this means anything. The night seems rather quieter than last, not so much machine gun firing. Saw a German observation balloon today.

March 14th – Telephone duty nearly all day; had a very busy time midday. We have such a kind old French woman near our billet; we take her bacon and eggs and rice to cook, and she never thinks of letting us pay. We always go to her for coffee. Her husband also is very friendly. They are Roman Catholics, as nearly every one round here is; their walls are covered with pictures of the crucifixion and the Virgin Mary. They have a nice, comfortable kitchen, and they never mind our dropping in to a meal. I am going up to the trenches tomorrow night; wonder how I shall get on. Till now, as a regiment, we have only had one casualty: Garner, of 'B' Company, wounded.

March 15th – Was on telephone duty till 5 p.m., when we were relieved by a party back from the trenches. They came back with some rather thrilling stories of how they had been shelled on the way back, and how they had only just left the shelter of a house when it was demolished by a shell. I was in charge of the party, and we together started on the journey with rather mixed feelings. On the way we met fellows who told us we were 'going through the mill,' so we did not have very much to cheer us up. We heard the machine guns, so put on rather more speed, and eventually arrived quite safely. We found the signalling office is a snug little place, sandbagged, and, I hope, pretty safe. We did not have to do any work, but just lay down and had a chat with the corporal in charge. He had been through Neuve Chapelle and had some good stories to tell. I liked what he said about Sir Douglas Haig.[301] Bert and I slept in a dugout by ourselves, and had a good night. The signallers here say they had an awful shelling near headquarters in the afternoon. From our billets we heard them shelling Fleurbaix.

March 16th – Woke up about 6.30; after breakfast, which was rather a rough affair, we went down to the trenches with the corporal. We first entered the communication trench, which leads to the firing line. These were nice and dry, owing to the boards laid down the bottoms. We saw the various stations, which seemed very comfortable, if a little cramped. The firing itself seemed very secure, being sandbagged heavily. The German trenches are not more than 80 yards away in places. I very much wanted to see the German trenches through a periscope, but did not have the opportunity. While we were in the trenches, the Germans were firing a small gun, quite close to their firing line. Some of our aeroplanes were observing, and were shelled. We took shelter in a dugout, lest some falling shrapnel should find us out. I have just seen three men brought in wounded, one an officer.

March 17th – We received our first mail since leaving England. What a treat it is to hear. Everyone seems well, which is a great thing. Last night I took over a company station for our 'C' Company, which is holding a part of trench on its own for the first time. I am glad to say we are going on well. The work is really simple, and provided we don't have too long a spell, I think we shall all be pretty satisfied. Our dugout is nice and roomy, but seems to want rather in furniture. If I were staying here for any length of time, I would soon have an alteration. The floor is corrugated iron, which is none too soft to lie on! We had a little exchange of shells this afternoon; a cheeky little 18 pounder of ours, which seems to have been annoying Fritz[302] terribly, underwent a bombardment, but once more escaped. It has been there now for some months. I am making this diary up at 11 p.m. It is generally done at this time; I have more time than when on duty. One of our land mines has just gone off, and quite made our dugout sway for a moment or two.

Sunday, March 19th – I had a lovely long sleep until nearly six this morning. There was a very violent bombardment to the south last night, somewhere near Neuve Chapelle. How differently my dear father and mother will be spending this day from what we are experiencing here, but the same God is over us here as there. Lord, do look upon us as the Friend of sinners, and do keep us from our indifference to thee.

> Come not in terrors as the King of kings,
> But kind and good, with healing in thy wings,
> Tears for all woes, a heart for every plea;
> Come, Friend of sinners, thus abide with me![303]

… We left the trenches about 3 o'clock, and were not at all sorry to get away. We had a hot march back, but managed to get some coffee near our old billet. We arrived at our new billet at Sailly about 6 p.m. after a safe journey out. It seems to be a great relief to be away from the trenches. A sniper had been very active near our dugout for several hours, and I was glad to be rid of his attentions. As we neared our billet I heard some men singing, and found the sound came from a Soldiers' Club [*YMCA*]. I got my pack off and went in, and thus attended my first service on French soil. I was glad, I think very glad, to attend a place of worship after all. We had some nice hymns, and the chaplain prayed very earnestly, but I am afraid the address was rather wrong at times. One thing was about universal salvation; he said that if he did not believe that he could never be a parson. It seems very sad that there is no one to preach the truth to these men, just back from facing death, and even then within sound of the guns; and yet at times he said some better things. We turned in about nine o'clock, and had a decent night's rest.

*March 20*th – Could not get the breakfast cooked till 9.30 a.m.. What a lot we are! We are leaving tonight for Fleurbaix. It seems rather strange we should be going there, as it is such a mark for the German guns. We feel rather nervy about it, but, as dear father writes:

Not a single shaft can hit,
Till the God of love sees fit.[304]

Later – Have arrived at our billet, which is a dwelling house, situated quite near the front. French mortars are making a great noise. As soon as we arrived, I was put on duty as usual, till 12 p.m.

March 21st – The first day of spring; rather misty here, but everywhere the hedges and trees are bursting into leaf. I had the morning 'off,' but could not do much, as no one is allowed out of town without a pass. The town is considerably knocked about. We are nearly on the outskirts, and in a fairly comfortable billet. We work in shifts as usual, four hours on, and twelve off. Our officer wanted us to do eight hours on, and eight off, but we jibbed rather! I tried to get a bath, but could not. Went and had supper with Lawrence. Heard from Arthur,[305] and had a parcel from home. Had a decent rest.

March 22nd – Rose at 4 a.m. to go on duty. Heard today that I am on headquarter's staff, settled. Am very glad and relieved, as I did not fancy the company work. Bert is also on headquarters, and a pretty sensible lot of men, too. Tomorrow we are leaving this place; so far we have been kept safe. About five o'clock this morning heard a sound of explosion; think it was an aeroplane, dropping bombs, as the anti-aircraft guns were in action. Am feeling very relieved we are leaving here. Heard from mother. Have been at work from 4 a.m. till midnight, though a little rest this afternoon.

March 23rd – Spent in much the same way. Made preparations for leaving. Some of our guns fired in the vicinity, but was thankful the enemy did not retaliate. Left Fleurbaix about 5 p.m. Had rather a tiring march; lost our way and had to wait about while our officer tried to find our whereabouts. It was very cold. Found our billet about 10 p.m. – it was a big barn. We soon tumbled in between the blankets, and as we were nearly dead tired, soon fell asleep.

March 24th – Woke about 10 a.m., after a fine sleep; cooked my own breakfast, after making my eyes water horribly. We are having a rest today, as we are on the move again at two in the morning. Am now going to see how I can cook my dinner. (Later: This has turned out very well considering the conditions!) About 6 p.m. I was warned to take charge of a party, and had to take them to the headquarters of the 9th Cheshires,[306] who are billeted at a place called Robarmetz. I found it all right, and was billeted for the night in a barn.

As I was lying down to sleep, I think I felt I wanted a little to thank the Lord for giving us the comforts he has done. Lord, do keep me from coldness and indifference.

A Cheshire officer was very kind to us, and gave us some supper, which was very welcome, as we had been rather short of food the last day or so.

March 25th – Heard from Legh.[307] We are always on the lookout for a letter. We find ourselves billeted in a small, low-pitched stable, which is anything but nice and enjoyable.

March 26th – I woke up this morning feeling anything but happy. It is Sunday again, and we have been brought through another week. We have been in danger, but have been preserved. Last night I read in the little book Auntie Martie gave me these words: 'The sufferings of this present time are not worthy to be compared with the glory which shall be revealed in us.' It seemed very nice, especially as I had been feeling rather 'down.'

Near here are several graves of soldiers. The French people seem to take care of them in some cases, which speaks well for them, but some of the native people seem very close and objectionable. I suppose really we cannot wonder, but the man in charge of the farm here is about the limit; he would only give me nine eggs for a joint of beef, about ten to twelve pounds [*weight*]. Needless to say, he didn't get it!

March 27th – Woke up and found it was rather a better day as regards weather. What a difference the weather makes to our feelings! Was on telephone duty from one to five o'clock, and as one of our men was sick, went on his turn from 9 p.m. to 9 a.m. Tuesday morning. It was a very dismal time, as the night was wild and windy. The signal office here is a very draughty place, with an ill-fitting door and broken windows. I was very glad to leave in the morning.

March 28th – Left off duty at 9 a.m.. Went back to the billet and had a good breakfast; afterwards lay down and had a decent sleep, until nearly one o'clock. A little buzzer practice in the afternoon, and at 5 p.m. once more went on duty. Received a lovely photo of father and mother as a birthday present from them. Am very pleased with it.

March 30th – My birthday. The second I have had since joining the army. I hope very much this will be the last. I had a nice lot of letters and parcels, which I think I was very fortunate to get on the very date. I am more than pleased with the photo of father and mother. Arthur and Legh sent me some of the always welcome chocolates, and the Lockes sent me a decent little present, too.

I hear that we are moving early on the morrow, but I think we are not going farther than Merville. I went there this afternoon, and find it much like the rest of the older French towns in this part. The square, bandstand, and town hall reminded me very much of Hazebrouck. There is a very fine church there, far more stately than some of our cathedrals. The town seems quite intact, and not to have suffered from the war at all. The YMCA has a hut here, and it was nice to go in one again, and get some tea, etc. The weather is getting quite mild. The last evening or two have been beautiful. The stars here seem very brilliant and large. I saw today a map of the British Front; we are quite close to La Bassée and Neuve Chapelle.

March 31st – Was on duty all the previous night, and wrote several letters during the time. We left Merville about 9.30 in the morning for this place, Vieux Berquin. It is very much prettier round here, and we are fortunately billeted in a nice barn, quite different from the place we have just left.

April 1st – Beautiful, spring-like day. The country seemed very nice and peaceful in the sun. Our life seems to run in one groove just now. We do practically nothing when not on duty, so cannot say we have a really hard time. There was a most beautiful sunset this evening. I went out for a little walk by myself.

April 2nd – Sunday has come round once more. I don't know how I shall spend it ... I would like to get right away from my surroundings for a few hours.

We had a church parade this morning, but I was unable to attend as I was on duty. I am afraid that being on headquarters we shall miss these parades. Though we don't hear much, I think it is right to attend. I hear the band playing the hymns in the distance. The country all round is dotted with churches, some of which are fine buildings. It makes one sad to think of what is taught in them. I noticed the people, dressed in their Sunday best, going out for walks this afternoon, just as they do in England. I have felt a great wish and longing for home just lately. How little I realised what blessings I had, when home before the war. I often wonder how long it will be before we are home together again. The Lord bring it about, if it be his will, and make it work for our good and his glory. We get some good letters from home. I very much wish I could write and tell my dear parents about that *one thing*, but I dare not, yet. When I write in these books, and look back and read what I have written, I wonder how I dare do it. I hope I shall never write but what I feel.

April 3rd – 4.30 a.m., I have sinned against thee, do in mercy remember me. I am continually sinning. It seems to me that those people who know the Lord as their Saviour cannot sin as I sin, nor be nearly as bad; yet the reason they love him is because they know he has forgiven their sins. Oh, 'remember me … with the favour that thou bearest unto thy people.' 'Blot out my transgressions', and let me not live an indifferent life towards thee. More often my sins don't trouble me at all.

I like to read of the woman in Luke 7, who was a sinner. It ended with all she could wish for. I remember reading somewhere Bunyan says, 'Let it not go off my heart, but in the right way.' I so soon forget, and get cold and careless.

> Convince us of our sin,
> Then lead to Jesus' blood,
> And to our wondering view reveal,
> The secret love of God.[308]

There are, in a soldier's prayer which the chaplain uses at church parades, these words, 'Let the assurance of thy presence save us from sinning.' Hymn 593 (*Gadsby's Selection*).

The day was spent as usual. Very warm weather. Was fortunate in being able to get a nice warm bath in the afternoon, and in getting a clean change of clothes for the first time in France. Early this morning I was able to watch the sunrise. It rises at Greenwich at 5.34 a.m. It threw a good distinct shadow at 6 a.m. this morning.

April 4th – Am able to get hold of some fine, fresh eggs, and thus can get some good breakfasts. We live now very well, not having had the army biscuits for some days. I don't dislike them when they are three or four days old, and the hardness has gone out of them a bit. Am very glad to learn from the papers that another Zeppelin is destroyed; they seem to be going one by one. Heard from Legh today, and am expecting a parcel from him.

In the evening went out for a short stroll with Lightfoot of 'A' Company. There was a pretty big bombardment on the front near us – we could see big gun flashes as it got darker; also heard machine gun firing. It seemed rather sad to hear it, as the evening was so peaceful and calm where we were. Heard from Arthur, he also sent some photos.

April 5th – Had to get up soon after 6.30, as I was on duty at seven o'clock. It was a beautiful morning. Didn't do much all day. There are some fine chickens here at the farm where our signalling station is; some decent little bantams especially. There is also a goose which makes quite a noise. We can get eggs here at 1½d apiece, which is not dear. They come in handy for breakfast.

April 6th – Not much to write about … My name comes out in orders as paid lance corporal.

April 9th – Yesterday afternoon I went for a walk in a big wood or forest that is close by, with Lightfoot. It was very decent: a fine lot of primroses and violets, also lady's smock and periwinkle were out, and the woods looked a picture. In one place we saw a deer, which was in all probability wild. I could not see it so as to distinguish it, but Lightfoot saw it and traced it along with his eyes. I saw something dashing through the trees. Coming homewards, or rather coming back, we dropped into a cottage, where we consumed six cups of coffee between us. We came back by the village of La Motte. The Roman Catholic church is a very painful structure. Opposite it is a shop where candles are sold for their altars. The French Government have their seal, or stamp, round the base of the candles. It seems very sickening, all this fudgery. I did not have to do my late, all-night shift, as Sergeant Woodward volunteered to do it for me. I was very glad, naturally, to get off the job and get another night in bed. By the way, I did sleep in a bed for the first time since being in France, though it was not long enough to stretch one's feet in. We heard from home today.

April 10th – I noticed how very brilliant the stars and moon were this evening. They seemed to shine just like diamonds out here. The moon seemed brighter than I ever remember to have seen it before, though only half of it was visible. Today I had a look through one of our telescopes, and tried to read the time on the clock of Merville church. I could see the minute hand, but couldn't manage the smaller hand. The distance was about five miles. We hear unofficially that we are likely to stay here for another fourteen days. I hope so, for some things. Heard from home today, also from aunties. How I long to get home, and for the end of the war. Sometimes I think it won't be long before the war draws to an end, but when I look at it in a different way, I wonder whenever it will end. The nations do not seem to be turning to God as their Helper, much less anything closer; but how can I criticise, while I am what I am? I am a puzzle, and do not know how to write it down. I get so very, very indifferent to everything that is good and right, but one thing I did feel a little tonight was, that if the Lord does love me, and love me even through all the sins I have committed, it is a *very great* thing. I don't know whether I am right to even write this down, because I have no real hope that he does, whatever, and in a few hours, or even minutes, may be thinking of the most worldly things.

The country round here is beginning to look very nice and green, fruit trees blossoming, and the hedges all in leaf, the woods being a picture. It has made me think that Watts must have written that hymn somewhere in early spring, after winter:

> There is a land of pure delight …
> There everlasting spring abides,
> And never-withering flowers.[309]

April 15th – Since writing last we have once more shifted, being now in a village called Locon, not far from Béthune. We can easily see the town from here, and it looks a big place. We had a very tiring march from our previous billet, it taking somewhere about four or five hours. We came through Merville, and passed over La Bassée Canal, and walked along the side of it for over a mile. Near here we saw the first real hill we remember to have come across since being in Flanders. The country is more picturesque and prettier round this part than in any other part we have yet come across. The march was made a little worse by the cold wind, especially when we stopped for rests and took off our packs. Didn't eat very much all day, except on arriving at Locon, where we raided a French girl's basket of cakes. The cakes are awfully small for one pence, and the chocolate was an even worse swindle.

We are now very much nearer the firing line; today we once more enter the trenches, and take over our portion as a battalion. From what we hear, we are in a hot part, so I think it is rather an honour for us to be put there. Since being at our last billet, a change seems to have come over me as regards fighting; I have even at times felt I want to actually go for the enemy. Fortunately, the feeling does not always last … We hear that the trenches we are to go to are about eight kilometres distant. Am glad it is not very far, as my feet are rather sore. The rats and mice are a great plague here. When I got up at twelve o'clock some mice were having high jinks in someone's haversack.

April 20th – On the next day we went on the final stage of the march up to the trenches. We passed signposts pointing to well known places, such as La Bassée and Festubert. The weather was rather cold; it came on to rain at times, which made it rather worse. After about two hours' march, we struck the famous La Bassée Canal. We marched up the side of it for over a mile until we reached our destination, headquarters. The shells had made a terrible mess of the houses round here. I had never, of course, seen anything like it before. Our billet was anything but what we had pictured – a ruined house, hardly any roof and no door; altogether a most unsatisfactory place to live in. The signal dugout, however, was quite different, and about the best of its kind I have seen.

In the afternoon I went down through the trenches to have a look round. I thought they looked as if they had had rougher usage than those we had been in at Fleurbaix. I had a look at the German lines through a periscope.

On the Sunday, the day after we came in, we suffered a good few casualties, and it was not very cheerful to hear of fellows whom you knew being wounded and killed. Sunday, however, was the worst day, the others being comparatively quiet.

The four days we were in the trenches went quickly. I had a rather sore throat for the last two days, so was glad for more than one reason to get into a more comfortable place. On the Tuesday, I think, we left for the rest billet, a big chateau at Gorre. Some of the men say it is the one the Crown Prince plundered.[310] It certainly does look as if the paintings, etc., had been pulled off the ceilings especially. It was not, however, my idea of a chateau, though, of course, it must have looked very different in peace time. While here we had a pretty easy time, and were fortunate in getting a fairly decent room for sleeping. We were a bit crowded, but we never do get things quite our own way.

Easter Day – We once more find ourselves in the trenches, or, strictly speaking, at our headquarters. Find it the same scene of desolation and ruin; but, to my joy, I find that our old billet has been condemned – whether as unsafe, insanitary, or unfit for human habitation, I do not know. It is a beautiful sunny day, with a bright blue sky and big white clouds, but we find it a job sometimes to appreciate the beauty. There has been constant anti-aircraft firing, both at hostile and British aeroplanes, since we have been here this morning. What a pleasure it will be to have the last shot fired and done with!

April 24th – There seems nothing much to write

A group of signallers serving with the Banfield brothers. It is believed that Arthur (possibly middle, front row) and Bert Banfield (possibly far right, middle row) appear in this picture

about. We have received several letters and parcels from home lately. We try to send them as many letters as possible, as they must feel anxious at times. The weather still keeps fine. It would have been more than depressing to have had all that rain and wind whilst in the trenches. The casualties keep pretty low, which is something to be thankful for, though Lieutenant Tayler was wounded yesterday. I expect he will be sent home, as he was wounded in three places. He will be missed, for he is an officer really liked.

April 25th – I heard the cuckoo several times today. It seems strange to hear it right up in the firing line. It is so very different from what I pictured. 10.15 p.m. Have just seen our artillery bombarding to our right. Rather a fine sight, though awe-inspiring. It seemed very incongruous to hear the guns blazing away, and to see the flashes, and then to look up and see the beautiful, peaceful stars in the sky. All the same, I hope the Germans have had something to remember, and I think they have.

April 26th – I hear that one of our signallers has been recommended[311] for mending the wires under shell fire. Also hear that three of our company signallers are *hors de combat*.[312] ... I think we leave the trenches tomorrow, but only to go into stand-to billets about two hundred yards from our present headquarters; then I hope after that we shall be able to get right back for a bit more rest. Have just been watching two brown field mice eating. They were very pretty little things, with big black eyes, and kept trying to get a piece of rasher rind into their hole. It was too big for them, though!

April 27th – Yesterday we once more left duty in the trenches, having been brought safely through, though we are only in stand-to billets about two hundred yards from our trench headquarters. We hear we are going in a few days' time to Locon for an eight-day rest. It will be rather a relief to get out of the fire zone. I saw this evening that the Germans are dropping a few light shells on our communication trenches; hope they won't do much damage.

Hear today that the 11th Battalion have sent all their packs back to the base or somewhere. Hope *we* send ours away soon; they are a bit too much to carry about this warm weather. Our billet here is very low-pitched, and the heat gets very oppressive in the evenings. We have to keep the windows covered up to keep the light in, or I expect we should soon become a mark for the German artillery.

April 30th – Sunday has come round once more. Have a little opportunity to be quiet, and as we have some grass near here, can lie down and rest. It is a beautiful day, with a little breeze. The sky is very blue, and what with the green leaves and spring flowers it is very nice. It is strange like this, so near the firing line; but just down the road there is desolation such as I have never seen before.

Friday evening – I read the 91st Psalm, and think it is so nice, verses 4-7. What wouldn't I give to know the Lord so regarded me.

An hour or two later we suddenly heard a hooter sounding on our right, and the next minute we were given the order to turn out with our gas helmets, as the enemy were launching a gas attack. We all felt rather nervous, especially as it was night time. I found the gas helmet rather stuffy, and was not at all sorry when, a few minutes later, we were allowed to put them up, as there was not any gas near us at the moment. After about three hours we were allowed to go in and sleep. In the morning I looked again at the same Psalm, and thought those words were specially suitable, 'Thou shalt not be afraid for the terror by night; nor for the arrow that flieth by day; nor for the pestilence that walketh in darkness; nor for the destruction that wasteth at noonday … but it shall not come nigh thee.'

Last night we were again held in readiness, as we had information that the Germans had got the gas cylinders ready in their trenches opposite us. Oh, that I could *know* that I am thus watched over. Lord, open my understanding, and let me know.

Tomorrow we leave here, and go back for eight days' rest, I think everyone will be more than pleased.

May 2nd – Last night we all safely left the trenches. We came away along the canal bank. A little way down I heard a nightingale singing; it seemed very strange to hear it, when the star shells were going up so near. We came by Gorre and Locon, and reached the billet about two o'clock in the morning. I soon turned in, and had a decent rest until just on eight o'clock, when I had to go on duty again. We like it here very much; it seems a great relief to be away from the firing line and the desolation. I don't think we shall mind it much if we keep having a break like this. The canal here looks very pretty, though un-English.

May 12th – Find I haven't written in here for nearly a week again. I haven't felt much like writing, feeling rather unsettled and careless. Last Tuesday night we left Hinges for the trenches, this time at Festubert. We had a fairly comfortable march up here till getting to the stand-to billets; after that it was positively painful. It came on to rain, and as it was just getting dark it was not at all pleasant. The star shells kept going up; we were fortunate indeed to get in without a casualty. The soil here is clay and gets very slippery, and for every step we took we slipped back nearly a half. As we were loaded up with signalling apparatus, etc., we were glad to get safely to headquarters. We found this a very comfortable place, by far the best we have yet been to. The dugouts where we sleep are also in the way, rather, when we lie down, but we manage to wedge ourselves in. It is hopeless to try to turn, and though our hips get rather sore from the hard ground, we manage to sleep soundly. I had a specially good sleep last night, nearly 11 hours, and only awoke once … The other night I was able to watch our artillery bombarding a point in the German lines. Through the glasses the explosions looked very near. The headquarters here are in the old British line, and our front line right ahead of the old German line. It is interesting to be in the very place where an advance has taken place. Tomorrow we go back to the battalion in support. I think it is rather a hot place, a few hostile shells dropping in that direction yesterday evening. There is not nearly so much aeroplane activity here as at Givenchy, but what aircraft there are flies remarkably low. The Germans fire chiefly by rifle at them, but don't do any damage apparently. Anti-aircraft guns seemed everywhere at Givenchy, but I have not seen many here. The authorities are getting extremely fussy, requiring us to have clean boots in the trenches; it is very sickening, and difficult to understand. We have had a few casualties here – considering where we are, remarkably few. One poor chap died of wounds yesterday, and two more were wounded.

It is wonderful what a lot of birds live out here. A skylark has been singing over our trenches this morning, and the first thing yesterday morning, about three o'clock, I heard the cuckoo in some trees close by. The country reminds me very much of near Buxted,[313] just behind our trenches. How I wish I were there. It also reminds me of those walks we had while at Hempstead Farm. Some St. John's wort in the fields behind reminds me of those days.

May 13th – Have just heard that poor Sergeant Harriott has been killed. He was shot by a bullet from a machine gun in going up to the trenches.

May 17th – This is the last day of a four days' rest, and tonight we once more go into the trenches. We have had a nice rest in a very comfortable billet, quite the best sort of place since being out here, I think. We have wooden huts, which almost remind us of Witley. The huts are in an orchard, and as the blossom is full on the trees, it looks very nice. Sometimes we almost forget there is a war on, so used have we become to the occasional boom of the guns. In the next field are two heavy guns, the report of which, when in action, shakes our hut. They are also in an orchard, one gun being under a fruit tree in full blossom. In the same field I noticed some cows grazing, but tied up so as not to stampede when the guns are in action. We have now lost our signalling officer, the sergeant being in charge. I don't know whether it is for the better or not. Last night I was awakened by some anti-aircraft guns in action quite close to us. I think there must have been a Zeppelin or something near, as the gun firing was so rapid. At about six this morning an enemy shell dropped quite close, but failed to explode.

Tonight we go into the trenches again. It is unfortunately full moon, but I trust the poor chaps going up to the 'islands'[314] will get in safely. I also hope we have a more comfortable time going in than last time.

May 20th – We all arrived safely in the trenches on Wednesday night. I think our party had some rather narrow shaves coming in. Some bullets whistled quite near enough to be unpleasant. I remember one, especially, that smashed into a bush close on our left. We find ourselves in the same places, and are still having as comfortable a time as possible. We have had fewer casualties so far, though Elliott,[315] our signalling officer, was badly wounded last night, and is hardly expected to live. He was shot in the forehead. We feel sorry for him; he had only left us when in the trenches before.

This morning, for the first time, I saw an aeroplane fall to earth. It was unfortunately a British one and shot down by a German. The shot, whatever it was, took the tail off the machine, and I suppose then there was no chance. The pilot did all he could, and from the way the machine came down, I should not think he was killed. It came down turning over and over, just like a fluttering leaf.

May 21st – Sunday has once more come round. We are relieved today, our battalion going back to stand-to billets. Poor Mr Elliott died last night at 6.30. We all feel very sorry for him now, and everyone has forgiven him. [316] He never would have made a soldier, and the army would never have been his home.

It is a beautiful morning, just the sort to be out for a stroll, but, of course, it is no good to think of such a thing in the trenches. Last night we saw a daring

British flying man; he came down very low and fired at the German trenches with his machine gun. The Germans were also firing at him with machine guns, and there was quite a fusillade for nearly a quarter of an hour. He got off scot-free in the end, and must have caused the Germans some wasted ammunition. We have built up a barricade across the gangway outside our signal office, in the hope that it will stop the enfilading bullets that come whistling along each night; think it does to a certain extent. We find a great difficulty to get washing water here, but suppose we cannot expect anything else while in trenches.

We hear that the colonel starts the leave next Friday. How fine! We naturally wonder when our turn will come; I don't think it takes as long as I thought. He goes away with his servant first.[317]

May 22nd – We left the trenches once more quite safely. We had a terribly hot march coming out. Find the stand-to billets not so bad. The country is quite pretty, the foliage on the trees striking me as being very heavy. The billet is rather knocked about, no glass in windows, and no doors; but there is a sound enough roof at present, though *that* bulges in, in one or two places rather ominously. I don't think we are allowed to move about much here in case we are spotted by the enemy. The 11th Battalion adjutant seemed to be in an extremely agitated frame of mind (though he did wear the Distinguished Service Order[318]) about our moving in too big parties.

There are some good drawings on the walls here, done by the various regiments that have been billeted. In the farmyard is the grave of 14 unknown men of the 21st London Regiment, also the grave of an unknown Canadian. Bound at the back of the billet is a decent-sized orchard, a good deal overgrown. I see there is a hammock in one of the trees, which I hope to sample.

We had several 'whizz-bangs' over today, which came quite near enough to be unpleasant.

May 24th – The time goes very quietly here. There was a good deal of artillery activity yesterday on our part, and at about eleven o'clock last night it grew very violent on our right. I thought we might have to stand-to, but fortunately we were allowed to sleep. More details to hand about leave. The commanding officer *does* go on the 26th. Fancy being in England on Friday!

May 26th – We came safely out of the trenches and stand-to billets yesterday. We had a very tiring march in the dead of night. To add to the misery of the march it was wet, and we had to wear our capes. We arrived at Hinges, in our old billet, about 2.15 a.m. We are going to be billeted in another barn, but I think it is a better one, and I hope we shall sleep warmer than last time.

We had some very disturbing rumours, just before we left the stand-to billets, that we were going over the top, but fortunately we were able to leave near midnight quite safely and peacefully.

May 28th – Sunday has once more come round. Am having a rest on the bank of the canal. Have just read one of Mr Popham's sermons, which I remember he preached six years ago, though I can't say I remember much of the sermon itself.

Yesterday from nine o'clock to four o'clock in the afternoon we were busy trenching. This is, I suppose, what the army considers a rest. I think the best rest we get is in the trenches. We were paid yesterday, which was welcome, as I had been without cash for nearly a fortnight.

The woods around here are rather nice. There are a lot of nut trees; I also noticed some young self-grown oaks. There have been a lot of barges passing up and down the canal this morning.

May 29th – Sunday afternoon we suddenly had the order to move, and take over a section of the trenches. It is rather hard that we should have to leave these rest billets, especially as we were looking forward to a little rest from the trenches. I had to go on in advance of the rest of the signallers. We went all along the canal bank. On the way we passed through Béthune and found it rather a decent place, old-fashioned, narrow alleys. We did not go near the main streets. Saw several big army stores on the canal banks. The number of barges there was very large, and they made rather a picturesque appearance, with the old church and the sunset for a background. Notice that the owners keep chickens on board, the fowls running on board by means of a plank. Some of these barges are rather decent affairs, with nice little cabins, well fitted up. The owners also generally keep a dog on them. Noticed that several of the barges were marked 'Dunkerque.' Also noticed a big hospital at Béthune; expect it was in that building that poor Elliott died. There is one big artificial piece of water, and I could see the Royal Army Medical Corps fellows boating. They seem to have a very easy time of it. We followed the canal up past Gorre. Noticed that we have practically pumped the canal dry near the front, I suppose to prevent the enemy bringing up stores by boat, and also to prevent them from pumping, and flooding our trenches. We eventually reached headquarters about 10.30, and found them pretty comfortable. Find that we buzz the messages here, different from Festubert, where we speak them. Had a busy morning on the 'phone. We relieved the Argylls,[319] a fine set of men, I thought.

May 31st – Things seem to be going very much the same here as elsewhere in the trenches. We have to spend most of our time, however, in the dugout. The brigade sergeant major, if he sees us outside, makes a great fuss of it. Our dugout is very secure-looking, and has great wooden beams, and small trees for a roof, besides the sandbags on top. It is a very long affair, like a miniature tunnel blocked up at one end. We have not really room to stretch our feet at night. My 'Premier' stove is very useful, and I have been able to fry some eggs for supper. I must be getting experienced, as they have turned out well.

Have just heard from our adjutant that the commander of our army corps has congratulated our brigade on coming up to relieve the one that was in the trenches. Last night there was a raid on our front lines, the Germans getting in and taking two rifles and some ammunition. One of our sergeants was missing in the morning, and later brought in dead, with a dead German. A land mine going up, too, last night, caused 15 casualties to 'C' Company.

The wires seem bad, very bad for the regular army. I have never had such a night of it, messages being delayed for some hours through careless mistakes. The tunnelling companies and trench mortar people seem to make a bother with their wires. Am afraid our dugout is 'chatty,' as we say; everyone is complaining of livestock on their persons.[320]

June 2nd – How the year is going! In a month's time

we shall be commencing the last half of the year. Everyone wondered if 1916 was to be the year in which peace was to be proclaimed, at the beginning of the war, but am afraid it is as big a question now as ever. Yesterday we left our trench headquarters, and moved into support. We are, however, still in trenches, but are in comfortable dugouts some 12 feet deep in the ground. We spend a lot of our time underground nowadays: up at the trench head-quarters we had to spend most of the time, night and day, down in the dugout. It was very dark and stuffy, but I suppose we ought to be thankful for the place, as it was very securely made. Last night there was a heavy bombardment on our right towards Loos. Am afraid I am getting very tired of all out here, but it cannot be wondered at. Our poor 'C' Company have had a rough time of it this time. A big mine went up near them, making fifteen casualties straight away. Our adjutant, when he heard of it, said to me, 'Well, Banfield, there is an advantage in being at headquarters sometimes, isn't there?' Another of our officers, Lieutenant Cornwell, of 'B' Company, has been killed, shot in the same place as Mr Elliott. I am afraid that the casualties are mounting up, though a draft came out, we heard, yesterday. I wonder if Arthur is ever likely to come out here; I hope not. I saw a dead German sergeant whilst in the trenches this time, one whom we had seen lying out in 'no man's land.' Lieutenant Fabian was responsible for bringing him in, which was rather a good bit of work, as the Germans must also have seen him, and would naturally try to get him. We found out from the intelligence officer that the German was a Wurtemberger. He was a big fellow, 6ft. 3in. Our adjutant got a ring off his finger as a souvenir; it sounds very rotten.

June 3rd – Just lately there has been a tremendous amount of aerial activity on our side. Have seen six, or even eight, of our aircraft up at a time, observing. The difference between our airmen and the enemy's is very marked. Our men are absolutely daring, and seem to care nothing whatever for the anti-aircraft shells, though I have seen those put up literally by the hundred. Our gunners have just to put up a shell somewhere near a German aeroplane, and she will generally turn back at once. I don't write this because I am an Englishman, but it is a marked fact, and we often remark about it to each other when watching the aeroplanes. There are very few German aeroplanes to be seen about this part; all the while we were at Festubert we only saw one. There was one over us this morning, but right up above the clouds, where I should think he had a job to see anything. I suppose the pick of the German aircraft is at Verdun.

We had a very interesting letter from Arthur, describing a walk he had with Legh and Postlethwaite over the downs, down to Fulking, and then to Henfield, via Woodmancote. I wonder how long it will be before we can once more get out to those places. Woodmancote church reminds me very much of the beautiful little hamlet of Westmeston, at the foot of Ditchling Beacon. I very often think of that place, out here.

June 4th – Last night I took a message from brigade, on the telephone, to the effect that the German Navy had got a good trouncing; also that the Canadians had made a move up at Ypres. We are anxiously waiting for details.

Found out an estaminet[321] at Givenchy where I bought some eggs, chocolates and oranges. It was nice to find such a place, though I wonder anybody can live there. Everybody seems to think they must be spies, but nothing is done to them. …

Have had a rotten night of it on duty. Was very busy up to twelve o'clock with messages, but since then the time has dragged very much. Some of our artillery has been active during the night; the report of the guns makes an ear-splitting noise in the signal office. Am now looking forward to a decent sleep, as I feel almost dead tired.

Later. What a beautiful hymn 'Abide with me' is. May I pray the prayer that the hymn is. We hear that the news is not nearly so good about the North Sea fight,[322] and we also hear something about the enemy getting a hold on part of the western trenches. I feel rather 'down' naturally about the news. The navy always has been our one strong point. We are anxious to hear the whole news.

June 8th – Have just had some letters and papers, which give an account of the North Sea battle. The results were, I think, pretty even in the end, though on the face of it the Germans look to have the best of it. We are still in the trenches, but come away tomorrow. I think we go back to a place called Annequin, which is somewhere in the vicinity of the divisional canteen. The night before last the 13th Sussex earned the distinction of being the first regiment in the division to enter the German lines. We had a small bombing raid under Lieutenant MacRoberts; nearly every man was wounded, I believe, but it was supposed to have come off all right. From what I could hear on the 'phone, the Hampshires[323] were indulging in one last night. We hear to our disgust that all leave is once more stopped, but trust it won't be for long.

June 10th – We are now back in reserve, in a comfortable barn, and are able to sleep on some rather decent beds, made of wood and wire netting. We leave here, however, tonight, going once more to Hinges. Am rather tired of the place and hope we move somewhere else soon, if we don't have to go into the trenches at the end of eight days. Went for a nice walk down to the salvage to get a bayonet replaced. Went through the fields. It was very nice; the crops look very well kept. Women do all the cultivating; they keep at it until it is pretty well dark. The weather now is cold for June, and we get a fair lot of rain. There is near here a big slag heap, which looks very like a pyramid. The Germans are shelling near it this morning, with some pretty big stuff.

Heard on the 8th of the death of Lord Kitchener.[324] It seemed difficult to believe it true, but it is so. We have now lost since the war began two of our greatest soldiers.[325]

June 11th – Once more back at Hinges – we hear for twelve days. Had a very tiring march from Annequin last night. The road along the canal is very rough, and well we knew it in the dark. We feel very much relieved in getting away from the trenches for a while; we had had practically 32 days in them on end. We hear that after this we once more go up the hateful canal to Givenchy. I don't like the place, but suppose it does not rest with our wishes.

June 14th – Hear we are leaving here again for the trenches tomorrow. This will be the second time our rest has thus been broken. Think we are going to a place called Richebourg, just the other side of Festubert. We don't feel altogether pleased about having to go, naturally, though we are tired of this place. Our sergeant has been up to the trenches today to have a look round. We are rather anxious to know what it is like; hope it is not like Givenchy – we had quite enough of that.

June 15th – Heard yesterday that we are not after all going up to the trenches, which is very nice. We hope we may after all spend our whole time here. Our band played outside by the bridge yesterday, which was quite a treat. The Marseillaise[326] was quite a pleasure to the French people, and the people in the estaminet opposite were very generous with their beer afterwards. It was nice to hear 'Sussex by the Sea' again, reminding us of the days at Cooden. They also played 'Till the Boys come Home,' which will always make me think of Detling, where we were always hearing it played on the piano at concerts in the YMCA tent. The effect of the Marseillaise on the French is almost electrical, and I think it pleased them to hear it played.

We still hear little or nothing about our leave, though the officers keep going.

June 17th – We arrived here last evening about 6.30. The headquarters looks as if it had been a sort of farm originally. The signal office is a sandbagged affair against the side of a house, and is not particularly comfortable. Some artillery fellows are in one corner of it. The weather has suddenly changed very much warmer, which is a welcome change. Our sleeping place is not so bad, but I am afraid it is overrun with vermin.

June 19th – Yesterday was a very strange sort of Sunday, passing just like an ordinary day. In the evening I went down to the front line, which I found was pretty good and well kept. We had rather a trouble with some armoured cable, but were fortunately able to find the fault. Had a look at the German trenches through a periscope. They don't look particularly formidable, but are evidently not what they look. I expect ours look very much the same from the German side.

June 24th – We are now out of the trenches and in some good billets at Vieille Chapelle. The place has some decent little shops, though only a village. The church is absolutely gutted; the inhabitants say that the British did it, as the Germans when here had machine guns in it. Bert has gone today on a signalling course at Locon. I should like to have gone with him for some things.

June 25th – Sunday has come round once more. I was able to attend an outdoor service in the evening. We are shortly going 'over the top,' from what we hear everywhere, and I think everyone felt it rather. The chaplain was new to me, but he seemed rather a nice sort, and one or two things he said I liked. One thing he said was that he felt his prayers were very poor. I noticed the little Irish chaplain whom I like. I was late so did not hear all the service, and was attracted to the place by the singing of one of the hymns. We sang the hymn, 'O God, our help in ages past,' while I was there. Yesterday afternoon we had a sort of rehearsal of charging the enemy's trenches. Am afraid I didn't like it much. I hope I shan't have to take an active part in the actual fighting. I hope Bert will stay where he is until this is all over.

Went up the ruined church tower this afternoon,

but didn't think very much of the view. It makes me think of that beautiful view from the top of Staplehurst church tower.

Had a nice batch of letters yesterday. Hear that dear father is nearly done up; do hope he can soon get away for a rest. Feel a little down about the news that we are shortly to attack. May I look to the right place for comfort and help. Lord, once more give me strength and wisdom for whatever may be before me, and grant that I may give satisfaction. Our work will be extremely important, and, maybe, many lives will depend on it. I wish we had a more capable sergeant, but I trust the men will turn out well. I don't know yet what position I may have to take.

June 26th – A little more news to hand about our coming attack. Hear that we shall all have to go over, but must await further developments. It is a serious time, but I don't feel at times as I should. I don't know how to write it down, and perhaps it is best that I should not, but may I be able to take the whole matter in prayer to the Lord. I think I did have a little encouragement the other day. I had mislaid my rifle, and could not find it anywhere. It worried me rather, as it is a serious loss. Just before dropping off to sleep, I tried to ask that it might be found and restored to me. No sooner had I finished when someone called my name, and asked if so and so number was my rifle. He had come all the way from one of the companies to give it to me. It appeared that one of the company men had taken my rifle in mistake for his own.

Note: There is now a long gap in the diary. The expected attack was made on the 30th June, 1916. This attack was a diversionary attack designed to distract the Germans in preparation for the battle of the Somme which was to follow. The brigade, of which the 13th Royal Sussex formed part, gained the enemy's trenches and held them for a time, but was subsequently forced to return to their own lines. It has been described as "the day Sussex died," due to the disastrous nature of the advance. In less than five hours the regiment lost 17 officers and 349 men, and 1000 were wounded or taken prisoner. The 13th Battalion was all but wiped out by the day's events. Marcus accompanied the attacking party, and regained the British trenches in safety. The Germans, however, commenced shelling very heavily. One shell struck a dugout in which Bert, a sergeant, and an artillery officer were, covering them in debris and soil, and Marcus dug them out, though exposed all the time to the shells dropping around. A little later he was wounded in the right arm and right leg by fragments of a shell. As a consequence of this wound he was sent back to England, and was in hospital at Portsmouth until mid-September. After a short period of leave he was then briefly at Newhaven, and finally, on the 21st October, he was sent to the much-loathed Aldershot, before being again drafted overseas on December 11th, 1916. The diary re-commences at this point.

✍ We left Aldershot about 2 a.m., Monday morning, December 11th after a rather stormy parting with the 97th Training Reserve.

We travelled, as far as I could make out, via Guildford and Tonbridge, down to Folkestone, arriving there somewhere about six o'clock. I managed to get a fair amount of sleep, so didn't get off very badly. On arriving at Folkestone we were billeted in a private house until about 1.30 p.m., when we were marched to the quay. It was a lovely morning, but towards noon it turned quite dull, and I noticed with apprehension that there was quite a respectable swell on the sea. We found our transport was a paddle-steamer, though not small in size. There were three transports in all, and they all went across together, ours being the second to start, but the last to get across. We had an escort of three destroyers, and the journey took about two and a half hours. I got over without feeling the least bit bad. We disembarked at Boulogne, a very slow affair, and then 'fell in' and marched up a very steep hill to a rest camp, I believe called St. Martin's. Here we were fortunately able to get into a hut, though a good many had to be content with tents. We were issued out with two blankets apiece, and were soon in bed and asleep.

This morning it has been snowing a good bit, and is very much colder; it reminds me rather of when we came out here before. There is, fortunately, a good Expeditionary Force canteen here, and a YMCA hut, so have been able to have some good hot tea.

We paraded about 1.30 p.m., ready to march off. We stood about in the rain for a good half-hour, as usual, waiting for the word to move off. Eventually we *did* move, and soon got warm marching down the hill into Boulogne. From what I saw of it, I think it is a pretty decent sort of town, the harbour being naturally very interesting. We marched to the station, and of course, had to wait nearly an hour. It would be quite impossible for the army to get things to work in a really organised way, I suppose. Saw a massive French railway engine belonging to the Nord railway; noticed that the lamps on the engines are oil, and have glass chimneys just like a reading lamp. Found we were to travel in the same old way – cattle trucks – and I was quite glad to reach Étaples.

Find this a tremendous place. Before arriving at our tents we were issued with our rifles and bayonets, very quick work, but evidently not quick enough for those in authority, for they snapped at us like a lot of dogs. We drew here a gas helmet and two blankets, and were soon in our tents and asleep. The next morning we had the usual kit inspection, also a medical inspection. In the evening I stumbled across Whitcomb, and was awfully glad to see him. Was very interested to hear of all the signallers' doings up to the time he left them.

Experienced the 'bull ring' this morning (a name they give to the square here). Can't say I minded it much, especially as we had a decent Scotch sergeant as instructor – I think of the Camerons;[327] but the time will never come when I shall be enthusiastic about drill, etc. We went into the poison-gas chamber, a rather novel experience, but of course had on our gas helmets; also the weeping gas, which promptly made us all weep!

Half the canteens and YMCA's here are taken over by the Australians, which makes it an awful job for us to get into one in comfort. Still, the places are a great blessing, and the way they are patronised would make one think the army was half-starved. I can't say the grub here is the best or the most plentiful, but I suppose, being on active service again, we must not expect the same rationing as was obtainable in England.

Today, the 16th, we have been trying our new rifles on a short range, and I think mine is as true as can be wished for. So far, we have not had a very strenuous time here, but am looking forward to going up to the old 13th again. Yesterday I went up the orderly room and found that the sergeant was quite willing to put me down for the 13th. He was a very decent sort, so was the regimental sergeant major, who, I found, was the king's piper – whatever that was.[328] Hear today that we are going up the line, or rather to our battalions, on Monday.

December 17th – Spent the morning from 8.30 a.m. to one o'clock at the 'bull ring'. Had a rotten time, as may be imagined. Find it very difficult to think that the day is Sunday. Feel very fed up with things, and don't feel up to much in myself.

Read these lines yesterday in a little text-book: 'The LORD shall preserve thee from all evil: he shall preserve thy soul. The LORD shall preserve thy going out and thy coming in from this time forth, and even for evermore.'

> He guards thy soul, he keeps thy breath,
> Where thickest dangers come.
> Go and return, secure from death,
> Till God commands thee home.[329]

I don't know what is before me, but I must believe that God has helped me in the past and heard my cries to him. May he indeed go with me where I go, and keep me, not body only, but keep and preserve my never-dying soul, keep me from my great indifference. May he also give me all the wisdom and strength that I shall need to do my work here.

December 21st – Had my first letter from home, and was naturally awfully glad to hear. Yesterday went down to the specialist about my knee – rather think he has advised an operation, but must wait for the report. Very wet this morning, and things are not exactly pleasant in our tent; rain comes in pretty freely. Still, it is better than being in the trenches with no cover at all.

December 23rd – Have heard nothing about my medical report yet, and we still hear nothing about moving away from here. We are making up our minds to spend Christmas here. Very windy today, and several squalls of rain. Some of the tents came down, but fortunately ours stood the shock.

December 24th – Went on church parade: service was held in the cinema here. Don't like the chaplain very much. In the evening went down to a service in the old cinema; was far better than the parade service of the morning. I think it was a Presbyterian minister who preached. There was a big congregation, and I don't remember ever seeing such an attentive body of soldiers before.

December 25th – Christmas Day. My second in the army; may it be my last! We had an apology for a church parade in the morning, but I was glad to have it over. We did not come off badly, really, as regards the meals, a very good pudding and mince pies being given.

December 29th – 7 a.m. The draft that I came out with from England have just gone up the line. Yesterday it was settled that I am to go back to the good old 13th Battalion, Sussex Regiment. Am awfully pleased, as may be imagined. Find I am to go before a travelling medical board about my knee. Can't understand it, and am very doubtful about going before such an august tribunal. Expect, if they decide on an operation, it will delay my getting back to the 13th. May I feel, however, that these things are not in my hands, but even in *his* hands who knows the end of all things.

December 30th – Moved yesterday from the old tent up to the 'casual' lines. Went this morning before the board, but managed to get off without the doctor sending me to hospital. It will suit me very well, and I hope it is the right thing.

December 31st – Understand I am marked 'active,' which, of course, means that I am for the line again. It is Sunday again, and the last of the old year. It has been a momentous year, much having happened, but through God's mercy I have been brought through it all.

I suppose that now, 11.20 a.m., my dear father and mother are at chapel. How different were those peaceful Sundays to the rush and tear of these out here! Practically no difference is made out here, even though at the base, where I think, at any rate, the training could be dispensed with for the one day. Of course we have a church parade, but from what I can see we are only allowed to attend on one Sunday out of two.

In the afternoon we went for a stroll through the woods that surround our camp, with Whitcomb, and I think we both enjoyed it. It was a relief to me to get away from everything military for an hour or two. The woods and sand hills reminded me very much of Whitley district; but on the high ground it very much resembled the fine old South Downs at home. The round haystacks reminded me of those we used to count up at Patcham. Saw the sea for the first time today, and suppose I was looking out towards England. In the evening went to a service in the Church Army hut, and got on fairly well. We opened the service with 'Jerusalem the golden,' sung to the tune of 'Ewing,' and closed with that grand hymn, 'O God, our help in ages past.' The chaplain gave a good address.

January 1st, 1917 – New Year's Day. Went to the 'bull ring' today, and listened to lectures on the edifying subject of barbed wire and wiring, also of repairing trenches that have been smashed by shell-fire. Afterwards practised the inevitable bomb-throwing and bayonet-firing.

Had a letter from Arthur and Auntie Martie. Very glad to have them. How nice it is to hear from home. Corporals Pook and Mockford left today for the 13th. Very much wanted to go with them, but it has been ruled otherwise. Arthur seems to have had a pretty decent Christmas on the whole. Am glad, as I was afraid the Aldershot surroundings would give him the 'blue pip.' Am still wondering how Bert came off.

January 4th – Was paid 10 francs today, after rather an unpleasant exchange of words with the pay sergeant. He didn't like to own up to a mistake of his. Hear rather disgusting news about my going back to the 13th. The pay sergeant will have it I belong to the 7th. Hope, however, all will come right, but it makes me feel very unsettled. The matter is, however, not in my hands, and those men can by no means do what they like. God sees the end of this, and though my thoughts about it are constantly changing, it is still the same with him. May I feel that he knows best, and be enabled to leave it with him.

Heard from dear mother today; they are disappointed I am not yet with Bert – think the letters must have miscarried somewhere.

January 5th – Had a long talk with Whitcomb last

night about the Church of England. He evidently does not take everything that is told him for granted, which is a good thing. Unlike Lawrence, he agreed with me on a good many things, and I with him. I wonder where Lawrence, is and, if I get back to the 13th, whether I shall see him again. From the newspapers this morning I see that the enemy artillery is reported very active at Ypres. Shall be interested, if I join the old division, to see the famous place; but it has always been known as a place for very hot fighting. Have shifted this morning to a new tent, and am to take charge of it. This afternoon went for a route march, and enjoyed it after a style.

January 6th – Was awakened at 4.30 this morning, as I was on a ration fatigue for a draft of men for the West Kents.[330] Got back and finished by 8.30 a.m., so have not been hard worked.

January 9th – Was awakened by the sergeant at 5.30 a.m. to go down to the station with some officers' kit. Got the job done all right, but was caught in a most violent rain squall and got my overcoat sopping wet. Later in the morning received the news that I am at last to go up to the line, and thankful to say to the 13th. Have shown kit and had the usual medical examination, and got even wetter still hanging about in the open.

January 13th – Have at last left Étaples. Woke at 4.15 a.m. Had to give in blankets and get breakfast,

Signallers mending telephone lines at the front during a gas attack

so as to be ready for marching off at 6.10. The day was fortunately finer. Found we were to travel in the old '40 hommes 8 chevaux,'[331] as usual. Found that the regimental tactical officer, or someone, had put us down for the 12th Battalion. It seems that they make mistakes over the simplest things here. We got two fires going in our truck, so were as comfortable as the crowded state of the truck would allow. After being rushed up at 4.15 a.m., we naturally expected the train would move off about 8.30 or nine o'clock, but we eventually left Étaples at 4.15 p.m.! We read a lot in books on the East that there, time is no object; it evidently isn't here. After travelling (via Calais) for about ten hours, we disembarked at Hazebrouck, and I thus renewed my acquaintance with that town. We marched up to the rest camp, which was a disused convent, where we were left in peace to try to sleep, as our train was not going to Poperinge till ten o'clock the next morning. I could not secure a palliasse,[332] so had to be content with sleeping on the stone floor, with just my overcoat between. I was naturally soon too cold to sleep, so I got up, and soon had some decent hot tea and biscuits and jam for breakfast. About 9.15 a.m. we left for the station; we found the train all right, but it was not very punctual in leaving. Was interested in the country, as very soon we were in Belgium. There is quite a Dutch sound about all the names here, very unlike the French. I suppose we arrived at Poperinge somewhere about midday.

Here we were met by a guide, who had the haziest of ideas whom he was to guide, but eventually we reached a collection of huts called 'F' Camp. Here we were seen by an adjutant, one of the best of fellows, who very soon had everything put right about our going to our own battalions. We had a little hot tea and some biscuits and cheese, and then started off to find our battalions. Everyone we met had different views as to the direction we were to take, and for some distance we did not find an English soldier to direct us. Eventually we reached a battered sort of village where we found a 12th Battalion man, and a few yards farther on I came across the quartermaster sergeant of 'B' Company, who soon had us on the right track. I reported to the sergeant in the orderly room, who was very surprised to see me, and also very pleased, I think. Then I went on to the signallers, and found them all well and as lively as ever. Found a few new signallers, but daresay shall soon be used to them. Bert being away on a course, I haven't yet seen him. Slept like a top the first night, but water drips through the roof of the dugout in rather an unsatisfactory way, so have decided to move my belongings to a better place for tonight.

January 15th – Am settling down to the old life again now. Found a few new instruments, but they are tolerably easy to get on with. About five o'clock yesterday evening we left the support lines for the line again. Proceeded down a pavé[333] road, which had very evidently been shelled by Fritz, shell holes being very unhealthily near. We reached the dugout safely, however. One part of our way took us through a wood, which has been knocked about very considerably, big trees lying all over the place.

January 19th – We left the trenches safely on the night of the 16th. Had to wait a few hours for the sergeant, and then marched off for our billet. This we found was in the remains of the city of Ypres. This place, and especially the village before entering Ypres, is absolutely gutted, and it makes me feel quite sick to see the buildings, or what is left of them. Our billet is a cellar, and I think fairly safe. We are able to have a fire, which is a good thing, as we have had snow for some days, and the stone floor of our cellar would make it otherwise unbearable.

January 22nd – We have left the cellar in Ypres, and are now in the trenches once more. Headquarters is dugouts, and I am fairly fortunate in my choice, but it is frightfully cold at nights owing to the dugout having no door. The Germans put some heavy shells over this morning, which came quite close enough for my liking. Hear that they have knocked our communication trench in. Am afraid my nerves are not quite the same as they used to be, but may I be enabled to leave everything in God's hands, and believe that nothing can happen of itself.

January 24th – Keep spending very cold nights here and have had about enough of it. The rats are a plague here; altogether it *is* a life. This morning a large shell dropped quite close to the signal office, the concussion of it blowing out the candle. The next few, however, dropped further off. Artillery has been rather active on both sides since we have been here.

January 25th – Left the trenches once more safely yesterday afternoon. Found that Fritz was shelling Ypres pretty heavily. Was glad to reach our billet and get near a warm fire once more.

January 26th – Very little doing. Have been able to have a good fire going all day. About 8 p.m. the gas alarm went, and we had our respirators on for about twenty-five minutes. Find them more comfortable than the old sort, though these are none too nice.

January 31st – We left Ypres about 10 o'clock on the 27th, and went up to some monastic-looking buildings.

March 17th – Wish I had kept the diary up, but will now try to do so once more. Since last writing I have been in some pretty tight corners, but am thankful to say have been preserved. Had a decent ten days' rest at a camp in huts – enjoyed ourselves there very much – after that, proceeding to a village near Bollezeele by rail. We were billeted in a barn. This rest was supposed to be the fabulous divisional rest of a month's duration, but after about ten days of it we were trained back to Poperinge. Next night we were in the line again, headquarters being in underground saps.[334] Though fairly quiet generally, Fritz gave us a bit of trouble at times.

Spent another decent little rest at St. Lawrence. By this time Bert had reported back. How decent to see him again, looking so well, too!

Am at present on a short signalling course at Boesheepe, and am having a pretty comfortable time. Am learning about P.B.s and amplifiers. The village boasts some decent little shops, for France, but where will you see anything like the English ones? There is a decent view from the hill here, which in a way reminds me of the good old views from the downs at home.

March 29th – Left St. Lawrence about 8 p.m. last night, arriving here at supper after a most awful journey. We had our usual experience of advancing in ten yard rushes; in short, the distance of about two miles must have taken over two hours.

April 2nd – Have now spent my third birthday in the army. Received a lovely cake from home, and letters from all. We are now in the trenches again, and in the old tunnel. The quarters are far from comfortable, and I was not feeling at all easy about coming in this time, as the enemy has shelled it and knocked it in, in one place. I think I can say I have felt a little comfort from the fact that all is in God's hands. May I realise it more and more, and feel that he is my only Refuge. The other night read that 91st Psalm, when it seemed a comfort to me.

When I see a bombardment, it makes me very, very afraid, but oh, to know that God controls it all! Read these words the other day in that little text-book: 'Like as a father pitieth his children, so the LORD pitieth them that fear him. For he knoweth our frame; he remembereth we are dust.'

April 3rd – Still in the trenches, but hear we are shortly to be relieved from this sector. Feel very glad, as the place seems very warm as regards the fighting. Hope we shall be leaving the Ypres sector altogether. Find I have written somewhere in this book that I should like to see Ypres, but am sure I shall be better pleased to leave it.

April 4th – Saw our artillery strafing on the famous Hill 60 the other day; rather a good sight, but am glad it was not opposite our front, which is perhaps selfish.

April 8th – Are now back at St. Lawrence; arrived here the day before yesterday. Our future movements seem very doubtful, but think we have now left these sectors for good.

April 14th – Are in a new sector near that awful Eki.[335] Find it very hot, and shall be glad to leave. Some of the signallers had to leave their dugouts owing to the insufficient shelter … What a great thing to know that God has a controlling hand, however, even over the furious fire the enemy sends over. Oh, may I realise it, and find comfort in it!

April 19th – Have been back to St. Lawrence for a couple of days, and now find ourselves in support on the canal bank. Very decent accommodation in dugouts, and up to now pretty quiet. We hear rumours of going back for a rest, and once more they have taken a lot of names for leave. Yesterday poor Lieutenant Rayner was killed in the front line; it seems very sad, for he was a nice fellow, and everyone seemed to respect him.

April 24th – We find ourselves once again in the line, but we hope not for long … Lovely spring weather at last – cold at nights, but a welcome change. The aeroplanes on both sides are taking full advantage of it, and we are continually warned to take cover from observation. Fine view from our headquarters looking on battered Ypres and right away to the hills beyond Poperinge. The other day saw two swallows skimming the canal, and today hear the skylark singing away, evidently quite oblivious to the ghastly surroundings on the earth.

April 29th – Left the line last night; came out pretty comfortably.

May 3rd – Left camp early in the morning of the 1st, arriving at a village just outside St. Omer about four o'clock in the afternoon. Left this place again about seven o'clock next morning for our final destination, a fairly clean village going by the name of Quercamps – quite the best looking place I remember to have seen in France. It is very quiet, however, barely boasting even a shop. Our own dry canteen will therefore come in handy.

May 10th – We have now been here just over a week. Have been out nearly every day from about 7 a.m. till teatime, pretty stiff training. Have been feeling very seedy with rheumatism in my knees, but feel quite different this morning. Had a decent morning signalling in the woods yesterday. Hear there was a wild boar shot in the forest the day before yesterday. The place is a picture with the violets, cowslips, anemones, etc.

May 17th – Left Quercamps last Sunday, and have today finished a three days' march. The weather has fortunately been cool, or I should have been rather apprehensive of the result … My feet were a bit sore, and I didn't look forward to the third day, as it was the longest march of the lot; however, I survived, though it was raining all the time, and we had to wear our waterproofs. Arrived at Wormhont at 10.15 a.m., and after marching about another eight kilometres, found our billet soon after 3 p.m. It is a big loft, holding all headquarters. Can once more hear the sound of the guns quite distinctly. This morning is much finer; everything is beginning to look beautiful and fresh. The fruit trees are a picture everywhere, being a mass of blossom.

June 7th – Are now in the line. Awful bombardment this morning; somebody must have 'gone over.' Weather is very hot; the trenches seem stifling. Have got a pretty decent and comfortable dugout, with very little on top, however.

June 10th – Very quiet this morning, such a difference from the violent cannonading of the previous days. Hear great news of the doings near Messines, etc. Hill 60 is evidently ours at last.

June 22nd – We are going out tonight, all being well. Shall indeed be glad to get away in safety and peace. Have had a warm time, but have once more been spared. God grant me to realise that I am a subject of his care!

June 24th – Midsummer Day, and beautiful weather. Am writing this in a hayfield near our billet. Cannot help being struck with the beauty of the country, the trees, of course, being in full foliage. A lovely blue sky. What a difference after the sickening desolation of the line, where everything is so uncared for. There seems such a peace here, not a sound of a gun, only a distant aeroplane reminding one of the war (I forget, however, a rifle range not far away; I can hear the firing now and again). The country reminds me very forcibly of the ragstone ridge in that lovely part of Kent just south of Maidstone, and the fields round Staplehurst; how I should like to be there now. There is a church close by, a big one. How I would go there this evening if it were other than Roman Catholic. We had a church parade this morning, and though it was what the chaplain called a 'scratch' service, owing to the fact that we were minus books and band, and he minus surplice and cassock, it was one of the best services we have had out here. I like the padre, and his sermon about the care of God for us was good. Oh, may I be given a thankful heart for the mercies that he does so shower upon me; may he give me a grateful heart. He does indeed preserve and keep me. Have today received a letter from dear Dad, in which he mentions the 91st Psalm. It seems made for any who are on active service. May I be of that number who trust him, who are his, for they *alone* are happy. Do make me to truly feel my need of thee, Lord Jesus.

Have just read the 91st Psalm, and have been very much struck by the seventh verse, chiefly by the clause, 'and ten thousand at thy right hand.' This is exactly the official number of casualties published in the papers of the Messines Ridge battle. This was just on our right at the time. And it goes on to say, 'But it shall not come nigh thee.' O God, number not my soul with those who care not for thee; 'be not silent to me,' lest if thou be silent 'I become like them that go down into the pit.'

July 2nd – The year is now half over. We shall shortly be having the third anniversary of the war. We are having a fairly good time here, having been this day on a signalling stunt with aeroplanes.

Keep hearing rumours of our taking part in an attack. Hymn 352 (*Gadsby's Selection*) seems very nice. How often we used to sing it at home:

> But they that in the Lord confide,
> And shelter in his wounded side,
> Shall see the danger overpast,
> Stand every storm, and live at last.

O God, thou knowest that these things are not always absent from my thoughts. Do grant me to be of that happy number that are thine own. Lord, do 'remember me … with the favour that thou bearest unto thy people.' I can't tell how I envy the lot of God's people.

Dear Legh has now to join the army, and father and mother will be left alone.[336]

July 22nd – It is Sunday, and just about 11 a.m. I expect father and mother are at chapel. This morning read hymn 480 (*Gadsby's Selection*), which is so nice:

> O might I once mount up and see
> The glories of the eternal skies,
> What little things these worlds would be;
> How despicable to my eyes.
>
> Had I a glance of thee, my God,
> Kingdoms and men would vanish soon;
> Vanish as though I saw them not,
> As a dim candle dies at noon.
>
> Then they might fight, and rage, and rave,
> I should perceive the noise no more
> Than we can hear a shaking leaf,
> While rattling thunders round us roar.
>
> Great All in All, eternal King!
> Let me but view thy lovely face,
> And all my powers shall bow and sing
> Thy endless grandeur and thy grace.

September 16th – I find several weeks have elapsed since writing anything down here. A lot has happened, chief being the attack made on July 31st. How can I be thankful enough for having been preserved through that ordeal.[337]

We attacked just before dawn, but it was still dark enough, so that we could not see where we were going. The roar of the guns was terrific, and the flashes of our own shells as we followed the barrage up gave us an idea where the enemy lines were. We missed the Boche barrage, and were soon in the remnants of his first line. Soon after this I got lost, and who can describe the chaos which the dawn produced. Hardly a yard of ground that was not overturned by our barrage. The German lines were battered in, in places, so much that you could not take them for trenches, their concrete dugouts alone standing the deluge of shells. I eventually found my party wandering about, and in the end we all found our destination, where we had a little breathing space. By this time we were experiencing a little of the enemy's fire, his 5.9s[338] being prominent.

We soon had the order to advance, and then began the worst part. We had to get through the enemy barrage before getting to our second headquarters, and this was extremely heavy, so much so, that we all (about 20) had to take what shelter we could find in a gigantic shell hole. I should say we stayed in that crater for nearly two hours, and the times the shells came so close as to take our breath away were too numerous to mention. I think I felt at this time that God was watching over me, and preserving me. Soon after we were ordered to get on, as the fire had slackened, and though dead-tired I managed to reach our headquarters and get a bit of rest and a portion of tinned rations. Here we were under observation from the enemy, and we were soon made to know it. Just before reaching here, a violent sort of shrapnel burst so close that the concussion absolutely stung my face, but still not touched, I was able to reach the comparative safety of a concrete dugout. We had to stand-to several times, as we were rather expecting counter-attacks, but our artillery put up a good barrage.

The next morning arrived very wet. I was thankful to get a good sleep (how much more fortunate than the men in the front line). But being so much under observation, we had orders to shift a little below the ridge into a big concrete gun pit. Here we stayed for the remaining two days, wet through, but eventually came out safely. About 15 minutes after I had left the gun pit, a shell came right into the mouth of the pit and killed over 12 outright, and wounded the remainder. I feel at times that God has been very condescending and gracious. Oh that I might be given a grateful spirit, that I could thank him as I ought. It seems very wonderful that though we had many shells near us during the 48 hours we were in the gun-pit, not one had exploded on or in it. I don't think I shall ever forget the walk out – the anxiety lest we should be spotted, our nerves unsettled by the strain of the last few days, the terrible mud, and the broken, uneven road. When about three-quarters of a mile back, and near our guns, the enemy started replying to our fire, and we, of course, came under fire again; but, am thankful to say, came through again unscathed. How welcome it was to see once more familiar ground, and to remember how far off it seemed when in the line; and then getting back to the *now* good old canal bank; to get into some dry clothes, have a hot drink of tea and rum, and then a good sleep. I lay down, reserving a place near me for a chap I liked very much, young Albert Ball; but, on enquiring, found that he was one of those killed by that last shell. He had stayed behind on his own account, issuing hot tea to the men of his company, and so had met his death. I have felt it rather, as I took to him and he to me, but I think I had made an idol of him. O Lord, I am unworthy of thy goodness. Keep me from the sins that do 'so easily beset' me, and 'be not silent to me,' lest, if thou be silent, 'I become like them that go down into the pit.'

For the last five weeks I have been on a signalling course at Contay; this is in the Somme district, and is not very much of a place. There is plenty of work, however, to keep one occupied, and next week (the last of the course) is all examinations.

October 3rd – Have now been back with the battalion several days. Had a journey back which covered nearly seven days. Stayed for one night at the rest camp at Étaples. Visited a few of my old haunts. Find I have passed my examination all right, and have now an assistant instructor's certificate. Am very glad, for I was a bit doubtful, as I was feeling seedy at the time.

November 4th – Have not had an over-eventful month since last writing here. Have only been in the line once for four days. We have not, however, been out of Belgium the whole time; it is not exactly a comfortable country to live in, these times. Bert has at last been on leave. Am now out of the line, though the battalion is in; hear I am to take turns with Sergeant Dudman in going in. There was a big strafe on this morning, but hope all our signallers have come through all right. On coming back from my course was very surprised and grieved to hear that four of our signallers had been killed in action – Tommy Lansdell, Gough, Reg. Collins, and Fish are all gone, poor chaps. We are rather depleted now, and we miss them, having been such a time together. This is an awful part of the front, and we all hope we are shifting.

This was the last entry in Marcus's diary. The following was written by his parents:

✍ Shortly after writing the foregoing, our dear boy came home on what proved to be his last leave. Returning to France on December 23rd, 1917, he was in the great German offensive of March, 1918, when he and his brother had a very rough time in the retreat. At this time he wrote and told us how good the words had been to him, 'Like as a father pitieth his children, so the LORD pitieth them that fear him. For he knoweth our frame; he remembereth that we are dust.'

He was relieved on March 30th, the day his brother was wounded,[339] and sent near Ypres again. He wrote from there that he was back at the old spot, and he was feeling God had been very good to him; he could say God heard and answered prayer.

We hoped that having been removed from the scene of the first great German thrust, he would now have a season of comparative quietness, but this was not to be. Scarcely had he arrived in the Ypres region than the second enemy offensive started, and his battalion was involved in the fighting, and on April 26th, during a German attack, he was mortally wounded and died a few hours later.

His body rests in Bandaghere Military Cemetery, Haringhe, Belgium, in sure and certain hope of a joyful resurrection.

'He asked life of thee, and thou gavest it him, even length of days for ever and ever' (Psalm 21: 4).

The following letter of sympathy was written to Marcus's parents by Mr John H. Gosden when he received the news whilst serving in France:

✍ My dearly beloved and esteemed elder brother,

I have just now received the sad news of the death of your dear boy Marcus. By reason of the love I bear for you, to whom I venture to claim (if I am not presuming) fraternal relationship in Christ, this is a heavy blow to myself, as I realise a little how naturally overwhelming it must be to you. God forbid I should harrow your feelings by anything I say. I would fain write you a word of sympathy and, by the Lord's help, of comfort.

And as your hearts, dear friends, are torn by your son's death, perhaps I may not be wrong or trifling if I should remind you of that love of the Father which brought him, according to eternal counsel, to give up to suffering, scoffing, desertion and death his dear, well-beloved, only-begotten Son. You were given your dear Marcus, and have enjoyed his filial love and devotion some 20 years. But the eternal Father had in his bosom eternally his eternal, holy, equal Son. And as the love of God is infinite, so must the Father's heart, so to speak, have felt infinitely that separation and pain to which, through electing love to his church, he delivered up his dear Son. I know that it would be unscriptural to think of the Father as human, and it is written, 'It *pleased* the LORD to bruise him.' But the terrible sacrifice of divine, paternal love seems to exhibit the wonderful height of God the Father's love to his church, as the coming of the Son of God and, in his sacred humanity, his suffering and dying for his people exhibit the eternal Son's love to his church. Yet these two loves, with the love of God the eternal Spirit in forming the humanity of Jesus and in revealing him to his church, are all one great, infinite love, the love of God.

I hope and believe that you will not deem the remembrance of these things irrelevant to your sad loss. For is it not that love in which you desire, above all else, an interest? Have you not had assurance that you are indeed the objects of that divine love? And are you not in your hearts assured, as it is said in the Scripture, that nothing shall separate you from it, but that *all* you meet with comes from that special redeeming love and care of your heavenly Father and Triune God?

Further, have you not reason to hope that that same love is fixed upon your dear boy, and is not this hope better than all else you could desire for him, yea, even than life itself? Consider then, my esteemed, sorrow-stricken friends, that thousands of people are daily losing their sons who know no divine consolations themselves; whilst many a godly parent has the unutterable sorrow, added to the loss of a child, of an entire absence in the child of evidence of life divine. May the consideration inflame in your hearts wonder and love, and beget real peace and submission to the Lord's solemn stroke in permitting your lad to be thus taken from you; because that you both have been, and you have good reason to believe that dear Marcus was, subjected to the saving grace and effectual call of God. And may the suggestion that all these things are against you, which you may find in your mind, be repelled by a manifestation afresh of the love of God to your souls. The God of all comfort and consolation bless, console, comfort your hearts. I am grieved and afflicted with you, but helpless to do you good. *God can* and, I believe, will.

The Lord in mercy bless Arthur, Legh, and Bert, give healing mercy to the latter, and his grace to each.

With true sympathy and Christian love,

J. H. Gosden,

France.

18. 5. 1918.[340]

Further letters written by Mr Gosden appear on page 325.

Douglas E. Bradford

As a young man, Mr Bradford joined the Merchant Navy. He was on service in the Merchant Navy in 1914 when the war broke out. After the war, with his health deteriorating, Mr Bradford was pensioned out of the navy. The Lord never purposed him to pursue a career at sea as he had been doing when war broke out, but instead placed him in a higher calling. In due course he was baptised, and sent into the work of the gospel ministry. He was for many years the beloved pastor of the church at Ebenezer Chapel, Matfield Green, Kent.[341] He wrote of his war time experiences as follows:

> ✍ I made another voyage to South America, which was my last in the Merchant Navy. We were lying in the docks at Montevideo at the entrance of the River Plate. This was in August, 1914, when the solemn news came through that England was at war with Germany. On hearing this the first thought that came into my mind was, 'Oh! to get home and be able to do something for my country and loved ones!' On the voyage home, having the confidence of my captain, I mentioned this to him. He said I should be doing just as much for my country by remaining in the merchant service as joining the navy. Also he said, 'You are doing very well and your prospects are good,' and kindly added he would be sorry to lose my service. I had always in a secret way been ambitious to get into the navy and this seemed to be the way, and indeed by the permissive will of God it proved to be so, but how little did I then know the mysterious way God was over-ruling my life, and how I have entered into the pathway of dear Cowper:

God moves in a mysterious way
His wonders to perform;
He plants his footsteps in the sea,
And rides upon the storm.[342]

All the way home my captain tried hard to persuade me against leaving the ship, but my mind was made up.

I shall never forget the last part of that voyage home as we entered the Channel. When I came on the bridge at midnight to take over the watch from the third officer, it was a lovely starlit night and a perfect calm, what we sailors called a 'dead calm.' I had not been on watch more than about a quarter of an hour, when suddenly we were enveloped in a complete blanket of fog and visibility was reduced to nil. This necessitated reducing the ship's speed to a minimum just to keep steering way, and sounding the fog horn every three minutes. This brought the captain on to the bridge. He was rather deaf and could not always catch the direction of other ships sounding their fog horns. At first this rather agitated me as I realised he was somewhat distressed. However, I was helped to overcome my feelings and he left the manoeuvring of the ship to me.

The night wore on and still the fog persisted. Most of the passengers got up and walked about the decks. The time came (4 a.m.) for me to go off watch and for the chief officer to take over. To my surprise the captain asked if I would remain on watch until daylight (6 a.m.) as he said, 'You have got the situation so well in hand.' I was dead tired, but knew I could not sleep in the circumstances and was glad enough to remain on duty. As I have already shown, I was not without prayer to the God of providence, and I tried to ask that the fog might clear. Six o'clock came and with it the dawn of day and, marvellous to say, with it the sudden clearing of the fog. 'Whoso is wise, and will observe these things, even they shall understand the lovingkindness of the LORD. (Psalm 107: 43)

We were granted a safe passage up Channel and docked in London. Home again, but what a change since we left! Now it was all war excitement and the awful preparations, and the ultimate sacrifice of the flower of our young men as the price of man's covetousness and wickedness.

The Word of God exhorts us to remember all the way the Lord our God has led us. The good hymn writer says:

> All my times are in thy hand,
> All events at thy command.[343]

I said farewell to my kind friend the captain of the good ship *Highland Brae*. As I walked over the gangway I wondered if it was right to leave this ship and almost I was tempted to go back, but why did I not do so? God had ordained it otherwise! The next voyage this vessel made was her last, as she was sunk without warning in the South Atlantic by the German cruiser *Kronprinz Wilhelm*, with the loss of all hands.[344] Thus we 'remember all the way' and the truth of the above hymn.

After about a week at home (this was October 1914) I went up to the Admiralty and offered my services and was given a lieutenant commission in the Royal Naval Reserve. Within a few days I received

Douglas E. Bradford

orders to proceed to Portsmouth and join *H.M.S. Excellent*, the gunnery training ship. After a short course here I was posted to Scapa Flow (Orkney Islands). Here, in this land-locked harbour, lay all the might of the navy, 'The Grand Fleet.' What a sight this presented, these massive great battleships and battlecruisers, destroyers and many auxiliary vessels, all with steam up and ready at a moment's notice to proceed to sea and engage the enemy.

As I viewed this great assembly of ships a rather awesome feeling stole over me. Was it fear and dread of what lay before me? Had I after all done wrong in leaving my old ship? Ah! No! God must have directed my steps and saved me from a watery grave. How true are the divine words: 'O LORD, I know that the way of man is not in himself: it is not in man that walketh to direct his steps' (Jeremiah 10: 23).

My first night at Scapa Flow was spent in the depot ship, which was crowded with officers waiting appointments. I was told there was no cabin accommodation and that I should have to sleep in a hammock. This did not worry me much, having had two years of this as a cadet on the old *Worcester.* I was told to report at ten o'clock next morning to the commanding officer who would tell me of my future appointment. As soon as dinner was finished, I slung my hammock. I was tired out after my long journey and soon fell asleep. How needful this was to calm my fears and strengthen me for the coming day's interview – 'When thou liest down, thou shalt not be afraid: yea, thou shalt lie down, and thy sleep shall be sweet' (Proverbs 3: 24).

Well, the time arrived for me to be interviewed by my commanding officer and I was duly ushered into his presence. He was sitting at his desk, and without looking up said, 'Take a seat please.' He was looking through some papers in a folio and on the cover was my name. To me he was a very imposing man, with four gold rings on each arm (a captain)! Suddenly he looked up and without saying a word seemed to search me through and through, and then again reverted to his folio. I thought, why does he not speak? Then suddenly the silence was broken, and looking up he said, 'So you are a navigating officer,' to which I meekly replied 'Yes, sir.' 'Well,' he said, 'you are just the man I want!' which remark was accompanied with a smile that seemed to break down all the ice of officialdom. 'I want you to take command of one of our armed trawlers.' He went on to explain the patrol would be rough, being north of the Shetland Islands. I should have the original crew, also a naval signalman and gunner. I replied in the affirmative to his question of my willingness to take the job on. He wished me well and every success.

I served for about a year in this vessel. It certainly was a tough life as my commanding officer had said. Very little fair weather did we have in those high latitudes, and long dark nights in the winter. Certainly one experienced the literal aspect of Psalm 107: 25 – 'For he commandeth, and raiseth the stormy wind, which lifteth up the waves thereof.'

My service in this little ship was abruptly brought to a close. I had boarded a vessel and was coming down the side on a 'Jacob's ladder,' as they were called. It was very rough, and halfway down I slipped, fell into my vessel alongside and broke my ankle. In looking back I can see there was much mercy in this, for, had I fallen into the sea, how different the issue might have been. There was now nothing left but to bring my vessel back to the depot at Scapa Flow and report, which I did, and after a few days I was put on board a hospital ship. To leave this little vessel under these circumstances caused me a certain amount of sadness. I had got to know my men and they knew me, and we were happy together. The skipper was an honest Scotsman with a very broad accent and sometimes, when he got a bit excited, I could not understand a word he said. He always used to call me 'Mr. Lieutenant.' The hospital ship (a chartered Union Castle liner) was bound for Portsmouth. We sailed with all our lights fully on at night, and two large red crosses on either side fully illuminated. This, of course, was to let the German submarines know we were a ship of mercy, but, alas, they did not always respect this and did sink some of this class of ship without warning. On arrival at Portsmouth I was transferred to the naval hospital at Haslar. After about three weeks I was sent on convalescent leave for about two months.

At the expiration of this period I was appointed to *H.M.S. Fisgard* at Portsmouth, a boy artificer's training ship. My duties were to instruct the boys in physical culture and to keep an eye on their health generally. I very much liked this work and found it most interesting and a healthy occupation. However, after a time I felt it was rather a dead end and not furthering my prospects of a permanency in the navy, which was always uppermost in my thoughts for the future. Ah! How I was to prove the truth in Isaiah 55:8, 'For my thoughts are not your thoughts, neither are your ways my ways, saith the LORD.'

After I had been about six months on this ship, it came to my knowledge that the Admiralty were short of navigating officers and invited Naval Reserve officers to apply for this class of work, with a prospect of permanency in the navy at the end of the war if they had given satisfaction. Now, I thought, was the door open for the fulfilment of my life's ambition, but again I was to prove, 'He that openeth, and no man shutteth; and shutteth, and no man openeth.' I was to learn in a remarkable way in the future the experimental truth of this text in my own experience.

Well, I applied and was accepted for 'navigating duties in the Submarine Service,' and was appointed to *H.M.S. Dolphin*, the submarine depot ship at Portsmouth.

I felt leaving my boys on the *Fisgard*, they were well disciplined lads and no trouble at all, and I was very fond of them.

After a three weeks' course on the gyroscopic compass, a mariner's compass used particularly on submarines, I was appointed to the submarine *J2* There were six of these vessels and they were the latest and largest type of submarine in the service, and great things were expected of them, but they proved to be most unseaworthy and most sluggish in diving and coming to the surface.

I well remember the first time we proceeded into the Solent on trials. We had on board the Admiral of the Portsmouth Dockyard and not a few high officials. Our commander was full of zeal and intended to show the virtues of his vessel. Proceeding along at a good speed in our exercising area, the order was given to 'dive' but to the bewilderment of our captain and the dockyard officials nothing happened, when suddenly, instead of going down at a graceful angle, she stood on her head! This could have been very dangerous but mercifully we were able to get her on even keel and back into the dockyard. I did not realise then, as I do now, that the Solent might have been my 'watery grave.'

Well, after a good deal of investigation and trials, we were pronounced seaworthy and were given orders to proceed to the submarine base at Blyth (Northumberland) for patrolling duties in the North Sea and Baltic.

A J-Class submarine from the war

We were usually at sea for about two weeks, and then in port for the same period tied up to our depot ship, the *Titania.* It was during the summer months that we were on this patrol which meant spending many hours submerged, diving at periscope depth, as being in enemy waters it would not be safe to be on the surface during daylight. It can easily be realised that after spending 18 hours below the surface, oxygen would become scarce resulting in much labour for breath. Our duty in the Baltic was to watch for the enemy coming out of Kiel and working her way through the Kattegat and Skagerrak and thence into the North Sea, the German Navy's 'back door', as we used to call it. Dangerous indeed were these waters, infested with U-Boats (German submarines), and overhead those monstrous beasts, the Zeppelins, to say nothing of hidden minefields. It was said of Jonah, 'Out of the belly of hell' (that is in the midst of the seas) 'cried I, and thou heardest my voice' and this is why I am able to write this account.

I never spoke to my commanding officer about prayer, but somehow I cannot think he was altogether a stranger to this, for the following reason. When possible on a Sunday he would take his vessel to the bottom of the sea and then hold a brief service from the Prayer Book, and always this prayer:

'O eternal Lord God, who alone spreadest out the heavens, and rulest the raging of the sea, who hast compassed the waters with bounds until day and night come to an end, be pleased to receive into thy Almighty and most gracious protection the persons of us thy servants and the fleet in which we serve. Preserve us from the dangers of the sea and from the violence of the enemy, and that we may return in safety to enjoy the blessings of our land, and with a thankful remembrance of thy mercies to praise and glorify thy holy Name, through Jesus Christ our Lord, Amen.'

To me this was a help, although at that time only for the preservation of my life which was dear to me, but with no concern for the danger of my soul.

On one occasion we spotted an enemy destroyer coming out of Kiel. 'Action stations!' rang out the command, 'Stand by to fire number one torpedo!' Then to our horror our vessel 'broke surface' and we were spotted by our enemy, who closed in towards us at great speed, and the escorting Zeppelin proceeded to manoeuvre into position to bomb us. 'Take her down, flood all tanks, full speed on the engines,' was the urgent command. All too long it seemed to us in our anxiety she trembled on the surface, and then suddenly like a stone she crashed to the bottom, as the destroyer roared over us, and there we lay with the bombs from our enemy on the sea and sky falling all around us – but not one hit. Why? Was it an answer to prayer? Surely it was, but we know now that our time had not yet come, God had to show us 'greater things than these.'

Now the breaking of the surface and the sluggishness of our vessel in diving showed us there was a dangerous weakness which we had to report, and various alterations were made. From time to time on our trips other things developed which shook our confidence and we felt our submarine was a 'white elephant,' which was the experience of the officers in the other five J-class submarines, and in the end they were all taken out of commission.

I was now appointed as a navigator to an E-class submarine based at Harwich. This vessel was much smaller than the J-class, but a beauty to handle and trustworthy. I remained in this vessel until the end of the war and experienced many wonderful deliverances.

Our patrol was the North Sea and the coast of Germany. This particular area was a mass of minefields, our own and the enemy's, and this made navigation very difficult, especially in relation to submarines, as by day we were submerged and we could only plot our position by star sights. In bad weather the stars never appeared, as Paul speaks of in Acts 27, and we were left to 'dead reckoning.'

Perhaps here it would not be out of place to relate a few experiences in 'dangers oft' and God's wonderful deliverances.

With six other submarines we were sent on an emergency patrol off the German coast; news had been received that there was a good deal of activity in the German fleet. For six days we lay stretched along the coast, but no sight of the enemy. During the whole of this time the weather was very tempestuous and we were unable to obtain sights. In those days, of course, there were not the facilities of modern times such as directional wireless and radar. Thus our position was only on 'dead reckoning,' always precarious. This, of course, would be the case of the other submarines.

Well, one afternoon we were at periscope depth when suddenly there was a heavy scraping noise all along the hull, causing us to heel over quite a bit. First of all we thought it might be a mine, but we soon dismissed this idea as the impact was too heavy. Finally we concluded we had struck a submerged wreck. We returned to our base, mooring alongside our depot ship, and then noticed another submarine with her conning tower badly damaged and the periscope buckled. We got in conversation with our fellow officers and then the mystery unfolded. They said on a certain day at a certain time something passed over them causing the observed damage. Day and time exactly corresponded with the experience already described – we had passed over this vessel!

How different the issue might have been had we been a few feet lower in the water! Surely by experience we learn:

> God moves in a mysterious way
> His wonders to perform;
> He plants his footsteps in the sea,
> And rides upon the storm.[345]

When in port we were not idle and would proceed out of harbour for exercise. This chiefly consisted in making a dummy attack on one of our destroyers. During one of these attacks the destroyer approached too close to us, altered his course to avoid us and crashed into our bows, making a deep hole through which the water rushed in, flooding our fore compartment and taking us down to the bottom. We tried to surface by blowing all our ballast tanks, but to no avail – our fore part was stuck in the mud. Was this the end? Surely in some respects our position was akin to Jonah's: 'For thou hadst cast me into the deep, in the midst of the seas; and the floods compassed me about: all thy billows and thy waves passed over me' (Jonah 2: 3).

We reversed our engines in the attempt to suck ourselves out of the mud, but she remained fast. If having one's mind up unto God is praying, then I prayed. The hours passed. We could not use our engines much more as the battery would be exhausted and our lights would fail. Our only hope seemed to be that the changing tide would shift the mud in

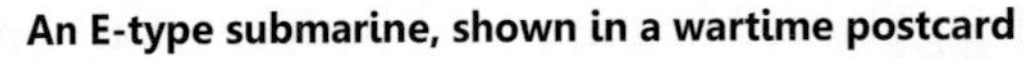
An E-type submarine, shown in a wartime postcard

which our fore part was buried, and this, through the mercy of God, is just what happened! Six long, awful hours had passed and hope seemed to be at its lowest. Suddenly the vessel seemed to quiver from stem to stern, there was a sucking noise, and then we realised the tide (God's) was doing her work. Once more full speed astern on the engines, and then O! who can describe the experience as she released herself, rose to the surface and leapt out of the water! Surely God 'vomited' us out of the water as in Jonah 2: 10. I think I was as near to tears of joy as a man could be and deep gratitude.

At Harwich (our base) there was stationed a fleet of six light cruisers and destroyers, and very efficient they were. Often as I used to see them steaming out of harbour they seemed the very epitome of Great Britain's naval strength (in those days) – alas now no longer great or the 'mother of the free,' but in bondage to other nations.

One beautiful summer morning, it was the Sabbath, we were patrolling the German coast, and were proceeding at periscope depth. I was on watch and spotted six cruisers and reported same to my captain. He came to the periscope and said, 'Oh that's all right pilot' (the nickname for navigating officers) 'they are our Harwich flotilla.' On occasions this officer could be humorous and as he looked through the periscope he said, 'I can see you but you can't see me,' but suddenly he realised his humour was being turned to awful reality – they had seen our periscope and were coming straight for us, [*mistaking us for an enemy submarine*]. Then once more we heard the awful urgent command, 'Take her down, take her down!' and down we went as the first destroyer roared over us, dropping his deadly depth charges, followed by others. To describe one's feelings is impossible. I can only remember standing motionless and feeling death was imminent, but strange to say all fear was taken away and my thoughts were up unto God. This attack lasted about ten minutes as these vessels of death passed over us dropping their deadly cargo, but through the mercy of God there was not one direct hit.

Our captain, thinking the attack was over, kept us down at about 100 feet. However, such was not so as they were returning to renew the onslaught and we heard the roar of their propellers as they closed in on us. Now our captain did the only thing that (humanly speaking) could save our lives, and the order rang out, 'Blow all tanks and bring her up,' and then as we surfaced our friends opened fire on us. Our commanding officer grabbed a white ensign which he waved as he opened the conning tower hatch, and then these destroyers realised their awful mistake! Well, although we were not hit by the depth charges, the blast had caused considerable internal damage and external by the gunfire, also the morale of some of the crew was badly shaken. In these conditions the only thing to do was to limp back to our base accompanied by a destroyer. What a demonstration this experience was that:

> All my times are in thy hand,
> All events at thy command.[346]

It was recognised that the Harwich submarines had a very dangerous patrol operating off the enemy's coast, and our losses were heavy; many submarines never returned to port again. Sad it was to see the poor wives standing on the pier gazing out to sea in the hope that the missing vessel might return. Mostly it was never known how our missing comrades met their end and we were never allowed to speak about this outside our own base. We never knew who was going to be the next! Why were we spared? Why was I? Well:

> God moves in a mysterious way
> His wonders to perform;
> He plants his footsteps in the sea,
> And rides upon the storm.[347]

I think we shall see the truth of these beautiful words as we try to unfold our little narrative.

Another very remarkable thing happened when we were off the Dutch coast. We sighted a German merchant steamer and closed towards her. We surfaced and fired six rounds at her, all of which hit. Then we observed the crew abandoning ship, so our captain put a boarding party on her under my charge. (Here I must break off this account for the moment. In September, 1908, I had joined the four masted barque, *Marlborough Hill*, in Rotterdam. I crossed from Tilbury in a Dutch vessel called *Batavia II*. Now to return.) Imagine my surprise that the ship I boarded was none other than the one in which I had crossed to Rotterdam nine years ago, and she was now under German charter. I had orders to get *Batavia II* under way and proceed to sea. Progress was slow as our gunfire had caused a leak and the steering was defective. A little later I observed two Dutch destroyers steaming towards me which signalled me to stop. An officer boarded me and said I was to consider myself a prisoner and await orders. This, of course, was not very pleasant news to me, and as this officer spoke fairly good English I asked for some further explanation. He said we were carrying on warfare in territorial waters, to which I replied that I had boarded her outside territorial waters, but that she had drifted in while I was trying to get her under way, and my captain would verify this, which he did. *Batavia II* was now sinking, which no doubt was due to our gunfire. I informed my captain (by hand semaphore) of this, and he replied, 'Open all sea connections and scuttle her, and abandon ship in *Batavia's* lifeboat.' This turned out to be no easy operation owing to the heavy list the ship had taken. I was concerned about my crew, whether they could swim! However, after an anxious time we managed to get our lifeboat into the water and pulled away to safety. We returned to our submarine, and the last we saw of *Batavia II* was just her masts sticking up out of the sea.

At times we were sent on the Dover patrol and this was very dangerous and exacting. The Germans had defeated Belgium and taken over all their Channel ports and made them bases for their submarines. We used to leave Dover at dusk and take up our position as near as possible to one of these ports. We then submerged with just the top of our conning tower above water, and there we stood and kept our watch until dawn, waiting to make an attack on any submarines we spotted coming out. We were so near to the coast that we could see the flashes of guns, those of both our army and the Germans, in the bitter conflict on land. Twice we intercepted the enemy and scored a hit but never really knew if the submarine went to the bottom as, for safety, we also went to the bottom and lay there. O! how bitter and cruel is warfare! I shudder now when I think of these things, and the terrible sacrifice of millions of young lives on this altar of blood! Godly inspired Isaiah and Micah wrote: 'They [*the nations of the earth*] shall beat their swords into plowshares, and their spears into pruninghooks: nation shall not lift up a sword against nation, neither shall they learn war any more' (Isaiah 2: 4; Micah 4: 3). When?

We would return from these 'stunts' (as we used to call them) to arrive off Dover at dawn and await for a destroyer to flash his searchlights at intervals to guide us into harbour, for while the war was on all our coastwise lights were extinguished. During the day we would try and get a little rest, which was not easy owing to continual air raids. Three weeks was the limit for this patrol, after which we returned to our Harwich base and were given a few days' leave.

Well, the war dragged on and the awful price was still being exacted among our flotilla – 'Submarine E is overdue,' and then the sad verdict – she must be considered lost with all hands, and yet my unworthy life was spared, whilst better and more efficient men were cut off. But why? I had to learn by experience the two-fold dealings of God in Psalm 107 – providence and grace. The former in my life I was not a stranger to: 'They that go down to the sea in ships, that do business in great waters; these see the works of the LORD, and his wonders in the deep' (Psalm 107: 23-24). The latter I was being preserved also to experience – grace, God dealing with my soul in 'deep waters.'

Over three years of submarine life in war conditions was now beginning to tell upon my physical and nervous constitution and I wondered how much longer I should be able to continue in this service. Some of my brother officers had been given a little 'rest' in lighter and less exacting duties. I kept this to myself – what of the future if I gave up? The door into the navy would be shut and all my ambitions also. Ah! I did not realise then God was going to shut the door and to open another. I had to learn what I then did not know, but what I now know by experience: 'O LORD, I know that the way of man is not in himself: it is not in man that walketh to direct his steps' (Jeremiah 10: 23).

Well, I was enabled to continue until hostilities came to an end in November, 1918. With others I was now employed in bringing in some of the surrendered German submarines. What a sight was this! The Harwich harbour was packed with these vessels as we moored them one alongside the other. Their crews were put on our destroyers and taken back to Hamburg. A rather pathetic incident took place when I was bringing in one of these U-boats. The captain had his binoculars slung over his shoulder and then, taking them off and putting them over my shoulder, he said 'Here you are, you English lieutenant, take these. I shall never want them again.' I still have them. The German 'Grand Fleet,' as they called them, were surrendered to our fleet in the Orkney Islands and sunk. Those massive battleships and battlecruisers, like the Spanish Armada, were sunk beneath the waves. Oh! what a deliverance God had wrought for us. Would it be wrong if we quoted the words of King David? 'How are the mighty fallen, and the weapons of war perished!' (2 Samuel 1: 27).[348]

Ezra John Buck

Ezra Buck was a remarkable character. Brought up in a godly home, he turned his back on the religion of his parents and lived a worldly and irreligious life. Although he saw many remarkable deliverances during the war, he was hardened under them. In later life he recalled how one day he was out attacking a German machine gun nest. The British had made a good advance on the German line, and when Ezra attacked the German machine gun nest he found that the Germans had all been shot. One of the Germans was kneeling with his hands clasped in the attitude of prayer with a bullet through his head. Mr Buck never forgot this incident, yet even such open reminders of religion made no impression on him at the time.[349]

After the war he married, and continued to live a worldly life, until the Lord was pleased to call him by grace while he was gambling on the Lord's Day, in 1930. He told his worldly wife that he had to give up the world, and that she was free to leave him if she wished, but that he could not give up his religion for her. Although they remained married, after he was baptised and entered the ministry, she placed every possible barrier in the way of his ministry, yet he felt he could never leave her. In later years, after his wife's death, he remarried, and his second wife shared his love of the Saviour. He was a member at Gower Street Chapel, London, though in later life he resided at Edenbridge in Kent. The following account was written by him in 1962:[350]

> ✍ As the Holy Ghost is pleased to help me I will try to relate what I feel to be my own experience before and after my call by grace. I was born in sin, 22nd February, 1900. Strictly brought up in a godly home, I had no desire for religion, being not so much as a stony ground hearer. My flesh was delighted when I was able to see the back of it and enjoy freely the common sports and pleasures of the world, and there I remained until I was thirty.

Ezra J. Buck

After the 1914 war broke out, as soon as I was old enough to serve in the army I was off, as I had a real passion for shooting. I served with the First Battalion of the Rifle Brigade in France. In my first engagement my Lewis gunner was killed at my left shoulder as we advanced toward the German strongholds.

On another occasion, one night the sergeant came round for volunteers to locate a German machine gun post which was giving trouble and could not be located by any form of day observation. Eventually I made one of the party of five or six as it was an adventure for me to meet a German, not having the fear of man. We bypassed our Lewis gun team until we came to the canal, and waded in shallow water until we came to an island where trees and bushes were growing. I spoke to my officer who, I noticed, gripped his revolver hard, and he brought us back. Then we approached the island by walking up to a green verge. There was a gulley between us and the island about four yards wide, and while I probed about in a ditch to my right, a blast of bullets passed my left jaw. The heat was like a hot poker. We soon realised where the German machine gun post was! We were well trained to fall flat when under such fire, and while doing so a stick bomb came over and fell between me and a brave Irish lad, but neither of us was hit by the explosion. As we had no orders to capture the gun, the officer and two other men made their way back. By that time the Germans had organised themselves for defence, although by their eyes glaring out from under their helmets they felt very uneasy. They could not see us two under the firing of the gun. The Irish lad said quietly 'What shall we do?' I said: 'I will give you a Mills bomb,' but when I felt for it in my pocket I realised I had left them in the dugout. This made us rely on our rifles and we were just about to send a hail of bullets into them when someone got hold of my shoulder. I naturally thought it was one of the Germans behind us, but it was my officer, who had come back to see what had happened to us. He was a very brave man. He spoke quietly and said, 'Come out of it, you fool,' and left us to make our way back.

When we had all arrived back safely, our officer brought us before the captain or major and he commended us on our success. But I was so disappointed that we were not left to make a good job of it by returning with the gun and the German crew. No doubt the artillery made short work of this once we gave them the position. My officer explained afterwards, when he saw how grieved I was over it all, that we were sent to locate the machine gun but had no orders to take it. He also said that he had been in France since 1914 (this was 1918) and had never seen a man delivered from death at such short range as I had been that night. He concluded by saying that only an act of God's providence could do it.

There were three men with me who had premonitory experiences that they would be killed, but one lived. He was Sergeant Mainey from Leicestershire, a very courageous man. We had taken the village that day, and sent all the Germans back through our lines. As the evening was approaching, the German shelling made us sit uneasy, especially as there was no sign of the lighter guns appearing. But after a long time they came galloping over the ridge and soon swung into action. I noticed Sergeant Mainey pacing up and down, so I went over to see what was wrong. With my youthful spirit I chafed him and said, 'Your wife wouldn't know you.' He abruptly answered, 'And your mother wouldn't know you, Buck.' Still feeling very disturbed with his manner, I said, 'What is the matter Sergeant Mainey?' He said, 'I have a great fear of death, Buck.' I said, 'Come and turn in with us in a shell hole.' He said, 'I think I will, because you are specially preserved.' My men were very tired, so I promised to do sentry duty throughout the night. I was helped to do it although I nodded frequently owing to my own weariness. It was a frosty night and I heard several thuds around my shell hole. When dawn was about to break I awakened the sergeant and men. As Sergeant Mainey looked around he took off his steel helmet and with real gratitude said, 'Did I not tell you that you were specially preserved?' Thus his life was spared through the providence of God, for he would have been killed had he slept where he had intended.

The other man was my right-hand man on the Lewis gun, and as we were going over the top he said, 'I don't care much about coming over with you, Buck.' Within a quarter of an hour a German shell killed him beside me and I was blown over toward a building, speechless, without a scratch, although some spare parts in a bag I was carrying were shattered by shrapnel, also a civilian nearby was killed. As I examined the broken pieces of metal in the bag, a Cockney lad looked at me and said, 'You lucky devil!' I replied firmly, 'I shall never get killed in this war.' I felt the loss of my gunner as all sensible men do.

The next man came from Ipswich and we were going over the top at midnight, but all the day before he was restless and careless, exposing himself to German snipers. I tried to persuade him to come over with me but his reply was, 'It does not matter who I go over with, I shall stop a landowner.' By this he meant he would be killed, and that was his fate, as I saw him no more once we engaged the Germans. So deadly was the machine gun fire, and within a sixty yard range, that one of my men reformed from using bad language.

On two occasions the brave stretcher-bearers came out to find us, expecting to pick us up in pieces because they thought the German shells had blown us out of our gun position in a slit trench. But we were wonderfully preserved.

The final engagement came with our battalion on 1st November, 1918, when light guns were wheel to wheel. At 3 a.m. on a long front, 5000 guns opened deadly fire into the Germans. Prisoners were taken in a short time, but the Germans fought back with fresh troops and caused our battalion heavy losses. While in a slit trench with my Lewis gun team, a shell exploded at my end of the trench. It partly buried me and wounded my right buttock, but three others were wounded badly. The brave stretcher-bearers found us about 5 a.m. and dressed the wounds. After the men moved off, it was my turn to be dugout. From the force of the explosion my left leg remained lifeless, and I said to the stretcher bearers, 'I have lost my left leg.' Ripping up the trousers with their jackknife, they said, 'Your leg is on!' Being so helpless and not able to stand, one bearer held me upright in his arms waiting for the other man to dress my wound. While doing this another shell burst and severed half his head from the shoulder. This brave stretcher-bearer had given his life for me. His comrade moved towards us to dress my first wound, but recoiled at the sight. Once recovered from this he bravely said, 'I will get you away.' I insisted that he should not worry about me as I would drag my body across the field, and strength was given me to do this until I reached a river. The river lay before me which I must cross to reach the casualty clearing station, but there was only a narrow plank on which to cross. Although a born swimmer, my limbs were useless, but my mind was fixed to grasp each side of the plank, and so I reached the other side. My next obstacle was dragging myself over dead and wounded Germans, but eventually I reached the dressing station. A cheerful voice received me kindly, 'Where have you got to, Buck? Here's a cup of tea.' They attended to my dressing, and placed me in a room on a rough, wire netting bed. As I looked around I saw four or five English lads had died from their wounds. German shells hit the dressing station, and I received another shrapnel wound in the thigh. This was dressed, and it was my turn to be carried off, but a married man came along and I said, 'Let him go first.' Then another shell fell and I never saw this man any more nor the Germans who were to take him away.

The same shell blew the doctor right into the room I was in and hurled him against where my head lay. I feared he was dead, but grabbed his tunic collar and shook him and said, 'Are you all right sir?' To my surprise he opened his eyes, and with love and energy said firmly, 'I will get you away.' This doctor found two German prisoners and they carried me away from that dressing station where love and loyalty were shown to the wounded without regard to their own lives. The Germans laid me down as their own shells burst around us, and covered me with their own bodies, taking the weight on their hands and toes. This continued until a wagon came to take us further down the line clear of shell fire.

All through these preserving mercies I knew not God, neither did I want his Christ, who was to my carnal wisdom 'a root out of dry ground.' As Mr Kent says in hymn 76 (*Gadsby's Selection*):

> Judgements nor mercies ne'er can sway
> Their roving feet to wisdom's way.

Hymn 64 explains every experience of a child of God both in grace and in providence. Since being called by God's sovereign and invincible grace I have been called to fight on another battlefield, where Satan's shot and shells are made of another substance – the powers of darkness. His fiery darts sometimes come in like hail – just as quick as the bullets from the German machine guns. This great enemy we fight by faith, and there is no discharge from this battlefield until 'death that puts an end to life will put an end to sin.'[351] A child of God's worst enemies are found within, but the remedy is in the holy blood of God's dear Son. These things I have related, not to advertise my experience, but because when I was born the Lord made it clear to my godly mother that I was for the work of the ministry, and the Lord assured her of it again as she came near the gates of death.

James Charles Burgess

Mr Burgess was called by grace as a young man, and was baptised in the open air in 1908, joining the church at Dauntsey, Wiltshire. After fighting in France in the war, and surviving serious injury, Mr Burgess was sent into the ministry whilst still serving in the army. He later became pastor at Mount Zion Chapel, Bournemouth. He died on 6th May, 1974. Three letters written by Mr Burgess after he was injured in the war are given on p. 294. One of the letters concerns his call to the ministry. The following extract is taken from his obituary:

> ✍ Called to serve in the army at the outbreak of the 1914-18 War, and being an excellent marksman, he was given the dangerous task of a sniper. One Sabbath morning, he went into a cornfield alone before an attack, to beg the Lord that if he preserved his life he would go to preach. His life was preserved. On another occasion, a bullet was coming straight for his heart, when his Bible in his tunic pocket deflected it, saving him from death.
>
> Later that year, he was so severely wounded by a grenade that the medics almost left him for dead, but two stretcher bearers, thinking he might be alive, took him to the field hospital. At the dressing station he was placed among the dead with a sheet over him. Later, a doctor walking amongst the dead noticed a tiny movement from a sheet and drew it back, finding him alive. He was taken from the front to Abbeville and from there he was brought to Christchurch, only five miles from the place he was one day to be pastor. Such was the pain caused by his wounds that he had to be kept on morphia, until the time came for the doctor to ask him to try and do without it for a night. He did; and though he gnawed the end off his pillow, he was favoured with such fellowship with the Lord in his sufferings that he fell into a sweet sleep and in the morning his pain was gone, much to the wonder of the doctor. He was later moved to Hull and Newcastle, and it was about this time of his suffering that he was exercised about the ministry, which exercise was confirmed by the word, 'I shall not die but live, and declare the works of the LORD' (Psalm 118: 17). Although so weak, he was gradually strengthened and eventually received the consent of his church at home to speak in the Lord's Name, whilst still serving in the Army.[352]

James C. Burgess

Stephen Clark

Stephen Clark was brought up to attend Jireh Chapel, Newick, Sussex. After his war service he moved to attend Mayfield Chapel, Sussex, under the ministry of Mr Caleb Sawyer. The following account of his war experiences was published after the war under the title of *God's Mercy and Goodness, as manifested to Stephen Clark of Mayfield, during the Great War 1916-18*:

Stephen Clark

✍ It was not a pleasant feeling that I must take my part in the Great War, but such was my lot on July 6th, 1916, having presented myself at the recruiting office. Leaving my wife and a baby of two months, the comforts of home, the privilege of the Lord's Day, to mix up with all sorts and conditions of men, I say, it was far from being pleasant. However, I trust I had a desire to do my duty to my king and country, believing this to be right and Scriptural.

My first night in camp was at Chichester. Though in a hut with several others, I was able to rest fairly comfortably. The following morning I, with several other men, proceeded to Dover. On my arrival there, I was posted to the Breakwater Battery, Royal Garrison Artillery. This battery consisted of two 6 inch guns, manned by about 22 men. These men I found very respectable, including amongst them a mayor's son, shop assistant, and businessmen. These, having joined earlier, were accustomed to their task; at first I found my duties, which were carried out on the breakwater, very difficult. This, I must explain, is a pier running across the entrance to the harbour. It was after my usual training for the day was over that I could get alone to read my Bible and *Gadsby's Hymns*, which I trust I valued, for these contained the source of all my comfort and hope. At times I was enabled by the Holy Spirit to draw with joy 'water out of the wells of salvation.' Many of the Psalms were made a comfort to me, and knowing so little of divine things, the hymns were a great help, for they often expressed the feelings of my heart.

Sunday came. We had a service, but having no chaplain attached to us, the officers took the service; but it being so formal it did not touch my case. I wanted the Holy Spirit's teaching which alone can bring real comfort.

After a stay of about two months, the order was given to pack up for Dover Castle. The Admiralty tug came over for us to proceed to Dover Castle, where we stayed the night before starting on our journey to London; and just as I was preparing for rest, an alarm was given that a Zeppelin was over the Channel. But our guns made her alter her course, and kept her over the open sea. I heard after that this monster was seven miles out. I then tried to commit my all into the Lord's hand, and returned to rest. Morning came; I felt refreshed. After thankfully praising God for his watchful care over me through the night, we entrained for London – Bostall Heath Camp. Here I was to meet fresh company, fresh officers, strange companions; and some here, I must relate, rather opposed to the truth. It was my usual habit to read my Bible and hymn book in bed. I remember one evening I was asked, 'What chapter tonight?' I very willingly told them. I have often thought of it since. No doubt the Devil wanted to stop it; but, bless God, I was able to stand all such sneers that came my way. The camp was made up of hutments, each hut holding about thirty men. My first task when off duty was to find a place of truth, not knowing my way about London. The nearest chapel was Plumstead Tabernacle. Here I found food for my soul, the word often being an encouragement to me. I well remember the deacon giving out Hymn 1075, *Gadsby's*. I felt this was just what I wanted. I could love Charles Wesley. But how soon the birds of the air took it away.

To return to barrack life. The company of ungodly men was a real trial, and having upon my mind that I must soon go out to take part in real fighting, this was indeed very hard. However, I was spared for a while yet. Having spent three months at Bostall Heath, the camp moved to Winchester, which, while it lasted, was worse than the previous one, there being no place of truth there. The camp was five miles from Winchester. I might say here it was only once that I ventured to walk that distance. Though denied hearing a good gospel sermon, I had the best book in the whole world, and when applied to my heart and conscience, I could say it was 'the power of God unto salvation,' and sometimes could acquiesce in all the Lord's dealings, and say:

> Sovereign Ruler of the skies,
> Ever gracious, ever wise;
> All my times are in thy hand,
> All events at thy command.[353]

The time came when there was a draught to be picked for France, and feeling unhappy with regard to the East,[354] I boldly asked if I might be sent to the Western Front, which request was granted. I had been having short leaves to see my loved ones, but the time came when I must have my last before going to the front. I attended Newick Chapel the next Sunday evening. My late pastor, Mr. Stubbs,[355] though not knowing that I should be there on my last leave, was led to take for his text the wonderful promise to Joshua: 'Have I not commanded thee? Be strong and of a good courage; be not afraid, neither be thou dismayed: for the LORD thy God is with thee whithersoever thou goest' (Joshua 1: 9). This put new strength in me. It was a very encouraging time; I believed it was a message from God himself, though feeling like Jacob of old, not worthy of the least of all God's mercies.

The time came when I must leave my wife and son, and all kind friends, to face the many dangers seen and unseen; spending my leave, which was very brief, at the house of my mother-in-law. Human nature is very weak under such circumstances. I had my last look at home and surroundings, not knowing if ever I should return. But, praise God! I not only returned, but with all my limbs and faculties, and in perfect health. The many mercies that I was the recipient of I shall try and speak of later.

So on the morning of March 19th, 1917, we made our way to Southampton. It was usual at the docks for clergymen and others to distribute portions of Scripture. A clergyman came over to me and asked my acceptance of a little booklet. To my pleasant surprise, there was the text – the word to Joshua, which I always called my last leave text.

After waiting some time at the docks, we were marched on board the troopship. I was given to understand it was the *King Edward VII*, though the vessel was nameless for this reason, that spies should not know of our movements. When I stepped on board, the words of Paul, while on his journey to Rome, came very powerfully to my mind: 'And now I exhort you to be of good cheer: for there shall be no loss of any man's life among you … God hath given thee all that sail with thee.' Through having to bear much discomfort, owing to the fact that we had on board rather more than we ought, and not daring to leave my kit-bag – if I did I may not have found it again – I felt more and more the need of some encouragement to bear me up. His good word that I had had on stepping aboard the boat proved that 'As thy days, so shall thy strength be.' The Lord enabled me to commit my way unto him, who alone was able to bring these precious promises to pass.

We sailed out of Southampton about 6.30 p.m., it being a very cold, wintery evening; when, having reached the open sea, it was not long before we were alarmed by a German submarine following us. Not a man was allowed on the top deck. Though having to alter our course, and having to keep close to our escort, we safely eluded the enemy, and thus we safely reached the shores of France – Le Havre. At the end of the journey, I tried to thank God and take courage, and by the mercy of God all were safe, though many of the men were seasick, myself being spared. But our troubles were now only beginning, for after we got to Le Havre, we were told we must march about four miles to the base camp. This was not a very pleasant journey; however, we arrived tired, very glad for a rest, if only on the hard floors of dining rooms for a few hours. When morning came we were allotted tents; but O what company! – the company of the ungodly. The Lord had been faithful to his promise, in that he had spared me from a watery grave; but now I had to experience a much longer trial of the promise that God would be with me whithersoever I went. This was a trial all through, sometimes more marked than at others.

My stay at the base did not last long, for in about three weeks I was among the draught for the fighting line. We were paraded before the officer commanding the base. But previous to this the order went forth for every man to have every bit of hair cut off. No doubt this was done for cleanliness, for it would be some time before we should be able to have our hair cut again. I am sure we did not look a very pleasant lot of men. However, the order was carried out. Often did I wonder what would be my lot; should I be spared to see home and England? or should I have a soldier's grave in a foreign land? However, through the mercy of God, I was spared. On our way up to the line we stopped at a rest camp, but found this already filled with men going up the line like ourselves so had to find what shelter we could to rest our weary bodies. It being dark all we could find was an old barn, with as many tiles off as on, but it was somewhere to lie down. The next morning we were off to make our way towards Arras, where I received my baptism of fire. I felt thankful that I had reached my journey's end, though feeling very low in spirit, and so destitute of any real spiritual things. I was posted to the 35th Heavy Battery, Royal Garrison Artillery. This was a peacetime battery, only recently come over from abroad. The British troops had just taken over this part of the line, and previous to my arrival had fought the second battle of Arras. Here the Lord very mercifully preserved me. I was off duty, or rather our guns were not in action. Knowing it was mealtime, I went over to where it was being prepared, when I heard a shell burst, and on looking round saw one of our men hurt very much. Needless to say, I did not wait for my meal, but returned to the little dugout, which was made of corrugated iron for the top, about two feet down in the earth, with a couple of steps just deep enough to crawl in. Here I was but a few moments before, sitting where the young man was when he was wounded, but I was spared. We were able to get a stretcher, and after making him as comfortable as we could, sent him off to the dressing station. I had very solemn thoughts at this time, and felt the truth of Cowper's hymn:

> God moves in a mysterious way
> His wonders to perform.[356]

My stay with this battery was short, as some of us had to make good the losses to other batteries. My next companions were the men of the 38th Heavy Battery (Welsh). These men were miners from the coalfields; the non-commissioned officers were Cardiff policemen. The men were excellent singers, as well as fighters; but, alas, their talents were not used to sing the songs of Zion. But their friendliness towards a newcomer to the battery was very noticeable, which made it more comfortable for me. I must say here that this position was the most dangerous that I had been in, for it was not safe to rest our weary bodies, only as we did so in a six foot trench.

One summer's evening, in the month of July, there were several of the German balloons up for observation purposes, and towards eight o'clock the enemy commenced shelling a field battery just in front of us. These men were given the order to clear. This order is generally given if not in action; if the guns are in action, then we had to carry on. However, in this case the order was given, 'Every man for himself.' I was having a wash at the time, and noticed these men passing our guns. No sooner had they reached our battery than the enemy opened fire on us; so we had the same order, 'Clear out.' As I said, I was having a wash. It was difficult to dry ourselves unless we could get out in the open. This I was able to do, and to another man, doing the same as myself, I said, 'We must get to a safer place;' and just as I was getting to a communication trench a shell burst between us, and a large splinter from it went through the heart of this mate and killed him, and I was this time spared. It was a crime if found without our gas masks. I suddenly remembered I had left mine just outside my dugout, and ventured back to get it, and that was how I knew this young man had been killed. This man was hoping to go to England to be married, but not so; instead of this we reverently laid him in a soldier's grave, there to await the resurrection morning. The words of the Psalmist came very powerfully to me: 'There is but a step between me and death.' 'Praise God, from whom all blessings flow.' The Lord had covered my head in the day of battle.

I must return to that never-to-be-forgotten evening. After I had told the N.C.O. that I thought one man was killed, they went back, but just to make sure it was so; then to seek safety for themselves. We were obliged to go some distance, and there wait till the shelling was over. It was about eleven o'clock when we returned to the guns. What a dreadful feeling having to go back again, but we did, and to add to my grief, I was on guard. But, bless God, we were never shelled again that night. Next morning our commanding officer sent a message to headquarters that if the colonel valued our lives, we must be given orders to pull out. I am thankful to say that we did pull out, and were given three days' rest at Arras. Needless to say, it did us a great deal of good, both mentally and physically. We could sleep more comfortably, knowing we were out of so much danger. Praise God for this.

The three days' rest was over all too soon, and we were then sent to a position on our left flank to the old place, but a much quieter part of the line. It was not often we had a service behind our guns, but one Sunday afternoon a chaplain came along, and asked if he might conduct a short service. Only on such occasions did we know there was such a day; but this Sunday was a special day for me. We got together in a gun pit, and after singing a hymn, the chaplain read a portion of Scripture, and, to my delight, I heard an extempore prayer. After praying for our safety of body and soul, and an honourable end to the serious conflict and victory to our armies, he gave a short address, encouraging us to seek that life which is in the Lord Jesus Christ, who is Eternal Life. I have said that sermon was the most profitable of the whole time. I felt a little refreshed for the hard times that were ahead of us all.

While at this position, one of our officers came to me and asked if I would like to go down the line with him for a fortnight. The officer was to take a course at the artillery school. The name of the French town was Abbeville – a fine place for its buildings, but notorious for the superstition of the Church of Rome and for the priestly element. In this matter I had my choice, for no man was expected to be a batman against his will, but feeling that a change would do me good I consented. Next day the officer and myself set out for our new billet, feeling thankful to go away from the noise and dangers, knowing that we should have better nights at that time! Little did we know it was the means of preserving me from many a hard day and night. For the most part I had a quiet time, but just when we were expected to go back to the battery, the Germans had made their big push, and instead of returning to the battery, we had word to proceed to Étaples, a typical French town, but now more British than French. Here we remained for another fortnight, the lines being used all the time for new and fresh troops from England. In this way the Lord was pleased to preserve me by his overruling providence.

Now the time came for us to proceed to the nearest railhead, and being an Englishman, I felt sad that the enemy had been permitted to advance, the new railhead being some miles nearer. However, having found the battery again, I continued my duties with the officer, who was most kind to me. When I was in need of money to buy anything extra I could always have it. Then at another time I was able to return that kindness. On one occasion, after having censored one of my letters for home, he spoke to me, and said he admired the way I wrote respecting my trust in God, which made me wonder and hope that there might have been some good done by reading the many letters from the troops to England, or even the turning of some to look heavenwards. Who can tell?

I must now relate how the Lord mercifully preserved me from certain death. We were holding the line at a village named Ashicourt. Like most of the French villages, there were cobbled streets. Our battery was just across the road from a French farmyard; there were three of us billeted in the farm building. This particular morning we had been shelled rather more than usual, and the major's servant suggested going to a safer place behind the village. To this I agreed, thinking it would be the wisest course to take, and we remained there about an hour; being officers' batmen we were allowed a little more latitude than the other men. At length we thought it time we made our way back to our duty, when the major's servant asked me for a match to light the fire for preparing the officers' lunch. I said I was sorry I had not any, but I might have some loose matches in my haversack; and while I was getting the match – I had only gone about six steps – to my surprise, a shell burst on the spot where I had been standing only a minute before. Part of the building that I was in was demolished, and it was with difficulty that I got out. The old farmyard was so full of smoke and brick dust, I had to grope my way as best I could to safety. There were large doors at the bottom of the yard, and I found to my surprise the despatch rider had left his horse tied up in the yard. The animal had broken away, and was standing at the bottom, our only way out, shivering and bleeding. I was able to take the horse with me to safety. Now I am sad, remembering that the other two men were killed outright. How solemn! these men hurled into eternity, it seems, without any warning! Thus was I preserved by the goodness and mercy of God. I felt I could not praise God enough for his delivering mercy. It is true my nerves were in a very bad state, but my life was preserved. Many may perhaps say that a match saved my life. I quite agree, but it was the means the Lord was pleased to use. It was a most trying time having to go back to the place, where I must carry on alone, but the Lord helped me.

One day the officer came to me and said, 'We are going to another part of the line,' for which I was very thankful. There I was able to rest better, which was most beneficial to me. When one is enabled to look at the cause of all wars that the world has felt or seen, the suffering that has come in its train, it is well that we can confess our sins as individuals, as well as the sins of our beloved nation, our forgetfulness of God, denying the inspiration of the Scriptures, denying the blessed atonement, also the desecration of the Lord's Day. These things call forth the judgements of God upon us.

I now come to another part of the line – the Ypres sector, the scene of many a hard battle. It was on a ridge, called Pilckem Ridge, that we took up our position. Here I must relate how, through the overruling providence of God, I was kept from making a decision like one of our men was left to do. Our sleeping place was a gun pit, with a gun sheet for a covering. One of the men thought it was not safe, so decided to make a little place just for himself. There not being any firing for the battery that night, we turned in. Just about twelve o'clock we heard a shell burst, and then a groan. A splinter from the shell had cut through both of the legs of the young man. Had he remained with the other men, he would have been safe; but it was not to be. We soon bound up his badly wounded legs, but before we could get him to a dressing station he died through loss of blood. I always remember this man for his advanced socialist views. Oh the mercy of God as extended to me! I have often to express myself like the poet: 'Why me? Why me?'[357] Was I any better? No! I often have to say I am the worst of sinners. I was spared; spared to see the good hand of God made bare on my behalf.

On another occasion we had gone to a fresh position, where, as usual, we made our own dugouts. One man had just put the finishing touches to the place where he hoped to rest his weary frame. The guns were not in action, so he lay down, never to rise again; for a shell dropped almost on top of him and he was killed. Truly,

> Not a single shaft can hit,
> Till the God of love sees fit.[358]

Often feeling very destitute of any spiritual thoughts, yet in the midst of dangers, and having a worldly spirit, this was a grief to me. One can understand a little the state of my mind; tried with regard to the safety of my body; tried for the safety of my soul.

On another occasion, I had just finished my midday meal, and was sitting by the dugout, when a shell just missed my head, dropping in a shell hole. Bless God, it didn't explode; this was what we called a 'dud.' Had it exploded I should have been hurled into eternity. How thankful I felt for the Lord's sparing mercy.

Another trial I had. It was decided that we should change over with another battery in a different part of the line. All the officers and men had gone except one other and myself. The last night at this position was really the worst, for we were shelled all night with gas shells, and I was alone in a dugout. How thankful I was in the morning to be alive and none the worse for the gas. I was thankful when we had handed over the guns to the new men.

I now come to November, 1917, when our troops were to attack in conjunction with the French, the objective being the town of Cambrai. We advanced to a village named Ribicourt, but here we came to a standstill, and on two occasions had to retire a few miles back. We were almost cut off by the enemy, we having formed what we call a horse shoe, being exposed to shell fire on both flanks as well as from the front. However, it was thought best that we take up a position at Havincourt Wood. Here we spent the 1917 Christmas. I shall never forget this. The officers were billeted in a 40 foot dugout, made by the New Zealand troops. It was usual for us to take our turn waiting at table, there being eight batmen. Unfortunately the lot fell on me for Christmas Day; there were eight courses to serve, which was very tiring. Thankful I felt when the day was over. It was my duty; it had to be done. For a time this position was fairly quiet, and we were fortunate to have a deep dugout to sleep in, though it was infested with rats. It was my experience with others to have the rats run over us while asleep. This we could bear; we were safe for the night. After a while orders were given that we take up a position six miles to the left, to enable us to fire in Burlong Wood, which was like a fortress. Many guns of all calibres were taken, as well as stores of all kinds. I remember having to take a message to another battery; I was able to see 'no man's land.' Having delivered my note with difficulty, being compelled to crawl over a certain point so as not to be seen, I commenced my return journey just at the time the enemy started to make an attack on a village named Fontaine, and to assist them the enemy shelled our artillery very heavily. While getting back to my battery the shells seemed to follow me, but, through the mercy and goodness of God, I arrived safe, not a minute too soon. Our battery was in a sunken road, our dugout being close by. About a minute after I had got back, shells came pouring over and around us. My billet was just opposite to some of the other men's, when one man shouted for me to come in with him, and less than a minute a shell burst right on my sleeping place. How thankful I felt that the man called me, thus proving again the overruling providence of God. I could say with the poet:

> All my times are in thy hand,
> All events at thy command.[359]

Not long after this we were told there would be a big battle, and we must take our guns up close to the trenches, which was usual before an attack on a large scale. This is done so our guns can fire a good distance on the enemy. When the morning came for the attack to be made, all our guns opened out to support our troops going over the top. Thank God, we had no casualties at this place. I remember on one occasion we were shelled by six German batteries of all calibres. In about half an hour there were 300 shells dropped around us; some went over, some dropped short of us. We were in a trench; but again, praise God, not a man was hurt. This was at a place called Hendicourt. Others, like myself, used to sleep in a trench the shape of a grave, just room to lie down.

I must now come to the last great advance. How I tried to pray that I might be spared to see my loved ones and my home again. It was a great trial to me. I had this thought that I had seen the Lord's protecting hand on the right hand and on the left. Should I be spared now I had been brought to the remaining stages of this great conflict, to see all my friends and all that was dear to me, to enjoy again the blessing of hearing a good gospel sermon, the privileges of the Lord's Day; or should I stain the soil of a foreign land with my blood? God in his rich mercy was pleased to bring me through, proving his faithfulness to his promise that he would be with me whithersoever I went. The later stages of this great conflict were most trying; though the enemy was beaten and retreating, yet occasionally I had fears as to my safety. During October, just before the end, our time was occupied in trying to keep up with the enemy.

I now come to the last day of the war, November 11th, 1918. Praise God for hearing the many prayers of his people! The fight was at an end with victory on our side. But what a price! Many good and gracious men had fallen in battle; many were made widows;

children made fatherless; and mothers mourning the loss of sons. I say, what a price! I felt I could adopt the language of the Psalmist when he says, 'O give thanks unto the Lord, for he is good: for his mercy endureth for ever' (Psalm 107: 1). I had been spared. It was a great relief to know I had been preserved thus far; yet we felt the need of being spared in other ways. We had to travel the road the enemy had gone, and many dangers were still to be faced. No one knew if any mines had been laid in the roads or bridges.

It was my lot with many others to march into Germany. We were told to pack up, our destination being Frechen, a village near Cologne, marching by day and taking our rest by night. What a happy change – trenches were exchanged for nice warm beds. We could sleep soundly after committing soul and body into the hands of him who neither slumbers nor sleeps. We were allotted comfortable quarters for the night in villages on our way. It took three days to complete our journey. What a strange experience! We arrived at the German village of Frechen, where we made a stay of nearly four months. The line, or the towns that our troops occupied, was about six miles in front of our battery. These positions were taken up just as if we were still at war, although only as a safeguard. This line ran through many prominent towns, such as Solingen – the Sheffield of Germany – a town famous for its German steel, and Düsseldorf, another large town, the scene of much unrest owing to the Communist element there. Like in all towns and villages, there was much agitation as to who caused the world war. Just think of enemy forces pouring through the towns and villages. This was a bitter experience for some of the inhabitants; but on the whole we were welcomed, especially by the burgomaster (a mayor), he being responsible for law and order.

During my stay in Frechen I came in contact with many of the business men of the village, as my duties made it necessary for me to go among them. They paid their respects; partly, no doubt, they thought it the better way. Often having to go about my duties alone, I felt my need of the Lord's protecting hand, and many a silent petition has gone up to heaven to this end. True, the war was over, but one must remember I was in a foreign land. My officer came to me one day and said we were to move, and go over the Rhine, to take up our duties in a village named Schlebusch. Those who have seen this wonderful river say that it is one of the best. To see the beauty of it, and the little villages on its banks, one must take a trip in a steamer. This village is about eight miles from Cologne. Though small, it had its trams; all you had to do was to jump aboard, and you were soon at the station. My officer chose a doctor's house for his quarters. This was very interesting to me, for there were two children, who, when asked if they could speak English, said they could. As I was able to speak a little German, we soon made friends, and by the time I had to leave I was able to speak their language fairly well. It was a grief to me to see the desecration of the Lord's Day, young people going off for the day out in the country. Probably many go to Mass early in the morning, then adding to their sins by spending the remainder of the day in pleasure. I often desired to bless God that I was an Englishman, and I do hope that he has given me a real religion of justification by faith.

The time came when I must leave this village. It was very interesting to move from one village to another, the Rhineland being a very picturesque country. One day a message was sent to me to pack up, for the officer and I must go on to Bonn University, where the officer was to take a course in agriculture. This town, known all over the world as a seat of learning, is a very wonderful town for its buildings. Many people that I was able to converse with showed how indifferent they were to the religion of the Scriptures; the offspring of Romanism, many of its inhabitants being brought up in the Church of Rome.

My stay in Bonn was short, I having word that my papers were through for my return to England and home. What a wonderful word that was to me! I had been longing for the day to come when I should return to my own country. I must now proceed to Cologne, where I, with other men, should take my leave. It was decided that we should go down the Rhine by steamer to Rotterdam. This was most interesting. I thought of this, that I had seen France, Belgium, Germany, and now I was to see Holland, of which I had often read of the noble stand they made for their Protestant faith during the siege of Leyden.

On our way down the Rhine, of which the Germans were very proud, and rightly too, it filled me with some pride, being an Englishman, to see our own naval men guarding this wonderful river. This guard consisted of naval launches with a small gun aboard, mostly a Hotchkiss. These little vessels were used to prevent any unauthorised shipping, all traffic on the river being stopped at sunset. This we had to do. Our steamer dropped anchor alongside several barges, where we slept the night. Here I must say, these barges were purposely placed, especially for our men, it being impossible for all to sleep on the steamer. Next morning, after I had tried to thank God for his goodness and watchful care through the night, and after committing our way unto the Lord, we sailed for Rotterdam. One soon saw that we were in Holland by the quaint dresses of the inhabitants. There are many wonderful buildings in the town. Unfortunately we were not allowed to go through this Dutch town, but had to confine ourselves round about the harbour. This was my last night in a foreign land. By the mercy of God, we should be sailing towards our coast by the time the sun peeped over this Dutch town. The vessel that was to take us home was lying alongside the quay. We went on board, and soon we heard the ringing of the telephone bells, as the captain gave, 'Full speed ahead!' I had been across the Channel quite a number of times, but not across the North Sea. It was rather rough, like it usually is just outside the harbour; but taking the advice of one older than myself, I gladly accepted a small biscuit, and found a resting place for the whole journey. I felt thankful on our arrival at Harwich I had been spared the ordeal of seasickness.

While our vessel was making its way through the long rows of battleships, the men on board shouted to us that the railwaymen were out on strike.[360] On our arrival at Parkstone Quay, we soon heard the sad news. This was sad for me, to see our train that would have taken us to London standing without her engine. 'What shall we do now?' was the question asked on all sides. After waiting a while we were marched on to Dovercourt hutments. When turning in for the night,

I felt like one of old, when he said, 'Hitherto hath the LORD helped us.' 'O give thanks unto the LORD; for he is good.' I trust I felt it to be a sweet time in returning thanks to God for all his watchful and loving care over me, preserving my life in the midst of great dangers on land and air and sea. I also trust he preserved that life in my soul which is born from above; that God had been my refuge in times of trouble, and they who put their trust in him, he will never forsake.

My stay at Dovercourt lasted about a fortnight. This place joins Harwich, a suburb where most of the naval officers make their homes when on shore; and it was England! While many of our men found pleasure in attending concerts and such like amusements, I felt it a greater pleasure in reading the Word of God. I was able to attend the chapel in Harwich; a good size building, and comfortable, but, sad to say, poorly attended. Each morning of my stay, when getting up, the question was asked by all: 'Is the strike finished?' The time came, however, when an officer came in one morning and told us to be ready at such a time. I was in a party to go to Fovant, in Wiltshire, to hand in our rifles and accoutrements. This day was a special one to all. We should soon be at our homes. On our arrival at Fovant we lost no time in disposing of all that belongs to war; but it is not so easy to dispose of the spirit of covetousness in the heart of man – no doubt the main cause of the late war – only God can do this. We can see it today; unrest among the nations of the world, and the many evil influences abroad in the earth, are proceeding from the old man of the heart. We have to prove daily that 'the heart is deceitful above all things, and desperately wicked;' and often we bring trouble upon ourselves. Those who truly fear God prove like Bunyan, that:

> A Christian man is never long at ease:
> When one fright's gone,
> Another doth him seize.[361]

But, bless God, there is a throne of grace, where we are enabled to make our wants and wishes known. This is the only source of relief. The writer has found this to be true for his comfort; it is the way we must go to enter the kingdom.

But to return to Fovant. We were about all night. I can say this, I did not mind in the least, it being the last night that I should wear the king's uniform. When morning came, I was handed my railway pass and some rations for my journey. I was soon on my way to Salisbury station, to take the train for London and Lewes, then home! Praise God the promise had been fulfilled in my experience: 'Have not I commanded thee? Be strong and of a good courage; be not afraid, neither be thou dismayed: for the LORD thy God is with thee whithersoever thou goest.'

I look back over the years of the world war, and the many dangers to which I had been exposed; the temptations of the enemy, and of those I came in contact with; the many temptations to join the company of evil-doers, coupled with my own wicked heart; the enemy often coming in like a flood with his taunts, together with my doubts and fears. It was then I felt my need of the Lord's help to lift up a standard against them.

And now in 1932 my need is even greater. I trust the Lord by his good Spirit has deepened the work of grace in my heart, I having had some deep and sore trials, which the Lord has been pleased to sanctify for my soul's good. I look back to the time when I was unable to hear the gospel of God's grace. But now I am favoured to meet among the people of God, to attend the services of his house, where I trust his honour dwelleth, where the Lord is pleased to make himself known. I say, what a change! Since coming to Mayfield, and sitting under the ministry of my present pastor, Mr Caleb Sawyer, who so ably breaks the 'bread of life' to us, the Lord has blessed his testimony to my soul from time to time. Though sometimes having to experience the pulling down, there has, I trust, been the building up in the precious truths of the gospel, and, by the grace of God, I can say with Ruth of old, 'Thy people shall be my people, and thy God my God.'

In conclusion, to any who care to read this brief account of the many dangers and merciful deliverances, the Lord's care over me, and the fulfilment of his promise that he would be with me whithersoever I went, I say, 'Give unto the Lord the glory due to his name.'

> A sovereign Protector I have,
> Unseen, yet for ever at hand;
> Unchangeably faithful to save,
> Almighty to rule and command;
> He smiles, and my comforts abound;
> His grace as the dew shall descend;
> And walls of salvation surround
> The souls he delights to defend.
>
> Kind Author and ground of my hope,
> Thee, thee for my God I avow;
> My glad Ebenezer set up,
> And own thou hast helped me till now.
> I muse on the years that are past,
> Wherein my defence thou hast proved;
> Nor wilt thou relinquish at last
> A sinner so signally loved.[362]

Caleb Sawyer

Joseph Chapman

During the years of the First World War, Joseph Chapman may be described as 'having no hope, and without God in the world.' He saw some remarkable providences and preservations, but sadly had to conclude that they left him spiritually unmoved, as the Lord was not pleased to sanctify it to him. From *In the Service of the King,* the little book he wrote detailing his experience up to the time of his baptism, which took place while he was serving in the Second World War, the following has been extracted:

> ✍ Life in the army was very congenial to me. I took great interest in all that went on, and my love of sport had full scope. I also gained rapid promotion, reaching the rank of sergeant in ten months. I was captain of the battalion football team, and all this success turned my head. To get on, and to be thought well of by men, was my sole ambition. My success as an instructor led to my being kept in England until January, 1918. I served at Bedford, Halton Park, Bucks, Hertford, Mill Hill, Chelsea, Hythe, and Crowborough, Sussex. While at Chelsea Barracks the first daylight raid on London took place.[363]
>
> About this time my wife's sister was taken ill, and after a short and very painful illness she died, leaving five young children. She was a member of Hope Strict Baptist Chapel, Westoning, and without doubt is now in heaven. But this sad event left me unaffected, as did a narrow escape from drowning when returning from a short time in France. When finally I was sent to France, and was brought face to face with danger and death, my only thought was for the body, and I planned what wonderful things I would do, and the good time I would have. After being in and out of the line several times, our battalion went in for special training, with the object of taking a German strongpoint. But we did not go back to that part of the line, as the German had attacked first, so our battalion missed the first onslaught. When eventually our battalion was thrown into the battle, only about 30 came through unscathed. We were a composite battalion, composed of survivors from all units of the army.

Joseph Chapman

The enemy was advancing rapidly, and we were ordered to strengthen a weak place in the line. But I never reached it, as just before our platoon reached the line a shell fell close to our left, and I received a piece of copper in my right elbow. As I flung myself down I had turned to my right; if I had not done so, that piece of copper would have entered my side, and I should probably have been launched into a boundless eternity without hope. The thought now makes me tremble.

I made my way as fast as I could to the dressing station where I received attention, and lay down to rest. Just before nightfall, everyone who could walk was ordered to set out for the casualty clearing station. I walked all night until daybreak, when quite exhausted I sat down by the road side where I was picked up by an ambulance, and taken the last few miles of the 15-mile journey, arriving about 6 p.m. The civilians were then fleeing from their homes. The Germans captured the dressing station that night. Yet these things, and my merciful deliverance from death and later from captivity, did not move my heart to thank God for his goodness to me.

I eventually got on an ambulance train for the base hospital. We had not proceeded far before we came to a dead stop. Later we found the cause of the delay was that enemy planes had blown up the track at Amiens Station. The remainder of the journey to the base hospital at Étaples was uneventful, except for the sad spectacle of civilians fleeing back for refuge. I was marked for England, and after staying one night at the base hospital, I came over to Folkestone, where we arrived after a calm and comfortable trip at 7 p.m. on 'Good Friday.' That I felt relieved, my readers will understand, but I did not recognize the hand that had delivered me from the jaws of death, nor did I have one thought concerning what Good Friday was a reminder of.

I was taken to a hospital at Nottingham, where, after an operation to remove the piece of copper, my arm turned septic, and the surgeon feared he would have to amputate. I felt very ill, and had to keep to my bed for some time, yet his fears proved groundless. He told me I should never be able to use my arm again, but it has become stronger as time has gone on, though it is permanently shortened. I am once more serving in the army, from which I was discharged on February 19th, 1919. I still have the piece of copper at home, which is three-quarters of an inch square and a half-inch thick. I was granted a disability pension which has been helpful to me.

It seems necessary to relate all this to make plain the Lord's dealings, and to show that he had a purpose of grace towards me. Yet how ungrateful I was, and though I had been so mercifully preserved and restored far beyond the expectations of the surgeon, I was too ignorant and blind to see that only the Lord had done it.

During the stay in hospital, services were held in the ward where I lay every Sunday morning, but these left me unmoved, and when again able to get out, I plunged once more into sin and pleasure with a new gusto after my enforced absence. There were plenty of opportunities for this in a city like Nottingham, and free tickets to places of amusement were given to myself and fellow patients, the donors blindly believing they were doing us good and helping the war effort. May God in mercy open their blind eyes, as in years later he opened mine, to see that these things only lead to eternal damnation both of men and nations. So my affliction did not cause me to turn to God. He was not pleased to sanctify it to me.

Do we not see the same thing with our nation today? Despite sore afflictions, our national sins increase, and far from turning back to God, who made our nation great and honoured before all the world, the people deny him more and more. Oh how I pray that God the Holy Ghost would convince them of the folly of their ways, break their hard hearts, and bring them as poor beggars to plead for mercy at mercy's door. My readers may say, who am I that I should write thus? Well, I feel myself to be the chief of sinners, but … the Lord dealt with me in convincing me of sin and ruin, causing me to wonder how there could possibly be mercy for one so unworthy and undone.[364]

After the war he continued in the same course, being taken up with football and Labour Party politics. In 1932, the "appointed time rolled on apace," and the Lord was pleased to call him by grace. When war was again declared in Europe in September, 1939, he re-joined the army, but in a very different state to how he had served in the First World War. His obituary states: "He found a continual struggle to hold on to a hope of obtaining mercy and the forgiveness of his sins. Satan reproached him and his army companions mocked him when they knew how he spent his Sundays."[365] Yet, in the midst of these painful trials, there was a period of great blessing, and he was enabled to apply to the church at Providence Chapel, Bedford, for baptism (the pastor, Mr Rutherford Hunt baptised him there on 25th July, 1940). He was later a member at Westoning. He died on 18th June, 1957, aged 63 years.[366]

George Crowter

George Crowter

George Crowter was born in Brighton, and called by grace under the ministry of J. K. Popham at Galeed Chapel, Brighton. After serving in the war he returned home and married, working in various parts of the country before moving in 1933 to live in Coventry. He was baptised at Rehoboth Chapel, Coventry, in 1933, and afterwards served as deacon there for 22 years. In 1968, he and his wife retired to Brighton, transferring their membership to Galeed Chapel. He passed away on 5th April, 1987, aged 92.

The following is taken from his own writings, as published in his obituary in *The Gospel Standard*:[367]

✍ I joined the army in September, 1914. After three weeks intensive training at Aldershot, I was sent to Colchester in Essex. Owing to my abnormal height, several months passed before a uniform was provided for me. During this time I was sent with another soldier to the headquarters of the 1st London Territorial Division, then stationed at Crowborough in Sussex. When the staff officer to whom I reported for duty saw me in civilian clothes, he hastily remarked, 'I sent for a soldier.' I endeavoured to explain the reason for my lack of uniform, but he obviously took a dislike to me, and in six days sent me back to Colchester with one word on my papers, 'Useless.' I felt my position painfully, but in due season had to prove it to be amongst the all things that work together for good. It was at Colchester that I met my dear wife to whom I was married over 50 years. Also, I had been in France some months in 1915 and had been promoted to the rank of warrant officer, when the 1st London Division came out to France. The officer who had so humiliated me took two soldiers of his staff in a car to find a suitable place to store gun parts, etc. He left the men sitting in the car while he surveyed the area, only to find them both headless upon his return through a shell or bomb. I could have been one of those men had I remained on that officer's staff.

In the autumn of 1915, alone in the night during heavy gun fire, I felt to be in great danger, when it pleased the Lord to apply with power that precious word, 'He that keepeth Israel shall neither slumber nor sleep,' which caused a sweet calm to soul and body.

One Sunday when we were back at rest, I was in a hut crowded with troops, trying to read a sermon my dear father had sent me, when a warrant officer senior to me entered and called aloud the most dreadful blasphemy concerning the birth of the Lord Jesus Christ. I could not be silent and reproved him openly. He said, 'Who are you talking to?' I replied, 'To you, for if that name means nothing to you, it does to some of us. I cannot stand your remarks.' I feel this experience was used for my comfort after my return to civilian life. The first time I heard Mr George Whitbread[368] preach, his text was Luke 23: 42, the dying thief's petition to the crucified Lord Jesus. Mr Whitbread said, 'Before the thief petitioned the suffering Redeemer, he rebuked the other thief saying, "We (suffer) indeed justly … but this man hath done nothing amiss." If you are one of these petitioners, you will not want your Christ to be evil spoken of.'

George Whitbread

The following is a transcription of Mr Crowter's war diary which he kept on the battlefield throughout 1916.[369] It tells of his involvement in trench warfare in both Belgium and France, and in particular his service during the battle of the Somme. It has additional interest from a military history point of view, as it contains an eyewitness account of the first use of tanks in warfare:

✍ **January**

4 Tues, Four shells fell within 40 yards.

16 Sun, Eight days leave started. Armentières[370] to London.

17 Mon, Met Kit[371] at Liverpool Street, journey to Brighton.

18 Tues, Chapel, first time for eight months.

24 Mon, Journey from London to Folkestone to Boulogne. Night at Boulogne.

25 Tues, Left Boulogne for Armentières 8 p.m..

26 Wed, 9.2[372] in action. Arrived Ponte de Nieppe, Armentieres 2.30 p.m. A day's work and great worry. Letter home.

27 Thur, 'Lord reigneth.' Kaiser's Birthday. Presents flying both ways.[373]

28 Fri, Letter to Kit. Letter from home. Heavy bombardments plus casualties. 9.2 busy. 'Rainbow.' 'When I see.'[374]

29 Sat, Much activity. Four shells in yard of trenches. 9th Division, six horses killed and four men wounded. Letter from Kit.

30 Sun, Letter from Kit. Letter to Kit (2)[375].

31 Mon, Machine guns and rifles busy during night. German 8 inch[376] causes casualties.

February

1 Tues, Artillery activity. Letter home (2).

2 Wed, Great activity. Letter from Mr Polley.

3 Thur, Continued activity. 3 German futile attacks. 11 inch shell within 40 yards and fails to explode.

4 Fri, Fairly quiet. Visit to Houplines with Len. All's well. 'Slow to anger, and plenteous in mercy.' Letter from home.

5 Sat, 'Plenty doing.' 9.2 very busy, Fokkers up.[377]

Letter home.

6 Sun, Spasmodic artillery fire. Letter to Kit (3). Letter (2) from Kit.

7 Mon, Exceptionally quiet. Letter from home.

8 Tues, Quiet. Strong Roumon.[378]

9 Wed, Heavy artillery fire. 9.2 in action. Huns[379] shell Nieppe. Visit to Nieppe. Letter from Kit. Letter to Kit (4).

10 Thur, British and Hun heavy artillery in combat at night. Letter to Harold.

11 Fri, Heaviest artillery activity yet experienced. Seven shells within 300 yards. Armentières, Erkenhem,[380] Nieppe and Pont de Nieppe receive Hun attention. Baths.

12 Sat, Still increasing. Pont de Nieppe and Armentières received artillery attention. Bridge hit! Letter home (4).

13 Sun, Renewed bombardment from aeroplanes and artillery. Letter from home.

14 Mon, 'The God of peace shall bruise Satan … shortly' (Romans 16: 20). Letter to J Woodman. Less severe artillery action here. Roar at Ypres.

15 Tues, Terrific artillery fire by both sides at night. Letter to Kit (5).

16 Wed, All's quiet. Letter from Kit. Letter to Mr Polley.

17 Thur, Firing at night. Heavy artillery fire at 4 a.m..

18 Fri, Fairly quiet day, with 9.2 in action at night. Heavy fire towards Ypres. Letter from Aunt Charlotte. Letter home (5).

19 Sat, Slight artillery action and machine guns and rifle fire at night. Letter from Harold and mother parcel.

20 Septuagesima Sun, Considerable artillery and aerial action. Letter from and to Kit (6).

21 Mon, Terrific artillery, machine gun and rifle activity at night. Anticipated attack. God is merciful. Letters from J Woodman and home.

22 Tues, All continue active. 6.20 p.m. gas reported by 60th Brigade to the north.

23 Weds, Shell and machine gun fire. Houplines church steeple brought down. Three letters from Kit. One to Kit (7).

24 Thurs, Quiet day. Plans for night attack. Letter to 'Uncle' Phil.

25 Fri, Night attack after heavy bombardment. Failure. 'Come on, Come on.' Quiet day. Snow.

26 Sat, Quiet day with heavy bombardment at night. Letter home.

27 Sexagesima Sun, Heavy bombardment from Huns all round. Letter from home. Parcel Kit.

28 Mon, Letter to Kit (8). Heavy fire by 9.2. Move cancelled. Relieving Division Verdun? Letter from Kit.

29 Tues, Aerial and artillery activity. 'Like as a mother.' 'Come out from among them.'[381]

March

1 Wed, A quiet day. Letter from Kit.

2 Thur, Quiet day with very heavy artillery fire at night ?Ypres. Letter to Kit (9).

3 Fri, Heavy guns in action.

4 Sat, Heavy bombardment by both sides. Shells fall Nieppe, Pont de Nieppe and Armentières. Colonel Daniels killed. General Jacobs wounded.

5 Quinquagesima Sun, Fairly quiet. Letter from and to home. Letter from Kit.

6 Mon, Heavy gun fire on Lille?

5 Shrove Tues, Quiet day. Letter from Kit and Mr Polley. Letter to Kit (10).

8 Ash Wed, Calm. Letter from Kit.

9 Thur, Shells at bridge.

10 Fri, Normal day. Machine gun fire at night. Letter to Mr Polley.

11 Sat, Fairly quiet. With renewed machine gun fire at night. Letter to Kit (11).

12 Sun, Artillery action at night. Letter from Kit.

13 Mon, Quiet day. Artillery fire at night. Letter home.

15 Wed, Fairly calm. Aircraft busy. Letter to Kit (12).

16 Thur, Big Lizz blown up – premature shell.[382] Aircraft busy.

17 Fri, Oh! Sinful man that I am, who shall save me from the body of sin and death?[383] Letter from Kit.

18 Sat, Fairly quiet. Letter from Kit and Mr Polley. Letter to Kit (13).

19 Sun, Letter from home. Letter to home. Bombardment.

20 Mon, Letter from Nicholas. Periodical bombardment. Prepare to move.

21 Tues, Move from Pont de Nieppe, Armentières to Merville for rest. Old thatched barn.

22 Wed, Rest.

23 Thur, Letter from Kit.

24 Fri, Letter from Kit. Letter to home. Letter to Kit.

25 Sat, Letter home.

26 Sun, Cold.

27 Mon, Letter from home and parcel.

28 Tues, Letter from Kit. Letter to Kit.

29 Wed, Preparation for march.

30 Thur, Left Merville for Arras.[384] Lorry break-down. Stay at Aire for night.

31 Fri, Left Aire for Amiens. Stay at Amiens for night. Leave Amiens for Ribemont[385] (Arras). Letter from Ruth. Letter from Kit.

April

1 Sat Arrive Ribemont. Taube[386] drop bombs before arrival.

2 Sun, Letter to Kit. Brigade in action.

3 Mon, Artillery activity at night. Letter home.

4 Tues, Stores arrive.

5 Weds, Visit to artillery. Letter from Kit.

6 Thur, Visit to infantry and artillery [*at*] Albert.

7 Fri, Visit to artillery. Letter from Kit.

8 Sat, Quiet day.

9 Sun, Visit to artillery. Letter from Kit.

10 Mon, Artillery action. Letter home.

11 Tues, Very heavy artillery and machine gun fire.

12 Wed, Fire at night. Visit to artillery.

13 Thurs, Night bombardment. Letter to Kit.

14 Fri, Letter from Kit and J. Woodman.

15 Sat, Zeppelin and aeroplane over at night.

16 Palm Sun, Infantry relieved. Visit to infantry and artillery.

24 Easter Mon, —.

28 Fri, Continual arrival of heavy artillery and troops.

29 Sat, Germans bombard and attack with gas. Eyes smart.

May

2 Tues, Letter from Kit. Letter from home. Journey with smoke helmets to infantry.[387]

3 Weds, Night journey to infantry with helmets. Letter to Kit.

4 Thur, Bombardment of infantry area. Letter home.

5 Fri, Letter from Kit.

8 Mon to **10 Wed,** Preparations for offensive commence. Moderate artillery firing.

11 Thur to **14 Sun,** Preparations continue. Night raids by British.

15 Mon to **17 Wed,** Still going!!!.

18 Thur to **21 Sun**, Preparations in full swing, almost complete. Terrific heavy guns arrive.

22 Mon – 24 Wed, Heavy guns continue to arrive. Artillery active.

25 Thur to **28 Rogation Sun,** Preparations everywhere. Heavy guns placed in position. Others keep arriving.

29 Mon to **31 Wed,** Shells and artillery arrive.

June

1 Thur to **4 Sun,** Divisions of infantry arrive. Many guns.

5 Mon to **7 Wed,** Things coming to a head. 2000 rounds of ammunition per 18 lb gun stored up.[388]

8 Thur to **11 Whit Sun,** Feverish heat. Division after division arrive. Guns placed in position.

12 Whitsun Mon, Artillery.

13 Whitsun Tues, Infantry.

14 Wed, Machine gun and trench mortar.

15 Thur, 79th Brigade of Artillery transferred to line for ordnance. Now 79th Brigade Royal Field Artillery, 96th Brigade Royal Field Artillery, 64th Infantry Brigade etc.

16 Fri, Ammunition arrives in endless streams.

17 Sat, Many preparations. Boards for crossing trenches etc.

18 Trinity Sun, Very busy.

19 Mon, Huns shelled with 6 inch howitzer.[389] Parade and instructions for offensive. Water to be taken from dead men. 'No retreat'.

20 Tues, Terrific work. French artillery 75s arrive.[390] Enemy shells, 6 inch howitzer.

21 Weds, French cavalry arrive. Endless streams of troops.

22 Thur, Huns shell 6 inch again. Everybody and they 'fever heat'.

23 Fri, Many troops and cavalry arrive. Terrific bombardment starts 4 a.m. Guns honeycomb the place. 'Work'.

24 Sat, Unexampled bombardment and with innumerable British and French guns. British heavies. Terrible work and worry.

25 Sun, All night and two days on duty. Heavy bombardment. Letters to Kit and home.

26 Mon, Felt very queer, very little sleep. Terrific bombardment.

27 Tues, Still queer and no sleep scarcely. Continued bombardment of every gun.

28 Weds, Infantry advance postponed, weather wet. Uninterrupted shelling of Hun lines.

29 Thur, Increased shelling. Springs a trouble, still feeling very bad.

30 Fri, Infantry prepare to go over following morning. Another night up and very busy. Gun out of action for springs. Infantry brigade[391] consists of 9th King's Own Yorkshire Light Infantry, 10th King's Own Yorkshire Light Infantry, 1st East Yorkshire Reserves, 15th Durham Light Infantry, 126th Field Company Royal Engineers, 4th Company 21st

Division Train, 64th Machine Gun Company, 65th Field Ambulance, Field Guns 64th Infantry Brigade, Field Guns 96th Brigade Royal Field Artillery, A Battery 96th Brigade Royal Field Artillery, B Battery 96th Brigade Royal Field Artillery, C Battery 96th Brigade Royal Field Artillery, D Battery 96th Brigade Royal Field Artillery, 64th Light Trench Mortar Brigade.

July

1 Sat, Great attack commences at 7.30 a.m. after 1 hour's hurricane fire. Infantry advances and take Mametz and Fricourt village.

2 Sun, Held up at Fricourt wood. Captured after heavy losses.

3 Mon, Held up before Mametz Wood. Prisoners roll in.

4 Tues, Heavy losses, wounded pour in. Slight advance. Division brought out. More prisoners.

5 Wed, Sent back to Belloy-sur-Somme for rest.

6 Thur, Casualties in 64th Infantry Brigade about 30%. Commanding officers of 1st East Yorkshire regiment (Major Stow), 9th King's Own Yorkshire Light Infantry (Colonel Lynch) and 10th King's Own Yorkshire Light Infantry, casualties.

7 Fri, Order to go to Cavillon. Very heavy work.

8 Sat, Go to Cavillon.

9 Sun, Orders to return to battle line.

10 Mon, Preparation. Lovely country.

11 Tues, Go to Méricourt. 20 miles of cavalry passed on Amiens road.

12 Wed, 64th Brigade go into action. Take on with 79th Brigade Royal Field Artillery. Heavy bombardment.

13 Thur, Much work and worry. Infantry advance. Artillery puts up endless rain of shells. Prisoners.

14 Fri, Casualties heavy. Terrible sights. High Wood captured.

15 Sat, Very heavy fighting. Bloody scenes and sufferings. Battle rages with unabated fury.

16 Sun, Artillery keep up incessant fire (shells).

17 Mon, Felt ill. On battlefield, Fricourt, Fricourt Wood, Mametz. Dead lie about, ground churned up, trees bared of leaves. Villages razed to ground.

18 Tues, Artillery and infantry casualties heavy. One gun blown up. Infantry continue to advance. Good number of prisoners. Very trying times.

19 Wed, Infantry come out of battle. Good work, but casualties heavy. Heaviest of all bombardment. Huns counter-attack. All guns firing.

20 Thur, Orders to go back to Cavillon for rest. Another gun blown up. Very irritable. Can't eat.

21 Fri, Rest cancelled. Order for 3rd Army. Many casualties. Wounded, agony, death. Graves – officers and men side by side. 54 in one trench 12x6 foot. Weary of earth and myself.

A contemporary postcard produced by *The Daily Mail*, showing a funeral at the front

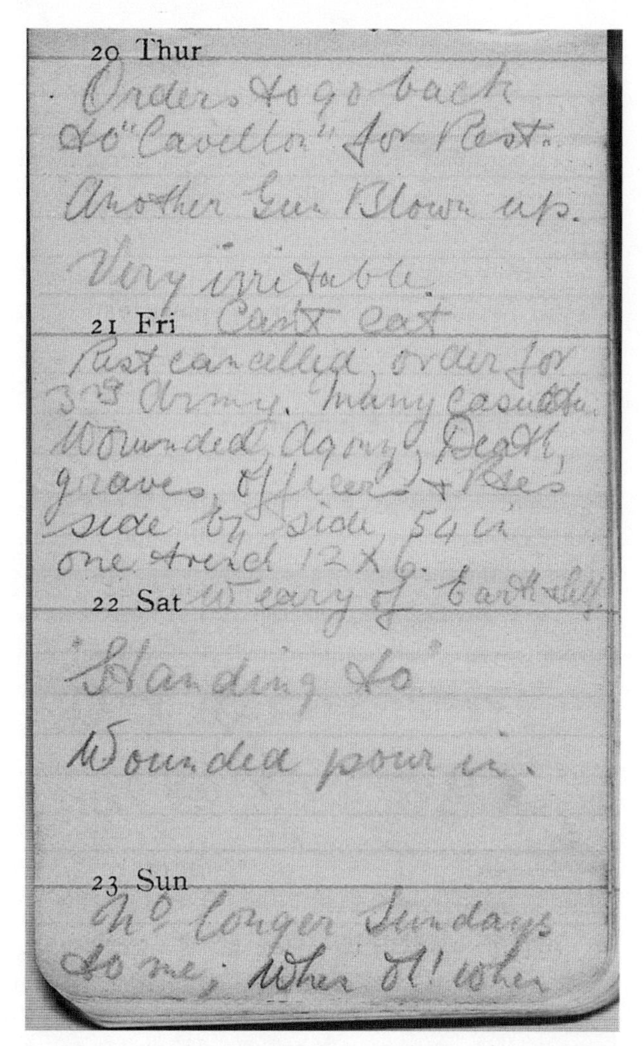

20 Thur
Orders to go back to "Cavello" for Rest. Another Gun blown up. Very irritable.

21 Fri [illegible]
Rest cancelled, order for 3rd Army. Many casualties. Wounded, Agony, Death, graves, Officers & Pte's side by side 54 in one trench 12 x 6.

22 Sat Weary of Earthly
"Standing to"
Wounded pour in.

23 Sun
No longer Sundays to me; When Oh! when

A page from George Crowter's diary, the Somme, July 1916

22 Sat, Standing to. Wounded pour in.

23 Sun, No longer Sundays to me. When, Oh! when.

24 Mon, Go to La Caroia.[392] All quiet once more.

25 Tues, Start to re-equip division. Heavy work.

26 Wed, Continued.

27 Thur, So-so.

28 Fri, And again.

29 Sat, Still it comes.

30 Sun, Move up to line. Duisans, Arras.

31 Mon, Work heavy. Guns very active. Trench warfare again.

August

1 Tues, Many orders about secrecy etc.

2 Wed, Reminds one of Armentières. Star shells[393] and other sorts.

3 Thur, Guns active both sides. Aircraft very active.

4 Fri, Work continues and Germans and British bombard.

5 Sat, Germans kill and wound men in adjoining field. Hit observation balloon just over head. The occupants jump with parachute.

6 Sun, Huns and our guns go ahead. Anxious at night.

7 Mon, Huns bombard Royal Engineers dump. German observation balloon plainly seen with naked eye. Heavy firing at night.

8 Tues to **13 Sun,** An occasional bombardment, though in all pretty quiet trench warfare. Battle of Somme audible at times. Heavy work.

14 Mon to **20 Sun,** Things begin to tell a bit. Seven days a week, month after month, and trying circumstances make one feel weary. God is very merciful.

21 Mon to **27 Sun,** Many visits to my infantry. On the whole things trying.

September

1 Fri, Germans raid our trenches. Take 16 of the 10th King's Own Yorkshire Light Infantry prisoners,

1 machine gun and 1 trench mortar.

2 Sat, Go to Arras at night upon horseback. Weird scenes. Twenty minutes wait within 100 yards of German line.

3 Sun, Orders to move.

4 Mon, Relieved by 38th Division and go back to open training.

5 Tues, Pursuit Division. Go from Duisans to La Caroia.

6 Wed, Re-equipping.

7 Thur, —"—.[394]

8 Fri, —"—.

9 Sat, —"—.

11 Mon, Preparing to move.

12 Tues, Under orders.

13 Wed, Leave La Caroia for Heilly via Amiens.

14 Thur, Journey from Heilly to Ribemont.

15 Fri, Batteries and battalions move into line. Tanks used 1st time.[395]

16 Sat, Go to the Somme battlefield, Fricourt, Mametz, Contalmaison. 64th Brigade in action with 41st Division. Big gains.

17 Sun, Into the Somme.

18 Mon, Heavy casualties in 64th Brigade with 41st Division and guards. Everywhere guns, troops, desolation, death etc. Journey up to Contalmaison is Death Valley. British and Huns shell.

19 Tues, Mud over knees. Wind up. Rain continues. Battle slackens in fury owing to weather.

20 Wed, Weather better. Troops covered with mud. Guns on the go again. Division prepares for action.

21 Thur, Regular bombardment and with all sizes of guns. Ground drying but still very bad.

23 Sat, Heavy shelling. Inferno of shells. Huns around by aeroplane at night, drop bombs, kill four, wound men and horses. Dead! Dead! Dead!

24 Sun, Huns use liquid fire.[396] We use new gas shells.

25 Mon, Hurricane and terrific bombardment. Infantry go over 2 p.m. Guards and 21st together with 6th. Take 1. Gueudecourt, 2. – ,[397] 3. Thiepval. Prisoners.

26 Tues, Brilliant success. Thiepval, Combles and Le [—][398] taken. Losses heavy but heavier for Huns. Huns counter attack.

27 Wed, Bombard Fricourt. Hold captured ground and push forward. Tanks play a great part. Huns' losses heavy.

28 Thur, Shelling! Prepare for further push!.

29 Fri, 1 p.m. 48 howizters bombardment commences. Heaviest yet experienced. All guns in action.

30 Sat, Incessant shelling throughout night. Toothache! Rain falls heavy. Brigade comes back. 2000 sets of clothing etc. to brigade. Busy day.

October

1 Sun, Re-equip brigade.

2 Mon, Orders to leave Somme for third time. Rain continues. Bombardment slackens.

3 Tues, Leave Somme for Abbeville. Day's journey.

4 Weds, Resting! All quiet! Leave artillery in battle.

5 Thur, Orders to leave for trenches. Lorry comfortable.

6 Fri, Standing to.

7 Sat, Move, long day journey to X (Heaux-les-

Manes)[399].

8 Sun, Rest at X.[400]

9 Mon, All quiet.

10 Tues, —.

11 Wed, —.

12 Thur, —.

13 Fri, Move to Labourse.

14 Sat, French area.[401] Lens! Hulluch! Loos etc.

15 Sun, Quiet.

16 Mon, Hardly know a war was on!

17 Tues, —.

18 Wed, —.

19 Thur, Heavy shelling and exceptionally heavy machine gun fire at night.

20 Fri, Shelling at intervals throughout day and very heavy bombardment at night. Machine guns busy Loos sector.

November

25 Sat, Germans shell heavily. Apparently 6 or 8 inch shells passed over head into Béthune. Activity in the air.

December

3 Sun, Cold, mud, water, yet much to be thankful for.

11 Mon, German aeroplanes over low followed by bombardment with shrapnel. Shells fall very near, a large piece enters roof of one tent. 'God preserveth man and beast.'

22 Fri, Huns shell.

23 Sat, Again.

24 Sun, Again.

25 Mon, Quiet.

28 Thur, Move.

Firing a heavy howitzer in France

Jesse Delves

Jesse Delves was born and brought up at Warbleton, Sussex, but as a young man he moved in providence to Brighton, where he sat under the ministry of Mr J. K. Popham at Galeed Chapel. There he found a spiritual home, and was baptised in 1916. He was exercised about the ministry during the war, commenting, "I had had an abiding impression that if I was brought home from the war, it would be for some purpose, though often the whole thing seemed impossible."[402] After the war, and further considerable exercise about the matter, in 1929 Mr Delves was sent out to preach by the church at Galeed. He was for many years the beloved pastor at Ebenezer Chapel, Clapham. His faithful ministry made room for him, and for many years he held respected offices in the charities associated with the 'Gospel Standard' churches. Mr Delves did not readily speak about his war experiences. All we have been able to glean is the following excerpt from one of his sermons:[403]

> ✍ Not long after entering the army in the last war, I was severely shaken with regard to what I hope I received from God, being assailed by fiery temptation even with regard to the reality of religion altogether. I believe the Lord then made that Scripture in John 14 a strength to my soul: 'Yet a little while, and the world seeth me no more; but ye see me: because I live, ye shall live also.' That was it: 'Because I live, ye shall live also.' O what a blessedness there is in covenant union with Christ! His life is our life. And union with him is the secret of all gospel fruitfulness. That is the source and secret of all fruit bearing. 'The branch cannot bear fruit of itself, except it abide in the vine; no more can ye, except ye abide in me.' But the searching point is just this: if no fruit is borne there is no evidence of union. So let us examine ourselves as to how we stand in regard to that point, where is our fruit?

Jessie Delves

Stanley Delves

Stanley Delves, brother of Jesse Delves, was for 54 years the pastor of the church at Forest Fold Chapel, Crowborough, East Sussex, until his death on 4th March, 1978, aged 80 years. Mr Delves was just seventeen when the First World War commenced. He was called up to fight, but was initially rejected on health grounds. Later, during 1917, the need for men had become so desperate that he was again called up, and thus at nineteen years of age he joined the army. After a spell in Ireland, Mr Delves spent most of his service in Russia as part of the North Russian Campaign, which lasted from 1918 to 1920. This campaign was not fought against the German forces, but against the Bolsheviks (Communists) in Russia. Following the Russian Revolution in October, 1917,[404] Russia withdrew from the First World War. However, the Bolsheviks did not have the support of a significant part of the Russian populace, and in 1918 an armed resistance broke out in Russia, resulting in civil war between the Bolsheviks (the Reds) and their opponents (the Whites). Britain (joined by the USA, Japan and France) sent troops to support the Whites in their rebellion, with the aim of protecting their own interests in Russia. Ultimately the opposition was unsuccessful – the Imperial family of Tsar Nicholas II was murdered, and Communism, under Lenin, was established. The following extracts are taken from Mr Delves' writings as published in his biography, *Preaching Peace*:[405]

> ✍ When I entered military service I was stationed near to Canterbury for some months and from there I went to the south of Ireland. I was attached to a mobile unit and travelled to Dublin, Limerick, and in both the north and south of Ireland. Here I saw what the Roman Catholic Church was at first hand: I saw both the poverty of the people and the power of the Roman Catholic religion over them. From Ireland I was sent to Archangel in Northern Russia and was there for 12 months, and had ample time to observe the Russian Orthodox religion. Although the latter repudiates some of the practices of the former, I saw little to choose between them. Most of the time in Russia was spent by the River Dvina, and all through one winter, so I knew what the severity of an Arctic winter was. I was preserved from some mysterious dangers there whilst others who were with me lost their lives. I will mention just one of a number of occasions when the Lord preserved me from death, which I feel would certainly have befallen me if the Lord had not overruled my circumstances.
>
> When I was in Archangel I was attached as a signaller to a unit with an officer, and the whole company was detailed to go on a certain expedition. But I was taken from them because another officer needed a signaller more than the one that I had been attached to, so I and the captain were sent on another expedition from which we safely returned, but the other company to which I really belonged and the other officer had run into an ambush. They were nearly all massacred, and the officer I had served was amongst them – I never saw him again – he was dead and nearly all those who were with him. Humanly speaking, if I had not been taken from him and attached to another officer, it would have been my end, for hardly any of the company came out of that danger alive.

Stanley Delves

Dr P. M. Rowell, Mr Delves' biographer, wrote of another wonderful deliverance:

> ✍ On one occasion he and a friend were in a hut on a hillside which came under attack. He ran out of the hut and up the hillside, but his friend ran down the hill only to he killed instantly by a shell. He said that he felt to be sovereignly preserved and was filled with most solemn feelings as he gave thanks to God for his escape.

Mr Delves also writes of the spiritual exercises which accompanied his time in Russia:

> ✍ Now all the time I was in Russia I was in a very dark and desolate state spiritually. Very much so. All my sacred enjoyment of spiritual things, the nearness of the Lord and that heavenly peace all seemed to go. Of course, there was no companionship spiritually, there was no ministry, and there was no difference made between Sunday and any other day. It was a very bleak time with me spiritually, but I vividly remember one Sunday evening after landing at Archangel I went into a YMCA and the soldiers were singing that hymn of Newton,
>
> How sweet the name of Jesus sounds
> In a believer's ear.[406]
>
> and I remember how my spirit softened to the sound of that name, and though I was so desolate spiritually I felt there was still that in my heart which could respond to the sweetness of the name of Jesus Christ.
>
> Occasionally I would feel a softening of my spirit especially when I thought of the Lord's people in sanctuaries at home, the ministry, and my desolate state, and my feelings were just like those of Israel in Psalm 137: 1, 'We wept, when we remembered Zion.'

Dr Rowell also writes of how Mr Delves found the Lord's people amongst the Russian people:

> ✍ He went into a cottage belonging to a poor Russian family and there on the table he recognised a Russian Bible. In spite of the spiritual desolation he had been feeling, his heart was immediately touched by a deep sense of love to the Scriptures. By pointing to the Bible and making suitable signs he managed to

convey to the family his feelings for the Word of God, and to his joy it was perfectly evident that these were their feelings too.

Mr Delves remained in Russia for some months after the Armistice in November 1918, as the fruitless attempts to prevent the spread of the Communist revolution continued. Then, before finally being demobbed, he spent some time in Scotland. This period of army service after the end of the war was not, however, a barren time for Mr Delves, but the Lord used it to deepen his exercises concerning the solemn work of the ministry. Mr Delves explains this as he continues his account:

✍ I was in Russia for 12 months, from the middle of 1918 to the middle of 1919, then I returned home.

For some time I was in Scotland with very little to do, for the war was over and we were awaiting discharge, and I had ample opportunity to pursue what was in my mind. Well now, it was there in Scotland that I began to feel the call to the ministry. And it came to pass this way.

When we came back to Scotland the Lord was pleased to revive my spirit again. This was not through any particular means, because although I went from church to church in Irvine, I never heard anything that was of a profitable nature at all. The sermons were dry and the ministers simply read them like essays. There was neither life nor power in them to me, so I used to take my Bible and read that instead. I had plenty of time so I took my Bible and went out on the moors where I could be all alone and read. In that way the Lord returned to me, drawing me back again to himself, and my old feelings of faith and hope and love revived again. But something else came with it. For one thing, I used to find my mind directed to the Epistles of Paul to Timothy, and as I read those Epistles to Timothy which, as you will know, were very largely bearing on the ministry, it seemed to me as though Paul's directions and admonitions were like a living voice speaking to me in those Scriptures. Such as these, 'Preach the word; be instant in season, out of season.' 'Let no man despise thy youth,' and Scriptures like that. Others that do not just now occur to me seemed to me like a living voice. I do not exaggerate when I say that it could not have been more so if those epistles had been verbally directed to me instead of Timothy. They were so personal. And that was not all. As I used to read and ponder over the Scriptures the precious truths of the Gospel were opened up to my understanding in a way and with an effect I had not felt before. They were not new doctrines to me, but they seemed clothed with a new fullness, and depth, and power, especially such a doctrine as the Trinity. Oh, the fullness and the blessedness and the glory I seemed to see in the Trinity, and the person and work and atonement and sacrifice of Jesus Christ. These truths seemed opened up to me with a fullness that I had not seen before. This produced in me a strong urge to preach those truths. Indeed, whenever I had any fresh entrance into the doctrines of the Gospel it was sure to have that effect upon my spirit, and I felt that I would be called to preach those things. I think it could be said quite honestly that the substance of my preaching over the past 50 years was shown to me and taught to me when I was all alone in Scotland with nothing but my Bible: no minister, no books, nothing but the Bible and prayer.

So it seemed to me as though the words to Timothy were a call to me to preach, and the opening up of those deep and blessed truths showed me what I was to preach. I was to preach those things. And then there was something else. There was the insistence of this word upon my mind in such a way that I could not but feel that it was from the Lord. 'Behold, I have set before thee an open door, and no man can shut it.' If the Lord speaks through any particular word he will give us to appreciate what application that word has to us, and taken in conjunction with the other exercises that I have mentioned, I felt no doubt as to what the purport of that word was. The continual insistence of it on my mind made me feel sure that it was not just an act of memory. I did not just recall it, it was insistent. It spoke to me like this – that although I had been in such a dark and desolate state during the 12 months that I was in Russia, yet the Lord had given me a little strength so that I had never given way to temptation, such temptations as beset a soldier's life and especially in a foreign country, and which the other fellows ran into greedily. The Lord had given me enough strength to resist those temptations, even though I was personally allured to them by others, and I had never denied his name nor denied my faith, nor that I was a Christian. 'Thou hast a little strength … and hast not denied my name.' Now then, 'I have set before thee an open door, and no man can shut it,' which seemed to speak to me this way – that when I was discharged from the army the Lord would open a door for me into the ministry to preach those things that had been shown to me in Scotland, and that there might be some attempt to shut that door, but that 'no man can shut it.' All of which came to pass.

Well now, that is one side of the matter, but there was another. Because of my extreme shrinking from publicity and my nervousness, the thought of preaching appalled me, and I felt that I never could face up to it – to the publicity of it and the responsibility of it. It seemed altogether too much, and I tried to quench and smother those urgent feelings in my heart and mind by every consideration I could think of – my youth, my inexperience, the solemnity of the ministry, the responsibility of it and the like. O! I tried to pile it all on to my mind to overcome the urge that I felt with regard to the ministry. And I remember those words of the good old prophets of the Old Testament, and how well I understood them myself, 'And Moses said unto the Lord … I am not eloquent, neither heretofore, nor since thou hast spoken unto thy servant: but I am slow of speech, and of a slow tongue.' And that was very true in my case because I was, and the first time I was asked to speak in public prayer in Rehoboth Chapel [*Tunbridge Wells*] I stood up, and I was so overcome with embarrassment and confusion that I said something or other and sat down without being able to pray at all. I was so nervous. And I sometimes think when our young men commence to speak in prayer at the prayer meeting, they all do better than I did. I could not pray at all. I stood up, muttered something and sat down, I was so overcome with confusion. 'O Lord, I cannot speak,' I used to say, 'I am not eloquent, I have no tongue to speak.' And that word of Jeremiah, 'Ah, LORD God! behold, I cannot speak: for I am a child.' And the Lord's answer came as well, 'Say not, I am a child: for thou shalt go to all that I shall send thee, and whatsoever I command thee thou shalt speak.' In my concern I felt this word, 'I have set before thee an open door,' was capable of proof whether it was from the Lord or not. I felt, 'Now I will say nothing whatever about this. I will keep my counsel, because if this word really is from the Lord, he will open a door for me into the ministry without my touching the matter.' And I thought, 'If I say anything, or give any indication that I am under this exercise, I might be very well asked to preach, and then I shall never know whether the Lord opened that door or not.' So with these feelings very urgent on my mind and spirit I was discharged from the army, and I came back to Hailsham to live with my mother.

Mr Delves goes on to record how he had only been home a very short time when he received an invitation to preach at 'Little Dicker' Chapel. This event was the fulfilment of the exercise he had been under in the army and the start of a ministry which lasted over 50 years.

A wartime postcard showing the earliest tanks in use at the Somme

William Fay

Mr Fay was brought up to attend the Strict Baptist Chapel at Reading, Berkshire. He was baptised in 1905 by Mr Obed Mortimer, the pastor at Broughton Gifford. He married a young lady from Norwich in 1908, and subsequently spent a few years there before moving to Guildford, where he was when the war broke out. Despite having made a profession of faith, Mr Fay recalls how that for a year or two prior to his enlisting in the army, he had slipped into a state of declension. The Lord was pleased to return to him during his war service, as he recounts in the following extract from his autobiography:

William Fay (left) & Obed Mortimer (right)

✍ It would be, I think, sometime in 1918, whilst I was in the army, that God put his hand a second time to the work. Most solemnly and painfully did I know what it was for many months to be in heavy bondage and great darkness, and under the felt frown and hidings of God's face. How did I call everything into question, and shame, the burden of guilt, and apparent lack of spiritual life caused me many a groan in secret. To this soul trouble was added a weakening of my nervous system, in consequence of which I was sent to a military hospital, where I remained ten weeks. My health improved, but the doctors said there was something they could not touch. Truly this was the case, for none but the Good Physician could heal the disorders of my soul. After my return to barracks the cloud gradually lifted, and hope revived just a little. This was, however, only a temporary relief, for some months later I was again sent to hospital and eventually discharged as medically unfit.

I remember one night in particular while in the hospital at Aldershot. Lying awake most of the night, for I could seldom get any sleep without drugs, I saw the other soldiers fast asleep and I envied them. I was crying to the Lord that he would appear for me in my distress, when the words dropped into my mind: 'Have not I chosen you twelve, and one of you is a devil?' This was like striking the dying dead, and my feelings can be better imagined than described. My distress was very great at that time. One of the deacons from Guildford came to see me, and was so perturbed about my state that at the evening prayer meeting at his return he mentioned my case, and special petitions were put up on my behalf.[407]

After his return from the front, while still in the army, Mr Fay received an invitation to preach, which he accepted, and this led to invitations to preach at several other places in reach of the military camp where he was stationed. He preached on these occasions in his uniform.[408] After the war he joined the church at Guildford, and was formally sanctioned to preach. He took the pastorate at Norwich in 1935, and remained there till his death on 25th December, 1965, aged 81.

Sydney Alfred Garnham

Mr Garnham was for many years a faithful minister. He was born to godly parents in Hackney, London. While he was a young man his father was paralysed, and his mother died from exhaustion at the hard work of trying to keep a roof over the family's head. The family was broken up, and Sydney was sent by guardians to a Church of England school in Kent. He left chapel, and went into the world. It was during the war that the Lord introduced a godly friend into his life, which was to be the means used to return Mr Garnham to chapel attendance, and ultimately to be called by grace. He was sent out to preach among the 'Earthen Vessel' Strict Baptists, and called to the pastorate at Derby Road Chapel, Croydon, in 1942. In 1964, he moved to take the pastorate at Abbey Chapel, Abingdon. There, contention for the distinctive witness maintained by *The Gospel Standard* brought conflict, and in 1970 he was forced to resign the pastorate. In his latter years he continued to preach, being a member at Grove Chapel, Wantage, till his death on November 14th, 1980. The following is an extract from his obituary:[409]

Sydney Garnham

> ✍ In 1917 he was called up for the army but a weak heart confined him to 'home service.' This period he would have liked to pass over, being painful to record. He describes in much detail how rapidly he was drawn into many evils, a willing slave, when he felt he was nearer actual hell than ever before or since, although since then knowing something of the 'believer's hell' in experience. Looking back on this time, he writes: 'The lines of the hymn fully describe my case:
>
> Why was I made to hear thy voice
> And enter while there's room?[410]
>
> and this fills my heart with wonder, love and praise.'
>
> A God-fearing companion was raised up while still in the army, who seemed to know something of his state. Through this means he again began to attend chapel services and, surprisingly to himself, this continued after new postings separated them and, more surprisingly, he began to loathe his old companions and his evil ways, though not yet completely. He was transferred to Cambridge and attended Tenison Road Chapel, where the pastor took an interest in him and this, he believes, was used to keep him from many snares. It was during this year that his afflicted father died and he felt sadly alone. His army service as a shorthand typist at the General Headquarters of the Grenadier Guards came to an end, and when he was demobilized in September, 1919, his commanding officer's reference states: 'He is painstaking, hard-working, efficient and reliable in every way and I have a high opinion of his capabilities.'
>
> It was now the Lord began to manifest a work of grace in his soul and he felt the first true conviction of sin; attended with most strange and mysterious teaching bringing him almost to despair. He records of this season how he tried to pray, then ceased to

pray, the devil telling him, 'You are too sinful for your prayers to be heard;' then a little *something* which urged him to seek again. At this period in his experience he first became acquainted with a young lady who attended Homerton Row and who later in God's appointments became his dear wife, a union which continued for 56 years. This acquaintance was the means in God's purposes of constraining him to attend the house of God regularly, though at first only to please her. However, the Lord was performing his own work 'little by little' and although space does not allow the detailed leadings, encouragements, falls and restorings, yet the teaching was deep and effectual.

Our dear friend was united in marriage on May 13th, 1922. Under a sermon preached from Genesis 24: 31 he was constrained to follow the Lord in the ordinance of baptism on Lord's Day, October 28th, 1923. Writing of this favoured season, he exclaims, 'What mercy, what love, for the Lord God omnipotent to look down on such as me in all my sin, degradation and wickedness and deal so bountifully with me! Instead of the torments of hell which I richly deserved, he gave me his love; instead of being an heir of eternal destruction, I was made an heir of God, joint-heir with Christ. I can truly say that from this day, "He brought me up also out of an horrible pit, out of the miry clay, and set my feet upon a rock." "What shall I render unto the LORD for all his benefits toward me?"'

Thomas C. Gibson

Thomas Cecil Gibson

Thomas Gibson was brought up at Ebenezer Chapel, Luton. After the war he married, and moved to attend Barton-Le-Clay Chapel, Bedfordshire. He passed away in August, 1980. The following is his account of his war service, as written by himself. It is taken from his obituary in *The Gospel Standard*:[411]

✍ I was favoured to attend the means of grace and the Sabbath School until I was 25 years of age. It was then that the First World War commenced and I had to join the forces. I had many fears and forebodings when I considered the life I should have to live and the company I should be surrounded with. Many cries went up to the Lord at this time that he would undertake for me and be with me. We had but a short period of training, only three months, and then we had to proceed to France. One instance I would name relative to this time. One day, feeling much cast down with many fears both inside and outside, I felt I wanted to know whether the Lord would be with me. So I turned aside to a quiet spot and took from my pocket a little Gadsby's hymn book and opened it, and it opened on John Berridge's hymn, 1113: 'How watchful is the loving Lord!' It was indeed like pouring oil on the troubled waters and was made, I hope, a strength and comfort to me.

Well, our period of training soon came to an end and I was placed in a draft for overseas, and almost immediately we received orders to proceed to France, which was on a Tuesday. On the Sabbath previous I cycled home for the last time, and as I went to Ebenezer Chapel that Sabbath evening I shall never forget the many dark and gloomy fears I was bowed down with. Would it be the last time I should ever meet in the house of God? Would he preserve me and bring me back? Or should I have to face the hour and article of death? And if so, how would it be with me as I entered into eternity? I do not remember anything particular about the hymns or the sermon, but I shall never forget the chapter that Mr Kemp[412] was led to read that evening. It was the 91st Psalm, and what a strength and comfort it was to me! How it seemed to sink down into my very heart, although in after months I had to prove it had to be sorely tried!

There are two instances I feel I must mention at this time. Having soon arrived in the front line, we had in front of us a wood which was very heavily shelled by the enemy both day and night, so that it could not be occupied in the daytime with any number of men, but every night about half a dozen men had to go forward into this wood on outpost duty. On this particular night it came my turn to have to go. As there were no trenches, two shell holes had to be occupied with three men in each. I well remember as I was just about to slide down into this shell hole in the darkness, not knowing whether I should be hurled into eternity before morning, how sweetly and blessedly these words dropped: 'Though I walk through the valley of the shadow of death, I will fear no evil: for thou art with me; thy rod and thy staff they comfort me,' and remarkable though it may seem, I do not think one shell fell into that wood during that night.

The other thing I would mention is as follows. Having to relieve those in the front line, we had to parade for this purpose about half past four in the afternoon to reach the front line about eleven o'clock. It was a dull and dreary November afternoon and I felt surrounded with everything to cast one down both within and without, feeling I wanted some word from the Lord. In this condition I stole away for a few minutes and opened my little pocket Bible, and it opened upon the last chapter of Daniel, and I shall never forget what a comfort and strength it was to me at that time as my eyes fell upon the last verse: 'But go thou thy way till the end be: for thou shalt rest, and stand in thy lot at the end of the days.'[413]

It is now my humble desire to make mention of the loving-kindness of the Lord in his providence towards me, in sparing my life and not cutting me off in the midst of my days, and for this reason I record the following. It was toward the end of November 1917. Our company had to relieve a company of another regiment in the front line. After a very difficult journey in pitch darkness we eventually arrived there between eleven and twelve o'clock. After searching around for some time, trying to find the company we were to relieve, we came across one officer and five men. We asked him about the positions and where his men were, but he replied, 'Positions there are none, and this is all that remains of our company – myself and these five men. All the rest lie buried round here.' As there was no cover of any sort, nothing but the utter desolation of shell fire, we were spaced out in shell holes, three men to each about 12 yards apart. Thus we had to pass the remainder of the night. As soon as it was daybreak, an enemy plane appeared over us and returned. This we knew only too well to be an omen of trouble. Soon after this, and suddenly, a most devastating torrent of shells rained down upon us without intermission until three o'clock in the afternoon. As we lay crouching in our shell hole, expecting to be blown to pieces any moment, a large shell dropped only a few feet from us. I was completely buried alive; nothing but complete and silent blackness, unable to move even a finger and a terrible weight of earth on top of my head which forced my steel helmet down over my face, and I was unable to breathe. In the providence of God, although both my companions were wounded, one was only partly buried and was able to free himself. I myself had almost lost consciousness and had given myself up to death, when all at once I felt a blow on the top of my head, which was my companion digging with his entrenching tool in an effort to free me. He was soon able to uncover my head and arms and then I was able to extricate myself. Although not so much at the time, I could afterwards see the wonderful providence of God; that same God who delivered Daniel from the mouth of the lions had also delivered me out of the very jaws of death. How true are the lines of the hymn writer:

> But see how heaven's indulgent care
> Attends their wanderings here and there![414]

Also his faithfulness to his word in the 91st Psalm: 'A thousand shall fall at thy side, and ten thousand at thy right hand; but it shall not come nigh thee.'

There are many other instances I could relate of his wonderful care and preserving mercy over me, but I do not wish to enter further into this painful period, ... through mercy I was spared to return home.

The author of the obituary notes: "Mr. Gibson omits to mention an act of conspicuous bravery. One of his colleagues had fallen wounded, but Mr. Gibson, though under fire from the enemy, went and carried him to safety."

Frank Luther Gosden

Mr Gosden was brought up under the ministry of Mr J. K. Popham at Galeed Chapel, Brighton. He was the younger brother of Mr John H. Gosden, who for many years was editor of *The Gospel Standard.* After the war Mr Gosden was sent out to preach by the church at Shover's Green. He held pastorates at Ebenezer Chapel, Broad Oak, Heathfield, and at Galeed Chapel, Brighton.

✍ In the years 1915 and 1916, the Lord granted me the favour of a closer walk with himself than I have had since for so long a time together. In those terrible days of the war he remembered that I was dust, and he granted me to 'go forth unto him without the camp, bearing his reproach.' He enabled me in a little measure to honour him before men, and he covered my head in the day of battle; and while in France, where there were no means of grace and none of his people (at least none that I came into contact with), he drew me near to himself. During the whole of 1916 he favoured me; he enabled me to seek him and often to find him. I believe that my experience through his rich mercy at that time is expressed by Jeremiah: 'I remember thee, the kindness of thy youth, the love of thine espousals, when thou wentest after me in the wilderness, in a land that was not sown.'

In October, 1916, when, through exposure, my health began to fail, before I was invalided home, in reading Psalm 91 I felt the lovingkindness of the Lord and a desire to be brought back to meet again among his people. And I made a vow that if the Lord brought me back safely, I would, as he might so enable me, walk in the ordinances of his house. At that same time the thought of preaching entered into my mind. That was the beginning. I want you to take particular notice of this, the *thought* of preaching entered into my mind. Do not set any more value upon that than is due because under those peculiar circumstances (when the Lord had, as I believe, pitied me even as a father pitieth his children), under such circumstances it is quite likely that many might have had such thoughts come into their mind; the *thought* of preaching. I will not call it the commencement of *exercise* with respect to the ministry, but the *thought* began there.

At one time in the war, 1917, after a very bad time in France, I was in an army hospital and then sent to England in a hospital ship. When discharged I had a long walk in heavy snow, and was weak in body, but I felt God was *very near* as my Father. As I walked along I said, 'My Father's snow, my Father's moon; all is his' (c.f. Psalm 147).

Frank Gosden

I came home, and in 1918 I was enabled to pay my vow. The friends asked me if I would speak at the prayer meetings, which at that time were very well attended. In the first place I refused, but on one occasion when our late dear friend, Mr. Nicholls (Sr.), asked me if I would speak and I told him I could not, I had never spoken, in the middle of that prayer meeting he called upon me. I read the 1008th hymn (*Gadsby's Selection*),

> Come, Holy Spirit, calm my mind,
> And fit me to approach my God,

and then tried to speak in prayer. I believe the Lord there blessed me and gave me access and communion with him.[415]

Edgar Robert Gosling

Edgar Gosling was brought up to attend the Church of England in Abingdon. When he was called up to serve in the First World War he was in an unregenerate state, yet during the war there appear to have been some stirrings of life in the soul. After the war, Mr Gosling was remarkably brought out from the Church of England to attend the Plymouth Brethren, among whom he was baptised in 1925. Eventually, in 1939, he came to attend the Strict Baptist Chapel in Albert Street, Oxford, joining the church there remaining a member for 11 years. He is one of the few men detailed in this book to have served in both world wars, and was able to contrast the experience of serving in the first in unregeneracy, and the second as one called by grace. The following account comes from his wife's writings and includes reflections on his service in both world wars. He died on 2nd May, 1951, aged 62.[416]

✍ My husband was born at Abingdon, Berkshire, in 1898. He was brought up to attend the Church of England, but at the age of 14 he went to live in Reading with his grandmother, and for the next two years he ran wild, attending no place of worship at all. At this time he joined the army, stating that he was 18 years old, instead of 16. It is wonderful how the Lord kept him from falling into many open sins during the days of his unregeneracy in the army. I have often heard him express his thankfulness to God for this. He did, however, drink heavily, and he describes himself at this period of his life as a wild ass's colt, although he often attended church services voluntarily and had a reverence for religion. He had no idea of what a Christian life consisted of but he knew he was not living as he ought, often resolving to be different and excusing himself from doing so whilst a soldier. He thought when he returned home it would be an easy matter and intended then to make a supreme effort to be 'truly religious.' He has often told me sadly how that during the 1914-1918 war, when he was in France with death and danger surrounding him, he never prayed. Yet, through the Lord's great goodness, he was brought safely through, with only two slight wounds.

After peace was declared he returned home and now he began to prove his inability to 'live a better life.' In fact he seemed daily to become worse …

Having detailed his call by grace, and how he came amongst the Strict Baptists, the account continues:

✍ About this time [*during the Second World War*] my

husband was unemployed, and it was suggested that he should join the army again for one year as a clerk. Looking back over this period of his life, he saw two reasons for this year in the army; first, to put right the wrong concerning his age[417] and, secondly, to show him that through the Lord's enabling, it was as possible to live as a Christian should in the army as it was at home. This year was one of the happiest of his life. During it the Lord spake unto him 'as a man speaketh unto his friend.' These words were given him as he entered upon this period of army service: 'They shall fight against thee; but they shall not prevail against thee; for I am with thee, saith the Lord, to deliver thee.' In a very remarkable manner, he proved by experience the truth of the two following texts: 'My God hath sent his angel, and hath shut the lions' mouths,' and: 'When a man's ways please the Lord, he maketh even his enemies to be at peace with him.'[418]

Bertram John Gurney

Bertram Gurney was called by grace during the war. After the war, Mr Gurney settled at Ashwell, where he held the office of deacon until his death on 7th April, 1958, aged 58.[419] The following record is from his obituary which appeared in *The Gospel Standard*:[420]

✍ In the providence of God [*Bertram*] moved with his parents to Luton in 1912, as yet unconcerned as to his state as a sinner before God. Though not left to enter into gross outward sin, he gave every evidence of his state by nature. The great war of 1914-1918 meant his being called to national service about

Bertram J. Gurney

the end of 1917, and it was while thus engaged the Holy Spirit's conviction of sin was wrought in his heart. While under a bombing attack in France the solemnity of his condition before a holy God was impressed upon him, and 'he felt without hope and knew not what to do.'

An entry in a small diary kept by him while in the army reads: 'Do have mercy upon me and forgive all my sins.' Other entries through the book give evidence of the continual exercise of his heart toward God, and the leading of the Spirit, teaching him well his need of mercy. The closing entry was: 'But we see Jesus' (Hebrews 2: 9).

Frederick George Gurney

Frederick Gurney, brother to Bertram, was called by grace as a young boy, and was baptised at Providence Chapel, Biggleswade, when he was 16 years old. Shortly afterwards, the family moved in providence to Luton, and in 1914 he transferred his church membership to Bethel Chapel, Luton. Mr Gurney remained at Luton for the remainder of his life, serving for 40 years as deacon there. The following is taken from his own writings:[421]

✍ The Great War broke out and several of the young men belonging to the Bible class and chapel were called to national service. I myself being weakly, though being called to register, was eventually passed C3, which meant I was quite unfit for the forces. I was at this time working with my father, who still carried on in a small way with his trade, and also helping my mother in a little drapery business which she opened, and was getting on nicely with.

As the war went on, the need for more men for our country was pressing. I was again called for examination and, my health now somewhat improved, I was passed B3, which meant I could at least be attached to a regiment and be useful. My first journey was to Bedford, where I was issued with uniform, and the first night in barracks I remember – how I feared I had not grace sufficient and that I should give way and be ashamed of Jesus! Yet I believe he gave me strength to kneel down by my trestle bed ere going to sleep, but how barren I did feel! Eventually, in about a week's time, I was sent to Edinburgh and was joined to the King's Own Scottish Borderers.

I had about three months' training in soldiering and had another medical examination, and again passed unfit for abroad so was made a worker in the cookhouse to be trained as a cook to the regiment I was in. I was then sent to Ireland with the regiment and remained there until after one year and 50 days I was discharged as medically unfit for service. During this time my greatest earthly comfort was to receive the kind and loving letters of the one of my heart.

Frederick G. Gurney

I cannot speak or write much of my spiritual exercises during this time. They were mostly cries to the Lord for sustaining grace to live before him. O the barrenizing influences of the army! I was slighted and 'given the cold shoulder' by most of my fellows, but the Lord saw to it I was not without one or two who were friendly. At Templemore, Ireland, the young Methodist minister opened his schoolroom for us to meet at night to read or write as we required. Templemore was steeped in Roman Catholicism, priest-ridden. The poverty and filth of part of the place was appalling. If the priest walked down the street, the people would come out and curtsey to him.

We used to get our writing material from a large stationer's in the town. I was one day looking through the books in the shop and seeing some Roman Catholic publications, picking up one on the Virgin Mary, I felt I must speak against the teaching in it. I said to the assistant, 'You don't think the Virgin Mary can save you, do you?' Immediately she ran to the manageress and said, 'This soldier has spoken against the Virgin Mary!' The manageress in horror said, 'Don't speak to him, don't speak to him!' and I left the shop. I told the minister of this incident and he spoke seriously to me and warned me never to go into that shop again, saying, 'You don't know Irish Catholics as I do.' I fear in those days I had a good deal of zeal, not always according to wisdom. I did not remain very much longer in Ireland. I was taken ill and ordered for a medical, when, as already recorded, I was discharged.

Coming home I gladly felt I was now to dwell among my own people. How gladly did I look forward now to being able to meet at Bethel, and to my beloved's company! I was enabled and strengthened to take up my duties at home, and at the chapel and Sunday School.

Reginald James Honeysett

Reginald Honeysett was brought up to attend Grove Road Chapel, Eastbourne. After the war, Mr Honeysett was baptised at Eastbourne, by his pastor, Mr Henry Popham. Sent out to preach in 1929, he was called to

Reginald Honeysett

the pastorate at Providence Chapel, Cranbrook, in 1942, holding that office for 42 years, until his resignation in 1984. He passed away in June, 1985.[422] The following is his account of his war service, as included in his autobiographical writings:

✍ It was on an evening walk toward the end of 1916, when I was eighteen and a half, that I well remember first expressing deep concern and exercise of my soul. One friend was speaking of her concern for her brother, who, like myself, was expecting to be called up for military service in the First Great War. I said to her I knew that if I was called up and had to go to France on active service, it would mean much hardship, but my greater concern was, if I should have to lay down my life. Where should I go?

I was called up for military service in February, 1917, at the age of 18 years, 10 months. From Eastbourne I was sent to Chichester Barracks, which was a dispersal centre for new recruits, to be sent to other camps for training. It was a Friday, and after being fitted out with uniform we were free. I was a stranger in a strange land, but here, in a way I should not have chosen, the Lord was to begin to unfold some of his purposes. I have often looked back and admired his wisdom and overruling and praised him for it. On the Saturday morning all new recruits had to parade at nine o'clock. The sergeant in charge picked out four men, myself among them, and dismissed the rest; two were sent to the 'wet' canteen, and two to the 'dry' canteen, to scrub tables and floors etc. Old nature began inwardly to resent having to do such work, while others were free. However, I saw the goodness of God in not being put in the 'wet' canteen amongst alcoholic drinks, but in the 'dry.' While the other lad [*Alfred Cheesmore*] and I were absolute strangers, we soon found we had something in common, a respect for the Sabbath Day and the Word of God. A friendship began which was only broken by his death in France at the end of that year. On the following Monday we were sent with others to Newhaven for training. One day he informed me his two sisters were coming to see him on the following Sunday and he wished me to join them. At first I declined, but he pressed me to go. When we met it proved that one was a twin to him and they being much attached to each other, left me with the other. This also was no mere human design, but in the all-wise purpose of God she proved to be the one who was eventually to be my beloved wife for nearly 49 years.

Alfred Cheesmore

My training period was rather brief, being only three months, and I was sent to France in May. My friend did not go with me as during that period he had fallen ill with measles and was behind with his training. He went out later, was wounded in November, and died of wounds on Boxing Day. We have reason to believe it was well with him.

Now, in France there were many hardships and dangers to endure and sometimes death all around. The first six weeks were particularly trying, as my letters did not reach home and they feared I was killed. There were some remarkable escapes from close danger. On one occasion, when in the forward trenches, I was sent with others on a night party to fetch rations. While I was gone a shell dropped in the bay where I should have been – one was killed and others wounded. Thus throughout I was often mercifully preserved. There was much wickedness and I have to confess to my shame that I was not always as consistent as I ought to have been, but God mercifully kept me by maintaining a measure of holy fear in my heart and by the good influence of other Christians.

About the middle of October, 1918, we had come out of the forward trenches to reserve positions, and were preparing places for shelter and protection, when a shell dropped in the middle of the field. I received a shrapnel wound in my left hand, affecting three fingers, the middle one deep enough to injure the bone. Others were wounded more severely. I was sent down from the line and after two or three days journey, with rests at various dressing stations, I arrived at a large hospital at Rouen and was put in a marquee in the grounds. My thoughts were that the wound would soon be healed and I should be back up the line, but God had ordered otherwise as the sequence of events will show.

About 6 p.m., when I had only been in bed an hour, a doctor examined me and, to my surprise, marked me for England to leave at 9 a.m. the next morning. This involved a train journey to Le Havre, a night journey in the hospital ship to Southampton, and from there back to Chichester, but this time to Graylingwell Hospital, arriving on a Friday. On Saturday morning I was examined and marked for Eastbourne Convalescent Camp, to go the following Saturday. Thus, through the Lord's overruling, instead of being sent to the other end of the country, as was sometimes the case, I was only five minutes' walk away from my home, this about a fortnight from being wounded. The wound healed in a month, but the bone of the middle finger, being injured, caused much hard swelling around the joint and was quite stiff, so I had three months on massage. We were allowed out of camp after 2 p.m. and I could therefore attend the services at the chapel.

Another favour was that, after a time, my old employer obtained permission for me to help him in the printing works as he was short staffed, and for this I was granted a pass out every day after 9 a.m. Thus I had the threefold privilege of services, my home and my usual work. The Armistice was signed on November 11th and I was demobilised in February 1919. So out of two years in the army I had 17 months of active service in France and four months home, wounded.[423]

George Humberstone

George Humberstone was born and bought up in Yorkshire. Although his godly mother attended the Strict Baptist Chapel at Leeds, he quickly gave up chapel attendance. The Lord convicted him of his state as a sinner when he was idling time away reading a New Testament while tending a machine at work. Subsequently he joined his mother and sister attending the chapel at Leeds. In later life he was a well-known supply minister. He ended his days in membership at Blackboys Chapel, East Sussex. Mr Humberstone's account of his experience during the war was serialised after his death in *The Zion's Witness*; from where the following is extracted:

> ✍ I had volunteered for service very early in the war, but was, time after time, rejected because of my short stature, being only five foot in height. But in 1915, latter part, I was accepted and placed in a battalion of the West Yorkshire Infantry, and not long after I was in France and Belgium.

George Humberstone with his wife

I well remember going the last time to the chapel at Leeds before going into the army, when an old lady, a member I think, said to me, 'Don't forget your Bible.' Oh, how indignant I felt, me forget my Bible! I should never do that! but I did forget it, to my shame. Oh what a backsliding state I soon got into in the army; I never met with any one I could converse with on spiritual things all the time I was in the forces, neither in England nor abroad. One man, who was a Wesleyan, a quiet person, seemed to want my company. Although I told him my beliefs he still stuck to me, and we kept together friendly. This was a means of escape from the dreadful language all around us. I soon found a natural liking for the army life – parades, drills, and the whole round of military duties I became quite interested in … The open air life I loved, and it did me good physically. I soon learned all the drills etc., but as all these things grew stronger upon me, religion began to be neglected, indeed hardly thought about. Outwardly I kept very upright, but inwardly, indifferent and careless as to the state of my soul before God. That God who had shown me such mercy.

After a few months of training we were shipped off to France, without even a leave home. It was 18 months before I saw home again. The abominable language of non commissioned officers and privates I was mercifully preserved from. On active service there was everything to deaden anything of a religious nature. Sunday was just like any other day, and when away from the line of war, we were in the midst of Romish idolatry and awful wickedness. How many narrow escapes from death I could not count. Pieces of shell made my steel helmet ring on my head. Once it was knocked off my head, yet I was uninjured. Pieces of shrapnel hit the edges of my boot soles, but my skin was preserved. Bullets whistled by my ears, yet I was preserved. Horses, mules, men and houses I saw blown to fragments, and in the midst of these dreadful things, my poor fallen nature became as hard and callous as if I had never known anything of divine teaching in my heart. In a few instances, though, I did feel the awful solemnity of my life being in such jeopardy.

On one occasion in June, 1917, when we were about a mile behind the front line, supposed to be having a rest, a beautiful clear morning, we were sighted by the enemy. Shells began to just rain upon us; there was no cover, it was just open country. We all fell flat on our faces; oh! how many were killed and wounded. What a terrible feeling came over me, 'Shall I be the next to be hit?' when, all at once, the words seemed spoken powerfully within me,

> Plagues and deaths around me fly;
> Till he bids, I cannot die;
> Not a single shaft can hit,
> Till the God of love sees fit.

This also followed it, 'I shall not die, but live, and declare the works of the Lord.' All fear left me, and a solemn persuasion came that I should be preserved through the war, get home again, and one day I should preach the Gospel. I began to help with the wounded around me until we were ordered from the place. But even after this, oh, the awful backsliding inwardly, and to a great extent outwardly too. How I learned my utter helplessness, in spite of conscience doing her work. Mercifully I was preserved, when out of the line and sometimes billeted with the French or Belgian people, from the wretched immorality all around me. There was no thanks to me that I was kept, for my heart was as evil as sin could make it. This has often been a wonder to me since.

Passing over much that would not be profitable, I was preserved until the Armistice, November 11th, 1918. About this time I had such a wonderful manifestation of mercy that I feel I must mention it. We were granted leave home at this time, and a Jew from Leeds and I set off together for home. This Jew was a very decent chap, and we agreed to meet at the end of our 14 days leave and return together, which we did. But on our arrival in Belgium, where we had left our company, they had moved and we were some days before we found them. We had lifts on lorries, but also had to tramp along miles of muddy roads. I had felt one of my feet very sore as we trudged along; oh, what a relief when we did find them. But on taking off, at last, my boots, I found I had a blister on the sole of my right foot, covering the whole sole. It had burst and was terribly painful; I washed and bandaged it up as well as I could, wondering however I should manage duty next. But the next morning, to my astonishment, our company sergeant major asked me if I would be his batman. Oh how thankful I felt, I could hardly believe it, for this meant I should have none of the duties of the company to do. I had just to stay in camp, see after his meals, polish his equipment, etc. It was the first time I had been offered a position like this in all my war service, and coming as it did, just when I so needed it, I saw the goodness and mercy of the Lord in it; my heart was softened and repentance was given. I wrote home at the time, I remember, putting in my letter, 'What shall I render unto the LORD for all his mercy to me? I will take the cup of salvation, and call upon the name of the LORD.' For some time after this I was kept more tender in spirit.

Demobilisation began after the Armistice. Employers could appeal to have their men returned. In my case, and in many others too, we were not applied for trade was in a bad way, so I was kept in the army until 1919. Units were all broken up, and a very mixed lot were then sent to look after prisoners of war, salvaging brass and iron in the devastated areas around Ypres in Belgium. Finally I was demobbed, but what a dreadful state things were in. Thousands were unemployed. I was too. The place I had been employed at before the war was almost closed. What a time I passed through. I learned to drive a car, but I soon found, at that time, there were far more drivers than cars. I felt the Lord was dealing with me in solemn chastisement for my wretched backsliding in the army. My way was hedged up in providence, and in my soul too. Oh the trouble within as the Lord frowned on all my efforts to get work. At the chapel there seemed to be nothing for me. Some there found fault with me because I had conscientiously refused to take a job with Sunday work. Truly the backslider was filled with his own ways. I remember in my simplicity asking a good old member if any of the Lord's people died of starvation spiritually whilst seeking him (for truly I did seek him). I was favoured with longings in my poor soul for him, but all seemed shut up against me. How I longed to hear his voice in the preaching. The answer the old member gave me was this, 'No, lad, keep on seeking.' This I was obliged to do out of sheer necessity, my case felt so desperate, but now and then the Lord mercifully began to give me a lift in hearing.

Previous to being in the army, I had been often exercised about baptism, and I had a longing to follow the Lord, I believe in love to a merciful Jesus, who had done so much for me, but I could never move in this solemn matter before the war. Although on one occasion a good old minister in the North, Mr Hacking, preached from Hebrews 13: 13-14. 'Let us go forth therefore unto him without the camp, bearing his reproach, for here have we no continuing city, but we seek one to come.' Mr Hacking spoke very solemnly of how Christ suffered without the camp or city, and of the blessedness of being led to him for salvation. Then of the poor sinner being enabled by grace to bear his reproach in an ungodly world; he then spoke of baptism, how sweet to be led by the Spirit to openly profess Christ. Lastly he spoke of the vanity of everything here below. Oh how my heart was softened as he spoke. What a love I felt to the Lord Jesus. What a love and a longing I felt to follow him in a public profession of his name and cause.

The above ends Mr Humberstone's own writings. Mrs Humberstone completed the account as follows:

✍ After he came out of the army, he was out of work for two years. Work was very scarce in the North of England, but during that time a promise was spoken unto him with power, 'Seek ye first the kingdom of God' etc., which promise the Lord gave him grace to fulfil, for indeed he was kept alive in the things of God, and always, all through our married

> life, it was 'first things first.' It was during those two years that he passed through many heavy trials and temptations. It was whilst passing through these things he had been to visit some godly friends, and on his way home he had to walk on a very lonely common, but he was led by the blessed Spirit into Christ's sufferings all through his life and on the cross, and in the garden of Gethsemane. Oh, as he related it, what a blessed time it was. He hardly knew how he got home, so taken up with what Christ endured, he felt how light was his pathway. After those two years, a way was made for him to work down the coal mine. He had not worked down a mine before, but chose it rather than be out of work. Whilst working down the mine he had one or two miraculous escapes from death, but his life was preserved, because he had yet to preach the everlasting gospel. The exercise about the ministry was still in his heart, especially when Jesus was made precious to him.[424]

Mr Humberstone was baptised in 1920 and married in 1926, but it was not until May 10th, 1953, that the exercise concerning the ministry, commenced on the battlefields of France, was bought to fruition and he was unanimously sent out to preach by the church at Gower Street Memorial Chapel, London.

Spencer Grey Wakeley Hunt

Spencer Hunt was born in Brighton and sat under Mr J. K. Popham's ministry at Galeed Chapel. After the war Mr Hunt married and attended West Street Chapel, Croydon. He was baptised there by Mr Walter Croft. In later life he was a member at Ebenezer Chapel, Clapham. He died on 10th December, 1971, aged 82. The following is taken from his obituary in *The Gospel Standard.*[425] It was written by Mr Jesse Delves:

> ✍ In the providence of God, during the First War our friend was posted to Chatham, and having relatives there who attended the chapel, he was shown much kindness, and their timely influence was graciously sanctified in preserving him from breaking the Sabbath except for one particular instance which became a great grief to him, as he felt that he had sinned against light and knowledge.

Spencer G. W. Hunt

About this period a younger brother was killed on active service and this was a sad blow, although there was a good hope of his brother; yet it occasioned much heart searching, as he felt that he himself was not prepared for that solemn change, and if his life had been taken, hell would have been his just desert.

While on active service in France, the soldier who took our friend's place through a last minute change of plans, was killed instantly by a shell. This remarkable preservation so affected and amazed him, he felt himself to be such a guilty wretch as before God, that a 'Who can tell?' was raised up in his heart that he would yet see 'greater things than these,' and he was encouraged still to plead for mercy and pardon.

After being invalided out of the army and returning to business life, he had to endure some trials and persecution in the company he had to associate with. About this period he was much helped under a sermon preached by Mr Tobitt of Hastings from the words: 'It is finished.' Our dear friend was much blessed at this time, feeling to be raised up to that good hope through grace which never left him, being as an 'anchor of the soul' for the remainder of his life. Shortly before he died, when a friend quoted this to him, he said, 'That is my text.'

Percy William Jempson

Percy Jempson was for many years the deacon at Bethel Chapel, Rye, until his death in 1981, aged 86 years. His brother Harry, also a member of the congregation at Rye, served in the war as well. During the First World War Percy served in the Royal Sussex Regiment, seeing service in France. The following brief account of some of his war experiences is extracted from his obituary in *The Gospel Standard.* [426]

✍ On one occasion, approaching the front line in a communication trench, under heavy fire from the enemy, I felt the presence of an angel by my side. It was a blessed feeling and caused a calmness whilst others were falling round me. Added to this, it being a Sunday morning, sweet was the thought that at Bethel prayers were going up on my behalf.

Percy Jempson (standing) with his brother, Harry

He was wounded in the arm and returned to England. On recovery he was sent back to the Ypres front.

✍ One special time I was in charge of seven men. We had spent four days without sleep and hardly any food. The runner brought news that the enemy were advancing toward our post. It was pitch dark; I trembled from head to foot; but immediately a cry ascended from my heart, 'Lord, help me.' It was the Holy Spirit's inditing. A calm came over me and I placed my men, fearless of the enemy. We were all ready for the attack, but to our amazement the enemy stopped at the barbed wire and no shots were fired either side. The marvellous work of God! Many, many times did I marvel at the Lord's preserving mercies when death seemed certain. Psalm 91 was my experience.

Alfred Levell

The following account of Alfred Levell was written by his son, Alfred, who never knew his father. The Levells lived in St. Michael's, Kent, and attended the chapel at Bounds Cross, Biddenden.

✍ My father had to join the army a week after his marriage in June, 1915, and for the next three years was in much of the fighting in France and Salonika. Early in 1916 he wrote: 'Isn't it a mercy the future is wisely hidden from us? We know not what an hour may bring forth, but One who rules and reigns knows what is best. Let him do what seemeth him good.'

Towards the end of 1916, recovering in Nottingham Hospital from wounds, he gives this account of the event that brought him there: 'I had a sweet Scripture brought to my mind the day we went into the trenches: "Be not afraid" "The Lord thy God is with thee in all places whithersoever thou goest." I said: "Lord, thou hast been with me in many rough places and thou canst be with me here." I was blown off the parapet and buried (he was dug out unconscious by his comrades). I was hit on the shoulder earlier, but stopped at my post as I had those words: "Do your duty bravely; 'fear God. Honour the king.'" I had no fear in the trenches I can honestly say, but it was an afternoon I hope never to witness again, one never to be forgotten. But still, isn't our God good in sparing such a vile unworthy sinner as me? ... I feel to come far short of all his mercies to me.'

Alfred Levell (Sr.)

In 1917, writing to a sister-in-law and referring to the painfulness of a parting from his loved ones, he says: 'My dear wife comforted me by saying when I left her: "If it is his will to take you, he can take care and provide for me and the boy"' (and indeed the writer can say how this trust has been fulfilled over the last 50 years). On his last leave in 1918, my father appears to have had some premonition that he would not come home any more. Having left his loved ones and gone down the road, he returned for a few minutes to tell my mother this – that he felt he would never see her again. He was killed in action a few weeks later on 18th October, 1918, aged 32, and buried at Le Cateau. Some months afterwards my mother discovered that Hymn 591 in the hymn book he had used abroad was side-marked, against the last verse being written, 'Very sweet to me,' and giving a date a short time before his death:

The time is now fixed, and soon it will come,
When Christ will his messenger send,
To fetch him from Meshech and carry him home,
And then all his sorrows will end.[427]

Thus was the righteous 'taken away from the evil to come' (Isaiah 57: 1). His death was a great blow to my mother, but she was supported and brought to that place where she could feelingly say it was 'not in anger, but from his dear covenant love.'[428]

Ebenezer Oliver

Ebenezer Oliver

Ebenezer Oliver was born and brought up at Egerton, in Kent. After the war he was baptised at Bounds Cross Chapel, Biddenden, Kent, by Mr John Kemp (Sr.). He was chosen as a deacon in 1924. In 1957 he moved to Wiltshire, joining the church at Manningford. He passed away on 16th September, 1983, aged 92.

The following account was written sometime after the war, when Ebenezer was working as a crane driver. He spent his quiet hours writing about his life. Instalments from these writings were published in *The Friendly Companion* in a series titled 'Thoughts in a Crane Cabin:' [429]

✍ Well, as before mentioned, we were married, and the happy event took place at Bounds Cross on

December 5th, 1914. We lived in a cottage right opposite the little watermill. The war had begun, and as time went on it was impressed on our minds that there would be a painful separation. How our hearts began to droop! …

A device called 'Lord Derby's Scheme' was set on foot to get young men to join voluntarily, and it was put in this way by those who went round canvassing: 'If you want to keep out of the army, join Lord Derby's Scheme;'[430] and I was caught. Ah, how deeply I regretted it, for had I waited until conscripted, I should have had another 18 months at home. Well would it be if such painful lessons had not to be learned again and again. The dreaded day came, April 7th, 1916, and I was given no choice, as infantry men were needed. So we had six months' training in 'The Buffs'[431] at Crowborough in Sussex.

I attended Jarvis Brook Chapel when possible, and found several kind friends there. One Sunday I had a feeling that I might try to get all day at chapel, and was able to walk boldly out of camp with little trouble, only being questioned once. 'Where are you going?' asked the last guard near the road. 'Church,' I replied; and he said, 'All right.' Strictly we were not allowed out of camp on Sundays until 1 o'clock. It so happened that they were having reading services all day at the chapel, and on each occasion Mr Philpot's sermons were read. In the morning the text was: 'And the Lord said, Simon, Simon, Behold, Satan hath desired to have you, that he may sift you as wheat: but I have prayed for thee, that thy faith fail not: and when thou art converted, strengthen thy brethren' (Luke 22: 31-32).[432] In the afternoon it was: 'Light is sown for the righteous, and gladness for the upright in heart' (Psalm 97: 11).[433] The sermons made a mark in my mind, and I put an interpretation upon them. How little I knew of real things; how little I know now, but when I was a child I spake as a child. It was the morning especially that abode, and I concluded that I should have to go right into the fighting, which I thought was Satan's sieve, but that I should be brought safely through; and in this natural way I proved right.

Just one closing incident before I commence on my experience in France. We had our last fortnight of training at Dover, where we were finally equipped for the front. On October 23rd, 1916, our draft was paraded and inspected by an old general. He had a kind genial face, and spoke encouragingly as he passed between the ranks. We were then brought to 'Attention,' and he spoke loud enough for all to hear: 'The parade is about to move off, but if any man wishes to speak to me, let him stand fast.' I remained stationary, the only one, and the sergeant major marched me up to the general, and I told him just simply how things were at home, promising faithfully I would be back in the morning. He put his hand on my shoulder and said: 'I am sorry for you, my lad, but you leave here tomorrow at three o'clock.'

On the following day, that little strip of water separated the large draft of men from home and loved ones, some never to return. Cruel, cruel war!

> Oh thou hideous monster, sin!
> What a curse hast thou brought in.[434]

But to those who are taught to know him, it shall work together for good. Two days later, at Étaples in France, a postcard informed me that our firstborn –

a baby girl – had arrived. How I wept, partly out of relief, partly out of sorrow. Oh how I rued the day that I joined Lord Derby's Scheme! But thus our gracious God permitted, and mercifully overruled all.

Whenever possible I got alone, and sometimes I thought there seemed some nearness to the Lord. True, they were providential trials, and can it not be easily understood that, realising that we should shortly be face to face with war in all its grim reality, it was no light matter. Death was a solemn thought.

> Who, except Jesus smiles within,
> Can look the monster in the face?[435]

Nor was my old matter cleared up – had I really felt myself a sinner, and had I really realised pardon? That was the point, nor could I find a satisfactory answer. But a verse that had begun to be my prayer was quickened while undergoing these things:

> Lord, make this heart rejoice or ache,
> Decide the doubt for me:
> And if it be not broken, break.
> And heal it if it be.[436]

We were not suddenly brought into imminent peril, but it was very gradual. This has been the Lord's way with me in various ways all my life, and I am inclined to think that in the experience of his people generally it is so. Doubtless there are sudden appearings, but they are very solemn. At last the dreaded day arrived, about July, 1917, and there were a few hours that sunny afternoon to contemplate the sad scenes through which I felt we should now be called upon to enter. I was in real earnest, for it was great trouble; but I seemed to get some nearness to the Lord in pleading this word: 'Hide not thy face far from me; put not thy servant away in anger: thou hast been my help; leave me not, neither forsake me, O God of my salvation!' With that feeling there came this thought, that if the Lord would indeed hear my poor prayers and bring me safely through, I would walk in the ordinances of his house on my return to civilian life.

I had my first leave in December, 1917, the next a year later, and another in May, 1919, and was demobilised in July, 1919; but perhaps one or two things might be mentioned.

At one time when working outside a dugout, a great deal of self-pity was uppermost. There was not another brother having so rough a time, and why should I be singled out? It did seem hard. I did not know this was rebellion working in my heart, but have thought on it since. See now what a compassionate Saviour, to come to me in such a state and soften that hard heart; but so it was, for gently, quietly, that hymn of Miss Steele's came to mind, verse by verse:

> Peace, my complaining doubting heart,
> Ye busy cares, be still.[437]

But as the last verse came, I knew that really and truly I could not pray it:

> But oh, indulge this only wish,
> This boon I must implore;
> Assure my soul that thou art mine;
> My God, I ask no more.

I did seem to want to be spared to come home.

Once, just before going 'over the top,' I felt inclined to read and pray with the seven men in my charge. I read Psalm 91, and in taking part of the Hindenburg Line[438] by sectional rushes, I thought on the 7th verse ('A thousand shall fall at thy side, and ten thousand at thy right hand; but it shall not come nigh thee'). The prayer was heard and answered, and we were preserved. After the war I had a letter from one of the seven. He worked in a brush factory, and his name was Dedman. In the letter he referred to that occasion and said he would never forget it, and he also sent me some brushes with my name on them.

The captain of our company on one occasion, while in the front line at Ypres, would not pass a letter I had written to my brother. He did not approve of some remarks I had made concerning a sad affair that had happened the previous day, saying, 'If you had your leg blown off, you would swear, and so would I.' Shortly after he was mortally wounded. The two stretcher-bearers of our platoon took him off the battlefield. So I had an opportunity of speaking to them later, and enquired if Captain Hill spoke after he had been hit. They said, 'Yes, we just got him on the stretcher, and he turned over on his side and said, "O Lord! have mercy upon my poor soul!" and died.'

Our lives are brought through adversity and prosperity, sorrow and joy, trials and deliverances, and now the scene changes. The long-looked for day arrived – though fears had run so high that it would not come; but it did – when freed from army life. I stepped into our little cottage one sunny July afternoon in 1919, to set out afresh on the journey of life. I believe our hearts were moved with humble gratitude to the God of all our mercies, as we bowed our knees together to return thanks.

Reuben Stanley Paul

Reuben Paul served with the 13th Battalion, King's Royal Rifle Corps during the war. He was the brother of Mr Sydney F. Paul, editor of *The Gospel Standard* (1964-1970). Reuben was killed in battle in France, August 26th, 1918, aged 25, and is buried in Bagneux British Cemetery, Gezaincourt. Two other of his brothers also served on the front during the war.

Reuben was highly decorated for bravery, receiving both the Distinguished Conduct Medal (DCM) and the Military Cross,[439] and his bravery was recognised in France by the award of the Croix de Guerre.[440] The citation for his DCM in the *London Gazette* of 25th June, 1918, reads: "For conspicuous gallantry and devotion to duty during an enemy attack. Though the enemy penetrated into the support line behind him, he maintained his position in the front line trench under intense fire, and used his Lewis gun with great effect. He displayed magnificent courage and leadership."

The following obituary was written by his parents, John and Hannah Paul. It is supplemented by extracts from letters Reuben wrote home while on active service, and followed by some extracts from the writings of his sister, Grace, showing how she coped with her brother's death, and the way the Lord blessed the ministry in sanctifying the loss:[441]

> ✍ We trust that this our great loss is our dear boy's eternal gain, and hope that the following extracts from his letters may be of some use and encouragement to praying parents. When he was a few weeks old, we were trying to ask that a name might be given for him. This was given with some

power, 'Let Reuben live, and not die,' accompanied with a persuasion that he was a vessel of mercy afore prepared unto glory. His tender, affectionate walk was consistent with this hope, and though nature would have loved to hold him here, we desire to give God the praise that he so instructed and prepared him for that inheritance which he was so early to enter into. We believe the Word of God was his guide in every difficulty, and he searched it to find direction and guidance. His nervous temperament naturally shrank from joining the army, and in this the latter part of Numbers 32: 6: 'Shall your brethren go to war, and shall ye sit here?' helped him to decide; also 1 Peter 2: 17: 'Fear God. Honour the king.' We desire also to render thanks to God for this comforting word, 'Like as a father pitieth his children, so the LORD pitieth them that fear him.'

In 1912 he obtained a situation in London, and from that time frequently wrote home expressing his anxious desires that he might find divine guidance in every step, and that he might know that Christ died for him; with sometimes a good hope that the Lord would be with him, and in his own time reveal himself as his Saviour. He was much affected by witnessing a bad air raid in London in Sept., 1915, and in Oct. wrote, 'I suppose you have seen the King's letter this morning. I think that should appeal to everyone; it made me think of the scripture, "Fear God. Honour the king."' This led him to volunteer, and on November 20th, 1915, he entered the 18th King's Royal Rifle Corps. He would often mention hymn 64 (*Gadsby's Selection*):

Sovereign Ruler of the skies, etc.

and once said the last verse seemed engraven on his mind:

Not a single shaft can hit
Till the God of love sees fit.

In June, 1916, he was sent to France. His letters in the next two years show the constant exercise of his faith and hope in God, many times passing through terrible things in which he realised special preserving mercies. Only a few extracts can be given. It pleased the Lord he should at length be fatally wounded, and without regaining consciousness he passed away a few hours later from this vale of tears to be for ever with the Lord on August 26th, 1918, and his body was buried in a British cemetery near Doullens.

The following are brief autobiographical extracts from his letters, selected by his parents and appended to his obituary in *The Gospel Standard*:

✍ *June 13th, 1916* – I am glad to be able to say I feel quite ready to go abroad. I believe it is the Lord's will, and so must be for the best. Although going from the country, I am not going away from him. I got a late pass on Sunday, and went to Gower Street. Mr Prewett was preaching; he read the 3rd of Exodus, and the first part of verse 12 seemed to fix itself upon my mind: 'Certainly I will be with thee.' I could not think of anything else all the evening, and felt it had its meaning which only time will prove.

France, June 18th – It seems a very long time since I went to Gower Street, instead of being last Sunday evening; the passage Mr Prewett read seemed very encouraging and quite as if meant for me. It is exactly what is wanted, for if he is with me, what is there to fear?

July 12th – I realised last night, I think for the first time, the deepness and beauty there is in that verse I quoted some time ago:

> Plagues and death around me fly,
> Till he bids I cannot die.[442]

Gower Street Chapel

July 22nd – The night before we left the trenches, Fritz gave us a terrible time for a while, but fortunately, I must say marvellously, we only had a very few casualties. If ever I have felt that there was a God in whose hands I could leave everything, I felt it then, and that verse was an enormous comfort to me. If I had not had a God to go to then, I feel certain I must have lost myself entirely ... I feel the strain is very great. But, however, let us still remember hymn 64 (*Gadsby's Selection*), and keep on our minds that these things shall end when the appointed time arrives.

July 29th – Since your last letter, I have seen various places and scenes and been in various positions, but all movements and circumstances have only tended to prove one thing, and that is – the truth of the text, 'Certainly I will be with thee.' He has been and is with me, I do believe, if I never before realised that – 'with God all things are possible,' and 'without him we can do nothing,' – I think I have done so now. If I had no God to go to, I think I should have been obliged to give up all in despair long ago. I thought I could realise what those words meant (hymn 64) when in London, especially during the time of the air raids, but I didn't know half then of what I do now, I mean in the value of them.

August 5th – Every day, in fact, every moment gives an opportunity of thanksgiving for safety; this time I have more cause than ever to remember his preserving mercies. What a wonderful story it will be, if I am spared to see the end!

August 13th – Woolwich Hospital: I am afraid the postcard would startle you, but I must tell you it is not at all serious. The piece of shrapnel came out of itself, missing the bone, so am spared the pain of having it searched for and removed, for which I would be thankful. It is not the only thing I have to be thankful for, as the sight on Wednesday morning was terrible in the extreme. I was one of 16 picked out to occupy an advanced bombing post. First the man on my right and then one on my left were wounded. I led them back, and afterwards felt something similar to a heavy kick on the thigh, which knocked me over, I did not realise what had happened, but still kept looking for the Huns. The other man was running about the trench not knowing what to do, and came to me; he was immediately wounded in the hand. I then took him back. The sergeant asked me if I could stick it out; I said, 'Yes,' and got three more men, and stopped until 3 a.m. It was not till nearly then that I realised I was wounded, and began to feel the loss of blood.

September 13th – It is hard, very hard sometimes, even to think that good can ever come out of such terrible things, and even harder still to see it; but I think it has brought me very near to the Lord several times, or brought him to me.

October 11th – It is quite possible that I shall get my draft leave very soon ... I have not forgotten the verse Mr Prewett read at Gower Street, before I left for France; 'Certainly I will be with thee.'

> His skill infallible,
> His providential grace,
> His power and truth that never fail,
> Shall order all my ways.[443]

Hymn 295 (*Gadsby's Selection*) is very true.

November 22nd – The text at Sheerness Chapel last Sunday night seemed to strike me as something particularly meant for me: Isaiah 43: 2, 'When thou passest through the waters, I will be with thee.' It seemed to be very encouraging for the future, although at the same time very strange.

April 15th, 1917 – I am glad to say I am feeling fairly well, but very weary after 3 days' strenuous fighting. It was our part to take a village; it was done, but very costly. The sights were fearful beyond description; hardly anyone expected to come out alive; but through God's mercy I am safe, and to him be given all the praise.

April 15th – It has been a terrible Easter. The enemy retreated fast, but not too fast to cause us an exceedingly anxious and trying time. I would like all to join with me in giving the Lord all the praise for bringing me through such a terrible experience, a veritable valley of death.

May 12th – We have been very busy since Easter Monday both in and out of the line. It was hard and dangerous in the extreme, but through the unspeakable mercies of God I was able to carry through. Psalm 140: 7 has been made true in my case; he has certainly covered my head in the day of battle, and to him I would give all the praise. I feel so unworthy of such great mercies, and what is worst of all, I seem so utterly unable to give him anything like sufficient thanks for his great kindness. The best attempt is so very weak and poor I feel ashamed of it, to think it is all I can do in return for what he has done; but yet I am not satisfied. I feel to want something more than even such great mercies; they are relative to this life and things of the present. But what of the future? When death comes, as it must someday, how will it be? I fear I do not think sufficiently or seriously or often enough.

July 12th – I believe I may say I have obtained some benefit from the terrible things happening around me. It has driven me to the mercy-seat more than once; I have read my Bible, perhaps I might say, have searched it for comfort, and have sometimes found it; and surely I have learnt to pray from the heart, if I never knew before. The psalmist says, 'It is good for me that I have been afflicted, that I might learn thy statutes.' Again in Psalm 57: 1: 'Be merciful unto me, O God, be merciful unto me: for my soul trusteth in thee: yea, in the shadow of thy wings will I make my refuge, until these calamities be overpast.' These and other similar verses have, from time to time, cheered me up and encouraged me. Soon after I first went to London, you wrote, quoting the hymn: 'God moves in a mysterious way.'[444] He has indeed done so, for I believe it was then that I commenced to look seriously at these things.

October 13th – We have had one of the worst times that any of us have known, but once more, all the praise is due to him who has again 'covered my head in the day of battle.' It will indeed need all eternity to thank him for all his preserving mercies, I do wish I could realise more what he is doing; nothing is impossible with God.

October 31st – We have had a very rough time recently; the days we were in the lines were the worst any of us have ever known. Those who are spared to come out of it have something to be thankful for indeed; I hope there are a few who realise it. I have wondered often how I could face all that I have done without the helping hand. I believe he has from time to time given a word of encouragement and promise. The first was at Gower Street, the last Sunday I was there. Mr Prewett read Exodus 3. The whole of the service was blocked out by part of that verse, 'Certainly I will be with thee.' I do believe it was a promise which has been kept by One whose word never fails. Again, last March, before going over the top for the first time, I was greatly encouraged by the word – 'O God the Lord, the Strength of my salvation, thou hast covered my head in the day of battle.'

Reuben arrived home for his last leave on 27th December, 1917.

✍ *January 27th, 1918* – The night I left home after my leave was not a happy one, but certainly not so sorrowful as it might have been. I felt inwardly that I was deliberately being led and guided by the unseen hand of One who is, 'too good to be unkind' and 'too wise to err'; he has, as I have proved more than once, 'covered my head in the day of battle.' But I'm afraid I am very much like Huntington[445] was; he says he used to pray over and over again when in danger, but when out of it, he left off. I find, when out of the line and away from danger, my thoughts and mind rush away to other things less profitable, in fact many times grossly unprofitable. I do wish God would give me the true spirit of prayer, and draw me to himself; lift me up as it were, out of all these carnal things, temptations and sins.

March 12th – As you have probably seen in the paper something which will cause you to worry, I hasten to get a few lines off. I am sorry to say that the mention does refer to us, and I consider that it is most marvellous that any of us are alive or not prisoners. I would desire all to join with me in giving all praise to the Lord for his great preserving mercies. It was without doubt the most terrible time any of us have as yet experienced, and I pray God to grant, if it can be his will, that such a terrible day is not allowed again. I think I realised a little of that Psalm: 'What time I am afraid, I will trust in thee.' I cannot imagine what a man felt like who knows not God; it must have been truly awful, for there was not a man who could help himself, much less another. I feel with E— L— thankful that I have praying friends who always plead for me at the seat of mercy. The bombardment put on was absolutely terrific and continuous for 12 hours.

April 15th – I have received the DCM[446] for sticking to and keeping my gun in action during the late bombardment. There is one thing I am afraid of, and that is, it will tend to increase pride. But I do try and pray God to continue to bless me, and preserve me as he has done in the past. Oh! that he would be pleased to intervene on our behalf. It seems to me we have reached the extremity now, and God only can save us. I wish the authorities would realise their position and dependence on the Lord. It would be well if this were the means of bringing them to their senses, and to seek his help and guidance, instead of saying, 'We are going to do this and that, and then we will do something else.'

May 20th – I felt very sorry yesterday that there was no church parade, it being the first Sunday out after three weeks in the line. I think a service should have been held. There seems to be less regard for God than ever there was. I fear for the inevitable result, for the Scriptures tell plainly what is the result of this sort of thing.

June 4th – There is apparently no seeking of God or his will. It seems almost as if he is applying to us the word: 'He shut their ears, lest they should hear and be saved;' (c.f. Isaiah 6:10) but he will hear and answer the prayers of his people, and I believe they are many, and often put up. May it please him to hear those prayers, and speedily send answers of peace, and deliver us. I had what might be called a marvellous escape a few nights ago. A few of us were told off for a special and important piece of work, which might have proved highly dangerous, apart from the ordinary danger of shells, which are not plentiful here, I am thankful to say. I was on for six hours during the night with a corporal and two men; and the night before last it was suddenly decided, as I was getting ready, that I need not go as there would be enough. During the night a salvo of six shells burst quite near, and killed the corporal in the place where I should have been had I gone. I think it is yet one more case to add to the numberless times that I have been covered and delivered by the great unseen hand. May he help us to give him all the praise and glory and honour.

June 22nd – It is now just over two years since I first came out here, and what things have been passed through in that time! God himself alone knows how many times he has delivered me, and I am sure it will need all eternity to praise him for all his mercies. But still I am not satisfied. I wish I could know more of him and feel that I walked more in his ways.

July 31st – The news lately has certainly been good, and one wonders what the result will be, but I don't think the end is in sight. The Lord only knows when and how it will end, but of this we are certain, he will bring the end in his own way and time.

August 10th – Two years ago today I arrived at Woolwich Hospital, which you will doubtless remember. What wonderful and marvellous things have happened since! What great cause have we to praise and thank him who has shown such great mercy so many times! Truly,

> God moves in a mysterious way
> His wonders to perform;
> He plants his footsteps in the sea,
> And rides upon the storm.[447]

P.S. You can please yourself about putting the letters DCM after my name, but I am entitled to it, and officially should have it; but I hope I want something better than a name or title.

The following extracts from the diary of Reuben's sister, Grace Lilian Paul, give an insight into the impact the war had on the families left at home, including the way in which the Lord blessed the ministry at the time as a comfort to their souls:

✍ *April 23rd, 1916* – Reuben home on final leave before going abroad in the war, and John to join the army on the 27th.[448] Mr Popham spoke of Christ as a Brother born for adversity. A very suitable subject, and felt while he was speaking helped to cast the burden on the Lord, who is too wise to err and too good to be unkind. On the Monday morning, before seeing dear Reuben off, Hymn 277 (*Gadsby's Selection*) was such a help and support and continued through the week.

Reuben S. Paul's grave

May 7th, 1916 – Heard Mr Popham from Psalm 102: 17, and felt he came into my case. He said we are as a nation and as a church under heavy judgements, and these circumstances can be made the means of God's drawing near to our souls. When one can really feel and say he deserves all, then the Lord is not far from helping and returning to that sinner. No well-formed prayers are needed, but a few cries and sighs he will attend to.

August 30th, 1918 – Had the overwhelming news of dear Reuben's death from wounds received in action. It is indeed a heavy blow, but O what a blessed exchange for him! Deal gently with us, Lord, and remember we are but dust. The Lord has been very tender and pitiful and I believe drawn me near to himself. The services seem so exactly fitting and I believe he has enabled me at times to fall into his hands and know no will but his. It has indeed been very hard to nature in losing my dear youngest brother of whom I was so fond.

September 11th, 1918 – Heard Mr Caleb Sawyer very well indeed. It was the first time he preached at Galeed and he knew nothing at all of our sorrow and loss, and his remarks were most fitting when he spoke of rejoicing in Christ as a Brother born for adversity, and said it might be in some heavy blow, just as if he had known our case.

May, 1919 – Our pastor spoke from John 11: 15: 'I am glad for your sakes that I was not there' etc.[449] It was a remarkable discourse on Christ delaying answers for our good and his glory. He said: 'Could not the Lord have prevented this trouble, this death? Yes, but it is better that he should not, better for you and glory will come to him.'

Mr Clayton

George Preston

As the following obituary of George Preston largely concerns the war, we have inserted it in its entirety. It was originally published in *The Gospel Standard*: [450]

✍ George Preston, a member of the church at Blackpool, entered into his eternal rest on April 22nd, 1922, aged 43. His godly mother died on March 21st, 1915, and up to the time of her death, George gave no evidence of any desire for religion. He never entered the house of God or paid any attention to the Scriptures, following only the pleasures of the world, and delighting in the company of the ungodly. On the Lord's Day following the funeral of his mother, he attended the chapel with the rest of the family out of respect, but without the least intention of altering his course of life. The Lord, however, had other purposes, and employed his servant, Mr Clayton,[451] to stop his sinful course. The text was John 14: 18, 'I will not leave you comfortless: I will come to you' and while he was preaching, the arrow entered his heart. The change made was evident to those who had previously known him, though he said little about it.

In November, 1916, he was called to the colours, and in the following January sailed for Egypt. During this passage an alarm was raised (which proved to be false), and all the men were called on deck. It was the Lord's Day, and the men were card playing, singing foolish songs, and following all kinds of worldly amusements. George was thinking what a state they were in if it should be the Lord's appointed time to cut them down, when he heard a voice from behind saying, 'If there is *one,* I will not destroy.' Not being very well acquainted with the Word of God, he could not understand what it meant, but the words never left him, and he was led to meditate on them afterwards. While in Egypt, the Lord was pleased to lay on him his afflicting hand, and to deepen the work in his soul. He was taken with haemorrhage of the lungs, which brought him to the border of the grave; and whilst lying in hospital, he received a *Gospel Standard* for May, 1916, containing a sermon, 'Remember now thy Creator,' by Mr. Popham.[452] This brought him to the bar of justice, and he pleaded guilty, suing for mercy as a lost, ruined sinner.

Being now unfit for the army, he was invalided home in November of that year. Many times did he fear, when on the ship, that he would not live to reach England; especially when another man died at Gibraltar, and was landed for burial; but he safely reached London, and was placed in hospital there for a few weeks, reaching his home at Blackpool on December 5th, 1917. His great desire now was to be in the house of God, whenever the doors were open. On one occasion at the prayer meeting he was asked to give out a hymn, and he intended giving out, 'Immortal honours' (No. 667, *Gadsby's Selection*); but being rather confused, he gave out No. 668, where the line is repeated, 'But pleads the blood that did for sin atone.' When he read the hymn, he was quite broken down, and saw the hand of the Lord in directing him to it. He was very tried about the pardon of sin, but the following Easter (1919), when in his garden thinking on the love of God, his burden was suddenly removed, and pardon, peace, and love flowed into his soul. He felt to have been completely turned round (to use his own words), and as if he were dreaming (Psalm 126). Not feeling quite sure of the reality of his experience, he that night asked the Lord, if it were true, to confirm it on the following day (Sunday). The minister gave out the hymn: 'Hark! my soul, it is the Lord,' and these words were powerfully applied to him:

> Thou shalt see my glory soon,
> When the work of grace is done.[453]

This satisfied him, and he was enabled to walk in the liberty of the gospel. He had the ordinance of believers' baptism laid on his mind, but in that December was laid aside with another attack of haemorrhage, and he feared he was going to die without being able to follow the Lord. It pleased the Lord, however, to restore him, and he was baptised on December 21st, by Mr Booth,[454] without taking the slightest harm, although considered to be in a delicate state of health.

Towards the end of 1921, it could be seen that he was rapidly declining; and about a week before he took to his bed, he had such a time in reading and meditation that he declared nothing could exceed it, except glory. Up to the end he had the impression he should recover again, and spoke hopefully of returning to the services of the Lord's house; but the Lord willed otherwise, and took him home to himself on April 22nd, 1922. He was interred in the chapel graveyard at Garstang by Mr Dunderdale[455] (in accordance with his own wishes), close to the grave of his mother, whose many prayers for him had been abundantly answered after her death, to await the resurrection morning. His widow and family, the church at Blackpool, and many who knew and loved him deeply, feel the loss. Truly this was 'a brand plucked from the burning.'

Harry Salkeld

Mr Salkeld's account of his involvement in the war, published under the title of *The Vital Year*, is well known, and still in print. Here we include a slightly different account of Mr Salkeld's wartime experiences, taken from another book he wrote, *The Night Watches*. After his return from the war, he was baptised and joined the church at Sale, Cheshire. Sent into the ministry, in 1947 he became pastor at Bradford on Avon, Wiltshire. He resigned his pastorate in 1960, returning to itinerant preaching. In later life he settled in the congregation at Chippenham, Wiltshire. His ministry spanned more than 60 years. He passed away on 14th July, 1995, aged 96 years.

✍ I joined the army in March 1917, and together with about 50 other raw recruits from Bristol began hard training on the edge of Salisbury Plain, a few miles from Warminster in Wiltshire.

Having been issued with – and trained in the use of – the army rifle, one evening several of us were detailed to set off for Warminster Railway Station, adjoining which was a large area of railway sidings, used as an open goods yard. Here there were several large haystacks which belonged to the army authorities, and were for the army horses, as these creatures played a very active and important part in the war of 1914-1918. There were three of us detailed for duty under a non-commissioned officer, to act as a night patrol to guard the haystack, in case of any attempt at robbery or incendiarism. Each man was expected to do two hours on duty, and two hours off. I well remember how, when my turn of duty arrived and I marched off with my companion in charge, my thoughts were concentrated on the prospect before me of two hours alone in the gathering darkness. It was certainly a weird and rather eerie experience, patrolling between those bulky haystacks, whose dim outlines were only just visible in the surrounding darkness. The only sounds were from small nocturnal creatures and occasionally an owl, but each little sound seemed magnified, and tended to fill one with a dread of the unknown. It was a test for the nerves, as no doubt it was meant to be – but it was also a trial for faith, and although young in years, and unlearned in the deep things of God, yet it brought out the prayer of felt necessity and an urgent cry for help, which, under God, allayed the present fears. Before setting out for this night watching duty, the officer in charge had warned us that an officer might appear before us during the night – on inspection, and demand that we hand over our rifle to him to look it over. This, we were told, we must on no account do, although bidden by a superior officer. I was certainly troubled in mind as to how to react if so accosted, but mercifully this trial did not materialise.

This first night patrol helped to strengthen and fortify for those severer trials still to come. These came soon enough, when, having been drafted overseas, first to France and then to Belgium, the hard and dangerous business of trench warfare was experienced.

To reach the trench system involved a slow journey in single file along a narrow (duckboard) track, which was often slippery in wet weather. One slip could often mean plunging knee deep into a nearby shell hole, half filled with muddy water. These journeys were always made after nightfall, which added to the hazards, and as no lights were allowed, it was necessary to keep within touching distance of each other. This particular route led through what had once been a pleasant wooded area, known as Sanctuary Wood, with undulating ground, and in peacetime it must have been quite attractive.

Now, however, the devastation caused by modern warfare had played havoc with those beauties of nature, and constant and incessant shelling had reduced the trees to bare stumps about 5 to 6 feet in height with jagged and splintered tops. To walk through this area was a strange and uncanny experience, especially in moonlight, when the torn tree stumps almost seemed like human beings, and I believe most of us were relieved when this part was left behind.

When eventually the wooden duckboard track came to an end, there was a space of about 50 yards to be traversed over open ground before the beginning of the trench system was reached, and it would have been almost impossible to cover this stretch in the darkness without some help and guidance. This had been provided by the Royal Engineers, in the form of a line of luminous tape, which shone out in the dark like a glow-worm. It was literally a 'kindly light' to 'lead amidst the encircling gloom' and following this glowing tape we entered first the communicator trench, and then the second line, and found ourselves in the very front line trenches, with only a stretch of no-man's-land separating ourselves from the Germans, our enemy.

Harry Salkeld

The first night-watching experience in the front line was a testing experience, as it rained all night long, and how we longed to see the first streak of daylight appear, with the hope of a clearance in the weather; which did eventually come about as the day wore on. However, daylight brought activity from the German side, and a number of their trench mortar bombs came over, one of which fell and exploded among a section of our men, to the left of my position.

One man was killed and all the others were wounded. The next day a similar incident occurred, this time to the right of us, and one was killed and others suffered injury. Looking back many times upon these solemn incidents, the words of the hymn have often followed,

> Plagues and deaths around me fly;
> Till he bids, I cannot die;
> Not a single shaft can hit,
> Till the God of love sees fit.[456]

'Night-watching' in the front line trenches was a great strain, because when naturally we should be asleep, we had to be wide awake all night long, and not only for one night – but for several in succession. Of course, sometimes weariness of body and mind did get the upper hand, and then it was a case of dropping off to sleep momentarily, standing on our feet. Because of this, we got into the habit of prodding one another occasionally through the night, so as not to be caught off our guard by the officer of the watch. Sometimes a few picked men were employed at night to patrol in what was known as 'no-man's-land,' i.e. the empty space between the opposing lines of trenches. It was a very hazardous and dangerous task, but it was adopted by both sides, with the object of ascertaining possible enemy movements and signs of preparation for an attack. At times during the night, one side or the other would send up into the sky, a star shell or Very light, planned to drop in 'no-man's-land,' which could light up the whole area for a few moments, and then the night watch men on patrol had to lie low and keep still.

The ordeal of front line night-watching in the First World War did produce certain effects, one of which was a longing and yearning to see the daylight appear in the east – even though we realised only too well what trials and dangers the light of day could bring in its train.

If one particular night was clear and starry, this would provide added interest, because as dawn appeared, first one and then others of the starry lights disappeared from sight until one bright star alone remained, and seemed to reign supreme in the sky – the 'morning star' – the beautiful herald of the dawn. To wait and watch through a long, dark night out in the open, feeling cold and weary, and then to witness with one's own eyes that glorious star of promise, is something one will never forget. But, what a mercy to know something of the vital, spiritual truth enshrined in it. As Charles Wesley so well describes it,

> Christ, whose glory fills the skies,
> Christ, the true, the only Light;
> Sun of Righteousness, arise,
> Triumph o'er the shades of night;
> Dayspring from on high, be near,
> Day star, in my heart appear.[457]

The army division to which I belonged was moved

from the Ypres area to a sector further south, near St. Quentin – in northern France. When this changeover took place – one dark night – the Germans were evidently aware of it, and as we set off along the duckboard track, they shelled the area continually. We had been urged to spread out as thinly as possible, so as to avoid heavy casualties. Two of us were walking one behind the other, when the scream of a shell sounding very near made us halt abruptly. At that moment the shell pitched close to the track only a few yards in front of us, and buried itself in the earth without exploding. It was a 'dud.'

We both heaved a sigh of relief, and tried to acknowledge the goodness of God in this merciful deliverance. The rest of the journey back to camp passed without further incident, and our night-watching in the trenches was now at an end, but many other 'watches in the night' were to follow in due time, and for some of us they were to be very strange and unexpected.

Not long before the extensive troop movement mentioned above, an incident occurred in connection with the Company of Light Infantry in which I was serving which was unusual and happily rare, although at the time, most alarming. After we had spent our allotted period in the front line trenches, we returned to a base camp some miles in the rear, and engaged in training exercises during the day and also occasional working parties at night, which consisted in carrying various materials such as duckboards, rolls of barbed wire, etc. from the Royal Engineers stores up to the trench system.

On one such occasion, during the night watches, the whole battalion of four companies was employed in this work. The load which each man was expected to carry was quite heavy enough, and difficult, especially if it was a roll of barbed wire on the end of a pole – remembering that it had to be done at night on a narrow wooden track which could often be slippery in wet weather. All of us made one journey, and on returning to the 'store dump' we expected in our simplicity that the night's work was done and a return to the base camp would follow. However, our hearts sank when we were faced with another load waiting for us, and told we would all have to make a second journey. When this was finally accomplished, not without very tired bodies and legs, three of the four companies were allowed to return to the base but the fourth (D) company, to which I belonged, was held back by the officer in charge of the stores, who told us that as there was still some material yet to be moved, we would have to make a third journey to complete the night's work.

It was here that grave trouble arose, because all of us were feeling almost at the end of our strength, and there was a sense of unfairness in allowing some to go back to camp whilst we alone were being forced to make a third, loaded, journey. Most of us, however, realising it was wartime and we were under military orders, would have undertaken the task under protest, but about six of our number resolutely refused to obey, contending that the order was wrong and in their view, utterly unfair. This placed us all in a dilemma, and the young officer, a lieutenant, who was in charge of us, spoke straightly and earnestly to the six objectors, showing them the seriousness of their position, and urged them to fall in line with the rest of us. Unhappily this had no effect, and so, in a desperate effort to avoid damaging results with serious consequences, several of our own men decided to approach the six hard core rebels, and if possible to change them over to reason and orderly obedience. However, this last effort was no more successful than the first, and so we were left earnestly debating among ourselves what was best for us as the next step: this was something none of us had ever anticipated, and the outcome of which none of us could foresee. Thus, under the open canopy of heaven, in the darkness of a dark night, and fraught with circumstances still darker, we reasoned together as to our best course. If we, the majority, decided to obey the order and make the third journey ourselves, and leave the six objectors behind, we hardly dared contemplate the final outcome, which might well have been the extreme penalty for some, if not all of them. As we argued and reasoned together, the sense of comradeship in wartime undoubtedly weighed heavily with us, and it was finally agreed that if we joined together as one, there was more hope of saving them from the firing squad than if we left them in isolation. It was a solemn and serious step to take, and the consequences for all of us were no less so. Thus, we all took part with the six objectors, and returned to the base camp as a whole company, having disobeyed a military order in time of war.

During the evening we learned that a possible means of punishment, and as an example, would be to have 10 of us picked out at random and shot at dawn. It was with this on our minds that we went to bed that night, and sleep was impossible. In one's own simple way, many a cry went up to God during the night watches, that he might grant deliverance and save us from the extremity which seemed to be threatening. Through the Lord's goodness and mercy we were spared, but nevertheless, severe punishment was meted out, first by being ordered to undergo a route march of 10 miles with full pack; and all pay and leave to be withheld for the remainder of the war.

Finally, we were subjected, on one particular day, to the semblance of a court martial. The rest of the battalion were drawn up fully armed to form a large square. We, the erring company, stood outside the square, unarmed and in fatigue dress. At a given signal we were commanded to enter the square, running into the middle, led by our young officer, and there we stood at attention. Facing us, and sitting on a fine horse, was the brigadier general, who then addressed us in forceful words, reminding us of the duties and obligations of serving soldiers in time of war.

The motive which moved the majority of us to side with the minority in this case was a strong desire, as comrades-in-arms, to shield the rebel six from the severity of punishment which might well have followed. It is said that there is safety in numbers, and no doubt it did in some respects influence the result. But nevertheless, I believe that above all it was urgent secret prayer to Almighty God which was heard and answered on this occasion.

It was dark indeed during those night watches, and fraught with dangers and forebodings with us all, but relief and deliverance, and light out of darkness appeared in due time, though we all had to learn our lesson the hard way, and certainly the lessons of life, so learnt, are usually the most abiding and useful.

It wasn't long after this episode that we moved out of Belgium into northern France, and settled in a pleasant country district close to the small town of Nesle, a few miles from Amiens, and about 10 miles from the front line. We were now part of General Gough's 5th Army, which bore the brunt of the huge German attack of 21st March, 1918.[458]

During the very early hours of that morning the enemy began a massive bombardment of our front line position, and from where we were billeted, 10 miles away, it sounded like one continuous roll of thunder. After an early breakfast we clambered into army lorries and were driven towards the advancing Germans.

On the way we passed large numbers of French peasants fleeing from the enemy, and trundling prams and handcarts, and some with young children – it was a touching sight. At the village of St. Simon we got out, and having collected spades and pickaxes from an army stores, we soon arrived at the Crozat Canal and began a march along the towpath, spreading out as thinly as possible. Then orders were given us to commence digging sectional trenches, each trench to be sufficient to hold four men; and the distance between the sections to be about 15 yards. In this way the whole battalion covered about a one mile stretch of the canal. As the light began to fail and the darkness of night came on, we were still digging when our colonel came along to inspect and to encourage us. He said, 'Now you young men of England, you are just a thin khaki line of resistance against the enemy, and I look to you to oppose him to the utmost of your ability.'

We learned later that all our artillery, both large and small, had been withdrawn to prepared positions some miles back, and so very literally we, the infantry, were left to oppose, resist and delay the Germans with their massive armaments and manpower, against which we had only our rifles, bayonets and a few small Lewis guns.[459]

The first night watch along the canal towpath was peaceful, and most of us managed to snatch a little sleep. The following day began with a thick mist, but as it cleared German shells began to crash over into the woods on either side of the canal, and one fell into the canal itself right opposite our trench, sending up a huge fountain of water, giving us all a drenching. We realised that the enemy had located our position, and that the German infantry must be close to the canal itself.

That second night watching was not at all peaceful, but found us full of anxiety and apprehension, and very much on the watch. During the night some of the enemy infantry, having reached the opposite bank of the canal, were able to cross over, assisted by the foggy conditions; and a few of our own men, who had managed to escape being overrun, came to us in haste and almost breathless to warn us of the danger we were facing if we remained on the canal towpath. It was clear that we could not stay any longer, and so an immediate retreat was ordered, which meant getting through the thick woodland behind us, and the only way through was by a narrow wooden gangway, raised up and supported by posts above the water below.

As we commenced our journey in single file along the narrow track, a German machine gun from the opposite side of the canal opened up against us, splintering the tree trunks on either side. It was nothing short of a miracle of divine mercy that none of us was hit, and so we plodded on until eventually emerging on to an open field, where we joined up with other British troops, and then moved on together.

A fast flowing stream had to be crossed, the water being about knee deep in the middle, but such was our emotional stress and strain at the time that we hardly realised our legs and feet were wet.

From this point we came upon a large ploughed field, and began to go across, though not without difficulty and it was hard going. Here, however, a striking incident occurred, which has remained indelibly impressed upon the memory since it occurred – 66 years ago.

As we moved out into the open field, several German machine guns on the edge of the woodland behind us began to sweep the field with devastating effect, and I am afraid our casualties were heavy. Then, all of a sudden, from among our ranks, a young soldier called out in a loud, clear voice, saying, 'Friends, isn't it a shame to have our backs to the enemy? Let's turn round and face him!'

To all of us who heard, the effect was viral and spontaneous. With a momentary sense of shame there came a surge of courage, and so we all stopped, made a right about turn, ran back for about 50 yards, lay in the prone position, and opened up against the enemy with all we had, which was chiefly the rifle.

Apart from short breaks for reloading, we kept up a continuous fire, and only ceased when there was the realised danger of running out of ammunition. When we finally stopped, we were relieved to find that the Germans had ceased to fire also, so that our brief counter-attack had been effective, and had given us renewed courage.

We are told in Psalm 78: 9 that: 'The children of Ephraim, being armed, and carrying bows, turned back in the day of battle.' Sometimes the people of God are sorely tempted to do the same, when opposed by the powers of darkness, hell, sin and Satan, and their own treacherous hearts: yet if the Lord is pleased to speak to the trembling, fearful soul, as he did to Joshua, and say, 'Have not I commanded thee? Be strong and of a good courage; be not afraid, neither be thou dismayed: for the LORD thy God is with thee whithersoever thou goest' (Joshua 1: 9), then out of weakness felt, that soul is surely made strong – in the Lord.

Continuing over the ploughed fields now unmolested by German gunfire, we came upon a deep railway cutting, which afforded welcome rest and relief. However, it was deemed unwise to stay there long in case we should find ourselves cut off by the enemy, so proceeding across the railway line, we came to another large ploughed field, and as the shades of evening were upon us, it was decided to dig sectional trenches here before nightfall – to afford as much shelter as possible, and await events as daylight appeared. The spades and pickaxes had to be abandoned on leaving the canal, and so we had to rely upon the small entrenching tool which each serving soldier was provided with.

These were useful in their way, but meant much harder work and the job took considerably longer. In consequence, it was almost midnight before we had finished the task, and feeling very hungry we had to fall back on 'iron rations,' consisting of some hard biscuit and 'bully beef,' kept by each man for emergencies.

By early dawn everything was shrouded in thick mist, but as it gradually cleared, a German plane flew low overhead, and we feared that our position had now been located. This proved to be only too true, and before long the enemy artillery began to rain shells around us, and to such an extent that we all realised our position was fast becoming untenable. The only officer among us then gave the command: 'Every man for himself' (the only time one ever heard such an order), and we scrambled out of the trenches and made for whatever building offered the nearest shelter. Several of us made for a large farm with numerous outbuildings situated somewhat to the right of us, not realising that it was already in German occupation, and on entering the courtyard we found ourselves surrounded by armed men and became prisoners of war.

Led out into a nearby road, we were joined by others of our kith and kin who also had fallen into the hands of the enemy, and after marching several miles and the daylight fading, we came to a halt by the roadside, and moving onto some waste ground with German guards around us we spent that first night of captivity in the open, sitting and lying on the cold, rough ground, with no warm greatcoats, and glad to huddle as close together as possible for some extra warmth.

Of all the night watches one had known, this was the strangest and most unusual of all. There was no sleep that night, and the mind was flooded with a multitude of thoughts, the chief of which was the wonder of still being alive and thus spared through the rich mercy of God, to whom one's humble thanks went up with a truly feeling heart. Had we then known what lay before us our hearts might well have sunk in dismay, because over the next three days we were to march over 50 miles with no food or drink to sustain us and hardly any sleep.

Not until we reached Landrecies on the evening of the third day was there food provided (soup and black bread) at a large prisoner of war compound. From this place, within a few days, we set off by train for Germany, crossing the Rhine at Coblenz and travelling up the beautiful Lahn valley, stopping one night at Giessen, a small and fashionable university town, and having a brief view of Eisenach, with the Wartburg Castle on the hill among the trees, so famous in the life of Martin Luther. Our final destination was Chemnitz in what was then known as Saxony, and here a former German cavalry barracks had been turned over for the use of prisoners of war.

There must have been several thousands of us at this place, including Russians, French, British, Italians and Serbians, and working parties were sent out from here to various destinations. Some of us were detailed for work at a large surface coal mine in lower Saxony, not far from the Austrian border. The small prisoners' compound here was occupied by several nationalities, and the wooden hut in which I slept contained British, Italians and Russians.

The hours of work were from 6 a.m. to 6 p.m. for six days a week and half day on Sunday. We were roused each morning at 4.30 a.m., out of a deep sleep, as the German postern came and poked us in the ribs with the butt end of his rifle, and called out: 'Stehen sie auf, stehen sie auf,' in other words, 'Get up, and get out.'

Among the night watches at this place, one stands out still as a memorable occasion. We had all got into our bunk beds about 8 p.m., feeling tired and weary, when I remembered my small pocket Bible, given by Christian friends at Norwich before leaving for France. I kept this Bible under the pillow, so pulling it out, I sat up for a few moments and read in the Psalms, afterward putting the book back under the pillow. Then a man in a bed near to mine stretched out his hand and touched me saying: 'Excuse me, but what was that little book you were looking at just now?' I pulled it out again, and held it up for him to see. 'Ah,' he said. 'I thought it was,' and putting his hand under his own pillow he drew out a small Bible, similar to mine, and said: 'You see, I have one too! and, my friend, what should we do at a time like this, under these hard conditions, had we no precious Word of God to turn to!' 'Indeed,' I answered, 'it is like a lifeline, and a light in a dark place.' Our mutual love and regard for the Word of God drew us together and I count that memorable experience as one of the outstanding memories during captivity.

Working alternately one week on day shift, and the next on night shift, we found it hard and laborious work with pick and shovel, and looking back on it now after all these years, one can only say: 'Who could have held me up, but thou.'

Later, some of us were transferred to Leipsic, working this time at a corn and forage merchants in one of the suburbs. This involved a long walk through the heart of the city, which is certainly an attractive place, and the railway station is very handsome and is one of the largest I have seen.

Then in October, 1918, a few of us were moved to a small township a few miles from Leipsic to work at a sawmill and timber yard. The number of prisoners here was comparatively small, equally divided between British and French, and we shared a communal dining room.

On the morning of 11th November, 1918, we went to work as usual, and everything seemed normal until soon after dinner time. Then in the early afternoon came running towards us a woman who said she understood on good authority that an armistice had been signed between the combatants in France, and that the war was over. The British and French forces had gained the day, and the Germans had been overcome. It was a day of rejoicing, and we Britishers who were working together gave a hearty cheer, but the Germans were quiet and glum, though they must have been thankful to see an end to the conflict, for their shops were almost bare of food due to the blockade of their ports by the British Navy.

Late in December transport was arranged to take us back to England, and a British light cruiser, returning from the Baltic Sea, called at Stettin to pick up the last 500, which included myself. We marched from a camp about three miles away, and arrived at the dock gates in the evening and well after dark. As the gates were opened we marched in seemingly into inky blackness. Those night watches were dark indeed. But then, in a moment, everything was transformed and the place was lit up with brilliant light. About six naval searchlights were suddenly shone up into the air, all of them meeting together at the top of a masthead where, proudly fluttering in the breeze was the Union Jack – our national flag, and symbol of freedom and liberty. To us it was a unique

> occasion, and as we tried to raise a hearty cheer, tears of emotion streamed from our eyes. This was among those night watches to remain deeply impressed upon the memory.
>
> The journey through the southern Baltic, and the straits, and across the North Sea, took about three days, and we finally disembarked at Hull, going on by train to Ripon, and then from there to our various destinations. Such a homecoming, with such a background of trials, hazards and dangers, can be, and certainly was, highly charged with emotion, but the prevailing feeling was a humbling sense of God's mercy and goodness in preserving life and sparing such an unworthy sinner.[460]

Ernest Shaw

Ernest Shaw grew up in the congregation at Rochdale Road Chapel, Manchester, where his father, Henry Shaw, was a deacon. During the war he served in France and was also part of the force sent to Salonika, in neutral Greece, in May, 1915, in an attempt to relieve the Serbians. He was awarded the Military Cross for his bravery in 1917.[461] After the war Ernest was baptised, with his sister, in 1919 at Rochdale Road Chapel, Manchester. Then in 1924 he took a post with the Dewsbury Corporation as an engineer and surveyor. This resulted in him moving from Manchester and he transferred his membership to the church at Ossett. In this position he was responsible for the building of the bridges at Savile Town and on Slaithwaite Road, Dewsbury. Both bridges are still standing today, and when he died an article in the local newspaper was titled, "Two Bridges are Monuments to his Skill." In 1928 he was sent into the ministry, and was a faithful minister in the north of England until his sudden death in 1947, aged 57. He served on the committee responsible for compiling and publishing *The Companion Tune Book*.[462]

Ernest Shaw

The following is his account of his war service, as was published in his obituary in *The Gospel Standard*.[463] The editorial comments within the account (given in italicised text) are those of Mr William Griffiths Vaughan, the pastor at Bradford, who took a part in Mr Shaw's funeral service:

✍ In November, 1915, I was called to go overseas with the Royal Fusiliers. I went with the constant prayer that the hand of God might be with me in a marked way, either to be brought back in safety to praise him for it, or if cut down in action, to comfortably realise a sweet union with Christ and prove the support of his everlasting arms of love in Jordan's icy flood.

On December 8th I found myself in most trying conditions in the support line at Festubert ... My spirits sank to a very low ebb and I feared that God had cut me completely off into darkness. It was a terribly discouraging condition of things from a physical standpoint, but my greatest burden was that I was surrounded with such deadness, darkness and desolation in my soul and mind as to feel at the end of everything but trouble, as if the accuser should say: 'Prepare to die, for there will I spill thy soul' (Bunyan). Almost mechanically I took out my Bible and my eyes fell on Psalm 27: 'The Lord is my light and my salvation; whom shall I fear?' My heart began to warm and melt, and I read on: 'Though an host should encamp against me … in this will I be confident.' Truly the word was a lamp unto my feet and a light unto my path. Nay, it was a very fire in my soul. My eyes streamed down with tears; in a moment such sweet contentment stole into my soul:

> My soul was in my ears;
> My heart was all on flame;
> My eyes were sweetly drowned in tears,
> And melted was my frame.[464]

Such an unction! And the next verse very sweetly and solemnly rested upon my spirit as a sacred vow unto my God: 'One thing have I desired of the Lord, that will I seek after; that I may dwell in the house of the Lord all the days of my life, to behold the beauty of the Lord, and to enquire in his temple. For in the time of trouble he shall hide me in his pavilion.' I felt persuaded that the God of Jacob was my God, and that I should be a spiritual overcomer; and if the Lord should be pleased to bring me back in safety it would be my privilege to pay the vow and walk and enquire diligently in his temple. A sweet and solid peace entered my soul, and I knew that I had not come into this wilderness for nought. I could see the truth of what the Lord said by Hosea: 'Behold, I will allure her, and bring her into the wilderness, and speak comfortably unto her. And I will give her her vineyards from thence, and the valley of Achor for a door of hope.' I felt during those few minutes, if called upon to lay down my life, that the gate of death would but prove the portal of immortal bliss.

A few days later the full significance of those words, 'For in the time of trouble,' etc., was brought forcibly to my mind when the dugout collapsed upon myself and a few companions ... Truly I proved that in the time of trouble God had hidden me spiritually and providentially in the pavilion of his overshadowing and covenant love. How I felt that God had turned away from his fierce anger in respect of my sin! How I should have liked to have retained the confidence and assurance of that sweet season! But the very remembrance has since, at times, been as a little dew on the parched branch. Much has come to cast me down, but the full burden of guilt never has returned.

After relating a time of weakening in faith and love, he tells of a sweet confirmation of the continued support of his God when his company was being relieved near Givenchy in 1916.

As I was coming down a communication trench, the shelling became very intense and was concentrated on a spot where the troops were crowded together; it seemed impossible to pass. With misgiving I begged the Lord to give me another token of his special presence. Almost immediately the words dropped into my mind:

> Amidst ten thousand dangers,
> Which everywhere abound,
> The pilgrims and the strangers
> Alone secure are found.[465]

I was at once melted with gratitude, and felt if the Lord should again bring me through, what a comforting evidence! Yes, I felt sure of it. A stranger? Yes; rather, a fellow citizen with the saints in my soul's experience. Not a stranger to the knowledge of God, but a stranger to the old things and supports of the world. Such a calm came over me and I felt it would be well in life, and well if the silver cord were loosed and the golden bowl broken. Yes!

> In every state secure,
> Kept as Jehovah's eye,
> 'Twas well with me whilst life endured,
> And well if called to die.[466]

But soon I had to prove that it is one experience to feel for a few moments to have a religion with which to die, and another experience to have a constant fear of God in act and exercise in the soul, which will weather the subtle temptations of a bewitching world, of the devil, and of our own turpitude.

Being recommended for a commission he was sent back from the line, and when removed from immediate danger he was concerned to find an indifference and lukewarmness creeping over the mind. He feared that his experience when in great danger was only a hypocritical emotion brought on by the fear of death. How exactly Gadsby's words fitted his feelings!

> *O make this heart rejoice or ache,*
> *Decide this doubt for me;*
> *And if it be not broken, break,*
> *And heal it if it be.*[467]

A ministerial friend enlightened him as to the probable cause of his dark state – a backsliding spirit, forsaking the way of truth, neglecting the throne of grace, a tardiness to read God's word. He analyses this and quotes much from Bunyan's Holy War where Mr Godly-Fear cannot make merry at the feasts of Mr Carnal-Security, for in all his darkness there was still kept alive, even as 'an odd flicker,' a certain unctuous fear, and the breathing of his soul when he came to himself was,

> *Return, O holy Dove! Return,*
> *Sweet messenger of rest;*
> *I hate the sins that made thee mourn,*
> *And drove thee from my breast.*[468]

Then in Macedonia, after being commissioned, his account continues:

May 1917 – I found myself in the midst of preparation for the second battle of Doiran.[469] As was customary with the prospect of an engagement, I set myself to write a few things as a comfort to the home people in the event of death in action. But there seemed such darkness, such reluctance to write that I became beset by two very conflicting thoughts. I believe one came from the very devil, and it was this: That I knew myself to be a hypocrite, and there was at least in my mind the desire not to deceive others and leave a false impression. The second thought was the sweet comforting one that my God would once more appear and I should be brought safely through the coming fight, and so consequently no written account was necessary. How I longed and prayed for some solid promise from God which would decide the matter beforehand for me! In reading my Bible the day before the engagement, my eye was directed to Jeremiah 46: 'And Jacob shall return, and be in rest and at ease, and none shall make him afraid.' The matter was decided in a moment, and I could look forward with confidence and equanimity to the issue of my part in the impending battle. My faith laid hold on the promise, and my heart overflowed with gratitude. So it was that amidst ghastly scenes, the presence of God spread such a calm in my being that I was enabled to carry on my duties cheerfully and unmoved. Truly the work of righteousness was peace, and the effect of righteousness, quietness and assurance ... I returned from the field faint in body but in mind as a giant refreshed. The sweetness of that deliverance lasted many days, and on one occasion the thought dropped forcibly into my mind: 'My witness is in heaven; my record is on high;' and this comforting verse followed,

> His love in time past forbids me to think
> He'll leave me at last in trouble to sink.[470]

He was awarded the Military Cross for skilful handling of a difficult situation when many officers had been killed. But of this there appears no mention in his own narrative.

The following two brief extracts from letters Ernest Shaw wrote to his sister (who was baptised with him in 1919) from the front, were included with his obituary in *The Gospel Standard.*

✎ January, 1918 – I read with a soft heart and brimming eyes your account of the Lord's dealings with your soul ... How many times have I longed for a word to assure me that I have really had a beginning in the path of experimental knowledge! ... Sometimes the solemn scene of being deceived has rent my very heart and I have pictured myself in despair at last, crushed by the sentence of the divine Judge: 'Who hath required this at thy hand, to tread my courts?' And despite solemn warnings, I have felt at times such indifference, such a coquetting with worldly things and secret sins, that I have had to ask: 'Can ever God dwell here?' But I cannot give up, satisfied with a worldling's peace. I cannot assuage the uneasiness of spirit. I cannot settle down in a fake confidence ... They are only well supported, well kept, whom God keeps. He alone can speak peace to the troubled soul. If he speak peace, who then can bring final trouble? Real religion is, as J— used to say before he died, a matter between God and the soul. The soul whom God wounds, that soul he finally heals, because it stands immune from penal wrath in the Person of the Son. Therefore it is said of the poor sin-bitten and bruised soul, in respect of the judgement of a holy God: 'Though he cause grief, yet will he have compassion;' and the guilty sinner fearfully cries: 'Lord, look upon the face of thine Anointed (Christ), and send down answers of peace.' What a mercy our unworthiness is no bar to sovereign mercy!

May, 1918, from a convalescent camp – I find it true: 'None can keep alive his own soul.' But then again, although the heart is often drawn after strange vanities, they bring us no comfort and we are only content when we get from the enchanted ground to the Rock of good hope, and in our right moments we say:

> Hence, vain, intruding world, depart;
> No more allure nor vex my heart;
> Let every vanity be gone;
> I would be peaceful and alone.[471]

I have felt like one of old at times: 'I had rather be a doorkeeper in the house of my God, than to dwell in the tents of wickedness.' ...[472]

At sea on a naval vessel

Charles Alfred Smith

Mr Smith was, in later life, a faithful minister of the Gospel and for over 30 years the pastor at Jarvis Brook Chapel, Sussex. He died on 7th January, 1983, aged 86. The following details of his experience are gleaned from his own writings, as published in his obituary in *The Gospel Standard*: [473]

✍ At the age of 18 I had to join the army and, having a desire to hear, I used to attend Aldershot chapel and sometimes on a weekend off at Brockham Green, where I had friends. Mr Haddow,[474] who was then at Brockham Green, often used to send me home mourning over my sins.

It was not long before I was sent overseas, and soon found myself out in the Atlantic in a very severe storm which crippled our ship and tossed it about like a cork. I was ill with sea sickness, and now felt the Lord was about to make an end of me and perish I must, soul and body. It was very real and no way out, and here I believe the Lord put a spirit of prayer in my poor soul that he would have mercy on us and calm the troubled seas.

The next morning was a bright, sunny morning, and I felt the Lord had heard my cry and spared our lives. Now how I tried to live a better life, walk more holy, lead a life more pleasing to God, but I feel the poet expresses me better here:

> The more I strove against sin's power,
> I sinned and stumbled but the more.[475]

So I went on a miserable man, mourning over my failings, but this sometimes brought a cry out of my heart for mercy. It was on Christmas Day, 1916, when, very weak after an attack of dysentery, I, with three others, set out to visit Mars Hill in Greece, but I had to fall out on the way and was left alone resting, to await the return of the others, when I believe the Holy Spirit came and preached Jesus into my soul as the Saviour of sinners. It came through these words of the Lord Jesus himself: 'Foxes have holes, and the birds of the air have nests; but the Son of man hath not where to lay his head.'

Here I believe the Lord gave me a faith's view of Jesus Christ and all he is to a poor, lost sinner in despair: his sacrifice, his atoning sacrifice; the efficacious power of his blood – whom I once despised – to atone for sin (yes, for one so vile as me), was made precious. I can never describe the feelings and joy I felt. I have often felt the Holy Spirit came and preached Christ to me in the wilderness when I had not one companion to whom I could talk of these better things.[476]

One other wartime experience which Mr Smith related on more than one occasion when preaching in later life was as follows. One fine Lord's Day morning, sailing on a ship through the Straits of Gibraltar, Mr Smith was attending the morning service, which was being held on the deck of the ship. As they passed the Rock, they sang Augustus Toplady's well-known hymn, 'Rock of Ages, cleft for me.' For a moment he was lifted above the view of the Rock of Gibraltar they were passing and he was blessed with a sense of safety in the Rock which is Christ Jesus. It was a never to be forgotten time for him.

John William Tyler

Mr Tyler was born in London in 1887 and as a young man attended the ministry of Mr Eli Ashdown at Zoar Chapel, Great Alie Street. Not long before the war, he married Miss Dann from Zoar Chapel, The Dicker, East Sussex. They set up home in London, and their son, John (later known as John William Sperling-Tyler), was born in 1912. During the war, with service inevitable, Mr Tyler moved his family out of London to Sussex to live near his parents-in-law while he was away fighting. He saw action in Egypt, Salonika and the Balkans.

Mr Tyler's account continues to include details of his return home and resettling to civilian life. Like many

Mr Eli Ashdown (left) with his wife (sitting, right) and family

men he had no job, and even home was uncertain. But as with so many of the Lord's people, Mr Tyler experienced the Lord's provision in both these regards. In later life, Mr Tyler was a deacon at Zoar Chapel, The Dicker, and in time his son, John, became the pastor there too. He passed away on 27th May, 1985.

✍ In 1914 the war broke out and I knew in time I should have to go into the forces. My father-in-law wrote saying if I had to go, it would be nice for my wife and son to be out of the raids. He had a cottage we could move to, and feeling it was the best thing to do, we tried to sell our business, but without success.

So we closed down and moved to The Dicker.

In a very short time I was in the forces and stationed at Woolwich Barracks, which was as a hell to me. The first opportunity I had to get out was to find Mr [*Robert*] Webb's[477] chapel at Plumstead. When I got there it was a prayer meeting, and it was like heaven to my soul. After a time Mr Webb looked up to where I was sitting and called on 'the young man in khaki' to pray. That meant I did not know how to go again through fear, though I believe the Lord helped me.

I was soon shifted to Oswestry, and well do I remember going home for weekend leave. I was in a barren state of soul and did hope to have something under the ministry. But no, my trouble seemed to increase, and I said to my dear wife, 'Nothing right anywhere, providence or grace.' I went to bed in that frame of mind, when I hope the dear Lord drew near to me, and without a word being spoken so blessed my poor soul and shed abroad his love in my heart. I said to my wife, 'Nothing wrong anywhere, everything right.' I got up in the sweetness of it and had to leave early in the morning under the sweet enjoyment. But as soon as I got to the camp I had such a blow (I believe it was the devil), and I said, 'Nothing in it all, only emotion.' But through mercy I was enabled to go before the Lord, and said if what I had experienced was real, would the dear Lord confirm it. The following Sunday afternoon I lay down with *The Gospel Standard* and read Mr Popham's monthly piece, 'Communications from Christ's fullness,' wherein he so blessedly described what I had felt.[478] The dear Lord granted the sweet confirmation I had prayed for, and my heart was broken under a sense of his goodness to such an unworthy sinner. So I proved the devil to be a liar and wept at the mercy of God.

After a few weeks I had a weekend leave, when two friends were baptised at The Dicker, and was

**John W. Tyler with his wife and son,
later John Sperling-Tyler, the pastor at Dicker Chapel**

made sweetly willing to follow the Lord in the ordinance of believer's baptism. But the dear Lord knew how I was placed and was soon going abroad for three and half years; and how I was tried as to the reality of what I had passed through! It was not long before I had to leave all my dear ones to go to Egypt and to Salonika. While at the base there I felt really awful spiritually. I saw that there was to be a Church of England service held in a marquee, so went and heard the Scriptures read, which was food to my soul. Afterwards I received a letter from home which said that my father-in-law had me so much on his mind at the prayer meeting that Lord's day, and I felt the Lord answered that prayer in my behalf. O how I longed for home and dear ones and the house of God! But such is the path, tribulation in so many ways, but as I write these lines I realise I have never lacked anything that was necessary, due to the goodness of God.

As we were trekking up to the line, we had a pouring wet day, and in trying to get a little shelter in a shed at night I met a man who attended Zion Chapel, Tonbridge, whose name was Will Clarke. We went up the line together and then lost sight of one another for 18 months. We met again at Aljack and he used to come round to my dugout and we had some very nice seasons together in reading the Word of God and prayer. Sometime after I was looking forward to going on leave but was taken very ill with malaria. How I longed to see my dear ones once more, but instead the dear Lord drew so near and shed abroad his love in my heart that I felt all natural relationships removed, and I longed to be gone, so willing for the dear Lord to take me home. From that time I began to get better. O the sweet mercy of God to a poor sinner! It seemed at times impossible that I would ever see home again. I came to within a fortnight of leaving for home when all leave was cancelled, and we were sent over the mountains into Serbia and Bulgaria. Before leaving I read a portion of Scripture which was so sweet to my soul, but have never been able to find it since. But I do know what a gracious help it was to me, and was enabled to commit myself into the hand of God. I was again very ill with malaria but was given strength to carry me through. After a while we sailed along the Bosphorus to a very beautiful spot where we stayed for six months, which was the means in the hand of God of building me up. It was in one of the forts here that a Rev. Kennedy used to hold a little service, and nice little meetings they were. I believe he was a good man.

I was soon on my way back to England and arrived home at the end of July, 1919. It was a wonderful reunion as at times I never expected to see home again, but friends believed I should be brought through and there had been many prayers in my behalf. It was a great disappointment to me to find we could not stay in the cottage at The Dicker. However, I felt it to be a great blessing to be again favoured to go to the house of God, with the desire that one might be enabled to honour the dear Lord.

I now became deeply concerned as to what to do to earn a living. I was told of a little shop to let and paid a deposit on it, but deeply resented the thought of such a thing as it had been a butcher's shop with irons hanging around, a butcher's block for a counter, and marble slabs in the window which one would have for display of shoes. Mr Seth Pack preached at Dicker on the Sunday, and he so went into my exercise that I was fully persuaded that I was to open the little shop and I could see it was my pride that was against it. Mr Pack said, 'Poor soul, this is the way you are to go, though it will be a rough way but right.' However, I went the next day to try for a position as manager of a shoe shop at Eastbourne, but when I got there the vacancy was filled, which I had expected. On my way home, feeling very guilty, I met with an accident and sustained a broken rib. O the folly of going against the Lord!

As soon as I recovered we began to make a move and to get the shop ready for opening. I took the shutters down and customers began to come in to buy footwear and bring repairs, so that I soon had as much as I could cope with. How I had to prove that the Lord was in it all, and that the hearts of all were in his hand. After some time a shop in North Street, Hailsham, with living accommodation was offered to us and we moved in, observing the Lord's leading and goodness to us. We stayed there until we retired from business.[479]

Jethro West

Jethro West was a member of the church at The Dicker, East Sussex, when he was called up to serve in the army. After his return from the war he was made a deacon in 1919, and served until his death in 1965 at the age of 83. The following is extracted from his obituary in *The Gospel Standard*:[480]

✍ During the First World War he was called to army service and had to close down his business,

Jethro West

except what could be done by his wife and their two sons, then at school. Whilst overseas he wrote: 'There is one who can sustain us and help us to trust him where we cannot trace him; but it is grace and faith that we are short of. O how we prove from day to day that we cannot help ourselves! But when we are favoured with a spirit of prayer, how good to feel a little nearness in trying to pour out our trials and complaints, and when we feel we can tell the Lord *everything.* He can manage for us, and preserve us and strengthen us in body, soul, and mind. Yes, one night this week I lay in my "kip" and felt I could trust the Lord with *everything,* to do as he sees fit with us each and all, and that he will do better for us than we could for ourselves; and I felt that if he would give us health and strength I would try and bear what he was pleased to lay upon us, which would surely be for our good.'

His life was several times wonderfully spared during his army service in Palestine and France, and he often reflected on two singular interpositions which took him out of the battle just before his company was practically destroyed. Once while feeling perfectly well, he was sent some hundreds of miles back to the base as a malaria suspect. Later, while lying on top of the trench awaiting the order to attack, he was wounded in the arm, which compelled his retirement as his comrades went into the battle. Very few of them returned. Of this he wrote: 'How many times I have tried to thank the Lord for allowing me to be wounded in this particular way and at this time, and for strengthening me to get back alone quite two miles without any human help amidst shot and shell, from which I had to take cover three times. Another thing that is so remarkable is that the night before we went over (the top of the trench in readiness) I went back to battalion headquarters with some empty ration cans, so that enabled me to know exactly where to make for when wounded otherwise I might have wandered about for a long time, it being still dark. So you see how everything worked for my good, and I think nearly all the way back I was trying to thank God that he wounded me so gently, and at the same time asking him to preserve me from further harm. But I didn't know then that it was bad enough to get me back to England. Well, "the Lord has done great things for us," and I desire ever to thank him as he enables me.'

Andrew James Woodford

Andrew Woodford was brought up to attend the Strict Baptist Chapel at Downton, Wiltshire, but as a youth turned his back on the things of God and lived a worldly life until he was 38. On the outbreak of war he joined up in order to have a good time, but the Lord began a work in his heart while he was serving in the Far East. This he describes in a paper he wrote in 1934 entitled *The Lovingkindness of the Lord to a Miserable Sinner.* The following extracts are taken from that paper.[481]

✍ I decided to join the army and get to France where I might have a 'good time.' What grief this caused my wife and dear mother! But the Lord's hand was in it all. I had to be shown and made to bow at the feet of a mighty God and cry for mercy and pardon for past and present sins. I could see that I was to face death, and after death the judgement; which made me cry for mercy, knowing and feeling myself to be a hell-deserving sinner. What I thought would be a time of enjoyment in worldly pleasures turned out to be three years of prayer. I can truly say that I was brought, as Paul says, to 'pray without ceasing.' On the way to Singapore how I begged for a token or a word that the Lord would pardon my sins. I sometimes hoped he heard my cry, and I felt a little peace; but not for long. Psalms 33, 91 and 121 were a great comfort to me. Returning from the East, I was sent to France, and what fighting! Truly the Lord 'covered my head in the day of battle.' I believe the Lord heard me and spoke to me one night. Those words dropped into my soul as if spoken to me: 'Fear not, for I am with thee; be not afraid, for I am thy God. With long life will I satisfy thee and show thee my salvation.' I laid me down in peace, trusting, I can truly say, in a crucified and risen Saviour, believing the Lord was with me. The times he saved my life! I prayed that if he did not see fit to spare me, he would have mercy on my soul. I can truly say the watchful eye and tender mercies of the living God have attended my path. How I thanked his holy name! I hope I can truly say: 'Once I was blind, but now I can see what a sinner I am before a just and holy God.' I also believe the Lord has spoken to me: 'Be of good cheer; thy sins be forgiven thee.'

An anonymous medic

We conclude this section of personal experiences during the First World War with the following piece which was published anonymously in *The Friendly Companion* in 1926. It was titled: "He withdraweth not his eyes" – Gleams amid the Glooms of the Great War. It describes the experience of a medic, possibly not a Strict Baptist, serving in Salonika, Greece, in the aftermath of the Serbian retreat. Following the invasion of Serbia in October, 1915 by the German, Austrian and Bulgarian armies, the Serbian army was forced to retreat through Albania. It was disastrous and an estimated 240,000 retreating Serbs died in the process. Allied reinforcements arrived too late, as described in this account.

✍ 'The Angel of the Covenant' has shielded me through many nights and days. How often have I re-echoed your remark: 'What must those days have been to the boys who sheltered not beneath his outspread wings!' Those two lines,

> Where'er they seek thee, thou art found,
> And every place is hallowed ground,[482]

are very real.

Many times, when in sheer desperation because of my utter need and loneliness, I have knelt out on the open hillside or in empty dugouts and poured out my heart to God. And now *I know* those lines are true. I do love hymns, and in connection with my army life there are so many that will for ever be precious. I think just now of the early days of active service. We arrived in November, 1915, just in time to get our hospital overfilled with the boys from the retreat from Serbia.

There were no nurses in those days, and we were 'full up' before half the equipment was unpacked. I had a surgical ward of 14 patients, for whom I had to do everything. I was allowed one bucket of water per day for drinking and other purposes. (This allowance was due to the fact that the water supply was six miles distant, and had to be fetched in a water cart for 1,000 patients and the staff. A little later on, even this supply froze up, and we had to depend on the snow for about a fortnight.)

It was grand work, and I was very happy, but 14 hours a day, seven days a week, gets wearisome to the stoutest heart. My duties included stretcher-bearing, night and day when necessary, over a bog where the mud was knee deep on the track and waist deep off it. Often I was away from my patients for four and five hours at a stretch, during which time no one went near them.

One morning I got up at five as usual, feeling as though I had not been to bed at all. (We could not undress owing to the caked mud on our clothes.) I was seeing to my patients, and wondered what day it was. After a little argument we remembered it must be Sunday. Oh what a thought! What would a Sunday at home be like? As I went for the patients' breakfast, a walk of half a mile through the snow, I started singing the hymn: 'Sweet day of rest! the pearl of days,' but when I got to the lines:

> My weary limbs and aching breast,
> Alike enjoy the sweet repose
> Afforded by the day of rest
> Sweet day! on which the Saviour rose,[483]

it was too much, and my heart overflowed. But through the rest of the day I was so wonderfully conscious of the prayers of dear ones at home that my heart was at peace.

I could tell of a hundred such incidents, and every one is a standing monument to the unfailing faithfulness of God. *God is real: the one Blessed Reality!* Through the day he has walked by my side, and at night I have rested in his everlasting arms. Again and again I have faced death with him, and through all the days he has never failed. So often I used to feel: 'If I am spared to return home I will never cease to tell of God's goodness,' *but* – how easily we forget. How little I have ever told! and what words *could* tell? How often it seems that God's great blessings come by way of sorrow; but to those in Jesus Christ, sorrow is not an evil, but just his gift.

> O could I tell ye surely would believe it!
> O could I only say what I have seen!
> How should I tell, or how can ye receive it,
> How, till he bringeth you where I have been?[484]

The East Kent Regiment at worship

Letters

Letters

Many who had experienced the horrors of the front were very reticent to say anything about their experience after the war had ended. Consequently it is in letters written during the course of the war that we find the most immediate records of the events of the war, including the spiritual exercises which accompanied those events in the souls of the Lord's people. The mercies and the judgements of the war, therefore, come across in this section of the book at least as fully and clearly as in any of the other sections.

Here the war letters are subdivided into sections. The first section is comprised of letters written by men serving in the war. The second section consists of letters written by others describing the battlefield experiences of friends and family. Two sections of letters written from home to those in service follow; the first are letters sent by families to their relatives serving in the forces; this is followed by a group of letters written by Strict Baptist ministers to those away from home serving in the war. A final section contains letters describing the war on the 'Home Front'.

These letters have not been edited except to provide abbreviations in full (where known).

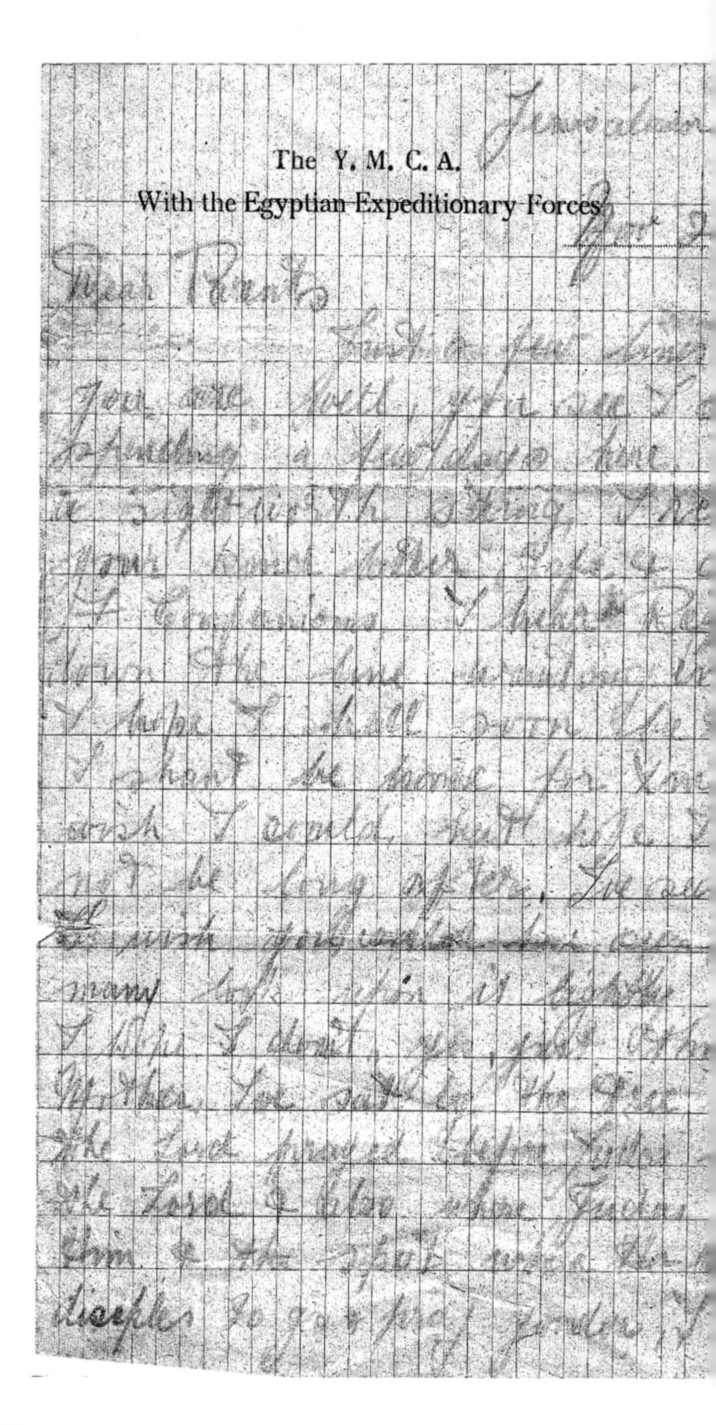

The Y. M. C. A.
With the Egyptian Expeditionary Forces

Jerusalem

Dear Parents

Letter sent by George Doel to his parents from Jerusalem, 25th November, 1917 (see p. 321)

Letters written from the front

Arthur Atkinson

Nothing is known about the author of the following letter. It was originally published in *Zion's Witness* during the war. The letter describes the events of the opening day of the Battle of Arras, on April 9th, 1917:

> ✍ Dear Mother and Dad,
>
> Through the mercy of God I am alive and well. I have been to the gates of hell, but have returned in safety. On Easter Monday we went over the top to the attack, and fought one of the most terrible and awful battles of this dreadful war. Men who have been through the Somme and other big battles agree that the one we have just gone through was the worst. In my platoon, after the fight, when the roll was called, only three lance corporals and seven men answered their names. I cannot give you our losses, but they are very, very heavy. I will try and tell you my personal feelings, and how God in his mercy took me through it all.
>
> We went into the trenches on Saturday, and we knew that on the Monday we were going over the top. The best part of Sunday night I spent in prayer, and while I was reading, these verses (Exodus 14: 13, 14) were impressed on my mind, 'And Moses said unto the people, Fear ye not, stand still, and see the salvation of the Lord, which he will shew you today: for the Egyptians whom ye have seen today, ye shall see them again no more for ever. The Lord shall fight for you, and ye shall hold your peace.' I could not seem to make out what they meant, but I was comforted by them.
>
> Somewhere about 11.30 the order came to go up and over. I got out of the trench without the least fear, and all through the fight I can truthfully say I did not know what fear was. That was one prayer answered, for I was so afraid I should show the 'white feather,' but I was as cool as if I was out for a walk. Well, we had not been out long before the Germans let us have it; men were falling all around me, but we went on, and advanced about two miles. The shell fire was terrible, but nothing stopped us. We get up to the German trench, but could not get through the wire. How long I laid on the ground with the bullets whistling just over me I cannot tell – I just had to lie there. The Germans turned the guns just in front of their trench; they started from the left and swept the front. I turned my head and saw a shell hole on my right, so crawled on my stomach towards it. I shouted to my chum to make for it, and when the machine gun stopped I made a rush for and dropped into the hole. I turned round to see if B— had followed me and was just in time to see a shell burst within a yard or two from him; whether he was hit or killed I did not know. I then made another dash to where my corporal was, and had got to the shell hole with him when we received word to get back, and it was a case of every man for himself. How any of us got back alive I never can tell. The machine gun and artillery fire were tremendous. The sights I saw that day were too awful for words, but they had no more effect on me than you who never saw them. When I tell you that I held a man's shattered hand while another bound it up, and my hand was quite steady, you will

understand. This is not patting my own back, but to show you how God answered my prayers. I think I prayed every step I took – not with fear, for, as I said before, I knew no fear. We got back about 600 yards to a sunken road, when orders came to dig ourselves in, which we did with the shells dropping round us. About 3 a.m. we were relieved, and went back in supports. We had not been in the sunken road more than an hour, when, to my delight, I saw my chum, but he was deaf through the explosion, and was suffering from shell shock. We had a little talk, but only by signs, and the stretcher-bearers took him off. Poor B—, he is the best chum a chap could have, and I feel lost without him. Poor Charlie! up to the present I can find out nothing about him whether he is wounded or killed. Although we did not capture the German trenches we heard next morning that they had retired, which was good news. With regard to our officers, I can only say they were splendid; but my company officer was shot through the breast, and when the sergeant major went up to him to ask what orders, almost with his last breath he said, 'Carry on!' He was only a young man about 21 or 22.

Just about an hour before we went to the attack I had a letter from you and dear Cis. We are back, resting, which we badly need. I must draw to a close; and can only say that if anyone's prayers have been answered, mine have; and I feel I cannot thank God enough for his mercy to me. So now, goodbye, with fondest love to you and Dad.

Your loving son,
Arthur Atkinson,
British Expeditionary Force, France.
April 4th, 1917.[485]

Lance Corporal Joseph Baker, Manningford

Joseph Baker had served prior to the war in the Wiltshire Regiment, and at the outbreak of war was in the National Reserves. He responded to the call to sign up, joining the army on 7th September, 1914. He was sent to Egypt in January, 1916.

✍ To Mr S. Hawkins, Reading.[486]

My dear friend,

Joseph Baker

How very pleased I was to receive your kind and welcome letter last night. Letters from the people I love are very welcome to me (especially from the ministers of God's gospel). O if I could only say your God is my God. I am very pleased to say at this critical time my only comfort is the pure Word of God and the words as I have heard from time to time by ministers. I was reading the Psalms the other night, the words I heard you preach from at the dear little chapel at Manningford once, 'There is a river, the streams whereof shall make glad the city of God.' Yes, dear friend, I believe the seed is sown deep into my heart, and if so, I have much to be thankful for, for I can only say, 'It is the Lord: let him do what seemeth him good.' My prayer is daily, 'O God, be merciful to me, a vile sinner, let the light of thy countenance shine upon me and create in me a clean heart, O God, and renew a right spirit within me, hold thou me up and I shall be safe;' and yes, I often sing that beautiful hymn:

> There is a period known to God
> When all his sheep, redeemed by blood,
> Shall leave the hateful ways of sin,
> Turn to the fold, and enter in.[487]

I was sorry to hear my dear wife was not able to get to chapel on the 12th. I know how delighted she would have been, but what a mercy she is still able to get out a little when the weather is fine. I hope God in his mercy will spare her life until my return – if it's in accordance with his divine will. He is able to do all these things for us, bless his holy name.[488]

I received a nice, welcome letter from Mark Perry. I am pleased the dear friends don't forget me in their prayers, and I shall be pleased when this Great War is ended. I am pleased to say I am keeping fairly well up to the present, thank God, and I hope I shall. Now, dear friend, as my time is limited and I have to write to my dear wife, I must draw to a close, hoping dear Mrs Hawkins and your son and daughter are all quite well. Accept my kindest regards and best wishes. Hoping you will write again when convenient to do so.

Believe me, yours most sincerely,
Joseph Baker,
British Expeditionary Force, Egypt.
31st March, 1916.[489]

William Samuel Beeken, Cranbrook

William S. Beeken

William Samuel Beeken (or Sam as he was generally known) attended Providence Chapel, Cranbrook. During the war he volunteered to serve with the Royal Army Medical Corps. At Providence Chapel, the young ladies who were left at home were encouraged to write to the men of the congregation serving in the forces. The girl who wrote to Sam Beeken would later become his wife. When these letters were originally published in *The Friendly Companion*, they were accompanied by a note from William Beeken's sister which read:

> ✍ My brother is now stationed at a large college in Armentières, France. At present the beautiful building and grounds are untouched by the shells, which, however, fall on other parts of the town. He was previously for six weeks in a convalescent camp near Poperinge, from which town he once thankfully escaped with his life. This verse has been given him: 'But they that in the Lord confide,' etc.

[1]

> ✍ My dearest M.,
>
> It is a great mercy that we have all been brought safely through thus far; I believe in answer to the prayers of those we have left behind; but, oh, what patience it needs to comply with all the various rules

and orders. We are all tired and sick of it, but make the best of it and keep as cheerful as possible. Anyway, I don't wish you to worry about me, for it is 10 times worse with some. We sleep on beds and live very well. We club round on Saturdays, and 10 orderlies collect five francs for the cooks, and so get tea after dinner and a little extra bacon for breakfast if any to spare. One day we bought flour and made three roly-polys; rather heavy but a rare treat. I should like to have been at 'Providence' (Cranbrook) on the 16th inst., and also to hear Mr Tiptaft.[490] Between January, 1899 and December, 1914 I missed attending our chapel only once (through illness), and now have not had the privilege for over six months. I do not want promotion out here ...

Your loving son,

S.

June 26th, 1915.[491]

[2]

✍ My very dear M.,

As you may be sure, my thoughts have travelled home many, many times today and this week, and to the sad time we were passing through last year.[492] And oh! what changes since; and to think this very night I am watching at the bedside of a seriously wounded, and perhaps dying comrade. But, as L— said in her last, '12 months of eternal rest and happiness,' taken from the evil to come, and God's judgement now o'er our beloved land. Thanks so much for yesterday's letter and enclosures. Mr W—'s leaflet very good. O that it may impress many, for it is too true; I am lending it to G— P—. Please give love and remembrances to all friends who think and speak so kindly of me. I don't feel worthy of it all, but I do at times feel to need a real friend out here, and especially on Sundays long to be in England. I have not seen Frank Boorman[493] for some time, though being in the 27th Division he cannot be far away as we all move together; but the école is at the far end of A—. Have had heavy rains this weekend. Friday afternoon it poured in torrents as if a cloud had burst asunder, and made a terrific noise on the glass roof ... May we all be spared to live in peace and happiness many years after this murderous war is ended. Four poor fellows, brought in last night, wounded by a sergeant's folly or mistake I believe.

Ever your loving son,

Wm. S. B.

June 28th, 1915.[494]

[3]

✍ My dear sister,

Am sure you are wondering where I am. Last week was a very busy, very tiring and exciting time, commencing with a race over ploughed fields and corn crops, to see the descent of the German aeroplane at 7 a.m., Monday 13th – both pilot and observer killed through firing on our troops, a K.R.R.[495] killed. The plane was scarcely damaged and nearly new (a valuable prize; and promotion no doubt for our airman that helped to run him to terra firma). In the heat of the day we had a very long route march; next morn, struck tents, moved away. 2 p.m. arrived at our first billet, at seven o'clock slept in a barn, next two nights in tents. Another long march on Friday, sleeping in trucks at a small village station. Loaded transport next morning, left at 8.30, arriving at our train journey end at 6.30. Left at 9 p.m., arrived 11.30, slept under a tree, tired from head to feet. Arose at 6 a.m., pitched tents and stayed one night; next day a short march, pitched tents among some trees near a range of hills. Ambulance divided up yesterday noon. C Section in an école once more, where I hope we shall stay some weeks; but what a hole! A decent billet now, but an enormous quantity of dirt, as usual, to be cleared away and burnt. There is a church opposite. Villagers live in mud and clay cottages; and being '*le premières troupes Anglaises en*' this district it is almost impossible to get anything at a reasonable price. We are amongst lovely scenery, and it was a most delightful railway journey, all along the rivers lined with millions of birch trees. At one place we passed several acres of allotments, worked on the intensive system, not a waste inch of ground, and each surrounded with water wide enough for the owners to travel round in a punt. The country is grand with autumn putting on her garb. One of our party considers it like Cornwall. The people are more uncivilized than any we have met and do not know a word of English.

Kind remembrances to all friends.

Your affectionate brother,

S.

September 22nd, 1915.[496]

[4]

✍ My dearest M.

We certainly have not settled at a very agreeable spot. Most think it the worst place we have been at, but we may not stay long. We are a sort of flying ambulance ... We are thankful to hear of the success along the line, and may have to march into Berlin. How delightful it would be to have Christmas, 1915, in Cranbrook! This is an advanced dressing station. We have not yet had a rush of patients, and we send away two and three times a day. A few serious cases. One officer died on the way from the aid post to here; he was only 27. Is it not awful to think of the loss of our brave officers and men? Roll on peace. Also what a number of deaths at home since I left. I have enjoyed some lovely tomatoes; the folks must think us rogues, they always serve us at the window; but we are settling down and getting a little more contented with our lot. Our wants will soon be better supplied in the village; everything very dear. The ground is not cultivated; very chalky. The roads are in a dreadful mess after two days' rain. I rather dread the oncoming winter, but we may not be here. How I think about you all, and should delight to be 'somewhere in England.' I hope you are all well.

Your loving son,

S.

September 28th, 1915.[497]

British and French troops were deployed on the Macedonian Front against Bulgaria, which was supported by some German and Austrian troops and had declared war on Serbia in the autumn of 1915. In the next letter Sam Beeken details his move to Salonika in Greece as part of this opening up of the South Eastern Front:

[5]

✍ My dear ones,

I do hope you will not get over anxious about me, though it does seem now that I am quite cut off from all friends; but my thoughts travel home quite as quickly as when in France. I wonder what is before us when we land? I hope I am thankful that the nine days journey through the perils of the sea has ended in safety. Through a thick, cold mist we have been anchored nearly all day; we are not far from port.

7th December – We arrived in harbour just after breakfast. Have had a fair view of the town and hills in the background. My glasses are very useful and in great demand by passengers. I wish I could tell you more of our surroundings. I want to get ashore to receive news from home.

8th December – It is possible this may not reach you by Christmas. I sincerely hope you will spend a very happy time together, and may God's rich blessing rest on each; and may we be kept in health and strength looking forward to that happy gathering when peace has been declared. How I long to hear news to that end.

11th December – We left the steamer yesterday at 2.30, thence by a large steam tug to the docks, landing in a very interesting Grecian town. Marched through it at top speed to a large camp about six miles away, arriving at 6.15. There was a dense fog. We had to hunt up a motor lorry, unload, and afterwards pitch tents; so it was about 11.30 when 15, with kit all round, cuddled down in a small circle to sleep, and found the benefit of an extra blanket each, the ground being very wet and dirty. Arose at 7 a.m. then a two hour course of physical and company drilling. We miss ship's menu and are sure to go a bit short. Small biscuits and Bovril for dinner, jam for breakfast and tea. I should like to spend a week around here in peace time. The natives, hundreds of pack ponies, yokes of oxen, and women carrying pitchers of water, remind one of Bible history and various texts. I fear we are in for a rough time, 'bully'[498] and biscuits, etc., but hope to do better when settled, if we ever do settle again. I have some washing to do. No mail since November 22nd until last night, when there was a general rush, nearly everyone had a letter. I was disappointed, was longing to have yours; it may be in the town. We are having a bread issue tonight.

14th December – Left camp Sunday midday, over some of the worst roads we have ever travelled, rough, with several inches of mud, loaded with a heavy valise and two blankets. I am glad you could not see me or you would have no rest. 2nd mail last night. No news. Longing to hear. Parcels were smashed up.

Ever your loving son,
W. S. B.
December 6th, 1915.[499]

[6]

✍ Dearest Mother,

Thirteen months of active service concluded. We left our camp on the mountains on the 18th at 10.30 a.m. Imagine going through a lane after a heavy fall of snow, then thaw, and following dozens of transport limbers. About three miles on we commenced going down the mountain sides; very narrow, crooked and slippery at places. I was brakesman; the mules are marvellously sure footed. We were glad to get to the bottom and rest, for it was very warm. We then travelled over a rough track beside a beautiful lake, about seven miles by two; pitched tents at 5.30, the distance was 18 miles. I was soon asleep after a mug of tea. Next day half the party went on another 12 miles; we get more amongst the uncivilized at every move. There are only nine of us.

24th January – We left camp yesterday, Sunday, at 10.15 and landed at our destination, 10 miles away, at 2.15. It is rather pretty country but I was not thinking much of the beauties of creation, my mind was at home all day. We are situated between the mountains and hills which are covered in heather, furze and very small holly bushes. It must be lovely in summer. The sun is warm in the day, but nights are usually frosty and cold. Must leave principal news till we meet; it is not likely I shall have leave until the war is over.

January 21st, 1916.[500]

[7]

✍ How fast the days flit by when we have plenty to do. I am glad of a fair share of work so that I can go to 'bed' tired. We are expecting to leave tomorrow for a camp nearer the sea. Yes, we landed at the place you mention (Salonika) but are now about 60 miles away, nearly on the opposite side I imagine. We know very little of the war. As we are taking over the sick of the division, there is plenty of work; immense marquees are being erected at our next halt. I and a mate are 'on our own,' having the care of a patient who is not well enough to be moved for a day or two. It is fine; no early parades and no 'lights out.' Glad cards reached home; I think they are worked in Paris. Some of the work is very fine; the lace-making would interest you. I should like a few days in France after the war.

11th February – 3 p.m. A very heavy rainfall this afternoon, and slight storm; we have to shout to each other. I wish I had a memory for good things; but then I might remember more of the bad that I hear every day. The sunshine is lovely; we shall soon want sun-bonnets. Yes, it is a very great mercy to have been brought through in safety thus far. The boat behind us was torpedoed, nurses and others drowned, the *Saturnia* and others damaged on the way back. The 83rd travelled from France to Greece in this boat. It was crowded with troops. Good wishes to all friends.

From your loving son in khaki,

Samuel.

February 10th, 1916.[501]

[8]

My dearest Mother,

This has been the best week I have spent on active service. I wish you could look in at the tent door. The M.O.[502] has kindly lent his 'Primus' on which I fry bacon and bread and cook rice, oatmeal and potatoes; we always have a cup of tea after dinner. I also draw our loaf each morning at the bakery. We shall both be sorry to leave the camp. I feel at times there is a special providence over me by night and by day. Really this place is preferable for many things to Dover and other bombarded towns on the East Coast.[503] It is truly a time for mourning in our country. As to the termination of the war, I see little hope as yet of returning home this year. At the commencement 'K'[504] spoke of a three years' engagement; but we know God still reigns and can bring the conflict to an end in as sudden a way as it apparently began.

Yes, I went to Ypres, but not on duty. A bombardment was preparing, and shells were rather too free to be pleasant. I was glad to get back again. There were some terrible sights; it is marvellous how our S.B.'s[505] escaped in May with so few casualties. Though the medical work is very monotonous, it is better than seeing our chums murdered and butchered as they were then. We have missed much of the bad weather this winter.

9 p.m. – Just a line, now in bed. We are living like officers; toast and sardines for tea, and arrowroot for supper; the best is to be our own masters for a week. It is a glorious moonlit night.

William S. Beeken during his service in Salonika

18th February – Find I have missed the mail. Have this afternoon read again Daniel Herbert's hymn you so kindly copied, 'Acknowledge me in all your ways;'[506] it did me good. You can't think how I long at times to sing those wonderful hymns, and again meet in God's earthly courts. I hope when this war is ended to put off khaki for ever. Kind remembrances to Mr Rose[507] and all kind friends. From your loving son,

Samuel.

February 15th, 1916.[508]

[9]

✍ My very dear M.,

Letters from home again, how welcome. I have been moved with four infectious cases. There are nine marquees, each to hold 24 patients on stretchers. I expect the cost of each is nearly £50. If we had one in the garden there would be little room left for vegetables. We are miles and miles from the enemy. I took a walk down to the beach a few nights ago and tried to fancy myself at a small English resort, but could not. It was grand to see the moon shining on the little waves. Frogs were croaking tremendously in the rushes, and nightingales were singing.

'God bless you now and till we meet again.'

W. S. B.[509]

[10]

✍ Dear Mother,

We have been busy since the 21st, which was anything but a Good Friday, clearing the hospital and moving the whole camp six miles back ... We marched off yesterday in the rain at 3.15 p.m., arriving at six; quite a race along very bad slippery tracks. We were all tired out. Paraded at 7.55 for orders and rations for a three day trek and manoeuvring over the hills. It rained hard all night and our tents were not trenched. We had to be out at 7 a.m. and went off at 8.20; not allowed to carry cape or coat, only ground sheet down which the rain ran on to our legs. We went a mile and then found the march was cancelled for an indefinite period; I wish for ever. Eight of us have been sleeping or lying on stretchers while our clothes are drying in a marquee. We are higher, but have lost sight of the sea; a lake is near. We see a few puff adders with fangs, but those caught are usually gentle ones, a good specimen this morning, about 5 foot. There are also poisonous centipedes, 4 inch long, awful creatures. Much less jam now; cheese issue stopped. Many write more than I and use much stronger language, but I am sure a week at home will make up for all the discomforts and treatment we have received during 17 months ...

I must be looking older, as a patient put my age at 40! I hope my strength will not fail. Pray for me, dear M. May the thousands of prayers that ascend to heaven for the termination of the war soon be answered.

We have been on another march, passing through a few very old villages that might have been inhabited in Paul's time. Some of the narrow passes were nothing but rock and stones. I always like to hear of friends; what a number of people I shall never see again. Young and old are taken, and so many unprepared: 'Prepare me, gracious God,' etc. I have not found one amongst the hundreds I have come into contact with that thinks as I do.

Love from your affectionate son,

Samuel,

Salonika Force.

April 27th, 1916.[510]

[11]

✍ Dearest M.,

Yesterday we had a warm, exciting experience; a fire broke out about three miles away, a very strong wind blew the flames towards the camp and along the side until it reached the top of the hills, some six or seven miles. We had to move all the patients out and carry them away by hand. We quite expected to see a part if not all the camp down, but the fire was confined to one side and practically no damage was done, as counter fires were made just in time. We were all back again by dark. It was the first time most of us had seen such an immense bush fire, a sight not readily forgotten. Thanks for particulars of meetings. You occasionally mention unsettledness in Greece; it does not affect us in the least yet.

From your affectionate son.

Later – We are kept busy, as the hospital fills rapidly and we get but little rest; in fact, we have been ever since the middle of February. We ought to be thankful that no serious disease has broken out. The climate is more trying than in Egypt. It is certainly preferable to cold and wet if we have good health, but our rations are not conducive to that. It is a marvel how little we can live on; we have a good supply of water. It is a lovely moonlit night. Please give kind remembrances to all at Providence Chapel, and other places. I have had 19 months of active service, and I believe, through your prayers on my behalf, I shall still be kept and preserved to the end. There are many in worse places than this. Goodbye dearest,

Samuel.

July 7th & 13th, 1916.[511]

[12]

✍ My very dear Mother,

I am getting behind in writing, but have thought none the less of home, indeed, you have been more on my mind than usual, for did we not hope the war would have ended before this and that I should have had my Xmas pudding from your table. Instead, we have been in this country 12 months, and the outlook is not very bright now. Somehow I feel rather in the dumps today; the weather has affected us all a bit, for last night the wind and rain were terrific. Some tents blew down, some were washed out of their bivvys, but I have kept dry; it would have been worse but for a full moon. The roar of the water at midnight was tremendous, the billows sounding almost like the rushing of a train; it is really grand to see them. It is much warmer and brighter this afternoon, and the ground will be nearly dry tomorrow. I have just been down to a stream and had a good wash, so you see what a strange climate it is.

Later – So many thanks for letter arriving yesterday in the first Xmas mail, a large one, but not *the* mail which we hope will arrive this week. How delightful could I have been one of the leave party of eight; we are rather down again through having to move our camp, only about a mile. I dare not entertain hopes of leave in case we are disappointed as usual, but what a privilege it would be to meet all my dear ones again ...

How sad is the loss of the two worthy men, Mr Ormiston and Mr Thomas;[512] O, how the few faithful are being called home. So many prayers less to ascend to heaven on behalf of our guilty land. Have just seen a picture of the Bishop of London blessing a war shrine; and practically no one to protest! Your ever loving son,

Samuel.

December 18th, 1916.[513]

[13]

✍ My dearest Mother,

I have now spent three birthdays on active service and have not seen you for nearly 26 months. How many changes during that time; and how I wonder where we shall be in 1918? At times I can really feel,

> My God, I would not long to see
> My fate with curious eyes;
> What gloomy lines are writ for me,
> Or what bright scenes may rise.
>
> In Thy fair book of life and grace,
> O may I find my name
> Recorded in some humble place,
> Beneath my Lord the Lamb.[514]

It seems ages since I had the privilege of singing, 'How pleased and blest was I,' etc.[515] I hope I have not lost the little love I had to God's earthly courts, and that it was not all form in attending.

We had a fall of snow on Jan. 25th, and rain since. One day I was nearly blown and washed out of my bivouac, which was incomplete at the time. I expect E. has experienced severe weather on the East Coast, yet I rather envy him. It will indeed be a mercy when the end of the war comes; but a greater mercy to be prepared for the end of life. Two officers were recently killed in an aeroplane accident, and a chaplain and officer were killed by an enemy bomb. I am so glad to receive all your loving letters and wishes.

Please give my kindest regards and best wishes to all friends. Very fond love from your ever affectionate, unworthy son,

Samuel.

February 1st, 1917.[516]

Ebenezer Boorman, Canada

Ebenezer (born 1887) was the son of Mr Arthur Boorman, a Strict Baptist minister, who held a number of pastorates, but at the time of the war was living in Maidstone, Kent, and attending Priory Chapel.[517] Mr Arthur Boorman had two more sons in the forces, Percy (born 1885) and Frank (born 1893). Both Percy and Ebenezer had emigrated to Canada prior to the war and, according to *The Christian's Pathway*, they both served during the war with the Canadian forces. Letters written by all three brothers follow:

✍ Dear Parents,

I was very glad to hear you are all well ... We are camping in a beautiful little wood; if it was not for the guns continually going one would not realize there is a war on, it is a glorious day. I had a letter from Percy two days back, he is well ...

I don't get much time to myself now, it seems to be all work and sleep, but I don't forget you all. My feet try me quite a lot, the roads are very hard. I have been trying to find out where Frank is, and from what I can gather he is only about two or three miles from where I am. I don't think Percy is near here.

With much love from your loving son

Ebb.

June 1st, 1917.[518]

Driver Frank Boorman, Maidstone

The following series of letters were written by Frank Boorman, who served in the Army Service Corps in France. Frank's father, Arthur Boorman, wrote to *The Friendly Companion*:

✍ Our eldest son at home joined in September, and has been sent over to France just lately. We received a letter from him this morning, of which I enclose a copy, thinking perhaps you would insert it in the February *Friendly Companion*, as it is interesting reading, and it has been censored. I can say, for one, in my waking hours my poor cries are almost continually going up to the God of heaven to soon deliver us in every way, and soon bring about peace on a solid basis; that is, as far as anything of an earthly nature can be called solid. More than ever I have felt of late the sweetness of dear Hart's hymn commencing, 'The moon and stars shall lose their light,'[519] especially this,

> But they that in the Lord confide,
> And shelter in his wounded side,
> Shall see the danger overpast,
> Stand every storm, and live at last.

Arthur Boorman and his wife

[1]

✍ Dear Parents,

I suppose you will not be loath to have a few more lines from me, although I have not yet received any reply to my letter of last Monday. We are still at the same place, although there is talk of a move tomorrow. Christmas passed off with little incidents for us; how did it go at home? We had a change from 'bully'[520] for dinner, having beef, potatoes, carrots, and all who liked had an allowance of beer. As I have told you, the Army Service Corps[521] arrived on Christmas Eve at a very late hour; it was quite a treat to see the boys again. I was fetched out of bed before one o'clock on Christmas morn, along with two others of the transport, as the stable guard were having trouble with the horses. We transport chaps do no picket,[522] a guard being drawn from the regiment. In the evening we all assembled at the barracks where our company is stationed and had a dinner together – beef, potatoes and greens; us attached chaps could not stay for the *Daily News* Christmas pudding,[523] as we had to be within our own barracks by 8.30 p.m. We got a liberal helping next day, however, with the Gloucesters.[524] It was good, quite like the real thing. They gave us some rum, too, on Christmas night; I had a little of that.

We all received yesterday a card from the King and Queen, and Princess Mary's Christmas gift. For smokers, this was a pipe, tobacco, 20 cigarettes, a card and a photo in a souvenir box; for non-smokers, a box containing acid tablets,[525] also a wallet containing writing materials. All troops also had either 48 cigarettes or two ozs. of tobacco and a box of matches, the latter a commodity which it is almost impossible to obtain here.

This is a very quaint old town, all streets of cobblestones; pumps, which all use, about every 100 yards or so. There is practically no drainage system, and people throw their waste water and very often their refuse out into the street. You see women street cleaners, bakers, etc.; women driving cattle and pigs, screwing their tails. The other day I saw a large farm wagon loaded with hay and drawn by two horses; on one sat a man, on the other his wife holding up an umbrella. One also sees dogs drawing little carts, and boys of quite tender age, seven and upwards, with pipes and cigarettes on. There is a fine old cathedral here, it is splendidly decorated inside. The Army Service Corps is to have a church service this afternoon in the barrack room. I was talking to two motor drivers who have been in the first line transport since the commencement of the war; they say the Allies have the situation well in hand and that the worst is over.[526]

Now good-bye. Best wishes for a Happy New Year.

Your affectionate son,
Frank.
British Expeditionary Force.
27th December, 1914.[527]

[2]

✍ Dear Parents,

Thanks very much for yours and Mary's letters, which I received a few days ago ... I am now on very active service, having moved up to within two or three miles of the trenches, and I have had very little time to myself so far. We of the 81st Brigade left the town where we have been since Dec. 22nd, and after about a 20 kilometre trek the Gloucesters stopped at

C— for the night, and I, after unloading, went on in the dark to a town another 6 kilometres along the road to rejoin the Army Service Corps. After much waiting, about 9.30 p.m. we got to kip in a room formerly used by the Germans for the same purpose. 140 Warwicks[528] were killed in the village some time before, and were buried in a field opposite to where our horses were picketed. The Germans had four machine guns in the church tower, but the place was finally taken at the point of the bayonet. Up betimes in the morning and, after waiting from 9 till past twelve o'clock to get loaded up with supplies, we started on again. Just before entering the next town saw a shell burst for the first time; this was soon followed by several from our guns. After passing through the town saw six of our aeroplanes in a field. There were hundreds of lorries from all parts of England on the road loaded with supplies, shells and ammunition, beside Red Cross motors, and all sorts of wagons. The roads were very bad all the time, cobbles and ruts at sides. We crossed the frontier into Belgium about 2 p.m., the roads then became chronic; they, in fact, beggar description. In most places just a cart track of cobbles in the centre and then often a drop of nearly a foot into thick mire; woe betide any wagon that gets off the cobbles. Every time that happened we had to get a dozen or so on the wheels, and sometimes a trace horse. In places the engineers are repairing the roads, using logs on which is placed rubble, Canadian fashion.

Then began what seemed like never-ending waits, in a cold driving rain till dark, so that we should escape being shelled, then we would move on a few yards and wait again. About two or three miles from our destination we spent some six hours, my seat and legs were wet through, and although I have a large sheep skin lined Canadian coat with a collar that reaches my cap, I sat there and my teeth chattered. The sky was constantly illumed by the flares thrown up by the Germans – these are used every night – but I think their artillery had been silenced early in the evening. It was a terrible job driving along those roads in the dark; one had to be continually on the alert or you were in a rut or ditch on either side.

The country is very flat, water lying in hollows everywhere, and quite a lot of windmills help to make up the landscape. The moon came out before we started again; it helped us considerably and we finished our journey at 5.30 a.m. on Friday 8th. I tried to get some sleep in a loft in the morning but was twice fetched out before I got off; the second time I had to harness up and go back about five or six miles for supplies. The quartermaster and myself came back alone and, after being held up for over an hour by a lot of artillery till nearly dark, got to within two miles and then found a wagon stuck in front of us. There we had to wait for another hour or two and we reached our place about 9.30.

Yesterday (Saturday), I saw three aeroplanes, shells were bursting all round them. Today I saw about four French ones chasing a Taube,[529] but it escaped both them and a hot shell fire. The Frenchies also were peppered at hot and strong, but flew around in seeming indifference. Last night I and another chap had to take our wagons and horses back to the company, about 9.30; it was pitch dark and I can tell you it's an eerie business driving along roads like we have here under such conditions. I am now sleeping in a barn on plenty of straw, but have to be out early; we start off about 7 a.m. for supplies and are gone the best part of the day ... My boots and socks are always wet through and it's such a job to get feet warm. The Belgians seem a decent lot. It's strange to see teams of two, three or four dogs drawing little carts about. The booming of the guns continues day and night; we can see the shells burst often. When with the Gloucesters we were within range, shells have fallen a few hundred yards from their place today. Please continue to write to same address. Souvenirs (shell cases, etc.) are plentiful but not possible to carry about.

Love to all,

Your affectionate son,

Frank.

Driver F. Boorman, 97 Company, Army Supply Corps, 27th Division. Train, British Expeditionary Force.[530]

[3]

✍ Dear Uncle,

My best thanks for rubber boots. I now shall be able to stodge about in the mud pond where our horses are picketed in comparative comfort. The mud about here is of a very sticky nature and you fairly have to stand and tug to raise your feet at times. An oilskin coat would indeed be a boon; there is no objection to us wearing them; indeed many battalions have had Macintoshes issued to them. I have two coats, my cloth one and a Canadian canvas coat lined with sheepskin; this has a collar that reaches above my ears, so it is all right for warmth. It has one disadvantage however, as it is not waterproof. If it is not imposing too much on your good nature the oilskin will be very acceptable and I think I shall then be able to face any weather. Nobody in England can imagine what the troops in the trenches have to endure in mud and water up to their knees and often to their waist for 48 hours at a stretch. The authorities try to ameliorate the men's discomfort by all means in their power, providing pumps, waterproof boxes and tubs for the men to stand in. And today have issued 200 pairs of jackboots to each battalion (a battalion is 1,000 to 1,200 men). It is a sight to see the poor men after leaving the trenches caked in mud and hobbling like old men. Their feet swell to an incredible size and turn blue, and boots and socks of many have to be cut off. I have seen lots with bare feet; sometimes one not so affected carrying a comrade on his back. The largest percentage of cases treated by Royal Army Medical Corps are bad feet; the lads will not mind the work in better weather which I also hope will not be long in coming ...

Goodbye. Thanking you again, with love.

Your affectionate nephew,

Frank.

January 21st, 1915.[531]

[4]

✍ Dear Uncle,

The weather has certainly improved the last few days, it not having rained for almost a week. Our artillery still keeps going strong; there has been a terrific cannonade today. There is a certain amount of liveliness around this neighbourhood, as there is ground to think there is a sniper in the vicinity. Our sentry the other night reported that he was shot at whilst near the horse lines; a night or two after an artilleryman was pinked[532] through the wrist, and others had reported that they had had bullets ping by them. Our company organised a hunt yesterday. We covered a large area but the only find was a British rifle that was in a drainpipe.

You would be interested to see some of the huts used as habitations by some of the troops; you would almost imagine they were the work of savages. They are just span-roof affairs with the floor dug out for 2ft. or 3ft. and built of logs cut from the woods and from the large poles that support the wire-work of the hop fields. These are thatched with straw and have a tarpaulin over all to assist in making them waterproof. The peasants live very simply; their diet consists chiefly of dark bread, buttermilk and potatoes. Dogs do quite a lot of work, drawing carts and turning a large wheel, treadmill fashion, to make butter, etc. I must now close, with love to you both, etc.

Frank.

January 26th, 1915.[533]

[5]

✍ Dear Parents,

Your welcome letters have just arrived, so will answer them while I have time. We have just had divine service in an orchard that adjoins the farmhouse; it is glorious out today. I am on picket at 6 p.m. I am sorry that so much of my last letter was obliterated ... By what you say, the idea that we are to get leave seems very prevalent in Maidstone; for myself I do not think there is a particle of truth in the tale. I should rather have the whole thing finished and done with before going home, the coming back business would not be at all to my liking. Stan Brown was not injured, nor in fact any of our company. A drumhead service is one in which a drum is used instead of an altar; a drum is also used for field court martials. Your parcel arrived two days after your letters, but alas it had been in the wars ... The contents were good, however, and enjoyed by our little clique; I finished up a mixture of cake and tarts with the aid of a spoon. We had snow on the 19th and 20th, previous to that we had had some splendid weather, and today again it is grand, in fact a real spring day. The ground has dried up nicely, and the side boards on each side of the road are becoming quite hard and firm. There are dozens of aeroplanes out today, have been scouting since quite early this morning. Several Germans have been over and been subjected to a hot shell fire. Hundreds of shells must have been fired; the sky looked like a piece of 'spotted dog'[534] in places where the puffs of powdery smoke were suspended in the atmosphere. I watched three of the Allies' last eve; they were continually patrolling to and fro over the German lines regardless of the shells which seemed to burst all around them.

Frank Boorman

German shells can be distinguished by the dark smoke that is emitted on bursting; their shrapnel smoke is mostly white however. There are also three balloon kites up for observation purposes, two of ours and one Allemand.[535] We have had a lot of night work of late, having to take the rations up at night as the road is often shelled in the daytime. Last Sunday night there took place the most terrific bombardment I have ever heard, or anybody else I should think. We had to stand by all night. We were just ready to start at 6.15 p.m., and our horses had to remain hooked in till next morning. I made a fire and sat by with several others until 1.30 a.m., and then spread a waterproof in the village graveyard, and I and another chap slept till 4.30 a.m. when we awoke feeling very cold. We then had a walk round, and finished our sleep under a tarpaulin that covered some stores. We took the supplies up at 7 next morn by another route. All is now fairly quiet again.

I will now conclude, thanking you again for parcel and letters, your affectionate son.

Frank.

March 21st, 1915.[536]

[6]

✍ Dear Parents,

Your letters arrived safely today. I was wondering if I should receive them ... On Easter Sunday we left the billet where we had been for 10 weeks and shifted six or seven miles away. Soon after we were installed

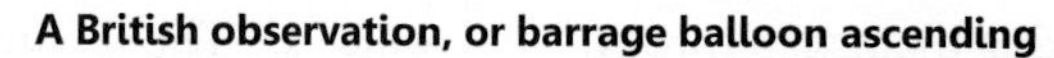

A British observation, or barrage balloon ascending

there about a dozen shells screamed overhead, and next morning I saw the front of a house, about a mile away, that had been demolished by one of them. The regiment that I was attached to is in Belgian barracks, in a town that has suffered very severely from bombardment some four or five miles farther on. Thither we have to go every other day to draw supplies, take them about a quarter of a mile and then return to the company ... On Friday we moved a mile or so farther back. There were numbers of French holding this part of the line, but they very soon shifted after our division arrived. I have seen much that was fresh and of interest. Armoured engines and motor cars, French 75s,[537] and searchlights and anti-aircraft guns mounted on motor cars. There are two aerodromes quite near to us, and aeroplanes are almost continually manoeuvring overhead. Two observation balloons have also been aloft today; one was forced to descend as several German shells burst in its vicinity. The Belgians have erected and are erecting miles of splendid trenches, dugouts and barbed wire entanglements fronting a fair-sized town that we are close to; I hope they will never be needed. It is glorious today, although last week it rained almost continually. I had never seen much of the effect of concentrated shell fire till coming to these parts. The town where we draw supplies had some fine old buildings such as a cathedral and a cloth hall; these are now nothing but a heap of ruins.[538] There is hardly a house that is not scarred by shrapnel and has not all its windows broken. I don't think there would be a lot of 'slackers' if they saw some of these things. I hear that the London Rifles, to which A. Hoare belongs, are in these parts, so must keep a sharp look out. Friday was washing day with me; I did a shirt, vest, drawers and three handkerchiefs. I may perhaps write to O— again later and do him a sketch or two. Now goodbye. Love to all.

Your affectionate son,

Frank.

April 11th, 1915.[539]

[7]

✎ Dear Parents,

There was dirty work being done again last night; about 6.30 p.m. a most terrific cannonade commenced, continuing almost incessantly all night. In the intervals one could hear the rapid machine gun and rifle fire. The Gloucesters did well, capturing five rows of trenches; our brigade took over 800 prisoners. In Sir John French's despatch of last Thursday you will read of the battle that I have told you of which took place on March 14th.[540] I think the cannonading which took place then was almost equalled by that of last night. A German plane was fetched down about 9.30 this morning; one of our aviators got 'top dog' and gave him his quietus. One was brought down by shell fire last evening, and on three successive days at the beginning of last week one was brought down ... There are quite a lot of troops in this quarter; the Canadian Division arrived on Friday; you may depend something will soon be shifted. I had letters from John and Percy[541] last week and have answered them. Percy also sent me one of the snapshots the same as you received. Have the trees started to bud yet? They have not out here although the hedgerows have, and swallows have been flying about since the 9th. I have not seen any primroses out here, but instead a bloom somewhat between that and the cowslip called by the natives 'Pascal bloom.'[542]

Love to all.

Frank.

April 18th, 1915.[543]

[8]

☙ Dear Parents,

This has been a week of events, our time has been very much occupied ... I daresay you will see a little of what is happening by the papers. The censorship forbids that I should enlighten you, but eventually you will learn that the fighting which commenced on Saturday, 17th April[544] and has been continuing with almost unabated fury ever since, has been some of the heaviest of the war, and I sincerely hope the beginning of the end. We have to be prepared for any emergency, wagons loaded, and have to sleep fully dressed, ready to move off in case of an advance or retreat as the case might be. The kiddies will understand that I cannot write them letters. I have not had a chance to get them postcards. We have been having lovely dry weather; it rained a little last night, the first time for quite a spell ... I saw a French aeroplane gun at work a few evenings ago; it was rather a thrilling sight. It hit the German biplane that it was firing at, making it very wobbly for a time, but not sufficiently to bring it down; the German meanwhile threw out various starlights,[545] these being some signal to their lines. The Germans did not make a big bag at Sittingbourne did they?[546] I reckon their Zeppelins have caused them some chagrin.

Your affectionate son,

Frank.

April 25th, 1915.[547]

[9]

☙ Dear Parents,

Circumstances unforeseen prevented me writing yesterday. Our division, which was out for a few days' rest, was called up to the supports towards the middle of last week owing to the Germans breaking through by the aid of their infernal gas.[548] They were soon pushed back. The effect of the gas was felt five or six miles behind the line, it making one's eyes and nose run. The troops are all supplied with respirators that cover the whole face, also a waterproof bag to carry them in and to keep them moist after being washed in an alkaline solution. The pattern made and sent out by the civvies were found of little use, and, having been condemned, will be burnt. All regiments are being supplied with a spraying device which forces the gas out of the trenches. It is being manufactured by Drake & Fletcher of Maidstone, and two or three men of each battalion have been trained in its use. The tackle is also being rapidly prepared to give them a dose of their own medicine. Things were a bit warm when taking supplies up to the supports, some of the big Krupps[549] making a noise almost like a train as they hurtled over. I have never seen so much artillery. There were batteries all round – English, French and

Belgian – and guns of all sizes. The troops were not needed there long, however, and on Friday marched away to another part of the line. The move lasted three days, and we now find ourselves out of Belgium and in one of the busiest, and I should say best parts of France. It is a welcome change; there has been practically no fighting for months, and the large town where the troops are billeted when out of the trenches, although within 2,000 yards of the trenches at one point, has suffered hardly at all by shell fire. It is a slight difference to Ypres, which was a veritable inferno, and is now a heap of smoking ruins. There is a nice river close to us as wide as the Medway.[550] A lot of us, including Lieutenant Green, had a grand swim on Saturday after our arrival. There are a lot of woollen mills in this district; it is a veritable hive of industry. Have you received the parcel of souvenirs yet? I will now conclude as I have to go on picket. Love to all.

Frank.

May 31st, 1915.[551]

[10]

✍ Dear Parents,

It gives me great pleasure to hear you are keeping well ... In these parts we do not find the difficulty in obtaining good water that we did before moving. In the town the water is conveyed in conduits, the residents drawing their supply from standards which are placed at frequent intervals along the thoroughfares. Our horses are watered from the river. All our water is supposed to be boiled before drinking, besides being treated with chloride of lime in the water cart; this imparts rather a peculiar taste to the tea. We roll out at 4.30 a.m., have stables and breakfast and start off by 6.30. We have to be in by 8 p.m., lights out at 9. This part of the line remains very quiet. The last few nights we have heard heavy firing on the right, they must be going it La Bassée way; there was also a tremendous blaze in that direction last night, the sky was illumined very brightly; the aeroplanes of both sides are very active. We have orders to take cover when an enemy machine is overhead and is being shelled; shrapnel bullets have often fallen near us. Two armoured trains are in action almost every day.

Your affectionate son,

Frank.

June 6th, 1915.[552]

[11]

✍ Dear Parents,

Fancy a marauding raider flying over Maidstone. I am very pleased that it did not loose any bombs on the dear old town. I have not seen an airship since I have been out here. We had quite a lot of rain a day or two last week, a great relief after the intense heat we had been sweltering under for a week or so. The crops look grand this way; I trust we shall have a fruitful year. It may make all the difference to the decision of the war; it certainly will affect the food prices which are so abnormally bloated. All of us are now supplied with respirators which always have to be upon our persons and are inspected once daily.

The spraying device makes the gas more volatile causing it to lift from the trenches. There is another mixture which dissolves it, the product of the chemical combination being a salt which falls to the ground. No, we are not in billets but are still bivouacking, which is much preferable this weather. The town you asked me of had a population of from 20,000 to 25,000. As soon as the bombardment began we used to see streams of the people with a few of their cherished possessions tied up in a bundle leaving the town; it was a touching sight. Many stayed on loath to leave their all, and in this way many were killed. There may be still a few existing in cellars and suchlike places. I never neglect the chance of having a swim when possible. We obtained a football and had a game of water polo a few days back ...

Your affectionate son,
Frank.
June 13th, 1915.[553]

[12]

✍ My dear Parents,

Yours came to hand yesterday. Storms have been raging on and off all the morning after a week of comparatively nice weather. Harvesting is well on the way towards completion, nearly all wheat being cut and much of it stacked. The situation continues very quiet, except for last Sunday night and early Monday morning, when the guns were at it hammer and tongs. This was the occasion of the British gain at Ypres. One afternoon last week I had to take a load of pit props from the Royal Engineers' pack up to a battery; they are used in constructing dugouts. One would hardly believe the peaceful nature of the surroundings; a peasant or two were getting on with the harvesting using reapers and binders, and this although they were not much over 1,000 yards from the actual firing trenches. Some of the farms and cottages, of which there was a sparse sprinkling, had suffered somewhat from shellfire, but most of them had their occupants with the little kiddies running about outside. I passed several batteries on the way up very cleverly concealed beneath trees; the one I had to go to was firing when I reached there, and as some of the guns were aimed right across the road I had to wait while the order was given to 'cease fire' before taking the load in. One thing that struck me as being rather ludicrous was that Venetian blinds were fitted to the front of the gun-pits. A day or two after I saw a couple of 9in. 2's in position;[554] they were monsters, firing a shell of about 1¼ cwt. It seems at present as if we are living in a fool's paradise; I expect the terrific upheaval will come with a bloodthirsty vengeance before very long. I should like to see Russia doing better; she may yet recoil upon the invaders. I don't think there is any more for me to ramble on about this time, so will close with fondest love to all.

Your affectionate son,
Frank.
August 15th 1915.[555]

[13]

Dear Parents,

... Since last Friday we have shifted three times, and expect to commence another two or three days' move tomorrow morning ... Our first day's move took us to a village where we had spent two nights five or six weeks before. That eve I lost a pal that has been with me right from Winchester (December, 1914), my good mare Dolly; for a week or two she had been suffering with a growth on the coronet,[556] and the vet said this could only be cured by an operation, so she was taken to a depot of the Army Veterinary Corps. I hope she will be replaced by another animal as good, and the sooner my pair is made up the better, for one gets messed about so much when spare man. Next day, Sunday, with my other horse we did well over 20 kilometres. Our horses were there stabled in the remains of an old water mill, and all the men were billeted on the top floor of what was once an old convent. Whilst there I made the acquaintance of a very nice little French boy who spoke English quite passably. He was one of a family of refugees from Armentières[557] where they left on Christmas Day as the shelling was getting too warm; he said he had learnt all his English from the troops. I began to think here was a good opportunity to pick up a little French, but alas, we only stayed

A Holt tractor hauling a Howitzer gun to the front

there two nights ... At the next place we were all billeted in a rather fine house which had been spoilt by troops. It was in a filthy state, there being straw and muck about a foot deep in every room; it took us quite a while to clean it out. I shall be glad when we are settled down again, one gets no time for anything, least of all for a bath and clean change. Another of my mates went on leave this morning, so my turn must be drawing closer. I am hoping to see you all before many weeks are over.

February 10th, 1916.[558]

[14]

✍ I am on picket tonight and having already done my first turn am writing this between whiles. A wild, wet night it is too, one of many that we have had to endure of late, gales of very wild wind and rain. Of course, as we have been moving nearly all this time, you will understand that things have not been quite as comfortable as we should have liked. On Saturday, 11th, the company packed up again and trekked a distance of about 28 to 30 kilometres. My one horse being lent to another fellow, I footed the whole distance, reaching my destination about 5 p.m., and was not overlong before getting down to it. We kipped in an old barn, but slept well nevertheless. As I daresay you will surmise, all these journeyings have resulted in us finding ourselves once more in the firing line, the troops going into the trenches soon after their arrival, that is within a day or so. Four German aeroplanes came over and dropped 10 bombs, but did little damage, and met with a warm reception from the French anti-aircraft guns, one of which I saw in action. It really is curious how soon the enemy gets wind that there is a move on. We only spent two nights at that village, one of which was spoilt for Woodie and myself by a cracked tile that let a stream of water into our kip and made us get a hurried move on. On Saturday the company moved to a village about seven kilometres distant, the horses being stabled in shelters that had been erected by the French. As we were in the wrong billets we moved again to a part of the village a few hundred yards away, and put our horses into fresh shelters. There is a lot of mud and water around these, and if you step off the narrow path of faggots you find yourself in slush nearly up to the knee. I think our wanderings are now over for a while, at least I hope so. We get a very long day, starting off for supplies about 8.30, returning late in the afternoon. If we were allowed to go upon the main road we should not be nearly so long, but have to go a roundabout route that cannot be observed by the enemy. Three more chaps went on leave last Thursday. 'Roll on,' says I.

Your affectionate son,

Frank.

February 18th, 1916.[559]

[15]

✍ Dear Parents,

I find it is well over a fortnight since I last wrote to you, but really I have not had an opportunity until now ... One thing I am glad to say, the weather has been very favourable, it not having rained once since

... It has been exceedingly hot at times, and one has been chewing dust all day when on the road. The tremendous amount of motor traffic has fairly pulverized the roads in this district, and as the lorries and motor ambulances pass you, you are almost blinded and choked by the clouds of dust that arise. 'O, for a corporation watercart!' I believe that during the last few days I have seen more of war and its preparations than I have hitherto done, and that is saying a lot; and from appearances, we should see a deal more during the next week or so. A few days back, I saw over 400 German prisoners and two officers being marched back; and that was one night's bag. On the whole they were rather a scruffy-looking lot, with here and there some fine specimens of manhood. Besides these I have seen lots of small parties being brought in, and a lot going down with our wounded. Farther back they were to be seen at work, under armed guard, repairing roads, etc. Our artillery is wonderful, and in conjunction with the French gave the Boches last night a terrific milling. Despite our proximity, it is very difficult to obtain any authentic information as to the progress being made. I believe it is quite a week since I last saw a paper. Thanks for the very nice parcel you sent me, and I assure you the edible contents were greatly enjoyed ... Tell J— that I had my first swim this year on Thursday; it was in a small and very fast-flowing river that we camped close to. We are not a great way from the same river now, so hope to have further dips in the near future. I am on guard and night is closing in, so will conclude with love to all.

Frank.

July 29th, 1916.[560]

[16]

✍ Dear Parents,

For the first time for over a week I have a little time to myself, so will write you a letter. I must thank you all very much for the good wishes and splendid parcel received on my birthday. The cake was very nice, and reminded me of the old custom at home of each having a cake on our respective birthdays. The writing material was also very acceptable, all my envelopes being prematurely closed for some time now, I suppose from the damp weather chiefly. Today I had a parcel from M—, I also had letters from T— and Auntie M— on the 20th. I was very sad to hear of Frank B—'s death in action.[561] B— dropped me a few lines informing me of it; I feel very sorry for them all. I expect his mother is very much upset. During the last week we have been working all night, usually getting in about 3.30 a.m. I am very glad this business has ceased, as we got no time allowed in the day for a bit of kip. It began to tell on me; I believe I could have slept standing up. I know I used to keep nodding all the time whilst on the horse's back. To cap it, the weather was excessively wet and cold, and we had some rare old cants in drawing the loaded wagons over muddy tracks, and torn up so thickly with shells that it is a job to dodge the holes in the daytime, let alone on a very dark night. You can guess the lead pairs were much in requisition ... With best love, and thanking you all again,

Your affectionate son,

Frank.

September 23rd, 1916.[562]

[17]

✍ Dear Parents,

It is Christmas Eve. One hardly seems to realize that Christmas is here again, despite the paper decorations suspended over my head – I am writing this in our messroom. Anyway, we have much to be thankful for, a good spread having been arranged for tomorrow. Of course, we shall have our duties practically the same, excepting perhaps the stables and harness cleaning may be cut down a bit. The feed is on rather a liberal scale. There will be roast beef and pork – 100 lbs. of the latter having been purchased, several vegetables, D.N.'s duff,[563] custard, a barrel of beer, lemonade, and such extras as dates, oranges, apples, figs, pears, cigars, etc. However, I shall be thinking of you all at home, and hope that next year under happier circumstances, I shall be once more within the family circle.

... Now I must thank you very much for the parcel which arrived quite intact, some days since; I have been saving the edible contents for tomorrow. There is no pudding like the real home-made article. Now mother, I was very sorry to hear of your rather severe fall, and hope it will not prevent you from having a good time; a mercy not to break any bones. I have some rather unpleasant memories of those selfsame steps, having gone down them on several occasions when a kiddie. What weather we have had this last week, continuous rain and very high winds. It has been grand today, however, and we must hope for a continuation of this sort. It is getting late and I am feeling chilly, so will draw to a conclusion. With best love, etc.,

Your affectionate son,
Frank.
December 24th, 1916.[564]

[18]

✍ Dear Parents,

I am already several days late in writing. I hope you received the cards, etc. I am enclosing a photo of the company taken last week. We have been having it cushy the last ten days, about the softest time since we have been out here. The weather has been glorious, and one is never happy unless in the open, and several of us sleep in a field with the sky as a canopy, keeping a wagon sheet handy to pull over us if it should rain. There is a fine canal near our camp, and we have a bathing parade several afternoons per week ... Whilst here we only go out on duty about once in three days, so take the horses out for exercise and grazing nearly four hours daily. On our return we ride them through a pond, and I can tell you they begin to look in the pink. Their coats shine like silk after a good whisping down.[565] I have a fine pair of animals now, splendid workers. I drive the company supply wagon; will send you a photo showing the full 'rig out.' Fondest love to all,

Your affectionate son,
Frank
June 1st, 1917.[566]

Percy Boorman, Canada

Percy was another son of Mr Arthur Boorman, and brother to Ebenezer and Frank, whose letters precede these. Percy, along with his brother Ebenezer, had emmigrated to Canada prior to the war, and, according to *The Christian's Pathway*, they both served during the war with the Canadian forces.

[1]

✍ My dear Parents,

... At church parade this morning we played the tunes to the grand old hymns, 'All people that on earth do dwell,' 'How sweet the name of Jesus sounds,' and 'Fight the good fight,' etc. I wondered if you would be singing either of them today, and tried to contrast the conditions: you would be in the beautiful chapel at Priory Road,[567] where serenity would doubtless reign; and we on the outskirts of a wood on the side of a hill, our attention occasionally diverted from the service by a big gun sending its message of death to our enemy – Fritz – whilst the preacher was speaking to us of the Prince of Peace; it all seemed rather incongruous. One hardly knows what the censor will strike out, which makes it rather difficult to speak even of oneself, as the individual movements are of necessity governed by those of the battalions; but I guess I may say that there'll be something doing here soon. We have witnessed lots of air duels lately. Fritz seems to be anxious to know what's going on around here, and obviously we are as anxious to keep him in the dark. I hope this will find you all well.

With love to you all from your affectionate son,
Percy.[568]

[2]

✍ My dear Parents

I thought that you, doubtless, having read of the doings over here and the part the Canadians have taken in them, would be anxious to get a letter ... We, the quartet, assisted the YMCA[569] at their 'forward' or 'advanced' stalls to give out free coffee, biscuits, chocolate, etc., to the weary soldiers and the wounded; also the prisoners as they came out of the line. If you could only see how the boys appreciate it, you'd understand the sense of satisfaction we felt in the work. I'd be thankful that we were safely brought through, though at times Fritz seemed to resent being forced back so keenly that he made us hop about pretty lively, but then you no doubt understand how very close up the 'Y'[570] gets on such occasions, in readiness to alleviate, if possible, to some extent the hardships of our gallant troops.

We had very interesting chats with some of the prisoners as they came to our stall; in fact two of them were detailed to assist us the first day, and they did work well. We use some of the prisoners as stretcher bearers, etc. One thing struck me, the very amazement with which they accept the hospitality at the hands of the YMCA, also the spirit of almost comradeship, shall I say, manifested towards them by our own boys. The Fritz has a horror of being taken prisoner because their authorities tell them the awfullest yarns of what will be meted out to them when once in our hands. One lad told me in French, pidgin English and sign language, that he fully expected to get his throat cut; instead he got from our stall hot coffee and biscuits. No wonder his amazement!

Well my dear ones, I won't stay to write more now ... I feel I ought to say that I realize today more than ever, the wonderful gift it is to have godly parents at such times as this, and to know that their prayers are going out on one's behalf day and night, and I believe I realize to a small extent the kind protection afforded to one quite unworthy these last few days. It has always been a source of, or perhaps I should say, a feeling of protection, to know that at home there is continual supplication made to the 'Giver of all goodness,' and to him that is able to protect, though a thousand deaths lurk all around.

With love to all, your affectionate son,
Percy.
British Expeditionary Force, YMCA
August 18th 1917.[571]

[3]

✍ Dear Parents,

... Yesterday we had a long route march, landing back near to where we were a month ago. We are now bivouacked in the open, which is healthy and pleasant in this lovely weather. We made a dug out sort of place to sleep in, and for a little protection in case of shrapnel pieces from a stray shell from our anti-aircraft guns. Also, it does rain over here occasionally, and without somewhere under cover to get in we might be uncomfortable ...

A few months back this place was under Fritz's observation, but now there is nothing but transports, bivouacs, tents, and all sorts of war material as far as the eye can see; which speaks volumes for the recent British successes, and is a happy augur for the future. Old Fritz has been throwing an occasional shell on the slope ahead of us this morn. I guess it's to keep us from getting too stuck up. So long as he doesn't lengthen his range too much I expect we won't lose much sleep. Well, with love to all at home,

Your affectionate son,
Percy.
September 2nd, 1917.[572]

Gunner Ebenezer Samuel Burfoot, Newick

Ebenezer Burfoot served in the Royal Field Artillery. He was wounded in battle on December 8th, 1917, and passed away a few days afterwards on 15th December. He is buried in Lijssenthoek Military Cemetery, Belgium. He was a member of the church at Zion Baptist Chapel, Newick, Sussex.

Ebenezer S. Burfoot

[1]

Extract from a letter to his pastor, Mr J. Stubbs:[573]

✍ I must say, although I have missed the privilege of meeting among God's people and many comforts I have had, and have had some trying things to pass through, yet I would not be without these things. ''Tis the right way though dark and rough.'[574] I find the Psalmist's experience true, 'They that go down to the sea in ships, that do business in great waters; these see the works of the LORD, and his wonders in the deep' (Psalm 107: 23-24), and that the deeper their sorrows the louder they will sing.

[2]

The following is the last letter he wrote to his pastor:

✍ One more Sunday in France. I wonder when I shall be meeting among you again! I am especially thinking of you again today and believe I felt a real soft heart. We had a service and sang a lovely hymn on the sufferings of Christ, the wounded side and the crown of thorns. 'Oh,' I thought, 'what love, what indescribable love to those who desired him not!' How I love these times when I feel all my troubles are very light compared with his, and then he bore the hidings of his Father's face. Oh, how we ought to love

Zion Chapel, Newick

him! I do pray he will keep me from grumbling, and yet how hard is my heart oftentimes, to prove 'that in my flesh dwelleth no good thing.' Yes, your text, 'In all thy ways acknowledge him, and he shall direct thy paths' (Proverbs 3: 6), will do for us. I do want him to direct all my steps. I often have prayed, 'Decide this or that way for me, I'm too ignorant to choose for myself.' I had another letter from Tom.[575] He is better and is returning to the battery, and seems on good ground, for he says, 'Surely goodness and mercy have followed me all the days of my life,' etc.

Lord's Day, November 4th, 1917.[576]

His widow wrote the following in a letter to Mr Stubbs:

✍ I do hope and trust this great sorrow will not be in vain. I want it to be for my soul's good and I trust for his honour and glory, then I shall truly say it was good for me to have this affliction. I love to think of my dear husband blessing and praising his Saviour, which he often longed to do even in health and strength. In his last letter he said, 'Seek more durable riches that will never fade away.' His letters lately were so resigned to the Lord's will, and how much he longed to love and praise him, for I see now quite plainly he was being prepared for a better world. How I long to be prepared to go too! But I must have patience, and, as he used to say,

If in his crown we hope to share
Why should we grudge to bear his cross?[577]

Truly the three testimonies confirm the Lord's faithfulness to the following promises, 'When thou passest through the waters, I will be with thee; and through the rivers, they shall not overflow thee' (Isaiah 43: 2).

James C. Burgess, Dauntsey

When these letters were written, Mr Burgess was stationed in Yorkshire following a serious injury at the front. During his stay there, it would appear that Herbert Sawyer of Hull, the editor of *Zion's Witness*, was instrumental in Mr Burgess venturing into the work of the gospel ministry. The first of these letters was written to Mr Sawyer, in reply to a request to preach. In later years Mr Burgess served as pastor at Bournemouth. For further details of Mr Burgess see p. 180.

[1]

✍ My dear Friend,

Thanks for your letter. Although it was unexpected, I felt it to be seasonable. When on Sunday you asked me if I had been exercised about speaking in the Lord's name, I did not expect you to ask me to attempt; why you were led to do so I will not question. I will now try to give you a fuller account of my exercises in this matter as the Lord will help me, as I do not feel it would be right to take such a solemn step without first acquainting you with all I can tell on the matter.

The first thing that moved me to think about preaching was when the Lord was pleased to liberate my soul from darkness and shed abroad his love within. I felt, oh, how I would like to 'tell to sinners round what a dear Saviour I had found;' this I believe was the beginning, and this has been the desire of my soul, at times, ever since, when the Lord has shone upon my soul. How I have felt when so blessed that I could endure any hardship in his service to speak well of his name, love and mercy. This is one side of the exercise of my mind; there is another, the dark side, temptation. Satan has come in upon my soul with this – What! you preach, a poor arrant fool like you, to whom the word of God is a sealed book. I had better think nothing more about it, it's only preaching fever, a frame produced in all Christians when under the effect of his blessing. I would then try to forget about it, and as soon as I attempted to do this, something would stir it up and my soul would again be tossed to and fro in the matter; I could not seem to get any word from the Lord in the matter. I felt I dare not breathe a word to a fellow mortal about it, even the companion of my life, my wife, to whom I spoke of most of my exercises. I feared lest in speaking in prayer at chapel I might let a word drop that they might find out and would think I wanted to preach. I tried in every way to keep it to myself, and yet when I thought I had been successful one of our members came to me in the chapel after prayer meeting, put his hand on my shoulder, and said, 'Yes, my friend, the Lord has a greater work for you to do, you will have to preach.' Oh, how I felt I could have sunk through the floor. I saw that what I attempted to hide the Lord was able to publish abroad. That man could never let me rest, although I loved him for the truth's sake. I feared to meet him, I shrank from him; the Lord was pleased, soon after, to take him home. About this time I was led to pray that if these exercises were not real ministerial exercises, that the Lord would take them away. If they were, that he would give me some clear proof, and that he would give me a clear call in which I should feel I had no hand in. But the more I prayed – that it would be taken away – the more agitated I seemed to get. This brings me to another instance of the Lord's ministers speaking to me about it; he is a hairdresser by trade, and in my business I call there once a week and usually have a shave when there. About nine months ago he quite suddenly asked me what I thought of the ministry, was my mind exercised that way. I told him about the same as I have told you, that I wanted the Lord to make it clear to me if they were of the Spirit of God or of the flesh. He has been very encouraging to me; he told me he felt on our first acquaintance that the Lord had a work for me to do, and in speaking on these things when we parted previous to me joining the army he said, 'It may be that the Lord is going to take you away from us to make use of you elsewhere.' But to go back to my experience. In the latter part of last year, sometime in December, I felt I could not keep it to myself any longer. I felt I must speak to my father, which I did. I told him just how I felt about it, that I did not want to preach, but I wanted to know the meaning of all this agitation within concerning it. He did not cut me off; he said he felt it was his duty to speak to the deacon about it, which, at that time, he had not the opportunity to do, being away on Sunday, and too busy to be out Wednesday evening. This brings me to the time of my going before the tribunal and being given a month to arrange my affairs, so the matter had to rest.

Since speaking to my father I have felt at rest; I felt whichever way the people decided I could feel it was the Lord's will, and I could rest upon it.

Now my friend, I think I have given you an outline of these things; I leave them to your judgement. I do not want to presume; I shrink from the work. I fully realize the responsibility, yet if it is the Lord's will and he has moved you to speak to me, how can I hold back? I have written to Father and enclosed your letter, asking him to lay the matter before our people amongst whom I have been since boyhood, and who should be able to form an opinion upon my fitness to undertake such a step. What the reply will be I will immediately let you know, that it may be an assurance both to me and you by which spirit we are led. May the Lord pour upon us the spirit of prayer. It is our only safeguard and source of strength. I must close now – I'm afraid I shall not be able to come Thursday, no passes issued this week.

Yours sincerely,

J. C. Burgess,

62180 C Company, 7 Hut, 85 T.R.B., Sutton-on-Hull.[578]

The following letter was written to Mr Burgess by his father. It is a reply to a letter seeking advice as to what he should do following Mr Sawyer's invitation to preach:

[2]

My dear son,

I received your letter this morning, also, Mr Sawyer's letter, which I very much like. It seems to have the distinct and certain sound of his dear father's religion.

Now, with the subject of contents. It is certainly a call to the work which you have been so exercised about for a long time. Now, you ask my advice. My advice in the first place is to consider what hath the Lord commanded thee in those matters. Also be very careful to obey and do them, lest the dear Lord use more powerful means to compel you to walk in his ways. I would ask you to read Exodus chapter 3, verses 7 and following, also chapter 4, verses 10 and following. I also might refer you to many other good men, but must refrain. It is the Lord's work. You could do no wrong in opening your mouth before the people if it is their desire, leaving the rest with them and the dear Lord. You may say with Jeremiah, 'I am a child,' but his grace is sufficient, who hath made man's mouth. Then my son, 'venture on him, venture wholly, let no other trust intrude.' I will lay the letter before the church, and when I have their decision I will write again.

I remain, your affectionate father,

H. W. Burgess,

Dauntsey Wharf.

March 22nd, 1917.[579]

James C. Burgess and his wife in later life

[3]

My dear friend,

I am sorry we missed each other on Monday. I expect to be back at S— in three weeks' time, when I hope to meet with you again: it is a favour I much look forward to. At times I wonder why I am subjected to these bonds, and isolated from all the Lord's people in the habitation of wickedness. How strange are the paths some of the Lord's people are called upon to pass through! But I feel I can rest at times, even in this perplexing path, upon this truth – that all our steps are ordered by the Lord.

> All his dealings wise and good,
> Uniform, though various;
> Though they seem, by reason viewed,
> Cross, or quite contrarious.[580]

We need grace to say with Paul, 'I have learned, in whatsoever state I am, therewith to be content.' I feel that I need the outpouring of the Spirit to keep alive the spirit of grace within, to enable me to commune with him. I feel dependent on him for every spiritual motion – to read, to think, to pray, with any sense of his favour, or to feed upon the Word. At times I feel the Word drop with much sweetness, and it fills my soul with a sense of the Lord's goodness to me. There are moments when I feel I can leave all things concerning me in his hands. This, my dear friend, is no mean favour – I feel thankful for it. What the Lord's will concerning me is, I feel I have no wish to pry into, and can say:

> My God, I would not long to see
> My fate with curious eyes;
> What gloomy lines are writ for me,
> Or what bright scenes may rise.[581]

One thing we must expect is tribulation. I have thought how comforting were the words of our Lord, 'But be of good cheer; I have overcome the world.' It matters not what the saints of God have to pass through, nothing can mar their inheritance; and every trial and conflict they endure will bring them closer to him, and make them look for that kingdom not made with hands, eternal in the heavens. If it were not so we should become satisfied in our nest. I believe that every child of God is brought to say,

> Weary of earth, myself, and sin,
> Dear Jesus, set me free,
> And to thy glory take me in,
> For there I long to be.[582]

The soul has to be prepared for the inheritance prepared for it. 'The preparations of the heart … is from the LORD,' and all things work to this end in his dealings with us. Let us, therefore, 'lay aside every weight, and the sin which doth so easily beset us, and let us run with patience the race that is set before us, looking unto Jesus.' There is much to beset us, and unbelief often beclouds our sky and bedims the eye of faith; but let us look to the end of our profession, when we shall lay aside this tabernacle and enter that kingdom, which, at times, the eye of faith gets a glimpse of. And if the sight we get at times now gives such enjoyment, what must the entering in be, where we shall be continually. Truly the anticipation gives abounding consolation!

I remain yours in hope of such a reward,

J C Burgess,

No. 62180, C Company, 85 T.R.B., Mapleton, nr. Hornsea, East Yorkshire.

April 14th, 1917.[583]

[4]

✍ My dear friend,

I will take the opportunity this afternoon of replying to your letter. The way, as yet, has not been opened for me to get to you; I had hoped in the past week that I should be able, but it was not the Lord's will. I could have got a pass, but I was warned for guard tonight: if possible shall get one for next Sunday. I feel, in truth, that I long for the company of those who fear God, as one sings:

> With long desire my spirit faints,
> To meet the assembly of thy saints.[584]

The Lord is still pleased to support and keep me in a quiet frame. Although at times much exercised with eternal things, he helps me to endure my lot. Knowing what an unexercised frame is, and a rebellious spirit, my desire is to praise his holy name, and say with one: 'Not unto us, O LORD, not unto us, but unto thy name give glory.' I feel it a great mercy in the midst of tribulation to be able to be submissive in his hands, and know no will but his. It is in this frame we can quietly watch his dealings and observe the little things which have directed our course. In looking back upon the past few months, I feel I could easily fill a book with these little circumstances which have brought me here; and one great thing I can say, his presence has been with me until now; and, however hard and trying my lot may be in the eyes of natural men, so far, his presence in it has more than made amends for all. I would not have missed the trial he has been pleased to bring me into because of the consolation which has abounded. Oh, how gracious is the Lord to us in tribulation; he afflicts and consoles, and the consolation is far beyond the affliction. My soul at times seems too full to contain, when I think of the love and mercy conferred on me. Only in the past week he has given me great encouragement concerning my brother; he is in deep trouble concerning his lost condition. In my letters to him of late I have been bold to touch upon these things, and, in his replies, I read the language of the convicted sinner who longs for release. He can no longer keep it to himself. In a letter from mother, she enclosed one she received from him in the same strain. You will be able to imagine my feelings better than I can describe. He has been the burden of my prayer for years. At times, I have felt I could not give him up but felt I must pray for him. Now, to feel the Lord has put his hand to the work, and is doing effectually what all persuasion on our part could not do: to hear him craving the thing he has always treated with contempt, and loathing himself for the things he once delighted in, are indeed great things to us. I have felt very humbled and softened in spirit at the Lord's goodness. As a family I feel the Lord has done great things for us: we have great cause for gratitude and thanksgiving. There are moments when he is pleased to give it, and what a gift it is! I feel this war will be sanctified to the saints of God, but whether it will find me in time or eternity remains at the Lord's will.

Sometimes I feel that I shall he brought through, and shall again be enabled to speak well of his name, at other times I am at a point, and wonder if it is the Lord's will to take me to himself. These things are in his hand; but, feeling that the Lord has led me thus far, I feel I can leave all things to him.

I will now close, hoping you are in good health.

I remain yours in the bond of an everlasting covenant,

James C Burgess,

62180, Det. C Company, 85 T.R.B., Mapleton, Hornsea, East Yorkshire.

April 22nd, 1917.[585]

J. Butler

We do not know anything about the writer of this letter. It would appear that the recipient was Ebenezer Littleton (Jr.) (1857-1934), who would in 1928 become pastor at Rehoboth Chapel, Portsmouth.[586] He authored a daily portion book, *Day unto Day* (1906). His father, Ebenezer Littleton (Sr.) (1833-1920), was pastor at Crowborough, Sussex.

Ebenezer Littleton (Sr.)

✍ To Mr Littleton.

My dear friend and brother,

In addressing you under this heading I desire to do so in sincerity and truthfully. To be a brother to another person it follows we must belong to the same family; and I believe we can honestly claim this relationship through Christ Jesus our Lord. What a blessing to be the humblest member in this family whose Father is God. In my daily life I have to so often come like the prodigal, 'I … am no more worthy to be called thy son: make me as one of thy hired servants.' 'I have sinned against heaven, and before thee.' I am plagued with unbelief and sin; my carnal heart and desires lead me away from instead of unto a precious Redeemer, so that I am in trouble, sorrows press me sore, and those things which my inmost soul delights in get, as it were, out of sight behind the cloud of transgressions and sins. I try to pray and cry to God for those things which are so desirable, and he seems to turn a deaf ear. What could we poor carnal creatures do if he did not remember we are but dust? We read that the Saviour of sinners was in all points tempted as we are, sin excepted. What a mercy he does not allow us to be tempted beyond what we are able to bear, and has promised with the temptation to make a way for our escape.

A few nights ago I was feeling unwell in body and sick in soul. I was out on a working party; it was a night shift and we were working in a deep dugout. I was sitting in the tunnel which connects up the entrances. I took out my little Testament and Psalms and I read the last Psalm (150). It commences with 'Praise ye the LORD,' and ends with 'Let every thing that hath breath praise the LORD. Praise ye the LORD.' I was not feeling much like praising God, but more under the influence of self-pity than anything else, and ready to cry out, 'how hard's my lot.' As I was helped to reflect on the praise of God, this verse came to my mind, 'Praise waiteth for thee, O God, in Zion.' I could see he was waiting to be gracious, and he brings us into the position to value his help before he bestows it, lest we should play with it like a child with a toy. I could see many things which he is daily 'loading' me with, which call for praise. I do love to reflect on a word when it fastens itself upon my conscience; and I was favoured to do so as I went on with my work and after I got home. It helped me, although I cannot feel my earnest desires after a particular manifestation of the help of God on my behalf in a special matter relating to my daily life are being answered.

Please forgive me if I pen just a few thoughts which I could see in this word 'praise.' The first letter is P, Perfection; 2nd, Righteousness; 3rd, Ascension; 4th, Intercession and Interest; 5th, Salvation for sinners; 6th. Eternity.

1st. Perfection. Every work of God is perfect, both in nature and in grace. Every detail connected with the birth of a child in nature shows the perfection and handiwork of God; and every child of God, born again of the Spirit, is in accordance with the perfect work of the covenant of grace entered into before the foundation of the world. What could show forth more of the perfection of that covenant of grace than the plan of salvation?

2nd. Righteousness. The righteousness of the flesh is as filthy rags. I can see where I have tried to cover my poor sin-spotted soul up in those filthy rags and endeavoured to believe they covered up my uncleanness; but God has stripped them off and shown me all things are open and naked before that God with whom we have to do. Also, God out of Christ is a consuming fire, and he burns up my carnal righteousness; and if I offend in one point I am guilty of all. But blessed be his holy name, on the second Sunday morning in September, 1913, he gave me faith to see I was interested in the precious blood of Christ and clothed in his robe of righteousness. It was a never-to-be-forgotten Sunday.

3rd. Ascension. Every poor sensible sinner is brought to praise God for the ascension of a precious Christ. It is not sufficient that he came down and was born of a woman to suffer, bleed and die, but he rose again and ascended to the Father. And what is he doing there? We get it in the next letter.

4th. Intercession. He ascended to the Father and

is continually making intercession for his saints, his choice, those whom he came to save. And cannot I praise him for a felt interest in him? What is the blood of Christ to me if I am not interested in its efficacy? I must be interested in the plan of salvation to receive benefit thereby. I must be interested in his glorious robe of righteousness or I cannot be,

> Rendered fit with Christ to sit,
> And be the guest of God.[587]

5th. Salvation. What a field opens up here, in the plan of salvation. God the Father, God the Son, and God the Holy Ghost, each one interested in this glorious plan! I cannot dwell on this letter, time and space forbid it, but I feel certain your soul enters into the praises of God for the plan of salvation for sinners.

> Sinners can say, and none but they,
> 'How precious is the Saviour!'[588]

6th. Eternity. My soul, where wilt thou spend eternity? Will it be praising God, or will it be in the confines of hell? It will be one place or the other. Blessed be God he has given me a hope beyond the grave. My soul sometimes 'rejoices in God my Saviour;' and I can say, 'If he meant to destroy me he would not have shown me these things.' And we can each say, 'Eternity will not be too long to praise and bless a three-one God, whose almighty arms are underneath to bear us up, lest we should make shipwreck of faith.' How I long at times to be with him in glory, and

> To bathe my weary soul
> In seas of heavenly rest,
> And not a wave of trouble roll
> Across my peaceful breast![589]

I have only just skimmed the surface of this grand theme 'praise;' but God can help you to dive deep beneath the surface and to go on your way refreshed and edified.

I am sorry you were given so much trouble in getting your letter over. Please thank your dear father for his kind wishes and desires. I know he will not mind me replying to his son; what a favour for father and son both to be interested in each other's natural welfare, and both to be taught by the same God, and both ministers of the gospel of good news to poor sinners. May you each be granted many seals to the ministry and souls for your hire. May grace, mercy and peace from God be multiplied towards you. May Christ be felt within you; no doubt you are, like me, bound to confess from time to time, 'without him we can do nothing.' But 'with Christ in the vessel, we smile at the storm.' My Christian love to you both. Your brother, in hope of salvation by Christ Jesus alone,

J. Butler,
British Expeditionary Force, France.
September 22nd, 1917.[590]

Ebenezer Clark, Barton

Mr Clark was born in 1894. He left school at the age of 13 and spent four years apprenticed to a bricklayer. His work took him to London in 1913, and he was there when war broke out in 1914. He soon joined up and was placed in the Life Guards, serving at home as a bodyguard to the king, riding postilion to his coach in processions. Seeing men called up to serve at the front, Mr Clark asked his superiors if he could be transferred to active service. In 1916 he went out to France and, in his own writings, admits that he "went out to France in 1916 without God and without hope in the world, and hardened in sin."[591] Such was his state until 'out for a rest' at Christmas 1916, after six months at the front line, his heart was arrested by the words, 'it is appointed unto men once to die, but after this the judgement.' His fears for his never-dying soul, and the Lord's gracious and sparing mercies to him, are reflected in the letters which follow, as well as in his wartime diary[592] and his later writings. He served on the front during the remainder of the war, becoming known as a highly skilled sniper. It seemed to his superiors that there was "watching care over him" as when a dangerous task was to be undertaken, they would say, "Send Clark, he will come back!"

When the Armistice was signed, he was amongst the longest-serving men of his regiment still out in France. He was, therefore, entitled to an early demobilisation, provided he had work to go to. The problem was, though, that he could not remember the job, nor the name of his employers in London. As an alternative he was offered an opportunity to join the police force. However, as he later recalled:

Ebenezer Clark

✍ I said no to that; no more uniform for me now. I want to be a good soldier of Jesus. I remember retiring after this among the bombed buildings and the heaps of bricks, very cast down, feeling so hopeless, not a penny in the world. I tried to kneel out of sight and tried to pray the Lord to have mercy on me and appear for me, and it was as if a voice spoke, 'Every beast of the forest is mine, and the cattle upon a thousand hills.' I cannot forget the effect it had; the power. I said, 'Lord, everything is in thy hand, gold and silver,' and I believed he would make a way for me, and felt the Lord with me, such an unworthy sinner.

Shortly afterwards he was called for and told that a builder had written to say he wanted Ebenezer Clark to work for him. He was, therefore, soon on his way home, arriving at Barton on a Sabbath, recalling, "I was very pleased to creep in and worship; very fearful the people would see through me."

Back home he was much exercised about baptism and making an open profession of faith. At a church meeting on 5th July, 1919, he gave his testimony and was unanimously accepted by the church, and was baptised on July 19th, along with his cousin Agnes.

Just over a decade later, on 24th July, 1931, the church at Barton met to consider Mr Clark's call to the ministry. Members of the church and congregation and others had observed the Lord's work in exercising him for the ministry, and much prayer had been made on his behalf. The church received his testimony and unanimously wished him Godspeed, sending him out to preach. After he had been preaching for a few years, on 18th July, 1935, the church at Barton wrote to Mr Clark inviting him to the pastorate, a position which he accepted and fulfilled faithfully until his death on 8th November, 1978.[593]

The following is the correspondence between Ebenezer Clark and one of his sisters (probably Mary Pearce[594]). Unfortunately, the letters that we have do not appear to be the complete correspondence between the two.

[1]

✍ My dear Sister,

I feel I must write you a few lines in answer to your most kind and affectionate letter, which I was pleased to receive, unworthy though I am. It did me more good than anything has, and I thank you from the bottom of my heart. When I read it, I cannot express my feelings in words; but I said to myself, 'Oh blessed sister, to be able to write like that!' Black as I am, filthy as I am, it gave me hope. You do not know what it set before me, for I have been very wicked. It grieves me to look back upon the past years, how I did not want religion, wanted to enjoy the wickedness of this world. Often I have said to myself, 'The Baptists think they are right, and not everybody else.' Oh I was hardened in sin! You do not know one half what I was like; did not want anyone to mention anything about it to me. So you will not wonder what I have to suffer for it.

When you wrote to me before, I well remember those words of yours, how they struck me: 'What a mercy it was to be out of a deserved hell.' And I said, 'Yes, for nobody deserved it more than I did.' I then saw my past sins as it were, and thought of instances. Oh, if the Lord had cut me down then! It's a wonder the roof had not fallen down upon my head. And I had to cry to the Lord for mercy. Oh how I did feel – all day I was trying to pray: 'Lord, do forgive me if it is possible.' I began to read the Bible M— gave me, which I had not touched before. I read because I hoped to find hope of mercy, and to see if there were sins too great for forgiveness. I believed he was a merciful God and would have mercy upon whom he would; but all the time it was on my mind: 'You would not have fallen so low if the Lord had intended to take you into his keeping; so you need not keep praying or asking for forgiveness.'

But your letter was a great comfort to me, for I am truly grieved and hope I truly desire to forsake the past, and pray the Lord will keep me. I have felt I dare not say a word, until I read a few words about a fortnight ago. I was greatly distressed in mind, did not know what to do; walked about, tried to cry to the Lord for help, tried to read the Bible, tried to write; could do nothing. Then I went into the tent and read again. Then I picked up a *Little Gleaner* and read a piece in that, and these words were in it that I cannot forget. They struck me and made me feel I could cry to think they were really true; and I did: the Lord came, 'not to call the righteous, but sinners to repentance.' 'Though your sins be as scarlet, they shall be as white as snow; though … red like crimson, they shall be as wool.' And I thought, black as I am, low as I feel, there must be hope.

Now I have searched the Bible and hymn book and cannot find it in either, not the last part. I found the first; they were his own dear words. Can you tell me where the others are? You said in your letter such blessed things. I feel I do desire to say that: 'O Lord! how can I serve thee aright, for I am so helpless?' It is true we cannot do anything in and of ourselves. What help we do need! It was thoughts of dear Mother that first caused me sorrow. How I thought of her, and how she would have grieved to see me in such a state. How I had run from her teaching. Many things came to me, but it would fill a book to write all. I do hope and pray the Lord will have mercy on my soul, for I feel, as you say, what are the pleasures of this world for a season, compared with everlasting joy! Oh that word 'everlasting,' what it means! Nobody knows but those who feel they are to suffer for ever and ever. Of course, nature would say the same; but it is different when one realizes that without God's mercy, unless some great power unseen changes their filthy state, they are for ever lost. That's what I feel, and can only pray the Lord will have mercy on me.

Dear Sister, I hope when you read this you will not think me as I often think myself, nothing but a hypocrite. I have just sat and written how and what I feel. I have suffered in body, and I have not said anything because I felt I must bear it myself; but I have told you now. I have been in the depths of sin and wickedness; one cannot express their feelings. Now I thank you again for your letter. I believe there is something in true religion, and that religion I truly desire and would like to feel more of it. Your words were very encouraging. May the Lord teach me, for I feel I can do nothing. I have read much of the New Testament today. Oh his love and mercy to the people! I felt he was the same God and has the same power to work miracles now as then; for I think sometimes, if he has mercy on me it will be one.[595] But I do hope he will, and keep and guard over me through this terrible war. Oh that men would praise him more for his goodness, and for his wonderful works to the children of men!

I must close, leaving all to a merciful God to deal with me as it seemeth him good. I hope I say it sincerely, for once I was hardened and I kicked; but now it is far different, I hope. Now, dear Sister, I hope you will understand this. I have just sat and written as I have felt. I have written before, but could not send it; but will send this, and you will understand a bit, for I have been greatly troubled and afraid I am wrong. So I will close with love to all, hoping there is hope of salvation for the vilest sinner out of hell,

Your loving brother,
France.
March 18th, 1917.[596]

[2]

✍ My dear Brother,

I was so pleased to receive your letter. Before I got up that morning I was thinking about you, and this verse came to my mind:

> Did ever a sinner sink to woe,
> Thirsting for pardoning grace?
> Ten thousand voices answer, No;
> None die that seek his face.[597]

I'm sure I felt after reading your letter that I could praise the Lord, to think that in some measure he had healed your wounds which sin had made, for which I earnestly entreated the Lord on your behalf. I hope the Lord will still go on to be gracious to you and bless you abundantly. I fear some are hardened in sin, but they say it is a long road with no turning. I hope the time will come when they will be brought to see their folly. How sad to know right, and then be bent on the wrong! That is how we all are by nature. I know I have said, if the Lord took me to heaven, there was hope for the most wicked wretch on the face of the earth. I used to feel so bad inwardly, everything that was wrong. And there should I have gone, had it not been for God's preserving care over me. I should have been as bad as the worst.

I felt so very down and out of the secret in January. I remember saying many times that I wanted Jesus only, and these words were a great comfort to me: 'It is your Father's good pleasure to give you the kingdom.' For a few minutes I did feel such love to the dear Lord that I said, 'What more can I want than the promise of his kingdom?' You know we don't always feel we love him, but I do like to know that there is something secret working inwardly.

I do hope you are feeling better; also that the Lord will spare you to meet with us all again. Time flies very quickly. We shall soon have had three years of war. Oh that it would stop! We have had a lot of snow again. I do feel the Lord's judgements are abroad in the earth, and fear sometimes what will be the next calamity. Oh that the nation would be more looking to the God of all their mercies, who could soon cause a famine, and then the people would know where their help must come from! He has wonderfully supplied our need up till now. We have never wanted for necessaries of life. I shall be very pleased to hear from you again. With much love to you from us all,

Your affectionate sister.

April 1st, 1917.[598]

Interior of Barton Chapel

[3]

✍ My dear Brother,

I was so pleased to receive your last letter that I thought of answering it at once, but I have let a fortnight go. It was good news to me to think that the dear Lord should condescend to visit a poor soldier in France. I did try and thank him for it, for do you know I had prayed, I should say to be honest, every night, that the Lord would bless your soul abundantly, and take care of your poor body. I felt he had somewhat answered my poor prayers, so that it quite broke my spirit down. For I feel the most unworthy of sinners, and cannot expect the Lord to hear a sinner like me; and yet as you say, they are sinners he came to save and take to heaven, so that we shall have to sing, 'Not unto us, but unto thy name give all the glory for ever and ever. Amen.'

Well, I do hope that the Lord will still go on to bless you and keep you in his fear, which we so much need daily, so that we do not bring trouble on our head. I often feel ashamed of myself, and if we were rewarded for our deserts, the Lord would never smile upon us again. Oh that we may endure to the end, for the same shall be saved! I know but little, and feel but a child in divine things. Mr Curtis[599] was preaching at our chapel today.[600] It was about Philip and the eunuch. I would have liked you to have heard him. I am sure you would have known what he said about Philip preaching Jesus unto the eunuch. I always think of you when they talk of the sinner being laid low in self-abasement. I am sure you have been at the right school, and have been brought to feel your sins a mighty load, and to lay them at his dear feet. But how nice to think he has borne with you, and cast your sins, as it were, behind his back, and never more to remember them!

I do hope you will be spared to come home, and all of us meet again. Oh that this dreadful war would cease, and all the poor fellows return to their homes! Mr Curtis did pray so nicely about it this morning. We are signing a petition to send to the Prime Minister for a day of prayer and humiliation to the Lord, that he would interpose on our behalf as a nation. But alas, the wickedness! There are people pleasure-making on the Sabbath, and I fear England is far from what we should like to see it.

Well, I hope you had a comfortable Sunday, although you can't get to chapel. The Lord isn't confined to means. He could make it a real Sabbath indeed to you. We do think about you; especially I also wonder if you get any sleep at night. I must close as it is before breakfast, and no one up but myself.

With much love to you from us all,

Your affectionate sister.

June 10th, 1917.[601]

[4]

✍ My dear Sister,

I would like to answer your letters in full, as I do not want my letter to cause you grief or undue concern. I hope you are kept from the awful, wayward sinfulness I was in. I dare not say a word. I feel there are none so wicked as I, and it is a great concern to me often, if I am deceived or not, if I am rightly taught. Ah, no one knows the weight of such matters, only those who pass through them! But I hope I understand you. I know, dear Sister, good works will not obtain salvation, and we need more than that. What a mercy, I feel, that it is not of works, for it could never reach me if it was for our deserts or merit. Ah, I know what nature and our hardened hearts think or feel; and the world, for I used to feel the same. They say God is unjust and unmerciful. Oh, but how different it is to us now! They do not think of what they are and who they are, that he is an Almighty God, that it is he that first made man and has all power over him, so that he could destroy the whole world; yes, be just in doing that. For so great is its wickedness that it is great love and mercy that he has saved a remnant; that it is a great mercy he has said he will have a people, 'and they shall be my people, and I will be their God,' and that he saved them for his holy name's sake. Oh he is a very just and merciful God! It has been wonderful to me, for I hope I have felt his love and mercy, and I cannot help speaking of it.

I often feel I will not say a word, for sometimes I have thought it is only presumption, and what a hypocrite I have been. I feel like you, so ignorant of such things. So I was and am now, and if I know anything it is, I hope, the Holy Spirit's teaching. Oh that is the great point! It is hoping with much fearing and trembling. You say you wish you were sure you were of that people. All I can say, dear Sister, to you is, if I may, wait patiently, hoping and trusting, for his time. It will be his time and not before; but I know what anyone says to you will do no good, but perhaps sometimes harm. I know I am not one that can say a word, for I need much teaching; but the Word of God is my teaching, blessed by the Holy Spirit, I hope. I have enjoyed reading it of late. Oh it is full of precious promises sometimes! For there have been times when one has read a portion and seen nothing in it. Then at another time it has seemed to melt one down with love and been such a sweet feeling. One likes to get out of the way and read and pray, or try to pray, for one is continually looking up to the Lord, for we do so need his help. One is brought very close to danger, so that things are very solemn. I am very thankful I have been upheld and preserved until now, and I desire to put my trust continually in the Lord and say, 'Thy will be done.' One has to be brought very humble at his feet and stripped as it were. Ah, it is a sweet place!

But I must close now ... Sometimes we are apt to

feel lonely, as you say, and have hard thoughts, but we could not but be thankful for many mercies. My two earthly friends are my Bible and hymn book. I hope we shall meet sooner or later, if it is the Lord's will. We cannot say; we know not what a day may bring forth. It is a very solemn fearing time for me, but one has got through thus far. My love to you all,

Your loving brother,
France.
June 14th, 1917.[602]

Ebenezer Clark and his wife in later life

[5]

✍ My dear Brother,

I saw R— at chapel this morning, and she said that she had received a letter from you, and thought you were very downhearted. She couldn't forget you whilst she was in chapel. You know this is Easter Sunday, which is supposed to be the day of the resurrection of Jesus Christ. Well enough to know he did die and rise again, but was it for *our* sins? Did he suffer that we might *live*? I hope he did for us both. I remember when young how I used to hate to hear of the judgement day. I feared it so much that I thought I would much rather be dead when that comes. But now I love to hear a minister talk about it in the pulpit. You know in our hymn book we have a few hymns about the day of judgement, and we used to have some solemn tunes, and I used to stand, and shiver, and tremble; it did seem so dreadful and solemn. It will be a most blessed day to the Lord's people, for him to say, 'Come, ye blessed of my Father.' But the wicked will hear, 'Depart … ye cursed, I never knew you.' How they will tremble and call for rocks and hills to hide them from the presence of the Almighty. Won't it be something wonderful if you and I are in the, 'Come, ye blessed'? I have a faint hope we shall be. I quite believe you will be there, and we shall feel that there is no one that can sing redeeming love and grace so loud as we. When you look round and see your fellow creatures sunk so deep in sin and left there, it makes you feel,

Why me, why me, O blessed God,
Why such a wretch as me?
Who must for ever lie in hell,
Were not salvation free.[603]

I am sure, my dear Brother, you have great cause for hope to think the Lord hasn't left you to go on in sin and have no concern about it. You might have done so, and never had a thought about eternity. You know, hundreds do, and then, poor things, to find themselves in everlasting punishment! If the Lord hadn't intended to save you, he would never have shown you yourself and what there is in your heart. And you know,

> Whom once he loves, he never leaves,
> But loves them to the end.[604]

I know he must tell you from his own dear lips, and then you will believe. I should like to do you good. I feel so for you out in a foreign country where God is hardly known. God is sending us some very cold wintry weather. To the people that have set their seed on a Sunday, the Lord has sent the frost, so that I should think it has frozen in the ground. I do hope he will remember us in mercy and hear the praying few, so that there may be food for man and beast. We all hope that the war will soon be over. Oh that in his mercy he would hasten the time of peace! We were getting a bit anxious, as a week had nearly gone and none of us had heard from you. We are afraid you will have to join your regiment again. I know you don't feel like fighting. The Lord can preserve you and bring you back to us again, if it is his dear will ... With much love to you, hoping you can say, 'Though he slay me, yet will I trust in him.'

Your affectionate sister.[605]

[6]

✍ My dear Brother,

It seems wonderful how you get through amidst the many dangers. Although we think of you, we cannot enter into your feelings facing death. I do feel I should be a coward, but I believe, dear, you often feel the Lord's presence. You know he is always near his dear people. 'His children shall always have a place of refuge;' even if they are taken from this earth there remaineth a rest for them. I do hope you will be helped through and be brought back to us in safety ...

I heard last night that G— S— was killed instantly in France. Oh my dear, to be cut down out of Christ, how terrible! Although we do not know how many hearts the dear Lord has changed, we know that he alone can do it. We cannot give our hearts to God, as some tell us. If he condescends to draw us to him, then we can say, 'Here's my heart, Lord, take and seal it,' as we used to sing.[606] Pleased to hear you get a little time for reading; also that the sermon was a help to you. Ah dear, fear is one of the graces. Now I must leave off.

Much love from,
Your ever loving sister.
July 7th, 1917.[607]

[7]

✍ My dear Brother,

Received your kind letter last Saturday, and many thanks for it. I quite look forward to them, and so enjoy reading them. Not, my dear, that I rejoice because you feel so low in mind; but it is a mercy to have enough religion to be tried. Your being so exercised is not a mark against you. All those that have got to heaven have had to walk the same path. I wish I could write and cheer you up, but I know your best Friend must come himself. To feel, as you say,

Jesus Christ precious in the want of him; that is nice. He has blessed your soul abundantly, and he will come again, because he is an everlasting Lover. You would not mourn over your sins and desire these better things, if you had not got spiritual life.

Paul, writing to the Ephesians, says: 'And you hath he quickened, who were dead in trespasses and sins.' Was it not so with you, dear, also me? I feel afraid to say much about myself. I can see your marks of grace, but do not feel I have had such a deep law work as you. They were indeed solemn words you mention: 'Man, know yourself.'[608] Were they the first words that were the means of convincing you of your state? I was pleased to read you had some nice helps when in that dangerous position. You see, the Lord gave you special help in a time of need. How we should love to see you and talk to you. I should think you will soon be having leave. You have been there 18 months.

I hope you received that little book with a portion for every day. I have read them for years, and they always seem fresh. I thought when you had not much time, they might be a little help to you. They are short and sweet ... A— has got conditional exemption again. Many apparently have had to go in a worse condition than his. I feel all I can say is, 'What shall we then say to these things? If God be for us, who can be against us?'

Now, dear Brother, I must close, trusting the dear Lord will take care of you, soul and body, and keep you ever looking up to him. I heard a minister say once we have need to pray to be kept if we only walk down the street. If left to ourselves we soon get into trouble; we have got such wicked hearts. How many times I have heard dear Mother[609] sing:

> We oft bring mischief on our heads,
> By some unwary step.[610]

How I understand some of her remarks now! I heard her say once, she was taunted with pride. Oh, she meant the pride of her heart! We have to experience the same things to understand. Good-night dear; I wonder if you are back in the trenches again.

Your loving sister.

July 23rd, 1917.[611]

Barton Chapel, as originally built

[8]

✍ My dear Sister,

I have written letters to you before, but could not send them. Oh I feel now I know not how to write! I do not know what you will be saying of me. Oh I am a wretched, vile sinner, richly deserving hell! It is a great mercy I am out of it. Great has been the anguish of my soul. Oh dear Sister, it is very solemn, very weighty! All I can cry is, 'God be merciful to me a sinner;' 'behold, I am vile!' Oh what shall I do! Oh that the Lord Jesus Christ would appear and deliver me from that horrible pit!

I have read your letter and have tried to look back. When I saw, as it were, the Lord Jesus Christ on the right hand of Almighty God, receiving his people, seeing, as it were, God looking down on vilest sinners, in love, in and through a Saviour's blood, even his only-begotten Son. Yes, it is all free and sovereign grace that sinners were saved. Oh, how then I did hope! Yes, that is the only way. But dear Sister, are we of that chosen people? 'Many are called, but few are chosen.' Shall I be without a wedding garment? Will the Lord say, 'Bind him hand and foot … and cast him into outer darkness?' Oh, for ever in hell! These things have been so heavily on my heart. Ah, it is a mercy I am kept as I am! Often I have been near to utter despair. I have tried to pray, but my wicked heart and all my sins rose up against me – sins I had forgotten. Oh how I have grieved over them! Then the wickedness around me, and when I look at myself within I see nothing but filth and evil. Then there is a great conflict, for the Word of God seems full of condemnation of such. If I was born again, if the Lord Jesus died for me, if I was of that people I had hoped I was, I should not be like this. Oh but what unbelief!

I have just written you a few lines of what a state I have passed through. I feel I cannot speak or do anything, for it will be some evil. I feel now full of sorrow, weighed down with a load of sin and guilt. Ah, those that feel it will know it, that to realize that there is hell or heaven for their never-dying souls, and many say that much; but oh to see and feel they are deserving of it, and feel no hope, that all before is only head knowledge, that they have been deceived! Oh, I cannot write too solemnly of it! Just now and then I seem to see some slight ray of hope in reading. Will the Lord reveal his mercy?

> Thy Spirit must the work perform,
> For it is all of grace.[612]

Oh, I feel I do so want to know feelingly the gracious presence of the Lord! Oh for faith to trust in him, that he would keep me from temptation, from hardness over our lot, grace to stand against the many temptations and hardships, both of body and our spiritual welfare; for we do need it. When my comrades are full of drink and saying at times hard things, all I can do is to ask the Lord to keep me, and say, but for the grace of God I should have been with them. I have proved that.

Oh man, know thyself! Oh that the Lord would make us to know! 'Teach me thy way, O LORD!' 'Create in me a clean heart … and renew a right spirit within me.' We feel now that we must come with much prayer and supplication, begging of a precious Christ for mercy; for Christ is the only way. He says,

'No man cometh unto the Father, but by me.' This is Sunday, and I have been begging, crying, and trying to lay my sorrow at the foot of the cross.

> Nothing in my hand I bring;
> Simply to thy cross I cling.[613]

I can say feelingly that if I do get to heaven, no one will sing louder, or have cause to, than I, of redeeming grace, sovereign love. I feel now I'm saying the language of my heart feelingly: Lord, 'my soul fainteth for thy salvation.' 'My soul is continually in my hand.' Yes, that the Lord will bless me with a blessing of love. It is a point I want to make sure – have I an interest in that holy covenant?

I do hope you will forgive me for not writing before, but it would have been wrong; for I was greatly troubled. But now it appears more again to me that salvation is of God through the blood of a dear Redeemer, Jesus Christ. Sinners vile as I are saved. Oh that the Lord will show me the way to go, for as the Apostle said, in and of ourselves we can do nothing. Oh it will be a mercy if we are taught of the Holy Spirit! And that is our heart's desire. Dear Sister, I am quite well in body; much to be thankful for. I hope you are. If you have bread to eat, you should be. Accept my love,

From your unworthy brother,
France.
28th July, 1917.[614]

[9]

✍ My dear Sister,

I feel I must write to you again for several reasons. You have been much upon my mind; I also must thank you for your letter and parcel; also I am afraid you will be upset at my last letter. Well, I cannot fetch it back if I wanted; but one has been very low in spirit. Feeling somewhat better now, I felt I must write to answer your letter, for it did me good to read it, and that night I felt helped on my knees, pleading at a throne of grace, and in thanking the Lord for his mercy in providential things. I felt humbled and able to pour out my full heart, as it were. But I want to write in sincerity and truth of such things, to know and realize in a right sense the weight of them. Oh that we may!

Well, dear Sister, I am afraid I have been a bad one in answering your letters with too much self! Perhaps when I was at home I did not appear to show much feeling, but, my dear, I do think of you. How it hurts me to know you are suffering for me, all of you, and Father too! Oh, I am sure I try to think of you in my poor prayers, that the Lord will help you all, as well as me, to be able to keep from hard or too sorrowful thoughts of our lot, and give us strength to bear up and to be able to feel it will be for our soul's good; for I feel I do not want to complain a word, but to be ever kept humbly submissive. I know it takes a lot of grace to say it:

> Let that grace, Lord, like a fetter,
> Bind my wandering heart to thee.[615]

For without him we shall not go one little step

aright, not even a right thought or desire.

Ah, dear sister, as you said, I should have liked to have heard Mr. Carr[616] speak from those words, trying Peter's faith and grace. But oh what a mercy, what a blessing, to be able to say and feel: 'Thou knowest that I love thee!' Yes, he knows all who love him, because he first loved them. Many perhaps like me will say, 'Lord, thou knowest I desire to love thee.' If not that, a desire to have that desire to love him. When I read it over, it seemed to me that it was the same as when a poor sinner has such a felt sense of his lost condition, what he was, what he is by nature, of his wicked past, and then the Lord asking him, as it were. What grace, what faith it needs! Only the felt presence of a precious Redeemer, a sweet drawing inwardly or in prayer, will enable a poor sinner to say, 'Thou knowest I do' …

May the Lord bless and be with you all, and also with me; fit and prepare me for all, keep me while I have to be out here. Oh that he may be my strength, that he will teach me and guide me by his Holy Spirit, and keep me humble at his dear feet. Much love from,

Your loving brother,
France.
17th Oct., 1917.[617]

[10]

✍ My dear Sister,

I am thankful to say I am as well as can be expected in body, and I hope better in spirits. I have enjoyed reading lately, what little time I have. I am sure I have had some nice sermons to read. One feels encouraged at times. You little think, perhaps, how encouraging your letter was to me. It perhaps may not appear so to you, but if you knew all you would understand it. It was your having no minister last Sunday night. I felt so drawn out. I looked at the time, and my thoughts ran out: 'Oh yes, if there is no minister, Uncle would be engaging in prayer at that time, and if I receive a letter to say it was so, I shall not be surprised.' And as you know, it was so, and I felt I must write and tell you. M— will perhaps know how encouraging such a thing is. One does not want to write presumptuously or anything like that, but to record the truth. Ah, we have treacherous hearts! Oh to be kept in sincerity and truth in all things!

Well dear sister, do not pity me or think I am hard done by, or suffering too much, for I might be much worse out here. I am out of it all and quite comfortable. The people where I am staying are very nice and kind. The weather has been rather wet and cold, but it is better sometimes than others. It is a great favour to be able to forget these discomforts, and have our mind and thoughts on better things in prayer and supplication and thankfulness. Nature would not have it, left to our own strength. It is full of hardness and self-pity, but what a mercy to be enabled to keep from it! Oh to be enabled to put our trust in the Lord! Oh that I might trust him more, as I was reading a sermon the other day and seeing what a wonderful thing it was! And the dear man quoted two lines that some might say:

> O could I but believe,
> Then all would easy be.[618]

And I thought the same. If I could but believe

really and truly, that I had a part in this, it would be so; but have I? Such a wicked, evil-hearted wretch as I? Yes, it is for such; but they would not be so bad as me now. They would not have such evils rising up daily. One has to prove he has nothing good in and of himself.

Ah, solemn things to write of! Oh that the Lord will teach us his ways, lead us and keep us, that we may serve him humbly and truthfully. You know not half my thoughts, not half my fears. Sometimes I fear to write a word. But this I say, I do not desire to write one good thing of myself, for I have not one. What a sad thing it is to be a professor and not a possessor, or as I was reading, having a religion of self-righteousness. Oh to be kept from it, and presumption and vanity! ...

Thank M— for her encouraging words, 'As thy days, so shall thy strength be.' Oh for more grace and faith! Much love from,

Your loving brother,
France.
October 19th, 1917.[619]

[11]

✍ My dear Sister,

I am very thankful to say I have been favoured again out here, and have been mercifully kept out of it. I was thinking this morning of you all, how you might be thinking of me. I felt I must write and tell you that I had been mercifully kept out of all. You do not, perhaps, quite understand how, and I cannot tell you now, but I quite expected to be in it this time. All I can say is, I am not, and I am quite all right as regards that. Of course, it is not much at the best out here in the way of comfort. It seems to get worse; or else it is me. But we do not want to complain of the rough life, if we are spared the other terrors.

I was thinking this morning over it when it was snowing a bit and the wind very cold. How thankful I felt when I thought of my mates and where they might be! I felt, 'Lord, it is all thy goodness. I desire to give thee all the thanks and praise for thy mercies towards such an unworthy wretch. Oh, if it is thy holy will, do bless my soul! Give me some token of thy love, some token, Lord, for good. Draw me with the cords of thy love.' Oh for grace and faith to trust in him! I had felt sure I should be in it by now, and I had desired to leave it all with him. He has done more than I could either ask or think.

Well, my dear Sister, I do hope you are well; also Father and M—. May the Lord bless you and comfort you; also Aunt and Uncle. Give my love to them. Do not worry too much about me. I hope I may have strength to bear all. Sometimes the body is very poorly, but as you put it, may it please the Lord to stand by us, and to keep us and bless us ... Oh that it were the Lord's will I might soon be with you, to stop you from worrying, and me, as we know not what we may have to endure as it goes on! Much love from,

Your loving brother,
France.
December 2nd, 1917.[620]

[12]

✍ My dear Sister,

I will try and write you a few lines to let you know I am quite safe and as well as one can expect, and as you are about to spend another Christmas with me away ... We thought last year we might be together, but it is not so, and we do not wish to murmur or complain. You say, tell you all; but I do not wish to. It may only lead to self-pity, and you more worry.

I want to write only the truth. I know the flesh is very deceiving. There are times when one has felt nearly done up, lost heart, and thinks it will be more than he can stand or bear. But it has not been so up till now. May it please the Lord that we may have grace and strength to bear all, to overcome the many evils that beset us, and I would say as I have felt, that while you are in the comforts of this world, you may also enjoy the comfort and blessing of the Holy Spirit; and if it is his will, that he would make up to me in blessing me with his felt presence and the forgiveness of my many, many sins, shed abroad the love of a precious Saviour, Jesus Christ, in my heart. I would like to be able to write more assuredly of these blessed things.

I have passed through a very solemn time with the felt weight and burden of many, many sins, but I have enjoyed some reading and been enabled in some humble measure to pour out my heart to the Lord. I had felt as the Psalmist in the 38th Psalm. Oh the many sins, indwelling sins of nature! We are nothing but sin and vanity in and of ourselves. Oh how one has to be humbled! How we feel so undeserving of the least of his mercies! One cannot write all the things, to feel one's want and misery, and the fullness of grace in the Lord. These are deep things. Ah, and I feel at times the devil will say it is not true! Is it real? Oh, we hope so! For one has said, you may know by the heart if it is or not; the grief at so many sins, the felt sense of our own inability to overcome them, and to fear one is lost, and be brought to cry mightily to the living God for mercy; to feel, 'Though he slay me, yet will I trust in him,' knowing and feeling that you deserve hell. He would be just in sending me there, yet to believe in reading his holy Word and other good books that he is a God of mercy.

I have just read a sermon, and I cannot say how I did enjoy reading it. It spoke of that which makes a child of God cry out of his misery unto a Deliverer. 'Oh,' I said, 'have not I felt these very things?' Yes, it seems to run with my very experience. And it spoke also of that Deliverer. Ah, I have passed a day or two, yet it has greatly encouraged me. I had so felt those weighty things. I had been much on my knees crying to the Lord, begging that he would bless my soul with some token. I so wanted an assurance of a part in the blood of Christ, that I must keep on until I had it. I felt that the only comfort to my troubled breast would be the sweet assurance of some humble place beneath his throne. Then I came in, and when I got in bed thought I would read; and I picked up the *Gospel Standard* Arthur[621] sent me, and one passage that was blessed to me when I read it, and melted me down, was: 'A sure token of a child of God is, if the news of eternal life, and that thou shalt never be condemned, is the only matter of thy consolation.'[622] 'Oh,' I said, 'that is it; that is what I have been crying for, that I might not be condemned.' You can read the sermon;

it is very solemn, but truth. Oh to be led by the Spirit of Christ! Ah, it picked me up in some ways! I am afraid I was trying to get consolation by keeping the law, or felt, as the dear man says, disheartened and faint because of the corruption of nature. We would honour God and serve him better than we do. Is it not often our prayer, especially if we feel a little favour: 'Oh that I might serve him better'?

But one has proved there is only one weapon to fight with, a spirit of prayer, to fight in the battle between the flesh and the spirit. Oh that we might be more often at the throne of grace, instead of trying to overcome them ourselves! For we only get worse off. But to have a humble spirit of prayer. I have thought I would rather spend this Christmas in prayer and supplication than as I did last year. It has been somewhat the cause, for when one looks back he is apt to say, 'Look at yourself last year. Does such a wicked wretch as you expect forgiveness for those sins?' But what a difference to see the blood of a precious Jesus! Is it not enough to humble one? And he says, 'Yes, it is all free grace, and will be the greatest mercy and blessing.' We do not want to be presumptuous, but humbly thankful. Yet I think it is all hope. There may be times when one can say he is sure; but it is soon, 'I hope I can.' Oh, I would like to be more free from that sin of unbelief! For I thought when I read that sermon, I had been too backward or too much encouraging unbelief and the devil.

I trust the Lord will give me grace and faith to walk through these many trials and hardships honourably, that we may keep a clear conscience; for one thought of sin will mar our peace. The Lord knoweth all our thoughts. There are two things in that. One makes us tremble at times, and at another time it is a source of comfort; or at least I have found it so. At times it has made one shudder to think the Lord knows our inmost thoughts, all our evil thoughts; and they have to be accounted for, and are as committed in his sight. On the other hand there is comfort to know he knows all, and one has said sometimes: 'O Lord! Thou knowest all our hearts, knowest all our desires, how they would be up unto thee! Thou knowest our circumstances, the things we have to bear with.'

But I must close, feeling he has helped me to write this. So if there is anything good, may he bless it to you, and he have all the honour; for it is, he says, all for his honour and glory that he has a people. May he keep you and bless you, one and all. I beg you not to worry much about me this Christmas, but would have your prayers and sober thoughts. Oh that I may feel his presence and his love, to take hold by faith of that glorious salvation! I have much reason to thank the Lord for his goodness. I am still out of it, although I may spend Christmas in those terrible scenes. If so, may his grace be all-sufficient for me. We desire to leave it in his hands and be submissive to his will. Much heartfelt love to you all,

Your loving brother,

France.

December 14th, 1917.

P.S. That sermon is in *The Gospel Standard* for October, 1917: 'There is therefore now no condemnation, etc.'[623]

[13]

✍ My dear Sister,

If I can I will try, with the Lord's help, to write to you in answer to your kind and affectionate letter. I have felt very destitute, and as it were no life in me as to better things. You have been much on my mind, and I have much to thank you for, as I did feel the Lord in his goodness has heard and answered your prayers on my behalf; and if it is his will and I am spared, I hope when I meet you again I may be enabled to tell you more about it.

Well, as I picked up your letter, feeling very low in mind, I read that hymn you spoke of ('Why should I yield to slavish fears?'; no. 981, *Gadsby's Selection*), and I felt greatly helped. I look back now and feel, 'Oh that I might experience it again!' I have been greatly tempted that it was not real. I was [*tempted*] the next morning, I remember; it seems to come back again. May the Lord seal it in my heart and soul, and bid the tempter flee. One day, when suffering somewhat from cold and hunger, feeling very heavy and weighted by the solemnity of death, my own wickedness of the past and present, a wicked evil heart, and much more, I was walking into the mess room when those words of the poet came with power, I hope: 'Not all the blood of beasts, etc.' Oh, what came, as it were, in a flash? No, but the blood of a dear Redeemer in Gethsemane and on Calvary, and all the wonders of salvation's plan. Oh that night I hope not to forget! I cannot write it, but I did not want to go to sleep. I did not know what to do, but said, 'What, for me?' What an unspeakable mercy for such as I, seeing as it were the glories of heaven and for ever singing praises! What love ran out to a precious Saviour! And what was so blessed that night was Hymn 993 ('O Zion, afflicted with wave upon wave'; *Gadsby's Selection*). Oh I cannot describe the humble, melting feeling when I read those verses, never doubting, but feeling they were being said to me, really were for me! What I saw, what I felt, I hope never to forget!

Yet that which grieves me is, I have doubted them. Things seem to come and say, 'If that was all true, you would not feel as you do.' And I think, 'No, I should not.' Ah, that is our own wicked, deceitful heart, leaving the way we should go and running after evil and idols, something of our own, something vain, or seeking our own honour, something that brings shame upon our heads! Oh for grace and faith, and a humble spirit of prayer! Oh that I may be kept alive as to these solemn things and the concern of my never-dying soul! I was thinking tonight, when one is greatly concerned, he is grieved over his state, and when not feeling concern and nothing in him, grieved for the lack of concern and felt deadness. Ah, it is as you say, up and down! Oh that I may be enabled to say, as David did, that I have a part in that everlasting covenant, etc.! …

Well, dear Sister, I am in a solemn place, never knowing what may happen. May the Lord, if it is his holy will, prepare me to stand before his throne, if he sees fit that I do not return. I do not know, but would desire to say, 'Thy will be done, O Lord. I am a wicked wretch and deserve nothing; but we read in thy holy Word and believe that thou wilt have mercy on whom thou wilt. But if it is thy will, remember us in mercy for thy holy name's sake! Thou hast said thou wilt save thy people with an everlasting salvation.'

As you say about that Hymn 981 (*Gadsby's Selection*), sometimes we feel, 'Would he show us these wonderful things and leave us at last?' Oh, we pray not! Oh that he may give us strength equal to our day! May grace the victory get. But I must close. If the Lord spares me, may it be for his honour and glory. He is the Potter; I am the clay. And he ruleth all our ways. Yes, it is true we cannot do anything ourselves, either spiritually or naturally; for the Apostle says, 'With God's help, I will.' And that's what I desire to say. Oh that I may be able always to do that, and to take all to him in prayer! I feel that is best. I have much to be thankful for. Hope you are well. May the dear Lord keep me and you all. May it please him to shine upon my heart and soul with the light of his truth. Much love from,

Your loving brother,

France.

February 8th, 1918.[624]

[14]

✍ My dearest Sister,

Just to keep you from worrying, as no doubt when you hear I am having a few days in hospital you will be wondering how much is wrong. Well, I hope not much to get anxious about. I hope to be all right after a week's rest. Of course, we cannot say. I am not feeling too bad now, having milk food and rest; but I feel afraid if I was to do much knocking about, it would not keep down, as I still have sickly feelings. So I hope now you will understand and be thankful, as I would be in my right mind, that I have not a lot of pain to suffer and that I am having a needed rest, as I am for my body.

I have been very dark in mind over all, very wicked thoughts, self-pity, and much more; but it may be to try us, and, let us hope, to refine, if it is his will. I was thinking last night, when you read my first letter, what a wicked fellow! Oh, I did feel in a sad state! I tried to pray, but could not; did not know which way to turn. My poor head was bad for thinking; bodily affliction is painful. But I felt the state of my heart and soul was worse. Oh that the Lord will appear, and shine forth to show beauty in salvation's plan, and that the Lord Jesus may be all and in all to unworthy me! I feel with all my sickness and loss of all worldly pleasures, I can only be happy with his felt presence and a hope in his mercy, to feel his sweet drawing to those beautiful, better things. Oh for faith to fully believe, and lay hold of all we read in the Word of God! And may we be enabled to trust him and leave all to him.

Well, dear Sister, I cannot write all, for what I have passed through in mind is more than I can write. Oh how wicked I feel, and how unworthy I am if ever he does have mercy! Oh that we may never be left to give up, but if it is the Lord's will, may he keep us seeking and looking up to him! We have to prove we can do nothing. No, we may try; but everything will go if we do. Oh to be made willing for his salvation, whatever course he sees fit to take! I feel now, what a mercy he has not laid a heavier hand upon me, for I deserve it!

But I must close. I hope you will bear with me. I hope you will not be expecting me home. I am afraid my case is not bad enough for that. May the Lord keep and bless us both in body and soul. With much love to you all from,

Your loving brother,

France.

February 16th, 1918.[625]

T. Cottingham, Halland

The following letter was probably written to Mr C. H. Matthews, the pastor at Halland Calvinistic Independent Chapel. We know nothing about the author. It probably, strictly, falls outside the scope of this book, not being written by a Strict Baptist. However, the letter made an impression on the compiler, and as it was published in a Strict Baptist magazine, we have included it here:

✍ My dear Pastor,

I have thought of writing to you several times, but have never started to do so before; so tonight I will endeavour to begin.

It is nearly eight months since I was called up; how the time flies! It is a month and two days since I started for France. We had a very rough passage; in fact the vessel turned round once to put back, but the captain changed his mind and went on again, and by God's goodness who holds the winds in his fists and the waters in the hollow of his hand, we landed safely on the following morning. Then I spent two weeks and four days at the base, and at the end of this time was picked out, put on draft, and sent up the line.

We were wandering about trying to find our division for nearly a week before we came to it. When we found it, they were out for a short rest, but we soon came up here, and it is about the liveliest of the fronts at present. We are informed that we shall not be here long as they have had a good turn here before.

I am sorry to say that I have been parted from all my good Christian mates, to whom I got greatly attached in our training. I am sorry to say I have found only one here, and I am now with him in his small dugout where he sleeps, writing this, but I am very pleased to say that my Saviour is continually with me, and I find his word very precious to my soul. Sometimes his word comes with great sweetness to me when none else is near me. I had quite a refreshing time yesterday while standing on the road with my horses on the way up to the line, while old Fritz was sending over some of his gas shells; it was quite a melting time. I tasted of his love, and like the church in the Song of Solomon I could say, 'I am my beloved's, and my beloved is mine.' He is 'the chiefest among ten thousand,' 'yea, he is altogether lovely.' I am so glad that he sought me, and taught me my need of him before I came out here, and that he led me to see in him a beauty so that I desired him, and he led me on to find in him my soul's satisfaction.

I also feel that we owe a debt of gratitude to God for sending you into our midst. I am sure God has made you a great blessing, especially to the young men and women in the Bible Class. I feel there has been a good work crowned with God's blessing. I well remember seeking to know Jesus as my Saviour in your Bible Class, and how often I got great encouragement during those precious hours in your dining room.

I had a letter from Jack Clough; he is well and sends his love to all at Halland. He also is rejoicing in a precious Christ.

Now I must close and soon get between the blankets. I hope you have been blessed in your labours today and been made a blessing. I often pray for you and all the dear ones, that you may be blessed together.

Now may God bless you all abundantly, and soon join us together again if it be his will.

I remain,

Yours in the best of bonds,

T. Cottingham.

November 18th, 1917.[626]

C. H. Matthews

Private William Harold Cripps, Swindon

William Cripps served with the 12th Battalion, the Gloucestershire Regiment. He died on 3rd October, 1917, and is buried in Lijssenthoek Military Cemetery, Belgium. His last letter was sent by his mother to Mr Tryon, the editor of *The Little Gleaner*, with the following accompanying letter:

✍ Dear Mr Tryon,

As letters from soldiers that have appeared in *The Little Gleaner* have been found very helpful, I thought you would like to read one from our own dear boy, who has been killed in France, and who all his life-time was a real lover of *The Little Gleaner*.

I may say that he has for a long time given practical proofs of a work of grace going on in his soul, and I verily believe the Lord had been preparing him for 'the great change,' as months before he joined the army he often said, 'If I ever go to France, I shall never return, for the Lord will take me home.' In some of his letters from the front he has said, 'Don't worry, I am quite prepared to go.'

Truly indeed 'the child shall die a hundred years old,' for to my mind the language in his short note is that of an aged child of God. He was 19 years and 3 months old; he used to attend the Sunday School at Providence Chapel, Swindon. He was born at Devizes, where we lived when I was a member of the late Mr Hemington's church. His name was William Harold and we always called him 'Willie.'

Below is a copy of the last letter he ever wrote; this was written just before going into the trenches. When we received it he was dead, but we did not know it.

Yours sincerely,
G. T. Cripps.

✍ My dearest Parents,

I am enjoying a sweet peace that none can understand save the children of God. I am perfectly happy, and my soul is at rest, because I know he is mine.

Your ever loving son,
Willie.[627]

George Jacob Doel, Trowbridge

The following letter was written by George Jacob Doel. George survived the war and lived to reach the age of 89, passing away on 25th September, 1979. He was baptised when he was 83 years of age and was the deacon at The Halve Chapel, Trowbridge for the last five years of his life. His obituary recorded:

George was first blessed with an exercise of soul when serving with the Wiltshire Regiment under General Allenby in Egypt in the First World War. As a stretcher bearer, he helped carry an injured soldier into a hospital tent, when the Lord gave him a sudden realisation that this case could have been himself, and how would he have faced eternity? This never left him. When he joined the church he referred to these years and said, "I cannot say much," but he added, "One thing I can say, 'I believe that Jesus Christ is the Son of God.'" When he had retired to await the church vote, Mr R. Kinderman (chairing the meeting) remarked, "What more do we need, friends?" [628]

George J. Doel in later life

The letter below was written to his parents from Palestine during the war. A picture of the original letter can be found on p. 265.

✍ Dear parents,

Just a few lines, hoping you are well. You see I am spending a few days here; it's a sight worth seeing. I received your kind letter, also *The Friendly Companion.* I hear Reg. is down the line waiting embarkation; I hope I shall soon be too ... I've seen what I wish you could have seen. How many look upon it lightly, but I hope I don't. Yes, just think, mother: I've sat by the tree where the Lord prayed before Judas betrayed the Lord, and also where Judas sat with him; and the spot where he left the disciples to 'go and pray yonder' (Matthew 26: 36).[629] I feel it to be such a sacred place. Many other things I hope to tell you when we meet; may the Lord hasten that time. I think I'll close. Hope all the friends are well.

With love from your son,
George,
Jerusalem.
November 25th, 1918.[630]

Sapper Alfred Muskett Dye, Rowley Regis

Alfred M. Dye

Sapper A. M. Dye was the only son of Mr Alfred Dye, the pastor at Rowley Regis. He was baptised with his wife in 1910, and at the time of being called up was superintendent of the Sabbath School. The first of the two letters which follow was written before he was sent to France, while he was still in training in England. The second letter was written to his parents from hospital after he had been wounded in France.

[1]

✍ My dear Father,

I was very pleased to receive your letter of the 19th inst. I forgot you were going away when I wrote.

Well, dear Dad, I am going on very comfortably; still it is, as you say, 'very hard to leave a dear wife and children.' I try to look to the right source, and I am sure I have been enabled to, for I feel such submission, and, up to the present, I cannot grumble – this is a mercy, because I am such a grumbler in and of myself. Fancy dear Aunty L— going to write to me – I should be pleased. Still pray for us in this heavy trial, dear Dad. I have made no associates, but kind and civil to all; and as regards religion I say nothing, but try to keep it between myself and God – I feel he will bring me through. May he still strengthen dear Pheobe;[631] I know she feels it very hard, and my dear children. O I do hope they may live to know him whom my soul loveth, and 'whom to know is life eternal.'

I hope you are well. I have had my second inoculation – am going on very well so far. Thank you for all your good advice; I am sure I wish you well, and a safe and profitable journey in all senses, and your heavenly Friend's company whenever you are proclaiming his precious Word.

Now I must draw to a close. Hoping to see you again someday, and that we may praise God for all I have passed through, for he has graciously upheld me till now. Cheer up! dear Father, we all have a cross to carry, but a precious Saviour to assist us makes all the difference.

I am, your only, loving son,

Alf,

235651, I.W.T., R.E., Hut D.H., C Company, Stonar Camp, Sandwich, Kent.

February 21st, 1917.[632]

[2]

✍ My dearly loved Father and Mother,

I feel such inclination to write to both of you; after lying in bed for 12 days I don't feel fit for much writing yet, only I know you will be pleased to hear from your only boy, who is so far from you all. I have been reading some *Zion's Witness* my beloved wife has sent, and how I have enjoyed the contents and felt God's blessing still resting upon unworthy me. I have read them all through, and felt refreshed from the words, 'I will also leave in the midst of thee an afflicted and poor people, and they shall trust in the name of the LORD.' How beautifully it was set forth by the late Mr Wilcockson, and how true what the poet says – 'Poor and afflicted, Lord, are thine,' etc. This is food the world partakes not of. 'Thanks be unto God for his unspeakable gift.' I feel in such a sacred place these last two days, and God is blessing the means used on my behalf; I am feeling better each day, though still in bed. I have such good nursing and nourishments, and above all, a spirit of prayer felt in my poor soul, and gratitude arises; then everything is in its right place – my dear wife, children, and all I am passing through. The first few days I was so dark, yet felt I must still keep wrestling in prayer; and *that* 'can force a passage through iron bars and brazen gates,'[633] can it not?

I have had such good letters from my dear wife; she has been helped in earnest prayer on my behalf, and the dear Lord has heard her cries. Oh may he still bless and strengthen her. I need to thank him a thousand times for such a godly partner; may he spare my life to live many years yet in such comfort and happiness as in our former years, and bless my beloved children and plant his fear in their young and tender hearts. It is indeed a great mercy to be called when young, and to be especially kept when getting on in life. How I long for my usual Sundays and think of the special times in the [*Sabbath*] school. The other day that verse came so forcibly into my soul:

> What peaceful hours I then enjoyed,
> How sweet their memory still, etc.[634]

I must draw to a close, as I cannot do much at writing yet. Dear Parents, may God bless you both. I long to see you all again, but I have proved France to be Immanuel's land, and if it had not been for his holy appearance, at times I should have sunk, but such a prop can hold the world and all things up. Yes, though the world is so full of trouble. I trust all our dear chapel friends are well. Kindly remember me to all of them, and especially to the [*Sabbath*] school; how is that going on? I do hope I shall someday be found with them again; I loved the work and I miss it very much now. They have my best wishes; I hope they do not quite forget me. I had a lovely letter from Miss C—, I must try and answer it later on, it did me good to know there are some young seekers at Rowley Regis Sunday School that seem to have benefited under unworthy me. Bless God for *that.* I trust you are all well; thanks for your nice long letters, dear M. May God bless and strengthen you and dear F., and bless his preaching, is the sincere wish of your only son. Fondest love to all,

Alf,

Sapper A. M. Dye, Hospital, France.

October 8th, 1917.[635]

Gunner Alfred James Ellis, Heathfield

Alfred Ellis served in the Royal Garrison Artillery, being sent to the front in July, 1916. Within three months, however, he was wounded and returned home to England. He was married with four children at the time. The letter below describes how he was wounded. It is supplemented with an account he wrote some time afterwards of his experience during his stay in hospital. In later years Mr Ellis was sent into the ministry and served as pastor at Worthing. He died in 1953.[636]

✍ My dear Aunt,

You will be surprised to hear I am so soon in England again. We were taking our guns up to the firing position – shells were bursting – we were very near our position, it was dark, and my left hand got caught in the couplings and broke one finger in two or three places. I was sent to the field hospital, then to the base, and late on Saturday arrived here. I am

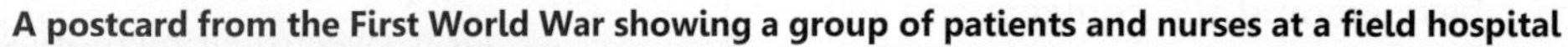

A postcard from the First World War showing a group of patients and nurses at a field hospital

well cared for. God moves in a mysterious way. I still prove him a prayer-hearing and prayer-answering God. The 8th chapter of Romans was sweet to me on Sabbath morning. Hope you are well. Remember me to all friends.

Your affectionate nephew,
Alfred James Ellis,
Edmonton Military Hospital.
October 30th, 1916.[637]

The aftermath of the injury resulted in Mr Ellis spending a considerable time in the military hospital at Ripon. His injury was complicated by sepsis and the finger remained virtually useless afterwards. It was, however, a time of blessing, which he describes as follows:

Alfred J. Ellis

✍ One night on my bed, first my awful state as a sinner in the sight of God was revealed. Oh! the depths of sin and iniquity I saw and felt, original sin, actual sins, and heart sins. Now a spirit of mental prayer was given to me, and how I pleaded with the Lord, through Christ, to pardon me again; to bring me nigh. Oh! the confession, the self-abhorrence and self-abasement! I was then led to meditate on the Father's choice of his Eternal Son to become man: 'Behold my servant, whom I uphold; mine elect, in whom my soul delighteth; I have put my spirit upon him.' In this verse I plainly saw the Trinity set forth: the Father in choosing; the Son as chosen; the Spirit as being put upon him. I was *made* to believe, and willingly too, that I was an object of his everlasting love; that I was a subject of his free and sovereign grace. Thus I was sealed, and the effect it produced was better felt than described.[638]

John Hervey Gosden, Brighton

The following letter was written at the end of the war by Mr J. H. Gosden, later the pastor at Priory Road Chapel, Maidstone, to Mr Jesse Delves, who would later become pastor at Ebenezer Chapel, Clapham. At the time Mr Delves was still waiting to be demobbed. As already mentioned (p. 22), Mr Gosden served in the war with the Royal Army Medical Corps and was decorated for bravery at the front. One other letter of Mr Gosden's written during the war appears on page 164.

✍ My dear Friend and Brother,

It seems selfish of me not to have written for so long, seeing you are still in a foreign land and isolated from all your friends, whilst I have been released from the army and am now, in that sense, a free man at home. They demobilized me under the scheme releasing all who had been in hospital 28 days and over. I feel it to be a great mercy and a very wonderful providence to have been brought through so safely. My leg is practically well, except for a very slight weakness which I shall always have but which does not affect me much, and is not worth mentioning.

I often think of you and sympathize with you. How thankful I am you have been kept safe! It is indeed a great mercy. You have, as you said in your last letter, been favoured in days past with sweet gospel liberty. If I may claim to have been so favoured in a small degree (and I trust it is not wrong for me to do so), I with you do truly want another such blessing. At times I am almost indifferent, but at other times feel I cannot go on without some renewed token of God's favour. It is an infinite mercy for us that he does not change as we do, but that he is faithful and true. And if he has reconciled us to himself in the body of the flesh of Jesus through death, he will never leave us to sink. He paid too high a price to lose one of his own. 'Ye are bought with a price.' But what we want, dear friend (is it not?), is a constant renewal with power of a sense of our interest in his love, the love which brought him to die for sinners. For sin so often defiles us and separates between us and our (as we hope, our) Redeemer, God. This at least is my sad experience, and no power on earth can bring nearness and cleansing again; only I do believe the blood of Christ can, as applied to the conscience. I wish I knew by experience more of what Hart sets out in those lines (concerning the blood of Christ):

> If guilt removed return and remain,
> Its power may be proved again and again.[639]

I hope it is well with you, and that my barren state will not be conveyed to you by this note. Remember me, if you can, in your prayers. I am a poor fearful creature, and need in many ways the help of God. The Lord bless you and prosper you in your soul, and bring you home again soon if his holy will.

With Christian love, my wife joining,
Yours sincerely in gospel bonds,
John H. Gosden.
February 7th, 1919.[640]

John H. Gosden with his wife

G. G. Graham

We know nothing of G. Graham, except that the second of the two letters below was written to his Bible class leader:

[1]

✍ My dear Friend,

... I take this opportunity of writing to you ... No doubt you are wondering how I spent Christmas. Well, I must say that, under the circumstances, I had a happy one, though very strange. We had a church parade during the morning at which almost every man attended; in the afternoon my time was occupied letter writing and reading. Since January 4th we have been in the firing line again. What has this New Year in store for us? I trust that God will remain with us, and that he will give us his peace and victory. How nice it is that our nation has been brought to a sense of prayer, and that a day was set apart for this all over England.[641] Around where we are in action the firing has been very wild of late, but we have at all times to be in readiness against any movement of any hostile forces. I pray that this war will be brought, by God's mercy, to a speedy conclusion.

Your very sincere friend,
G. G. Graham,
Expeditionary Force.
January 7th, 1915.[642]

[2]

✍ My dear Friend,

Writing this letter from my little billet in a wagon, I thank you very much for your last two letters, also for your kindness in taking the interest that you have done for my good and comfort during this war ... We are again in different quarters to when I wrote you last. Our battery has not been brought into any heavy combat with the enemy lately, but still, we may be at any time. Again I am sure that God has been with us during the past few dreary weeks. One poor fellow of our battery was wounded by a sniper the other day, whilst approaching the trenches. Apart from that casualty we remain, by Providence, intact. Much better weather of late, drying up the swampy districts that have been such a drawback to our movements. We have much to be thankful for; the change has brought about a decrease of illness. I long for the time when I may be privileged to return to England to have the pleasure of seeing all my friends again. Still, Mr Gillett,[643] I am quite satisfied with the position I am placed in, knowing that it is my place to be here; our country has been brought into the fight quite honourably, for the peace of Europe ...

I have received a lot of parcels, which have been very acceptable. I think I have had more comforts sent out to me than ever I had anticipated. I am very grateful for all that has been done for me.

Now I must close, still trusting that God in his mercy will remain with us all to the end ..., etc.

G. G. Graham,
126th Battery, Royal Field Artillery, France.
February 2nd, 1915.[644]

William Hatton, Redhill

The following two letters were written by William Hatton, the grandson of Joseph Hatton, editor of *The Gospel Standard.* William Hatton was born on October 18th, 1874, and attended Hope Chapel, Redhill. During the war he served in the Royal Air Force.[645]

[1]

✍ My dear Mother,

I hope you will not think it unkind of me to delay writing to you for so long ... Doubtless you, as well as all other friends at Shaw's Corner,[646] often wonder how the new style of life affects me. Blandford Camp was truly a terrible place, and this camp is little better. How I endured the fortnight's stay at Blandford, where almost everybody I came in contact with used the most abominable language, profanity, filth and blasphemy of the worst description, I cannot find words to describe; it was a living hell to me. I sometimes found a few moments' quietness in the evening, but could not leave the camp, as my army boots hurt my feet so much. During the day the work was exceedingly hard, but my health throughout was wonderfully good. It was no uncommon thing to see men fall out of the ranks in faints, yet my bodily strength never failed. Never shall I forget my first Sunday there. I was included in a fatigue party marched off to a part of the lines about a mile away, to pick up stones from the parade ground and arrange them neatly in a border adjoining! I leave you to imagine the rebellious state of my mind while doing such menial work, and on a Sunday, too. But when full of self-pity our Lord's humiliation was laid on my mind with overwhelming force. The thought that the Maker of heaven and earth should have left the abode of bliss to live a life of weakness and suffering, and with perfect willingness and submission, contrasted with my condition, was too much for me, and I thought my heart would burst. At that moment I said goodbye to wife, family and worldly prospects, and was willing to be sent to France, Egypt – anywhere. A week later I was posted to this Motor Transport Depot at Hurst Park, Surrey, where an unlooked for disappointment awaited me. My home being so near at hand I thought I could easily get off to see you all occasionally, but the rule of this depot is that any use of the main lines is prohibited to the men. So I can get no farther away than Clapham Junction, with a midnight pass issued for Saturday or Sunday after the duties of the day are ended. This rule does not apply to the electric railways running to any London suburb. There is no place of worship near here where I can feel at home, and I have no companions with whom I am united in heart. At times a feeling of unutterable loneliness oppresses me, and yet through all I often enjoy that sweet assurance of the Lord's help which I had at Shaw's Corner on the Sunday before I left Redhill. In the midst of much discouragement I have been upheld in a way which has surprised me.

Goodbye for the present. My best love to you all,

Your loving son,

Will,

R.A.F. Depot, Hurst.

Sunday, July 21st, 1918.[647]

[2]

✍ My dear Mother,

I was greatly pleased to receive your letter. Your quotation of hymn 105 ('When I by faith my Maker see'; *Gadsby's Selection*) did my soul good. In days gone by I have often read it, but with a feeling that I knew nothing of such an experience as there described. Indeed, until you mentioned it, I had forgotten that the hymn was in the book. Though I had but a glimpse of our Lord's humiliation and suffering, I found its effect overpower me; and even now find it hard to control my feelings whenever I think of it.

May the Lord help the church in these distressing times, and bless your decisions in regard to the pastorate and the trusteeship.[648] Especially remember me to Mr Popham. He will remember our little conversation in the vestry when he was last at Redhill, in the light of what I told you in my letter ...

Goodbye for the present and my love to all,
Your affectionate son,
Will,
R.A.F. Depot, Hurst Park, East Molesey.
Sunday evening.[649]

Lance Corporal C. J—, Devizes

Lance Corporal C. J— is known only by his initials. From the content of the letters we learn that he was married with children, and that just prior to signing up he had started to attend services at Devizes Chapel. These letters were written from the front to friends at home, and describe his early spiritual experiences soon after he was called by grace. The circumstances are described in the following note, which was published in *The Little Gleaner* by way of introduction to the series of letters by C. J.:

✍ Dear Mr Tryon,

The following letters have been received from a soldier now at the front. About a 12 months ago he attended the chapel at Devizes occasionally, and was at that time convinced of his sinfulness, but was not then able by grace to leave the City of Destruction and set out for the Celestial City. He wandered about to different places of worship, and latterly was not able to come owing to weakness in the arch of the foot, his home being at a distance from Devizes. In October last, he was called up to serve his King and country, and on the Sunday night previous to his leaving home on the next day for Weymouth, he and his wife walked in to chapel on a very wet night to hear the pastor preach. The text was from Jeremiah 45: 5: 'Thy life will I give unto thee for a prey in all places whither thou goest.' He was deeply moved by the text and sermon, as will appear in his letters. After the service two or three friends spoke to him, and one of these posted some gospel booklets to him that evening, receiving the first of these letters a few days later. I think they will be read by many with prayerful interest in and sympathy for the writer.

I am, yours sincerely,
E. S. S.
February 2nd, 1915.

Manasseh Tryon

[1]

✍ Dear M – ,

I am writing to thank you very much for the little books you sent me before I left home; I shall take them with me wherever I go. I cannot express my feelings as I am writing, to tell you how pleased I am that I came to chapel last Sunday night. I think of the text, and it seems as if it must be for me. I do pray that the Lord will make me conscious of my utter helplessness, and shew me what a poor sinner I am. I have heard Mr Wiles preach a good many times, but I never thought his sermon would move me as it did on Sunday. I do hope that God will bring me home again, so that I may see my dear wife and children, and more than that, that I may go to his house to listen to his gracious truths. I do pray that the end of this war will soon be here. Since I have been back I have been moved to the Draft Camp, and am now waiting to go to the front. I think, how many are there ready to die? It is awful to think about. What sin there is in the world; everywhere I look there is nothing but wickedness and often cloaked by different kinds of religion. I do pray that the Lord will guard me from all and every sin.

I must ask you to excuse the writing; it is the best I can do under the circumstances. God bless you for your kindness.

Yours very sincerely,

C. J.

P.S. I shall carry your books in my breast pocket, and may God help me to understand them.

Draft Camp, Weymouth.

October 30th, 1914.

[2]

✍ Dear M – ,

Thank you very much for the beautiful muffler you sent me. It is very kind of you to send it seeing that I am almost a stranger. What a comfort it is to me to know that although we are far away, we are being thought of and prayed for. I am quite conscious that others' prayers for me alone will not suffice unless I pray too. What a comfort to know that God answers prayer. What a merciful God he is to such a poor, vile sinner as I am, who am not worthy of the least notice. Since I have been here, I have felt the need of a Saviour more than at any time in my life. I do pray that the Lord will make me a true child of

God. I know it is no use for me to try to be good, for I should fail, but I do ask the Lord to save me, and to keep me from every sin.

While I am sitting in this tent there is much sin and wickedness going on around me. I do not wonder that God is punishing this country for the sin we are guilty of; it is awful to think of. I must thank you for the sermon you sent me. I cannot express my thoughts. What a lovely text, 'Fear thou not, for I am with thee.' It seems as if the Lord had spoken it to me; what consolation it gives me. I pray God that it may apply even to such a sinner as I am. I am thinking now of you at Devizes. I can picture Mr Wiles in the pulpit preaching the precious truths which are contained in the Bible, and with the thought comes a pang in my conscience to think that I did not attend when I have been able. Oh may the Lord forgive me for broken Sabbath days. I cannot tell you when we shall leave here; we are waiting orders. It might be tomorrow, it might not be for a week or two, but all I can say is I feel this morning that the text, 'Fear thou not, for I am with thee,' will go with me and that it applies to me.

Believe me to be, yours very truly,

C. J.

Sunday morning, November 8th, 1914.

[3]

✍ Dear M—,

I expect by the time you receive this we shall be in France, but I want to let you know I am trusting in the Lord, and I pray that he will be precious to me wherever I go. I shall not forget Devizes, and I trust I shall come back to hear the Word of Life in the dear chapel.

I have not forgotten the text Mr Wiles preached from, and I pray the Lord will strengthen me in his own truth.

Yours very truly,

C. J.

Tuesday night.[650]

[4]

✍ Dear M—,

I must just write a line to you tonight; it is Christmas night, and it is very quiet now. I wonder how many there are in England praying for us. We went out trench digging last night, and we could hear the Germans singing and their gramophones playing. It sounded rather weird on a battlefield. Tonight our chaps are singing carols, and one would not think of danger being near, but it is [*a situation*] of great peril, and we realise it, but we are cheerful and do our work with good hearts knowing it is for those who we have left behind. The Germans had fires lit up last night all along the firing line. One of our company was killed last night, and we buried him this morning. I am quite well, and I pray God to favour me with good health. We get rough and smooth times, and I can truly say God has helped me till the present time, and I know that he will be with those that trust in him. I pray for a clean heart, free from every sin. Sometimes I feel so full of sin and void of good that I begin to doubt whether I shall be saved or not. How often has that verse came to my mind, 'Fear thou not,' and I ask the Lord more earnestly that he will keep me in his fear. 'With Christ in the vessel I smile at the storm.' These words came to me yesterday – how sweet they are to a poor sinner like me! To think of a holy God condescending to look upon one who has broken all his laws, and who would be in hell were it not for his great mercy. I have to own my helpless state and aver, 'Lord, save me or I perish.' If I have to get home again, my one desire will be to glorify him in his house. I must close with my very best wishes for the New Year.

Yours sincerely,
C. J.
Friday, December 25th, 1914.

[5]

✍ To Mr J. P. Wiles,
Dear Sir,

I hope you will forgive the liberty I am taking in writing to you as I am a stranger to you, although I have heard you preach a good many times and I have one of your printed sermons with me now, which was sent me by —. It was preached on Sunday, September 6th. The reason, dear Sir, why I am telling you this is because the text you preached from has followed me ever since I read it. 'Fear thou not; for I am with thee: be not dismayed; for I am thy God: I will strengthen thee; yea, I will help thee; yea, I will uphold thee with the right hand of my righteousness.' I must tell you that previous to this I had been convinced of sin and of a judgement to come. For a long time I have felt my sin, and I knew that I was a condemned man. I was also shown by the dear Lord that nothing I could do would alter it. Then I cried unto the Lord in my trouble, and I believe he has heard me. 'Lord, save me,' was the cry, and the text, 'Fear thou not,' has been with me ever since. Sometimes I think of my past life, and then I get troubled. I think, Can I be saved, such a poor, wicked mortal as I am?

> Shall such a worthless worm as I,
> Who sometimes am afraid to die,
> Be found at thy right hand?[651]

Then the text. 'Fear thou not,' comes to my mind, and my fear is all gone. What a Saviour! I do pray that I may be kept from all sin in thought, word or deed. I had a nice letter from — the other day, and how thankful I felt that there was someone who knew my feelings, and who was doing their best to help and cheer me. How nice it was to get encouraging words from someone who knows the Lord. I have been favoured with good health since I have been out here.

> Not more than others I deserve,
> Yet God has given me more.[652]

I have dear Christian parents living, and I have told them of the Lord's dealings with me, and I am telling you, dear Sir, that you may know it too.

I first went up into the firing line on Monday night, November 23rd, and we have had it rough and smooth. Sometimes when I have been crossing a field and the bullets have been whistling along near me, then I have proved that there is no fear with God. May I be kept pure, that is my cry. Oh God, keep me from every evil thing. I do want to serve him with a single eye to his glory. I hope, dear Sir, you will be able to read this. I am sitting down in a barn with a candle, and I know it is a scribble, but I could not resist writing as it has been in my thoughts all day. We are going into the trenches again tomorrow night.

I remain, yours very sincerely,

C. J.

2nd Wiltshire Regiment, Field Force.

December 29th, 1914.[653]

[6]

✍ Dear M – ,

I was very glad to receive your letter tonight; how good of you to write, and how it cheers one up to get a letter out here. I am thankful to be able to tell you that I am quite well. God has been very gracious to me in giving me good health, and in preserving my life, although I know how unworthy I am. We came out of the trenches tonight, and we are staying in a big house that has been vacated owing to the war; in fact it is a small town but no one is living here. We are having three day's rest, and we can do with it as it is very wet. I saw the Germans dipping water out of their trenches this morning, and ours have been bad enough. It is wonderful how our men stick to it, sometimes wet through and covered with mud, yet there is the same good humour, and the same old spirit. No one will ever realize what our men have gone through during the past few months. I have stood the cold and wet better than I expected, and I am thankful to God for his lovingkindness. Oh, I would not be without a Saviour for anything, although at times I must confess I have forgotten him, but glory to his name he has not forgotten me, nor has he left me. If left to myself I should sink; who else can I trust other than a gracious God? This morning I prayed that there might be a letter for me, and I had two, one from my dear wife and one from you. All the men eagerly look for news from home, and perhaps none more than myself. One night I was lying down in what we call a 'dugout' in the trenches, and I asked the dear Lord for a token of his love, and these words came to my mind immediately – 'Thy sins, which are many, are all forgiven thee.' The tears fell down my face for very joy, and then came this beautiful verse –

> I fear no foe, with thee at hand to bless;
> Ills have no weight, and tears no bitterness.
> Where is death's sting? where, grave, thy victory?
> I triumph still if thou abide with me.[654]

What peace reigned within, but it did not last; Satan told me these words only came to me accidentally and doubt seemed to creep into my soul, so that I wondered if it was a delusion and felt very uneasy, but the thought that other poor sinners have felt the same encouraged me to still trust on. Who would doubt such a Friend? Oh blessed thought! that such a base sinner as I am should have an Advocate with the Father, even Jesus; I who have denied Christ, if not by words, by my deeds. These words come to me now –

> Shall such a worthless worm as I,
> Who sometimes am afraid to die
> Be found at thy right hand?[655]

I believe the Christian dies daily to the world; oh that I could be more dead to the world, and more alive to Christ. What an intense longing fills my heart to be more like him, and to feel that I am indeed dying to the things of this wicked world. I do trust the Lord and I want to serve him faithfully. If I live to come home what a difference there will be in me. How I shall enjoy going to God's house, and listening to his precious truth. I often think of you there, and my heart was filled tonight when I read in my wife's letter that she had been to chapel with the children. I hope they will be good, God bless them. I do pray that he will in his rich mercy bring them to himself. I must thank you for the book of Psalms, and the card, 'Prayer is the soul's sincere desire'[656] – what a sweet hymn! I have a New Testament; what a book full of promises for those who love the Lord! I must close now, as it is getting late.

Yours very sincerely,

C. J.

Thursday, January 14th, 1915.

[7]

✍ Dear M—,

I am writing to you again this morning as we are going into the trenches tonight, and I might not be able to write again for some time. It is a beautiful Sabbath morning. I have been on guard now three days, and I am sitting down to a table (quite a luxury) in a nice room of what was a gentleman's house. How pitiful! Nice pictures hung upon the walls and everything left in a hurry; the windows broken and a few bullet holes in the walls and ceiling. While I am sitting quietly writing, the big guns are booming all the way round. What a contrast to our home in England! I can picture Devizes now, and I should like to be there – the people going to chapel and church, and in my mind I can see the chapel with Mr Wiles in the pulpit, giving out the hymns, and other people who I know by sight. Why am I telling you this? It is because my heart burns within me towards God's own people, who I am sure are worshipping him, and because I know the truth is preached there. Why do I know it? Because I have felt it in my heart, and the Word has been made precious to my soul. Has not the Word spoken there made me anxious about my state? Yes, and I have gone away from that place feeling my load of sin and knowing that I must be born again; this has only been known to myself and God. I did not know where to go or what to do, and I am sure that sometimes my home has been made gloomy because my dear wife did not understand what was the matter. How many times have I resolved to think no more about it, yet it would return again. What a merciful God! How longsuffering and full of compassion towards a guilty soul! My heart seems full of gratitude this morning. What shall I render to the Lord for all his benefits? I have just read the 46th and 91st Psalms. How beautiful they are! Full of promises to God's own people. I know there are false doctrines and false prophets, for it is more in evidence out here than in anywhere else I have been. In every village there are big images of Jesus on the cross and the Virgin Mary, even at the crossroads, and in nearly every house. How thankful I am that I was born in a Christian home, and that I had dear Christian parents.

Thank God they are still living, and I have great hopes of seeing them again in this world. Can one wonder why this country has suffered when it is so full of Roman Catholicism! How glad I am to know that I have a living Saviour to worship, not an image, but a real living Saviour who is King of kings and Lord of lords, and who can hear his children's cry, those whom he has bought with his own blood.

Now I must close. I am glad to know prayers are made on my behalf at your prayer meetings, and I hope someday I shall be permitted to join with you at Devizes. This is my earnest hope. We have left the house where I wrote this letter and we are now in a barn.

Yours very sincerely,
C. J.
January 17th, 1915.

[8]

✍ Dear M – ,

I hope I shall be able to send this letter today, but it is uncertain. We went out trench digging last night, and we reached our barn again about half past twelve. Before we went our men sang a hymn or two. We were out about five hours and it was bitterly cold, snow and rain fell most of the time. The Germans sent up a few rockets to see if anyone was about. These rockets light up the country for miles and you can see quite plainly on a dark night. We always lie down when we see one of them. It has been snowing fast this morning and I am glad we are inside. We have some straw to lie on so it is not very bad. I expect we shall have to go out tonight. I prayed God to bring us all back safely last night and he did. I felt no fear myself, but was a bit startled when a bullet came pretty close; but I am trusting Jesus whatever befalls. Please remember me to Mr Wiles. Tell him I have just been reading the text he preached from the last Sunday night I was at Devizes, 'Thy life will I give unto thee for a prey in all places whither thou goest,' and it has cheered me.

C. J.
Monday, January 18th, 1917.[657]

[9]

After the battle of Neuve Chapelle.

✍ Dear M – ,

I am writing to let you know I am still alive and quite well, and that I have been a recipient of God's preserving care. We have been into action since I last wrote, and I have been kept safely by the mighty power of God, so that again I have proved that to believe in his precious promises is life to the believer. Amidst scenes of death and suffering he has not left me, nor has he failed to protect me. Our captain led us, and before we got far he was killed, but on we went and took the German trenches. Our company captured over 100 Germans and we treated them with respect, but they do not treat our men so; they captured one or two of our men, and stuck them with their bayonets, and I am afraid this will have a bad effect on our men in future.[658] I can truly say that my hands are clean of any inhuman conduct, but I do not wish to think of this; I have seen enough, and pray that I may never see such sights again. God has been gracious to me, and his precious promise has been, and still is with me, 'Fear thou not; for I am with thee: be not dismayed; for I am thy God.' Our general has sent us the highest praise for our work, but although this is an encouragement, yet I know that without Christ I should have nothing to cheer me. I do pray most earnestly that my mates may be led to know his saving power. He is mighty to save, and not only to save but to keep. I pray that I may be spared to come home again, and that my life will be a living witness for God. He alone is able to keep me from falling. I have written to my dear wife today, and I expect she is very much worried because she has not heard for some time from me. I pray that God will lead her to put her trust in him, and that he will in his own good time make her to feel the same as myself. I will tell you just one of many escapes we had during our engagement, which lasted four days. I was lying on a dead German in a trench we had captured with three more of my mates, and the Germans blew up the trench. I believe we were all praying, and not one of us were touched beyond being covered with earth. Some would have us believe this is luck, but I know I was kept by God's mighty power – with Jesus by my side nothing could harm me. What a deliverance, and thank God I realise it. One poor wounded German gave me a cigarette. I think he was afraid I was going to kill him, but when I smiled at him he lost his fear. I felt sorry for him, though I could not help him as we had to go on.

I am, yours sincerely,

C. J.

P.S. I had a letter from you a week or two ago, but cannot remember whether I answered it or not. I am very forgetful. I hope my dear little children are good in Sunday School, and that God will bless your efforts with the young.

> Jesus, thy blood and righteousness
> My beauty are, my glorious dress;
> 'Midst flaming worlds, in these arrayed,
> With joy shall I lift up my head.[659]

Monday night, March 15th, 1915.

[10]

✍ Dear M – ,

I was very pleased to hear from you last night and your letter was very cheering and encouraging to me. We came into the trenches last night after ten days' rest. We have had a lot of rain, and this does not improve our trenches, but still it's a good deal better now than formerly. It is very cold and frosty at night. I was pleased to hear that my little boy can remember some things he has learnt at Sunday School. I am thankful to be able to tell you I am well. I was sorry to hear Mr Wiles had been poorly, but I trust he is better and that he will be spared for many years to preach God's own Word. I was indeed pleased with the sermon you sent me, and it has been a source of joy to me. Why (some might ask) do I like this particular sermon? Because what is set forth there is my state, my hopes and my desires; in fact, I know that all I can or shall have is set forth in that sermon. I believe every word of it, not because a certain man said it, but because I know it is God's truth. I was reading it again tonight, and as I looked out of the trenches toward the west, where the sun was sinking, and where I knew lay the land of my birth, my heart was full, and oh! how I prayed, if not by words by a groan, and God hears our groaning, does he not? It is my desire that if I live to come home I may be baptised, and that I may by God's grace be enabled so to live before the world that they may see I have been with Jesus, and learnt of him. I expressed the same desire to my parents, and they have written telling me how pleased they are, and that it was my duty to do so. Many times I have heard it said one could be a Christian without being baptised, but I believe, as Mr Wiles says in his sermon on baptism, Christ says, 'If ye love me, keep my commandments.' These last few days I have felt down at heart; something seemed to be sapping out all the joy of my life, but since I have had your letter and read that beautiful sermon my faith has increased, and the words, 'I will not leave you comfortless,' have cheered me. I think a good deal of my lowness is through lack of faith, and I have to cry, 'Lord, give me more faith.' I feel so weak at times that I have to cry, 'Lord, save, or I perish;' yet it is scarcely a fortnight ago that I was the recipient of God's great mercy and goodness. How I loathe myself. I am like the children of Israel after God had made a passage for them through the Red Sea; they murmured and said God had brought them unto the wilderness to starve. I pray to be kept from trusting to my feelings. I have seen people shed tears, and have thought them penitential tears, but have found it was a passing emotion and nothing real. I want to lean solely on Christ crucified; I know that of sinners I am chief. What a mercy he has saved me! What love! What dying love! Nothing but dying love could do it. I need fresh grace from day to day, and it is only by prayer and supplication these needs can be supplied. To be without prayer is to be without Christ. 'Watch and pray, that ye enter not into temptation,' are Christ's own words, and I know from experience that when I feel tempted is when I have forgotten the Lord's dealings with me, or have been too much absorbed in the things of the world. Then Satan has tried to rob me of joy and peace in believing. My prayer is tonight, 'Lord, give me another glimpse of thy face, and of thy wondrous love.'

I must close now. Yours sincerely,

C. J.[660]

Friday, March 20th, 1915.

[11]

✍ Dear Sir,

I feel that I must write a few lines to let you know that I am still in good health and strength, which is to me a great token of God's mighty power both to save and to keep. After the battle of Neuve Chapelle I could indeed say, 'Lord, thou hast given my life to me for a prey in all places whithersoever I have been.' This text has followed me ever since I heard you preach from it last October. I remember it was a very rough and wet night, but as I knew it would be my last Sunday night in Devizes for some time at least, I and my wife came to chapel. I believe I told you before how greatly blessed I was. The following morning I received from Miss S— the book of the

Hebrews with the text written on the cover. I am very glad to be able to tell you that I still have it with me, although I lost my pack in the battle, yet I still retain this as I always carry it in my breast pocket. I need not tell you that it is engraven on my heart. I have also received several other sermons preached by you, and one especially is still fresh in my mind. The date is Wednesday evening, 1st October, 1913, and the text you took is this, 'Can any man forbid water, that these should not be baptised, which have received the Holy Ghost as well as we?' How precious this was to my soul as I read it! I do pray that I may be spared to come back so that by my life I may be able to show to those around me that I have been with Jesus and sweetly learnt of him. I know that being baptised with water will not save any poor sinner, nor dare I rest upon this. I have nothing to boast save Jesus Christ and him crucified. It has been and still is my greatest desire that I may follow the Lord in all that he has ordered us. Your explanation of the text is just what I believe, and it has been a source of great blessing to me. I feel myself unworthy, so dead and cold at times that I wonder whether I am really a child of God. At another time I am so full of joy and peace that amid all-time great excitement and bustle I am quite calm and nothing seems to disturb that peace. The day that we went into action at Neuve Chapelle, while we were waiting to advance, my heart was lifted up in prayer, and although I must confess I felt timid before we started, once on the move I did not seem a bit afraid, although shells were bursting all around and above us and bullets were whistling through the air, and men were dropping. I saw no fear. On we went till we came to the German trenches. Although I could not pray yet my heart was lifted upward, and my cry was heard and answered by the God who will always hear his people's cry. We were in action four days. I was supported in a wonderful way and manner. Nothing seemed to move me at the time, although I saw some awful sights. I myself was entangled in barbed wire in the darkness and shells were bursting quite close, other poor men being knocked down. But eventually I extricated myself, and a mercy to relate I was not touched. This was the first night, but we went through worse things than that afterward. My head seemed all in a whirl, and I really cannot quite remember what happened. The German dead were lying everywhere. I would not tell you this, but I want you to know how wonderfully the Lord has preserved me and kept me, even when I felt I could not live in such a murderous place. What a merciful Saviour! You cannot imagine what my feelings were on the Saturday night when we came out of action. I could not tell anyone. Although my nerve was a bit shattered, yet I could say, 'Praise the Lord for all his mercy and lovingkindness toward me.' I must tell you that we are now resting, but I cannot tell how long it will be. I do earnestly pray that this awful war may soon come to an end. I am sure there are thousands praying the same prayer. Tomorrow is Sunday, the Lord's Day. I shall think much of you at Devizes, and although we are miles apart, yet I know our united prayers will ascend to the same God. I do pray that my dear wife may be blessed at the little chapel. She told me that you prayed for us, and it encouraged me very much. I do earnestly pray that I may hear those same words spoken of poor me, poor in myself but rich in Christ – of this I feel sure, may God bless you all at Devizes – 'Can any man forbid water, that these should not be baptised, who have received the Holy Ghost as well as we?' My whole heart's prayer is that I may be spared to hear these blessed words spoken of myself for Christ's sake.

Yours very sincerely,

C. J.

Saturday, April 10th, 1915.[661]

Joseph P. Wiles

[12]

✍ Dear M – ,

It was a great pleasure to me to receive your letter which was handed to me on Friday evening, and I can truly say it has been the means of helping and encouraging me. I read the little book through, and then handed it to my chum, who is a nice quiet fellow. He comes from C—, and I knew him before we joined the army. We share everything, and I hope he has been brought to feel that he needs a Saviour. He always wants to read the verses you send to me, and I am only too glad for him to do so. There are a good many of our fellows, who, if they have never prayed before, do so now. One man from S— told me a few days ago that before he came out here he never used to think about a creator, but now he knows there is a God, and that he never goes to sleep without praying first. There are several in our company who, I believe, have been led to see their sinfulness, and I pray that God's love and mercy may shine upon them that they too will,

> Leave the hateful ways of sin,
> Turn to the fold, and enter in.[662]

I know nothing short of God's almighty power can do this, and that to be saved we must be born again. Oh that this cry was more in evidence: 'What must I do to be saved?' How good God has been to me! What blessings I have received at his hands! 'What shall I render unto the LORD for all his benefits?' I feel this morning this is my answer:

> Take my heart, and let it be
> Consecrated, Lord, to thee.[663]

Since I wrote the first part of this letter we have packed up, and instead of being in a barn we are now in a big house, and we are fairly comfortable. We must not take our shoes off, as we are liable to be shelled at any time. It is very dark tonight, and the lights of the star shells show up all around. Last night we were out trench digging, and the Germans had two great search lights which light up the country for miles. This is a very flat country, not hilly like Wiltshire, which would be a great relief to this part of the country. I have not seen a hill for nearly two months, and I am of the opinion that no place can beat our own country downs and vales. About two months ago we were in a town, billeted out in different houses, and the inhabitants were very kind to us. As we were going to this town we halted in a little village, and the people brought us out food and drink, which although not very nice to the taste was quite refreshing. I offered them money, but they refused, so I gave it to the little boy who was delighted with it. Our soldiers out here conduct themselves well, and so far as I have seen behave in a creditable manner. Although the houses have been deserted, our men have not looted them, though of course we have used their tables and chairs, plates and cups. When we reached the town which I mentioned, I was billeted in a house with another soldier, and the people were very kind to us, although their ways are quite different from ours. I asked the good woman to make some tea, and we could not help laughing at the way she made it, so I made the rest myself. We were there for a few days' rest, and they were the best I have spent out here. I had a very bad cold, and the husband came down in the night, and made me something hot to drink, and if ever I go that way again I shall endeavour to see them. They seemed sorry when we left them; they had seen a great deal of the war and felt safe while we were there. I should like to have been able to tell them the Germans would not trouble them again, but not being able to speak their language I had to shake their hands, and say, '*Au revoir*.' I can say a few words, and make them understand what I want, so I suppose I must be content.

I feel tonight that I have been very much favoured of God. I was laid up last year with rheumatism, and never thought I should stand the cold and wet as I have done, but I can see through it all the good hand of God, and I thank him with all my heart.

If anyone has cause for thankfulness I have, but as you say,

> I dare not trust the sweetest frame,
> But wholly lean on Jesus' name.[664]

How precious is that name to me! What could I do now without a Saviour! The most precious moments in my life are when I am communing with God, and I can say tonight, 'Lord, I only want thee. Thou art my refuge and defence, and I fear no foe with such a strong deliverer.' I desire to be in constant communion with my God, though I must own with shame there are times when I forget him. How sweet is that hymn you sent me, 'Prayer is the soul's sincere desire.'[665] Sometimes when I am walking along the road it is all I can do, just look up, but God knows what is going on and he can hear even a groan or sigh. When I have been tired and still had to toil on, only able to cry 'Lord, help me!' I have had all needful help, and have been able to finish what I have had to do.

I have heard with regret of the wicked crimes the Germans have been guilty of in killing poor defenceless people, and I remember the words, 'Vengeance is mine, I will repay, saith the Lord.' I also pray that God will in mercy look upon us as a nation and forgive us our sins, and that peace may once more reign on the earth. I am glad my dear little children are good at chapel. God bless them, also my dear wife, and all the kind friends at Devizes. I have the Epistle to the Hebrews you sent me. I have read the 1st chapter tonight, and the 14th verse has been very sweet to me. I must close, hoping that I may hear from you again. I cast myself, body and soul, into the kind care and keeping of Jesus my Saviour. I have nothing to boast of, but lean solely upon the merits of Jesus' atoning blood, which was spilt on Calvary.

Yours in Christ,

C. J.

Sunday, February 7th, 1915.[666]

[13]

✍ Dear Miss —,

I am writing a few lines to let you know I am still quite well. It is Easter Sunday, and I wonder how many realise its true meaning. I ask myself if I really know and truly believe in a risen Saviour. Last night I prayed that today might be a day of much blessing to me, but this morning I feel dead, lost in thought. May God revive my soul and make me rejoice as those only can who know Christ as their Saviour and risen Lord … We have been back again for a rest, but cannot say how long it will be. We have some nice billets in a town. I went into a Roman Catholic church the other night out of curiosity. It was a fine building. I looked at all the statues – beautiful workmanship! I saw a few persons there praying and counting their beads, and I felt truly sorry for them. These poor misguided people go there regularly, count their beads, burn candles, and bow to images. Oh the horrible thought of it all – what an impression it left on my mind! As I stood there my heart was lifted up in prayer, although in a Roman Catholic church. I do not wonder at the destruction which has been caused out here (but I must not judge). I pray every day for this dreadful war to cease. I see by the papers that drink is causing a lot of trouble in England; it is a sad thing people do not yet realise what a cruel war this is. Thousands of poor men who have wives and families at home are undergoing great hardships, while men at home are refusing to work. It is the chief talk out here, and our soldiers are very bitter about it. We have given up home comforts and have faced death rather than be subject to a cruel and hard nation. I hope Lord Kitchener will deal severely with the dock strikers on the Clyde.[667] They are not men. I am afraid I have spoken too freely, but you must forgive me.

Yours sincerely in Christ,

C. J.

Sunday morning, April 4th, 1915.[668]

[14]

✍ Dear M – ,

I was pleased to get your letter tonight, and I am

glad you have seen my dear wife. I wrote to Mr Wiles yesterday; I had thought about it for some time. We are still out resting, but I don't think it will be much longer. I awoke this Lord's Day with prayer. I read a portion of God's Word, and went for a walk with a comrade who is a stranger to me, but getting into conversation with him found he was looking to Jesus for strength. How I prayed that I might say something that would encourage him. We went for another walk tonight, and you would, I am sure, have been glad to have heard our talk. It was Jesus and him crucified … Since I have been here my thoughts have expanded. I have heard and seen things I knew nothing about before. Sometimes I get so absorbed in thought that I do not realise that there is such a thing as war. I feel the need of communion with God. I must every hour ask for fresh help and grace, and a greater zeal to serve him who I know to be the Mighty God, the Prince of Peace, and my Saviour. I want Christ in all I do, in all I say, and in all I feel – then my joy will be full. Lord, help me in everything, then shall I know that my whole life is hid in Christ.

Yours very sincerely,

C. J.[669]

[15]

✍ Dear M—,

I must thank you very much for the sermons and cards, also letter which I received safely. While I am writing shells are bursting all around, and I do not know when this letter will be posted. It is the Lord's Day, a day that was ordered to be kept for praise and prayer, and here we are fighting. What a sad thing – I have seen hundreds of poor wounded soldiers coming off the battlefield, and oh, I wonder how many have lifted up their hearts in prayer to God. And then comes another thought – do I feel the need to cry, 'Lord, teach me to pray?' I read one of the sermons this morning and what truths there are in it: 'A brand plucked from the burning.' And to think that Jesus has plucked me from the Evil One! How unworthy I am! When I would do good evil is present with me.

Sunday morning, May 10th, 1915

Here the letter was left unfinished and taken up a few days later:

✍ Dear M – ,

It is now with a thankful heart that I am trying to finish my letter to you which I started five days ago. We are back for a rest, and it seems like a paradise to be able to sit down and have a few moments in quiet meditation. You will see by the newspapers of the British advance. I have seen some awful sights again. The Germans shelled us very heavily; two of my mates were killed by a shell, and two others wounded, one on my right and another on my left, but I was spared. As we were going along, I came across a poor wounded man. I could not help him, but I said, 'God bless you, my friend.' How pleased he seemed just to hear those words, for he said, 'Thank you, thank you for that.' I pray that I may be used of God to bless and cheer some poor soul. One can hardly realise the awfulness of it all.

Again has the Lord been mindful of me, and again

have I proved his precious promises true, 'I will be with thee.' When the shells were coming from all directions dealing death and misery, such messages as these came to me: 'Not a hair of thy head shall fall;' 'Not a bone shall be broken.' How precious this was to me at that time! I believe there were a good many praying souls. I must confess I was a bit shaken, but all through I could say, 'Lord, not my will, but thine be done;' and be it to his glory I am again a living monument of his mercy, unworthy though I am and the chief of sinners. I am indeed a brand plucked from the burning, and to him be all the praise. God forbid that I should glory, save in the precious blood of Jesus Christ. I believe my hopes are to be fulfilled, and that my life is given me 'for a prey.'

I have found the sermons very helpful to me, and I pray that I shall yet hear the truth from the lips of God's own people.

Now I must close.

Yours very sincerely,

C. J.

Friday, May 21st, 1915.[670]

[16]

✍ Dear Miss —,

I was very much blessed in reading your kind letter which I received tonight. I am sorry to tell you I had to go to the doctor this morning as my heart has been bad. I cannot rest at night, but still I am thankful to God, for I know it might have been a great deal worse, had it not been for his tender mercies.

We are resting now, so I took the opportunity of seeing the doctor. I have to go to him again tomorrow, so I will write and let you know how I am in a few days. I have been very low lately, but still I can cry, 'Lord, in thee will I trust. Cleanse me from every sinful thought, and may my whole life be in accordance with thy divine will.' How true have his precious promises been to me, 'thy life will I give unto thee for a prey;' and, 'a thousand shall fall at thy side … but it shall not come nigh thee.' 'What shall I render unto the LORD for all his benefits?' I don't forget the chief of all these mercies, the gift of Jesus Christ, God's only dearly loved Son, who has shed his precious blood that sinners like me should be forgiven. I was much interested in your letter, and I pray with you that your efforts and the efforts of all who serve the King of kings to lead others to Christ will be greatly blessed, and that souls may be saved. How sad for a soul to die with no hope in the tomb. I am glad you told that young soldier of my deliverance, but it was all of grace. I shall never forget my experiences, and if I live to come home, I shall, by God's help, tell others of his saving power. What have I done that I should receive such blessings at the hands of a righteous God! I do pray that I may be kept humbled before God and a due sense of my nothingness. If I come home my life must be kept (by the grace of God) in accordance to his will. I long to show my gratitude by coming out from the world and following our Lord's footsteps in baptism. I believe God has pardoned my sins, and that he will in his own time fulfil the desire he has put into my heart. May God bless his own Word everywhere this day, and comfort every dejected soul. I thank God that he has given me kind Christian friends whose letters are a blessing to me. Hoping you will enjoy your visit.

A German gas attack on British trenches

I am, yours very truly in Christ,
C. J.
Sunday night, May 30th, 1915.[671]

[17]

✍ Dear M – ,
I am writing a line to let you know I am in a hospital in England, and oh! my heart goes out in thankfulness to God that I am again in my native land. I cannot tell you what it seems like to me. I got a taste of the dreadful gas, but I am getting better. I did not tell anyone about it as I did not want to upset my dear wife, but thank God I am getting better.

I am in a hospital where there are lady doctors;[672] in fact, everything is done by ladies. They wait upon us voluntarily; we get every possible attention.

I came across last Wednesday, and reached London about six o'clock. It took about four hours from Boulogne to London. I think that is a record. I am very shaky yet, but my whole heart and soul go out to my Saviour for the fulfilment of his gracious promise. The doctor has promised me a short motor ride as soon as I can stand it. Now I must close.

I am, yours very sincerely in Christ,
C. J.
Monday, June 14th, 1915.[673]

[18]

✍ Dear M – ,

I am writing a few lines this morning trusting this will find you well. I haven't been so well this last day or two, but feel brighter this morning. I am rather shaky. I must tell you I had quite a pleasant surprise yesterday. Mr Wiles came to see me. How pleased I was, and how good of him to come out of his way to see me. He stayed quite a nice little time, and before he left he had a little prayer which helped me very much. I'm afraid I appeared rather dull, but I was too overcome to say much. My heart went out to the Lord for his goodness and mercy toward me, and indeed I knew it was the Lord's doing that Mr Wiles was enabled to visit me. I was also very pleased to see my dear wife and little girl on Wednesday, but it was as much as I could bear. It seemed as if my heart would melt at the wonderful goodness of God in answering my prayers. I am sure I have the greatest cause for thankfulness; I have been greatly blessed in many ways since I have been here, and I have made friends with a good few. I get all sorts of things to make me happy, and in it all I see the good hand of God.

I am indeed a monument of grace. My life has been preserved thus far and the promise has been mine. I shudder now to think of the past eight months. I cannot forget them, and my nerves shake as I lie here, but not with fear, for I have not known what fear means since I have trusted the Saviour.[674] But the horrors of the battlefield are beyond description, and to me it is a divine revelation to know the wonderful manner in which the dear Lord watches over his children.

Although destruction was on every hand, and it seemed as if all the powers of hell were let loose, yet not a hair of my head was touched. If I told my story to some, they would say, 'Yes, but you got the gas.' I can easily answer that. I had enough gas to enable me to come home again, to see my loved ones. Answered prayer, nothing short of that, and I realize it fully though I am unworthy. I feel my utter helplessness, but praise God he is my All in all. Now I must close.

Believe me to remain,

Yours sincerely in Christ,

C. J.

I shall be pleased when I can come home, but that won't be just yet. I shall think much of you at Devizes today.

Sunday morning, July 5th, 1915.[675]

The following two letters appeared in *The Little Gleaner*, giving further details of their author:

✍ Dear Mr Tryon,

The writer of the foregoing letters returned home last Saturday, August 21st, after nearly ten weeks in the military hospital. He was at chapel last Sunday; our pastor being away, Mr Farmer was preaching for us. He thanked God very suitably on C. J.'s behalf, saying how amazed he would be at the goodness of God in bringing him home again, and preserving his life in such a marked way. C. J. took tea with me and my sister, and two or three incidents he related may be of interest to your readers.

On one occasion the Germans took their trench, and coming into the part where Lieutenant Corporal[676] J. was with six men, they asked one of the men certain questions, such as, 'How many troops have you behind?' etc. The brave man would not reply, and the officer ordered him to be bayoneted. Seven men thrust their bayonets through him to the wall of the trench. C. J. was close by and resolving he would die rather than reveal anything, when the Yorks[677] sent some shells into their midst and disturbed them. C. J. saw his opportunity, and leaping over the parapet of the trench, escaped. Later on our army recovered the trench.

Another touching incident was the death of their captain. When going on dangerous night duty he generally chose Lieutenant Corporal J. to accompany him. He would say, 'I want you to come with me, and take care of me,' so that there was a friendly regard between them (Captain Hoare knew that C. J. was a praying man and read his Bible. He, the captain, was a Presbyterian.) The day the captain was shot, as they rushed forward to meet the enemy, he shouted, 'Come on, J!' J. replied, 'I am close behind, sir.' Immediately a bullet passed through the captain's head, and poor J. had to rush over his dead body.

When the airman, Lieutenant Morgan, was killed, our friend rushed to the spot, forgetting the danger till he was fetched back again, but the Germans did not shoot, so that again his life was given him 'for a prey.'

When he was taken prisoner,[678] everything had to be given up but the little book of John's Gospel and Epistle to the Hebrews. This was returned, and though of no intrinsic value, yet it was prized by him for the words of life it contained, and as a memento of a Sunday night when, with a troubled heart, he and his wife walked four miles in pouring rain to and from chapel, and he received the first token of God's love through his promise: 'Thy life will I give unto thee for a prey in all places whither thou goest' (Jeremiah 45: 5).

Yours very sincerely,

E. S. S.[679]

✍ Dear Mr Tryon,

As a further proof of God's care I write to tell you that Lieutenant Corporal J— was ordered to go to Servia[680] with a draft from Weymouth last Wednesday. As his heart was still troubling him, and his paper said 'Home Service,' he and his friends felt it unfair to send him there, especially as he had not appeared before a Medical Board. Prayer was made in submission to God's will, which we knew was above the will of man. He left his wife and children on Tuesday last, his faith greatly tried, and as he writes, 'passed a restless night; on Wednesday morning going for his kit he was informed he was NOT to go with the draft.' I do not know as yet why he was spared, but a lady in W— would like to have him to help her in her work for soldiers and sailors, and we think she may have interceded for him. We feel sure 'the hand of the Lord hath done this,' and are thankful to him for it. Not that we want any to shirk their duty, but he has not yet recovered from the effects of the gas on the heart.

You may like to let your readers know this. Wishing you every needed blessing in God's service. I remain,

Sincerely yours,

E. S. S.

Devizes, November 12th, 1915.[681]

Private E. Jarvis, Luton

Private E. Jarvis was only in the army for about two months before he was invalided out because of a weak chest. The following letter detailing his struggles against the spirit of army life was published in *The Christian's Pathway* as an encouragement to others.

✍ To Mr Kirby.

Dear Friend,

I feel it may be a little encouraging to you, and perhaps to others who are lovers of the Lord Jesus Christ, and like myself have been called to serve king and country in this time of great trial, if I should relate a little of my experience since being called up. If any reader of your valuable magazine, *The Christian's Pathway*, should be sent to the above camp, or have a son or brother there, and would communicate to me at the above address, I should be very glad to find them out, as I feel like a sparrow alone upon the housetop, bereft of all friends except the Friend 'that sticketh closer than a brother.'

On Monday, June 19th, I was called up from Luton to go to Bedford the same day. Before leaving home on the Monday, I read with my dear wife and family Psalm 121, and after bending the knee and begging of the dear Lord to fulfil the language of the sweet Psalmist in preserving me and mine in this time of great trial, I promised my dear wife that I would read a portion of the Word and bend the knee before I retired to bed each night, and again in the morning, whatever the consequences should be. Little did I think I should have such a battle to fight the first night. I was confined to the barrack room with about fifty other men, all called up that day, and the drunkenness, cursing, smoking, song-singing and dancing carried on was too dreadful for words, and I thought, 'What could be said if God were strict to mark iniquity?' My poor heart ached within me to have to be in such company. Now came the trial for me. I had promised to read the Word, and as I sat on the so-called bed, I felt I dare not undress without fulfilling my promise to read the Word and bow the knee. I sat begging and crying to the Lord for mercy and help, when the enemy came in like a flood. He suggested that I dare not bend the knee in such a place, nor open my Bible – if I did I should get boots and curses thrown at me. With these and many other insinuations he came upon me and got me to the ground. Then he said, 'If you do not do it tonight no one will ever know, as you are a stranger to all;' and so, listening to his soothing way, I was about to yield, and he assured me that my wife would never know.

So I began to undress, but with a heavy heart, knowing 'the eyes of the LORD are in every place,' and feeling I dare not, must not get into bed without reading the Word. Yet, while I was in this great distress of mind, I opened the bed to get in, then Satan turned the other way upon me, and said, 'You, a Sunday School teacher, a member of a Strict Baptist church, a deacon too, and ashamed and afraid to read the Bible here – how does your light that you speak about shine before men? You teach the children to love and read their Bibles, and now you are afraid to practise what you preach.' Thus he assailed me till tears ran down my face, and among the many petitions I offered to the Lord, one was this, 'O LORD, do undertake for me, I am oppressed.' Then these words came with such power and sweetness, 'Call upon me in the day of trouble: I will deliver thee, and thou shalt glorify me.' I then fell on my knees, fearing neither man nor devil, and was enabled to pour out my soul in prayer and praise, and the sweetness and calmness I felt within filled my poor soul with praise, and when I got off my knees the man at the next bed, although drunk and one of the ringleaders, called out, 'Watch and pray,' but not another word or remark was made to me on the matter.

While I was on my knees the noise and song-singing quieted down, and I felt, 'Surely the Lord is in this place; and I knew it not,' and so precious was He to my poor soul that I got no sleep all night, but was blessing and praising God and meditating upon his goodness so wonderfully manifested to one so unworthy. I felt I could tell to all around 'What a dear Saviour I had found,' and about 4 a.m. I got up and dressed, then took my Bible and sat reading for over an hour, and felt I could say, 'Precious Bible! what a treasure,'[682] for it seemed full of precious promises wherever I turned and read. Each night and morning since I have read the Word and bent the knee in prayer, and never has anyone interfered or passed any remark upon it in any way. I always spend one hour with the Bible each morning, from five to six, and have found it very sustaining and comforting to meditate upon it when on parade or marching order. Should anyone who has been brought up in the fear of the Lord, especially among our young friends, be in such company and circumstances, do not neglect your Bible or fear to bend the knee in prayer. Remember the exhortation, 'Them that honour me, I will honour.'

Since being down here at Landguard Camp I have had the honour and privilege to meet with the Lord's people at Harwich each Sunday, although I have had to obtain a special pass. I feel it has been in answer to prayer, as it is three miles by boat, and I understood when I came here I could not get a pass each Sunday; but I believe the dear Lord gets it for me (by his wonderful influence), as I am the only one that goes over to Harwich. I should be glad to do anything I can for anyone who would like to meet with us there. Surely among the many thousands here there are some who love a free and sovereign grace gospel as it is in Jesus. Anything I can do I would do as unto one of the least of those who love and think upon his name, for, says the Word, 'They shall be mine … in that day when I make up my jewels.'

Yours,

E. Jarvis,

No. 30365, 7th Company, 3rd Battalion, Bedfordshire Regiment, Z 14 Hut, Landguard Camp, Felixstowe.[683]

Lance Corporal Alfred Edgar Jenkins, Brighton

Alfred Jenkins, who attended Galeed Chapel, Brighton, entered the army on April 11th, 1916, serving in the Wiltshire Regiment, and was sent to France in October, 1916. After 11 months' active service, he was killed instantaneously by a bullet through the head, while digging a new trench in front of the line, on September 4th, 1917, and is buried in Torreken Farm Cemetery at Wytschaete, Belgium.[684]

[1]

✍ Indeed, dear Aunt, this has been truly a great deliverance, and I do desire to truly thank the Lord for such love and mercy manifested to one so utterly unworthy, to so great a sinner. Yes, the truth is I have indeed suffered much, and when this move came, I was so weak that I feared a total collapse. I have told dear C. much about it, and I would say no more than that now; that I was brought to my extremity, and the Lord graciously made that his opportunity. I have many times, since being in France, walked in the experience of these words: 'Then they cried unto the LORD in their trouble, and he saved them out of their distresses.' Dear Aunt, may we have grace enough given us to thank the Lord both for what he is and what he does. 'O that men would praise the LORD for his goodness' (i.e. what he is), 'and for his wonderful works to the children of men' (i.e. what he does)!

You will readily understand that for several days after the relief came, I felt very near the Lord every day, and he also graciously made Jesus sweetly precious to my soul; so that it appeared to me that every step of my path was paved in tender love and mercy. 'Twas sweet indeed, and for several days I did walk in the fear of God day by day, watching every word, lest I should grieve the sweet Spirit. It has now gone, and I feel my cold state, and would have a return; but 'twas sweet indeed. Everything seemed to show me nothing but love, goodness and mercy. I found freedom in Jesus Christ, and liberty, which is better felt than spoken of.

Its absence proves to me how real it was. These words would keep pondering in my heart as I walked the streets of this town, and in billets at night too:

> O my Jesus, thou art mine,
> In all thy grace and power;
> I *am* now, and *shall be* thine
> When time shall be no more.[685]

I knew no trouble, all my sins seemed gone right away, nothing condemned me, all was peace, yea, perfect peace. Coupled to this, dear Aunt, I had a week's perfect rest bodily (my duties here did not commence until last Sunday), and though very weak, I saw the medical officer, and the Lord has been graciously pleased to bless the means, and today I feel much nearer to my real self.

There is another side to my experience, and black as it is, I must tell you, though I would refrain; yet I would be faithful. When I was at my worst, and feeling ill, and fearing a severe illness, my heart rose in open and fierce rebellion against the Lord; so much so that I told him he cared not what I suffered, nor did anyone else, and persisted in it, though he had before shown me marked deliverances, and had blessed me with the prayers and love of each of you dear ones at Tunbridge Wells, and many others elsewhere. Yes, dear Aunt, such was his goodness that even whilst I was thus rebelling, the means were being put in hand for my deliverance. Can you imagine how such a sinner can be so truly blessed? It is our mercy that while our Lord Jesus never excuses nor approves of our sinful rebellion and unbelief, yet he is full of tender love and mercy to *us* in our weakness. 'The spirit truly is ready, but the flesh is weak,' are his gracious words. And there lie forgiving love and mercy, the quality of which the world knoweth not, nor can our poor hearts conceive.[686]

January 10th, 1917.

[2]

✍ The Lord bless you and comfort your heart, and grant you peace in your soul by the sprinkling of the blood of Jesus Christ, sweet as it is indeed to have. It may be of some great comfort to your heart if I speak to you of God's great mercies to us since last I wrote to you; and I do desire to speak with his fear before my eyes, and in deep humility before him. Wonderful preserving mercies have been mine, and answers to your many prayers, I am sure.

The first I have to record is, that on a working party one night last week, I was standing talking to one of the men, when suddenly he fell down badly wounded with a bullet from a German sniper; he has since died. Had he not been in the way, the bullet must have entered my heart; it could not have been otherwise from the position in which I was standing. After he had been carried away, I took over his shovel, and carried on his work with very solemn feelings passing through my breast. I spared, he suddenly cut down, and, poor man, having a wife and six children.

The next I have humbly to tell you, though how I dread speaking of it to you, and I cannot say much. On Easter Monday our regiment went into action, and we were called upon to take a very strong German position, and through God's help and mercy we finally succeeded, and also advanced about two miles. It was a day of suffering to me, which I think I shall never forget as long as I live. Yet not a scratch did I receive throughout the whole of the battle, though hundreds were killed and wounded around me. As we neared the German position we received a heavy rain of shells from them, and our platoon officer, myself, and two others had to take cover in a large shell hole. Now here is my mercy, and praise God for it. We had scarcely been there five minutes when a shell dropped right in the midst of us, but it did not explode; and instead of being blown to pieces, we were only covered with earth. How solemn! yet how great are the Lord's mercies to me! O that I might live according to these wonderful mercies received! I saw some sad and terrible sights, and at the end of the day I was sick and weary.

These mercies occasion me very sober thoughts. First, I desire to praise and adore the wonderful goodness of him who so freely gave them to me. And then I am astonished that on such a miserable sinner as I should be bestowed such wonderful keeping care (Psalm 145). Our men behaved very well and courageously, and faced odds splendidly, and have been highly commended and praised by our generals. O that it may please the Lord in his infinite mercy, and if his sovereign will, to bring me back again to you! The mercies I have received of late are truly encouraging, though I fear to presume. God was my 'refuge and strength, a very present help in trouble.'

Praise God, from whom all blessings flow.

April 13th, 1917.[687]

[3]

✍ The days of great tribulation in which we are now living, and which are to get worse yet, are to be shortened for the elect's sake, whom God shall avenge, though he bear long with them. His Word declares this (Matthew 24); faith endeavours to lay hold of it. You will have much trial to bear, yet as enabled, humble yourself in the very dust before him, the infinite, great, I AM THAT I AM, committing your way unto him. It is my own personal conviction that our present bitter affliction may be prolonged; but the Lord seeth not as man seeth, and has delivering power and mercy, and ways and means continually at hand at his disposal. This *is* true. I, even this wretched sinner, have been favoured to prove this. I well remember how he came upon the troubled waters the day we went into action; so much so that my mind was kept all through quite calm and quiet, and though in the midst of death, my hope remained quite firm in our Lord Jesus Christ. You know I desire to say this very humbly indeed. I am not brought clearly into a full, clear assurance of the forgiveness of my many sins; and many dead works thus remain on my conscience, which is thus not clearly purged. I confess that I have daily need to be kept spiritually alive, and seeking for those great blessings which are indeed and of a truth treasured up in Jesus Christ for needy, coming sinners. It is a mercy to be made truly and daily to grieve at sin, and to repent, seeking healing virtue from the blood of Jesus Christ.

This fountain so dear, he'll freely impart;
Unlocked by the spear, it gushed from his heart.[688]

May the Lord truly separate both you and me from the world, which will ever be a burden to our spirits both in what we see and hear; because as he is, so are we in this world, and if we are helped to walk consistently to the gospel, the world will cast us out.

May 10th, 1917.[689]

[4]

✍ With regard to our many trials, how difficult it is to trust the Lord with respect to deliverance! What wickedness is in our hearts as to the time and the manner of his appearing for us! What sin on this point have I to confess, if God but grant me his free Spirit! How little we verily believe in his wisdom, and that out of evil shall come great good! Yet he bears with us in patience and love, and will not let our nature have all its own way. He can appear for us. He has done so in days past when we have greatly needed him, and never failed in our time of deep need.

O that my soul could love and praise him more,
His beauties trace, his majesty adore! etc.[690]

He sees the struggles that go on within. Remember,

His human heart he still retains,
Though throned in highest bliss,
And feels each tempted member's pains,
For our affliction's his.[691]

June 15th, 1917.[692]

The Moon Brothers of Southborough

One of the most tragic accounts of the war to appear in Strict Baptist denominational magazines concerned the Moon family of Southborough, Kent. They lost their four eldest sons[693] in less than three months during the summer of 1916. Their father, Walter Moon, spent much of the war in Bath Hospital. The local newspaper reported the loss as follows:

✍ SOUTHBOROUGH FAMILY LOSES FOUR SONS. Very great sympathy will be felt for Mr and Mrs Moon, 13, Western Road, in their terrible loss. They have indeed truly contributed their share in this great war, having now lost four sons in less than three months. Gunner Harry Moon was killed on June 2nd, and Sergeant Walter Moon in July, and this month two other brothers have given their lives. On Tuesday Mrs. Moon received a letter from Captain E. Williams, of the 6th Battalion Royal West Kent, in which he says: 'It with very deep regret I have to inform you of the death of your son. Corporal C. Moon, who died of wounds received in action. He was one of my best non-commissioned officers, and had been setting exceptionally good example under fire, and shall find it hard to replace him in the company. Please accept my deepest sympathy in your great loss.' Corporal Moon joined the 6th Battalion, Royal West Kent Regiment soon after the outbreak of war. He was previously in the employ of Mr H. Nicholson, of Bidborough Court, as footman. In a letter to his mother in June last, Corporal Moon enclosed a card he had received from the Major General commanding the 12th Division, on which he stated his pleasure at hearing how Corporal Moon (then Private) had distinguished himself by his conduct in the field. The gallant soldier was the third son of Mr and Mrs Moon.

On Saturday Mrs Moon received further distressing news in a letter from Lieutenant J. Gilliland, O.C., C Company, Anson Battalion, British Expeditionary Forces: 'Dear Mrs Moon – I am awfully sorry to have to write and tell you your son John was killed during bombardment this afternoon. I know how terrible this news must be to you, but in your great grief it must be a consolation to you to know what a splendid soldier your son has proved. He joined us on the 22nd March, and we all very soon got to know his cheerful and manly disposition. It will console you, too, to know his death was instantaneous, and that he had no suffering. He will be remembered by his friends in C Company, who are very numerous.'

Mrs Moon also received the following letter from the chaplain, Rev. W. E. F. Rees: 'I am deeply grieved at the death of your John, who was killed on the 14th August by a German shell in the front trenches. I took the funeral service, in which your son was accorded full military honours, and his comrades and officers attended. He was buried in a cemetery close behind

The Moon brothers

Sgt. W. Moon. aged 23. | Gnr. H. Moon. aged 22. | Cpl. C. Moon. aged 21. | Seaman J. Moon. aged 18.

> our trenches, and his name has been placed above the grave. After the war we shall able to tell you the exact spot of the grave. May God comfort you in your great loss.' Mrs Moon has also received a letter from Lieutenant Moir, who speaks very highly of Able Seaman J. Moon, and one from Petty Officer H. Gobling, who says how he and all the men of C Company greatly sympathise with Mrs Moon, and how much they all respected her son. Able Seaman J. Moon is the fourth son of Mr and Mrs Moon, and joined the Royal Naval Division a week after his eighteenth birthday, and he is not yet 19, and had been in France some months. Mr Moon has been ill himself for some months, and is now in Bath Hospital, where Mrs Moon will have to travel to break this terrible news.[694]

All four brothers are commemorated on the war memorial at Southborough. Walter's name also appears on the Tunbridge Wells memorial. The following are the known details of the four brothers, their deaths and burials.

Gunner Henry Moon died 2nd June, 1916, aged 22. He was in Canada when the war broke out, so joined the Canadian Field Artillery. A Canadian chaplain wrote to Mr and Mrs Moon the day before Henry died as follows:

> ✍ I know you will be very much disturbed and anxious to hear that Harry has been wounded. He asked me to write and tell you about it, as he will not be able to write himself for some time. The battery where Harry was, was heavily shelled today at noon, and Harry, unfortunately, was hit by a small splinter on the lower part of the chest on the right side. Our medical officer was away when the word came to our brigade headquarters only a few hundred yards away. I got the medical sergeant, and we went over with a stretcher. We put a dressing on his wound and carried him on the stretcher down the road, where an ambulance and doctor met us. The doctor redressed his wound and sent him off to the hospital, where I think they will operate to remove the splinter. He was very brave and bright, though he was suffering a good deal. He will probably be laid up for quite a while, but the doctors do not anticipate any danger.[695]

Henry is buried in the Lijssenthoek Military Cemetery, Belgium.

Lance Sergeant Walter Moon was killed 4th July, 1916, aged 23. He served with the King's Own Yorkshire Light Infantry and is buried in Heilly Station Cemetery, France.

Corporal Charles Moon was killed 14th August, 1916, aged 21. He served with the Queen's Own (Royal West Kent Regiment) and was awarded the Military Medal. He is buried in Warloy-Baillon Communal Cemetery Extension, France.

Able Seaman John Moon was killed 14th August, 1916, aged 18. After serving at sea, he had joined Anson Battalion, Royal Navy Division, and seen action in Turkey before moving to the Western Front. He is buried in Tranchée De Mecknes Cemetery, France.

Mercifully, the family were not without hope. The following letter was written by the bereaved father:

> ✍ Dear Friend,
>
> Many thanks for your kind letter; I was glad to hear you had arrived home in safety ... Yes, Friend,

ours is a bitter trial; but hitherto the Lord has helped us.

My dear wife came down to Bath and broke the sad news to me that our fourth boy had been taken. But we are comforted with the hope that they are all safely landed where wars and tumults are not known; so that does indeed make the trial more bearable. Oh what a mercy to feel the Lord showed them what they were as sinners, and brought them to his feet, seeking for mercy where alone mercy can be found! Of course, I nor their mother will ever get over these solemn and painful to the flesh bereavements. But we do feel that the lash is indeed steeped and softened with his blood,[696] and I trust we have been enabled to lie submissive at the Lord's feet and say, 'Thy will be done!' But they were four good boys, and for the most part very thoughtful, and very loving. But, like David of old, we hope we shall go to them, though they cannot come to us. The two lines of one of our hymns have been very sweet to me,

> Then thou presently wilt see
> Thou hast little cause to grieve.[697]

If they are now in heaven, and I believe, through grace, they are, we have indeed cause to bless the *taking* hand, as well as a *giving* hand. The Lord enable us to do so, is my desire.

I was able to get to both services yesterday, and sat down with the friends at the ordinance in the evening, and felt a little softness in the hymn we had where it says,

> Drop the soft tribute of a tear,
> For he shed many a tear for you.[698]

O that you and I may be favoured with much sympathy to him who has done such great things for us, as one has said, 'Who rather than lose us would shed his heart's blood.' Nothing but a felt personal interest in that blood will satisfy my needy soul.

My dear wife left Bath on Saturday afternoon, and I had a postcard this morning saying she had a safe journey to London; she is staying there till Monday, then I hope she will have a safe journey to Tunbridge Wells and home. She will let you have the boys' letters and then you will see for yourself what ground we have for hope that the Lord began a work of grace in their hearts. Mr Carr[699] has read the letters and he considered they were of the right ring; and said they were the sort we wanted to be brought into our churches ... I feel you will be able to do what is right if you are spared; we only want to do what is right. We want no praise of the creatures; and I feel the dear boys, if they could speak, would say, 'Exalt Jesus! Lift him up, for to him is all praise due!' I hope to be able to go to Trowbridge Anniversary on Wednesday, if I can get out. I've written a few lines to Friend B. to thank him for his kindness, and now I will thank you for yours, still asking to be remembered by you and the friends at 'Hanover.' Please remember me to all the friends.

I am, your friend and brother, I trust, in the best of bonds,

W. Moon,
Royal Hospital, Bath.
September 4th, 1916.[700]

The editor of *The Friendly Companion* commented: "What greatly supports the parents under the heavy bereavements is, the sweet persuasion that all four of them now behold his face in glory."[701] This testimony is borne out by the letters which follow, written from the front by three of the brothers. Unlike the other letters in this book, those that follow by the Moon brothers have not been arranged in alphabetical order by the author's name, but have been given chronologically as they refer to events in the family in sequence.

Sergeant Walter Moon, Southborough

[1]

✍ My dear Mother,

Just a line or two hoping they will find you well. Am very thankful indeed to say that I am safe and sound. Going through the wood on Sunday evening in company with another sergeant I was shot at. The bullet passed through my right breast pocket and wounded the sergeant. Poor fellow got a nasty hit in the shoulder. I got a bit of shock; felt the bullet strike me but did not know where it had gone. Next day I had occasion to get something out of the pocket and found the bullet had gone through my paybook and out the other side; in its passage it partly crumpled Lily's miniature up. You will understand it was a wonderful deliverance, and I know it was the Lord's doings. Going up to the trenches earlier in the afternoon these words were laid upon my mind, 'The eternal God is thy refuge, and underneath are the everlasting arms.' They were accompanied by the words:

> Why should I fear when guarded so,
> Or shrink to meet a deadly foe?
> His mouth is held with bit;
> I need not dread his utmost spite,
> Nor can he bark, nor can he bite,
> Unless the Lord permit.[702]

I do hope I shall be given grace to be truly thankful for so striking a deliverance. The 91st Psalm was what I had read in the morning.

Well, mother, I am not telling you this to make you nervous. Rather that you may know how I have been watched over. I had a letter from the M. friends this week. Strange that she should have written to you the night before receiving my letter. The rumour was round there that I had been killed in action, and they were rather anxious. Had a parcel from Aunt Eliza and also from a fellow-teacher at Gower Street. What cause for gratitude, and yet how prone to evil. Truly I must sing, 'His loving-kindness, O how great!' ... I could not refrain from letting you know this. With love to you all,

Your affectionate son,
Walter Moon.[703]

The event described in the foregoing letter were reported in the local paper as follows.

✍ His first experience under fire was at the Battle of Loos, when his battalion acquitted themselves most courageously. Soon after Sergeant Moon had a very narrow escape. While walking through a wood he paused a moment to speak to a sergeant of the Canadians, and a German sniper fired at them. The bullet struck sideways on a pocket book in Sergeant Moon's breast pocket, was deflected by the frame of a miniature in his pocket book, and wounded the Canadian in the lung. Our representative was shown the pocket book and the miniature with the mark of the bullet. Sergeant Moon is full of praise of the arrangements for the comfort and health of the men in the way of food, clothes and baths. He had only once been short of food, which was during the Battle of Loos, when it was impossible for the convoy to come up owing to the heavy fire. They had then to depend on the emergency rations carried with them, and Sergeant Moon says that that meal of 'bully beef' and biscuits was the best and most welcome he had ever had.[704]

[2]

✍ Dear Mr Gillett,

I feel I must write you a few lines ... I must thank you for the bound volume of the 1915 *Friendly Companion*; I am afraid I have been a long time doing so. I am in hospital again, yet I feel to be well favoured. I have had time to read some of the narratives set forth in the book. I could not help but entering into the experiences of the dear lad given in the January number.[705] Though only nine years of age, yet how he did long to rest assured that he was right for eternity. I am sure that there are many older that long for the same. I feel I can truly say that my desires are the same as his were. Yet how base and vile I feel and unworthy of the least notice. Yesterday, Sunday, for the greater part of the day I was in the isolation tent of one of our hospitals; there was only one other case in besides myself. How great a contrast did I feel it to be when thinking of Sunday in the dear homeland. I was led back and enabled to take a retrospective view of my past. Well, my dear friend, I could not help but praise the Lord for his preserving and guiding mercies. When I looked back and saw the way I had been led I could not but say 'wonderful;' I never merited so great and so watchful a care. I have read the memoir of dear Mr Newton,[706] and though not for one moment would I place myself beside him, yet I remember the time when I hated anything like religion, and only attended Sunday School and Bible Class because it was my father's wish. How I did long for the time to come when I should be free and able to go my own road. Truly I have had to prove that we are not allowed to map out our own path. Eventually the time came when I should leave home. Strange as it may seem, the thoughts that I was my own master and free from parental care did not cross my mind. Rather, and I can but remember it with a feeling of gratitude, it was laid on my mind before I had been in London many hours to seek out Gower Street Chapel. I attended there regularly, and it was not until Mr Dickens preaching one Sunday made mention of that particular feeling that I realized my position. By that time I believe I can truly say all desires to forsake chapel had left me. I can even now remember what a sense of the Lord's great watchful care was given to me. Going on right through three years since I can only see how goodness and mercy have followed me. I feel more and more that it is not because I merit it, but it is all free grace. I could not but feel yesterday that had I been left to myself it would have been no more than I deserved. I felt then, I hope, such a feeling of gratitude to the dear Lord for his continued mercies; that isolation tent was to me a chapel, and though far from home and dear ones, in a land where Sunday is held in little regard, yet to me it was a real Sabbath. I do hope I have not done wrong in writing these few lines, but I felt I could not refrain from doing so. I could write much more of what I felt, and how circumstances that I could not see have all blended together, but I should be making this letter too long for the censor to read. The text that has laid upon my mind so many times, 'He knoweth all the way that I take,' I have proved to be true many times. Now I must close, with kindest regards,

Yours sincerely,
Walter Moon,
British Expeditionary Force.
February 28th, 1916.[707]

Corporal Charles Moon, Southborough

[1]

✍ My dear Mother,

Thank you much for all your good wishes and the large parcel of good things ... Yes, dear Mother, at last I have come to the age most people long for [*21*] and think, 'Now they are out of control of parents.' But I hope and trust it is with me the time that I feel most need of them; though I am away and cannot see you, I need your prayers; and I trust that those put up for my brothers and myself may be answered. Yes, it may be a great day with some, but with me – may it prove to have been a day I shall be glad to look back upon. Father said in his letter that he would like to have given me a big present; but this I did not want, or even think of. I know I am a child of poor parents, but *good ones*; that is a great blessing and mercy, something to be thankful for. As F— wrote, 'May it prove to be the time that I am given faith and grace to know that I am born again, that I am among the chosen to inherit that kingdom which was prepared from before the foundation of the world.' If I get there, it is worth suffering for, worth waiting awhile. It may seem a rough road, but what a glorious end. O, to be found in it! There may be tears here below, but all will be wiped away there. We may have losses here, but there there is no separation; all is love and joy. It is blessed to get foretastes below, 'But what must it be to be *there?*'

Thus far the Lord has brought me, fed and clothed me; O, for a thankful heart!

> Plagues and deaths around me fly;
> Till he bids, I cannot die;
> Not a single shaft can hit,
> Till the God of love sees fit.[708]

... I am feeling very well; hope you all are too.

... Dear Mother, I know things are a terrible price, and what little money I leave you I do not want it spent on me. I leave that to help you, so I am going to ask you not to send any more parcels, though I have loved to have them and enjoyed them. But you understand. Don't be offended, will you? Many thanks again for all your good wishes.

Love to all,
Your affectionate son,
Charles Moon.[709]

[2]

✍ My dear Mother and all,

A few more lines, hoping they will find all well. I am thankful to say I am feeling very well, but at times feel very *down* when my thoughts dwell upon the loss of my two brothers.[710] I had a nice comforting letter from John, which I will try and answer. Strange to say, he tells me the words, 'Blessed are the dead which die in the Lord' came to him; and I have been comforted with the words, 'Precious in the sight of the Lord is the death of his saints.' What a mercy and favour it will be to be made one of the Lord's saints; not such as the Pope makes, no, nor what people term saints, but a poor sinner made one because the Lord loved him and had a favour to bestow upon him, not for what he merited, but because the Lord loved him with an everlasting love, knowing neither beginning nor end, nor height nor depth. What a mercy to be able to follow the psalmist and say; 'This poor man cried, and the LORD heard him;' and what then? 'Delivered him.' O, to have the holy Word revealed and set forth in the soul by the Holy Ghost as it is in Jesus! What does that precious name mean to our souls? That name which is above every name, and to whom every knee must bow! Does it speak to us? Is there an inward feeling that the Jesus I am trying to write of is *my* Jesus and *your* Jesus, *my* Saviour and *yours*?

> Sweet the moments, rich in blessing,
> Which before the cross I spend …
> Love I much? I've much forgiven;
> I'm a miracle of grace.[711]

Ah! we have the sweet moments, the sips and the tokens by the way, but not always, and not very long at a time. But the cheer and the love these moments bring to the soul give it hope and strength to go on its way rejoicing. But the Lord has promised that when we are passing through the fire or the waters he will be with us. Begone then, unbelief, which does so torment the soul and bring in so much despair.

I hope father will soon get to Bath, and that it may be the means blessed to restore him to his health and strength; and I hope he had a good time at the prayer meeting, though perhaps his soul was burdened on the journey down, and the devil may have caused him to reason, 'why all this trouble for me, and my wife and children.' That while in the little room he may have received such a blessing, and be made to say, 'Has not the Lord a right to do what he will with his own?' And that he may have had a sweet feeling that his two sons which *are not* are better off, that they are where sin and trouble are not! 'Still, I am left to struggle on until he bid me go.' Then to be made ready, and while here below to have said to us, 'This is not your home … it is polluted,' and to be given faith to look beyond the grave and view the home prepared for the saints of the Lord; but O, to get there!

> Then loudest of the crowd I'll sing,
> While heaven's resounding mansions ring
> With shouts of sovereign grace.[712]

Cheer up! Hope on! The Lord kills to make alive, and wounds to heal! Strange sentence to human eyes; but not so to the soul taught of God.

I received parcel, and enjoy contents very much indeed. Thanks for all your goodness and love shown to me as two good parents. I must soon close. I had a letter from Ethel. Tell her to seek on, though she may think the Word contains nought for her. The way of the chosen is a strange path; their love is sometimes hot and sometimes cold; and sometimes wonder if they have any love at all.

Give my love to all, and kind regards to all friends. Will close with love to all,

Your affectionate son and brother,

Charles,

'Hitherto.'

August 1st, 1916.[713]

Able Seaman John Moon, Southborough

✍ My dearest Mother and all,

I hope you are all quite well, as I am feeling 'A.1.' Was very pleased to hear from you again yesterday morning. I sent a D & D card[714] off to you on Sunday, so I expect you will get that before you receive this letter ...

Will now try and answer your first letter. Yes, as you say, it is a comfort to know that our dear ones are now far away from all suffering. I cannot make out how it is that you have not had any official notice of Walter's death ... So pleased to hear that you and Dad have been so supported in this heavy trial. It is nice to have a Comforter to whom we can go with all our sorrows ...

Now for your second letter. Was so pleased to hear that you had heard from Charlie and that he is still alright. He has had a rough time of it out here. I shall be very pleased to hear from you twice a week instead of once, and will let you have a line as often as possible. It is always a treat to get news from home out here. I wonder how it is that C. had not received your letter. Perhaps they have been so busy that they could not get the mail up to them.

Am thankful to say that I have been supported wonderfully well, though at first I felt deeply grieved. I was reading that sermon that you sent out, preached by Mr Jarvis.[715] These words came in, 'All things work together for good to them that love God;' also, 'For whom he loveth he chasteneth, and scourgeth every one' of them. Mr J. spoke of the chastening as being ruin in business, or the loss of a dear one, and I thought how suitable those words were for the present time, 'Whom he loveth he chasteneth.'

I have not received parcel yet, but will let you know as soon as I do. I should very much like you to send me out *The Friendly Companion* again, and also, if you can, another sermon. The words came in the text of Mr Jarvis's, 'When thou passest, through the rivers, the waters shall not overflow thee: and through the fire, thou shalt not be burned; and the flame shall not kindle upon thee.' What a sweet promise there is in those words; and how happy we shall be if we receive that blessed promise ...

I sent a card off to Bert for his birthday. I hope he will get it alright. He will be seven years old tomorrow. Guess he is getting quite a big boy now. How is Dad keeping now? Has he heard any more about Bath? I do hope and pray that he will soon get properly well again. Have not seen anything of Bill lately, though his battalion is not very far from where we are. Of course, we cannot go all over the place out here, but have to keep near our billets in case we are wanted. Should very much like to see Charlie, but am afraid he is too far away from where we are stationed.

Well, Mother dear, I do not think I have any more news now. Those words keep running through my head:

He is my refuge in each deep distress;
The Lord my strength and glorious righteousness...
In him I live, upon him cast my care;
He saves from death, destruction and despair.[716]

Now I think this is all; so, with fondest love to all, I will close.

Your loving son and brother,
Jack,
British Expeditionary Force.
August 1st, 1916.[717]

Driver John Moore, Ramsgate

John Moore died of colic on 13th September, 1916, while serving in India with C Battery, 220th Brigade of the Royal Field Artillery. He is commemorated on the Karachi 1914-1918 War Memorial, Pakistan. The following are excerpts from his last letter to Mr Kirby, the editor of *The Christian's Pathway*:

✍ Dear Mr Kirby,

I received your very welcome letter dated 26th July, and was very pleased to hear all concerned were well. Your letter cheered me up, and at the same time I received a letter from Mrs Sheppard. At the time of writing we have had immediate orders to undergo a medical inspection. I daresay we shall be on the move again shortly, that is why I have addressed my letters c/o Indian Office. I have been in hospital four days with colic, but I am better now, and have kept well except for that touch while I have been in India. I have seen a good bit of India, landing at Bombay on June 17th. From there we went to a small place called Deolali, from there Jubbulpore, from there to Mount Abu in Rasputana, from there to Bombay, where we were held in readiness for the Gulf, but had to return to Lahore, from there to Sialkot, N. India, 72 miles from Lahore ... I thank you for your kind advice, which is always a help to me, and I pray God to guard and keep me while out in this country and wherever I go. From yours truly,

John Moore

J. Moore.[718]

Driver J. Moore, 2203, A Sub., C Battery, 220th Brigade, Royal Field Artillery, Sialkot, India,[719] c/o Indian Office.

George Oliver, Hawkhurst

George Oliver was bought up to attend Egerton Forstal Chapel, but by the time of the war he was attending a chapel at Hawkhurst (not the Strict Baptist cause). He served in the navy during the war, and his experiences left him with nervous illness for the remainder of his life. An account of the wartime experiences of his brother Ebenezer appears elsewhere in this book (p. 229). The following letter is extracted from the family history of one of his relatives. It was evidently addressed to his parents and describes his experiences when his boat was torpedoed by the German navy, his rescue from a watery grave, passage to Canada and subsequent return home:

George Oliver

> ✍ I took the opportunity of going to Seaford by train and had a good view of the docks … They were busy putting cargo on … I saw a good sized motor picked up and put on just as easily as I could pick up a pin. After that we had to fall in and get our hammocks, and at 9.30 we were slung up. We were lying quite close which made it very hot. Some of the fellows rolled out, but I managed to keep in mine, but came over faint so I took my blanket and slept on a concrete floor … We found ourselves moving out soon after we went to bed, and when we went up on deck in the morning we were well away from shore. As we proceeded the scenery was grand; had a splendid view of the Irish, Welsh and Scottish coasts. I never saw anything so grand. It brought home very forcibly to my mind the greatness of the Creator; truly his handiwork is wonderful.
>
> About two o'clock we began to settle down a bit hoping we might be safe, but at four o'clock another torpedo was fired at us again, missing by a very short space. We were then put on guard all round the boat, about three feet apart, watching for periscopes. There was a special guard on duty that night and I was among them, going on duty at 9.30 and having to stay on duty until 5.30 the next morning. At midnight our captain came along and asked if I had my lifebelt on. I said, 'Yes,' and he wished us goodnight and passed on. At 12.15 the fatal shot came; I was knocked off my feet by the explosion but soon regained myself and with many others made a rush for our lifeboat. How I got there I don't quite know; however it was a wonder our boat did not capsize as one of the ropes hung up, but eventually we found ourselves tossing about in the Atlantic.
>
> The water soon started to rush in so I set to work and baled it out with my hat. Some of the boys rowed, some were very sick, some were crying and some were praying … Two of us got together and comforted each other with the fact that if our time had come we were ready to go, and we expected every minute to be shelled out of our boat. But the commander of the sub was a German gentleman. He could speak English well, and told us not to be afraid; he did not want us and hoped we would soon be picked up. We had eight hours tossing about. By the way, I am sorry to say we lost 40 dear fellows, our captain and the captain of the ship being among that number. About 8.30 we sighted a ship which turned out to be a friend. It was an old tramp, third class, a steamship for cargo only. The last cargo it had was oil and it was returning, so you can imagine the state that it was in, worse than

any coal van, but we were grateful for it. We rowed alongside her and soon climbed up the rope ladder. As I landed on deck I nearly collapsed. As soon as we were safely in and huddled up together in a heap, I said to the boys, 'Chums, we must thank God for this our wonderful deliverance,' and there and then we held a service of prayer and thanks. I was wonderfully helped through it. Some of the boys who had previously called me 'the religious bloke,' thanked me.

We were not allowed to walk on deck and for three days had to crawl on our hands and knees everywhere. This was a time of great privation; the captain had only rations for his crew and this is how we existed: one ship's biscuit per meal, an old tin of porridge for breakfast, with only one spoon to share between 40 men. I was number 17, so 16 men had a go before me. We were allowed three spoonfuls each, then we were allowed three spoons of coffee, out of an old cigarette tin, as there were no mugs. I was thankful we had our meals in the dark so that I could not see much about it, but just got it down. We had nine days of this and then put in to St Johns, Newfoundland, arriving there one evening. It was a treat to be anchored and have a peaceful night. The next day at three o'clock we were taken ashore in boats. When we stepped on land we all felt very weak and bad and suffering from rheumatism, as we had to sleep on deck with nothing to cover us. Those who had greatcoats shared them with those who had not any. As soon as the Newfoundlanders found out we were a torpedoed crew, they went mad with excitement. I took a chum who had no money and treated him to a cup of coffee, and as we came out of the shop a nice lad of 16 asked us if we would like a meal … He took us to his home, which was a nice one, beautifully furnished, with electric lights etc. We were shown into the drawing room where the grandma came and talked to us. I gathered from her

Men being rescued from a liferaft, their ship having been sunk, during the First World War

conversation they were Catholics, but that does not matter; they were indeed ministering angels. In about an hour we were shown into the dining room and there was a beautifully laid table; flowers, silver plate, and everything to make it look nice.

The first thing I did was have a good cry. My nerves were shattered and my heart filled with gratification. I soon got over it and did good justice to the meal.

When the corporation found out our condition on the boat they sent mattresses, blankets and food on board, and the ladies of the town presented each of us with a shirt and a pair of socks; of course we had lost everything. One gentleman gave me three dozen Sankey hymn books as I had asked him if he had any old books to sing from.

We spent six hours ashore, and left St Johns the next day amid much cheering and thanks.

In two days' time we arrived at Quebec. It was reported we were going to Montreal, but this did not come off. As soon as I got to Quebec I put in for 24 hours leave as it was only one hour's journey to Montreal, but I could not get a permit to go. Quebec is a very quaint French province full of Catholics and beautiful buildings. We had a rare time on the second day – we were taken by the ladies of the town in a special train to some wonderful waterfalls. Also nearby were some roundabouts and all kinds of fun. Our expenses were all paid, so you can imagine me going round on a horse bobbing up and down to the music. Then we were given a French tea; scones, cakes and ices.

The next day they arranged to take us all around the town in a tram car especially arranged for parties, with a guide in front shouting through a megaphone all the important places; this was fine. On the Wednesday morning I found the Baptist church. I was glad as they had a meeting. The minister was quite a young fellow, a student from Toronto College. I took part in the meeting and the congregation very graciously sent a message of greeting to our little church at Hawkhurst. After the service I was taken to a restaurant to select my supper at the pastor's expense. He then kindly paid for two sets of underclothing, socks and handkerchiefs.

On our last day in the morning – oh! I might say I telephoned to Auntie and had a little chat with her to persuade her to come and see me. So that morning I received a telegram to say she was coming, due Quebec at 3.30. We were not allowed out after 2 p.m., so I had to go before a captain and explain. He granted me as a great favour one hour with Auntie, so I went to the station and met her. One of the Canadian Pacific officials came with me onto the platform; I picked her out of the crowd. As we approached each other a Sankey hymn came to my mind: 'We shall know each other better when the mists have rolled away;' there was a mist of nearly 29 years. We had a very happy hour together. Is it not wonderful that I should have been granted this privilege? I know dear Father will be pleased. Auntie is getting just like him; I could see a very striking likeness. Of course, she is looking old, but she is bright; no doubt she will be writing to you.

Now I must begin to finish up. I am travelling in a very nice boat second class. We shall be in danger zone tomorrow but I am hoping and praying to get through. We were going to Salonika but this disaster has upset all plans. I don't know what will happen now.

Arrived back in Liverpool this morning … I am now travelling back to Burford. It is only five weeks today since we left. Four weeks today we were torpedoed and we have travelled 6,000 miles.

Am well considering all things and hope to get home shortly.

Your ever loving son,

George.[720]

Private John E. Parish, Manchester

John Parish served in the Royal Army Medical Corps associated with the 2nd Reserve, 1st East Lancashire Regiment. He was destined for the Dardanelles when his boat was torpedoed. This experience he recounts in the following letter:

✍ I am very pleased and thankful that, owing to the mercy of Almighty God, I am permitted to sit down and write a few lines which I hope will reach you in safety. We are at present in camp here, having arrived yesterday (Monday).

No doubt you will have read in the papers of the terrible disaster which befell our ship, the *Royal Edward*, on Friday last. I hasten to let you know that I was among the rescued, and now am safe at Alexandria, after a very exciting time. I was in my cabin at the time the submarine attacked us and fired the torpedo which struck us amidships, so that the ship sunk in less than five minutes. The torpedo was seen by our guard some distance away, and they fired at it with the intention of exploding it before it struck us, but unfortunately they were unsuccessful in their object. Personally, I never felt more calm in all my life. I was in my cabin, and just had time to fasten on my lifebelt and walk to the side down to the next deck lower, and seeing the water rising rapidly I plunged into the sea and swam away from the ship out to a lifeboat which had got well away. This boat contained about 28 men, and was so full of water that it was entirely submerged, but did not sink. Imagine us in this, with water up to our chests in a fair swell, with only one oar and only one bucket to bail with (I took off my boots and used them as ladles), and then you will see how we kept afloat for two hours, after which we found another oar. After four hours in this boat we were picked up by a French minesweeper. We were afterwards transferred to three different French boats, the last being a cruiser, which brought us in to Alexandria on Monday last. I cannot describe the kindness of the Frenchmen, who robbed themselves in order to make us comfortable. The sad part of it is the loss of so many good comrades. Out of our draft of 50 men and two officers we have only 31 men and one officer here, but keep hoping that some more may turn up yet. The only clothes I brought away with me were my trousers and shirt, but I am now fitted up again. I expect after a few days' rest we shall sail again, and I

John E. Parish

hope and trust with better results. I thank God for his preserving mercy towards me, and pray that he may protect me in the future as in the past.

Alexandria.

August 17th, 1915.[721]

R.M.S. Royal Edward

Lance Corporal John R. Parsons, South Chard

John Parsons served in A Section, 32nd Field Ambulance, 31st Brigade, 10th Division. He saw action in the Dardanelles, where he was wounded. The following two letters, written to his parents and his pastor, describe the landings at Suvla Bay, which began on 6th August, 1915. Their aim was to strengthen the Allied forces already in the Dardanelles, and enlarge the front there. The Dardanelles is the strait between the Mediterranean and the Sea of Marmara, the passage to the Black Sea being completed by the Bosphorus, and is controlled by Turkey. When Turkey joined the war in 1914 and sided with Germany, Russia was no longer able to use this route to obtain supplies into her Black Sea ports. In 1915, Britain decided to attack Turkey, believing they were weaker opponents than Germany, and that liberating the Dardanelles would help Russia by restoring her supply route. In the event, however, the campaign was a disaster.

John R. Parsons

[1]

✍ The landing was under shell fire, of course, but the 32nd Brigade got ashore quite safely. Since then, among the stretcher bearers we have had one killed and one wounded. I don't think we should ever have succeeded here but for the grand work of the navy … The noise of the guns is very nerve-racking, especially when the Turks are replying, and from over the hills comes the roll of musketry, sounding for all the world like a big pot of thick soup bubbling away in the distance. Last night the division came in for the highest praise from the General for all its fine work. The climate here is much better than at Lemnos,[722] and I feel quite fit and well, though tired of course. Many providences and mercies have come my way, and I want to thank him who has shielded me in some queer places. I feel that he is here indeed, and pray for continued help and guidance. I feel that this is my place till the war is over, in the thick of the work.

August 19th. The 32nd Brigade had a run of great good fortune with very few casualties till August 17th. On that date, in the early morning, a party of 40 of them advanced too far with their stretchers and got cut off by the Turks. At least five of them were killed and five wounded, and about ten are missing. So we are having a rest after ten days of work day and night till we were utterly tired out.

The Lord has once more been very, very merciful to me, and been indeed a shield to guard me from danger, so that I am still happy and well and shall be fit for anything in a week or two, for I must tell you that the 40 men were volunteers to take the place of the regular stretcher bearers who were utterly exhausted, and I was one of them. Yet here I am, safe, and thankful to him for his protecting power. I saw my poor comrades shot dead beside me; another was dying for hours beside me as I lay all that day behind a stone not daring to move, for the Turks were only 100 yards away. I was in the rear of our line as we advanced along the ridge, and, with another man, dressed a poor comrade whose leg was shattered, while another dashed off for a stretcher. He did not return, so the two of us made a dash to get one, and my comrade was shot through the lungs, dying seven hours later. I got a bullet through the fleshy part of the upper part of my left arm, and managed to crawl back to safety 15 hours later. The wound is doing very well indeed with the expert attention I am getting, for I get the best of everything here on our hospital ship, 50 miles from Gallipoli.

You can guess how wonderfully I was delivered when I tell you that I was not 100 yards from the Turks when they shot me, and as I was crawling away they tried to shoot me again, but an Australian sniper shot one just in time. I lay not daring to move for 11 hours, with shells and bullets going all around the place. It took me three hours to crawl a mile back to safety, under fire most of the way, but the Australian helped me along. In a trench halfway back I was dressed, and given some stimulant and one grain of morphia; I arrived at the advanced dressing station at 9 p.m. and got back to the ambulance that night. Lying out there with bullets whistling around me I read Psalm 46, and very good it was. Surely, 'God is our refuge and strength, a very present help in trouble.' Now I must write letters for the poor chaps who can't write, so goodbye for a while.

August 14th, 1915.[723]

[2]

✍ To Mr Thomas Dare.[724]

My dear Pastor,

I fear it is a very long time since I last wrote to you. Since then I have seen many things never to be forgotten; some among the beautiful sights of the earth, such as a sunrise and sunset in the Mediterranean, others horrible beyond expression. Strange indeed to reflect that I, a mere lad of 20, have had experiences which my parents never have, and which I hope will be spared to all whom I love.

Never, never will any man or woman who has not been in the actual turmoil of it realize just how awful and nerve-racking is war. Indeed, it is a most terrible punishment for any nation, and the worst of it is that the innocent seem to get all the agony of it … Some make their fortunes over and over again; while poor wives and children weep in their little homes over lives carelessly thrown away to gratify great men's ambitions. It is a great trial of one's faith to believe that God is really ordering and controlling all these horrors for some great and wise purpose. But when the awful battlefield pictures fill my mind's eye, it is a wonderful comfort to reflect on his great, omnipotent guidance of all things. I know that he has most marvellously guided me. It might seem, because I have been wounded, that God has not answered the almost countless prayers which I know have been offered up on my behalf by you and all my dear folks. But if you could realize (but you never will) how many times I have only just escaped being hit in a vital part; how many times another man has been laid low just where I was before, you would with me marvel at his great, boundless mercy in so protecting the weakest and most sinful of Christians, as I feel myself to be.

Another 32nd man, Biggs, of C Section, came here two days ago in another batch of wounded. He brought the news that only two of the party came back after myself from the ridge where we were trapped; as we have made no further progress at this point the fate of the others is wrapped in mystery. Biggs is one of a party wounded at the dressing station. Five shells pitched right into it and killed some of the wounded. Lieutenant Young, after all his valiant self-denying work, was badly wounded in the groin; Corporal Green in the abdomen; and Gowans and Biggs wounded; while Paul, a dear little married Scotch fellow, who was a universal favourite, was killed outright. On the other hand a fellow named Kennedy was hurled into the air by a shell bursting beside him, and when the dust cleared away, there he was quite uninjured!

Administering aid to a wounded soldier in the Dardanelles

My arm is now healing rapidly under zinc ointment treatment. The pains in my fingers are still very bad though, and I cannot bend the thumb and forefinger. The head surgeon thinks the nerves in the arm are contused, but will come right in time. The weather is becoming cooler, I am glad to say, though even now at 5 p.m. the perspiration is running down my body.

Your letter was most encouraging, and seemed a message sent to cheer me on the day I was wounded, and it was a strange coincidence that you should mention the 46th Psalm when it was so much on my mind. I may say that in body I feel much stronger, and my stomach is now very much better, and daily I extend my inquisitive explorations round the gardens. And now please give my love to all.

J. R. Parsons,
Hospital, Cairo, Egypt.
August 30th, 1915.[725]

Private Joseph Piggott, Horsham

The following letters were written by Joseph Piggott, who served with the 1st Battalion, The Buffs (East Kent Regiment), and was killed by a shell in France on 11th April, 1917, aged 24 years. He is buried in Maroc British Cemetery, Grenay. As explained in a comment in *The Friendly Companion*, Joseph's parents did not find out until after his death that there was good reason to believe he had been called by grace:

✍ Among the many families recently put into mourning by losses through death at the front, we learn of that of Mr H. J. Piggott, Horsham, whose second son has been killed by a shell in France. We are glad to learn they have hope in his end, which they have only learnt since. It appears that he had concealed from his parents any indication of what he felt within, fearing that if he came back he 'might drop back into his old ways.' ... The father had sent magazines to him monthly, but had not heard from him enough to satisfy their anxious minds, and only since his death have they found, from letters written to others, the clearer testimonies they longed for, and which have settled their minds on the all-important question.[726]

The letters that follow are the series of correspondence that gave Joseph's parents hope concerning his eternal state. It appears that most of these letters were written to a young woman who he was friendly with at home, identified in the correspondence by her initials, "L.S." No doubt many readers will share Joseph Piggott's trembling concern that his religion might have reality and not just be head knowledge.

[1]

✍ My dearest L – ,

Your letter struck a new note, which was a pleasure to me to read, as my own thoughts wander in the same direction; but what concerns me most is, I want a right beginning. I feel I think so little about these things, often only a few minutes in bed or when in danger. I feel I am not prepared to die, but hope that the words of the hymnwriter may be for me,

> Not a single shaft can hit,
> Till the God of love sees fit.[727]

They were very often on my mind when in tight places ...

Hope you are well.
Yours, etc.
Joe.
December 3rd, 1916.

Hope Chapel, Horsham

[2]

✍ My dear Aunt,

Your nice, long and welcome letter arrived safely some days ago, and as I have a few spare minutes thought I would write a few lines ... How desolate everything seems around here, and it seems awful when you see and hear the inventions of war. There are some shells you can watch almost from the time they leave the German trenches, powerful enough to make a hole which would bury a horse. It makes me value the prayers of my parents and friends as I never did in England, and I feel even the few days I have spent in the trenches that God's protecting hand has been near me. It is very kind of Aunt Rosa and yourself to think of me. Food from England comes as a very pleasant change out here. We get one advantage in this part, a hot stew for dinner, and it is very acceptable this cold weather. There seems very little sign of peace yet, does there? I hope things will soon take a turn for the better, and that God will graciously hear and answer the many prayers put up for that day to come. I hope you and Aunt Rosa are keeping well, and that Arthur will soon be returned home safe, as I am looking for myself.

Your loving nephew,

Joe.

December 14th, 1916.

[3]

✍ My dearest L – ,

I was very pleased to receive your nice, encouraging letter and I hope it has done me some good ... I want to put it down to another sign of God's directing hand in my affairs. For if we had not had that talk I should probably have dropped our correspondence, then I should not have had a sympathetic friend at the present time when I do feel to need one ... Even in England I have often felt that God was taking control of my affairs, but I still went on in my sinful path. My constant dread now is that my thoughts on eternity are only remembrances of youthful teaching revived by the nearness of death; and what is the use of these without being born again? It is mere hypocrisy, and I dread that more than a state of open sin. I hope I sometimes feel a longing to be made right, to be 'born again' as remarked above. I often fear, that being brought up under the sound of the gospel, I may only get the teaching without the power. Do you get those feelings, dear?

I was reading in *The Friendly Companion* a month or

two ago[728] (Dad sends it to me) about a little scullery maid who, not knowing what she said, repeated this prayer, 'Lord! show me myself;' and as he answered her, I hope sometimes that if my cries are only words, he may be pleased to hear them and commence his work in my heart. One of my fears is that I shall slip back into my old ways after the war and prove to be only 'a stony ground hearer.' Still, that fear may be my safeguard. When reading your letter about hearing Mr P—, it brought to my mind a quotation I once heard him use, and which I hope gave me a little confidence during a slight bombardment:

> The fictious power of chance
> And fortune I defy;
> My life's minutest circumstance
> Is subject to his eye.[729]

And how true that first verse in *The Friendly Companion* is to me out here:

> My God, I would not long to see
> My fate with curious eyes;
> What gloomy lines are writ for me,
> Or what bright scenes may rise.[730]

And I hope my prayer will always be the last verse, 'In thy fair book of life and grace,' etc. You are the only one I have written to like this, as I want to feel that I can honestly say I am a real Christian before saying anything in my letters home. But as you said in your letter, 'How wonderful if God is being gracious enough to make our paths identical, and if he has ordained that we shall walk the same path and be a means of encouragement to each other.' I have often hoped that God would be pleased to call me by his grace ...

Yesterday the shells were falling around, sometimes shaking the dugout; still I am preserved and I hope that your belief in my safe return will prove to be right. If only those words of the hymn were meant for me,

> Not a single shaft can hit,
> Till the God of love sees fit.[731]

I sometimes feel he will graciously bring me through all dangers; but oh! when I think of what I might have to see and endure before the blessed day of peace arrives! I had a letter from Mother a few days ago. I like to have hers now, while before they were 'too religious' for me. Our people started a bombardment last night, and we were expecting Fritz to retaliate, when a sentence she wrote came to my mind, 'The day and night are all alike to him;' 'He never slumbers nor sleeps.' What a blessing it would be to feel his arm is about you.

I was thinking yesterday, and hoped it was God who directed you to write as you did a few weeks back, as I feel if it had come previously I should not have taken any notice of it. E— said in her last letter, 'If you come home safe we shall have to sing "Count your many blessings."' How little she realizes the great blessing I have faint hopes I shall always have to thank him for; and I feel that if only as the means for saving my immortal soul, the war will not have been in vain.

I see by the paper that Fritz is getting sick of the war; my hope is he will soon be forced by a Higher Power to throw up the sponge. I do not think it will be done by fighting, but by God's great power working on our behalf. I shall now have to draw to a close, and hope that what I have said is my sincere thoughts, and that God will bless it to both writer and reader. I believe I can say I value the prayers offered up for me, both by you and my parents and friends at home. Trusting that God will see fit to bless our mutual correspondence to our souls' welfare,

Your loving friend,

Joe.

December 17th, 1916.

[4]

✍ My dearest L—,

Am glad to hear you are going home for Xmas. I hope you will find them all well. I can quite realize how you will notice the vacant chair. Still, I believe you have hope that he has gone to a better country; a blessing which I am afraid many homes will not be able to console themselves with. May our prayer be that we shall be made fit to meet there when our time comes. How I can sympathize with you when you say how little your thoughts go to God and eternity. Last night I was thinking how seldom I could say my longings were to be made right. Even when in the trenches it seems that my principal cry is for protection; yet, if I was made fit to die, what a difference it would make. Even if called away out here, it would only mean a quicker passage to heaven! Well, L—, I often feel that God himself must make the longing, and I can only hope that, although only infrequently we think of him and attempt to pray, that he is leading us slowly where another would proceed faster. I try sometimes to get hope from what I have often heard our ministers say, that God sees fit to lead his new born children along ways they do not expect. I fear I am rambling, dear, and even now dread that I have only written from the head, and am afraid that if I returned to England now it would be blown away as the seed cast on the 'stony ground.' But I have not yet returned, and pray that ere that time comes God will be graciously pleased to deepen his work, if he has begun it; or if not, to commence it and to make me feel what a sinner I am, and to give me his holy fear. Hoping once again that my pencil may be guided by him to our mutual eternal benefit,

Yours, with much love,

Joe.

December 22nd, 1916.

[5]

✍ ... I have read the New Year's address in *The Friendly Companion.* It is very good, isn't it? Also I was a bit encouraged with the mention of Mr Newton's[732] early experiences, who, although he had been a very wicked man, God saw fit only to start his work of grace slowly and quietly. O, that it may be that the same is happening with me! Do you ever see *The Little Gleaner*? There are one or two nice pieces in it this month. One in particular I should like you to read; a letter found on a corporal killed on the Somme, and addressed to his mother.[733] If I felt I could honestly write as he did many of my fears would be at rest. What a difference it must make to his parents' feelings in their loss, to know he has gone to a better place where wars and partings are unknown. I do not want to go to God for grace just to satisfy my parents, and hope that my cry is for myself, and that my longing to be born again is a right one, and not prompted merely by the perils I am at present in. Well, dear, I think I must draw to a close. I am afraid my statements to you on these matters are very samely and might be wearisome, but I do not seem to advance at all, and the same prayer has to be repeated time after time. Mother said in her last letter,

> A prayer-hearing, answering God,
> Supports me under every load.[734]

May we both be able to say that, dear. I often hope that these letters passing between us may be inspired in some small way by God to our mutual encouragement, and that we may not merely write on these things from head knowledge.

Yours, with much love,
Joe.
January 18th, 1917.

[6]

✍ ... Have heard again from Mother; but her writing (as all seem to now) falls on a hard and unreceptive heart. She writes to me so well, and yet I only seem to get further away from the things that matter. I feel sometimes like throwing myself back into my old ways and making myself one with my companions in the section. Now I feel an outsider, and yet hardly ever feel that I can hope I have started in the right way. For, as Mother says, it is not enough to abstain from outward sin. Yet, dear, I hope sometimes that my petitions, though weak and few, may be heard and answered. If only I could feel I was on the right path I would not mind ... Since leaving the part of the line where we were often shelled, I seem to have gradually lost those thoughts which I hoped were real, and am afraid they were only brought on by fear. Oh L—, I do feel that I need all my friends' petitions on my behalf, and feel that I have yours.

Now dear, I will close, as rambling on I shall only write to you from the head; but I hope that what I have said is sincere.

Yours, with much love,
Joe.
February 22nd, 1917.

[7]

✍ My dear Aunty,

It was with great pleasure I read your letter which arrived the day before yesterday ... It is nice to think we out here are remembered by those we love, and I hope that in my case the prayers of my parents and friends will be heard and answered. But it is constantly brought before me that it is not often God's will that the children of God's people are spared any more than others; but I sometimes try and ask to be made right before I am taken away, but if it is his will, that I may be returned safely home at the end of this dreadful war. Well, Aunty, I don't know why I am putting this as I have said nothing to any at home, wanting to feel sure I am made right before I say anything, as I do not want to buoy them up with false hopes, or find myself a hypocrite and so grieve them. So please do not repeat what I have written, but help me to ask for right guidance and a new heart ...

With love,

Joe.

February 25th, 1917.

[8]

✍ My dearest L – ,

I was pleased to again hear from you ... I have never realized the value of friends until I came out here, particularly those who attend 'Hope.'[735] But it would be nicer still if we could realize and say with the poet, 'What a friend we have in Jesus.' I am afraid I cannot go so far as to say, 'I can leave all my concerns in his hands;' but when in danger, I hope I sincerely say, 'Lord! Thou hast preserved me up to the present and canst still! Do protect me and prepare me for that change which must come sooner or later.' I have been encouraged by reading a piece in *The Little Gleaner*, entitled 'Lord, help me!'[736] I am sure you will enjoy reading it when I can send it to you. Our team had some close goes last night but are still alright, owing to Fritz being a very few yards out of his range; and I trust I feel a small spirit of thankfulness that it was so. 'Not a single shaft can hit,' etc.

Must now close.

Yours, with much love,

Joe.

March 6th, 1917.

[9]

✍ My dearest L – ,

I feel that I have great cause for thankfulness in still being safe and sound at the present time, as we have spent our last turn in the front lines in the worst position I have held up to the present. Although not able to feel that peace of mind I should have wished, yet I felt enabled as dangers presented themselves to go to God for protection ... Your reference to your 'Sunday evening's singing' recalls vividly many evenings at 28,[737] the remembrance of which has never faded. So far back as when they sent me straight to bed after chapel, I can recollect how I would lay and listen to their singing the 'Resolve;' I am sure Mirrie remembers it. I should like to hear Mr Hewitt again;[738] from what little notice I used to take when I had the opportunity of hearing him preach, I realize he is a very suitable man to encourage the young in the way. The chapter (Isaiah 55) is very nice all through. Verses 8, 9 was the first text that made any impression on my mind, and that was years ago ...

One day I saw the most beautiful rainbow I have ever seen. I have looked at them sometimes on sentry-duty, and realized that there is a God above; but you have only to look around the earth here to realize there is a devil as well. Hoping you are getting on well.

Yours, with much love,

Joe.

April 2nd, 1917.

[10]

✉ My dear Aunt,

Your letter, I hope, has been of a little help and encouragement to me; and it was not long before I had need for God's protection for my body, and have proved him to be a prayer-hearing and answering God several times while in the line, where I have had my most nerve-trying experiences out here. But I seem to have few such thoughts except when in danger, but I hope my religion is not caused by natural fear of danger and death.

We are having very changeable weather lately; snow, sleet, rain, sunshine and all sorts of winds; it makes it as trying as the severe frost.

Have just had a letter from Father; he says that Mother has kept much better than usual this winter. I am so glad John seems to be still enjoying himself in Egypt; I hope he keeps there. There is very good news from all parts now, isn't there? I hope it means the end is near.

This is only a short note. Hoping you are keeping well.

Your loving nephew,

Joe.

April 4th, 1917.

The shop in Horsham owned by Joseph Piggott's father. Joseph Piggott is standing to the right of the front door

[11]

✍ My dearest L—,

As I promised, I will try and write you a few more lines, although I do not feel very much like it. I think this part of the line is getting on my nerves, but am doing my best to carry on. We seem to move more like rabbits than men nowadays, we so often have to run about under the earth. In some places they have even got electric light fitted up. Am always pleased to receive your papers ... Now I am away from a town I am almost entirely dependent on your news.

I heard from J. a few days ago. He is still fond of army life, and says that once I get away from the war I shall like it and not wish to come out. But I don't, and anybody will be welcome to my khaki as soon as I can get a civic suit. For one thing, the talk you have to hear practically every minute of the day is enough to make me long to get away. I think sometimes the parsons out here, if they have any heart in their work, must be often very disheartened as so few seem to have any thought of God, except to take his name in vain. One of the services I have liked best of those I have heard out here was a Church of England meeting I attended two Sundays ago. I was undecided whether to attend it or not, but something seemed to say, 'Go.' The clergyman's text was, 'Confess ye me before men and I will confess you before my Father in heaven' (c.f. Matthew 10: 32). It was only a few days before that I had read the same passage in my Aunt's letter, and it seemed to come direct to me. But I feel I shall want much given strength to live up to it, and pray that I may not bring discredit on his name by my profession.

Must close now. Hope you are still progressing favourably. With the hope that our feeble prayers for each other often meet at the throne of grace, I remain,

Yours,

Joe.

April 5th, 1917.

[12]

✍ My dear old friend Joe,

Letters are always welcome out here as you are well aware, but I was particularly pleased to again read one from you ... What a day it will be when we meet again won't it, particularly if it should be in good old Horsham and with the world at peace ... Have you thought of the interest to Bible students of the attacks on the Turks, particularly in Palestine? We have been having regular March weather this year ... Joe, I don't think we shall look back on this episode of our lives altogether with regret if it proves to be the cause of a change of heart in us! But my fear often is that it is only a head affair brought on by dangers, and I often look forward to the days to come, when I hope once again to be a civilian, and wonder whether I shall not fall back into my old ways and prove myself to have acted the hypocrite! Yet sometimes, as you say, 'faith seems to rise up and a feeling comes to you that God is working in you.' Do you ever see *The Little Gleaner* now, Joe? In January there was a copy of a letter written by a young chap the night before he went over the top.[739] It was what I feel I should like to be able sincerely to say or write; but at present I feel far from that state of assurance ... L— S— was, I feel sure, guided to mention something on this matter some time ago, and since then she has been often a great help to me, both telling her of my doubts and fears, etc., and often receiving some little helps from her letters. We seem to have so many thoughts in common, and feel we are being led in much the same path although under such different conditions. I hope for many quiet walks and talks when (if) I return, and now hope that with you also I shall be able to have the same, and that we shall be enabled to talk one to another of what God has done ... Now Joe, I shall have to close. Wishing you all you may wish yourself, I remain,

Your old and sincere friend,

Joe.

August 24th, 1917.

Mr Jefferies commented on these letters in *The Friendly Companion* as follows:

✍ The letters from which our extracts have been taken were a source of joyful relief to his parents afterwards, and we trust they have been so to readers; they have manifested an anxious and tender feeling of 'the fear of the Lord,' which much commends them. His death would seem to have been not long after the date of the last letter.

There are some good 'signs following' that the Lord did not finish his dealings with the dear young man's death, but that in his wonderful counsel and excellent working, he has sanctified the solemn dispensation to two of his brothers, one now in Palestine, and the other, just 18 and expecting to have to join the army, has been received into the church. Of the one in Palestine, his letters show continual exercise of soul. Surely, 'Wonders of grace to God belong.' We have a feeling that the Lord is variously working in the hearts of many young soldiers, and 'his work is perfect.' Much of it may be hidden from man, and much may be of a gentle measure, so gentle that elders may scarce know what to make of it and anxiously wait and watch for clearer evidences of 'growth in grace.' The Lord gave much encouragement in these points by pointing to the wind's reality and effects being known by its movements and sound; but its source of origin and procedure were hidden from man's powers of definition or description at the time of generation or creation. 'So is every one that is born of the Spirit.' We believe only eternity will reveal many who have passed from the battlefields to glory; while the future time will reveal many who have been 'killed and made alive' by that eternal Being, passed from death unto life and been translated from the kingdom of Satan into that of God's dear Son in the same awful surroundings. May we reverently join them in their desires to 'worship God!' [740]

The following letter was written by Joseph's brother, Ben, who is mentioned as serving in Palestine. Mr Jefferies commented: "Many will rejoice with Mr and Mrs Piggott in having been the favoured parents of two such sons as Joe and Ben."

✍ Dear Miss Swinson,

It was a very pleasant surprise to receive a letter from you, and it is very nice to know I am not forgotten by the old friends although I am so far away. I value the thoughts and prayers of all who think of me, and hope the many prayers on my behalf will be answered, and that I may be permitted to return ere long if the Lord's will. Ah! what mercy has been shown to us in calling us from nature's darkness into his marvellous light. O, that I could praise him more for it! But I seem so ungrateful for it and at times feel so unable to live a life of godliness, so dead and cold to religion that it causes many heart searchings as to whether I am right or not. My devilish heart so easily seems to be led astray, so prone to evil, so averse to good that I wonder oftentimes if I have ever had a right beginning? O, that I could feel more love to him and to his ways; but I feel I can say,

> I hate the sins that made thee mourn,
> And drove thee from my breast.[741]

I have to prove that my 'heart is deceitful above all things, and desperately wicked.' O, that he would take possession of my heart, 'cast each hated idol down, and reign without a rival there.' Yet in spite of all my felt backslidings and fallings from him, I hope and feel that he still has a love for me. Ah! what a mercy that,

> Whom once he loves he never leaves,
> But loves them to the end.[742]

'Why was I made to hear his voice,' etc.[743] There was no free will in that, for I should never have sought him if he had not sought me first. I was contented in the world, or thought I was; I had no desire for God or godliness. I cannot understand anyone preaching free will; it is an insult to our Lord. I suppose the carnal heart likes to think it had some hand in it; but if we are really born again we can see our utter inability to help oneself. Only last night at our church parade the padre said that, 'God gave us free will so that we could accept him or reject him as we would; and that he would not force himself on anybody.' What a sad state to get into to believe that. It made me remember the words of the poet,

> 'Twas the same love that spread the feast
> That sweetly forced me in;
> Else I had still refused to taste,
> And perished in my sin.[744]

One time, like the prodigal, we filled ourselves with the husks of this world's so-called pleasures; but now we hunger for heavenly food, food which never clogs, never overfills.

> We hunger now for heavenly food,
> And our poor hearts cry out for God.[745]

I love the hymns, and the memory of the dear men who wrote them. They seem to contain my experiences, my desires. They have been a help and comfort for me many times out here, and a lot of them I know by heart with so often reading them, but they always seem fresh and with new meaning. How precious he seems to us when we are brought to a sense of our vileness and filthiness. What healing balm he is possessed with! Yes, the longer we live the worse we seem to become and the viler we seem to get. I have heard some people say that as soon as they believed all their sins vanished and they never had any more doubts of getting to heaven. I have never found it like that. I have found doubts and fears will continually rise, and I often have to question whether I am right or not.

Thank you very much for the sermon. I miss hearing a good sermon, and the written ones are very welcome. The sermons we get in the army are very empty for the most part. I was very glad to hear what a nice time you all had at Guildford at Easter, that you had such a good collection and attendance. I should have liked to have been there, but perhaps I shall be able to get there next Anniversary, if God's will. It is very nice to hear that the debt at Hope[746] is getting so low, isn't it? The dear friends at G— have helped us in reducing the debt very much; may the dear Lord reward them for their kindness.

Must close now. Hoping you and all the friends are keeping well, and hoping to see you all soon if the Lord's will.

With kind regards and good wishes from,
Yours sincerely,
Ben,
Palestine.
June 3rd, 1918.[747]

W. H. Pratt, Rotherfield

The following letter was written from Palestine by W. H. Pratt, to his pastor, Mr James Dickens of Rotherfield. W. H. Pratt was a grandson of Richard Pratt, the pastor at Forest Fold Chapel, Crowborough.

✍ Dear Mr Dickens,

Although so far from Rotherfield, I have not forgotten you all, nor have I forgotten the cause of truth there, so I am sending you ten shillings to help the cause, as a memorial from me. I wanted to send it in time for your anniversary, but could not do it, as one cannot always keep in touch with the post office here. I am out on the sands of the desert, not quite in the road of the children of Israel when they went out of Egypt, but am in the direct road that Joseph must have gone when he fled to Egypt with our Lord in the night. What a journey that must have been, over 200 miles, straight as one could go, for I am now at the coast of the Great Sea, as it was called, near Gaza where Samson was.

Richard Pratt and his wife

I am sorry to say that the sound of the truth is not heard here. I have not heard its sound since I was at Providence Chapel, Bath, on January 6th, when I taught a class in their Sunday School; but I hope and trust that I shall be spared to come home safe and meet with you all again at Rotherfield, also Hanover.[748] I miss Hanover greatly; but there is no Sunday here, it's every day alike. May the Lord bless and spare us so that we may meet again, is the wish of your unworthy friend,

W. H. Pratt.

June 1st, 1918.[749]

James Dickens

Eli Smith, Biddenden

Eli Smith was born in Headcorn in 1892. He attended the chapel at Bounds Cross, Biddenden, and his mother was a member there.

This letter was written to his parents, describing the experience of having to take cover in a shell hole, with a serious injury to his leg (which necessitated him wearing a prosthetic leg in later life). We understand that it was while he was lying there, expecting to die, that the Lord spoke to him regarding the work of the ministry. Shortly after his parents received the letter, they heard he had been taken a prisoner of war and was in Germany.[750]

After the war, in fulfilment of the exercise given him on the battlefield, Mr Smith was sent out to preach, and was for a few years pastor at Zion Chapel, Leicester. He retired from the ministry due to a problem with his voice, and is buried at Bounds Cross Chapel, Biddenden.

✎ My dear Mother,

I now have the opportunity of writing a few lines. I must say I have felt the Lord's presence with me in this time of trial and conflict. After I was wounded I lay in a shell hole for four days and nights, but during all this time I was sustained, and now am in comparatively comfortable surroundings. I have much to thank God for and so far I have found him very good to me, so do not worry as I am getting on as well as possible. I should like to know how you all are getting on, but I must be content and trust God you are all safe and well, for I cannot send you my address. My dear Mother, as I lay in that shell hole, those words kept coming to me which I told you of when I was reading one day, and they were fastened to my mind: 'I will bring evil upon all flesh, saith the Lord: but thy life will I give unto thee for a prey in all places whither thou goest' (Jeremiah 45: 5). Well, cheer up and trust in God, for your son is now away from the shot and shell, and God will one day bring me back to you safe and sound.

I will now close, hoping this will find you all well.

Fondest love and best wishes from your loving son,

Eli Smith.

P.S. God bless you and keep you safe.

May 17th, 1917.[751]

Eli Smith

Private George F. Smith, Colchester

Private George Smith was the son of Mr William Smith, a minister at Colchester, Essex. He served in 10th Battalion, Essex Regiment, and was killed on 26th September, 1916, during the battle of Thiepval. He was 24 years old and left a young widow. His name is recorded on the Thiepval Memorial as he has no known grave. His brother, Frank W. Smith, who is mentioned in the following letters, also served in the war. When the letters were originally published in *The Sower*, the editor, Manasseh Tryon, prefaced them with the following note from a friend of the family:

✍ Two of our oldest friends living in Colchester have their two boys in the army, one in Egypt, the other in France. The latter was reported by a friend as having been killed on 26th September; but the official report was that he had been 'wounded.' Not another word has been heard, neither from the War Office, nor from the poor lad himself; the parents are in painful anguish, fearing that if only wounded he must be dreadfully ill, as they know his first thoughts would be to send a message to them and to his anxious young wife. But in the midst of it all, they are rejoicing in the Lord's mercy to his soul. I spent a night with them recently, and they gave me some of his letters to read.

To these letters we have added the last letter his father wrote to his son at the front, and an extract from a letter from the grieving father, giving some further details of his son.

[1]

✍ My dear Parents,

Just a few lines, as I have a short time to spare, to let you know how I am getting on. Of course you will understand that I'm not allowed to state where I am, but I am thankful to say that through God's mercy I have up to the present enjoyed good health and spirits. Things are rough out here, but it is only part of the cross we are all having to bear just now, and I trust God will give me strength to bear all hardships without murmuring. I am further from home, but nearer to God than ever I felt in all my life, and I feel I need him now, and I know your prayers are often sent up on my behalf. I often think what a mercy it is I was brought up with God-fearing parents, but I must say I never thought of that until these last few weeks.

It is right that God should teach us a lesson as he is doing, and I trust and believe it will make a new man of me. If he spare me, I do beg I may be used in his good service, and I think this has always been the desire of your hearts. 'God moves in a mysterious way …,' and we know that while we trust in him all things must work together for our good.

I trust, dears, you will do your utmost to comfort dear — during my absence, and get her to spend as much time as possible with you. I firmly believe that when we were married God was answering your prayers in blessing me with a God-fearing wife.

God bless you all. Much love to you all, and hoping to hear from you soon.

Believe me,
Your loving son,
George,
British Expeditionary Force, France.
August 2nd, 1916.[752]

[2]

✍ My dear ones all,

I am thankful to say that through mercy I am still keeping well in body, mind and spirit, which is indeed a mercy. I get about a good deal with Ben. He is with me now, and one or two other young fellows in our regiment with whom I am able to converse on spiritual things. It is indeed nice to be able to talk together thus, and it makes us feel ashamed that we have neglected such matters until just now, but oh, how we do long to know more of God's mercy! We usually attend a service at night; in fact we do every night we are able to, where we sing hymns, some good old hymns, too, and the boys do sing. After that there is prayer and a short address. I never enjoyed a service as I do these; indeed, I value them. The other night the minister, a good man, took for his text Matthew 5: 6 'Blessed are they which do hunger and thirst after righteousness: for they shall be filled.' That is my case exactly, and how I need it! and I trust and believe I shall be filled. I have such a feeling, such as I have never had before, that God is indeed watching over me, and every day I can see his goodness towards me. You know as well as I do that I was always one to worry and look down, and yet since I have been here I have enjoyed such peace and comfort of mind as he alone can give, and I feel that it is only an answer to my poor prayers and yours.

I have a dear good wife. The letter I had from her today brought tears of joy to my eyes, and I could but thank God that he had blessed me with a partner in life who I believe is one of his chosen. I have a desire that if he sees fit to spare me, and I believe he will, I may be used in his service, and that is her desire also. When I think of what good parents I have, what a comfortable home I have, and what a good wife, I feel I can say as David did, 'Surely goodness and mercy have followed me all the days of my life.'

Holy Father, in thy mercy
Hear our anxious prayer,
Keep our loved ones, now far absent,
'Neath thy care.

Jesus, Saviour, let thy presence
Be their light and guide.
Keep, oh keep them, in their weakness,
At thy side.

When in sorrow, when in danger,
When in loneliness,
In thy love look down and comfort
Their distress.

May the joy of thy salvation
Be their strength and stay;
May they love and may they praise thee,
Day by day.

Holy Spirit, let thy teaching
Sanctify their life.
Send thy grace that they may conquer,
In the strife.[753]

We have been singing this hymn, and you don't know how I did feel what I was singing. I think it is lovely, don't you? I want you all to sing it together, and when you do, I need not say you will think of dear old Frank and me. I think of you all when I sing it, and never have enjoyed a hymn like it.

I will try to write again soon, and am anxiously waiting a letter from you. God bless you all.

Your loving son and brother,
George,
British Expeditionary Force, France.
August 10th, 1916.[754]

[3]

✍ My dear Parents,

I have just turned in for the night, and as it is not very late, I thought I would write to you after having written to F—.[755] I know how anxious you must be to hear from me.

Well, I am thankful to say that, through God's mercy, I am, in spite of many hardships, still in excellent health and spirits. God has indeed been good to me in thus favouring me. Our guns are again pounding away at the enemy tonight as I write.

F— tells me, Mother dear, that you are sending me a parcel this week between you. I was hoping to receive it this afternoon, as we have unavoidably been on short rations today. It sometimes happens that they cannot supply us some days as others.

Thanks, Dad, so much for *The Gospel Standard.* I was very pleased with it, and read it right through. I wish I could get more reading like that to pass the weary hours away. It is so nice to get buried in good reading amidst all the ungodliness which surrounds one out here. I went to a service at the YMCA here last night. There was a crowded attendance and I had a most enjoyable evening. These YMCA places are a great boon out here, and you find them almost everywhere; but what strikes me so much is the good men they engage to speak to our lads. Wherever I have attended one, and I have been to a good many, I have found their doctrine to be most sound. I often wish, Dad, you could hear some of these men speak. I feel their efforts are indeed blessed, and it thrills one to take part in the singing of some of the real good old hymns amidst all the turmoil. One tonight was, 'What a friend we have in Jesus!' Although there is so much ungodliness, there are many good men. You can tell it by the eagerness with which they attend these places.

Tonight we have a nice warm hut to sleep in and a decent bed, although up to the present I have not felt any cold; but it is quite cosy in here. The other night I could not sleep for the rats which ran all over me, even over my head. Rats abound everywhere, but they don't generally upset me much.

Well, I must close now, as it will soon be 'lights out.' Goodnight, and may God bless you all. I often think of you and wonder what it must be like to live in a decent house and sit at a decent table, but I trust that before long I may return to these blessings; blessings indeed they are, and you realise it out here. Don't think I am miserable and depressed. No! God has seen fit to place this cross upon me, and it is for me to submit to his will and not grumble. I have indeed felt his presence out here, and that takes off the sharp edge of the knife, I can assure you.

Dear F— tells me she feels very down sometimes but is greatly comforted by the words, 'Whatsoever ye shall ask in prayer, believing, ye shall receive;' 'I will never leave thee, nor forsake thee;' and, 'Fear not … be not dismayed.' She is a dear, good girl; her letters are beautiful, leaving no doubt in my mind that she is one of God's children.

Believe me, your loving son,
George,
British Expeditionary Force, France.
Thursday, September 21st, 1916.[756]

The following is the last letter that George's father, Mr William Smith, wrote to him in France:

✍ My dear George,

I cannot find words to express the pleasure your letters give us, and I feel very far from being able to make a suitable reply. I feel I need what I trust God has given you – the Spirit, even *his own* Spirit, to write; but I go about the streets, and sit in the home, and everywhere I am thinking of you, and am filled with longing for your spiritual and eternal welfare. And this is no goodness of my own, but all of his wondrous grace. The knowledge of God's special goodness to you, and to me in so blessing you, has humbled me to such a degree that I felt prompted to enquire why so great a favour should be conferred upon me, and it were as if he spoke to me, with his *still small* voice, these words, 'Them that honour me I will honour,' and the feeling that took hold of me was, 'Lord, wherein have I honoured thee? one so vile, so full of sin.' But still the answer seems to come to me, 'Them that honour me I will honour.' Well, my dear boy, if the life of God is truly in our souls, and we are called by his grace to seek him and to serve him, his honour and his glory will be our aim and our highest delight for time and eternity, though in the flesh, as the Apostle says, 'dwelleth no good thing.' It is the new creature, the new birth in the soul, that sincerely seeks and sincerely serves and worships him.

We have much cause for the deepest gratitude,

that, in the midst of vice and death and destruction, the fear of God and the presence of God is in you and with you, to keep you in remembrance of, and reverence for, his holy name.

Your letters to us are a great comfort in the trials of the way, and I like the lines you sent, and would encourage you to continue, if the spirit comes upon you, and shall be glad to receive a copy of any, so that I may make a special entry of them in a book. Don't be afraid; we are generally bold enough in that which is not good. I am, at least, to my sorrow.

We received a short letter from Frank by the same post as yours yesterday, and one for you and Florrie[757] from him, which she gave us to read, as she came up to dinner with us yesterday. I thought Frank's letter to you was very nice, and displayed a strong affection for you, which gave me great pleasure, and his concluding remark, 'This is how I *try* to pray,' spoke in unmistakeable language to my poor soul still further of the Lord's goodness and mercy to me. I dare say you have had the letter sent on by now. I posted a letter from Katie to you yesterday, which I hope you have received by this time.

We often speak of Ben, and we are glad you get a good bit of time together, and I am very glad you have as a chaplain a good, God-honouring gospel minister. May the Lord accompany his messages with his own divine power, and may you and Ben and your young friend, and many more, be brought (by the Spirit) into the banqueting house, under the banner of his everlasting love in your souls' experience, as you hear his testimony.

Kenneth keeps us from getting dull; his tongue is going all day long, but he is not a spoilt child, and we have very little trouble with him. Katie, I think, looks better than she has done for some years. Dorothy told us that Mr Crowther had a letter from you yesterday, and he was very pleased with it; I felt glad to think you had written to him. Through mercy we are all favoured in health, and trust you are still favoured with the same blessing.

I was glad to notice in your letter you spoke of yourself as a sinner, and of your poor prayers. If a person isn't brought to this, there isn't anything very sound in his religion; and the Lord must be all power, and we must be all weakness, to make the one (either way) suited to the other. Thus, when we are weak, then (in his strength) we are strong. It must be a putting on the whole armour of God (not a part of it), to come off more than conquerors through him that loved us, and gave himself for us.

That the Lord may indeed bless you, and deepen his work of grace in your soul, is our united desire. With much love from your affectionate father, mother, sisters and nephew,

20, Recreation Road, Colchester.
August 17th, 1916.[758]

An extract from a letter dated April 2nd, 1918, from Mr W. Smith, relating to his son George:

✍ After 11 months' painful suspense, we received from the War Office in August last the statement that he was believed by them to have been killed, September 6th, 1916.[759] A comrade, to whom he was greatly attached, called upon me and informed me that he was one of six men who formed a reserve section of machine-gunners at the battle of Thiepval, sent to obtain ammunition, and just as they had got out of sight an explosion was heard in the direction they had taken, and no sign of them or anything belonging to them was ever seen again. The enclosed acrostic, composed by him, was sent me shortly before he died. The pain to nature is often still great, but the abundant grace and mercy of God to him, and us in so teaching him, far exceed the down-castings of bereavement. In his letters to us he wrote much of the Lord's presence with him, and I am often filled with wonder and amazement, and humbled under the mighty hand of God, that he should so graciously distinguish one so vile and unworthy of the least of all his mercies as I feel myself to be.

Our only son is now in Palestine, having been with the Egyptian force over two years.[760] I was deeply exercised about him before he went out, in regard to danger from submarines, but the Lord gave me this promise, 'I will have mercy upon him.' In his first letter home he said, 'We have safely arrived, although our ship was chased by a submarine for about 200 miles.' So that God has taken one, and, so far, left us one – one we believe is with him in glory, and one with us at the throne of grace.

W. J. Smith.

G rant me, dear Lord, thine ever-helping hand,
E 'er I see war, in this far distant land;
O pen mine eyes, that I may truly see;
R ule thou my heart, that I may purer be;
G ive me the strength and courage that I need;
E ngage my mind, my faltering footsteps lead.

S hield thou my head when death is hovering round
M ercy I ask, Lord, for with thee alone 'tis found;
I cannot live without thou be my shield;
T ake thou me up, be with me in the field.
H ear Lord my prayer, and keep me at thy side![761]

Corporal Henry Smith, Haydock

The writer of the following letter, Corporal Henry Smith, died of influenza on 15th November, 1918, in Boulogne Military Hospital, aged 26. He had been serving in France with the South Lancashire Regiment. He is buried in Terlincthun British Cemetery, Wimille, France. It was said of him, that he was now a 'happy songster'[762] – that is, he had joined the choirs in heaven. He was a Sabbath School teacher at Haydock, and it had been hoped that on his return home he would prove a useful church member. Sadly, his sister died of influenza three days before Henry succumbed, and was buried on the same day as her brother (16th November, 1918), in Parr churchyard, St. Helen's. Their father, Evi Smith, had passed away in February, 1918. Their younger brother, Edwin, who had served in the Royal Fusiliers and narrowly escaped being taken prisoner at the Battle of Loos, was killed at Ypres on March 18th, 1916, and is buried at Lijssenthoek Military Cemetery, Belgium.[763] Such was the desolation the war brought to many families.[764]

Henry Smith

✍ Dear Joe,

You were waiting for my last letter, but what will you be doing for this? Perhaps you will have heard something of it before this reaches you. On April 1st I was sent to hospital, having poisoned my finger with a bully beef tin, and I thought I should lose the finger; but it is now well on the way to recovery. It has been very severe; prevented my writing.

I return kind remembrances to Agnes and Father; pleased to hear they are keeping well, and hope you are; thankful to say I am.

Dear Joe, when shells are raining over and about you, it is indeed a time for calling upon the Lord. The passages you refer to are very nice, and like you I have found sweet expressions in the Psalms. In times of dire necessity you can go down on your knees in bivvies or dugouts when bombardments are on and, with God's blessing, feel a calm unknown to the many. What a time they must have who know not God! But I, who profess his name to know, have such a lot that I see others destitute of, both temporal and spiritual, and yet am so unprofitable a servant, and hardly know what to make of myself when I think of it. Your referring to the teachers' prayer meetings brings to my mind a time when, being at some friends' home one Sunday afternoon, near Alton, Hampshire, they would have me read a portion of the Word, which I did, but they could not persuade me to do more, and when going back to camp (seven miles) Satan did harass me about it. Perhaps you will be leaving Gower Street shortly; where are you going?

Yours very sincerely,

Henry.

April 21st, 1917.[765]

Private Benjamin Snell, Carshalton

Benjamin Snell served in the Essex Yeomanry. As he seems to have been born in the third quarter of 1897,[766] he must have enlisted when he was less than 18, making him an underage recruit.

[1]

✍ Dear Mother, Father and all,

Just a line to let you know I am quite well. I am not now in the B Squadron, but in the Gun Section, which is much better, as we are nearer headquarters and get much better food, served up in a more civilized manner, with plates, knives and forks, etc. Have heard I am not to go into the trenches with the others today, but am to remain with the horses. It seems marvellous, because if I were still in the B Squadron I should certainly have gone up; it seems an answer to your prayers. I was not going to tell you about it to prevent your worrying, but it does not matter now.

We have been out since 7.30 a.m. exercising horses, and it is a beautiful morning. The trenches into which the regiment is going are beyond Ypres and are knee-deep in water, so I have thankfully avoided that. All the others who are going are greasing themselves with whale oil to prevent frostbites, so you can guess it is pretty bad. Numbers here are obliged to have their feet cut off because of frostbites; people at home don't know what it is like out here. I dislike Sundays more than any other day; it is not regarded a bit. We are at a distillery, and the old engines are rumbling away night and day, and Sundays too, just the same. I have heard a good many say they would not want to live in a Roman Catholic country, and I know I should not. I am now cook for the remaining six of our section, and am just going to make a currant pudding. The others left for the trenches at two o'clock, and I counted them as they formed up, wondering how many will return.

February 2nd, 1915.[767]

Benjamin Snell

[2]

✍ You might send me a *Little Gleaner* and a *Friendly Companion* or two when sending again. I am still cook, and got up this morning before 5 a.m., breakfast at 6, but I am not just now overworked. They want me to be cook regularly, but I don't think I shall, as I would rather be out and about. We have just heard of the German air raid over Yarmouth. We have only been up near the front once, and that was weeks ago. I should be very glad if it were all over and I could go back home in the quiet for a time. Second parcel just to hand. It is very kind of you all to take all this trouble for me. On guard tonight (Sunday); suppose you are all cosy round the fire. Hope you are all well.

Yours affectionately,
Ben.[768]

Benjamin was wounded while carrying ammunition to his gun section during fighting in the vicinity of Ypres, Belgium, on 13th May, 1915. Although his lieutenant initially reported to his parents that his death had been instantaneous, it later became clear that he in fact died a few days later, on 15th May, aged just 17 years. He is buried in the Bailleul Communal Cemetery Extension, Nord, near the French-Belgium border.

The following note was written on the 17th May by his mother, who had not then heard of his death.

✍ Dear Ben,

We send this cake and potted meat, and hope you may be enabled to enjoy same. Write when you can, dear son, and may the God of Israel protect you day and night, and enable you to seek his care for your soul and body, for none else is able to preserve you but the great God of heaven and earth. Best love from all. What you need, write and tell us.

Mother.

Families often found it very difficult to find answers to their questions about their loved one's death, and in some cases even confirmation that their loved one had actually been killed. The following is an extract from an extant manuscript letter written by Mark Ruse, who was a cousin of Ben Snell, to Ben Snell's brother, Willie Snell. Willie had obviously asked Mark to try and find out some details about his brother Ben's death.

✍ Dear Willie and all,

I have received both letter and parcel. It is kind of you and I wish to thank you all. I have not had much spare time lately. Have been away from the billet a fortnight cooking for a trench-digging party. We returned last Monday, packed up and moved into fresh billets about 21 kilometres away. We have had some trouble to get the horses under cover, but we are fairly comfortable now. The weather has been rough lately, plenty of snow and such cold winds. We are now in a very hilly district and the wind comes over the hills, enough to freeze your very bones.

Mark Ruse

I am glad you have plenty work in hand. Do you find money very scarce yet? The war is now getting to be a terrible strain on us financially and everyone will feel it. Wilfred[769] was telling me that it was a worse job each week to get the money in. Do you think that both Wilfred and George[770] will have to go? It will be bad for father if they do. I don't think you will have to go. It is not right that you should leave your family; there are plenty of single chaps yet.

I will try if I can find anyone in the gun section who knew Ben. As far as I can find out, the whole team of No 1 Gun (Ben's gun) was either killed or wounded on May 13th. A big shell caught the gun and the whole team was blown up. Sergeant Major Robins can tell me nothing more. They are now nearly all fresh fellows in the Gun Section. Harold Watts was a great friend of Ben's. He is in this troop. He can tell me nothing as he was back with the horses that day. Young Speller knows nothing as he is still in B Squadron. I am afraid I cannot help you much but I will try. You are right about fellows being so hard and callous. I have been astonished to hear them speak in such a way about those that have fallen … I know young Wakeling quite well. He told me that he was certain Ben was killed outright in the field. After all the different accounts one does not know which to believe. One thing I know, it is an awful thing to have to go through a charge. …

Glad to say I am well. Am rather surprised I am so well; quite a long while I have been unable to keep my feet dry, so much mud and water. It is worse since the snow. I have two photos of Father and Mother. I cannot tell you how pleased I was to get them. Sometimes I feel it very much being away from home and no one who I really care for. France seems such a desolate, cold place. However, we know its all for the best and I would not wait when our country is in danger … It is just eight days under the year since I saw poor Ben off at Woodbridge Station. I cannot say how I felt when I saw the train steam out of the station. When he was put in the Gun Section, something seemed to tell me I should not see him again … Mother sent me out a nice khaki Bible, pocket size. Wilfred sent me his but it was too large so I had to return it … The people about here are very good natured, some of the best we have seen. At our last billet they were very nasty. Well I hope you will be able to read all this scribble. Hope Mrs S— and the little folks are well. Little Mary must be a bonny girl now. Will close. Love to all and best thanks for your kindness.

Yours affectionately,

Mark,

1460 Waltham Abbey Troop, C Squadron, Essex Yeomanry, British Expedition Force.

Sunday, November 21st, 1915.[771]

KHAKI BIBLES AND TESTAMENTS,

For those on Active Service or in Training.

We can supply a small Bible on India paper, in Khaki Cloth, buttoned flap post free, 4/3. Also a cheaper Bible, without flap, post free, 2/9.

Testaments on India paper from 10d. upwards.

An advert for khaki Bibles, supplied by F. C. Farncombe and Son, that appeared in *The Gospel Standard*

Quartermaster Sergeant John Woodfield

John Woodfield served in the 9th Battalion, King's Own Yorkshire Light Infantry. He was killed on 22nd March, 1918, and is buried in the Péronne Communal Cemetery Extension, France. The following is a letter written by his father to *The Friendly Companion.* It contains extracts of letters from John together with comments by his father:

✍ Our dear son John joined the King's Own Yorkshire Light Infantry in September, 1914, at the age of 19, with Walter Moon, one of the four sons of Mr and Mrs. Moon of Southborough.[772]

One morning, after talking with his mother about the matter, he came to me and said, 'Dad, what do you think about me joining up?' I said, 'Well; I do not know what to advise for the best; but do not be in a hurry, consider it well first.' But although never before anxious to enlist, his mind seemed set upon it, so that I did not dissuade him further. When leaving home, he said, 'Mother, you know I am not doing this without prayer;' which surprised her, as he had never before said anything as to prayerful exercise of mind. He then left with his friend Walter Moon and went first to Pontefract, then to various other places nearer home, remaining in England 12 months, during which time they both attained the rank of sergeant. He went to France in 1915, and was brought safely through several severe battles, including Loos and Fricourt; in the latter, for his behaviour on the field, he was given the choice of a Military Medal, or promotion to Company Quartermaster Sergeant and ten days' leave. He chose the latter, and was carrying out his duties in this capacity when he was hit by a piece of shell; there was terrific fighting that day and he was found by a corporal lying on a stretcher, wounded and unconscious, having evidently been left as a hopeless case. The corporal remained with him until he died, about ten minutes after he found him. He was expecting, if spared, to be home on leave again in May, but the Lord has seen fit for it to be otherwise, and has taken him to be with that happy company, of which dear Dr Watts wrote:

> O what amazing joys they feel,
> While to their golden harps they sing
> And sit on every heavenly hill,
> And spread the triumphs of their King![773]

I will now give a few extracts from letters he wrote after leaving home. In one letter, written in answer to his brother Ralph, who is with the British Expeditionary Force in Palestine, he said:

'Referring to your remarks about there being a greater war going on than the war of the nations, speaking from a very little knowledge, and I must confess it is very little, I am quite aware that there is a very great battle continuously raging between the Spirit and the flesh, and like you, I feel the constant need of prayer to keep me from falling into the many different manholes and traps set for unwary feet by the Evil One. I know that God in his great and merciful providence has watched over me from the moment I was born, and I think I can say that, bad as I have been, and shamefully low as I have fallen, if it had not been for the wonderful grace of God I should have fallen even much lower in outward sin than I have. I don't think that there is a better guide for life than Romans 12. My prayer is that the Holy Spirit will enable me to live by the truths and precepts set out in that chapter.'

I may add that I believe he was so enabled, especially during the latter part of his life. In another letter to his mother and myself:

'It is a great mercy in these nerve-racking and terrible times that we have a sure refuge to whom to turn, in a prayer-hearing and answering God.'

In a letter to his sister Dorothy he says:

'Quite a lot of difficulty and disappointment are continually thrown across our path wherever we may be. I have found it so particularly since leaving home; but we have one great consolation in all our sorrows – the knowledge that a great, almighty God lives and reigns to answer prayer; yet I have the impression that you do not need any reminder of the sort from me. Quite possibly you have had experiences of prayers asked and answered yourself.'

John Woodfield

In another letter to us:

'We can only place ourselves in the hands of the Lord and pray earnestly for his guidance, protection and mercy. My prayer is that he will give me courage and wisdom to face fearlessly – we know not what. Often when I have felt myself faltering and giving way in 'the valley of the shadow of death,' I have asked the Lord to give me courage and to keep me from all harm, and I in my present state am a living proof of the answers to those prayers. Often have I wondered why I should be spared when thousands of far better men than me are cut down in all the pride of young manhood. But after all our thinking and wondering, we are only reminded that,

> God moves in a mysterious way
> His wonders to perform.[774]

Therefore, as I have already said, we can only place ourselves, body and soul, unreservedly in his hands, fully aware that,

> Not a single shaft can hit,
> Till the God of love sees fit etc.[775]

I will cheerfully do anything that may be used as the means to finish this terrible conflict. As I am called upon to face danger and perhaps death, so it is your duty to look the facts squarely in the face, and if it is God's will that you should give either Ralph or myself up in the interests of our country, to do so as willingly as possible, assured that it is his will, and that 'the LORD gave, and the LORD hath taken away; blessed be the name of the LORD.'

In a letter to Mr John H. Stonelake,[776] superintendent of Gower Street Memorial Sabbath School and minister of the gospel, he says:

'It has been proved to me personally more than ever before that the Lord is a prayer-hearing and answering God, and when we know this it gives us greater faith and courage to continue praying earnestly, and to push resolutely forward, entrusting ourselves completely to his care. I feel I can say, 'The LORD hath done great things for me;' and yet how ungrateful and thankless I am sometimes. There are times when I go about my duties, etc., completely forgetful of him who has watched over and protected me thus far, and then conscience says, 'It is only in times of danger that you remember the Lord!' O for more faith to trust him at all times, for all things; I wish I could do so more than I do.'

More might be added but there is sufficient to show that his life was mercifully preserved throughout unspeakable dangers while the Lord graciously carried on and completed the work of grace in his heart. And then 'he was not, for God took him!'

His friend, a fellow Company Quartermaster Sergeant, in writing to us says:

'It may comfort you to know that Ben was a son worthy to be proud of. He and I have been close companions for nearly two years. Always he made it his endeavour to live up to those ideals of life he knew to be worthy, never faltering from what he felt and knew to be the right. I sorely miss him.'[777]

Letters written by unidentified servicemen

The following letters were all sourced from denominational magazines. When they were originally published they were stripped of all their identifying features, and as a consequence it is impossible for us to state who they were written by with any certainty.

[1]

✍ My dear Mr and Mrs G – ,

Just a few lines to answer your most kind and welcome letter received this afternoon. I have no doubt you are all very pleased to hear that I am once again back in dear old England. It was indeed a great surprise to all my relations and friends, and I myself really did not expect such a thing to happen. I was very glad to see my mother and my loved ones again; I could almost have cried for joy. I hope that in a week or two I shall be well enough again to come home for a few days. The Lord has been very merciful and gracious to me the last few months of my life in guarding and protecting me through the perils of land and sea, and bringing me safely home again. The beautiful hymn,

> God moves in a mysterious way
> His wonders to perform,[778]

has been a means of help and blessing many a time to me while on the peninsula.[779]

The 6th of August, when my brother was lost – which I expect you have heard about – will be a day never to be forgotten in my memory. I felt the presence of the Lord very near. The shells were screaming and bursting all around us, who were anxiously waiting the word to charge. Something seemed to say to me, 'Be of good cheer, I am with thee.' At last the word came down the trench, 'Prepare to charge.' Then I offered up a silent prayer, and I believe that many more did the same; and I can say I never felt calmer in my life as over the parapet I was helped, not knowing what a few seconds might bring forth. But the Lord guided my feet in a safe path through that awful hail of lead and shells, while so many of my comrades were mown down like grass before a reaper.

Do you remember speaking one Sunday evening about two years ago, and saying that woodmen always marked the trees that were to be cut down next? Well, during those few minutes of the charge that same thing came to my mind. I thought to myself, 'Shall I be the next one to be cut down?' But the Lord had willed it to be otherwise. Next morning came the roll call. What an awful time was that! Everyone was saying, 'Have you seen so-and-so, or this or the other man?' Often the answer was, 'I have not.' I had no peace of mind, as you may well guess, when I found out that my brother was missing. This all happened on Friday and Saturday.

Sunday came with its usual toil and work, but my Testament was my constant companion, and I could always go to its pages for words of comfort and help. Sunday evening came, and with it the word to get ready for church parade. How glad I was to go I cannot in words describe, for I hoped to get relieved by its means.

The speaker started his address by saying that he did not know how to say anything to us after the events of the last two days, but he would give us the text, and leave it to speak its own message to us. It was this, 'Let not your heart be troubled: ye believe in God, believe also in me. In my Father's house are many in mansions: if it were not so I would have told you. I go to prepare a place for you. And if I go and prepare a place for you, I will come again, and receive you unto myself; that where I am, there ye may be also.' It was enough; I broke down completely; it was the exact message wanted, and you may guess the rest.

I hope that this short story may not have tired you; but I should like to add that out of a little over 900 men who marched into the trenches on Friday morning, only about 300, more or less, returned the following morning; so I have much to be thankful to the Lord for in sparing me through all these dangers.

I am very pleased to know that you are feeling much better after your long rest, and I hope that you will continue to enjoy good health. I am glad to hear that our old friend Mrs W— has reached her 100th birthday; she is indeed a monument of the Lord's goodness, and what a useful present it was you gave her. I want you to remember me to her and to all the friends at H— W—.[780]

I am pleased to say that I have been making wonderful progress since I have been here; the climate is all in my favour. I have bad dysentery, and such awful pains in my head, and two other complaints; but I am glad to say that the worst is over now, and I shall be allowed to get up in a few days. I am almost free from pain, and taking my food well. Well, now I think I will close, as this is about all I can say at this time. I must say that I have made myself rather tired, so I will now say goodbye for the present, hoping to see you all soon.

With all kind regards and best wishes, I remain,
E. H. R.,
War Hospital.
November 11th, 1915.[781]

[2]

✍ My dear Friend and Brother,

It is long since I received your kind and welcome letter; I have frequently been thinking of you, but for various reasons have delayed writing, and although now I feel most unframed for letter writing, I am anxious not to delay longer lest you should think I have entirely forgotten you. I have been on the look-out for your division, but up to now have been unable to find you. We have been in the 'push' which commenced on Wednesday last week, and have had a very busy time. I would acknowledge God's good hand upon me in his preservation amidst many perils, and would look to him concerning the unknown future.

I wonder if you have been in action lately, and if you are well. Mercifully the great influenza epidemic seems now to have nearly ended.[782] Through mercy, I am fairly well now, and am strengthened for each day's recurring needs. I was grieved to know that your wife had had rather a severe attack of the 'flu, and do hope by now she is strong again.

My thoughts went around the dear ones at Galeed[783] and to you, when this morning I was reading the account in Matthew of the Lord's first institution of the Supper. Tomorrow is the day for its celebration amongst us, and in being deprived of this means of grace, we are companions in tribulation. I trust it may never be that we become so accustomed to being isolated from the services of God's house as to get quite careless about them. I hope I may truly say that there are times when my heart longs, yea, pants, for the courts of the Lord's house. And although my nature is so carnal and dead, yet the wickedness surrounding one, the godlessness, and immorality, and blasphemy do sometimes grieve me exceedingly.

I wonder how my brother gets on in this matter. Oftentimes I feel guilty by reason of not being so separate as I should be, and altogether I have again and again to come to the conclusion that there is no hope of salvation, peace, or justification but in and through the work of the dear Redeemer. No merit, no help, no goodness can be found, when well sought, in self. In extremities the only refuge is the mercy of God in Christ. How comfortable it is to feel an interest in that work, so grievous to his human flesh, which he so willingly and lovingly undertook and accomplished. In the near view of it he said, 'O my Father, if this cup may not pass from me, except I drink it, thy will be done.' Dear brother, if you and I have an interest in that emptied cup, we are favoured indeed. Only we *shall* be ashamed that we cannot live more holily, that we cannot be more separate from that hateful thing, sin, which brought to the dear, spotless, innocent, and pure Son of God the keen sorrows, and pains, and hell which we deserved.

I am glad you were able to tell me again of that sweet gospel liberty you once were favoured with. I do sincerely wish, both for you and for myself, much of that sweet peace which flows from a sense of the cleansing virtue of the blood of the new testament applied to the soul. Now I commit you into the safe-keeping hands of a faithful, ever-present, omnipotent God. May he abundantly bless you.

France.

August 31st, 1918.[784]

[3]

✍ To my dearest Wife,

... At last I find a little time to write again, after about a week's hard fighting and marching, through which the dear Lord has seen fit to spare me; and I hope that I am thankful for all his mercies to me that least deserves it.

You will learn, I think, by the papers where I have been – the big battle of the Aisne, in which we came out best. We were there about a fortnight, but I am in a different part now; am not allowed to let you know where. We have had a still rougher time since we left there, and last night I think was the first real night's sleep we have had for about eight nights. We had to take a position and hold it for three days and three nights; I lost my other two 'messing chums' there, one killed and one wounded. It was at night that the last got wounded in the thigh; I tore up his trousers and bandaged him, then took him to hospital. Had to carry him over my shoulder part of the way, till I got him on a wagon. There were four of us originally; the first was taken away sick, the second shot dead, the third wounded. So, my dear, you see how much I owe to him who holds us all 'in the hollow of his hand;' and I feel what an ungrateful wretch I am more and more, and these words came sweet to me: 'With lovingkindness have I drawn thee' (Jeremiah 31: 3), and I only hope and trust that I shall never forget, although it seems impossible to realise what I do owe. O, to be able to thank him sufficiently!

Now dear, I have heard from dear M—, and received parcel and letter from Jack. I cannot write and thank them all now, so will you do so for me. I have not heard from you for a long time, and have written several to you. What is the matter? I do worry, and watch every mail. You are always in my prayers and thoughts.

You would have liked to see me this morning; had not washed or shaved for about eight days, and had been lying in mud and ditches. Am wearing a pair of German boots laced up at the side, about two or three sizes too large, no hat, and looked like an old tramp.

Write quick; kiss kiddies for their dad.

Yours always loving,

Will,

Private W. P. B., British Expeditionary Force. [785]

[4]

✍ My dear Mother,

I drop you a line before I leave England. I am under orders. I will let you have a line when I arrive, if in safety. I am not 'down' at all, for I know if it is his will he can preserve me. For,

Not a single shaft can hit,
Till the God of love sees fit.[786]

I can't feel assured that I'm going to be brought back safely, and I can't feel that my life will be taken; but I do feel I must leave it all with him, and know no will but his. O to lie submissive at his feet. I try to pray, but seem to have no prayer within me. There seems so much to take my thoughts from him, so that I love to know that I have a praying mother who tries to pray for her son; and surely he will not despise her prayers. If I am never brought back, and if I get to that happy land, oh! what praise will be there, to be away from all this wickedness. And I am as bad as others; I don't seem to have a good thing within me, and therefore 'wonder where the scene will end,' whether I shall ever get there? ... Love to M— and B— ...

Your loving son,

Driver B—.[787]

[5]

✍ My dear Mother,

I direct this letter to you, but as I owe so many letters to friends, you will please let all read it.

First, I express my delight to hear you are all so far helped in the journey of life, for a journey it is and the end must come.

I am looking forward to hear what has befallen Freddie, and to know what yoke has been placed upon him; by the way, I will here mention that in the yoke in the money order I sent home from Italy, you have a perfect picture of oxen and plough as I see them here, and it is instructing to watch how gently these oxen move forward in their labour. They seem especially careful not to jerk forward lest they hurt themselves, so they are oxen 'accustomed to the yoke.' So often while we are young and not used to hard labours, we are found to turn about and refuse the ordaining of God's providence. But so far I have found God has simply turned me about and led me another way to the same yoke, so that the last few years I have found it far better to walk tenderly and gently, and to move forward carefully, knowing the yoke of God's providing is upon me. It then does not matter so much where he leads us to or what labours, but for us to know with certainty God is behind my yoke. I can say, 'It is good for a man that he bear the yoke in his youth' (Lamentations 3: 27).

Since I wrote to the children I have moved six times and slept in six different places. So you see I am a wanderer, but not without a captain; I have only to listen to his orders. Last night on going to rest we expected to be called at 3.30 a.m. to move off; but breakfast was ready at 7.45 and we had never been called. We may move tomorrow. How uncertain is our journeying! Fifty of us have been billeted in a large farm for a week; it has been a week to be remembered. I should think there are six families in this building; all the young people work in the fields. By the way, I may say, 'the winter is past, the rain is over and gone; the flowers appear on the earth.' I am sending a primrose home; they are busy pruning the trees and tying up the grape vines, and the corn is a few inches above ground. We can get plenty of eggs at our farm about two pence each in English money; some of our men had a chicken for supper one night. Of course, I am beginning to speak Italian now, but I will not enter into this ...

I think now I will write about what I saw last night. I have told you there are mountains to the north of us. Well, last night as friend Needham and I were out for a walk, we noticed something red creeping down from the top of the mountain; afterwards we could plainly see what is a volcanic eruption.[788] I hardly know how to describe this to you, but from the top to about half way down in two places were streams of red-hot cinders. We had noticed a mist, as we thought, on top for several days, but it was evidently smoke, and of course today we see no fire but smoke issuing from all about the mountains. This is a great sight and leads us to great things. I could not help reading 2 Peter 5, where he describes how this earth is now – by God's word, 'kept in store, reserved unto fire against the day of judgement and perdition of ungodly men,' and how, on that great day of the Lord, the 'heavens shall pass away with a great noise, and the elements shall melt with fervent heat, the earth also and the works that are therein shall be burned up.' It all seems very solemn. As I was called out about 10.30 to see about packing up my paints, etc., I had to walk across two fields and I felt the air warm, like a hot-house, where it is usually bitterly cold at night. This plainly proves to us how the elements can be changed. Today I think if you were here you would say it was August, being quite hot; but there is a nice breeze. I think how soon God could work for or against a people with his elements!

I should think around this very mountain there are five or six different nationalities fighting, and they say in some places very near the eruption. But the future is still unknown while we look around and beneath, but if we look up we feel there is no uncertainty. 'The day of the Lord' is coming; we shall only want then what is necessary. Like us soldiers, when we are about to move, we dump as much as is unnecessary, we carry no useless or empty things on a march; but move so. As men enter the trenches, they even come to spending all their money, lest they have not another opportunity. But all this is nothing compared to looking forward to the appearing of Jesus Christ, and, 'unto them that look for him,' it is said, 'shall he appear … without sin unto salvation.'

There are many other things I should like to mention relating to this. In our farmyard is a well about 60 feet deep, and it is going all day nearly, as someone is getting up water, but the water is slightly warm. Now, as it is not warmed by the sun, it must be warmed from beneath. One more thing; the stones in the plain are all smooth; they are plentiful below the top soil, scarcely any above ground. The fields are a picture concerning this, generally about four feet of mould, but the stones are any size up to a child's head, but they are all smooth whatever their shape, like stones on the seashore, which made me feel that in bygone ages this plain was not quite as it is now, but was in much turmoil, with many waters: and who knows what yet awaits us who are prepared for the great day of the Lord?

There are many kinds of trees here in the private gardens which have been out in pretty flowers, have no leaves on, and the beautiful perfume comes from some of them. I only wish I could send you some of them. I have one of the large thorns which I hope to save. I may later be able to send it home.

Now I think this will suffice for this time, if I add,

> Thus far my God has led me on,
> And made his truth and mercy known;
> My hopes and fears alternate rise,
> And comforts mingle with my sighs.[789]

Wishing you all his continual favour through this 'waste howling wilderness.'

Your affectionate son,
Stanley,
Italy.
February 24th, 1918.[790]

[6]

✍ My dear Brother,

I will try and answer your letter of the 17th. Yes, I quite realize you have your hands full, besides the extra anxiety all these new rules must cause. As you say, I certainly should not know how to carry on if I were to drop in now. The flour you use certainly must be very hard to handle in the dough stage; plenty of room for the miller to work behind such a mixture for his own benefit, I should think. I should not think rye would be much of an improvement from the baker's point of view ... Really the baking trade is seeing a revolution; one wonders whether the war will see the end of these adulterants! I doubt it. I think, with you, that we shall more than likely see another winter campaign; when will it all end? ...

Well, as regards the Sunday question,[791] if you look at it entirely from one point of view, and leave the being of an Almighty God out of the question, you are no doubt right; but I feel that in doing so, as no doubt you feel, that we should be wrong. Therefore, 'to the law and to the testimony;' what saith the Scriptures? First; God 'rested on the seventh day' (Genesis 2: 2), 'blessed' and 'sanctified' it. In Exodus 15 we read how the children of Israel were provided with bread in the wilderness, and were not as much as allowed to gather it on the Sabbath; and if God could provide for them even in this dreary waste, do you think he would let the people go hungry that, in obedience to his command, refused to till the land on Sunday? On the contrary, he has said, 'Them that honour me I will honour, and they that despise me shall be lightly esteemed.' In one of the magazines, they were wanting men for the cricket match on the Saturday afternoon, and they pleaded with those that excused themselves on the garden question, that there was time on Sunday for that; and you quote the passage that, 'The sabbath was made for man.' Well, if you look up Exodus 16: 27-30, you will find there the account of the Lord giving the Sabbath day unto Israel, but *not* for them to do as they pleased in it. Exodus 20: 8-11 and Leviticus 19: 3 give just a reference to what I said on the last page. 'The LORD will not suffer the soul of the righteous to famish: but he casteth away the substance of the wicked' (Proverbs 10: 3). 'The labour of the righteous tendeth to life: the *fruit* of the wicked to sin' (v. 16). Or if you read Proverbs 1 right through, you will see how God promised to honour the righteous. Also, is not manual labour here quite the secondary consideration? To my mind it should be. Take, for instance, the week or so hard frost you had; this prevented both the weekday and Sunday labour; was it not the voice of the Almighty showing to man how helpless he is? 'Paul may plant, and Apollos water,' but it is for God to give the increase. Suppose you should get a dry summer, or a disease amongst the plants, man's Sunday work would then be vain. I hope that it will not be so; but I can assure you in good faith that these solemn truths are not mere sentiments with me, and if you read *The English Churchman* (not a Strict Baptist publication) you will find the same truths put there in a more clear and fuller form.

Well, my dear brother, we never know what may happen from one day to another here, and I can assure you last Whit Sunday morning you were as near losing me as is really possible. A shrapnel shell exploded between myself and the party with which I was working; but the pieces went both sides and over my head. Whatever may happen, remember that I have not written thus for argument's sake; but I do feel that if we, as a nation, are not humbled before God, he will punish us still more. I hope it will not be as was with the Egyptians, that the greater the judgement the harder Pharaoh's heart grew, till it ended in the destruction of both him and his host, lost in the Red Sea. Then there was the reference to Mr Lloyd George,[792] and you quote Oliver Cromwell; but let's go further back, to the old Book! You quote part of the Sermon on the Mount, about prayer; and I do not think there is a better place and standard for this part of our faith. But if you refer to Matthew 5: 14-16, 'Let your light so shine before men, that they may see your good works, and glorify your Father which is in heaven.' Also, 'In all your ways acknowledge him,' etc.

I do feel that as the victories are gained, and as our position is improved, God should have the praise; instead of so much boast in the strength of man, what these have done. What those have done? Remember, all men are in his hands; if he wished, he could allow this or that man to be afflicted, or disease to again break out in the munitions factory. Where again would be all the boasting? During the first year, was it not even acknowledged by the German naval men that they could not do anything on the sea; but what of it now? Have not they done a good deal, and brought us at least into a very low condition?

Now, just one word more. I have no wish to be any wider or any narrower in my views than the Bible itself. I am the last one to say all Christians, or, as you put it, all the 'goodness' is in the Strict Baptists, for I have not seen one since 22nd of December, 1914; at least not to recognize one as such. But I have knocked up against a good many other denominations, but *not one* I like better, or feel that they are nearer the truth as it is in Christ.

But to close. Remember, 'There is a way that seemeth right unto a man, but the end thereof are the ways of death' (Proverbs 16: 25). 'Enter ye in at the strait gate: for wide is the gate, and broad is the way, that leadeth to destruction, and many there be which go in thereat: because strait is the gate, and narrow is the way, which leadeth unto life, and few there be that find it' (Matthew 7: 13-14).

Well, my only regret is, when looking back, not that I have professed these things, but that I have not adorned the gospel of Christ as I should have done. I, like Paul, have found the law of sin in my members is warring against the law of my mind.

I think now you will have read enough perhaps; and it is dinner time, and digging tonight; also our guns are banging away just on my right; so farewell for the present!

Your affectionate brother.

P.S. May God in his mercy lead us and those dear to us to seek out what this narrow way is, and give us grace to walk therein.[793]

[7]

✍ My dear M – ,

I saw a funeral of a little child yesterday. The weird incantations of the priest made one shudder. Girls with white veils carried the coffin on a little stretcher, and the procession was headed by two acolytes[794] clothed with white and red surplices, and one bearing a cross aloft. Every few yards the priest lifted up his voice in a mournful Latin dirge, and one's spirit shuddered as he saw the procession wending its way, in the darkness of the mystery of iniquity, and in the labyrinths of the great apostasy. Outside the house where the dead child lay for a day or two was placed a wooden cross with a skull painted in relief in the centre. Such is the repellent and gruesome custom which Popery leads to in the hour of death.

We have had a proper rest at this place. It is pleasant to walk out in the quiet lanes in the evening, or to stroll over the fields. It is at such times especially when I take out the Word of God that I realize God's mercy to me at this time. I lament that sin does so easily beset me: but the spirit which says, 'There is no hope,' is that which angers God, so I say, 'I stand in awe of thy Word,' and, 'Lead me into the patient waiting for Christ.' When 'nation rose against nation, and kingdom against kingdom,' this was to be the beginning of sorrows, and Christ warns us of these times, against our hearts being overcharged with surfeiting and drunkenness and cares of this life, lest the day of his appearing come on us unawares. Therefore, I pray that God will prepare me, and I am thankful for the quiet lanes.

Your affectionate son,
G.,
France.
May 4th, 1918.[795]

[8]

✍ My dear Friend,

I now take much pleasure in answering your two most welcome letters. What a help to me your letters are, especially when I feel that all's against me, then I read your letters through and what a help they have proved to me. Ah! How my mind did run to you especially yesterday when in a dangerous position in the firing line, repairing some trenches very close to the Germans; and I think they had a clue that we were there, as they shelled our trenches and I thought every moment would be my last; how very solemn did I feel the position we were placed in. Well, a marvellous thing it was, only one man got hit and his wound was not serious; he was hit on the wrist with a small piece from a shell. A shell burst quite near to me, a piece falling in the trench; I was going to pick it up but it was red hot.

We, as a battalion, have been greatly favoured. Oh! that men would turn and give thanks to the Lord for his wonderful mercy towards us as a nation; but, dear friend, they go as it were headlong into destruction. When we were in a dangerous position they were very alarmed, but as soon as matters improved they were in the same place. It makes one's heart ache to see the wickedness of the world. What a lot I shall have to talk to you about. O, that I may be spared to meet you again! How often does my mind run back to the times when we were favoured to walk together.

Our occupation out here is not so hard, only we have to walk now so far from our billets to the trenches, six miles each way; how at times I have had to beg for strength to get home; I seem absolutely done right up. Last night, as I was returning, I felt that I should have to fall out by the way; then I hope I can say I begged of the Lord to give me strength to continue, and the words seemed to come so clearly, 'As thy days, so shall thy strength be.' 'Well,' I thought, 'that's for me,' although the enemy tempted me to believe it was all false; but nevertheless, my dear friend, I was enabled to get home and felt fresher than I ever had before. How often has my mind run to those lines dear Mr Daw used to quote,

Yes! it will be a wonder,
To see one black as I,
White without spot of blemish,
Among the host on high.[796]

Your affectionate Friend,
John,
4th Battalion, Coldstream Guards, France.
October 24th, 1915.[797]

[9]

✍ My dear Friend,

Many thanks for the — sent me, also your letter. I wish you and Mr J. God's richest blessings in this New Year. May it be a year full of special blessings, in which you can see the leading, guiding hand of our never-failing Friend making the path plain and the way straight, and above all leading you both into all truth. I prove the goodness of God daily to one who has sinned beyond measure. In my extremity, he makes his opportunity, and at the moment of my deepest exercise and trial, he shines into my heart with such light that I am astonished at his goodness and melted down by his visits. Thanks for sending me *The Gospel Standard*; I like to have them. I read part of the first sermon in the October issue, preached in 1605, and although it was pleasant reading, I did not enter much into it at the time.[798] In the night I awoke, and with a great flood of light, what I had read stood out in relief, and I got such a revelation of the two opposing forces of sin and grace. Then clearly did I see that although 'the evil which I would not, that I do;' 'it is no more I that do it, but sin that dwelleth in me.' I have never seen the battlefield of the Shulamite (Song of Solomon 6: 13) so clearly ... Prayer is very effective; I have never known it to fail. Only a little while ago I was in desperate straits to locate a position I had to report at, and after wandering about for an hour, 'In my distress, I cried unto the Lord, and he heard me,' for immediately a man came toward me who was going to the very place I wanted, and I was there in five minutes ...

Yours very sincerely,

Fred,

France.[799]

The following is not a letter, but rather a "meditation", entitled "Pick up all nails," written on the battlefield in France. It is included here as it may have been written by the author of the previous letter, although this is not certain.

✍ In following up the trail of war out here, one may often see the above notice, or one somewhat similar and to the same purpose. It is almost certain to catch your eye as it is written in bold characters and affixed to the walls of some ruined house. It certainly implies that nails are dangerous to most kinds of traffic. A small nail may mean a bad puncture; a puncture may mean a serious delay, and a delay may mean the loss of many lives. In this sense a train of thoughts started in my mind which I venture to pass on to 'Friendly Companions.'

There is a Scripture which says, 'Take us the foxes, the little foxes, that spoil the vines: for our vines have tender grapes' (Song of Solomon 2: 15), and I seem to see some connection between that word and the notice I have referred to.

There are things in our lives which start in a small way, comparatively speaking, and which if left just where they are will mean, sooner or later, a disaster. The great majority of people, when they hear the word 'sin' spoken think of some outward act of violence, some well-known crime; but when the Holy Spirit shines into the heart, there is revealed such a depth of hidden evils, some of which by their activity are the 'little foxes which spoil the vines;' and, of course, the 'tender grapes.' They are the nails which need to be picked up. Do you notice that in both cases the request to remove the dangerous thing is made to someone other than the one who is especially open to the danger? It is not expected out here that the motorist should alight to pick up nails. He asks others to do this for him. And so, when the Holy Ghost shines into the hearts of men and reveals the 'nails,' the 'little foxes,' he also indites a prayer to himself: 'Take us the foxes, the little foxes, that spoil the vines, etc.'

May the Lord so reveal truth to us, so shine upon the road we have to travel, that we may see the danger in time and be constrained to ask him to go before us and to 'pick up all nails.' He is the one to make a plain path. Out here trouble has been caused more than once because somebody has failed to comply with the request; but with him is all light, all wisdom, and all power. He cannot fail. Let us ask him to 'cast up the highway,' to 'gather out the stones,' or, 'pick up the nails;' to 'take us the foxes,' and in his strength, with him going before us, we shall get through well and come off 'more than conquerors' through him who has conquered.

There are nails that need to be gathered;
There are foxes that spoil all the vines;
There are dry spots that need to be watered,
And souls who are waiting for signs.

But the Lord, our God, he has promised
And his Word is one that never fails,
That comers to him, he'll not cast out;
Let us pray him to 'pick up the nails.'

Frederick Paul,[800]

British Expeditionary Force, France.
January 8th, 1918.[801]

[10]

✍ My dear Friend,

At last a few lines in answer to your looked-for letters. It is some time since we last met, but I have many times been talking to you when alone. I often wonder when we shall once more have the favour of renewing those good times. I wonder also what will be the end of this conflict.

I trust I was helped a few weeks since when walking alone in a very lonely place; I looked into the heavens, and this verse came so sweetly –

The God that rules on high,
And thunders when he please;
That rides upon the stormy sky,
And manages the seas.[802]

I felt such a melting of heart, could leave the war and all its troubles for the time being. I believe that night I was able to breathe out my troubles to the Lord. O, what a mercy to get safely through, and at the last to be prepared! How solemn to see so many of our comrades who seem to have no regard for better things. I am sleeping in the open; it is very nice this time of the year. One wakes up so much fresher in the morning.

I must close with love, and wishing you every blessing,

Your affectionate friend,
J. B.
May 25th, 1917.[803]

[11]

✍ ... I want to hear the truth preached, and want a word oftentimes to 'assure my conscience of her part,' etc.[804] We cannot rest and be satisfied with past tokens, but want to realize again and again that he is our salvation. I found, when reading Psalm 37: 39, 40: 'He is their strength in the time of trouble,' etc., what a mercy we have such a Lord to put our trust in at all times. How we need the Lord to keep us from looking to creature things, and to be kept in holy conversation. It says in 2 Peter 3: 11 that all earthly things shall be dissolved, etc. O to be kept in his fear and to grow in grace and the knowledge of him, etc. (v. 18). What a mercy to be able to say, with David: 'He is our God for ever and ever: he will be our guide even unto death.' ... How I wish I could meet with you all again and sit down at the Lord's Table. I often feel like as in hymn 393 (*Gadsby's Selection*): 'A crumb of mercy, Lord, I crave' etc. A beautiful hymn, so encouraging. May the Lord bless you with all spiritual blessings and favours,

Yours,

F. B.

May 6th, 1917.[805]

[12]

✍ Dear Uncle,

Many thanks for your most encouraging letter. Could you have only a little idea of my position when yours arrived you would say that something beyond human power caused it to be written. I had just been through two of the hardest trials – walking for miles on ground that is practically under water, sometimes sinking 18 inches at every other step. This we did carrying heavy packs, and to crown all under the worst shell fire yet experienced; this may not seem so bad, but it was about midnight and raining very hard. Yet going through this terrible ordeal I could not but see God's great mercy towards a poor creature in distress, for being a stretcher-bearer I was dreading to see a man hit. Everybody has thought it wonderful to come through such fire without a casualty; but what can I say? Here I remained silent. Can I tell them what God has done for me, and that he spared them at that time for my sake?

Quite a number of men in my own company were wounded just after, but they were not near me at the time, and I was not called upon to carry them away. A day or so afterwards I had a stretcher case, but the first two miles we had to manage the best way without stretchers, as it was impossible to carry it a yard. When we came to ground more solid we used a stretcher, but poor fellow, he jumped off just in time to save his own life. I laid flat on the ground, but was covered with dirt from the explosion. The poor fellow crawled on his hands and knees, without boots or socks on, through mud and water, and just after handing him over to the Royal Army Medical Corps, from where he would be safe.

I received your letter. Yes; I was ready to give up everything and would not ask to live any longer, but your letter to me seemed to point out my position and tell me it was the Lord's way for me, and that I must walk in it. Dear Uncle, you know what it is to sink so low, yes, without a soul to cheer you or give a helping hand. Indeed, I have had some trials in my life, and often wonder why so young a person should be called to pass through all; but if it is for God's own honour and glory, then I pray for grace and strength to hold on. You may think this letter a little gloomy; it certainly is so, but I must be honest in writing about such an important matter.

The above was written just after coming out of the trenches; since then Christmas has passed. I was thankful not to be in the trenches during that weekend; I had the pleasure of attending two services on Christmas Sunday, but regret I did not go anywhere the following day. I believe I gave way to a little feeling of sickness, and nobody seemed to know where service was to be held. It shows how ungrateful man is to One who has been so kind and true ...

With love, your affectionate nephew,

N – ,

France.

December, 1916.[806]

[13]

✍ My dearest Mother,

On arriving at Southampton, I was told off with 20 others for a fatigue party, and we had to unload the horses from the train. They were put aboard a ship which was in dock. I helped to lead one fine horse on deck. It is a magnificent ship, specially fitted up for cattle. When I went up the gangway into the ship leading my charge, I came across rows and rows of horses and mules already loaded. After travelling some distance, I delivered the good beast at his destination, the other end of the ship. It was laughable to watch the different antics of the horses on board, fighting by means of their heads, etc. There must be several hundred cattle. Contrary to what I thought, and to what many think, the boat left in broad daylight and we are now past the Isle of Wight, the sun still fairly high in the west, a glorious evening. On passing Cowes and Ryde, I thought of the enjoyable times we have had in the Isle. I am unable to tell you where we are going to land, although I know, and it will probably be about midnight. I am thoroughly enjoying the trip, and would do so more if there was not the constant reminder of what we are going for. The big ship is not at all crowded with men, like those that have passed us. One was crammed with troops on the top deck, scarcely room to move. The majority of our battalion is following in another transport. We have with us two escorting destroyers; they picked us up at — and I could distinctly see them signalling to us.

Well, Mother, it doesn't seem like Sunday. I wonder who was at Forest Hill and if he remembered *us*. If he forgot, I know you didn't. Now I must say, 'Goodbye.'

Much love to all.

Your ever loving son,

Edward.[807]

[14]

✍ My dear Mother, Father and Brother and Sister,

... I hope, if it be the Lord's will, to see you all again in the flesh one day. But his ways are not our ways, and we are being brought, we trust, by a way we know not, and should like to say, 'Shall not the Judge of all the earth do right?' Parting from those we love is no easy matter; but 'here we meet to part again, in heaven we part no more.'

> There shall we see his face,
> And never, never sin;
> There, from the river of his grace,
> Drink endless pleasures in.[808]

Bunyan says, 'The bitter must come before the sweet;' but, blessed with that great grace, how clear the way does seem. You can, when given a sweet feeling of his love to us, leave everything in our heavenly Father's hand; for,

> How can we sink with such a prop
> As holds the world and all things up?[809]

... Well might David tell Ziba, after deliverance, to do what he liked with the land. He knew that his God was more to him, and that earthly trash was nothing. May he in his mercy bless us and make us more fond of him and Jesus in our own eyes ... I hope you will all have what is needed for comforting your bodies; and may God grant you that grace so you can lay aside that which so easily besets you; and 'press towards the mark … of the high calling of God in Christ Jesus' for his dear name's sake. Remember me in your prayers, as I trust in my feeble way I have you at heart very much. May God in mercy bless and keep you all looking towards the hills from whence does come my aid, is the poor prayer of your ever affectionate son,

Clifford.[810]

[15]

✍ Dear Aunt and Uncle,

... This is life indeed out here. I do escort duty and guards. We get all sorts, sizes and characters. I had a Prussian Guard, a master printer, in one of my parties. He was a big fellow. The country is looking fine; no empty fields here. It is all cultivated; women and children all do their share. I saw a donkey harnessed to a plough; dogs in harness draw trucks about. All the streets in the towns are cobbled. All are Roman Catholics out here; the nuns do our washing if we wish it. I have seen the Channel many times, but it has not been clear enough to see Blighty yet. I met S— M— the week before last: he said he could recognize the language of Zion, and indeed I could. He led in prayer, and I thought to myself, 'You are a "S. B.,"'[811] so I followed him, and he thought the same thing, and we have had some good times since. I don't know when I shall see him again. Florrie keeps well so far; the Lord is good to us each, and we both enjoy tastes of his love in our hearts. He will never leave us, and truly I feel he will make us testify of his faithfulness to us, unworthy though we are. We are travelling in dark paths now, but his rod and his staff, they comfort us. Many times I have watched the flashing of the guns as I stand on guard at nights, and it makes one think of God's sovereignty. May he bless and preserve you, and make his face to shine upon you each.

Love to all,
Yours ever, in him,
J— F—.
June 2nd, 1917.[812]

[16]

✍ To Miss Weaver.

My dear Aunt,

Your letter arrived Friday from E—, which you sent to France, and I hope you will see those promises fulfilled. It must be trying and testing for your faith. What a mercy if we have a measure of that real, living, God-given faith, which 'laughs at (natural) impossibilities,'[813] and a faith that holds God to his word. For, as you know, there is such a thing as having something in faith, before we come into the actual possession of the thing promised, in regard to providential things. I have had things in faith before I was delivered, and though in darkness as to the Lord's mind and will, yet I have felt that he would appear, and he *did*. And is not the life of a child of God one of constant dependence upon God and his word, by faith? And that for all things we need in nature, in providence and grace? And what an unspeakable mercy to have a grain of vital faith – a faith that has for its main object the person and work of the Lord Jesus Christ, as very God and very man? And what a favour when in trials, troubles and tribulation, and in darkness, doubts and fears, to trust in him, to look to him and rely upon him, believing that though we fall, yet shall we rise again. And how do we rise afresh but by faith in a risen Saviour?

Lose sight of Jesus and his cross,
And soon we fall a prey, etc.[814]

How true. The sermon at home this morning[815] by the late Mr Philpot was very searching ... I have been troubled with indwelling and besetting sins of late; and what can slay these lusts but a sight of Christ crucified? ... As you sit at his table and partake of the signs today, may you enjoy the *real* substance by faith.

My finger painful at times. With Christian love,

A. J. E.[816]

February 4th, 1917.[817]

[17]

✍ Dear Horace,

Was very pleased to hear from you ... Alas! there is only one in the company that cares for the things that pertain to godliness. I have some very sweet times in reading the Word and in prayer. I take my Bible and go to some quiet spot, and there pour out my heart to God in *my* poor way, that he would bless me and my partner in life and body, which is to my comfort and refreshment. I have no other solid joy. I do feel that I am in the Lord's hand – that he has said in his Word that 'he that endureth to the end shall be saved.' I am glad you have experienced a little of these things. May God continue to show you what you are by nature, which I am sure will be for your eternal good. I have seen A— E—. I meet him at the Baptist meeting room; also seen J— B— ... I am very sorry that I can only get off to go to chapel one Sunday in three. We are in active service. God 'is able to do exceeding abundantly above all that we ask or think.' I have been here six weeks. Shall be very pleased to see my dear wife and boy ... I think I have told you all. May God bless us each. Hope you are well.

S— C – ,

Dover.[818]

[18]

✍ My dearest Dad,

As I am now having a few days out of the lines, on reserve, I write a few lines in answer to yours. Yes, Dad, I hope too that I feel very thankful to God for his many preserving mercies towards me, and wish I could get more of that feeling too, but one feels so much of the opposite within him at times, and so full of indifference, that one often wonders if we have any right feelings at all. Even with shot and shell all about him, one wonders at one's own indifference, but it's not always so, I hope. But he is able to take care of me, and this verse has come to me at times –

> Plagues and deaths around me fly,
> Till he bids, I cannot die.[819]

And this I feel sure of, that I am as safe here as at home. But there is little comfort in those words unless applied with power to us; and one often needs the comfort of application of some such passages when he is expecting almost every moment to be his last. I thought of what you said about killing another man the other night on a raid: 'Is he prepared?' Am I prepared? Mr Wiles quoted the verse,

> Pause, my soul! and ask the question,
> Art thou ready to meet God? etc.[820]

As I said to him, 'If I could answer in the affirmative I should indeed be a happy man.' But with the feeling of so much death and indifference one fears the opposite. Yes, the destruction of property is fearful – one really ought to have no feelings here – houses, land, furniture, gardens, crops. And there are some good wheat crops round here being trampled to pieces; and when one goes into the destroyed villages and houses it is past description, one cannot say what he feels.

And now, Dad, I think I'll leave this. With my best love, from your ever affectionate son,

Ebb.

I think of you Sundays and wish I could be home with you for the day. Kind regards to friends at Hanover.[821]

France.

June 21st, 1918.[822]

A subsequent letter, dated 14th August, 1918, read:

✍ I am still preserved through a most trying time, a monument of God's sparing mercies. I wish I could feel more thankfulness. Will you request from me for hymn 9 (*Gadsby's Selection*), 'Loving kindness,'[823] to be sung, and 'Praise God, from whom all blessings flow.' ... I should like your pastor, Mr Pack,[824] to publicly acknowledge and give thanks to God for all his mercies towards me, one so undeserving of it; but it is not for our deserts, or we should have to keep our mouths shut; etc.[825]

[19]

✍ My dear Mother and Father,

I am expecting several letters here today; some may have gone to the line, and some may have been returned to you. If the latter has been the case, I know it would cause a certain amount of anxiety; this I have tried to avoid by writing practically every day. I trust that my sickness (tonsillitis) has caused no great alarm, as it is nothing but a chill. Although a change has come so unexpectedly when I was just getting used to the work, it has not been in vain, but shows what a wonder-working God we have. Yes, a God who does not consult powers nor kings before he carries out his good works towards creatures, who are sometimes past hope, and unwilling to make the best attempt to save themselves. Yes, when least expected, undeserved, he stretches out a hand and lifts us out of a horrible and depressing life, and tells us that it is only for a short time. Then we look at the Saviour and his sufferings and try to compare them to ours (what a contrast); does this not give us cause to hide ourselves with shame when we think how we have been grumbling and complaining all through life? Even some of our fellow creatures suffer more and do not grumble half so much. There are times when our thoughts go back to those at home, with every comfort that life can give, and perhaps their happiness has not been marred by any sorrow; yet we would not exchange our lot for theirs while we have such a great hope in Jesus Christ. And when we think of this, how contented we are with our humble lot, and repeat the words,

> What a friend we have in Jesus,
> All our sins and griefs he bore.[826]

And to think that he will present us to the Father in a spotless raiment, not doubting that a blemish may be found, but certain of being received, for everyone that cometh unto the Father through the Son shall be saved.

The other day I was recommended by the doctor to go to England, but on appearing before higher officers my case was rejected. Of course, I was very much disappointed after coming so far, and while thinking of my case being thrown out and left behind when so many cases were passed and signed, the thought came to me, 'What if my God should reject me?' Then I felt this could not be so if his only Son had recommended me. This was a great consolation to me and made me willing to stay out here while others were homeward bound. In the same ward I am in one fellow had lost a leg, another had lost an eye, and I could not help but look to God with gratitude when thinking of myself, and how he has brought me safely here when so many have been cut down, and yet not one of my hairs have been touched. Why should I dread the future when this same God is still reigning, and his love is still the same, 'yesterday, today, and for ever.'

Yesterday we had a good day, two services. This is a great advantage of the base, and I would like to stay, but believe I must return to the line very shortly. God can keep me here if his will, but if not he will not leave me to the will of my enemies; and I believe he who has been with me thus far will not leave me, but comfort me in the hour of trial, strengthen me in the hour of need, and bless me with his outstretched arms in the hour of death. This is not written in anticipation of anything serious happening, but that it is my duty to let you know how I am feeling ... I will close; hoping all are well at home; with love to all,

Your affectionate son,
Norman.
November 27th, 1916.[827]

[20]

The following correspondence was described as being 'extracts from a brother's letters from the battle field;' an appended note stated that the writer was about 25 years of age.[828]

✍ ... I cannot write you a letter. I want nothing really, as far as the body goes; we have as much done for us as is possible amongst so many thousands; but I am sorely tried. Have been sustained till now, in mercy and through the Word of God. Yes, J—, I hope I have seen Christ in his beauty, once or twice since I have been in the army, but past favours are at present as sweetness remembered in a cup of gall. O to come through this furnace in such a blessed condition as those 'many' described in Daniel 12: 10! This has been to me a blessed chapter; also Galatians 4. There are those to whom I feel responsible in writing, to seek their comfort; but now I would drop my pen, and seek rest, wisdom, grace, and strength that I may endure to the end ...

Love to both,
Your ever loving brother.
1915.

✍ ... Although I am in a dark state of mind, and incessantly in a 'devilish' atmosphere, yet,

I love to meet among them now,
Before his gracious feet to bow,
Though vilest of them all.[829]

The Gospel Standard has at times been good reading to me…
1915.

✍ My dear Brother,

... We are expected to be in the trenches next week ... I much enjoyed re-reading the Opening Word in *The Gospel Standard.* What is in store for me temporally is not my chief concern. I am persuaded all else matters but little if only granted the felt presence of the Lord Jesus Christ, but I feel unworthy of this. I have flushed and blushed in taking out his blessed Word to read, and then how cool and unmoved I have been when his holy name has been abused! What a weak, unworthy, sinful creature I feel, to seek such a one to dwell with me! Many eyes are on my actions, and when in the hour of danger and terror, I do want to live then, not for a Victoria Cross, but to the glory of God, and his Word. But again, I feel too poor a sinner for such a display of grace. This is my desire as I go up yonder—

O for a closer walk with God,
A calm and heavenly frame;
A light to shine upon the road
That leads me to the Lamb.[830]

My dear brother, when you are granted access to the throne of grace, remember your poor unworthy brother. I do not ask for comfort, or life, but peace through the blood of Christ ...

Love to you both,
Your affectionate brother,
France.
1916.

✍ ... How I wish I was able to relieve the suffering out here! I am a poor, timid sort of soldier, yet through the mercy of God I have been brought through so far. The shellfire has been terrific ... Am on night duty tonight and appreciate an hour's quiet, but 'Oh that I knew where I might find him!' How lifeless and barren I feel, and faithless too. What a condition at such a time! It is 3 a.m. Lord's Day. May the Lord be with you and all who meet in his name. For the most part it is despised out here; yet may the cries of his dear ministers and people be heard above the roar of guns. How I long to meet among them, but I need an enduring substance that will live through this furnace, to his honour and glory. I feel unworthy of it …

France.
1916.[831]

[21]

The following are extracts from a number of letters by an unknown soldier.

✍ ... This ghastly war being the judgement of God against the sins of the nations, it seems that in the mobilisation of men there has been a concentration of evil and vice, and the outrages committed by some Germans are not beyond hundreds of our men. Therefore numbers of armies and 'weight of steel' will never bring success. I can only see victory in one way, viz. sovereign mercy and grace abounding over our sins, for the sake of those in the nation whose minds are stayed on Christ. This has caused me many moments of self-examination as to my position in the army. I was pleased to find many exceptions to the above characters when I was at chapel on Lord's Day. I do feel there is a duty which one can render to the nation. If favoured with grace and courage to live to God's honour and glory, and endure to the end, it may prove that I have been in the right place ...

1914.

✍ ... Christmas night I think I shall never forget. The fearful things I am now continually witnessing have at times caused me to seek refuge in Christ. O, what will be the end of these things? The end I feel I can leave, if only I am interested in Christ, and my poor soul clothed in his righteousness. O that in this death and hell the Lord would deal bountifully with me, that I might live and keep his Word ...

1915.

✍ ... I do feel at times an attraction to those who know and fear the Lord ... I desire to thank the Lord that he should incline your heart to commit me, so undeserving, to his care. Sometimes I believe I desire above all else an interest in that inheritance of the saints in light. I dare not say I have never felt a sweetness in these things, and have once or twice been able to say: 'How sweet the name of Jesus sounds.' But the shortness of those moments compared with that ever-present self with its evil propensities, and the fickle deceitfulness of my heart, cause me to seriously question the reality of the former ...

The love and union I have felt towards some of the Lord's dear people, together with the recollection of a good time I once had at —, have melted me to tears and will, I hope, be some comfort amid the desolation into which I am about to enter ...

I feel your letter expresses more my desires than my possessions, yet I would acknowledge anything that is manifested of the goodness and mercy of God toward me ... May the Lord make himself known in all his dealings with us! ... This is written under distractions ...

1916.

✍ From a military hospital

I did not know what a blessing to be enabled to endure to the end, and there to bear witness to the truth! ... The exercises of my mind and soul for a long time have been connected inseparably with sad, foul and ghastly things. Yet I would acknowledge the unspeakable mercy and goodness of the Lord which enabled me to endure until he was pleased to deliver me. My head had been covered, and during several engagements I hope I felt a measure of divine support and peace. I had felt a spirit of supplications before our first attack at —. The bays[832] were packed with the first, second, and third waves, my post being through a gap in the parapet which was difficult to reach. In the stillness of the morning and ominous silence, fear took hold of me and death came on my hope and peace. At 3.15 we opened a terrific bombardment, and the enemy replied with a still more violent one. For a time prayer seemed gone; the rain of high explosive shells was distracting; the stretcher-bearers got busy. But the Lord appeared with these words: 'Let your moderation be known unto all men. The Lord is at hand.' Hope and courage revived, and I was enabled to say: 'Choose thou the way, but still lead on.' ... Such was the goodness of God to one so weak, so fearful, so faithless ... [833]

[22]

As has already been noted, the spiritual magazines produced by the churches were often greatly appreciated by those serving on the front. The following three letters are but a few of a number of letters of appreciation that appeared in the various magazines.

✍ To the Editor of *The Christian's Pathway*.

Dear Mr Kirby,

Having seen the appeal in *The Christian's Pathway* for help towards the cost of printing your directory [*of chapels and ministers*], I felt I should like to send you a small contribution. Will you accept it as a thank offering (although an unworthy one) for the greatness of the mercy and goodness of a prayer hearing and prayer answering God. I feel that I can never be sufficiently thankful for his sparing mercy in bringing me through this war safely, and in making me sensible of his presence in times of great danger. Only those who have faced death on the battlefield can realise what a difference it makes at such times. I desire especially to place on record his goodness to me on the night of September 27th, 1917. It was then, in the midst of a terrible bombardment, when strong men cried out through fear and the fury of hell seemed let loose, that he drew near, as it were, and spoke a gracious invitation to my soul, drove away my fear, and made me feel prepared to face death. I hope I shall never forget that night, when, true to his promise, he made me feel that he was a tower of refuge to my soul; and as often as I remember it I want to feel very thankful for that experience. In closing, I would say that I hope your appeal for help may be very successful. I remain,

Yours very sincerely,

Gunner T. T.,[834]

Royal Field Artillery, Tourcoing (British Troops in France).

June 11th, 1919.[835]

[23]

✍ To the Editor of *The Friendly Companion.*

Dear Friend,

I am sending you herewith 15 francs,[836] 10 of which I shall be glad if you will kindly allot to your 'Gower Street Chapel Card,'[837] and the remaining 5 francs to the fund for 'Widow and Imbecile Son.' The Lord has been very gracious and merciful in helping, sustaining and protecting me during the last 12 months that I have been in the army, and in particular in hearing and answering prayer and granting me two signal deliverances. As I have been led to meditate a little on the goodness and mercy of God to such an unworthy sinner, it has melted me down, and the language of my soul has been 'Bless the LORD, O my soul,' etc. (Psalm 103).

It has been laid on my mind to send you the enclosed. May the Lord grant you all needed help and grace in the management of *The Friendly Companion* and continue to bless your labours, is the sincere desire of,

'A Reader of F. C.'

France.

June 14th, 1917.[838]

[24]

To the Editor of *The Friendly Companion*

Dear Sir,

It may interest you to know that your little book, forwarded to me monthly here, has many times proved a help and blessing to me, and I have passed it on to others whom, I've no doubt, have appreciated its encouraging contents. Some of the soldiers' letters you have inserted from time to time, showing how the writers have found 'him precious who hath promised,' have been most interesting and encouraging, and one cannot help noticing that the words that seem to ring through most of those letters are, 'O for a closer walk with God.'

Many of us have indeed been many times within death's shadow, and at such times our mother's and father's God has helped us when we cried to him. May he that has also blessed your little magazine and supported it for so many years, continue a blessing and encourage you in your work, which is his work for the extension of his kingdom.

Yours sincerely in him,

'One of the boys in Egypt.'

December 21st, 1918.[839]

Mr Jefferies, the Editor, added the following note:

✍ We have felt much encouraged by different letters received. Another letter told us of a soldier who had arranged to spend £10 on pleasure. When he saw our appeal for the 'G. S.' Christmas Fund, his mind was changed and he sent it there. May the Lord accept and bless such changes, and make known his loving kindness therein and thereby.

[25]

✍ To the Editor of *The Little Gleaner.*

Dear Mr Tryon,

I felt I must write and thank you for *The Little Gleaner*, for I have felt helped and encouraged several times through reading the little books. There was one letter in the number written from the front from a brother to his sister, which really did me good, for had I seen him and told him he could not have described my experience and feelings better.[840] He spoke in his letter of having been to a service, and said there was nothing for him, no food for a living hungry soul, and said how dead the place seemed, and felt so himself, with no one to converse with on spiritual things. How many time I have felt the same, and been tempted to think there was none of the Lord's people out here, but after reading a letter like that, it proves the Lord has his people in our armies and it is helpful to find they have been made to experience much the same things. I really felt after reading his letter I should like him to know, as it might be helpful to him, that although he has no one to converse with on spiritual things, the Lord is leading other of his people the same way and in the same country. I can sincerely join with our friend in hoping the dear Lord will soon see fit to end this strife, and bring us home again in safety, so we can meet as we used to do with his people in his house.

Yours in him,

R— C— E—.[841]

P.S. I am enclosing a ten franc note; please accept this small donation to help with the cost of printing.

January 25th, 1918.[842]

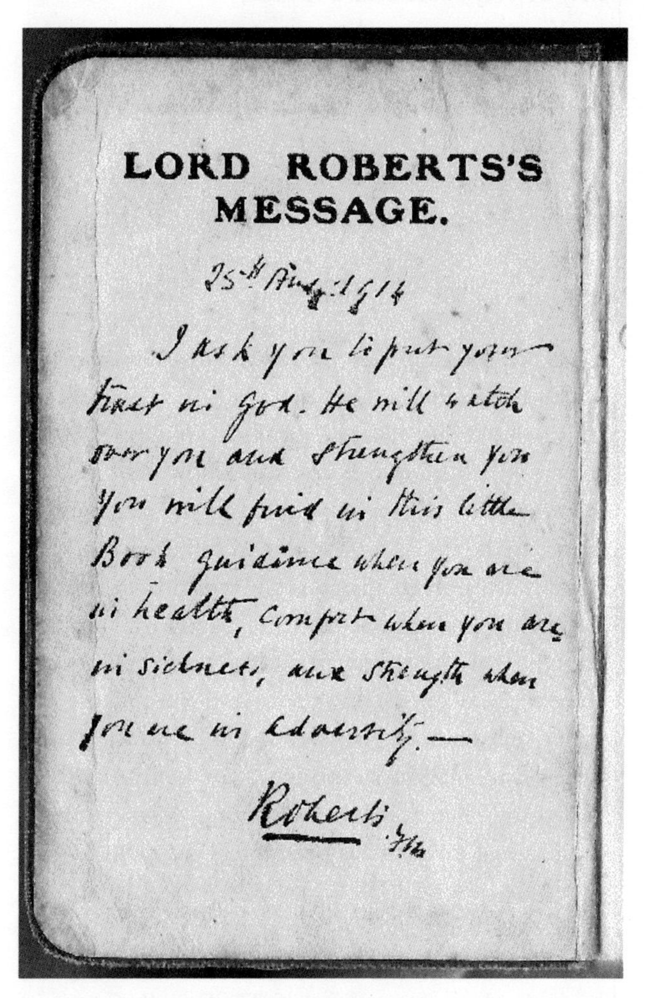

LORD ROBERTS'S MESSAGE.

25th Aug. 1914

I ask you to put your trust in God. He will watch over you and strengthen you. You will find in this little Book guidance when you are in health, comfort when you are in sickness, and strength when you are in adversity.—

Roberts. F.M.

The Scripture Gift Mission (SGM) printed thousands of New Testaments during the war, and these were issued to servicemen in all forces. These Testaments contained a standard message by Lord Roberts, the last Commander-in-Chief of the British Forces, exhorting the men to trust in God.

Letters from parents and friends describing the experiences of those serving in the forces

Mrs Buggs, Matfield

The following letter was written by Mrs Buggs of Matfield, on the death of her son, Frank Buggs.[843]

✍ Yes, dear —, my mind does often dwell on our dear Frank, but chiefly with more pleasure than pain. I thought much of him on the 11th, which was the day last year that he left home full of life and spirits. Whilst my memory is spared, never shall I forget the bitter trouble concerning him, then the blessing I had afterwards was so great, it seemed as much as my poor body could bear. I felt I could give him up to the Lord then, if only he assured me of his eternal safety; and from that time I had a hope it would be well with him whether he lived or died. When he came home on his last leave, I could not help thinking as he stood behind singing in chapel, it would probably be the last time; and yet I had such a peaceful time. Then again, after receiving his letter, saying he was picked out with a draft for the front, and had been served out with necessaries for active service, ending his letter by saying, 'Now, dear Mother, do not worry about me, simply leave me in the Lord's hands. He will do right.' I was wonderfully supported, and enabled to leave the dear boy in the Lord's hands. I felt I had given him up to him

Who is too wise to err, and O,
Too good to be unkind.[844]

That was so good to me. I told Mrs S— I had no promise that he would be brought home again; but did not like to tell any of you. Then again, after the news of his death came, each day I felt more confirmed of his eternal safety, and was enabled, in some measure, to enter into the blessedness of his position. But Sunday was a day never-to-be-forgotten – I wonder if I shall ever spend such another! I felt if I had ten thousand tongues they were not half enough to bless and praise the Lord God Almighty, and a precious Christ, who shed his blood to atone for the dear boy's sin, and for taking him to heaven to join in that new and never-ending song around the throne of God and the Lamb. 'Unto him that loved us, and washed us from our sins in his own blood … be glory, dominion and power!'

I have often thought how much mercy there was connected with everything concerning him; the health and strength given him to endure hardships (many we know nothing of) and not having a lingering illness, and some friend close by to send us word, etc. And what a blessed exchange to be taken from such a hell upon earth as the battlefield must be, to 'that holy, happy place, where sin no more defiles!'[845] I often think how dreadful it must be for our poor soldiers in the trenches now. There are no more weary days and nights for dear Frank now!

November 23rd, 1916.[846]

Mark S. Downing, Old Hill

The next letter was written by Mr Mark S. Downing, an itinerant minister amongst the Midland churches. He was a member at Spring Meadow Chapel, Old Hill.[847]

✍ My dear son, John A. Downing, born January 31st, 1899, was killed in action on September 6th, 1918.[848]

Previous to my dear boy's joining the army, my mind was much afflicted, and also his dear mother's. Having one already there it was a heavy burden indeed, but I had to say with Jacob, 'If I be bereaved of my children, I am bereaved.' The dear boy was willing to attend the service at the chapel, and the Sabbath school, and I thought for him to go from home would ruin him morally. Therefore my prayers were constant that he might be saved from the wrath to come. After my youngest had gone, my soul became more deeply concerned respecting his salvation, and that of each of my family. In my prayers the words, 'Preserve him, and prevent him, Lord,' were frequently used, and for each. The following words were an encouragement, as they would occur in my requests to God: 'For thou preventest him with the blessings of goodness.' I perceived the psalmist, in the spirit of prophecy, was speaking of God the Father, and his Son Jesus Christ, and of the provision in his Son for his people. Hence, I implored God, for Christ's sake, to grant the blessings contained in the text, if it were his will, upon my son and each of them.

On September 1st, my late dear wife[849] received a letter for me from a deacon, in which he quoted from Jude, 'Preserved in Jesus Christ.' The letter was a comfort to my beloved wife. From this time, whenever I thought, or cried to God about my son (who had been reported killed, though at that time we had not received the news of his death), the words, 'Preserved in Jesus Christ,' would occur to my mind. That which appeared essential to me was, did the Spirit apply them or not? Hence I was tossed upon the waters of trouble. My daily request was, 'Lord, is it *thy* voice?' After hearing the first report of my son's death, the words were again repeated, and in measure quieted my spirit. But I felt to want more power with the words. Therefore I waited upon God for more assurance.

When the second report came, it appeared clear that my dear boy had passed away, and my soul was in an agony as I read the news. Then my heart appeared to break, and the tears flowed. But now, the words 'preserved in Jesus Christ' came with more power than before, assuring my soul that his happy spirit had entered into rest. I enjoyed, for a moment, peace in my heart, believing the words came from God. I trust the Lord has heard and answered prayer, and I desire to ascribe all praise to Father, Son and Spirit. 'They that sow in tears shall reap in joy.'

Words quoted from dear John's letters: 'I read my Bible every night, and pray to God for strength and deliverance.' In another letter he writes: 'Praying to the Lord for salvation;' and when on the sick list, and apparently much depressed, he says, 'These words cheered me last night: "My grace is sufficient for thee: for my strength is made perfect in weakness."'

Mark S. Downing.[850]

Emma Littleton, Freemantle, Australia

The following two letters were written by Mrs Emma Littleton, who lived in Australia and used to write regular letters to *The Friendly Companion.* Mrs Littleton was the widow of John Littleton, a Strict Baptist minister who had emigrated to Australia.[851] His brother, Ebenezer, was pastor at Crowborough, Sussex, and his father, Thomas Littleton, had been pastor at Chippenham, Wiltshire.

Emma Littleton

[1]

✍ My very Dear Ones,

I received your packet of Mr Popham's sermons, and indeed thank you for them. I have already sent them on their way to some of the thirsty ones out here, who do not find streams of living water flowing from the crystal fountain of truth as you still have at home.

I am sure I posted to you a day or so after I received your last, yet it is no wonder you have not received it. The greater wonder is if you do; for danger lies all along the great sea road now. I keep a list of 'received' and 'answered' or I should not be sure. The number has been near 300 a year for many years; now, however, they will soon cease, for I find my strength failing fast; especially since August 4th, 1914, when this cruel, satanic war was declared. Day and night, night and day the burden presses sore, not only for one's own, but the whole world seems engulfed in the monster power in some way or other, and the poor distracted Jews are suffering heavily indeed. And who are the Jews? The natural brethren of our beloved Lord Jesus. We shall yet hear him say – 'These my brethren!' He was the Son of David; so are they. Read Jeremiah's Lamentations when you feel oppressed and sad ... Ask that the veil may be lifted from their hearts; that they may be brought to 'look upon him … and … mourn,' as the Lord has declared they shall (Zechariah 12: 10.). Seek a spirit of prayer for them, they are his flesh; and oh, their sorrows are unspeakable!

Now, I am wondering where your brother is? O Kate, we are all unworthy wanderers from the Father's house, and are not worthy to be called his sons; not one of us. Where is the poor lad? I have seven sons and grandsons eligible to be called out for service. Two are already out, and today I have given the last kiss to one, a truly exceptional lad, of whom his brothers say, 'He has no vice in him.' Indeed, I believe he has the deep fear of God implanted in his heart, and that, you know, 'is the beginning of wisdom.' His name is Charlie Littleton, and he is in our Australian troops. He may even cross your path. There are others also coming on. I may be called away any moment, for fainting comes on in a moment, and I know not how any one of these faints may end. I give you this information that you may be even looking out, for we are 26 in family here now, and one grandson married, and has one child. Six of them, sons and grandsons, have served in the army corps, and may, if the duty's call comes, be called out. I find it hard to pray that grand prayer, given us as a directory of thoughtful prayer, 'Thy will be done in earth, as it is in heaven.' Do you find it difficult? I do; yes! I do. Natural love puts its arms round the dear lads' necks and receives their warm kisses, for they all love me; they do, I assure you, and they show it; and then to think what one exposes them to! It is hard to say, 'Thy will be done.' Yet it must be said, from the heart too; and their younger mothers feel it perhaps even more than I do. Oh! dear ones, I cannot put into words how I long for 'his appearing' whose right it is to reign over this sin-distracted world. I am so, so glad he has given us a right to pray – 'Come, Lord Jesus; come quickly!' Come. Oh! that he would.

And now, dear ones, I would remind you of our only hope, and that is in the Word of the living God. Remember, we are past the latter days and are in the last ... It is our business now to study the world's history, lest 'that day,' the last, 'come upon us unawares;' and nowhere shall we find a true account but in the inspired Word of God; therefore, read it with its own keys. You find that the Most High elected a nation in one man, Abraham! ...

Read all the prophets, ask the Lord's eye-salve that you may see. These are the last days. And what nation has been used as the British have been to carry the news of salvation to a fallen world; as the city of London has to the whole known world; and there are the royal seed of the house of Israel! And there is the only hope of victory in this cruel, satanic, bitter, hateful war! Farewell, dear ones. Heaven and home is ours, through his precious blood.

Emmaus (Emma) Littleton,
Fremantle.
April 4th, 1915.[852]

[2]

✍ My dear Nieces,

I have just read your last and, thanking you for the precious sermons first, I will respond at once, for time is not at our disposal; we know not what a day will bring forth. The daily peril of war is affecting the greater part of our poor sin-desolated world. We here are in well nigh as great trouble as yourselves. Ships are bringing loads of wounded, our own sons are gone into the field of strife and death; there are few families free from the terror and those who are, are taxed to the utmost in every possible way. It is a great mercy England is so far spared from invasion, and it is our bounden duty, as those who know the Lord, to put our trust in him. The word is, 'They that know thy name will put their trust in thee: for thou, LORD, hast not forsaken them that seek thee.' Fear, love and trust are the fruit of knowledge, of divine intuition.

We may scarce recognize it ourselves, but there it is. Read Psalm 2 over and over again, till you have it by heart; you will find it a secret chamber for your poor distracted spirits; when you have no words to utter before the Lord it will be something like being hid, as Moses was, 'in a clift of a rock,' while the Lord Jehovah passed by him, declaring his wonderful name (Exodus 33: 32).

You tell me you don't know how to pray. Ah! dear ones, neither do I. No, I do not. I am dumb before the Lord. But let me tell you, I have found in the Psalms of David most blessed leadings and teachings for the expression of my soul in this overwhelming season of trial as I have never done before; I mean in heartfelt language in my utter helplessness and ignorance. I have studied them more than 50 years, but have not had the dire necessity of using the wonderful words they contain as I do now. In our morning worship Mary reads, and I say, 'Take the next psalm, they supply the longing as well as the distress of soul, with language for prayer, and help me more than ever before.'

Take this too: the sons of Reuben 'cried to God in the battle, and he was entreated of them, because they put their trust in him.' (1 Chronicles 5: 20.) There is something very beautiful in that. Think of a father passing with a happy helpless child through and over a dark dangerous passage. While he holds the little hand tight, if it is ever so dark the child feels safe, and steps out without fear; and our Father, God, has said, 'I, the Lord, will hold thy right hand, saying unto thee, Fear not.' 'I am the first and the last.' Then that includes all the life from first to last of all and each one of us; and this tremendous upheaval of nations is included too. O, should not this hush all our fear? What if life is taken with the enemy's crash; are we not taken 'to be with Christ, which is far better?' All who are in the covenant mercy of Jesus cannot even die! 'He that believeth in me shall never die.' Think of it; to be 'absent from the body' is to be 'present with the Lord.' It is an opening of the gate of transition to life that is eternal in the heavens. Having begun here, by the power of the Holy Spirit's renewing and regenerating breath, we cannot die ...

I have had to pray that my reason would not give way, for I often feared it must; my whole being seemed to go out in prayer, 'Be not far from me, oh my strength!' And do not ask me if that prayer was answered. I am yet a living witness of the wonders and condescension of the fatherly goodness and faithfulness of the Lord God of Israel. Yea, even to the love and care of a mother; he hath said, 'As one whom his mother comforteth, so will I comfort you;' you who need it, faint for it, seek it. He has indeed held my right hand, saying unto me, 'Fear not!' and he is saying it still to his host of distracted sons and daughters.

As to your daily danger, the Lord help you to go forth in his strength, knowing, 'The angel of the Lord encampeth about them that fear him, and delivereth them.' The gracious Lord help you to put your hand in his, and go forth, looking upward. 'I will lift up mine eyes unto the hills, from whence cometh my help.' 'When the poor and needy seek water ... I the Lord will help them.' The desert. Ah! that's the place to thirst, and there shall be water.

I will not say more. I am very weak; am not out of my room many hours now; cannot help others much, need hourly helping myself, and I have all that love can do in my children and my priceless nurse, Mary. So the gracious Lord has fulfilled his word, 'Even to your old age I will bear; even I will carry, and will deliver you.' What a wonder working God!

Still in love and hope,

Aunt Emmaus Littleton,

Tabor, Forest Street, Fremantle, West Australia.

July, 1915.[853]

Elizabeth Riseley, Carlton

The following letter was sent for publication in *The Friendly Companion* by Mr Alfred Dye of Rowley Regis. According to his covering letter, "Mrs Riseley, a widow, states that she has preaching in her cottage at Carlton, Beds. The son Jesse was about 12 years old when his father died; he has been in the Bedfordshire Regiment some time, and was sent to the front almost as soon as the war broke out." When Mr Dye was preaching at her cottage soon after, she told him of her faith that her son's life would be spared and that he would return home safe, and would be made manifest as God's child.[854]

✍ Dear Mr Dye,

I feel I must write at once, as you name my dear boy and your hopes that, according to my faith, his life will be spared.

I had quite forgotten I had told you of the words I had when he went away to the front. Well, those words came just as if someone spoke to me as I was walking in Reformatory Lane: 'I will make a way for his escape, and I will bring him back in peace and safety;' and they used to come to me many times in a day. And since, when I have been very much cast down in thinking about my poor Jesse, these words used to come so nice, 'Let not your heart be troubled,' etc. And a few weeks since I received a letter, saying he was in the hospital with bad varicose veins in his legs, and that they had all broken out. And on the following Sunday I received a post card saying, 'My dearest Mother, you will be surprised to know that I am in dear old England once more, and that I am going to Cambridge Hospital;' then a week after that he came home for a fortnight, and went back last Monday. Although he is not quite 'up to the mark,' they have again passed him as fit; but he does not know whether he is now for home defence or for the front again ... He is now at Felixstowe.

He was in all that heavy fighting at Ypres, 19 days in the trenches without a wash or change of clothes; and he says they were curled up in the trenches like hedgehogs, up to their knees in mud and water. His mate next to him was shot dead, and he had (poor fellow) a wife and two little children at Wellingborough, and the poor thing has been over to see Jesse in order to know if her husband was really dead, and to ask about him. It is terrible, and Jesse does hope he may never go there again. He told us that several soldiers shot themselves. The war is so bad, he says it is nothing unusual to see heads, legs and arms blown off; and he said he had had lots of men's brains blown on to him; and one day four of them were in a trench by themselves, and the three were shot dead and he escaped. He says he has wondered that he never was hit, as many times he had very narrow escapes.

When he came home I did think the Lord was kind to bring him to me. Yes, I do think he is kind, for what am I or mine that he should so shield him? But here is the trial again: I do not know if he will have to go back, and it troubles me; and will the Lord prevent it as the poor thing dreads it? ...

My eyes are up unto him who hath power to kill and to keep alive ... When he went away this time the words came again, 'I will make a way for his escape, and will bring him back in peace and safety.' And I said, 'Well, he is not got to the front again, yet.' And I might say the same day these two promises came: 'And I will be his God and his guide, even unto death;' 'And I will deliver him.' I did think it nice; but one wants the faith to grasp it. I have hope, but I fear; and so I did before. I will try and leave him now.

How is dear Mercy, and all at home? What a lovely letter there was in *Zion's Witness* of your son's wife[855] ... Your son is highly favoured, and you also, especially as I think she said you were her father in the faith, and this is very nice for you ...

Ever affectionately,

E. Riseley.[856]

E. Thomas

The following letter was written in response to a letter of sympathy sent to Mrs E. Thomas. She had recently lost her husband by death, and this was quickly followed by the death of her only son, Private F. A. Thomas, who was serving with 19th Battalion, The King's Liverpool Regiment. He was killed on 25th October, 1917, and is buried in Bailleul Communal Cemetery Extension, Nord.

✍ Dear Friend,

... I am left to mourn the loss of a godly loving husband. My loss is very great, and my loneliness I cannot describe to anyone on earth. My second bereavement is too cutting to say much of at present; but for the mercy and goodness of God I must have sunk in despair, but he has and does support me, and I have proved that 'underneath are the everlasting arms.'

What I passed through in my mind for a fortnight I cannot tell anyone, for the weight of my dear boy's soul was crushing to bear. But just over a fortnight after I had the notice to say he was killed in action, the Lord spoke words of comfort to me concerning him, and I can say that I have a good hope that he is now in heaven out of all suffering and pain; but this did not come to me before I felt that I was at my wits' end, and I could bless God that he had spared to me my reason. Now I do not wonder at people losing their reason when they have no God to go to. My beloved child was my all on earth as regards close natural ties. He wrote me four letters in October. The last was written on the 20th, I received it on the 24th, and he was killed the next day. He wrote whenever he could get time and always asked me to pray for him, as he said, 'I know I have your prayers, and I greatly need them. I do try to pray for myself, but there is everything so averse to that out here.' How he would beg of me not to worry, knowing how weak I had been for a long time. When he was home for his last leave, I had a feeling when he left me that I should never see him again.

He was out there just three months. In one letter he told me that while he was in the field, witnessing the firing of the guns each side, shrapnel bursting over his head, very forcibly the lines came to him,

> Plagues and deaths around me fly;
> Till he bids, I cannot die,[857]

and he said, 'All fear was taken away and I felt quite safe.' What a wonderful mercy I felt it to have the fear taken away in the midst of death! He was 23 the 17th February ... I am thankful to say I am much better in health, as I was so weak and quite ill at times for a year after my beloved husband died. The three months nursing night and day was a great strain on my body, but I felt truly thankful that the dear Lord granted me just strength to get through till after the funeral, then I had to go to bed. I felt I would gladly have gone with my dear husband if I had felt as he did, as he longed to be gone all the last week of his life.

Yours etc.,
E. Thomas.[858]

Unknown correspondents

The following letter was sent for inclusion in *The Friendly Companion* by Joseph Wilcox, the pastor of Fredrick Street Chapel, Birmingham.

Joseph Wilcox

[1]

✍ My dear Sister,

I thought you would like to know and rejoice with me at the Lord's goodness and preserving mercy to our dear Ernest up till the 21st of last month. It seems they were going to A— when they saw a submarine coming toward them. The captain told them nothing but a fog could save them, when, to their surprise, a dense fog came over them in three-and-a-half minutes, which lasted three-and-a-half hours, which hid and shielded them from the sight of the enemy. When the fog passed away and they saw they were safe, the captain called them together on deck and held a thanksgiving service for their deliverance. When I knew of it I felt melted to tears; the 103rd Psalm was so suited to my feelings. How it brought to my mind the children of Israel going through the Red Sea, how the cloudy pillar preserved them. The dear Lord still rules and reigns, and not a single shaft can hit till he permits. O that it could please him to hear prayer for the dear boy's soul, and make him manifest as a chosen vessel of mercy! This circumstance encourages me to still hope on; I know the Lord can still shield his head in the day of battle. All unite in love to you.

Your affectionate sister,
H— R—.
August 8th, 1915.[859]

[2]

✍ Dear Friend,

The young man that I told you lost his leg and expected the other would be taken off, is in England ... By what we can gather, he lost one leg, or foot, and the other leg is broken. He says our boy was standing close to him when the shell burst, and that it killed both our boy's horses. It struck our boy on the breast pocket and made a hole halfway through his letters, etc. O, mercy of mercies! I hope, if it can be the Lord's will, that he may return in peace and safety. He has certainly been mercifully shielded up to now; we have to leave the future in the hand of the Lord. It seems to me that England is one vast military camp; at the present time we have thousands of men and horses in our town, and I hear other towns are the same ... I fully believe that it is the prayers of God's own children, and prayers alone, that have saved us from invasion. I do not undervalue our brave men on land and sea; all honour to them. Yet I still believe that praying men and women have done more in this national struggle than many Christians are aware of. We find it was so in Scripture. O that the issue may redound unto the glory of God!

Yours, etc.,
W. G.,
Kettering.
April 3rd, 1915.[860]

[3]

✍ Dear A – ,

... We do well to consider ourselves immersed in national trouble. What effect it will have on us individually we see not yet plainly. If ever we had dark clouds hanging over us as a nation, it is today. If trouble would suffice to bring people to God, we have it now; but we have learned that something more is wanted. God may be convincing the world what use he has of salt; I mean, the best sort (Matthew 5: 13). It is a hard lesson for the world to learn; also for the 'salt' to believe it is themselves. Will God make use of prayer? If so, he must inspire prayer for that end, and give us faith to mix with prayer. 'Tis true, we have not now a Noah, or a Daniel, or a Job (Ezekiel 14: 14) to intercede for us, but there is One who is more prevailing.

Is it God's set time or not? Or is our house to be left unto us desolate? What work has God to do more in our once favoured land? If we have hope, must it not be 'against hope'? One says that if the Lord had not left us a seed, we should have been as Sodom and

Gomorrah. I believe God has a seed yet in the land: but who are they? God knows everyone. The worldly professor would be the first to say: 'I am one.' Jesus says the 'first shall be last, and the last first.' The Lord does not reckon on running fast. Are we in the narrow path where the world is not found – where the vulture's eyes and the lion's whelps are not found?

For a long time our country has been given to pleasure of all kinds, and as we sow we reap. People in all ages have said of threatened judgement, 'it is far off,' till it gets to their doors. They take no notice of Noah's building, not foreseeing the storm approaching. It is only the wise that shall understand (Daniel 12: 10). Many will pretend what will be done after the war. What will it profit them if they have their desire? One says: 'To me to live is Christ, and to die is gain' (Philippians 1: 21). Who so lives, need not fear to die. How busy the world is everywhere! but will everything be in its right place so as to suit everyone before the great trumpet is blown, saying, 'Come to judgement'?

I want to feel the importance of being right myself, so as to hold with a slack hand everything else. We cannot be too much like Mary, but diligence in business and fervency in spirit are joined together. Every precept is a good looking glass to find out our spots and shortcomings, and much tends to make us cry for mercy and the blood of Christ to pardon us. How thankful we ought to be for the furnace to purify us, as we have so much dross that wants separating. We need a hand to be continually pushing us down into the valley of humiliation, or our proud hearts would take us as far from God as Satan is. What a mercy it is that Christ has so much grace to give – with pardoning grace – as we daily stand in need of! It is one thing to need it, and another to sensibly feel the want of it, for his own glory. We need to have Calvary more in view, and to see the holy, willing Lamb nailed there by our sins. If this does not make us hate ourselves, what will? 'Tis cruel for us to have self-love when we owe our all to such a friend. Have I begun to love him? Yes, but not as I would. 'Tis time to awake out of my slumbering state. I should like all my children to serve Christ much better than I do. I do not know if they will be called to suffer more for the truth's sake; that must be left with him who reigns over all things. He has permitted some to be put in the fire, but he himself goes in with them. I do not think it is right for God's people to grieve for their young whom he has 'taken away from the evil to come.' Christ said in his day: 'Weep not for me, but weep for yourselves, and your children. For behold, the days are coming when ye will say: Blessed are the barren … that never bare, and the paps which never gave suck.' What if that takes place in our own land? Is it not so today in some other places?

I saw G— R— this morning. He is in the same mind with myself: it will be worse in the future, as there is no real crying to God for help; all looking to man, like the Babel-builders. May the Lord cause us to be like Josiah, whose heart was tender, to whom the Lord spoke comfortable words, but not to the impenitent.

Your loving father.

1916.[861]

Letters from home to those serving in the forces

Emma Dancy, Brighton

The following letter was written by Emma Dancy, who was a member of Mr Popham's church at Galeed Chapel, Brighton:[862]

✍ Dear E – ,

I constantly hear of you, and am thankful you have been thus far preserved. I have felt you are really as safe, though exposed to dangers, as you were at home, for you are under God's protection.

Not a single shaft can hit,
Till the God of love sees fit.[863]

My thoughts are with you often, both day and night, and the other dear ones who are suffering hardship that we may have the comforts of home. Prayer is a sweet privilege, a sure refuge, and a great comfort when the heart is heavy and sore oppressed; to find oneself helped to pour it out before God and to commit loved ones and all concerns into his kind and wise hands. May he sanctify to your soul's good and profit all you are passing through. May your loneliness but draw you nearer to him; he is an ever-present friend: may your weakness cause you to turn to Christ for strength. There is no need too trivial to go to him with, no extremity too great for him to help us in.

I have thought sometimes of that little word 'able' and all it contains in respect of Christ's power; the declarations and promises connected with it. 'Able to deliver.' 'What he promised, he is able also to perform.' 'He shall be holden up: for God is able to make him stand.' 'Able to make all grace abound toward you.' 'Able to do exceeding abundantly above all that we ask or think.' 'Able even to subdue all things unto himself' – our inward foes, our evil hearts of sin and unbelief that sometimes, yea, often, seem too much for us – even these God is able to subdue unto himself, lay them low, and bring into subjection every thought. 'Able to keep that which I have committed unto him against that day.' 'Able to make us wise unto salvation.' 'Able to succour them that are tempted.' 'Able also to save them to the uttermost that come unto God by him.' 'Able to keep you from falling, and to present you faultless before the presence of his glory with exceeding joy.'

The ability, the power, the omnipotence of God is to be employed for his weak, tried, tempted, helpless children throughout their lives. And his grace has made in Christ provision for their eternal blessedness. What a comfort there is in real religion! What a reality! To this great God sinners, weak, helpless, and burdened may approach – 'made nigh by the blood of Christ,' pleading his merits and his great name. 'For Jesus Christ's sake' is a prevailing plea.

... There is never a service at chapel but what you are all thought of and committed to God in prayer.

With love and every good wish.

Yours very sincerely,
Emma Dancy,
Brighton.
November 6th, 1916.[864]

Abraham Jarvis, Greenwich

The following was written by Abraham Jarvis to one of his nephews, a son of Stephen H. Jarvis, the minister at Blackgang, Isle of Wight. Stephen H. Jarvis had three sons known to have served in the war: Martin Luther Jarvis, Swynfen Jesse Jarvis and Stephen Herbert Jarvis. It is not specified which of these nephews the letter was addressed to. Abraham Jarvis's other brother was the well-known and well-loved Joseph Jarvis, the pastor at Devonshire Road Chapel, Greenwich, for 33 years, until his death in 1928. Abraham Jarvis was a deacon at Devonshire Road.

> ✍ My dear Nephew,
>
> I am very pleased to get your letter; and very glad to know that you have found friends among the Jireh people; also that you are able to help in the YMCA meetings, when you cannot get to Jireh. I spoke to an RAF man tonight at chapel, and found that I knew his father when I was a boy; so I was glad to make his acquaintance; and as he is coming to Deptford next week, I hope to see him often.
>
> I suppose you have heard about the Zeppelin raids? On Tuesday night they passed over us, and dropped bombs in the next road, which did not explode, and so, through mercy, we have been preserved until now. On Wednesday night I saw the shells from the Heath anti-aircraft gun exploding all around; and this lighted up the sky, like fireworks. It was a very solemn time, as we could not tell at any moment whether or not we should be launched into eternity. May it be our constant concern in these terrible times to know that we are ready to meet God, if called upon to do so. Are you seeking salvation by the sufferings and death of the Lord Jesus? 'There is none other name under heaven given among men, whereby we must be saved.' He casts out none that truly come to him.
>
> Now I must close. Shall be glad to hear from you, whenever you can drop a line. With love from all;
>
> Your affectionate uncle,
>
> Abraham Jarvis.[865]

Abraham Jarvis

The following account was written by Jesse Jarvis, one of the nephews of Abraham Jarvis, and possibly the recipient of the foregoing letter. It is probably autobiographical:

✍ It was in the dark days of the war. Saturday night, and a regiment was going into the trenches – some for the first time. Most of them were young lads, and going into the line was a much quieter operation than coming out. Mile after mile was tramped in silence over rough ground dotted with large shell holes, into which everyone managed to stumble occasionally.

Arrived at the trenches at last, the boys surveyed their underground dwellings, knowing they would stay there for at least four days and nights. They decided they were not too bad, when a voice proclaimed that No. 1 Platoon would proceed 100 yards nearer the enemy's lines and dig fresh positions. Now a platoon should be 30 men, but this particular one had been so decimated by the enemy that only 12 remained. They proceeded cautiously through the night, stealing nearer to the German lines, pausing only as the suspicious enemy fired a Verey light,[866] which he did every few minutes. Arrived at the new position, the word was passed, 'Dig in two by two, and get deep before daylight, as enemy snipers are in a row of trees a couple of hundred yards off.'

Between 4 and 5 a.m. Sunday morning, as the day broke, the positions were discovered, and at once a fierce attack was launched. Peeping out, the men saw three of their comrades fall wounded. Now three out of twelve only leaves nine, and those nine began to feel very uncomfortable about it, for against shell fire they could do nothing effectively, and there was a risk of the enemy making a hand-to-hand attack under cover of their artillery. One of those men called very earnestly to the God of heaven for help, and speedily it came, for comrades behind brought the heavy guns into action, and other infantry arrived on the scene, as we say, 'just in the nick of time.' How true the words, 'Call upon me in the day of trouble: I will deliver thee.' 'The LORD is thy keeper.'

A week later, another Sunday morning, from the positions on the edge of a wood, the troops see French civilians trying to escape the battle zone – old men, and also women and children, with all their belongings on an ox-drawn wagon. Seeing their plight, two brave English lads jump out of their holes and advance unarmed and with white flags to help the poor French, when, to the horror of all, the German army destroyed the whole party by shell fire, and started a big attack on the British troops. A terrible bombardment ensued, and the regiment was subjected to a most murderous firing. Crouching helpless in the mud, one of those soldiers passed another a copy of the Psalms, opened at the forty-sixth: 'God is our refuge and strength, a very present help in trouble,' etc. Again arose that earnest prayer to God: 'Lord, save us, we perish!' And did God answer by destroying the enemy? No; he does not always remove the trouble, but in the midst of it, over the consciousness the sweet feeling steals of the peace of God which passeth all understanding, and anxiety is allayed as each realises that God reigneth. 'A thousand shall fall at thy side, and ten thousand at thy right hand, but it shall not come nigh thee!' 'Trust in him at all times; ye people.' He is a rock and fortress. 'The blood of Jesus Christ his Son cleanseth us from all sin,' and by it we may be made ready to pass from death unto life, and ready to meet God when his time shall come.

O Jesus! when such terror springs
In church, or home, or soul.
Wake from thy patience at our cry,
And with thy word of majesty
Our enemies control.[867]

Jesse Jarvis,
Blackgang, Isle of Wight.[868]

George Lodge, Gravesend

The following two letters[869] were received by Percy Lodge, who was based at Portsmouth serving in the navy (see p. 40). They were written by his grandfather, George Lodge, who was a founder of the 'Gospel Standard' Strict Baptist cause at Gravesend. When George Lodge died in 1925, he had been deacon there for 49 years.[870]

Percy Lodge

[1]

✍ Dear Percy,

We received yours today and were glad to learn you were quite well, as by God's mercy we all are, with the exception, perhaps, of George who has a cold and cough. …

Now, with regard to the questions you ask about the garden. Yes, we have all the crops in and they are up and growing, so that if you are long before you get leave we shall have new potatoes.

You seem to be doing alright. I thought about you this morning. Your old buzzer was blaring 8.30 as I was going down the lawn, but I was pleased to think you were comfortable, the secret of which is, as I have already told you, contentment with our lot, obeying those who have the rule over us. I notice in yours you intend asking for leave soon. Do not build too much hope on meeting with success. You will not then be disappointed if it is not granted. Of course, we shall be immensely pleased to see you; in the meantime your pigmy of a brother is keeping your place warm and just rousing grandma's anger, then he has to haul in his weather brace pretty sharp, and he does it.

Mother asks me to tell you Allen Durling[871] and

co. think they will all have to go.

Now, how are you getting on at Salem?[872] Are you still able to go occasionally? Do you get the magazines?[873] I expect a reply to these questions when you write, for as John writes, 'I have no greater joy than to hear that my children walk in the truth.'

I beg you to remember the words of our Lord and Saviour, 'Them that honour me I will honour, and they that despise me shall be lightly esteemed.'

> Trust him, he will not deceive us,
> Though we hardly of him deem;
> He will never, never leave us;
> Nor will let us quite leave him.[874]

God bless you,
Your affectionate granddad.
P.S. Can't see, it is getting dark.
109 High Street, Northfleet.
10th May, 1918.

[2]

✍ Dear Percy,

I have yours of the 26th and am under an obligation to reply, which is not an unpleasing fact, especially when in the right mood.

Now I was glad to learn from yours that you have a discovery of the effects of the fall, viz. indwelling sin. Painful as this is, it is a knowledge that keeps us from being in love with ourselves, and teaches us experimentally the truth of the words, 'the flesh profiteth nothing.'

The young beginner is apt to think that in course of time he may grow better, but he will find all his pilgrimage that sin is mixed with all he does. The great thing is, does it cause grief? Do we hate it? Is it a burden? Because, as Mr Hart has it,

> To see sin smarts but slightly;
> To own, with lip confession,
> Is easier still; But O to feel
> Cuts deep beyond expression.[875]

George Lodge

But what a mercy for us that, he was made 'sin for us … that we might be made the righteousness of God in him.' Now I would have you call continually upon our Lord Jesus, that he would give you an understanding, that you may know him that is true.

I will not deceive you by telling you that the pathway is strewn with roses. It is a hard fight, but there is this consolation for all his true followers – victory is certain.

It was my intention when I began this to give you a good long letter, but after attempts failing, I am compelled to give up; time will not allow. We are all well, I am thankful to say, and hope this will find you so. Magazines to follow. I will write again as soon as time will allow. You will see by the above date I began this two days ago.

Yours very affectionately,
Granddad.
109 High Street, Northfleet.
29th May, 1918.

An unknown correspondent

✍ My dear Boy,

Just a line to say we received your letter and were very pleased to hear from you again, and to find you were still in the land of the living. At the same time I am thankful to say that we are all about as usual under the present circumstances; and you may be sure our 'better parts' do their part in the worrying line, but I tell them that that will not help matters in the least. We must hope for the best as long as there is hope. No doubt you find it somewhat different out there on the Sabbath from what it was when you were stationed at Nottingham, where you had the pleasure of meeting with a few of God's dear people at Chaucer Street,[876] and where you said you enjoyed the services of God's house. Well, my boy, we were very glad to hear it, because where there is a desire in the heart to be found amongst God's people in this life, it affords a hope of spiritual life within; these things come not from the bottomless pit, but from the 'Father of lights' from above, for our carnal hearts have no desire after spiritual things until such is created within by the blessed Spirit of God.

You did not say how you got your wound in the trenches. Glad to hear it is going on favourably. And now, my boy, I hope you are not ignorant of the fact that we must observe the good hand of our God in this matter. Although wounded in one of your members, see how he protected your body. Had the missile struck you in a vital part, doubtless it would have been sudden death. The Lord has preserved you thus far; we hope he will still be a guardian about you in the day of battle and a protection in the hour of danger. Read frequently the 90th and 91st Psalms, and. the Lord grant you may in a measure realize the blessings contained therein, that you may be favoured with a little meditation thereon at times, to seek his good hand to be with you to keep you in all your ways from future dangers. For we are conscious of the fact that you are in constant danger of your life whilst engaged in this terrible conflict. What misery and destruction have been on the face of the earth through the selfish ambition of one man and his military advisers! I hope the Lord will soon arise and put on his strength to subdue our enemies, and stay this terrible slaughter and sacrifice of life.

We hope we are defending the right, as we, as a nation, had no desire for these things; but as a land and nation we have sinned and dishonoured our God. It would doubtless have been better for us if the whole nation had been bowed in humility from the beginning, and sought the good hand of our God in the matter, without so much boasting of our own abilities and strength. We hope the time will soon come for the Lord to appear for us and give us success in this terrible conflict.

Now we must once more commit you into the hands of him who is able to do all things for us. As time is short with us in this life, may he grant that we may all be found amongst those upon whom he has set his heart's affections from before the foundation of the world. Then, my boy, if we ever reach that blessed 'house not made with hands,' it will be well with us. There will not be so much as a rumour of war there, much less the reality of it, nor will there be confusion, but all will be serenity, joy and peace in which to spend that never-ending eternity with him who has shed his own dear heart's blood to atone for our sins. May he in mercy lead you to meditate upon those things at times for your benefit, and grant hereafter we may be reunited around his dear feet in heaven, to join in the everlasting song and 'Crown him Lord of all.'

The poor petitions and desires of our hearts to heaven are that he may keep you, both body and soul, in his merciful hand, and bring you back in safety if consistent with his blessed will.

With family affections from all,
Your affectionate father,
H— P—.,
Eaton.[877]

Henry Bradford

Letters written by ministers to those serving in the forces

Henry Bradford, pastor at Eastbourne

Mr Bradford was one of the first people to be baptised in the chapel at Grove Road, Eastbourne, in 1865. He was later sent out to preach by the church there, becoming pastor in 1871. He resigned his pastorate because of ill health in 1912.[878]

✍ My dear Herbert,

As I have been favoured with one of your photos, I feel it devolves upon me to attempt to write to you to acknowledge the kind favour.

It is a splendid picture of you; we all think you have come out very well. When one's loved ones are away from us, it is very pleasing to have at hand their image. Your dear mother brought it here. I did not see her, as I was in bed at the time if I am not mistaken. But one is very forgetful, and forgetfulness is an affliction, but we cannot expect our mental powers to last always, or our physical powers either, can we? 'The days of our years are threescore years and ten; and if by reason of strength they be fourscore years, yet is their strength labour and sorrow; for it is soon cut off, and we fly away.' What strong language, and yet how beautiful! Hebrew poetry is very grand, very sublime, is it not? How very beautiful the Psalms are, and what a blessing they have been to our fellow men and women, and they continue to be the same. It is so nice to find the lamentations and the confessions of our hearts expressed in the beautiful language of the Psalms, and in them are to be found expressions of the gratitude of the soul very sweetly conveyed.

It may be that you for one have found some of your heart's best wishes expressed in the Psalms or in the hymns. And if you can find your heart in harmony with the hymns of prayer, of confession, and of praise, then you must know something of true worship, even if you should be silent, so far as voice expression is concerned.

Some of the hymns of prayer are so truly expressive; and the same may be said of the confessions of sin, and felt unprofitableness also. If you can think of a verse of a hymn or of a Psalm that expresses your heart's pulsation for the Lord's kind help, or mercy, or forgiveness, or eternal salvation, endeavour to think of such words, and seek to plead them in your mind, if you cannot express them with your voice or lips. I have read of one whose 'lips moved.'

Being a soldier of our king, you must of necessity be in the company of your fellows a great deal, but a kind God sees the motion of the lips and fully reads the inmost wishes of the heart. I hope you may not forget the merciful attention that is paid to those who wish that they could really pray for mercy, and for every needed blessing. It is a mercy for such poor sinners as we are that God is watchful; he always sees when good cometh from contrite and broken hearts. A sigh for mercy through Christ is worth having; it is a valuable thing, and there may be more prayer in that than in a multitude of vain words.

Do you remember the following words: 'From

heaven did the LORD behold the earth; to hear the groaning of the prisoners; to loose those that are appointed to death.' They are very encouraging, they express great divine goodness, mercy, grace and compassion, also condescension, and who is like unto the Lord God, who condescendeth to behold the things that are in the heavens and the earth?

God has ever been propitious to the sighs and groans of pour sinners who have realised their need of his gracious hand, help, pardon and power. If you are enabled to seek him for the good things that your condition and circumstances may require, there is no doubt but that you will have cause to praise him as the one who has been gracious to your heart's longings, for his gracious, merciful and necessary help. And he really is our chief necessity, for after all, what is man in comparison?

All that is necessary for our salvation is in the Lord, and with him all things are possible. He can give you all the wisdom you need, refuge, defence, success, support; deliverance and victory are all with him.

If you have him, you have all you need, wherever you may be called to go, whatever you may be brought into. He can lift up a sinking head, as well as compose a disquieted heart. 'If thou seek him, he will be found of thee.' 'Call upon me in the day of trouble: I will deliver thee, and thou shalt glorify me.' He can defend in all places, and make the needful way.

Your reward of two stripes is cheering; we do not know what may yet await you in the way of promotion. Look on high, especially if you are discouraged, cast down, feeling too bad for divine mercy.

See, here an endless ocean flows
Of never-failing grace;
Behold, a dying Saviour's veins,
The sacred flood increase![879]

May you be preserved in all places and at all times.
With united love to you and yours,
I remain, dear Herbert,
Yours affectionately,
Henry Bradford,
Eastbourne.
January 18th, 1916.[880]

Robert Brooker, pastor at Hastings

Mr Brooker was pastor at Ebenezer Chapel. Hastings, for 25 years, until his death in 1938.[881] His son, E. A. Brooker, was sent out to preach shortly before the end of the war, on 2nd June, 1918. E. A Brooker later held pastorates at Burgess Hill and Rehoboth Chapel, Tunbridge Wells.[882]

✍ Dear Friend,

It was kind of you to write; please feel free to do so any time. I have been glad to see you and other of your comrades at our Ebenezer, and am encouraged to hear that you have been helped at the services. May the Lord, who I feel has given you a real concern for the things of eternity, and a longing for a saving knowledge of Christ, make and keep you a humble suppliant at his dear feet. May his kindness to you be such that the exercise of your soul shall give him no rest until Christ be formed in your heart the hope of glory.

It is a mercy that he is seekable, and his own gracious promise is: 'Him that cometh to me,' thirsting, panting, desiring mercy, 'I will in no wise cast out.' That sweet hymn you mentioned, 'Emptied of earth I fain would be,' etc.[883] ... and which, I am pleased to hear, is still your desire, led me back many years. I used to rise soon after five o'clock in the morning, winter and summer, so that I could have my quiet read and prayer before I entered upon the business of the day. On a particular morning I was favoured to get near the Lord in prayer. (O how sweet that is! O that I more often were thus favoured!) When I arose from my knees, I opened the hymn book and my eyes fell upon the words: 'Emptied of earth I fain would be,' etc. The whole hymn was made so sweet; I have never forgotten it; it expressed the heartfelt desire of my soul. May the Lord be pleased to keep in lively exercise this desire in your heart and mine ...

I fear your surroundings are far from pleasant and have a tendency to rob you of that desire and feeling you love. May the Lord help you to be much in mental prayer.

> He understands a sigh divine,
> And marks a secret groan.[884]

May he shield you in time of danger, and preserve you in the hour of temptation. I am enclosing you a little Book of Psalms, which I pray may be made a comfort to you. Wishing you all good for time and eternity.

Believe me,
Your sincere friend,
Robert Brooker,
Hastings.
1915.[885]

Robert Brooker

Edward Carr, pastor at Bath

Mr Edward Carr knew something of the pain of war. When he wrote this letter, one son serving in the forces had been missing for several months. Concerning this,

Mr Carr said, "The suspense seems to be wearing out our hearts and lives." Another of his sons had already been killed, leaving a widow and two fatherless children.[886]

Edward Carr

✍ My dear C – ,

... Glad to hear you had been helped on in a spiritual sense. E— tells me you are desiring to hear from me again. I am so sorry to hear you are in such a foul atmosphere. It isn't at all for your spiritual health, is it? I thought of your words to me when I last saw you, *viz,* that you 'could never be anywhere where the Lord could not be with you.' He has said, 'Lo, I am with you alway, even unto the end.' (Matthew 28: 20) Oh! what a mercy. Though you cannot always feel his presence, yet he never leaves you; else, where would you have gone to long before this? We have a wicked heart that will take the devil's part, but there is a stronger than he that keeps the palace; 'He must reign, till he has put all enemies under his feet.' Till then there is the warfare between the flesh and the spirit, and we need to be clad in the whole armour of God, that we may be able to stand against the wiles of the devil and his fiery darts. You prove the dear Saviour's words true every day, I know, *viz.,* 'In the world ye shall have tribulation;' and, 'Without me ye can do nothing.' But what a mercy there is the bright side to the cloud: 'Be of good cheer; I have overcome the world;' and, 'That in me ye might have peace.'

Peace by his cross has Jesus made;
The church's everlasting Head
O'er hell and sin has victory won,
And, with a shout, to glory gone.[887]

As sure as the great Head of the church has won the victory, so sure shall all his dear people go, because they are united to him in ties of blood –

'Twixt Jesus and the chosen race,
Subsists a bond of sovereign grace,
That hell, with its infernal train,
Shall ne'er dissolve nor rend in twain.[888]

It was made very sweet to me some time ago. Read it, dear C—, and may the Lord make it just as precious to you. That sacred bond that it speaks of is so sweet. What a firm foundation for the saints to build their hopes upon. Oh! if it rested with us, our religion would be swept all away; as soon as the winds blew and the floods came, the foundation would soon be gone. But O, what a mercy, if we are in him, not all the powers of earth or hell will ever shake us off that solid Rock.

What a mercy to be brought up out of the horrible pit and miry clay and to have our feet placed upon that solid rock, Christ Jesus! The Lord has taught *you* that there is no help in yourself; all your self-righteousness is as filthy rags, and you have no hope in anything you can do, and can truly say,

> My hope is built on nothing less
> Than Jesus' blood and righteousness;
> I dare not trust the sweetest frame,
> But wholly lean on Jesus' name.[889]

This is a blessed place to be brought to. May the Lord enable you to rejoice in what he has done for you. The pathway is very rough for you, I know; you need the shoes of 'iron and brass.' May he keep you very near to him; keep you from sin, that it may not grieve you. We read of Lot, how the filthy conversation of the wicked vexed his righteous soul from day to day. May you feel the force of the apostle's words, *viz.,* 'What hast *thou* that thou didst not receive?' (1 Corinthians 4: 7); and while you hate their filthy talk and abominate their doings, may it lead you to adore that grace that has made you to differ, and may you have the spirit of prayer given you to plead with the Lord for them, that he would open their blind eyes and bring them to see themselves in the light of God's holy Word. May your life be an influence for good, that they may see what a difference there is between them and you. May he cheer and comfort your heart. He has said, 'As one whom his mother comforteth, so will I comfort you' (Isaiah 66: 13); 'Let not your heart be troubled, neither let it be afraid.' When he speaks these words home by his Holy Spirit, 'tis then his poor fearful child can take comfort. It must be sent home with divine power. How afraid we are when we look at ourselves, we have no strength, but the psalmist said, 'I will lift up mine eyes unto the hills, from whence cometh my help. My help cometh from the LORD,' etc. (121: 1-2) May you realize his help and strength daily and hourly.

I expect E— has told you of our good Sundays at the chapel, and of a prospect of the Lord bringing some of his dear people out. I must close now, my best love to you.

Your loving friend,
Edward Carr.[890]

James K. Popham, pastor at Brighton

This letter was written to the three Banfield brothers, Arthur Joseph (1892-1965?), Marcus Ebenezer (1894-1918) and Herbert Pitt (1895-1992), when they joined the army. Arthur and Herbert were spared during the war and returned home. Marcus, whose war diary is included in this book (see page 125), died of wounds on 26th April 1918, aged 24. For an account of Herbert's war experiences see page 165.[891]

James K. Popham

[1]

✍ My dear Boys,

Ere you leave home, let me say farewell. God be with you all. You have had in your home exceptional mercies and advantages in the love, prayers, and example of your father and mother. Keep all those blessings in your minds, before your eyes.

Now, for the first time, you are to meet and live in the midst of another sort of life and atmosphere. May you be preserved. If sinners entice you, consent not. You have read all your lives your Bibles; do not give up the good habit. But you may meet with much discouragement; pray for strength to persevere in the good practice. You will hear language you have never heard in your home; God keep you from becoming accustomed to it; flee from it whenever possible. You will be asked of what religion you are; may you be enabled to say exactly. 'Them that honour me I will honour.' Few opportunities for private reading and prayer will be found. Seek in all ways the Lord. Be it given you to pray; 'Those that seek … shall find.' Seek the all-covering wings of Christ, his most precious blood. Your new life will bring to light many weaknesses in your characters, but also make room for the mighty God of Jacob as your help. Oh, how happy you will be to find him so. 'Happy is he that hath the God of Jacob for his help.'

Farewell, dear boys, for a time, only for a time I hope. The all-surrounding, protecting, and supporting God be your portion, and Christ in you all the hope of glory.

So prays your affectionate friend,
J. K. Popham,
Normandien, Surrenden Road, Brighton.[892]

[2]

The following letter was written by Mr Popham on behalf of the church at Galeed Chapel, Brighton, to all the young men from 'Gospel Standard' churches who were serving in the forces:

✍ To the young men belonging to the 'Gospel Standard' denomination, who have so nobly gone forth to fight for their country, the church worshipping at Galeed, Brighton, sends all good wishes.

Dear young Friends,

We desire to send you a word through the magazine belonging to our churches. Our admiration of your courage and self-denial in leaving home and all its comforts for the hardships and risks of the battlefield, and our gratitude to you for so doing, would not be easily expressed.

But chiefly we desire to let you know we do not forget you when we get access to the throne of God's heavenly grace in private, nor in our public worship. You are missed from our congregations, and we earnestly long for the day when you will, by God's mercy, take your places there again. In your present circumstances you are brought face to face with death. Naturally this may cause some serious reflections and touch you deeply. But the teaching you have been accustomed to may have been, to most of you, sufficient to impress upon you the sacred fact that only the gracious work of God the Holy Ghost in your hearts can produce in you a right knowledge of sin and of your ruined state in the law, and bring forth a prayer for mercy; and also that that blessed Spirit alone can impart to you the knowledge of salvation by the remission of your sins (Luke 1: 77). And that you may be the subjects of that gracious work is our prayer.

We know there are some among you who fear God, and some are members of our churches. Into your hearts may the Lord pour abundant consolation by Jesus Christ, give you to realize that you dwell in the secret place of the Most High, and are abiding under the shadow of the Almighty, and that therefore no plague, no death, can come nigh your dwelling (Psalm 91).

We pray that the all-protecting hand of God may be the covering of each and all of you in each battle, in each hour of danger.

We, now assembled, send this word to you from our hearts.

On behalf of the church,

J. K. Popham (Pastor),

Brighton.

April 25th, 1918.[893]

The following is one of the replies that was received from a serving soldier, in response to the foregoing letter:

✍ To dear Mr Popham and the church assembling at Galeed, Brighton:

It was with mingled feelings of gratitude and encouragement that I read your very kind and loving letter to the young men of the Gospel Standard denomination who are now on active service overseas. I do hope that a feeling of gratitude was felt, in that the Lord has still a praying people at home, who do not forget us when coming before the throne of grace, and I am sure we feel to need much their prayers and to be remembered before the Lord God of heaven, as 'the effectual fervent prayer of a righteous man availeth much.' It has been often a means of encouragement that this is the case, and I did feel once again this encouragement in reading your letter to us, and thus I earnestly pray the Lord will graciously grant answers to your petitions on our behalf. Oh! that the day may not be far distant when your hearts, and ours also, may be gladdened, if the

Lord will, by our again taking our places amongst you. For it is a great trial to be deprived of this great mercy.

I, for one, hope that there is an echo in my poor heart to your prayer that we may be made the subjects of the Holy Spirit's work, that we may be shown our lost and ruined condition by nature, and be brought to confess our sin and shame, and led to see that our only hope of salvation is in the great redeeming work of the Lord Jesus Christ. May the solemn surroundings of our daily life cause us to cry earnestly that our minds may be impressed thereby, and we kept ever watching unto 'all prayer and supplication,' for we none of us 'know neither the day nor the hour wherein the Son of man cometh.' Oh! that we may be ready, that we may be prepared to meet him, and that we may enjoy the experience of being hid in Christ with God, and in our moments of danger feel that 'underneath are the everlasting arms,' and thus,

> Not a single shaft can hit
> Till the God of love sees fit.[894]

I desire, before I conclude, to acknowledge the Lord's goodness and mercy that he has caused to pass before me in this life. Oh! how good, how longsuffering is his mercy, and the writer how unworthy, how vile and sinful. I can feel with the hymn writer in the words:

> Indulgent God, how kind
> Are all thy ways to me.[895]

Oh! for a heart filled with love, praise and gratitude to the Lord for all he has done for us young men! I cannot (and doubt if ever I shall be able to) express fully what he has done, or ever be truly thankful, but such as I feel, may it be acceptable in his sight through the Lord Jesus.

In conclusion, dear Mr Popham, I pray that the Holy Ghost may unfold to you the great mysteries of the gospel of Jesus Christ, and that in your labour you may be granted all needed strength and wisdom, and find you have not laboured in vain, in that the hearts and minds of the hearers may be opened to hear and receive the word spoken, and the church of God blessed and encouraged. May the Lord also raise up more young people to the glory of his great name, and many sinners be brought into his fold by the power of the Holy Ghost.

May he grant unto you the peace and love of the Lord Jesus which 'passeth all understanding,' and grant that his blessing may rest upon and abide with you through your pilgrim journey here below, for his great name's sake.

I have felt constrained to write for some time past, and I hope it is out of love to the Lord and his people, and I do hope you will not think me too forward in thus writing, who feel the most unworthy, and I trust I write feelingly from my heart. Thus desiring ever to remain, your friend in Christian love and affection,

Private B. Jenkins.[896]

Henry T. Stonelake, pastor at Nottingham

The following is a copy of a letter sent by Mr Henry T. Stonelake, pastor of Chaucer Street Chapel,

Nottingham, to 15 young men connected with the congregation there. Others would join up subsequent to the letter being written, and in all 23 men from the congregation served in the war.

Henry T. Stonelake

[1]

✍ Dear Friend,

Feeling a deep interest in your temporal and spiritual welfare is the motive which prompts me at this season of the year to send you these few lines.

The hazardous duties which you have been called upon to undertake on behalf of your king and country expose you to many great and terrible dangers, and I should be lacking every sense of pastoral feeling and affection were I indifferent to the trials and anxieties which you must necessarily suffer, as a soldier in His Majesty's army.

I am sure you will be glad to know that much real sympathy is felt by the members of the church and congregation at Chaucer Street for you, and for all the other young men who have met with us in the past, and who are now serving with the colours. You are not forgotten by us when we meet together at the throne of grace to worship the Triune Jehovah, and without doubt the prayers of God's people have been heard and answered. Some have had most remarkable deliverances from the jaws of death. I know of several instances of God's miraculous interposition or providence manifested to one and another of my young friends. The Lord has in much mercy preserved and protected them, while many of their comrades have been cut down, and I now thankfully record the fact that, up to the time of writing, I have not heard of the death of any among our number. May we not truly say, 'What hath God wrought!'

I trust that the same kind and gracious hand which has thus far upheld and shielded you in the hour of danger, or in the heat of battle, will still protect and keep you in days yet to come.

I hope you have already felt the truth of the hymn so often sung by us at chapel,

> Not a single shaft can hit,
> Till the God of love sees fit.[897]

It may appear strange to some that he who holds the waters in the hollow of his hand should permit this awful war to continue, bringing with it such untold misery, and such vast destruction to human life. If we consider, however, the solemn and sad fact that very many of our fellow countrymen have, for a long period past, openly despised and defied their Creator, wilfully turning their backs upon him and upon his holy laws, disregarding his holy day, and saying: 'Who is the LORD that I should obey him?' it is a wonder that his indignation against us was not displayed long since. He has declared, 'Them that honour me I will honour, and they that despise me shall be lightly esteemed' (1 Samuel 2: 30). These words not only apply to individuals, but to nations and kingdoms likewise; 'For the nation and kingdom that will not serve thee shall perish; yea, those nations shall be utterly wasted' (Isaiah 60: 12).

As lovers of our land and nation we would ever pray for its peace and prosperity, for God has greatly favoured us in the past. We have had an open Bible, and many great and godly men have been raised up in our midst, men who have broken to us the bread of life.

I trust the Holy Spirit of God may give to you a desire to make the Word of God 'a lamp unto your feet, and a light unto your path.' Life with us all is short. A never-ending eternity is open before us. Let us then ask the important question:

Am I ready to meet God?
Am I made a real Christian,
Washed in the Redeemer's blood? etc.[898]

Remember, the promise reads, 'Seek, and ye shall find; knock, and it shall be opened unto you.' May we be found among the people 'that sigh and that cry for all the abominations that be done.' Such received God's mark of grace in their foreheads in the days of Ezekiel; and such the Lord will mercifully regard in this our evil day.

May we as a nation yet look to him against whom we have so greatly sinned for deliverance from our enemies, instead of looking so much to the creature and to creature things. God's heavy rod is upon us; but many times in the past history of our nation he has stretched forth his arm for our defence in answer to his people's prayers; and our eyes are up unto him, that he will be very gracious to us in this our time of need.

You are no longer able to hear my voice at Chaucer Street, but you are often in my thoughts, and my desire and prayer for you is that your present trials may be graciously overruled by the Holy Spirit of God to your soul's eternal profit. Then every trial will work for your good, and you will be able to say: 'It is well.'

Kindly accept this letter and enclosed card as a token of the sympathetic interest which I shall ever feel towards you, and I would praise the Lord for his wonderful mercy vouchsafed to you thus far. The Lord bless thee, and keep thee from all evil, shield and cover thee in the day of battle, strengthen thee day by day, and watch over thee night by night, sustain thee under all thy burdens, and ultimately bring thee home to thy relatives and friends in peace and safety, is the desire of,

Your affectionate friend and well-wisher,
H. T. Stonelake,
63 Gregory Boulevard, Nottingham.
December 12th, 1915.[899]

[2]

The following letter was sent to 22 men from the Nottingham congregation by Mr Stonelake, their pastor. There had been one death among the young men from the congregation who had joined up. Mr Stonelake commented that they were "not without hope that it is well with him, for I trust we have good reason to believe that he feared the Lord."[900]

✍ Dear Friend,

On behalf of the teachers, scholars and friends of Chaucer Street Chapel Sabbath School, I write to say that at our teachers' meeting it was unanimously resolved, 'That we send to our young friends now in His Majesty's army this small token, as evidence that you are not forgotten by us here in Nottingham.'

We hope that you are in good health and able to discharge with satisfaction the duties required of you in your present position.

The nations of Europe, including our own, are still engaged in a fearful war. Great and terrible is the conflict now raging in different parts of the world, and how it will end we know not; but this we *do* know, that 'The powers that be are ordained of God,' and under his divine control (Romans 13: 1). He can and will dispose of them as he sees fit, for 'all the inhabitants of the earth are reputed as nothing: and he doeth according to his will in the army of heaven, and among the inhabitants of the earth: and none can stay his hand, or say unto him, What doest thou?' (Daniel 4: 35).

When we consider the solemn events now taking place it becomes us to bow low before the Lord and say, in the language of the psalmist, 'He hath not dealt with us after our sins; nor rewarded us according to our iniquities' (Psalm 103: 10). Our country has not been invaded, our homes are continued to us, we are still supplied with food to eat and raiment to wear. How kind and merciful God has been to us in these matters. How good he has been to you, exposed as many of you have been to storms of shot and shell. Many of you have been in the midst of suffering and death, yet your lives have been preserved. Some of you have been sick and some have been wounded. How great has been his mercy to you who have been restored to health and strength; and to you also who have been hitherto preserved from injury and sickness. How wonderfully has God shielded you all in times of the greatest danger, as I well know from what I have heard from the lips of several of our young men.

This letter will undoubtedly reach some who have not yet been exposed to the painful trials and privations of actual warfare. May the Lord be your protector and keeper in whatever path he may call upon you to walk, and may you also prove that he hears and answers prayer, as several of your companions have already had proof. Many trials may be before you all; but, 'The LORD is good, a strong hold in the day of trouble; and he knoweth them that trust in him' (Nahum 1: 7). The Lord direct you to look to this strong hold, whether it be relating to the things of this life, or to the things of that life which is to come.

Few seem to know what it is to be in soul trouble; but if any among you should be in such a state, let me

Chaucer Street Chapel, Nottingham

remind you that 'whosoever shall call upon the name of the Lord shall be saved.' God's ear is ever open, for 'he will regard the prayer of the destitute, and not despise their prayer.' Look at the gracious invitation he gives to all such, 'Come unto me, all ye that labour and are heavy laden, and I will give you rest, etc.' (Matthew 11: 28).

> The vilest sinner out of hell,
> Who lives to feel his need,
> Is welcome to a throne of grace,
> The Saviour's blood to plead.[901]

How thankful we shall all be should it please the Lord to put forth his almighty power and cause this awful slaughter to cease; yet we must not overlook the fact that what he is now permitting to take place is but bringing about his own eternal purposes, both as regards the world and his Church, and that 'all things work together for good to them that love God, to them who are the called according to his purpose' (Romans 8: 28).

Much confusion of thought may possibly exist in our minds concerning the war, but it is not so with God. He knows all things from the beginning, and,

> He sits on no precarious throne,
> Nor borrows leave TO BE.[902]

Those who trust in him will not be confounded; may he enable us to rest here.

The clouds hanging over the nation are very heavy, and darkness covers the earth at the present time, 'and gross spiritual darkness the people,' but a brighter and better day is yet in store for the Church and the world, when 'they shall beat their swords into

George Ward (right), who was later pastor at Horsham, with his two brothers, Bert and Frank (sitting)

With many men, including several ministers, the only record we have of their service are photos such as this one.

plowshares, and their spears into pruninghooks: nation shall not lift up sword against nation, neither shall they learn war any more' (Isaiah 2: 4).

Let me remind you that your friends here do not forget you in their prayers. May the Holy Spirit teach and help you to pray for yourselves. May he make his Word your constant companion, and if he should graciously apply it to your hearts, it will be 'a lamp unto your feet, and a light unto your path.' It will be food to your soul, give comfort in distress, support in sickness, relief in pain and joy in sorrow.

May the Lord be with you in all your future steps, and grant you an interest in that everlasting favour that he bears to his people. We hope the time will soon come when we shall once more see you in our midst, and have the pleasure of welcoming you home again.

All our friends unite with me in wishing you every needful mercy and blessing, both for body and soul.

Your sincere friend,

H. T. Stonelake,

63, Gregory Boulevard, Nottingham.

June 20th, 1916.[903]

Letters about the home front

Alfred Dye, Rowley Regis

The following letter, written by Mr Alfred Dye, describes the bombing of the Midlands during the Zeppelin raid of 31st January, 1916. Nine airships were involved, intending to target Liverpool, but misnavigation meant that none of them reached Liverpool. They instead mistakenly dropped their bombs on random settlements in the Midlands.

Alfred Dye

✍ Dear Friend,

You are, of course, aware through the press, that we had a visit of the German Zeppelins. On January 31st we were holding our usual Monday night prayer meeting, when, about eight o'clock, as one of our friends was engaging, there was a heavy thud, then another, and another; indeed *many*. Our female friends soon began to show great nervousness, and of course I had to close the meeting ... There being several stone quarries near us, and being used to the blasting of the rocks, forgetting for the moment it was *dark* and the sounds could not be from the *quarries,* we did not at once realize the fact of falling bombs. Many bombs fell not very far from us; and flashlights also were seen, and the fire engine signals were given. We consulted then as to going to bed, and after I had tried to pray, we retired. But at midnight or just after they came again, and many very heavy bombs fell, shaking us; so we all hurriedly dressed and came downstairs. I advised them to light a fire and warm them. Having been very poorly myself for some time, I got into bed again.

There is what is called the Colliery about 60 or 70 yards from us, and the banksman declared next day that a huge machine hovered over this and our house and chapel. It seemed as if the occupants had lost their bearings, so hesitated, and suddenly it turned southwards. I have thought since that, unworthy as I am, as a poor, weak, erring mortal, it may be the great Jehovah Jesus heard my poor cries upon my bed, so caused the managers of the Zeppelin to suddenly turn away from us.

Another remarkable thing is, there are friends of God's truth about two miles off, members at —, and though (some say 13) bombs fell one after another *near* them, not one of them *burst.*

We have, as we hope, *grace,* and a well-founded

hope, so that we have not much trouble with the fear of death, it having lost its sting in our conscience many years ago; but these raids show us that we are but men, and that nature is very fearful and weak, and if we 'can do all things,' it is, as Paul saith, 'through Christ which strengtheneth us.'

Yes, *that* is the *point;* and with his most gracious presence, not a million Zeppelins, nor the removal of the earth, nor thc huge mountains being carried into the sea could make us fear; as the church saith in Psalm 46. Some words from dear Anne Steele's hymn were a comforting whisper in my soul,

> This only can my fears control,
> And bid my sorrows fly;
> What harm can ever reach my soul
> Beneath my Father's eye?[904]

Beautiful words, *unapplied* even, but *heavenly* words when the blessed Spirit applies them in a poor weak trembling heart. We have slept fairly comfortably since, but unless the Lord assures us, we, knowing not when the Huns may pay us another visit, are kept in fear. There are large munition works all around us, which, if exploded, one of them might ruin every building for miles around; yet, though they flew *over* them, not one bomb dropped on them, or near enough to do harm. Oh the mercy of a gracious God!

A young man, a *stranger* to me, walked to my gate with me. He told me his name, and that he used to work in the colliery here when he had his leg broken, and he said, 'I often think of what I heard you say at a funeral in your chapel. You said, 'If people did not pray when in trouble or afflicted, they were *dead* in soul to God,' and I believe you now, as I did then; and if this war don't make people think and try and pray, they are as you said, '*dead.*' I was pleased to hear this.

May God help us to pray, and may he have mercy upon England and crush the cruel Hun in his own time.

Alfred Dye.[905]

Henry Haddow

J. Illingworth

Written to Mr Henry Haddow, pastor at Brockham Green, Surrey, and Secretary of the Gospel Standard Societies. We know nothing about the author.

✍ My dear Friend,

It has been on my mind to write to you ... It does

astonish me why the Lord should take notice of me. It humbles me in the dust before him, and my daily prayer is to be kept from bringing any disgrace upon his holy name. But, good news, he 'is able to keep me from falling;' so all the honour and praise is due to him. But I want to tell you that the explosion took place not more than a mile from my little cottage; and I am very pleased to tell you that, while a very many had all their windows blown out and all their furniture broken into matches,[906] and had nowhere to sleep but in the open air all night, all the damage I had was my gas mantle broken and my milk so covered with dust that it could not be used. Of course I got a shaking, but I am no worse for it. O, it was a terrible sight to see and hear. The terrific explosions one after another. O, how the glass cracked and flew in all directions near my own door. O, what havoc it made a little lower down than my little cot; hundreds of houses not fit to live in; and the flames, fed as they were by the extreme combustible material with which the place abounded. If the children had not been on their holiday the loss of life would have been fearful, for the school is a complete wreck; and if it had taken place in the night it would have been fearful indeed, for hundreds would have been smothered in their beds. But it took place about 2.30 in daylight, so the people had time to flee, leaving the dough in their bowls and the bread in the ovens ...

Well, in the afternoon, the people were all ordered to leave their homes and go into a park or some other out-of-the-way place, as they were expecting a large gasometer[907] to explode, which it did. But I did not get to know, so I stayed in my little palace, with these words uppermost in my mind,

Plagues and deaths around me fly;
Till he bids, I cannot die;
Not a single shaft can hit,
Till the God of love sees fit.[908]

O, my brother, in looking back and taking a review of the circumstances attending this most exciting scene, with instant death staring me in the face, and that by explosion or fire, what surprises me most of all is the perfect coolness, peace, calmness and self-possession which were given unto me; for I felt that had the Lord there and then told me that that was both the time and the way of his calling me to my 'country house' above, I could then have really, truly, and cheerfully said, 'Thy will be done!' Now, I do not ascribe this to self; no, not in the least, for it was the Lord alone who was pleased to give unto me that calmness and peacefulness which I then felt in my poor soul. And it has left a blessed savour upon my heart; and I have been given to see by this one thing more clear than I ever saw before, that as far as human prudence and foresight reaches, our God looks that we should take care of ourselves, and if we will not, he suffers us to reap the fruits of our own folly. But, good news again, when we can't take care of ourselves, and that is just how I felt at that time, we have reason to hope and expect that he will take care of us.

They came round again about 6.15 and told us all to get out of our homes into the open air; they feared an underground explosion which would blow all the district up if it came. But it did not explode, as it was flooded with water. I shall not forget the sight of seeing the young and old, sick and lame taken out of their beds. Some had to be carried in chairs. O, what a sight! ... But believe me when I tell you that I did not feel half so comfortable, content, happy and peaceful in the park as I did in my one-roomed cot! For I was 'a sparrow alone,' and I could not help the words bubbling up within, and I did not want to, for they were sweet, grand and nice under the circumstances, for they came in a way of question, 'Is there a greater God in the park than in thy little cot?' And I at once said, 'No, Lord!' So I turned myself round and began to hobble back to my home, singing all the way, to the joy and comfort of my soul, and the grief and dismay of Satan:

> There is an over-ruling Providence
> That wisely marshals every circumstance.
> Heaven, air and sea, and this terrestrial ball,
> With their contents, are all at his control.
>
> There's not a particle of dust can fly,
> A sparrow fall, or cloud obscure the sky,
> A moth be crush'd, or leaf fall from a tree,
> But in submission to his wise decree![909]

And when I got back to my little home, where the ravens have brought me and my dear departed wife 'bread and flesh in the morning, and bread and flesh in the evening' for many years, this thought came, though I could still hear explosions going off, 'A good man will not deceive or forsake those who depend upon him; much less a good God.' Then I read Psalm 91, knowing and feeling sure that, since all events are in God's hands, we may leave all our affairs to our Lord to carry us through this world in the way he sees best. For we really felt in this solemn time that his glory and name was at stake, seeing that, by his grace, we had committed ourself into his hands. And we will say, to the honour of his great name, now that he has brought me safely through this terrible affair, while a very many have been taken out of time into eternity, and very many had no homes left to go back to, our God whom we serve, and sometimes glory in serving, is a skilful pilot, and his skill appears best in guiding our little frail bark among the rocks and shoals. Well might one of old say, 'LORD! what is man?' for this is what I felt at that exciting time, and still feel and find by daily experience. I had not been back long before my two sons came up, so we locked the place up and they took me to one of their homes ... When I got back to my dear little cot I found all safe and sound, and I could really and feelingly say,

> A Sovereign Protector I have,
> Unseen, yet for ever at hand.[910]

Perhaps you have plenty of troubles, sorrows and cares of your own, without me burdening you with mine, therefore I have been hesitating whether to tell you. Well, if my little palace was not blown down by the terrible explosions, it has got such a shaking from another quarter that, if a greater than man does not interfere, it will cease to be called 'Hope Cottage.' So you will see I am proving the words of John Bunyan,

> A Christian man is seldom long at ease,
> When one trouble's o'er another doth him seize.[911]

But let me tell you, sometimes I have so much faith given, and a good hope, that I can sometimes sing amidst all crooks in my lot and the cross things taking place down here,

> What though I can't his goings see,
> Nor all his footsteps find?
> Too wise to be mistaken, he,
> Too good to be unkind.[912]

But there are times when I am 'Joseph full-of-fear;' and I have learned another lesson by this I thought I had learned before, but I see I had not. I have been given to see very clearly that there is nothing so casual and uncertain so as to be exempted from the disposal of providence. O, is there anything more casual than a lot? And yet the wise man tells us, 'The lot is cast into the lap; but the whole disposing thereof is of the LORD' (Proverbs 16: 33). The Lord help us not to content ourselves with a general belief of God's governing the world; no, no! Whatever our state and condition here below, and when or wherever we have to flit or move our tent, or whatever good or evil comes upon us, may we be so favoured and blessed to receive all as coming from the Lord. So, if we be poor, and have our furniture put into the street, O, to be enabled to say with the God-man: 'The foxes have holes,' etc., or with good Eli, 'It is the Lord; let him' etc. ...

Well, our landlord gave me a month's notice to get out, although he promised that he would never disturb us. But I did not say a single word to him. These words came and stopped me, 'Be still, and know that I am God.' 'I will work, and who shall let it?' All I can do in the matter is to look on, like Manoah and his wife, and let the Lord work ... When we came to L— he told us to 'tarry at the brook until it was dried up,' and believe me when I say that when it is dried up, there is another ready for me, only I don't know where; but my dear Lord and Master does, and that is good ground for faith to rest upon, and I will let you know at once where it is, etc ...

Yours,

J. Illingworth.[913]

S. Spaldon, West Hartlepool

The following letter was written to Mr and Mrs Hugo Gruber. Mr Gruber was the pastor at Rochdale Road Chapel, Manchester. It describes the bombardment of West Hartlepool by the German navy on 16th December, 1914. The German navy literally turned its guns on the town and shelled it from the sea, damaging many buildings, including the town's Baptist chapel, and killing civilians. The bombardment continued until locally based ships of the British navy managed to put to sea and chased the Germans away.

✍ My very dear Friends,

Yours to hand of the 18th December. We desire to thank you, not only for your sympathy, but also for your prayers, for we know the prayers of a righteous man availeth much. I must begin my account with the morning of the 16th of December. Before I left home at 7.30 I asked God's blessing on myself and family, commending them all to his care and keeping, and I do believe he heard my cry, for not a hair of our heads was touched, although I and one of my sons were in the straight firing line. Oh, friends, I shall never forget it! I commenced my business with my men at eight o'clock, only a few minutes after the guns commenced firing. We, thinking it might be our naval men practising, continued work until the shells were flying on all sides of us. I exclaimed, 'Men, the Germans are here!' and that we soon found out to be true, so we took shelter behind a big stack of deals. The shells were coming over our heads five or six at a time. By the wind which we could fccl, and by the way they were coming, we soon found they were making for the West End, and I was troubled about my dear wife and family, but I dare not leave my hiding place. I said, 'Lord, we are all in thy care,' and I felt whatever happened it was he who permitted it.

As soon as the firing stopped a bit I made my way home, and found the youngest lad had conveyed his mother and sisters up near the park where thousands ran, but my eldest daughter only went part of the way. She said, 'I am going to see where my father is – where he is, I will be also.' On my way up I met her; she got hold of my arm, oh, how she did grip it! She seemed so pleased I was still preserved. One shell struck a stack of deals very near us; I wish you could have heard the crack. We jumped off our feet, but the pieces were prevented coming to us by striking another stack, and only a few pieces fell at our feet. We could see the gas works ablaze, also the broken tram wires; we do not know the number killed, but there were so many that they were burying them all day Sunday. The hospitals are full with the injured, some having to be taken away to other places. If the firing had lasted another hour at the speed we got it, there would not have been very much of the town left. Soldiers who are here invalided home say they did not experience anything like it at the front. One might think the clouds were breaking over one's head. One of my sons was at Hartlepool East up a ladder when a shell came close by him and knocked into a little church. He soon came down that ladder though not any the worse; he was facing the sea and could see the ships. I cannot tell you all the sad cases. Several have been killed close to us, but not one of our family was touched.

Hartlepool Baptist Chapel after the bombardment

My dear wife said that verse came to her mind:

> Plagues and deaths around me fly;
> Till he bids I cannot die;

Not a single shaft can hit,
Till the God of love sees fit.[914]

Two British warships were in the dock, also some torpedo boats, but it took them time to get out, having received no warning, for the Germans fired before our men saw them. But as soon as they got sight of our ships they fled off, coward-like. My dear wife has been ill for more than two years with bronchial asthma. She has such bad attacks from about two o'clock to six o'clock nearly every morning, then they pass off. My eldest daughter has taken entire charge of the house the last two years, the younger sister helping her.

My dear wife and family all join me in love to all. May the dear Lord be with and bless you all, for his name's sake, is the desire and prayer of your affectionate friends,

S. & F. Spaldon
10, Sheriff Street, West Hartlepool.
December 19th, 1914.[915]

A further note appeared in *The Christian's Pathway*: "Up to January 16th, the death toll numbered 115. One poor young girl is buried today; she suffered terribly, part of her face and part of her body behind being blown away. There are still more not expected to recover." Modern sources quote the final death toll attributable to this attack, and the simultaneous ones at Scarborough and Whitby, as being 137.

Some of the shells which were fired at Hartlepool

The structural damage done to homes in Hartlepool

A lady weeping outside the ruins of her home, with all her earthly goods packed into a couple of buckets.

War Poetry

War Poetry

The First World War is often associated with the writings of the war poets, the names of Siegfried Sassoon, Wilfred Owen, and Rupert Brooke being among the most famous. The impulse to respond to the war in poetic form was of course much more widely felt. It was a day when everybody wrote poetry, even when they had no gift for it. A number of poems written by Strict Baptists were published in the denominational magazines, either written by soldiers at the front, or by those at home. A selection of this poetry, of varied quality, is included here.

Poems written from the front

The following poems were all written by servicemen. Some of them were penned at the front and sent home to loved ones; for others the time of writing is unknown.

God is Love

Tho' troubles hedge my way about,
Tho' worries fill my soul with doubt,
Tho' darkness seems to blind my eyes,
This glorious knowledge still I prize,
That God is love.

Tho' oft my cup is filled with care,
And tho' I mourn o'er soul's despair,
Tho' sorrows like a river flow,
'Tis joy, a blessed joy, to know
That God is love.

Tho' battles rage and wars are rife,
Tho' all the world is filled with strife,
Tho' nations rise and nations fall,
'Tis plainly written over all
That God is love.

The purpose of his chastening rod
Rests with the counsels of our God;
But every movement does fulfil
His great design, and shows us still
That God is love.

But, oh, my soul desires to see
That Jesus shed his blood for me,
And as my blessed surety stood;
Thus it is truly understood
That God is love.

O may you know this precious truth
And learn to serve him well in youth,
And in the fall of hoary age
This glorious truth shall still engage
That God is love.

Private J. E. Jay,
Royal Army Medical Corps
(aged 19 years).[916]

J. E. Jay

Remember, Lord!

The following verses were composed by Lieutenant J. P. Williams, 5th Battalion, the night before he passed away. He was wounded at Gallipoli during August, 1915; returned to Australia an invalid, and died at home in Victoria, April 1st, 1916.

Lord, thou hast bid thy people come to thee,
To thee we come;
Bless thou our noble sons, across the sea,
Afar from home.
Be thou their guard, their comfort, and their might,
Remember, Lord, Australia's sons tonight.

Gone from the humble cottage in the dell,
From 'home, sweet home!'
Gone from the dear ones, whom they love so well,
To brave the storm;
Gone from the mansion, 'Lead, thou kindly light,'
Remember, Lord, Australia's sons tonight.

Some now are dying, 'tis the cost of war;
Have mercy, Lord!
Wilt thou prepare them ere they 'cross the bar?'
Have mercy, Lord!
Burst thou death's door, by heaven's august light,
Remember, Lord, Australia's sons tonight.

Be thou our refuge in the darkest hour,
Be thou our stay;
Stretch forth thine arm, reveal almighty power
In thine own way;
Thou, who didst still the storm of Galilee,
Speak peace to nations! Reign eternally![917]

At the Front

"At the front" you hear on every hand –
Shells roar and bullets sing;
Yet thoughtless mortals often stand,
Without a thought of *him,*

Who came poor wretched souls to save,
From all the pains of hell;
When death comes over, like a wave,
They lie just where they fell.

Their comrades near just glance at them,
"Poor Joe," and on they trudge;
That's all they think of those who're gone
To face a righteous Judge.

There are a few who think on God,
And to him try to pray
That he would come with power and love,
And take these hearts away;

Change hearts of stone to hearts of flesh,
His wondrous love make known;
To turn these men from ways of sin,
To learn to love his own.

It grieves them sore to see such men,
With not a care in life,
Without thoughts of eternity,
Or any afterlife;

With not a thought. Though death be near,
They rush to meet the foe;
A shell explodes, and down they sink,
In everlasting woe.

The favoured few are far between,
To whom God shows his love;
'Tis by his help that they hold on
And look to him above;

That when this world of sin and woe
No longer they've to rove,
He'll come and bear them up on high,
To endless joys above.

Sometimes a cloud obstructs their view;
And Satan then suggests
They've never known a Saviour's love,
Nor differ from the rest.

A fierce bombardment's starting up,
They feel they cannot die
In such a state; and then to him
They raise their mournful cry.

"Oh Lord! appear for me, and grant,
If it can be thy will,
Just one sure token of thy love
My troubled heart to still."

He hears; and gently to them speaks,
And whispers to their heart,
"Fear not! I'm with thee to the end;
Nor with thee will I part!"

Their hearts o'erflow with joy and love,
They feel all will be well
In life or death, nor can they see
More terror in a shell.

To "Climb the parapet!" they hear
The order passed around.
With Christ at hand they know no fear,
But firmly tread the ground,

Where death in every shape and form,
Presents itself to sight;
For death to them has lost its sting –
Christ is their one delight.

Thus life goes on from day to day,
Now hopes, now fears preside;
But they who put their trust in God,
God will for them provide.

Written by a soldier at Salonika to his sister, in August 1916.[918]

Clinging to Christ

A Soldier's Hymn

(Written chiefly by one returned from the front into hospital)

Clinging, clinging, closer clinging,
To our dying risen Lord,
Who to glory now ascended –
Lives our Advocate above.

There in one all-glorious person,
God the Son and God the Man,
In his people's cause is pleading
His own blood before the throne.

But consider what he suffered,
Struggling in his bloody sweat,
And on Calvary's cross behold him
Suffering in his people's stead.

There we hear him crying, "Father,
Why hast thou forsaken me?"
'Tis the hell he is enduring,
Due, poor soul, to you and me.

Hark! No, hear him cry, "'Tis finished!"
All the dreadful work is done;
Justice satisfied for ever
For the crimes that we have done.

Clinging, clinging, closer clinging,
To the finished work of Christ,
Seek the Spirit's witness, sinner –
This gives title to our bliss.

Oh! to sing his love for ever
In the sacred realms above!
Praise the Father, Son and Spirit,
Who have made us sons of God.

A. J. E., May, 1917.[919]

A Song of Peace

I sit and rest awhile in pensive muse
And cast my glances o'er a placid sea.
The shimmering surface mirrors landship views
Reflecting quiet thoughts of PEACE to me.

My mind would run to Grecian fables too.[920]
With their quaint symbols! who can clash, forsooth?
Beauteous and mystic, old, yet seem anew
E'en though they hold not solid concrete truth.

In vain for PEACE to Bacchus can I turn,
And though fair Flora fragrant odours showers,
Helpless alas! for solid calm I yearn,
E'en from her leafiest, dreamiest rosy bowers.

'Tis found not in the bower or in the chase,
The gift of Midas brings no lasting weal.
The joys of health, of fame, the pride of race,
Still I the sadness of disquiet feel.

I've stood at dawn and seen with mystic eye
How veiled Aurora, drawn by milk-white bay,
In rose-tint chariot flits across the sky,
And with her finger opes the Gates of Day.

Oft in the stilly night I awesome scan
The firmament's bright star-bespangled dome.
Bind Pleiades' sweet influence! Who can?
By whom, Orion's bands shall loose become?

Methought there was a quiet that Morpheus brings,
Which I might spend upon a dreamless bed.
Nay! Even here PEACE, calm, are nameless things.
I find, alas! clandestine fears instead.

I've roamed where creep the clusters on the vine,
Where pomegranates flower with scarlet bud,
Where crimson sunsets flashed with hues sublime,
But passing take peace home in fiery flood!

I lookéd thus for PEACE in sea and earth,
In sky, in health, in wealth, in sounding fame.
I turn away in sadness! All is dearth!
The worldling's peace is but an empty name.

I hoped for nature's peace in this light age.
Instead, I see Bernhardi,[921] Treitschke,[922] blood!
And slaughter writes for me a sorry page,
A world swept o'er by foul ambition's flood.

Truth! I shall reach a calm when battles cease,
And laid aside are armaments of war;

At best I only taste an outward peace;
My soul desires a PEACE more sweet by far.

Oppressed by wars without and wars within,
My guilt-afflicted soul its burden bears.
It fears that penal wrath the wage of sin,
And, weary, longs for freedom from those fears.

There is a PEACE which passes others by,
A PEACE by blood! In covenant promise laid,
Which reigns when earthly, mortal peaces die,
Because 'tis sealed eternally and paid.

Maybe in silent watches of the night,
A still small voice my anxious spirit calms.
And on the field of blood, in murderous fight,
A quiet PEACE steals o'er, and still alarms.

And as Gennesaret's sea lay quick becalmed,
The Prince of PEACE Almighty bids it rest.
So shall the soul, by Satan sore alarmed,
Like John find PEACE upon the Saviour's breast.

My soul would find her rest in pastures green,
And where Love's peaceful rivers gently glide;
On hills where Shiloah's waters flow between,
And there beside the sheltering Rock I'd hide.

Oh! lovely PEACE! Oh! matchless calm! With thee
I'd fain, for ever, seek a tranquil joy.
My weary soul, unfettered, "sans-souci,"[923]
Would taste those sweet delights that never cloy!

No real PEACE, until the soul mounts higher,
Methinks that here 'tis but a transient joy,
Reaching the only Haven of Desire,
The soul, in heavenly PEACE, shall find employ.

The Pilgrim, Salonika, April, 1918.[924]

Samuel Burton and his wife

A poem written to a soldier at the front

The following poem was written by Mr Samuel Burton, who was for many years the faithful and beloved deacon at Rehoboth Chapel, Coventry. They were addressed to his brother-in-law, Henry Herbert Foster, of Luton. In a covering letter to Mr Tryon, the Editor of *The Little Gleaner*, Mr Burton's wife wrote:

> ✍ The enclosed verses written to a dear brother, who is now (should his life be spared) taking part in the great conflict at the Dardanelles, I felt, though addressed to him personally, are suitable to many of our dear young men, who have left comfortable houses and godly parents to do their duty in preserving to us our country and our liberties.
>
> Though we are passing under heavy judgements,

and I feel even they are light to what we, a guilty nation, deserve, I trust it may be a time when many hidden ones, even on the battlefield, may be brought to light. I sometimes believe it will be so.

Lines to a dear Brother Serving his Country

Dear Bert, my thoughts oft wander
To yonder distant land
To which you have been drafted,
And now – in danger stand.

Exposed to many perils,
To sniper, shot and shell,
Death and destruction round you,
Far worse than many tell.

I wonder what your thoughts are,
Which only God can read,
If from your heart there rises
A prayer – the prayer of need.

If in your quiet moments
For mercy you now cry
With faith in the Redeemer,
Who understands a sigh.

And if the fight grows fiercer
If faced by desperate foes,
You'll find a Refuge stronger
Than any worldling knows!

I wonder if the leadings
Of Providence with you
Are to unfold a purpose
Of grace and mercy too.

The Word that never alters
Declares in language plain,
That none can enter heaven
Unless they're born again.

If this should be the period –
Of old known to the Lord –
For your soul to be quicken'd,
And born again of God;

If answers to those prayers
Prayed many years ago,
By one who dearly loved you
Since gone from all below;

Will now receive their answer
From God, who heareth prayer,
And you be manifested
An object of his care;

If in the day of battle
Midst cannon's awful roar,
You're led to seek his favour
Whose mercy's ever sure!

No creature now can help you,
Protect, sustain, defend.
May God almighty help you!
On him alone depend.

Your times are in his hands, Bert,
No harm can come to you
Contrary to his purposes –
I trust he'll bring you through.

He works by means mysterious,
Accomplishes his ends,

And when affliction's needful
He then his mercy sends.

I trust you may be favoured
To cast on him your care,
And should you thus be led, Bert,
He'll not despise your prayer.

And now I would commend you
To God, and to his grace,
And if his holy pleasure,
May we meet – face to face –

As monuments of mercy,
As objects of his love,
To sing on earth his praises,
Then dwell with him above.

S. T. Burton, Coventry, October 12th, 1915.[925]

Poems about the front and the men serving there

The following poems all describe various aspects of the front, and the diversity of the experiences of men serving there. They include a prayer for those serving in the navy and for prisoners of war.

At the Front

In the night, when bullets rattle
And destructions fly,
When our brave men in the trenches
Sad and silent lie,
God, and God only, knows what thoughts are born,
And who of his are saved 'twixt dark and dawn.

Youth and manliness with vigour
Tramp towards the foe,
Willing to be used; but, later,
In the trenches low.
God, and God only, knows how heaven's light
Falls on the by-past life in the dark night.

Danger in the mine beneath them,
Danger overhead;
Whispering to a well-known comrade,
But to find him dead;
God only knoweth then what prayers are worded;
These, in the letters home, are not recorded.

We poor sinners cannot fathom
Mercy's boundless way;
We can only bid our guardians
In the trenches, pray;
For God, God only, knows what way he takes
To seal forgiveness home when conscience wakes.

Through the dark nights godly parents
Clench their hands and pray
For the boys who shunned their teaching
'Ere they went away.
But the Lord only knows how many a son
Flies to his mother's God when day is done.

God be with them in the trenches,
With them on the sea,
Breathe confusion on the Kaiser
Where the battles be.

And when the night is dark and foes abound,
Jehovah with his hosts our boys surround.

M. A. Chaplin.[926]

M. A. Chaplin

The Christian Soldier's Prayer

Far from my home and all I love,
I lift my heart to God above;
Protect my loved ones is my prayer,
Lord, I commit them to thy care.

Still the same stars watch o'er my head,
Still the same moon lights up my bed;
Still the same God shall be my guide,
For still in him I will confide.

Far, far apart by land or sea,
I pray for them, they pray for me;
And as we humbly seek thy face,
We meet around thy throne of grace.

And when amidst the shot and shell,
The cannon roar, the rage of hell;
Still may I feel that thou art near
To shield my head and banish fear.

A noble courage would I feel
With arms of strength and nerves of steel;
I would espouse the cause of right
Against the evil powers of might.

Lord, what is man when left alone?
How he would spurn thee from thy throne;
But should the tumult still increase,
Oh, keep my soul in perfect peace!

Thou canst preserve on every hand,
Though midst a thousand deaths I stand;
Or shouldst thou will that I must fall –
I come to thee, my God, my all!

S. Adams, Blackheath.[927]

"Right About Turn"

Drill-Sergeant, Colour-Sergeant,
Corporal, have a care;
Though it be an awkward squad
Wherefore should you *swear?*
Can you wonder if the boys
Practise what they learn –
(What some never learned before)
When your backs you turn?
It is such a *useless* sin,
Such a *lowering* thing
In the eyes of decent men
About you gathering;
'Tis a *terror* to one lad,
And *disgusts* another,
And is thought of in the prayers
Of a godly mother.
Take my cautions kindly, friends,
Irksome though you find them;
Those who take God's name in vain
Store a curse behind them;
Think how England's safety needs
Jehovah's interference;
And of the swearing he so hates,
Be glad to make a clearance.

M. A. Chaplin, Galleywood, January, 1917.[928]

War!

Oh! dare we let our thoughts a moment rest
Upon the mangled forms of friend and foe,
Nor, shrinking, own the awfulness of sin
Which broods for ever over death and woe?

And such a death! Great God, in mercy stay
This awful carnage spreading o'er the land,
O'er forests vast, o'er cities fair to see,
O'er hill and dale, and seething plains of sand

It bubbles o'er, a cauldron vast of woe –
Seest thou the hearts bereft of those most dear?
Seest thou the forms who wait in patient love?
Hearest thou unuttered prayers and silent tears

For voices hush'e e'en now beneath the sod,
While wolves do howl and carrion ravens croak?
Seest thou the swaying mass of human freight
Fast hurrying onward o'er the storm-tossed main?

Behold the hearts by sorrow rent and dumb,
And hear, O Lord, each cry of human pain.
Ah me! full soon doth break each groaning day,
When moving millions meet in death's embrace.

O! hatred, fear and terror-stricken pain,
And blinding glare lights up each human face
'Mid battle fierce and clam'rous agony,
While famine dwells in each sad lurking-place.

And weary captives watch the passing day
'Ere stars beam coldly on earth's stricken race.
Availing Christ! With thine almighty voice
Bid wars to cease and save us by thy grace.

A. M. Brooke.[929]

Bless the lads

Our Father which in heaven art,
Above all earthly powers,
Wilt thou thy blessing now impart
Unto these lads of ours –

Who, separated from us, stand
To guard our native shores
Against a ruthless foeman's hand;
Lord, bless these lads of ours!

Thou hast been pleased at times to send
Thy blessings down in showers,
Wilt thou now cause them to descend
Upon these lads of ours?

O hear the loving mothers' plea,
As through the anxious hours
Their earnest prayer ascends to thee,
Lord, bless these lads of ours!

In Jesus' name we pray, that when
The front of battle lowers,
Thy presence may be with them then
To shield these lads of ours.

To keep them safe from every scourge
Which life and health devours;
When death's dark billows round them surge,
Lord, save these lads of ours!

And bring them back in peace, that they
May join their songs with ours,
To praise thy name, who to this day
Hast kept these lads of ours.

Keep them through life, and when at last,
Before angelic powers,
Thy people stand by thee confessed,
Lord, bless these lads of ours!

Thomas Heaton, Preston.[930]

A Prayer for our Sailors

God bless our sailors true;
God bless our boys in blue;
If it can be thy will,
Keep them from harm and ill.

Guard them where'er they be,
Fighting o'er land and sea,
Through the night watches drear
Be there to help and cheer.

When with home-sickness they
Yearn through each fearful day,
Soothe thou each aching moan
For father, mother, home.

Midst foe and shot and shell,
Be pleased with them to dwell,
Saviour and Guardian be
In each extremity.

Death lurks in every mine;
Torpedoes through the brine,
Menace both day and night,
These lads so brave and bright.

We sit at home and wait,
Yearning to know their fate;
When news is long delayed,
How soon we grow afraid.

Pardon each wailing cry,
As post by post goes by;
And eyes grow tired and dim,
With anxious fear for *him!*

Jesus, forgive our fears,
Wipe these so human tears:
Did not tears fall from *thee,*
Long since at Bethany

Over thy friend's deep woe?
Even though thou didst *know*
Lazarus should rise again,
Yet, for the sisters' pain,

Thy holy tears did fall
In pity sweet. We call
On thee, the same kind Friend,
To make this warfare end.

Oh! give us back our boys;
And peace with all its joys,
And quench the fiend of war,
For ever – evermore!

Mabel S. Good, Addlestone Moor.[931]

Prayer for Prisoners of War

Thou God of love, to thee we pray
For sons and brothers far away,
Who hear the sentry's watchful round
In prison-camps on hostile ground.

Dispose their foreign guards to shew
Due kindness to a captured foe;
And let the gifts which we impart
Supply their need, and cheer their heart.

And hear us when we ask that he
Who died for men at Calvary
May plead their cause in heaven above
And shew them his redeeming love.

J. P. Wiles.[932]

Crippled!

Our brother has been home again,
And eased our smart;
The same old loving sympathy,
The same dear heart;
But never more th' electric strength,
To man so sweet,
And never more the nimble tread
Of willing feet.

But still, our brother has been home,
And mother smiled;
It seemed just then he was to *her*
Her *only* child;
For, "one was not," and this one seemed
Back from the grave;
And so his longest company
We let her have.

Oh shattered men! and mothers too;
We – yet unstricken –
Mourn for the sorrows which have come,
And those which thicken;
And many a weary watcher turns
Aside to implore
The twenty thousand chariots,
God has in store.

Written o'er all, in capitals,
Is MYSTERY![933]

The patience of creation's Lord,
We cannot see;
But though man tortureth man, and keeps
The world in fright;
We *know* the Judge of all the earth
Is doing *right*.

M. A. Chaplin, Galleywood, January 1918.[934]

Amputees from the war

From every Mother to any Wounded Soldier

Where'er I go I always see
Some lad who's shed his blood for me,
To whom my heart impulsively
Cries, "Thank you!"

"O, thank you that you've borne for me
Those wounds that caused such agony;"
O, soldier-boy, most tenderly
I "thank you!"

For all those hours of cruel dread,
Among the dying and the dead,
Where blood like water has been shed,
I "thank you!"

For all the terrors of the trench –
The horrid dead and dying stench,
The sudden fear you could not quench –
O, "thank you!"

But for thy grand, heroic deed,
Our country now would lie and bleed,
A broken, Hun-polluted reed –
So "thank you!"

And God be thanked for all the skill,
Courage, endurance, strength and will,
He gave thee, laddie; O, I still
Must "thank you!"

And though long years of pain may be,
Dear soldier-boy, in store for thee,
A thousand hearts shall pray for thee,
And "thank you!"

O, tenderly with thee we'll deal;
Our tears thy sufferings shall seal,
While wives and mothers plead thy weal,
And "thank you!"

Let England blush if she forget
Thy sacrifice and painful sweat,
Or fails to pay the monstrous debt
She owes you!

And may the God who hateth war
Be pleased in mercy to restore
Peace to our land, and evermore
Repose you!

Mabel S. Good, Addlestone Moor.[935]

Poems about parents at home

The following poems concern the anxieties and cares of the parents of the men serving at the front.

"Pray for me Father!"

"*Pray for me, father!*" 'Twas the lad's request
At parting, and while stepping in the train;
Then something, like a swelling in my breast,
Responsive rose, moist'ning my cheeks like rain.

And then, as iron steed drew on away
Beyond my sight, bedimmed by flowing tears,
I felt in sweet affection *power* to pray
God would him bless, and take away all fears.

And thus I staggered home without my son;
Nay, *with* him in my very soul as *mine* –
Then, thanking God for giving such an one,
I begged our Jesus might upon him shine.

Might mercif'ly preserve his life, and bring
Him home again, to loved ones all, and where
Some humble souls preserving mercy sing,
And listen to the sacred gospel cheer.

His king and country called him, and he's gone,
As very many thousands have before;
And though I've felt that fact, *this is my son,*
Now gone to join the forces for the war!

This all the difference makes, 'tis grief at home,
Compared with what takes place so far abroad;
And oh! the grief – should Britain meet her doom
Beneath proud Germany's most cruel sword?

We fear not this, but illustrating thus,
Observed the difference close relations make;
Another's grief might well be borne by us,
Could we their nature, grace and places take.

Hence, *interest* will assert itself the while;
But O, for grace to bow before God's throne
Beseechingly, till Jesus on us smile,
And help us say – "Father, *thy* will be done!"

Alfred Dye, February 10th, 1917.[936]

The Editor of *The Friendly Companion* added the following comment to this poem when it was originally published in the magazine:

> ✍ Mr Dye writes that he is now *sharer* in the feelings of so many others who have had to part with their sons for the army. The son had the wrench so many others have also had in parting from parents,

wife and two dear children; also, which we sadly fear too many others have *not* felt, leaving *the means of grace.* (see p. 322). He had been baptised with his wife, mother and a sister in 1910, and was also Superintendent of the Sabbath School. Thus Mr Dye has, beyond most, reason for gratitude and joy in his sorrow. 'I never knew I loved him as my son in nature and grace as I did when assured of parting. The last words after kissing him farewell on the platform touched me. They were, "Pray for me, father!"' Doubtless that has been the often feeling and request of many sons during the war. Many, perhaps, have had more confidence in their father's prayers than in their own. Some perhaps never before felt the great importance of, and necessity for, prayer as they did then; and perhaps an earnest cry may have been wrung from their heart that their father's God might be their's, and the desire – 'pray for me, father!' may have been their own first prayer. May gracious parents have it much in their minds to so 'pray, without ceasing.' We fear an awful time may soon burst on the battlefields. May God cover our soldiers' and sailors' heads *then* and at all times and send speedy success. Pray, *pray,* PRAY!

A Mother's Anxious Questionings

When this cruel war is over
  And the troops return again
To their homes among the clover,
  Or the busy mart and main.

Will *my* laddie be among them,
  Or with fallen warriors lay,
Sleeping on the field of battle
  Till the shadows flee away?

I remember well his prattle,
  When he romped upon my knee;
Saying, "Mum, here comes my daddy
  Up the garden for his tea."

Now for king and country fighting,
  While I stay behind and pray
That the Lord will him deliver
  Till *war's* shadows flee away.

None can tell a mother's trials
  Half so well as she herself,
When she dusts her darling's photo
  Hanging on the wall or shelf,

With a wonder in her bosom
  If the post will bring today
News from him who's simply vanished
  Till the shadows flee away.

France and Belgium tell a story
  Different from the Dardanelles,
There we hear how Turkish triumphs
  End at last in hideous yells:

"Allah! Allah! come and save us;"
  But they may no longer play
Their destructive pranks on Europe,
  For *those* shadows flee away.

"Lord! Support bereaved relations,
  Send the wounded timely aid,
Say to those whose nerves are shattered –
  'It is I; be not afraid!'

Give our enemies repentance,
Make them know thy sovereign sway –
And forgive my poor dictating –
Let these shadows flee away."

Christian soldier, young or aged,
Thou art fighting for a King
Who will never, *never* leave thee
Till thou shalt of victory sing

In the highest courts of heaven,
Where he sheds his brightest ray
On the eyes of those that see him –
Shadows there are passed away!

W. G., Kettering.[937]

Anxieties of War

Will the lads I love be present
When the armies are removed
From dire scenes of strife and conflict,
Or among the missing proved?

These are questions wives and parents
Ask a hundred times a day;
Nothing less than card or letter
Can disperse their fears away.

Silence suddenly is broken,
They with joy and pleasure read,
How the boy received the parcel
When he was in greatest need;

Perhaps he never thought Jehovah
Had so marvellously appeared,
In his providence and goodness –
'Heard him in the thing he feared.'

Soon the wrapper is cut open,
And his comrades have a share
Of the portions freely sent him
By another's tender care;

They have helped him bear his burdens,
Carried half his heavy load,
When his feet refused their action
He upon their shoulders rode.

Christian soldier! here's a lesson
Certainly for you to learn,
When the Lord gives you a blessing,
Other hungry souls still yearn;

Go and share it with another,
Eat thy morsel not alone,
God will see there is sufficient
And the work of love will own.

W. G., Kettering.[938]

Poems about aerial attacks on England

A number of people wrote poetry describing the bombing attacks which Britain was subjected to during the First World War, and especially the raids of the Zeppelin airships. Among the poems, one describes the first shooting down of a German airship on British soil (see p. 67). Many of the poems refer to remarkable deliverances – the bombs dropped did relatively little damage.

Our Aerial Perils

Hark! the hooter loudly screams,
  Zeppelins are coming;
See the flashlight from the clouds,
  And the people running
To their homes, they left awhile,
  For an hour's pleasure,
Now they travel back again
  Spoilt of all the leisure.

Lighted streets and palaces
  Quickly wrap in darkness;
While the fog seemed, like a pall,
  To increase the blackness;
Women trembled, children cried,
  But the worst was over,
Not a bomb dropped on the tower;
  Thanks unto Jehovah.

'Oh, that men would praise the Lord'
  For our preservation!
We should surely bless his name
  For his intervention;
Oft, alas, our trust is fixed
  On the second causes,
Battleships and aeroplanes,
  Soldiers, sailors, horses.

We do not despise the means
  Given for our using,
  'Tis the horrid *trust* in them
Britons are abusing;

When the nation's made to see
  Human scheming hollow,
Feels about to find the Lord,
  Peace will quickly follow.

"Save us, Lord," we humbly pray,
  "Save the British people
From the enemies without,
  And from pope and steeple!"
All are willing to destroy
  England's constitution,
May true Protestants unite
  For her restitution.

W. G.[939]

To the German Huns

✍ Verses written after reading of the cowardly air raid upon the Norfolk coast,[940] and as Mr James Muskett,[941] my father-in-law, lies in a feeble state in his 86th year within about 150 yards of St. Peter's Church Square, where bombs fell, I felt somehow I *must* write.

And didst thou, O Hun, for the sake of some fun,
    Or from a mere maddened despair,
Soar up a great height, and take a long flight
    In darkness to frighten us here?

And, when nearing town, did ye flash a light down
    To see where to drop thy vile bombs;
Prepared by thine art, and from thy vile heart,
    Determined to upset our homes?

And are ye quite glad, when our mothers are sad,
    At losing their babies through thee?

Or at buildings destroyed are ye quite overjoyed,
And think, "O, how clever I be?"

Well, whether or no, thou most cowardly foe,
Thy bombs upon innocents say
How bad is thine heart, and how wicked thou art,
O German, and "woe worth the day."

Ye wanted this war, and ye long for our shore,
Yet cannot get armies across;
So in fell despair, in gross darkness glide near,
Inflicting on Yarmouth a loss.

And, maddened in sin, did ye fly to King's Lynn?
Over Cromer, and Sherringham near?
Then, after thy bombs had caused death in some [homes,
Did ye then for dear Sandringham steer?

And, in thy hot hate for King George's estate,
Did ye take little Heacham for it?
Then make for the sea, with an infinite glee,
Quite hoping the palace was hit?

Then didst thou alight on thy shores with delight?
And hath thy great Kaiser bestowed
That cross made of iron, because British Lion
Seemed frightened at bombs that ye throwed?

Well; thanks to thy fun, thou most cowardly Hun,
Our Lion is watching ye; aye,
And believe me, he roars, and his teeth and his paws
Shall win for us Britons the day.

Yea, all are amazed, and our anger is raised
At cruelties shown in this war;
And if this is culture, 'tis that of the vulture,
That spotteth its victims afar.

And, what is thy gain, since thou didst disdain
That poor 'scrap of paper' ye signed?
Not Paris nor Dover – although ye fly over,
But rather disgust of mankind.

Now believe, ye who boast, whatever the cost
In men, or in ships, or in gold,
Thine awful delight in a cowardly flight,
Thy strength and thine honour have sold.

And with them the boast of invading our coast,
To govern us Britons today;
So now we will sing, "God preserve Britain's King,
His throne, and our liberties aye."

Alfred Dye, Rowley Regis.[942]

Air Raid on January 31st, 1916

✍ The following verses were written just after German Huns had paid us a nocturnal visit, January 31st, 1916.

We've read of German bombs dropped near and on the
Of fellow-Britons round East Coast, [homes
But thought two hundred miles inland beyond the wiles
Of cunning quite, whate'er its boast.

But, when infernal wit, with envy boiling, sits
In consultation on a ride,
Poor modicums of sense, and every moral fence
In insignificance must hide.

Our common foe hates light, so chooses aerial flight
When darkness supersedes the sun;
Hence, lifted up with pride, Huns quite enjoy a ride,
And think, "O, what most splendid fun."

Thus, though "Black Country" lies so far inland, he flies
And droppeth bombs with hellish zest;
Hence, now our miners and the iron-workers stand
In the same danger as the rest.

Perhaps 'tis well to share some perils from the air,
To stir our sympathies with those
Who've suffered nearer shore, in this most awful war,
The "frightfulness" of coward foes.

And, what should we that know the Mercy-seat now do?
The only answer found is, Pray.
That sweet almighty power, preserving us each hour,
Remains the same at night as day.

Yes; devils, with all men, and air-craft 'bove our ken,
Are in the sight and hands of God,
Who bids the mighty deep within its bounds to keep.
And well obey his sacred nod.

One thing about these raids on adults, boys, and maids,
Reveals the limits of foe's wit,
And that one thing is this, they evidently miss
The objects they design to hit.

Hence Sheffield, Liverpool, designed as the goal,
Turns out to be South Staffordshire;
While each munition shed looks as a garden bed;
So treacherous is the misty air.

And, though some houses tell, with dismal funeral bell,
Destructiveness, and strike with fear;
The useless damage done shows disappointed Hun,
As also Jesus' watchful care.

Then, as sweet prayer, with faith in what our Maker
Is honoured most, when humbly we [saith
Before him prostrate fall, and importunate call.
Let us to this sweet refuge flee.

Yes, let each Christian pray, in this most awful day,
For patience, soberness, and nerve;
Christ Jesus is the same, ah! bless his precious name,
And will his praying ones preserve.

Yea, let our children try and heave a deep-felt sigh
To him who did invite such near
His sacred feet below, compassion sweet to show,
And little trembling hearts to cheer.

Indeed! let one and all upon the Saviour call,
Till cruel Huns with bruised crest,
Lick, serpent-like, the dust, as proud ambition must,
When nations call our Jesus blest.

And shall all nations bless 'The Lord our Righteous-
O yes; 'his precious name shall be [ness?'
Continued as the sun,' till nations every one
Sweet homage pay, with Germany.

Then coward raids no more will ever reach our shore;
Then 'pruning-hooks for cruel sword,
And plough-shares for each spear, and peace from year
So saith the Spirit in the Word. [to year'

And shall we live to see such peace and liberty?
I cannot say; but this I know,
Albeit unbelief with ignorance play thief,
Immanuel's kingdom here must grow.

Alfred Dye, February 2nd, 1916.[943]

Sudden Death of an Editor-Minister

✍ Dear friend,

We read in one of the papers that in a North-Eastern town one of the victims of the last Zeppelin raid was a man over 80 years of age. This appears, from a note, to have been Mr Arthur Wilcockson, editor of *Zion's Witness*. He was 86 years of age last February, had edited the *Witness* for 58 years, and was a minister of over 60 years' standing. Although he stood, as a minister, isolated, or independently of any denomination, as also showed an indifference to some ordinances, yet he was a most strenuous advocate for essential and eternal realities, and a true lover of all whom he received and believed were God's grace-taught children. And further; the kind Christian spirit he showed to me for quite 25 years, has left an indelible mark in my affections, therefore have I put the following thoughts into verse, and send them you for *The Friendly Companion* ... It seems such a sad thing that civilians should be murdered in time of war. It appears that Mr Wilcockson died from the *shock* of the bombs falling near his house. (A circular-letter by his son, Mr C. W., supports these statements, adding, 'He passed away as he would have wished, painlessly and peacefully, at the age of 86 years, actively engaged in his life's work.') Oh to be prepared for a sudden exchange of time for eternity! I have but little grace in my soul; and if any strength, it is in the *grace* that is *in* Christ Jesus our Lord.

Yours in the gospel,
Alfred Dye.
Bellend, Rowley Regis, August 15th, 1916.

Written on the death, through *shock* from Zeppelin bombs, on August 2nd, of Arthur Wilcockson, editor of *Zion's Witness,* in his 87th year.

Apart from *special revelation,* how
Uncertain is the number of one's days;
As also in what *form* grim death may blow
Away one's fleeting breath and end our days.

Nor can the righteous an exemption claim
More than the wretch whose crimes for vengeance [call,
Because, though *blest,* there are the very same
Calamities of life and death for all.

Our aged friend, who, more than sixty years,
Contended for the gospel of God's Son
Hath, after tribulation and its tears,
Just fall'n a victim to the cruel Hun.

Yet, as the aged sometimes fear decay,
And, as one consequence, dependency
Upon the care of others, wisdom may
From *frightfulness* a mercy sweet descry.

He had no partner to condole or nurse,
Nor needed one; nor, though his children weep,
They have no vigilance now to rehearse,
Because, forsooth, he quickly fell asleep.

And soundly too he slumbers, close by, bomb
Effects all round, just where he fainting fell,
As angels hastened from their heavenly home
To take his soul to bliss, remote from hell.

Nor had he an *afflicted* son to leave,
Dependent on a parent's loving care,

He predeceased him; and, as I conceive,
Like Francis Covell's did, more than a year.[944]

So, putting things together, with his age,
One sees the mercy of a covenant God,
In taking Wilcockson from off the stage,
While nations bleeding are beneath his rod.

And may it be *our* lot to move with *fear,*
As Noah did, in these most awful days,
Ere deluge comes, and thus for death prepare
In hope of life, as lasting as God's praise,

Where sin nor sorrow, death, nor war, nor pain,
Nor any darkness shall becloud our sun,
But where sweet peace and glory ever reign,
Afar from *frightfulness* of cruel Hun.

Alfred Dye, August 15th, 1916.[945]

A Raider Raided: September 3rd, 1916

✍ The following piece was written by 'Esther' after the first 'Zepp' had been brought down, but was delayed in sending until the lines,

Why should the wonders God hath wrought
Be lost in silence and forgot?

moved her to think, and *act* in sending it forward.

It was a man-constructed fly,
A monster, mounted very high,
Which buzzed and hummed as on it flew
Conveying deadly bombs and crew
O'er sea and land, o'er wood and wave,
Intent the Britishers to strafe.
Like bat or owl, it flew by night,
Preferring darkness to the light,
Forgetting, or in proud disdain
Ignoring, God, and all his train;
And man, with his inventive power,
Sought to evade at midnight hour.
But ah! the God of destiny
Is watching as you onward fly;
And faithful watchmen guard our shore,
In case such demons venture o'er,
To warn the watchers, far inland,
All ready at their guns to stand,
And caution people, though 'twas night,
Which way the Zepp steered in its flight,
That all might be prepared for raid,
In case the foe an onslaught made;
While many slept in peace at home,
Until they heard the great guns boom;
Then, starting from their sleep profound,
Were terrified, by flash and sound,
To realize the Zepps were here,
Discharging deadly weapons near!
They listen now with bated breath,
Not knowing whether life or death
Will be their lot in this dread raid,
To move or tarry half afraid.
Some venture to a window near
And say, "The monster's just up there."
The searchlights stream across the sky
And meet each other on the fly,
Which looks as if it's passing o'er;
The guns are firing as before.
But some afflicted helpless folk
Lie still, God's mercy to invoke –

"Good Lord! defend us!" one soul cried,
"Do stop the raiders as they ride;
Give skill to those who aim the shot.
Return in safety, let it *not!*
Lord! undertake; our weapons own
To stop its course, and bring it down!"
Flash, flash, bang, boom, tut, tut, tut, tut;
What's coming now? I know not, but
There's something happening I trow;
The monster's stricken, surely, now.
Flash, boom, flash, boom, now flames a light
Seen many miles around that night;
The people run from far and near,
Now clap their hands, and start the cheer,
"Hip, hip, hurrah!" and faster run,
"Hip, hip, hurrah! Well done! It's done!"
The horns and sirens on the Thames,
Sound long and loud as Zeppy flames;
The night seemed rife with varied sound
From folks and instruments around.
Now dies the light, the sounds abate,
The dragon-fly has met its fate;
And all its occupants, alas!
Without an exit thence to pass,
Held with infernal grip around,
Midst flames and terrors fall to ground.
Not as they mounted, full of life
To aim on us destruction rife;
But, as they thought to do to us,
They met their fate, or even worse;
Midst dire explosions, terror, flame,
Their hope expired, and down they came
In wreck and ruin, mangled, charred,
With none their death-shrieks to regard!

Whatever others think of this,
My heart would no instruction miss,
But learn of Jesus, night and day,
Watch his dear hand as well as pray;
For all his works his praise enhance,
Nor death, nor hell devour by chance;
The world he into being bade,
And for himself he all things made,
The wicked for the evil day,
His power and justice to display.
He rules o'er all enthroned on high,
Yet stoops to hear his people cry;
And though to answer he refrain,
Their lot he surely will maintain,
And sometimes, almost ere they call,
He extricates them from their thrall.
'Twas so that night, as many know,
His hand controlled the archer's bow,
As when Goliath in his pride
The armies of the Lord defied,
Till David, with a sling and stone,
By God's direction brought him down.
King Ahab also, though disguised, –
Who God's own prophet had despised;
A man, at venture drew a bow,
God sped the dart, and laid him low.
And so with this great Zeppelin,
And much explosive pent within,
A young man, taking steady aim,
God blessed the means, and down it came!
Then, he who gave the mortal blow
Turned his machine and homeward flew,
P'raps little thought of risk he'd run,
So glad to see the work was done.

But we who cannot work nor fight,
Should plead with Jesus day and night,
To bless all lawful weapons used,
And shield defenders thus exposed.
Now, God be praised! for 'tis his due,
Who heard the cries of not a few,
And, his rich mercy to display,
Delivered us in such a way;
Then gently hushed one off to rest
By sweetly whisp'ring in her breast –
"He will be very gracious: He
Will hear thy voice and answer thee."[946]

The Hand of God!

> ✍ Verses composed upon reflecting on a most remarkable providence on the night of October 19th, 1917, when nearly forty bombs fell around our district without injuring a single human being, or causing any destruction of property.

What! after nearly two years absence, Hun,
Another nocturn visit paid us here?
And didst thou count upon a murderous one,
Like those in London and its suburbs near?

Whatever thy commission or design,
Allow me now a verse or two of rhyme,
To just express, how providence divine
Prevented loss of life by thee this time!

The choice of district shows thy cunning well,
As all around us are munitions made;
While high explosive works and factories tell
How suitable for thy nefarious trade.

How is it then, O Hun, thou didst not split
One single factory or munition shed?
Nor dwelling-house, nor human being hit,
But simply grazed the skin of one cow's head?

In other words: How, after all thy bombs
Had dropped, so few exploded? and those few
Not near enough to injure any homes
Save panes in cottages where shrapnel flew?

Perchance, if one could reason with a Hun –
The height Zepps flew, in fear of anticraft,
Might be the cause of no more injury done
To cows or human beings, fore or aft?

It might be fog? It might be this or that,
To human reason, pampering well its wits;
But reason flits, as blind as any bat,
When disappointment all its cunning hits.

It was the hand of *God!* and his alone
In answer to his humble people's cries;
And 'tis the prayer of faith before his throne
That shall avert fresh dangers that arise!

And be it known to all who read these lines,
There are some "jewels" in our country round,
Some precious "salt" forsooth – if no divines –
Preserving well until with glory crowned.

Reflection, then, on preservation, when
Such missiles of destruction fell, declares
A Providence divine for praying men –
A God that hears and answers humble prayers.

So, go on Hun; exert thy skill the while
As best thou canst; there is a God above

Who shall not, cannot, on the wicked smile,
Although he tries the objects of his love.

Nay; go on Christian, in these solemn days,
Where'er thou art, and bow before thy God;
He listens to each soul that humbly prays
While nations writhe beneath his scourging rod.

Of course, the same afflictions may befall –
So far as this poor mortal life's concerned –
Upon some persons who on Jesus call,
As on some soul's whose life God's curse hath earned.

Yet, notwithstanding; importune in prayer
For spirituality of mind and faith;
Such souls are saved, though Zeppelins appear
And drop their bombs, and cause an instant death!

Hence, though we are preserved from harm this time,
And though it reads an omen that is good –
A providence most marv'lous and sublime –
Jehovah is a sovereign, all-wise God!

And though a single shaft shall never hit
Until his wisdom wills it, who dare say
Without especial faith, *what* he'll see fit
To use, to stop one's breath? *Hence, Christian – pray!*

Alfred Dye, October 30th, 1917.[947]

Poems about specific events of the war

The following poems were written about three specific events of the war. The first of these events was the massive loss of life at the Battle of Neuve Chapelle, France, in March, 1915. It is estimated that over 11,000 men were casualties of the battle. The second event covered by the poets was the execution of Edith Cavell on 12th October, 1915. Cavell was a British nurse, who worked in Belgium nursing wounded soldiers from both sides in the war. She was executed for her involvement in helping some 200 soldiers from the Allied forces escape from behind the lines in German-occupied Belgium. The third event was the loss of Lord Kitchener at sea, when the boat he was sailing on was sunk on 5th June, 1916. Kitchener was regarded by many as God-fearing, and a source of great hope in Britain.

War's Direful Cost

✍ The following verses were written after reading Sir John French's dispatch to Lord Kitchener, relative to the terrible loss of life at Neuve Chapelle, and adding the losses in killed and wounded, etc. of our 139,000 men – with those of the Germans, Belgians, French, Russians, Austrians, Serbians and Turks – since the commencement of hostilities, it seems possible that millions of immortal souls may have already gone into eternity.

The Roll of Honour, read now every day,
Betrays the price Great Britain has to pay
In this most dreadful war;
And while this gun-fire, bayonet-charges, shell,
Make what poor soldiers call "a very hell,"
Death satiates its maw.

Yea, though each forward movement fans the hope
The brave Allies well able are to cope
With their inveterate foes,
The loss of life makes battles *won* to cost
Almost as much as many battles lost –
Well, so Neuve Chapelle shows.

And, when one meditates upon God's Word –
Especially the precepts of our Lord,
How horrible is war;
When proud ambition spits its grim disdain
At peace, humility strives to it maintain
With justice evermore.

But men are *sinful,* and ingenious pride,
With unbelief and hardness, strives to hide
Its own deceitfulness;
Nor lays to heart amount of evil done
To neighbours, parents, friends, or anyone,
And winks at their distress.

Hence proud ambition's hold of reins controls
And sends its thousands, nay, its million souls
Into eternity;
And though a remnant may have reached that shore
Where peace is sung remote from horrid war,
As lost some millions lie.

Yea, put the evils of all wars in scales,
Then weigh the price, when peace again prevails,
And throw each victory in,
However grand the peace and glory seem,
The loss of *souls* makes former kick the beam,
And shows the *weight* of sin.

Of all the wars, since our first father fell
There is but *one* – waged by Immanuel –
In which *no* lives are lost;
He gave his own, in mercy souls to save,
Then rose triumphant from the lonesome grave,
And sends the Holy Ghost.

And did the nations *know* his lovely name,
By th' Spirit's teaching, 'twould their hearts inflame,
With fond desire for peace;
'Twould break propensity for strife in twain,
Make instruments of dire destruction vain,
And liberty increase.

Now, could I breathe in simple verse a prayer,
I would pray thus: "O, Prince of glory, hear
And put a stop to war;
Let providence, yea thine, with mercy now
Precede the peaceful Dove, with olive bough,
Proclaiming deluge o'er.

Yea, let me live, dear Jesus, a few years,
To witness answers to thy people's prayers,
And join in thankful song –
All glory to sweet Mercy, evermore
Rejoicing over judgement and all war,
And roll thy praise along."

Alfred Dye, April 15th, 1915.[948]

Another Fiendish German Murder

Or, German infamies crowned in the murder of Nurse Cavell, whose parents I knew in Norfolk.

☞ Mr Dye, in sending the following, tells us Swardeaton, Miss Cavell's home, is only two miles from Braconash where his father died. He knew them by sight very well. "Mr Cavell held the living there for 46 years; he was a 'low' Churchman, a good-living man, a Protestant." Our readers will know of the kindness of Miss Cavell in nursing soldiers, even some of the German wounded, which seems to have stirred the malevolent passions of the Huns to their deepest, so that in spite of all appeal or reason she was condemned to death and shot soon after midnight, before further appeal could be made on her behalf. Friends will have seen the account of her death in the newspapers.

Preparing, vile Huns, many years for a war,
Ye've acted consistently base;
And such the insatiableness of your maw,
Ye've branded yourselves with disgrace.

Th' invasion of Belgium and cruelties there –
Revealing insatiable greed –
Foreran thy sea murders, and Zeppelins here,
And show ye up monsters indeed.

Yes; monsters uncovered, such actions proclaim;
And history shall stand to attest
For ages to come, a most horrible name,
From North, East, and South to the West.

Now, crowning the most of your infamies vile –
Too awful to put into verse,
Ye have, in your cruel and hard-hearted style,
Just murdered a kind-hearted nurse.

A lady by birth, and whose parents I *knew* –
Ye callous and inhuman Huns –
A lady, so Christian, so kind, and so true,
Who nursed, with the British, *your* sons.

And what was her *crime,* insatiable Hun?
Befriended poor prisoners, I trow,
With a little advice, the best way to run
Afar from that hardness ye show?

And – say 'twas a breach, or abuse of the law,
To pity poor soldiers beneath
The heels of a monarch with whom there is war,
Why punish a lady with *death?*

Ye boast much of *Kultur*, of science, and faith,
And often make use of God's Name,
While cruelty practised pathetically saith
A solemn '*Amen!*' to your shame.

Beware then, ye Huns, of stern Justice incensed,
With Vengeance equipped by its side,
Commissioned till honour is well recompensed,
In blows on the crest of your pride.

Yea, believe me, ye Huns; the hearts of mankind
Are bleeding, and blood cries amain,
For vengeance on murderers, till Justice shall find
Redress for sweet innocence slain.

O yes; cruel Huns! that God we adore,
Is merciful, holy, and just;

And though judgement lingers, at the heels of this war
Prepare thou thy seat in the dust.

And there to reflect on the oceans of blood
Thy pride and ambition have shed,
Remember Nurse Cavell, so kind and so good,
Cries vengeance divine on your head!

Yea think, cruel Huns, of that horrible doom
Awaiting impenitent men;
Then ask – "When *Nurse Cavell* shall rise from the tomb,
How? How shall it be with *us then?"*

Alfred Dye, October 26th, 1915.[949]

"Greater love hath no man than this, that a man lay down his life for his friends."

✍ In honoured memory of Miss Edith Cavell, the brave British nurse who was executed by the Germans for assisting English, French and Belgian soldiers to cross the frontier into safety.

Merciless Hun, what hast thou done?
Black is thy day, eclipsed thy sun;
Adamant heart, unmoved to save
A noble woman from the grave.

This last black deed, this foulest blot,
Will never, *never* be forgot.
All England cries aloud to God
T'avenge this selfless martyr's blood.

Noble 'mongst Britain's womanhood,
Calm and deliberate she stood
Facing her cruel judges, who
Cried for her blood as bloodhounds do.

Fearless she laughed at martial laws
That would have checked her righteous cause,
And bravely worked while it was day
Knowing the price she'd have to pay.

With noble zeal she nursed her foes,
And sympathized with all their woes;
As though each foe had been a friend,
She nursed them kindly to the end.

And her reward? Words blush to tell;
They placed her in a prison cell,
Nor rested till the price was paid
Their *Kultur* charged! Oh! ne'er will fade

The deeds that have such halo shed
Around her brave, devoted head!
"Guilty" she owned herself to be –
"Guilty!" Ah, yes; of sympathy,

To save some mother's noble son
From the wild fury of the Hun.
And for *such* deeds she had to die –
What base, unheard-of infamy!

Happy was she her blood to shed
For her "dear country's sake," she said.
So, midst a storm of hate and spite,
Her spirit took its last, glad flight.

Murderous Hun, what *hast* thou done?
What *wilt* thou do in days to come?
When one stern voice thy heart shall touch,
And thou shalt hear the "Inasmuch

As ye have done it unto her,
Whose love thy hatred did incur," –

Thou'lt surely quail beneath *this* word –
"Thou'st done it unto *Me* – the Lord!"

Mabel S. Good, Addlestone Moor.[950]

Edith Cavell's Own Feelings

Would *we* avenge the death of Nurse Cavell?
Her gracious words forbid us. From her cell,
The message bears a noble soul's impress
"Toward my foes I feel no bitterness!

In time of war, my duty was to tend
The sick and wounded, whether foe or friend;
It mattered not whate'er their creed or race,
I gave my best to each and every case.

So busied was I in my arduous task
That when arrested and in prison cast,
I found ten weeks of quiet none too long,
Spent in communion with the Holy One.

I fear not death, for often I have seen
The dreaded phantom with a brow serene
Glide through the ward and, with a gentle sigh,
He kissed those first who knew not he was nigh.

Soon will the sentence passed be carried out,
And death's strong arm encompass me about,
'Where is death's sting? where, grave, thy victory?
I triumph still if *God* abide with me!'

Yes; I shall triumph over all my foes,
Happy to die for freedom's sacred cause;
'Heaven's morning dawns, and earth's vain shadows [flee,
In life, in death, Oh Lord! abide with me!'"

Heroic soul! thy earthly race is run;
In darkest night the Master called, "Well done!"
And England, too, proclaims that such as thee,
Hath made her what she is and still would be.

Never has martyr's blood been shed in vain;
Each drop of thine shall fall like gentle rain
In hearts well fallowed, causing them to grow
Valiant and strong to meet the common foe.

Men who will wade through blood, and march through [fire,
Inspired by thee, like thee shall they desire
To live for others and, if need be, die
Assured that right shall triumph bye and bye!

Martha Sowerbutts, Accrington.[951]

On the Death of Lord Kitchener

A soldier good,
Example of devoted duty stood;
They of a higher calling well might feel
Ashamed before his true and steadfast zeal
As soldiers good.

With ordered brain,
And high-wrought plans he journeyed o'er the main;
Death claimed the army's honoured able head,
His thoughts are perished on the ocean-bed,
With fertile brain.

And he is gone;
And men are asking, "Who shall carry on?"
O, let no Christian in the mighty trust,
But in the Almighty God, for men are dust,
And soon are gone!

God raises up the man,
And predetermines every earth-wrought plan;
Shows forth his glory in the exalted one.
Then lays him low, the destined purpose done;
And what is man?

M. L., Northampton.[952]

H.M.S. Hampshire, the ship on which Lord Kitchener perished

Lord Kitchener's Death

The hand of the Lord seemeth strange,
Where Reason usurps the control,
And striveth all things to arrange
Respecting this life and the soul.

Hence, Kitchener numbered among
The humblest poor seamen beneath
The billows, she turneth her tongue
To murmurings because of his death.

Says Reason, "Why was he not spared?
He who could so well organize
An army that always him feared
E'en when he but turned his eyes."

Yet, just as he'd marshalled a host,
Yea, millions, to combat the Hun,
He's gone to the bottom, and lost
Where now can we find such a one?

Well, Reason, let's reason awhile,
And more from a scriptural view.
Sweet meekness, so free from all guile,
Is better at reason than *you.*

Jehovah, in whom we all live,
And move, and have being today,
In mercy did Kitchener give,
Then sovereignly took him away.

Yes; Kitchener, born for our good,
Worked for it for many a year;
And Sovereignty, well understood,
Can all us poor mortals well spare.

And though we all grieve at the stroke
Befalling upon such a one,
Faith, musing on life and God's Book,
Sees Kitchener's work was all *done.*

And till a man's work is complete,
The man is immortal, I trow;
Then, let us all fall at God's feet,
And humbly submit to the blow.

Yea, in that humility pray,
Confessing each national sin,
Till faith, as well strengthened, shall say
"The Allies, with God's blessing, shall win!"

Alfred Dye, June 16th, 1916.[953]

Poems about the national situation

Much of the poetry written concerned the sin of the nation, and the need of national repentance. One poem highlights how much the people were apt to forget God, even in victories granted, rather ascribing them to secondary causes. A few of the poems were written around the concern over the command to desecrate the Lord's Day by agricultural work in order to feed the nation.

A Prayer for the Nation

O, what trouble's now abounding
In this our much favoured land;
Lord; wilt thou, our foes confounding,
Show thy great almighty hand?

Thou didst fight thy people's battles
In the days of old, we read;
Wilt thou now be with our armies,
Give them strength in time of need!

Guard those on the mighty ocean,
Perilous though their state may be;
May they prove thee their protector
On the land, and on the sea.

True, we are a sinful nation,
And deserve thy wrathful frown;
But wilt thou remember mercy,
And the 'man of sin' put down?

Long we have departed from thee,
And thy holy day forgot;
Going on in sin and pleasure,
Lived as though a God was not!

Now so many homes are mourning
For their loved ones, called to fight;
Doubtless many prayers are uttered
For thee to defend the right!

Many of our noble soldiers
On the battlefield will die;
Leaving weeping widows, children;
Lord, wilt thou regard their cry!

Sisters, brothers, friends and lovers,
Painfully are called to part;
Rich and poor in this are suffering,
Young and old must feel the smart!

Broken-hearted fathers, mothers,
Overcome with helpless grief;
'Tis a bitter cup they're drinking,
Oh that they may find relief!

Succour, too, those who are wounded,
Suffering agonizing pain;
If it be thy will, may many
Be restored to health again!

Give to those who wait upon them
Kind and tender hearts and hands;
May they feel while at their duties
They are doing thy commands.

And may we, a sinful nation,
Once again return to God;
And in true humiliation
Bow to thy correcting rod!

Wilt thou hear our poor petition –
On this ground our fathers stood –
May what seems to us most evil
Work together for our good!

Bless our King, our Queen, our rulers;
Give them wisdom, Lord, we pray;
May they look to thee for guidance;
Seek thy help from day to day!

Then, if thou shouldst give us victory,
May we, as a nation, raise
Unto thee, who thus has helped us,
A sweet song of prayer and praise.

M. A. H., Tunbridge Wells.[954]

Confession and Supplication

Almighty God! whose power upholds
This vast creation; who controls
All things in heaven, all things in earth,
Whose mighty word first gave them birth;
Who stillst the raging of the seas;
O God of Hosts – send peace, send peace!

Put down the wicked from their throne;
Their power destroy, their cause disown;
They've trampled on thy sacred laws,
And slain the helpless without cause;
Let not their brutal power increase;
O God of Hosts – send peace, send peace!

We've sinned against thee, O our God!
Justly provoked thy chastening rod;
O arm of strength, awake, awake,
We pray, for thy great mercy's sake;
Our cries to thee, Lord, shall not cease;
O, God of Hosts – send peace, send peace!

Our loved ones who are called to serve,
Most gracious God, protect, preserve;
Teach them to pray, to seek thy face,
O save them by thy mighty grace;
And shouldst thou will that life should cease,
Call them to thine eternal peace.

Vengeance is thine; thou wilt repay;
Thy truth and justice, Lord, display;
And by thy stern correcting rod,
Still teach the nations there's a God;
Till war, with all its horrors, cease,
And earth be blessed with peace, sweet peace.

S. Adams, Blackheath.[955]

"We Forget"

(After Kipling)

God of our fathers, who hast felled
The outposts of our battle line;
By whose permission we have held
Dominion over palm and pine;
We are in danger! Save us yet,
Though we forget; though we forget!

Far-famed, but little, is our fleet;
The moss has on our headlands grown;
Over our pomp a winding-sheet,
The threatening enemy has thrown;

Lord God of hosts; defend us yet,
Though we forget; though we forget!

The tumults and the shoutings grow;
The captains and the kings combine;
And who, in all the nation, show
That ancient sacrifice of thine?[956]
We lean upon our merits yet;
But we forget; Lord, we forget!

For the ungodliness which rules
In many a so-called house of thine;
For the idolatry of fools,
Who bow towards a tinselled shrine;
For bishops who ignore thy Word,
Thy mercy on the nation, Lord!

And for the comfort of our king,
The owner of a million cares;
For the proud sceptic, who would fling
Rank folly on thy people's prayers,
Be thou a God to England yet,
And pity her, though she forget!

M. A. Chaplin, Galleywood.[957]

"Let God arise, let his enemies be scattered."

(Psalm 68: 1)

Great God! in mercy now appear,
And fight for England once again;
To all the nation make it clear
That thou art God to rule and reign.

As thou didst once our shores defend,
And drive a boasting tyrant back;
His plots and schemes brought to an end,
With dire destruction in their track;

So now thy mighty arm make bare,
And cause this cruel war to cease;
Let us now in thy mercy share,
And shortly see return of peace.

'Tis true we cannot see or know
Thy secret purpose or thy will,
Yet in this time of saddest woe
Would have our eyes up to thee still.

Thou hast a few names in the land,
As thou didst once of Sardis speak,
Who now would for thine honour stand,
And for thy great deliverance seek.

O, bless our rulers, gracious Lord!
And give them strength, and wisdom too;
Make them to steer by thy own Word
In all they think, or say, or do!

Bless thou our king upon the throne –
For 'tis by thee kings rule and reign;
Teach all thy sovereign sway to own,
And so pure justice to maintain.

Our soldiers and our sailors bless;
Give courage, strength and valour too;
And in each hour of deep distress
Still guard and bring them safely through.

And O, dear Lord, amidst it all,
Our souls would for thy Zion pray;

Let richest blessings on her fall,
Renew her strength from day to day.

Do not our feeble prayers reject,
But listen when on thee we call;
Our favoured country still protect,
That we may praise thee, Lord, for all!

M. M., March 10th, 1917.[958]

A Prayer for Help

O Lord! Drive back these dreadful Huns,
Who're risen up 'gainst England's sons;
Subdue their rage, destroy their reign,
Nor let them rise in war again.

Cruel beyond all thought or ken
Throughout this war their deeds have been; –
Is it so, Lord! that thou hast left
Us of thy sympathy bereft?

Thy twos and threes still meet for prayer,
And sometimes hope that thou art there;
They pray that thou wouldst send us peace,
And cause this dreadful war to cease.

O, hear in heaven, thy dwelling-place!
Send to us fresh supplies of grace,
That we more earnestly may plead
In this our nation's time of need!

Could we but hear our rulers say –
"We now will set apart a day,
To supplicate the Lord on high;"
We soon should think war's end was nigh!

W. Leaman. October 24th, 1917.[959]

War's Wailing

Oh! bleeding's my heart with pain's terrible smart,
For anguish lies thick all around;
Earth's woe-song is sung to hearts that are wrung,
And there seems not a joy to be found!

Oh! the millions of tears, born of love's countless
For the dear ones engaged in the fight; [fears,
Legion hearts beat as one in this thing being done,
This infamous war – wrong 'gainst right!

Oh! the pity of it! Oh! the pity of it;
That some who are no foes at all,
But brothers in heart, must yet needs take a part
And help in a dear comrade's fall.

Oh! these are real woes; and nobody knows –
Save our Father – the false from the true;
Oh! then, let us pray, through this war's dreadful day,
For the would-be blood-guiltless ones too.

And for our loved who fall! Oh! we'll weave them a
Of honour, and courage, and glory; [pall
Let the sad widow's weeds write the brave, selfless
Of the true in our nation's grand story! [deeds

Oh, for peace! gentle peace! Oh! that war soon may
For ever, and ever, and ever; [cease
That master and man, and lion and lamb,
Be true friends and comrades together!

How I long for that time – that beautiful time,
When the Angel of Peace shall arise;
And, through sweet ages long, turn earth's sorrows to
And with smiles chase the tears from our eyes! [song,

Mabel S. Good, Ashford, Middlesex.[960]

None Good Save God!

It all gets worse and worse,
The war, yea, and the world;
A proof this of the weighty curse
Which God on man has hurled.

His laws are all defied,
His judgements all contemned;
Alas! the fact can't be denied,
Our nation seems condemned.

No penitence we find,
No humbling before God;
The young display a haughty mind,
The aged provoke his rod.

Though numbers have been maimed
Though millions have been slain,
It is the Almighty who is blamed;
Alas! this is too plain.

O, sad and awful state,
All mankind now are in;
Can it be even now too late
For to confess our sin?

Our Sabbath-breaking sins,
And pleasure-loving too; –
Idolatry, when it begins,
Worse things begin to show.

Look throughout all the land,
Crosses are now set up;
Rome showing thus her stealthy hand,
And millions taste the cup.

The vials of God's wrath
Are poured upon the earth;
Millions are now silent in death –
What gave these things a birth?

Our sins, our nation's sins,
Casting away God's Word;
This way a nation's fall begins,
As judgement from the Lord!

W. Leaman, Bournemouth.[961]

For the New Year

Another year has passed away,
Week after week, day after day,
In quick succession flown.
And, Lord, since war was first declared,
Our Empire and our homes thou'st spared,
What mercy thou hast shown!

This dreadful war is raging still,
We know not what may be thy will,
Nor when the strife will end.
We may be taken with surprise,
But thou art faithful, just, and wise,
And will thy own defend.

For thou dost hear and answer prayer;
In thy own time, thou wilt appear,
Thou makest wars to cease.
Prepare us for thy coming, Lord,
On this New Year, if such thy word,
Who art the God of peace.

The King of glory will descend
And judgment unto victory send,
When he shall come to reign.
In power and glory he will sway,
A peaceful sceptre in that day,
So soon to come again.

Look up, ye saints, rejoice and sing,
And wait the advent of your King,
Redemption draweth near.
As now we greet our friends today,
May earthly shadows flee away,
And brighter prospects cheer.

Ellen Booker, Bath, December, 1915.[962]

Three Years of War

Three years have rolled their solemn months around
Since Britain felt herself in honour bound
To enter the arena with the rest
And put vile Hun ambitions to the test.
But oh! what oceans of life-blood have flowed!
What awful cruelty the foe hath showed!
What breasts have heaved in agonizing pain!
What treasure lost beneath the mighty main!
Yet, though war rages still, sins still are great,
Men obdurate remain in every state!
Titanic wars great purposes imply,
And in the end – whatever atheists cry –
Reveal a God omnipotent and wise,
Albeit unbelief his grace denies.
Three things appear upon Great Britain's side –
Despite profanity and vaunting pride –
One is her constitutional law, so grand,
As pioneer of good in every land.
Another is her cause, so nobly just,
She fights injustice now because she *must.*
And *last*, not least, more godliness is found
In this our isle, than any nation round,
And here I as a Christian take my stand,
In expectation of a victory grand!
Yea, here I stood three years ago this day,
And on this ground we humbly watch and pray,
Reflecting much upon our Saviour's words –
As King of every king, and Lord of lords;
Who every evil and all worlds controls –
'In patience,' friends, 'possess your precious souls!'
Naturally *impatient* from our birth,
And sanguine, as a child that plays for mirth,
We thought, of course, Lord Kitchener was wrong
In saying that this war would last so long.
Three years? Dear me! its magnitude so great
Must soon exhaust resources of each state.
Yet still it rages, and must rage until
Omnipotence shall speak his – 'Peace, be still.'
And till he speaks, let us becomingly
Adore his awful and pure sovereignty,
And sovereign right to deal with nations all,
Till, 'dust and ashes,' *we* before him fall.

Alfred Dye, August 4th, 1917.[963]

Jehovah Shalom

O God our strength, to thee we cry,
The nations weep – the nations sigh;
Involved in conflict, fierce and strong,
Grant, Lord, that right may conquer wrong.

Hasten the end of strife so sore,
Give peace unto our lands once more.

O God our hope, stretch forth thine hand,
To guide and guard our native land;
Frustrate the evil schemes of men,
And bring our loved ones home again.
Hasten the end of strife so sore,
Give peace unto our lands once more.

O God our refuge – thou our head,
Give us each day our daily bread;
Be our strong tower – be our defence,
And save us in thy providence.
Hasten the end of strife so sore,
Give peace unto our lands once more.

O God of battles, who art strong,
Bid anguished sighs be turned to song!
Cheer thou the widow in distress,
And comfort all the fatherless.
Hasten the end of strife so sore,
Give peace unto our lands once more.

O God of peace, we trust in thee,
Maker and ruler of the sea,
May he who bade the waves, 'Be still!'
With calm assurance all hearts fill.
Hasten the end of strife so sore,
Give peace unto our lands once more.

E.S. (Her husband was serving in the army).[964]

God our Refuge

'Trust in him at all times: ye people, pour out your heart before him: God is a refuge for us.' Psalm 62: 8.

Oh! thou who in the ages past has been
Thy people's help, for us now intervene;
Once more, O God, thy mighty power display,
Be our defence this direful, ruthless day.

When numerous foes around on every hand,
Striving to conquer our beloved land,
Spread desolation, death, and misery,
Our homes destroy, us rob of liberty;

Lord! as a nation far from thee we've strayed,
Thy Word despised, its precepts disobeyed;
Dishonoured thee, our ears to error lent,
Profaned thy day, on pleasures fully bent.

Thy goodness day by day regarding not,
Thy mercies of the past we have forgot;
Thy servants' warning words, reproofs divine,
Alas, ignored, call for these strokes of thine!

Thine anger we deserve, thy scourging rod;
But since thou art a kind and gracious God,
Grant us humility, with grace to fall
Into thy hand, and own thee Lord of all!

Thy people mourn these evils in the land,
And own the justness of thy chastening hand;
Meanwhile this truth rich consolations yields,
'God is our refuge' still, our strength and shield.

Thou know'st the foemen's threats, their vaunting boast;
Frustrate, O God, the proud, ambitious host,
Who, slaughtering helpless ones, with sword and flame,
Claim thee their helper, thus blaspheme thy name.

Numbers to thee are nought; 'twas but a few,
With arms so strange, the Midianites o'erthrew,

Assyria's mighty host all fell in death
By the sharp blast of thy destroying breath.

We use our means, but ask thee, Lord, to bless,
To own the same, and crown them with success;
Prayer is thy people's sword, their helmet hope,
Their breastplate faith, 'tis thine to deal the stroke.

O thou who rulest the armies of the sky,
Whose word withholds or bids destruction fly;
No foe can move, no woe nor shaft can hit
To harm till thou, the God of all, sees fit.

Though dark the cloud, there is the silver line
Across it drawn of grace and care divine;
Once more thy great compassion is displayed,
Destruction merited is still delayed.

In war there's sorrow, suffering and ail,
While poignant anguish follows in its trail;
The widow's groan, the orphan's cry is heard
On every hand, in mercy, Lord, regard!

Our fathers' trust. They did commit their way
To thee; thou didst direct; lead us each day
Until this warfare ends. Bid conflicts cease,
And o'er the earth expand the bow of peace.

So shall the benefit be ours; be thine
The praise. To honour thee our hearts incline,
Enable us low at thy feet to fall,
Own thee the King of kings, and Lord of all!

Joseph Aldworth, 1916.[965]

Keep the Sabbath Day

Thoughts suggested on hearing of the nation being urged to till the ground, etc., on the Sabbath day. "Remember the sbbath day, to keep it holy. Six days shalt thou labour, and do all thy work: But the seventh day is the sabbath of the LORD thy God: in it thou shalt not do any work, thou, nor thy son, nor thy daughter, thy manservant, nor thy maidservant, nor thy cattle, nor thy stranger that is within thy gates." (Exodus 20: 8-10).

"Till the land on Sunday" do we understand,
Urged upon the people of our favoured land?
"Till the land on Sunday!" Christians, take a stand,
'Gainst the voice of Popery in this darkened land.

"Till the land on Sunday!" All will be in vain;
For we need the sunshine, we shall need the rain.
God must give the increase; if he rain withhold,
And no sunshine sendeth, where will be the food?

"Till the land on Sunday!" England, take a stand;
Six days God commanded man should till the land.
Heaven declares the Sabbath holy to the Lord!
Thus, expect no blessing, if you break his Word.

Keep the Sabbath holy, God will give the rest;
Nations that do honour him, surely shall be blessed,
Blessed in store and basket; but if we forsake,
God will on lands guilty surely vengeance take.

A. Edwards, Horsham.[966]

Confession and Supplication

The Summer's passing on,
The Autumn's drawing nigh,
The fields of corn we look upon
Doth cause us many a sigh.

The corn has ripened fast,
But rain and winds prevail;
Will it be spoilt now, at the last?
Our hearts begin to fail.

We have despised the Lord,
In these most solemn days;
The teachings of his Word ignored,
And walked not in his ways.

"Don't heed the Sabbath day;
The crops must be got in;"
God's Holy Word thus disobeyed
Became a national sin.

"Go, plough and plant the land;
We must have food to eat;"
Thus they despised the Lord's command,
And took the scorners' seat.

Both Church, yes, and Dissent,
God's laws did thus deny;
Not teaching sinners to repent,
But teaching to defy.

Disease, so we are told,
Is spreading far and wide;
If God his blessing doth withhold,
None else can e'er provide.

O, England; once so blessed,
In providence and grace,
God from us now his blessings wrests,
And O, doth hide his face!

Throughout this dreadful war,
His power has been defied –
His truth, and grace, and Scriptures are
By thousands all denied.

W. Leaman, Bournemouth, August 27th, 1917.[967]

Hymns for time of war

During the war, there was felt to be a lack of hymns suitable to the time in the standard Strict Baptist hymn book, William *Gadsby's Selection of Hymns for Public Worship*. In response to this, a number of hymns and poems were specially written. The following hymns were mainly composed by the minister, Mr Ben Warburton. He later published them in a booklet entitled *Hymns for Time of War*.

1.

King of kings! Defend the right!
Put the godless hosts to flight!
Bring to nought their power and skill,
Save us from each threatening ill.

Midst the desolating woe,
Teach us, Lord, thy will to know;
While the war-lust sweeps the land,
Keep us safe within thy hand.

Let thy wings be spread above
Every object of our love:
Stay each messenger of death,
Turn aside each poisoned breath!

In the hour of storm and stress,
Thou alone our souls canst bless:
Give us strength to bear each cross,
Sanctify to us each loss.

Bid the war-clouds, Lord, to fly!
Bid each Christless passion die!
Cause the cruel strife to cease!
Bring, O bring, thy lasting peace!

B. A. Warburton.[968]

2.

While war's dread conflicts shake the earth,
While thousands daily fall,
Lord, we would leave the worldling's mirth,
And for thy mercy call.

Our favoured land has turned aside
From truths once dearly prized;
And, lifting up her head in pride,
Thy blessings hath despised.

And now, in righteous wrath, thy hand
Doth on us sorely press;
And war, 'neath thy supreme command,
Sinks us in deep distress.

Lead us to search our hearts and try
Our ways, and turn once more
To thee, who hears the suppliant's cry,
O God of grace and power!

Thou who hast stricken canst alone
Our nation's sufferings heal,
And, turning from thy wrath, make known,
The love thou dost conceal.

Before thy footstool, Lord, we bend:
In mercy hear our plea!
From every ill our land defend,
And turn our hearts to thee!

B. A. Warburton.[969]

3.

O God of hosts, whose powerful hand
O'er all creation doth bear sway,
Look down upon our stricken land,
Be thou our sure defence this day,
O hear us in our time of need,
In war's dread grip our land doth bleed!

The nation's manhood, far and wide,
Has answered to the nation's call,
Thousands in our defence have died,
Thousands yet further still must fall,
O hear and help us, mighty God!
O stay the avalanche of blood!

Loved ones lie stricken 'neath the skies,
Loved ones lie buried 'neath the wave;
The widow mourns, the orphan cries
In sorrow o'er an unknown grave.

O hear us, God of might, and bless
The nation in its sore distress!

The sins that for thy chastening call,
Teach us contritely to confess:
And with true supplication fall
Before thee, craving thee to bless.
O hear us, God of might! Arise!
And drive the war-cloud from the skies.

Hasten the time thy Word makes known,
When nations shall learn war no more;
When godless might shall be o'erthrown,
And silenced be the cannon's roar.
Hear us, and cause all strife to cease,
And reign o'er all, O Prince of Peace.

B. A. Warburton.[970]

4.

O God of hosts, arise!
Hear our united cries,
  Make war to cease:
Its desolating hand
Doth press upon our land
O do thou take command;
  Lord, send us peace.

We own thy sovereign right
Our country thus to smite,
  For sins increase.
Thy Word, with wisdom stored,
Is mocked – thy day ignored,
Yet do have mercy, Lord;
  O send us peace!

Those who on sea and land
For our defence do stand,
  In mercy bless.
Teach them to look to thee,
Thou their protector be,
Grant speedy victory;
  Lord, send us peace.

Those who now wounded lie,
In quivering agony,
  Deign thou to ease;
Close thou the glazing eyes,
And hear the suppliant's cries;
O God of mercy, rise!
  Send, send us peace!

B. A. Warburton.[971]

5.

While the war-clouds round us lengthen,
  God of hosts, we turn to thee;
Do our faith and patience strengthen,
  May we watch thy will to see;
    Ever pleading
  Thou wilt grant us victory.

Bless our rulers 'neath the burden
  Which upon them now doth press:
Let thy wisdom be their guerdon,[972]
  Keep them in the hour of stress:
    Give them guidance,
  And their counsels richly bless.

Bless the peoples of the nation
  In the sacrifices made;

Prove that thou art our salvation,
Let our minds on thee be stayed.
God of mercy!
Grant us thy almighty aid.

Keep us, Lord, from all division,
Shield us from all party strife;
Let no godless, mean ambition
Prey upon the nation's life.
Be our guardian
While the powers of war are rife.

Thou the future wisely hideth,
Weal or woe is in thy hand;
Make us know thy mercy guideth
To the blessing thou hast planned;
When thy praises
Shall resound throughout our land.

B. A. Warburton.[973]

6.

God of mercy! God of blessing!
Deign to hear our heart-felt prayer!
While, our sins to thee confessing,
We commit into thy care
Loved ones on a foreign soil,
Struggling 'neath war's crushing toil.

Spread thy wings, O Father, o'er them;
Be thou their defence and stay:
Let thy presence go before them,
Keep them from all ill, we pray:
Guard them by thy mighty power,
When the battle-cloud doth lower.

Jesus, let thy great salvation
Cheer their souls in earth's dark night;
Gild the doom of devastation
With the rays of heavenly light.
Succour them in time of need,
Prove thou art their friend indeed.

Holy Spirit, grant thy sealing:
Breathe thy consolation kind:
Be each wounded spirit's healing,
Strengthen every heart and mind.
Bid the rage of battle cease!
Bless us with thy perfect peace!

Father, Son and Holy Spirit!
Thou eternal God of love!
Though deserving sin's demerit,
May we thy compassion prove!
Then our grateful songs of praise
We to thy great name will raise.

B. A. Warburton.[974]

7.

"God is good." All nature says it,
Daily bringing it to view;
All the Scriptures clearly show it,
Gladly we consent 'tis true:
If before his bar we stood,
Should we then say, "God is good?"

Long ere Israel had a being,
All their boundaries were known;
Not their wit, nor might, or striving
Were to shape their course alone.

From heaven's throne their ways were viewed,
Tried and tested, proved 'not good.'

On they went, in mad defiance
Of reproofs in mercy sent;
With the nations made alliance,
On their own self-seeking bent.
God's own prophets they ignored,
Mocked the counsel of the Lord.

Then his judgements fell upon them,
And the arm of flesh gave way,
Foes prevailed, and terrors seized them,
Sinking them in sore dismay.
Clear and just God's judgements stood,
And their ways were shown 'not good.'

"God is just." Today we own it,
Gathered in this house of prayer:
We have sinned, Lord, we confess it,
We, like Israel, greatly err.
Chastened, they thy mercy found:
May the same to us abound.

F. J. Kirby and B. A. Warburton.[975]

8.

Britain! Hear the voice of warning,
Hear, O hear, God's cry!
Ere beneath his outpoured anger
Thou dost lie.

Britain owes to him allegiance,
He her past did mould;
And her yet unwritten future
His hands hold.

Thou hast heeded not his statutes,
Thou hast turned aside,
Living chiefly for thy pleasures
And thy pride.

He has shown his sore displeasure;
Judgements heavier still
Lie before thee, if thou seekest
Not his will.

If repentant, he will save us,
And his grace display;
Nineveh before him pleading
Points the way.

Let us come, then, to his footstool,
And with sins confessed,
We shall prove that God in mercy
Will give rest.

F. J. Kirby and B. A. Warburton.[976]

Benjamin A. Warburton

Poems about victory

The following two poems were written after the signing of the Armistice and cessation of fighting on 11th November, 1918.

National Thanksgiving

Almighty God, with heart and tongue,
We now thy wondrous power proclaim,
We praise thy name with hymn and song:
And from our breast, with holy flame
And joy unknown, we Britons raise
Triumphant shouts and gladsome praise.

The war, with all its scenes of blood,
And fears and terrors by it caused,
Has now, at thy command, O God,
Made peace to reason's calmer force!
To thee we look! Rule thou for us!
The work of peace do thou complete.

Nations and kingdoms widely spread,
Have of their best most nobly given;
Our sons for freedom's sake have bled,
And parents' hearts with pain were riven;
But prayer ascended in those days
That thou thy power wouldst display.

Thou heardst our call, read our desire;
Emperors and kings thou didst control;
And all to which they did aspire
Was crumbled, broken; and their roll
Of crime, in breadth and length is stayed!
Our thankful songs to thee are raised!

The Armistice crown with final peace;
Thy kingdom come with power divine;
Thy will be done from West to East;
Empire and thrones be wholly thine.
Unto thy name we Britons raise
Our gladsome songs and notes of praise!

F. J. Kirby, November 15th, 1918.[977]

Thanks be to God which giveth us the victory

We praise thee, Heavenly Father,
For what thine arm hath done;
Our mighty foe is conquered,
The victory hath been won.
No more we need the bayonet,
The rifle, or the sword,
For peace proclaimed, and England saved,
We thank thee, blessed Lord.

Brought through the gloom and darkness,
Into the light of day,
Thine was the arm in danger's hour
That held the foe at bay.
We trusted not to numbers,
But looked to thee alone
To come to our assistance,
And "roll away the stone."

Our enemies were countless,
But what was that to thee?
Who saidst, "No further shalt thou go,"
E'en to the troubled sea.
Our men were given special strength

To stand the trying hour,
And now are more than conquerors,
Through thy almighty power.

All honour to our soldiers,
Who fought so well and brave;
All honour to our sailors,
Who braved the ocean wave;
We're proud to call such men as these
Our brother and our friend,
But most of all, to thee, our God,
Our thanks we would extend.

And now the conflict's over,
And peace proclaimed once more,
May the *Entente Cordiale*
Still reach from shore to shore,
And while we call Great Britain
The land of the free and brave,
Let's ne'er forget that God above
Alone can help and save!

William Calton, Southampton.[978]

A French postcard from the First World War showing British soldiers defending a position

Notes

[1] GS (1915) pp. 5-6.
[2] GH, No. 746.
[3] GH, No. 76.
[4] On his father's side, David Field (see p. 51); on his mother's side, Edward O'Kill Dadswell, who served in the Canadian Field Artillery as a driver. Edward Dadswell and was killed on 20th August, 1918, and is buried at Ligny-St. Flochel British Cemetery, France.
[5] GH, No. 1139.
[6] GH, No. 833.
[7] FC (1921) pp. 174-177. We have left this account as it stands, showing a contemporary understanding of the commencement of hostilities. There are however differing accounts in modern history books as to the exact order of events surrounding the German invasion of Belgium and Britain declaring war. Some agree with Mr Croft's account, others do not.
[8] See FC (1914) pp. 229-232, and GS (1915) pp. 5-10.
[9] The Strict Baptist pastor at Devizes.
[10] Henry Wiles was also a famous sculptor before his call by grace. His works are in the collections of leading British museums.
[11] *The Gospel Magazine* (1930) pp. 536-537.
[12] I am grateful to Mr T. J. Rosier, Mr John H. Gosden's successor as pastor at Maidstone, for clarifying Mr Gosden's view of the war.
[13] The stigma on conscientious objectors is seen from a Strict Baptist perspective in an article in *The Christian's Pathway*. See CP (1916) pp. 370-371.
[14] *The Birmingham Gazette* (1916) 2nd March, p. 3.
[15] *The Liverpool Mercury* (1916) 28th February, p. 6.
[16] *The Birmingham Gazette* (1916) 22nd March, p. 5.
[17] CP (1915) pp. 347-348.
[18] CP (1916) p. 292.
[19] At the start of the Second World War, Mr Gosden encouraged the young men of his congregation to sign up, saying that at least this war, unlike the First World War, was a *just war*. (Personal communication, Mr T. J. Rosier). For some of Mr Popham's thoughts on men, and ministers, fighting, see GS (1915) June wrapper, p. xii, December wrapper, p. xii.
[20] See *The London Gazette* (1919) 11th March, p. 3442. Mr Gosden served in the 6th Field Ambulance, No 500257.
[21] FC (1970) p.228.
[22] GS (1914) p. 382.
[23] GS (1915) p. 6.
[24] GS (2014) p. 69.
[25] The Annual Address, GS (1855) pp. 1f.
[26] CP (1917) pp. 45-47.

[27] C.f. CP (1916) pp. 128, 284.
[28] It is almost impossible to give a precise number as to how many Strict Baptists served in the war. The chapels represented in 'The Muster Roll' represent a very small number of the total number of Strict Baptist causes. It is also difficult to precisely determine the number of Strict Baptist chapels at the time. Dr Kenneth Dix cites 587 being open in 1900, but lists 31 of these as being closed by 1919 (Dix, K. (2001) *Strict and Particular: English Strict and Particular Baptists in the nineteenth century.* The Strict Baptist Historical Society, Didcot. p. 279f.) Some chapels are not represented in this list. The figure of 550 given in the text is therefore likely to be a conservative estimate of all Strict Baptist Chapels associated with the lists published by *The Gospel Standard, The Earthen Vessel* and *The Christian's Pathway.*
[29] GS (1954) p. 223.
[30] GS (1971) p. 319.
[31] Eighteen people were killed in this air raid.
[32] GS (1919) p. 294.
[33] FC (1918) p. 132.
[34] CP (1918) pp. 43-44. The quote is from the well known hymn, "Abide with me."
[35] Of the 638 names on *The Christian's Pathway* 'Muster Rolls', over half were listed as being privates in the army.
[36] CP (1916) p. 33.
[37] *The Times* (1911) October 3rd.
[38] Information gleaned from an undated and unidentified newspaper cutting, collected by Mr John Raven and pasted into his volume of Grey Hazlerigg's sermons, now in the author's possession.
[39] GH, No. 352.
[40] These details were kindly provided by Mr Saunderson's grandson.
[41] These details were kindly provided by Mr Julyan's daughter.
[42] CP (1916) p. 129.
[43] Catalogue for the sale of Orders, Decorations and Medals, held by Dix, Noonan and Webb on 29th March, 2000. Lot 908. With the exception of the Victoria Cross, the DCM is the highest award for bravery that non-commissioned officers and the junior ranks are eligible for.
[44] CP (1917) p. 175.
[45] GH, No. 241.
[46] GS (1985) p. 384.
[47] His promotion.
[48] This name was given by the British forces to a particular German gun.
[49] CP (1916) pp. 161-163.
[50] CP (1917) p. 204.
[51] GH, No. 64.
[52] GS (1964) p. 222.
[53] CP (1917) p. 228.
[54] GH, No.232.
[55] GS (1918) p. 126.
[56] FC (1915) p. 220.
[57] GS (1967) pp. 220-221. Notice of Mr Burfoot's brother, Ebenezer, who was killed in the war can be found on p. 292.
[58] Personal communication from Mrs P. Izzard.
[59] CP (1916) p. 196.
[60] FC (1939) pp. 142-143.
[61] GS (1976) p. 159.
[62] I am grateful to Mr Morris' granddaughter for this information.
[63] Extract from John Pack's war diary, kindly loaned to the author by his son.
[64] CP (1916) p. 58.
[65] FC (1915) pp. 263-264.
[66] CP (1917) p. 100.
[67] GS (1971) p. 350.
[68] GS (1975) p. 255. For letters written to Percy Lodge while serving in the navy, see p. 428.
[69] GS (1984) p. 349.
[70] CP (1916) p. 381.
[71] CP (1917) p. 128.
[72] CP (1918) p. 124.
[73] See GS (1931) p. 88f.
[74] See p. 328.
[75] We are fairly certain this is an error in the original, and should read 'Peebles Hospital.'
[76] GS (1972) p. 92.
[77] Salkeld, H. (1996) *The Vital Year.* Gospel Standard Trust Publications.
[78] CP (1919) p. 150.
[79] Vaughan, W. B. G. (1928) *For Jesus' Sake: the Life and Ministry, with Sermons, of John Booth.* C. J. Farncombe and Sons, Ltd., London. pp. 64-65.
[80] GS (1963) p. 126.
[81] GS (1988) p. 90.
[82] CP (1916) p. 128.
[83] GS (1977) p. 159.
[84] Marcus Ebenezer and Arthur Joseph. The fourth brother, Maurice Legh, joined up later in the war. See p. 126.
[85] GS (1992) p. 125.
[86] Exactly what a 'bar-way' is, is unclear. It is probably a term describing a gate.
[87] GS (1976) p. 254.
[88] By 'his own faith' he refers to being a Strict Baptist. CP (1916) p. 132.
[89] Honeysett, R. J. (1987) *Life and Experiences.* Privately published. p. 4.
[90] GH, No. 440.
[91] GS (1981) p. 156.
[92] *The Anzac Gospel Echo* (1916) September, No 1, p. 1.
[93] For Emma Littleton's obituary, see GS (1927) p. 313f.
[94] See Littleton, J. (1884) *To Him that Remembered me in my Low Estate.* F. Kirby, London. And, GS (1889) p. 141f.

[95] Probably Noah John Littleton, born 1875.
[96] FC (1917) p. 63.
[97] Further examples can be found in the obituary of Albert Golding of St Ives (See GS (1949) p.59) and of George Nicholls of Wadhurst (See GS (1948) p. 298).
[98] FC (1918) p. 32.
[99] See CP (1922) pp. 113-114.
[100] Curtis, S. (1928) *A Memorial of Samuel Curtis*. C. J. Farncombe and Sons, Ltd. London. pp. 43-44.
[101] See CP (1933) p. 36.
[102] See p. 52.
[103] GS (1918) p. 360.
[104] The Highland Cemetery.
[105] GS (1969) p. 160, and personal communication, Mr and Mrs J. W. Brooks, Brabourne.
[106] GS (1996) p. 290.
[107] GS (2003) p. 92.
[108] GH, No. 961.
[109] See GS (1972) p. 31; (2001) p. 127; (2012) p. 318.
[110] GS (2012) p. 318.
[111] CP (1917) p. 252.
[112] Wild, E. (1943) *Memories of a Young Brother Killed in the Great War, 1916*. Privately published. p. 75.
[113] Wild, E. (1943) *Memories of a Young Brother Killed in the Great War, 1916*. Privately published. pp. 82-83.
[114] FC (1918) pp. 142-143.
[115] GH, No. 4.
[116] These letters are included in this volume, see p. 369.
[117] I am grateful to Lydia's grandson, Mr P. Hanks, for the information which appears in this paragraph.
[118] See p. 40.
[119] For accounts of Archdale Palmer, see Paul, S. F. (1954) *Further History of the Gospel Standard Baptists*. Privately published. Vol 2 pp. 210-214 and GS (1932) pp. 96, 266ff. For an account of Lady Biddulph see: Hyde, M. J. (2010) *According to Mine Heart*. Gospel Standard Trust Publications. pp. 337-338.
[120] GS (1940) p. 118.
[121] CP (1914) p. 277.
[122] This is believed to be a reference to a letter from the Pastor included in each parcel, rather than to a supply of letter (or writing) paper.
[123] FC (1915) p. 73.
[124] Rhoda Brooker died young, of cancer. For further details of her life and other poetical writings, see Harman, R. (1929) *Letters and Poems of Rhoda Harman*. Brooker, Hastings.
[125] FC (1915) pp. 194-195.
[126] Personal communication from Mr and Mrs B. Honeysett.
[127] GH, No. 352.
[128] GS (1984) p. 189.
[129] Personal communication from Mr John Ruse.
[130] For details regarding Mr John H. Gosden see p. 22; for Mr Frank L. Gosden see p. 215.
[131] GS (1987) pp. 187-188.
[132] One of these was Mr George Humberstone, later a supply minister among the Strict Baptists. (See p. 100).
[133] GS (1975) p. 192.
[134] GS (1984) p. 190.
[135] GS (1984) p. 190.
[136] Buss, G. D. (2000) *The Hidden Pathway*. Gospel Standard Trust Publications. pp. 56-61.
[137] For an account of Mr Aldworth, see *The Sower* (1937) p. 169., and for Mrs Aldworth, see CP (1929) p. 52f.
[138] Buss, G. D. (2000) *The Hidden Pathway*. Gospel Standard Trust Publications. pp. 59-60.
[139] Broome, L. R. J. (1988) *Surely Goodness and Mercy*. Gospel Standard Trust Publications. p. 3.
[140] Personal communication from Mrs E. Beadle.
[141] LG (1916) pp. 37-38.
[142] CP (1915) p. 353.
[143] CP (1916) p. 293.
[144] ZW (1916) October, pp. 5-6; FC (1916) p. 260. See also: Wilcockson, A. (c.1866) *The Way He Hath Led Me*. E. Hannath, Hull. On Mr Wilcockson's death *Zion's Witness* nearly came to an end. However, the following note was circulated in the October, 1916, edition:
"To the readers of the *Zion's Witness*.
Dear Friends,
Although it had been decided to discontinue the *Witness*, the writer, who has been in close personal friendship with the late dear Editor for a number of years, intends, with the Lord's help, to conduct it for the present.
It may not be out of place to say, our dear friend intimated to him several times that he believed it to be the Lord's will that he should succeed him. Knowing, however, the liability of the best of men to make mistakes, the writer gave no encouragement to these intimations, wishing to see the hand of the Lord clearly himself.
When he looks at his natural unfitness and inability, not to mention his dreadful condition as a sinner, it seems little short of presumption for him to undertake so important a work.
It has pleased the Lord, however, in all ages 'to choose the foolish of the world to confound the wise, and the weak things of .the world to confound the things which are mighty, and base things of the world, and things which are despised, hath God chosen; yea, and things which are not, to bring to nought things that are: that no flesh should glory in his presence.'
Should our gracious Lord condescend to own and bless the feeble labours of the unworthy writer, it will be made manifest that all the power belongs alone to him.
Will the lovers of *Zion's Witness* still support it by their prayers, that it may be the means of humbling the sinner and exalting a glorious

Christ; that the spirit of the world and the flesh, together with all error, may be ever excluded from its pages.
Brethren, pray much for him who subscribes himself feelingly the weakest of all saints,
Herbert Sawyer, 36, Coltman Street, Hull. September 28th, 1916."
Mr Sawyer took up the editorship, the magazine survived Mr Wilcockson's sudden death, and it is still published today.
[145] FC (1916) p. 98.
[146] FC (1916) p. 72.
[147] Pack, J. E. (2000) *Tell it to the Generation Following*. Gospel Standard Trust Publications. p. 74.
[148] Windridge, F. (n.d.) *His Great Goodness*. O. Perks, Watford, UK. p. 123.
[149] GS (1978) p. 155. Mr Pither was the father of Mrs C. G. Hyde, the author's grandmother. For a photo, see p. 16.
[150] *Kent Messenger* (1916) April 29th, p.6.
[151] Fir or pine planks.
[152] CP (1915) pp. 61-62.
[153] Banks, A. (1975) *A Military Atlas of the First World War*. Heinemann. p. 296.
[154] The War Office (1922) *Statistics of the Military Effort of the British Empire during the Great War*. H.M. Stationary Office, London. p. 676-678. Also: Hersch, L. (1927) La mortalité cause par la guerre mondiale. *The International Review of Statistics*. 7 (1) pp. 47-61.
[155] For example, GS (1918) January wrapper, p. xv.
[156] Buss, G. D. (2000) *The Hidden Pathway*. Gospel Standard Trust Publications. p. 61.
[157] *The Coventry Evening Telegraph* (1914) 18th September, p. 2. During the war this fund was regularly advertised in *The Gospel Standard* and support for it encouraged by Mr Popham. See for example: GS (1914) December wrapper, p. xii.
[158] A type of self-propelled wheelchair.
[159] FC (1919) p. 119.
[160] CP (1917) p. 56.
[161] CP (1915) p. 123.
[162] Salkeld, H. (1996) *The Vital Year*. Gospel Standard Trust Publications. pp. 48-49.
[163] The old currency of Italy, prior to the introduction of the euro.
[164] FC (1918) p. 92.
[165] FC (1918) p. 115.
[166] Mr Popham appealed in the wrapper of *The Gospel Standard* for voluntary donations towards the cost of printing his monthly sermon: "As the cost of paper and labour has so much increased, we are now printing the monthly sermons at considerable personal loss, and rather than raise the price, we ask those of our friends, who have the means, to help us in this matter by their generous contributions, as has already been done by some." GS (1918) May wrapper, p. xii.
[167] C. J. Farncombe and Sons, the denominational printers, were forced to place an advert in *The Gospel Standard* to tell readers that "owing to the scarcity of paper we cannot now undertake the printing of a larger bill for Anniversary Notices etc., than 11 ¼ in. by 8 ¾ in. (half the usual size). We will accept orders for any number not exceeding 50, and we ask our friends not to take more than are absolutely needed, so that no paper is wasted." See GS (1918) August wrapper, p. xv.
[168] GS (1918) November wrapper, p. xii.
[169] For a further account of how the war affected a Strict Baptist business, see GS (1950) p. 92 and (1955) p. 252.
[170] See CP (1924) p. 59. James W. Tiptaft had a brother, William Tibetot Tiptaft, who was also a Strict Baptist minister at Mexborough, Yorkshire (see CP (1927) p. 245). Several of William T. Tiptaft's sons served in the war (see CP (1916) p. 225), and one, William Rutherford Tiptaft, was killed. He is buried in the Klien-Vierstraat British Cemetery.
[171] In later life, Norman Tiptaft stood unsuccessfully for election as a member of parliament and served a term as Lord Mayor of Birmingham. Sadly, he forsook his parents' religion, becoming thoroughly liberal. His autobiography, *The Individualist* (1954), contains interesting references to his childhood hearing of Mr James Dennett's ministry at Frederick Street Chapel, Birmingham (pp. 18-19).
[172] See Tiptaft, N. (1954) *The Individualist*. Norman Tiptaft Ltd., Birmingham. p. 65; *The Happy Jeweller* (1932) No 15, Spring, p. 3.
[173] See ZW (2006) pp.177-181. A number of pieces by him (sermons, letters, and poems, etc) appeared in *The Gospel Standard* and *The Sower* during the 1800s.
[174] See *The Sower* (1893) p. 186.
[175] CP (1918) pp. 42-43.
[176] A fairly lengthy memoir of Frank Buggs was published by his sister, Esther Wild. Given its length, and the fact that it is already in wide circulation, we have not quoted at length from it in this book. See Wild, E. (1943) *Memories of a Young Brother Killed in the Great War, 1916*. Privately published.
[177] See p. 415.
[178] FC (1917) pp. 139-140. See also: Wild, E. (1943) *Memories of a Young Brother Killed in the Great War, 1916*. Privately Published.
[179] Also see CP (1917) pp. 217-218.
[180] FC (1918) pp. 119-120.
[181] GS (1975) p. 126.
[182] GS (1914) p. 382. Mr Popham also suggested the churches join for prayer on 3rd January, 1915; see GS (1915) January wrapper, p. xii.
[183] GS (1999) p. 189.
[184] *Kent Messenger* (1916) January 8th, p.8.
[185] See Williamson, P. (2003) National days of prayer: the churches, the state and public worship in Britain, 1899-1957. *English Historical Review*. 128. pp. 323-366. Also: www.ucb.co.uk/british-national-days-prayer-twentieth-century [accessed 28th January, 2015].
[186] CP (1918) p. 68.
[187] GS (1916) February wrapper, p. xii.

[188] Windridge, F. (n.d.) *His Great Goodness*. O. Perks, Watford, UK. pp. 136-137. The same issue was in fact raised again during the Second World War, when Mr J. H. Gosden argued the same point, that the Sabbath is to be used for divine worship, rather than national concerns (GS (1942) Supplement, September. p. i.)
[189] FC (1917) pp. 267-268.
[190] FC (1921) pp. 174-177.
[191] Montgomery, A. (1920) *The Story of the Fourth Army in the Battles of the Hundred Days*. Hodder and Stoughton. p. 7.
[192] FC (1917) pp. 152-153.
[193] http://www.wscountytimes.co.uk/news/nostalgia/breach-of-4th-commandment-october-1914-1-6376823 10/01/15 [accessed 18th January, 2015].
[194] See GS (1953) p. 384.
[195] Told to the author by his grandmother, Mrs E. M. Field, daughter of William Savory.
[196] *Folkestone, Hythe, Sandgate and Cheriton Herald* (1918) 12th January, p. 8.
[197] See p. 357.
[198] *Sussex Agricultural Express* (1915) 26th February, p. 12.
[199] *Sussex Agricultural Express* (1915) 2nd April, p. 8.
[200] GS (1927) p. 66.
[201] CP (1919) p. 174.
[202] CP (1916) p. 238.
[203] See CP (1916) p. 347.
[204] For further information, see Hyde, M. J. (2014) *Gadsby's: The story of a hymn book 1814-2014*. Gospel Standard Trust Publications, Harpenden. p. 165.
[205] For further information, see Hyde, M. J. (2014) *Gadsby's: The story of a hymn book 1814-2014*. Gospel Standard Trust Publications, Harpenden. pp. 154-157.
[206] It was first advertised in May 1918. See GS (1918) May wrapper, p. xv.
[207] The only potential sources we have been able to trace are as follows: On the Tyne Cot Memorial, Passchendaele, Belgium, there is recorded the name of Benjamin Rowland, from Ecclesall, Sheffield, whose wife was Ethel Rowland. After Benjamin was killed in the war, his widow married George F. Allen, in 1920. However, militating against this possible source is that the preface to *The Companion Tune Book* acknowledges "Miss Ethel Allen," suggesting that Ethel Allen was unmarried. There was an Ethel Allen, a violinist, who was listed as a licentiate of the Royal Academy of Music, during the 1920s. It has not been possible to determine whether these are the same person.
[208] CP (1917) pp. 53-54 and 87-88.
[209] CP (1917) p. 87.
[210] CP (1917) pp. 104-110. James Pearson is buried in Sailly-Saillisel British Cemetery, France.
[211] GS (1969) p. 219.
[212] GS (1969) p. 219.
[213] There was controversy over this situation between *The Christian's Pathway* and *The Gospel Standard* magazines. See CP (1916) pp. 184-185 and (1918) pp. 13, 17, and 133; GS (1918) October wrapper, p. xii.
[214] GS (1918) October wrapper, p. xii.
[215] The Gospel Standard Societies publicly offered the services of their solicitor to ministers facing problems with conscription. See GS (1918) July wrapper, p. xii.
[216] GS (1960) p. 270.
[217] CP (1915) p. 383.
[218] I am grateful to Mr Morris' granddaughter for this information.
[219] See *The London Gazette* (1918) 17th May, p. 5986.
[220] *The London Gazette* (1919) 30th May, p. 6877.
[221] GS (1960) p. 380.
[222] *The Times* (1917) August 31st, p. 14.
[223] CP (1918) p. 123.
[224] GS (1944) p. 188.
[225] For an interesting account of Mr Stone, see CP (1933) p. 211. Mr Stone was called to the pastorate at West Hartlepool in 1916. It is reported of his call by grace that "he was arrested almost as marvellously as the Apostle Paul himself, for God met him in the main street of Sunderland, after he had attended a football match between Sunderland and Newcastle, and convinced him that what he was doing was not pleasing in God's eye. He was born in 1883, but never sat in a chapel until 1907. He was baptised in November, 1910 by John Smith, of Siddal, and preached for the first time on the first Lord's Day in January, 1912."
[226] *Newcastle Journal* (1917) 21st September, p. 8.
[227] *Liverpool Daily Post* (1917) 25th September, p. 7.
[228] *Kent and Sussex Courier* (1916) 11th August, p. 6.
[229] Mercer, M. (1957) *A Little One in Zion*. E. J. Harmer. p. 14.
[230] For an interesting review of this see MacLeod, J. L. (2007) The mighty hand of God: The Free Presbyterian Church of Scotland and the Great War. *BRIDGES*. 12 (1) pp. 19-41.
[231] For further information, see Reed, J. W. (n.d.) *He, Being Dead, yet Speaketh*. C. J. Farncombe and Sons Ltd., Croydon.
[232] CP (1914) pp. 357-358. Mr Popham and Mr H. T. Stonelake did similarly in *The Gospel Standard* for men attending Galeed Chapel, Brighton, and Nottingham Chapel respectively (GS (1915) March wrapper, p. xii and (1916) January wrapper, p. xii.).
[233] CP (1916) p. 353.
[234] LG (1915) p. 236ff. and (1916) p. 17ff.
[235] See Wiles, M. (2003) *Scholarship and Faith: A Tale of Two Grandfathers*. Biograph, Cambridge. p. 112. Harold Wiles' son, Maurice Wiles, was a renowned theologian, and held the office of Regius Professor of Divinity at the University of Oxford, although he was seriously heterodox on the doctrine of the Person of Christ. Maurice's son, Sir Andrew Wiles, is also a professor at the University of Oxford, most famed for solving Fermat's Last Theorem.
[236] GS (1975) p. 30.
[237] ZW (1978) June, pp. 281-283.

[238] GS (1980) p. 205.
[239] GS (1985) p. 59.
[240] GS (1958) pp. 190-191.
[241] See CP (1915) p. 259; and GS (1956) p. 323.
[242] See CP (1916) p. 196; and GS (1970) p. 320.
[243] See CP (1915) p. 290.
[244] See CP (1917) p. 249; and GS (1957) p. 192.
[245] GS (1978) p. 126.
[246] GS (1972) pp. 317-318.
[247] GS (1976) p. 255.
[248] GS (2001) p.330.
[249] FC (1918) p. 216.
[250] GH, No. 64.
[251] CP (1919) p. 100.
[252] Salkeld, H. (1996) *The Vital Year*. Gospel Standard Trust Publications. p. 64.
[253] CP (1918) p. 221.
[254] GS (1918) December wrapper, p. xii.
[255] The sermon is amongst the typescripts of the late Miss Sybil Baker, preserved in the Gospel Standard Baptist Library at Hove.
[256] Clark, S. (1932) *God's Mercy and Goodness, as manifested to Stephen Clark of Mayfield, during the Great War 1916-1918*. C. J. Farncombe and Sons, London. P. 20
[257] CP (1919) p. 123.
[258] FC (1919) p. 93.
[259] CP (1919) p. 118f.
[260] Probably J. G. Evans, the pastor at Rehoboth Chapel, Tunbridge Wells.
[261] Rowell, P. M. (1981) *Preaching Peace*. The Stanley Delves Trust. p. 20.
[262] CP (1919) p. 123.
[263] GS (1919) pp. 1-2.
[264] Rowell, P. M. (1981) *Preaching Peace*. The Stanley Delves Trust. p. 20.
[265] Health issues arising from the war were often long-term. When John Paul, a member at Brighton, Galeed, and brother of S. F. Paul, the editor of *The Gospel Standard*, died suddenly in 1926, aged 50, his death was attributed by his doctor to the stress of his war service. See GS (1927) p. 87f. and (1950) p. 42.
[266] CP (1916) p. 347.
[267] Probably a reference to Arthur C. Morley. See CP (1919) p. 100.
[268] Stonelake, H. T. (1924) *Words of counsel*. C. J. Farncombe and Sons Ltd, London. pp. 24-28.
[269] FC (1944) pp. 43-45; cf. GS (1946) p. 253 footnote.
[270] CP (1919) p. 103.
[271] CP (1919) p. 130.
[272] Wild, E. (1943) *Memories of a Young Brother Killed in the Great War, 1916*. Privately published. p. 82.
[273] FC (1922) p. 32f.
[274] Although the houses have since been demolished in the course of local redevelopment, the money arising from their compulsory purchase was invested and the charity still makes financial distributions from this to local cases of need.
[275] CP (1931) p. 310.
[276] Personal communication, Mrs M. Palmer and Mr E. Palmer.
[277] GH, No. 1139.
[278] GS (1980) p. 206.
[279] Possibly GS (1917) p. 57f.
[280] GH, No. 64.
[281] A light machine gun, designed by Isaac Newton Lewis in 1911, which was produced in England and used throughout the British Empire through the war and continued in service until at least 1942.
[282] GH, No. 480.
[283] GS (1993) p. 262.
[284] GS (1992) pp. 125-126.
[285] A hotel.
[286] Marcus and his brother Herbert.
[287] High church, as in Anglo-Catholic.
[288] That is, tag along with, or always attempt to be in the company of Marcus.
[289] William Thomas, of Loose, who died in 1916. See GS (1917) p. 161ff.
[290] Probably Arthur Boorman, who at that time was a member of the congregation at Priory Chapel. See *The Sower* (1930) p. 108ff.
[291] Edwin Picknell, pastor at Station Road Chapel, Redhill, who died in 1918. See GS (1919) p. 49.
[292] Possibly William Little, of Brighton, who died in 1916. See GS (1916) p. 295.
[293] Probably J. E. Hazelton, of Streatley Hall, London. See GS (1925) p. 185.
[294] Young Men's Christian Association.
[295] Medal ribbons.
[296] Meaning he was elevated a rank.
[297] Probably his brother.
[298] The exact meaning is unclear here. During the early months of 1916, there were increased calls within the military for unrestricted submarine warfare, i.e. German submarines could attack any ship without warning, even ships from neutral nations. On 29th February, 1916, Naval Chief of Staff, Admiral von Holtzendorff, withdrew previous restrictions on German submarines, and submarine warfare intensified. However, this was short-lived, as the German Command remained concerned about provoking America into joining the war against them, and on 4th May, 1916, Germany promised America that its submarines would keep within international law. Unrestricted submarine warfare did not commence again until 1st February, 1917.
[299] Probably a reference to General Gordon of Khartoum, as 'Abide with me' is always reckoned to have been his favourite hymn.
[300] Heavy artillery gun.
[301] As Field Marshall, Douglas Haig had overseen the battle of Neuve Chapelle, on 10th March, 1915.
[302] The Germans.

[303] A lesser known verse of the hymn, 'Abide with me' by Henry F. Lyte.
[304] GH, No. 64.
[305] His brother.
[306] One of the county regiments.
[307] His brother. See GS (1986) p. 320.
[308] GH, No. 27.
[309] GH, No. 1022.
[310] During the opening days of the Battle of Marne, when the German Crown Prince Frederick William was stationed in the home of the Baroness de Baye, he is reputed to have plundered her collection of art. However, Chateau de Baye is nowhere near Gorre, so Marcus was obviously misled in thinking this was the castle which had been plundered.
[311] For a medal, or promotion.
[312] Literally 'outside the fight' – a status given to those unable to defend themselves when the enemy overcame them, because of injury, or having to parachute out of an aeroplane behind enemy territory. A form of prisoner of war.
[313] A small village near Uckfield, East Sussex.
[314] The exact meaning of this is unclear. It is possible it refers to the advanced posts in No Man's Land, in front of the front line of trenches, manned by a few men and armed with machine guns.
[315] This is probably Second Lieutenant George E. Elliott, who died of his injuries, on 20th May, 1916, and is buried in Bethune Town Cemetery. He was the son of Rev. W. Hayward Elliott, Vicar of Bramhope, Leeds, and a graduate of Queen's College, Oxford.
[316] Quite what Mr Elliott had done to upset the men is unclear.
[317] At the time, high ranking officers still had the privilege of a servant while in front line service. These were generally known as a 'batman,' and would have taken leave at the same time as the officer they served.
[318] A medal awarded for distinguished service in war.
[319] A Scottish regiment.
[320] This is probably a reference to the lice, cockroaches, and other vermin, which plagued the men in the trenches.
[321] A small, shabby, French café.
[322] The Battle of Jutland. This was the only battle between the main battle-fleets of Britain and Germany, and, although indecisive, the German fleet returned to port after the battle, leaving Britain dominant at sea.
[323] One of the county regiments.
[324] See p. 40.
[325] It is difficult to know which other soldier Marcus thought so highly of. Sir John French had been forced to resign from high level command in December, 1915. History has not necessarily judged French kindly, although at the time he appears to have had some considerable support from the regular troops.
[326] The French National Anthem.
[327] One of the Scottish regiments.
[328] Probably the King's Bagpiper.
[329] Isaac Watts.
[330] Another of the county regiments.
[331] A box car, like a cattle truck, on the French narrow-gauge railway, so named because on the side they had stencilled, '40 hommes 8 chevaux,' meaning they could carry 40 men or 8 horses.
[332] A straw mattress.
[333] Marcus here uses the French word for pavement, presumably meaning a road with a hard surface.
[334] A sap was a tunnel built beneath the enemy, and filled with explosives, aimed to destroy the enemy's position. It uses the old definition of sap – to undermine.
[335] Unlocated, but obviously around Ypres somewhere.
[336] All four brothers, Arthur Joseph, Marcus Ebenezer, Herbert Pitt and Maurice Legh were now serving in the army.
[337] He refers to the battle now known as the Third Battle of Passchendaele
[338] A heavy artillery gun. The term '5.9' refers to the bore (or diameter) of the gun in inches.
[339] His brother Bert.
[340] GS (1918) pp. 279-280.
[341] GS (1981) pp. 285-288.
[342] GH, No. 320.
[343] GH, No. 64.
[344] The accuracy of this report is uncertain. It would appear that rather than being sunk immeadiately, *Highland Brae* was captured by *Kronprinz Wilhelm*, and only sunk a couple of weeks later, after all the cargo and supplies had been transferred. The exact fate of the crew is unknown.
[345] GH, No. 320.
[346] GH, No. 64.
[347] GH, No. 320.
[348] Bradford, D. E. (1987) *The Autobiography of Douglas Edward Bradford*. Ebenezer Chapel, Matfield. pp. 20-36.
[349] Personal communication, Mr S. A. Hyde.
[350] This is taken from Mr Buck's own manuscript. A reduced version was published in GS (1983) p. 30.
[351] See GH, No. 314.
[352] GS (1975) pp. 29-30. Also: FC (2006) pp. 196-197.
[353] GH, No. 64.
[354] Why Stephen Clark was reticent to serve in the East is unknown. It may have been because of the distance from home, but we cannot be certain.
[355] See GS (1930) p. 129 and CP (1931) p. 132.
[356] GH, No. 320.
[357] GH, No. 680.
[358] GH, No. 64.
[359] GH, No. 64.
[360] The National Union of Railwaymen staged a national strike of railway workers between September 27th and October 6th, 1919.
[361] John Bunyan.

[362] GH, No. 346. The original account was dated: Fir Toll Cottage, Mayfield, Sussex, February 11th, 1932. Taken from: Clark, S. (1932) *God's Mercy and Goodness, as manifested to Stephen Clark of Mayfield, during the Great War 1916-1918.* C. J. Farncombe and Sons, London. See also: CP (1918) p. 100.
[363] 13th June, 1917. It killed 162 civilians. See Banks, A. (2013) *A Military Atlas of the First World War.* Leo Cooper. p. 293.
[364] Chapman, J. (n.d.) *In the Service of the King.* Privately published. pp. 13-18.
[365] Further details of this experience are given in: Chapman, J. (n.d.) *In the Service of the King.* Privately published.
[366] GS (1957) pp. 318-320.
[367] GS (1988) pp. 90-91.
[368] Pastor at Rochdale Road Chapel, Manchester (see GS (1936) p. 209f.).
[369] This is a No 61, black Lett's Oblong Diary for 1916, still complete with its elasticated band to hold it shut. Inside it is inscribed: "George Crowter with the best of wishes from his loving Mother. Mizpah." It was kindly loaned to me for transcription by his descendants. I have written out in full all abbreviations used in the diary, and corrected the spellings of place names where their location is definite, as an aid to the reader. It is published here in its entirety, and entries become more spasmodic towards the end of the year.
[370] In Belgium.
[371] Kit was the name George Crowter gave to his fiancée, later to be his wife, Kate. For an account of Mrs Crowter, and a brief note of how she met him when he was stationed in Colchester and started to attend the Strict Baptist Chapel there during Mr Crowter's wartime service, see GS (1973) p. 31.
[372] A British heavy artillery gun.
[373] A light hearted comment about shelling from both sides, given it was the Kaiser's birthday.
[374] A reference to Exodus 12: 13.
[375] He appears to start numbering the letters he receives and sends.
[376] A German heavy gun.
[377] Fokkers were a make of German aeroplane.
[378] The spelling and meaning here is unclear.
[379] The Germans.
[380] Presumably meaning Erquinghem-Lys.
[381] Isaiah 66: 13 and 2 Corinthians 6: 17.
[382] Evidently a reference to an artillery gun. The shell must have discharged before it fired, destroying the gun.
[383] Romans 7: 24.
[384] Until this point he had been stationed on the Belgian front. Now he moves to the Somme region of the French front.
[385] Probably Ribemont-sur-Ancre.
[386] A German reconnaissance plane.
[387] He was carrying early gas masks out to the men in the frontline trenches.
[388] The British 18lb gun was a common field artillery gun in use by the British army throughout the war.
[389] A British artillery gun.
[390] French 75mm gun.
[391] The 64th Brigade, 21st Division.
[392] This location, though mentioned several times in the diary, has not been identified.
[393] Incendiary shells, designed to light up the front at night.
[394] Presumably signifying that the re-equipping stretched over the next three days as well.
[395] Mr Crowter here records being an eyewitness to the first ever use of tanks in warfare. Developed in secrecy, they must have terrorised the Germans as they saw them advancing over the trenches towards them for the first time. They allowed access over the barbed wire defences of no-man's land, and could drive over the enemy's trenches. Their greatest weakness was a lack of manoeuvrability, and their greatest enemy was the quagmire of French mud which covered the front lines at times during the war.
[396] A reference to the use of flame-throwing devices, which projected incendiary liquid into the enemy trenches, burning everything it came into contact with.
[397] Just a dash given at this juncture in the original.
[398] Just a blank in the diary: "Le   ", but probably Lesboeufs.
[399] It has not been possible to locate Heaux-les-Manes.
[400] A reference to Heaux-les-Manes in the previous entry.
[401] An area of the front line manned and commanded by the French army.
[402] GS (1981) p. 50.
[403] GS (1941) p. 352.
[404] November, in the Western calendar.
[405] Rowell, P. M. (1981) *Preaching Peace: A Biography of Stanley Delves.* The Stanley Delves Trust, Crowborough. pp. 17-22.
[406] GH, No. 135.
[407] GS (1966) p. 280. See also: Fay, W. (1969) *Waymarks.* Gospel Standard Trust Publications. pp. 24-28.
[408] GS (1966) pp. 311-312.
[409] GS (1981) pp. 156-157.
[410] GH, No. 440.
[411] GS (1982) pp. 284-286.
[412] Mr John Kemp (Jr.) of Luton.
[413] Daniel 12: 13.
[414] GH, No. 76.
[415] GS (1980) pp. 205 and 378.
[416] Mr Gosling also wrote a little pamphlet: *Free Will, the Root Error,* which is still in print and obtainable from the Huntingtonian Press, Hedge End.
[417] Mr Gosling lied about his age, stating he was 18 in order to join up in 1914, when he was in fact just 16 years old.
[418] GS (1951) p. 322.
[419] For further details of Mr Gurney's life, see Gurney, B. J. (1970) *Brought Forth as Gold.* Mrs G. M. Gurney.

[420] GS (1958) p. 222.
[421] GS (1981) pp. 147-148.
[422] See GS (1987) p. 283f.
[423] Honeysett, R. J. (1987) *Life and Experiences of R. J. Honeysett.* Privately published. pp. 4-5.
[424] Extracted from three pieces in ZW: (1976) *The Blessed Spirit's unmistakable work.* October, pp. 26-29; (1978) *A few particulars of the Lord's dealings with the late Mr Geo. Humberstone.* June, pp. 273-279; *Call to ministry.* June, pp. 279-281. See also GS (1978) pp. 125-126.
[425] GS (1972) p. 158.
[426] GS (1981) p. 381.
[427] GH, No. 591.
[428] GH, No. 758. Taken from GS (1969) pp. 159-160.
[429] FC (1982) p. 78ff.
[430] Lord Derby's scheme called for voluntary enlistment of men, prior to conscription. A portion of those enlisting under the scheme were given deferred dates for actually joining the army, and were sent home to their employment. It would appear that men hoped that by volunteering they would be spared active service.
[431] The East Kent Regiment.
[432] *The Gospel Pulpit* No. 219.
[433] *The Gospel Pulpit* No. 218.
[434] GH, No. 154.
[435] GH, No. 470.
[436] GH, No. 281.
[437] GH, No. 1086.
[438] A heavily fortified and defended series of German trenches running across the North Western Front.
[439] *The London Gazette* (1919) 24th January.
[440] Reuben Paul's medals were sold at auction by Dix Noonan Webb of London in 2000, where they were described in the catalogue as follows: "Distinguished Conduct Medal, G.V.R. (C-7740 Pte.-L.Cpl., 13/K.R. Rif. C.); Military Medal, G.V.R. (C-7740 Pte., DCM 13/K.R. Rif. C.); British War and Victory Medals (C-7740 Pte., K.R. Rif. C.); French Croix de Guerre 1914-1918, extremely fine." The hammer price was £900.
[441] The following is extracted from GS (1919) pp. 294-300. Obituaries of Reuben's parents appear in GS (1930) pp. 291-298 and (1950) p. 20ff.
[442] GH, No. 64.
[443] GH, No. 70.
[444] GH, No. 320.
[445] William Huntington, the famous Independent minister.
[446] Distinguished Conduct Medal.
[447] GH, No. 320.
[448] See GS (1927) p. 87f. John Paul's early death at the age of 50, in 1926, was attributed by his doctor to the stress of his war service (see GS (1950) p. 42).
[449] Mr Popham's Monthly Sermons, number 127.
[450] See GS (1923) p. 30-32.
[451] Possibly Charles Clayton, see GS (1940) p. 64.
[452] See p. 197f.
[453] GH, No. 968.
[454] Probably John Booth of Bradford, see GS (1928) p. 129.
[455] See GS (1925) p. 42ff.
[456] GH, No. 64.
[457] GH, No. 726.
[458] This is generally known as the opening of Operation Michael, with the Battle of St. Quentin taking place on 21st – 23rd March, 1918.
[459] A type of machine gun.
[460] From: Salkeld, H. (n.d.) *The Night Watches.* Privately published. pp. 2-17. See also: GS (1996) pp. 157-160.
[461] *The London Gazette* (1917) 28th December, p. 45.
[462] See GS (1948) p.35ff, and Hyde, M. J. (2014) *Gadsby's: The story of a hymn book 1814-2014.* Gospel Standard Trust Publications. pp. 198 and 206.
[463] A More detailed account of Mr Shaw's war-time experience can be found in his biographical writings: "The Valley of Achor, or The Door of Hope of the Stranger," published in *The Sower* (1949) January, p. 152ff. The pagination of the January 1949 issue of *The Sower* is incorrect, hence the odd page numbering for this reference.
[464] GH, No. 268.
[465] GH, No. 292.
[466] GH, No. 412.
[467] GH, No. 281.
[468] GH, No. 958.
[469] In which the Greeks and the British forces fought against the Bulgarian army. Doiran is in present day Macedonia.
[470] GH, No. 232.
[471] GH, No. 1085.
[472] From: GS (1948) pp. 75ff.
[473] Personal communication from Mr S. A. Hyde.
[474] Mr Henry Haddow, the pastor; see GS (1936) pp. 116ff.
[475] GH, No. 144.
[476] GS (1983) pp. 252-253.
[477] See CP (1923) p. 133.
[478] GS (1916) p. 123f.
[479] GS (1985) pp. 315-317.
[480] GS (1966) pp. 285-286.
[481] GS (1954) p. 223.
[482] GH, No. 1023.
[483] Origin unknown.
[484] Poem by F. W. H. Myers. Account extracted from FC (1926) pp. 162-164.
[485] ZW (1917) August, pp. 343-344.
[486] Mr Shadrach Hawkins was a supply minister from Reading. See GS (1943) p. 195f.
[487] GH, No. 76.

[488] Joseph Baker's wife, Louisa Baker, died of cancer shortly after his return from the war. Her obituary appears in CP (1919) p. 53.
[489] CP (1917) pp. 56-57.
[490] See p. 74 and CP (1924) p. 59.
[491] FC (1915) pp. 223-224.
[492] His father died on June 29th, 1914.
[493] See p. 277.
[494] FC (1915) p. 224.
[495] The abbreviation used for the King's Royal Rifle Corps, a regiment in the British army.
[496] FC (1915) pp. 308-309.
[497] FC (1915) p. 309.
[498] Normally a reference to something like corned beef.
[499] FC (1916) pp. 56-57.
[500] FC (1916) pp. 105-106.
[501] FC (1916) p. 106.
[502] Probably the Medical Officer.
[503] Presumably a reference to the bombardment of Hartlepool and other East Coast towns by the German Navy.
[504] Probably a reference to General Kitchener.
[505] Probably a reference to the stretcher bearers.
[506] Herbert, D. (1819) *Hymns and Poems*. Simpkin and Marshall, London. Volume 1, pp. 95-99.
[507] Mr George Rose, who at that time was pastor at Providence Chapel, Cranbrook.
[508] FC (1916) p. 134.
[509] FC (1916) pp. 192-193.
[510] FC (1916) p. 193.
[511] FC (1916) p. 284.
[512] Probably references to Rev. James Ormiston, the Editor of *The Gospel Magazine*, who died on 30th September, 1916; see *The Gospel Magazine* (1916) pp. 529ff. Mr William Thomas, of Loose, Maidstone, an itinerant minister, who died on 8th July, 1916; see GS (1917) pp. 161ff.
[513] FC (1917) p. 58.
[514] GH, No. 4.
[515] GH, No. 362.
[516] FC (1917) p. 109.
[517] See *The Sower* (1930) pp. 108ff.
[518] FC (1917) pp. 182-183.
[519] GH, No. 352.
[520] Normally a reference to something like corned beef.
[521] The Army Service Corps provided the food and supplies to the servicemen on the front, no doubt including the fresh food Frank mentions.
[522] Sentry duty.
[523] It would appear that *The Daily News* paid to provide all the troops with a Christmas pudding for Christmas 1914.
[524] Another regiment.
[525] A common boiled sweet of the time.
[526] Here Frank would have been expressing the common sentiment at the time – the buoyant optimism of the early war that it would all be over by Christmas 1914.
[527] FC (1915) pp. 49-51.
[528] A British army regiment.
[529] A German reconnaissance plane.
[530] FC (1915) pp. 83-85.
[531] FC (1915) pp. 102-103.
[532] To pink something is to punch a hole through it.
[533] FC (1915) pp. 103-104.
[534] A suet pudding.
[535] *Allemand* is the French word for Germans.
[536] FC (1915) pp. 140-141.
[537] A quick firing artillery gun commonly used by the French army.
[538] Possibly a reference to Ypres?
[539] FC (1915) pp. 168-169.
[540] This is probably a reference to the battle of Neuve-Chapelle, although this is generally dated 10th-13th March, 1915.
[541] His brothers.
[542] Probably the 'oxslip', *primula elatior*.
[543] FC (1915) p. 169.
[544] Probably a reference to the 2nd Battle of Ypres.
[545] Flares, used to light up the front for night attacks.
[546] On 16th April, 1915, a German Albatros BII dropped five bombs on Sittingbourne. The only victim was a blackbird.
[547] FC (1915) pp. 169-170.
[548] Gas was first used as a lethal weapon by the Germans at Ypres on 22nd April, 1915, but after that it was added to the weaponry of all countries. This is an historically significant eyewitness account of this event.
[549] German guns; Krupps was the German gun maker.
[550] The Medway is the river running through his hometown of Maidstone.
[551] FC (1915) p. 222.
[552] FC (1915) pp. 222-223.
[553] FC (1915) p. 223.
[554] The 9.2 inch Howitzer was a common artillery gun used by the British army.
[555] FC (1915) pp. 278-279.
[556] Part of the hoof.
[557] A French town near the Belgian border.
[558] FC (1916) p. 104.
[559] FC (1916) pp. 104-105.
[560] FC (1916) p. 256.
[561] Probably a reference to Frank Buggs from the congregation at Ebenezer Chapel, Matfield, who was killed on 7th September, 1916.
[562] FC (1916) p. 304.
[563] A plum pudding.
[564] FC (1917) pp. 57-58.
[565] Rubbing, or combing down.
[566] FC (1917) p. 183.

[567] A reference to the Strict Baptist Chapel in Priory Road, Maidstone. At the time, Mr Arthur Boorman and his family were attending there.
[568] FC (1917) p. 126.
[569] Young Men's Christian Association.
[570] Army slang for the YMCA.
[571] FC (1917) pp. 241-242.
[572] FC (1917) p. 183.
[573] See GS (1930) p. 129 and CP (1931) p. 132.
[574] Quote from Joseph Irons' hymn: 'Let saints proclaim Jehovah's praise.' The hymn appears in Denham's hymn book, No. 366.
[575] Tom was his brother, who had been wounded in battle. This appears to have been Thomas Benjamin Burfoot, who was later deacon for 25 years at Hope Chapel, Blackboys, Sussex (see GS (1967) pp. 220-221).
[576] CP (1918) pp. 95-96.
[577] GH, No. 873.
[578] ZW (1978) May, pp. 248-251.
[579] ZW (1978) June, p. 283.
[580] GH, No. 315.
[581] GH, No. 4.
[582] GH, No. 386.
[583] ZW (1917) Volume 69, p. 284f. It is likely that this letter was written to Mr Herbert Sawyer.
[584] GH, No. 369.
[585] ZW (1917) Volume 69, p. 339f. It is likely that this letter was written to Mr Herbert Sawyer.
[586] CP (1934) p. 115. In early life, Ebenezer (Jnr) had spent time working in India, see Littleton, E. (1908) *A Jubilee of Ministerial Mercies*. C. J. Farncombe and Sons, London. pp. 109ff.
[587] GH, No. 805.
[588] GH, No. 806.
[589] GH, No. 474.
[590] FC (1918) pp. 9-12.
[591] I am grateful to Mr P. Clark for access to the quotes from Mr Clark's own manuscript writings.
[592] These have not been included here, but it is hoped that they may one day be published separately.
[593] I am grateful to Mr P. Clark of Barton, for providing this information and the original quotes from Mr Clark's extant writings that I have included in this introduction to his letters.
[594] See GS (1931) p. 256.
[595] In other words, if God had mercy on him, it would be a miracle.
[596] FC (1962) pp. 44-46.
[597] Septimus Sears. This hymn is No. 386 in the *Clifton Hymns, A Service of God for United Worship*. Houlston and Wright, London. (undated, but the Bodleian dates it 1870).
[598] FC (1963) pp. 4-5.
[599] Probably Samuel Curtis, the pastor at Southill.
[600] Ebenezer Chapel, Luton. This has been identified by searching through the preaching lists published in the GS for 10th June, 1917.
[601] FC (1963) pp. 5-6.
[602] FC (1962) pp. 47-48.
[603] GH, No. 680.
[604] GH, No. 351.
[605] FC (1963) pp. 6-8.
[606] GH, No. 199.
[607] FC (1963) p. 8.
[608] Mr Clark mentions this expression in the following letter. The series of letters is obviously not complete, and it is also possible that the dates of the letters, as given in the magazines, are mis-reported.
[609] Their mother, Susan Clark, had died in 1911 (see GS (1912) p. 189f.). The 1911 census shows Ebenezer living with his sister, Emily Robinson, at Barton-le-Clay. Ebenezer appears to have been one of ten children. His father James' obituary appears in GS (1941) p. 160. Susan Clark's father, John Frost, was a most godly man; his obituary can be found in GS (1883) p. 315f.
[610] GH, No. 335.
[611] FC (1963) pp. 8-10.
[612] GH, No. 471.
[613] GH, No. 143.
[614] FC (1962) pp. 64-66.
[615] GH, No. 199.
[616] Probably Mr Edward Carr, of Bath. He had taken the "autumn services" at Ebenezer Chapel, Luton, on 26th September, 1917 (see GS (1917) September wrapper, p. vii.).
[617] FC (1962) pp. 66-67.
[618] GH, No. 278.
[619] FC (1962) pp. 67-69.
[620] FC (1962) pp. 84-85.
[621] His brother.
[622] GS (1917) p. 341.
[623] FC (1962) pp. 85-88.
[624] FC (1962) pp. 88-90.
[625] FC (1962) pp. 90-91.
[626] *The Sower* (1918) pp. 22-24.
[627] LG (1918) pp. 7-8.
[628] GS (1986) p. 219.
[629] The reference here would be to the Garden of Gethsemane, which is believed to have changed little since the time of the Lord Jesus Christ, and some of the olive trees there now may have been present then. However, to associate a particular spot in the garden with a particular event must be dubious.
[630] FC (1919) p. 25.
[631] His wife.
[632] ZW (1917) July, p. 319.
[633] GH, No. 397.
[634] GH, No. 958.
[635] FC (1917) pp. 272-274.
[636] For an obituary see GS (1954) pp. 125-127.
[637] CP (1917) p. 180.

[638] GS (1954) p. 126.
[639] GH, No. 155.
[640] GS (1981) pp. 54-55.
[641] A day of national prayer had been held on 4th January, 1915.
[642] FC (1915) pp. 101-102.
[643] Probably John W. Gillett, of Accrington Chapel, see GS (1945) p. 128.
[644] FC (1915) p. 102.
[645] For his obituary, see GS (1931) p. 88f.
[646] A reference to 'Hope' Strict Baptist Chapel, Redhill, Surrey.
[647] GS (1931) pp. 88-89.
[648] The church was at that time considering giving Mr John Raven the call to the pastorate. Mr J. K. Popham had oversight of the church.
[649] GS (1931) p. 90.
[650] LG (1915) pp. 60-61.
[651] GH, No. 938.
[652] Isaac Watts.
[653] LG (1915) pp. 80-81.
[654] Henry F. Lyte.
[655] GH, No. 938.
[656] GH, No. 1002.
[657] LG (1915) pp. 95-96.
[658] Unfortunately it was not always true that the British treated their prisoners with respect. Ebenezer Oliver (see p. 229 for more information) records how one evening at the front in 1918 he was standing guard with another man over two German soldiers, who had been captured. A Regimental Sergeant Major came along and said to them: "What are you doing here?" Mr Oliver told him that they were waiting authority to take the two prisoners behind the lines. To this the Regimental Sergeant Major replied, "We can't spare you on a night like this, shoot them." When neither Mr Oliver nor his companion moved, the Regimental Sergeant Major retorted, "Well if you won't, I will," and Mr Oliver states: "The lads dropped at our feet with a groan." Smith, E. M. (1990) *A Short History of my Immediate Ancestors*. Privately published. p. 19.
[659] GH, No. 103.
[660] LG (1915) pp. 118-119.
[661] LG (1915) pp. 143-144.
[662] GH, No. 76.
[663] Frances R. Havergal.
[664] GH, No. 1106.
[665] GH, No. 1002.
[666] LG (1915) pp. 160-161.
[667] These strikes by the dock workers on Clydeside were part of what has become known as 'Red Clydeside.' Radicalisation among the working class led to a number of high profile strikes. During the war a number of these strikes, aimed against legislation governing the work force and rent rises, were specifically anti-war.
[668] LG (1915) p. 227.
[669] LG (1915) p. 227.
[670] LG (1915) pp. 227-228.
[671] LG (1915) pp. 228-229.
[672] At this time there were very few female doctors, hence the surprise expressed here.
[673] LG (1915) p. 216.
[674] Note added in the original: 'He means here the fear of the natural man, as he had told me his faith was sometimes tried.'
[675] LG (1915) p. 216.
[676] There is probably some confusion here, as it would appear that no such rank has ever existed in the British Army. The letter probably should have read: "Lance Corporal."
[677] One of the British county regiments.
[678] It is unclear where exactly his imprisonment as a prisoner of war, which must have been brief, fits into the account.
[679] LG (1915) pp. 216-217.
[680] It is unclear if this is Servia, the town in Greece, or the old spelling for Serbia. It is most likely to be Serbia, although the Serbian Army was beaten before reinforcements (including British) could get there.
[681] LG (1915) p. 254.
[682] GH, No. 43.
[683] CP (1916) pp. 282-284.
[684] A record of his early experience was published in: GS (1919) pp. 148-153.
[685] GH, No. 801.
[686] GS (1919) pp. 194-195.
[687] GS (1919) pp. 196-197.
[688] GH, No. 155.
[689] GS (1919) p. 197.
[690] GH, No. 667.
[691] GH, No. 23.
[692] GS (1919) pp. 197-198.
[693] The 1911 Census shows that they had at least one other son, Herbert, born in 1910, and three daughters, Ethel (b. 1900), Ruth (b. 1902), and Nellie (b. 1905).
[694] *The Kent and Sussex Courier* (1916) 25th August, p. 3.
[695] See http://www.judithjohnson.co.uk/blog/the-sorrow-of-the-moons [accessed 12th December, 2014]
[696] GH, No. 871.
[697] GH, No. 273.
[698] GH, No. 824.
[699] Mr Edward Carr, the pastor at Bath.
[700] FC (1916) pp. 269-271.
[701] FC (1916) p. 269.
[702] GH, No. 1113.
[703] FC (1915) pp. 334-335.
[704] *The Kent and Sussex Courier* (1916) 18th February, p. 7.
[705] pp. 13-16.
[706] FC (1915) pp. 17-21.
[707] FC (1916) pp. 132-134.
[708] GH, No. 64.

[709] FC (1917) p. 224.
[710] Henry and Walter.
[711] GH, No. 158.
[712] GH, No. 938.
[713] FC (1916) pp. 271-273.
[714] This was a standard postcard on which a soldier could tick boxes and delete statements to send to relatives to inform them they had arrived safely at their destination.
[715] *The Devonshire Road Pulpit*, New Series No. 82, October 1914. Sermon preached by Joseph Jarvis, Lord's Day evening, October 4th, 1914. Text: Isaiah 43: 1-2.
[716] GH, No. 667.
[717] FC (1916) pp. 273-274.
[718] CP (1916) pp. 348-349.
[719] Since the establishment of Pakistan in 1947, Sialkot has been in Pakistan, and not India.
[720] Smith, E. M. (1990) *A Short History of my Immediate Ancestors*. Privately published. pp. 10-13.
[721] CP (1916) p. 58.
[722] A Greek island off the coast of Turkey.
[723] CP (1915) pp. 347-348.
[724] For an obituary of Thomas Dare, the pastor at Chard, see CP (1931) pp. 16-18.
[725] CP (1915) pp. 348-349.
[726] FC (1917) p. 153.
[727] GH, No. 64.
[728] (1916) p. 264.
[729] GH, No. 70.
[730] GH, No. 4.
[731] GH, No. 64.
[732] John Newton (1842-1914), the pastor at Hanover Chapel, Tunbridge Wells, Kent.
[733] The soldier mentioned here was Angus Cattanach, a member of the Free Presbyterian Church of Scotland congregation at St. Jude's Church, Glasgow. His pastor, Rev. Neil Cameron, wrote the piece in *The Little Gleaner*. See LG (1917) pp. 6-7.
[734] GH, No. 967.
[735] Hope Chapel, Horsham.
[736] LG (1917) pp. 21-22.
[737] Presumably a reference to the address where they used to gather on a Lord's Day evening.
[738] Probably Charles Hewitt, of Hungry Hill. See GS (1921) p. 163.
[739] LG (1917) pp. 6-7.
[740] FC (1918) pp. 85ff.
[741] GH, No. 958.
[742] GH, No. 351.
[743] GH, No. 440.
[744] GH, No. 440.
[745] GH, No. 673.
[746] There was a mortgage on Hope Chapel, Horsham, at the time.
[747] FC (1918) pp. 177-179.
[748] Hanover Chapel, Tunbridge Wells.
[749] FC (1918) pp. 194-195.
[750] See GS (1978) p. 352.
[751] FC (1917) pp. 217-218.
[752] *The Sower* (1917) pp. 22-23.
[753] The author of these lines was Isabella Stevenson (1843-1890).
[754] *The Sower* (1917) pp. 23-24.
[755] Probably Florrie, his wife.
[756] *The Sower* (1917) pp. 43-45.
[757] George's wife.
[758] FC (1921) pp. 11-13.
[759] Although the date of 6th September is the date given in the *Friendly Companion*, the Commonwealth War Graves Commission give the date of death as 26th September, 1916, which is the one we have chosen to use in the book. It is possible that this was a typographical error in the original source, or that this is an example of the difficulties families had obtaining information about their loved one's death.
[760] A reference to their other son, Frank W. Smith, who appears to have survived the war.
[761] FC (1918) pp. 142-143.
[762] GH, No. 333.
[763] CP (1918) p. 26.
[764] CP (1919) p. 55.
[765] FC (1919) pp. 24-25.
[766] Based on birth certificate records.
[767] FC (1915) pp. 196-198.
[768] FC (1915) pp. 196-198.
[769] Mark's brother.
[770] Another brother.
[771] Original letter kindly supplied by Mark Ruse's nephew, Mr John Ruse of Stotfold.
[772] See p. 356.
[773] GH, No. 481.
[774] GH, No. 320.
[775] GH, No. 64.
[776] See GS (1940) pp. 126-7.
[777] FC (1918) pp. 132-136.
[778] GH, No. 320.
[779] Probably Gallipoli.
[780] This is most likely to be a reference to Zion Chapel, High Wycombe.
[781] LG (1916) pp. 60-61.
[782] Sadly, this was not the case, and the epidemic would continue to claim lives up until 1920.
[783] Probably a reference to Galeed Strict Baptist Chapel, Brighton.
[784] FC (1958) pp. 23-25. The author is unknown, although it is suspected that this may have been written by Mr Jesse Delves; see p. 205.
[785] FC (1914) p. 324. Of this letter the editor wrote that it was: "... recently received by a niece of ours from her husband, who was,

like so many more, suddenly called upon to leave her and their three little ones, and comfortable home."
[786] GH, No. 64.
[787] FC (1917) p. 217.
[788] This part of the letter is a mystery. The fighting on Italian soil during this part of the war was in the north east of the country, where, to our knowledge, there is no record of volcanic activity. Exactly what is being described has proved impossible to determine.
[789] GH, No. 289.
[790] FC (1918) pp. 137-139.
[791] i.e. whether it was right to work on the Lord's Day, in order to maximise the war effort.
[792] The Prime Minister from 1916.
[793] FC (1917) pp. 254-256.
[794] An assistant to the priest.
[795] FC (1918) pp. 195-196.
[796] Source unknown.
[797] FC (1915) pp. 333-334.
[798] GS (1917) p. 339f. The sermon, on Romans 8: 1, had been preached by John Welch of Ayr.
[799] FC (1918) pp. 39-40. It is possible that the writer of this letter was Frederick Paul, and that it was addressed to his pastor, Mr J. K. Popham, who at that time was assisting Mr Jefferies (probably the Mr J. mentioned in the letter) with the editing of *The Friendly Companion*.
[800] This is likely to have been Frederick Paul, the brother of both Reuben, an account of whom appears in this book (see p. 232), and Sydney F. Paul, who would later become editor of *The Gospel Standard*.
[801] FC (1918) pp. 59-60.
[802] GH, No. 770.
[803] FC (1917) pp. 183-184.
[804] GH, No. 24.
[805] FC (1917) p. 216.
[806] FC (1917) pp. 64-65.
[807] FC (1917) p. 108.
[808] GH, No. 770.
[809] Isaac Watts.
[810] FC (1917) pp. 108-109.
[811] A Strict Baptist.
[812] FC (1917) pp. 216-217.
[813] From Charles Wesley's hymn: 'Father of Jesus Christ, my Lord.'
[814] GH, No. 564.
[815] Given the closing comment in the letter, it would suggest the writer had been injured and was recuperating at home. Evidently a printed sermon was read at this service in the absence of a minister.
[816] It is possible that this letter was written by Alfred James Ellis, later the pastor at Worthing. See page 324.
[817] FC (1917) p. 218.
[818] FC (1917) pp. 218-219.
[819] GH, No. 64.
[820] GH, No. 698.
[821] A reference to Hanover Strict Baptist Chapel, Tunbridge Wells.
[822] FC (1918) pp. 176-177.
[823] The hymn has the refrain in the last line of each verse: 'His lovingkindness O how ...'
[824] Mr Seth Pack, the pastor at Hanover Chapel, Tunbridge Wells.
[825] FC (1918) p. 177.
[826] Joseph M. Scriven.
[827] FC (1917) pp. 126-128.
[828] The author suspects they could have been from the hand of Mr F. L. Gosden.
[829] GH, No. 938.
[830] GH, No. 958.
[831] FC (1945) pp. 203-204.
[832] Possibly a reference to a landing of an invading force somewhere, likely to be the Dardanelles.
[833] FC (1946) pp. 40-42.
[834] It is possible this letter was written by Thomas Tingley of Scaynes Hill. See CP (1917) p. 155 and GS (1948) p. 179. His father, William Tingley, a supply minister, who was a member at Scaynes Hill, had died during the war on 22nd April, 1915, aged 69 years (GS (1915) p. 515f.).
[835] CP (1919) p. 157.
[836] The old French currency.
[837] This is a reference to the fundraising then taking place for a building to replace the old Gower Street Chapel, London, on which the lease was shortly to expire. See FC (1917) pp. 72-73.
[838] FC (1917) p. 241.
[839] FC (1919) pp. 25-26.
[840] It is unclear which of the letters in *The Little Gleaner* is being referred to here.
[841] Possibly Richard C. Edwards, of Swanwick Shore, see CP (1917) p. 225.
[842] LG (1918) pp. 80-81.
[843] See p. 55.
[844] GH, No. 7.
[845] GH, No. 850.
[846] Wild, E. (1943) *Memories of a Young Brother Killed in the Great War, 1916*. Privately published. pp. 77-79.
[847] See CP (1933) p. 36.
[848] John Downing is buried at Fins New British Cemetery on the Somme.
[849] Adelaide Downing, who was a member at Spring Meadow, Old Hill. See p. 52.
[850] FC (1920) pp. 153-154.
[851] See Littleton, J. (1884) *To Him that Remembered me in my Low Estate*. F. Kirby, London. Also GS (1889) p. 141f.
[852] FC (1915) pp. 286-288.
[853] FC (1916) pp. 25-29.
[854] For further details of Mrs Riseley, see GS (1926) p. 67.

[855] Phoebe A. Dye, see ZW (1914) November, pp. 63-64.
[856] FC (1915) pp. 85-56.
[857] GH, No. 64.
[858] FC (1918) pp. 68-69.
[859] FC (1915) pp. 263-264.
[860] FC (1915) pp. 141-142.
[861] FC (1942) pp. 25-27.
[862] See GS (1948) p. 58.
[863] GH, No. 64.
[864] FC (1948) pp. 74-75.
[865] Jarvis, S. H. (1946) *Wonders of Grace in the Salvation of a Large Family.* C. J. Farncombe and Sons, Ltd. pp. 114-116.
[866] Sometimes called a 'Very light.' This was a flare which was used to light up the front at night.
[867] Source unknown.
[868] *The Sower* (1926) pp. 185-186.
[869] Both letters were kindly provided for inclusion here by Percy Lodge's grandson.
[870] GS (1925) p. 284.
[871] Probably a reference to his future brother-in-law, named as Albert Allen Durling in the 1911 Census.
[872] A reference to Salem Chapel, Portsmouth.
[873] Undoubtedly a reference to religious periodicals, such as *The Gospel Standard.*
[874] GH, No. 746.
[875] GH, No. 806 Part 1.
[876] The Strict Baptist Chapel in Nottingham.
[877] FC (1916) pp. 239-240.
[878] See Paul, S. F. (1954) *Further History of the Gospel Standard Baptists.* Privately published. Vol 2, p. 124f.
[879] GH, No. 212.
[880] LG (1916) pp. 76-77.
[881] See GS (1938) p. 160.
[882] See GS (1954) p. 283f.
[883] GH, No. 991.
[884] GH, No. 765.
[885] FC (1948) p. 152.
[886] FC (1918) p. 32.
[887] GH, No. 925.
[888] GH, No. 405.
[889] GH, No. 1106.
[890] FC (1917) pp. 145-146.
[891] For his obituary, see GS (1992) p. 125.
[892] FC (1920) p. 14.
[893] GS (1918) p. 186.
[894] GH, No. 64.
[895] GH, No. 732.
[896] FC (1919) pp. 35-37.
[897] GH, No. 64.
[898] GH, No. 698.
[899] FC (1916) pp. 33-35.
[900] Probably a reference to Private Arthur C. Morley. See CP (1919) p. 100.
[901] GH, No. 527.
[902] GH, No. 4.
[903] FC (1916) pp. 229-231.
[904] GH, No. 1083.
[905] FC (1916) p. 69.
[906] Splinters.
[907] Gas tank.
[908] GH, No. 64.
[909] William Gadsby, see Gadsby, W. (1824) *The Nazarene's Songs.* Manchester. No. 256. (Recently republished by Gospel Standard Trust Publications.)
[910]GH, No. 346.
[911] John Bunyan.
[912] GH, No. 7.
[913] FC (1916) pp. 289-292.
[914] GH, No. 64.
[915] CP (1915) pp. 61-62.
[916] *Cheering Words* (2015) p. 19. Private Jay was from the congregation at Sible Hedingham.
[917] FC (1919) pp. 10-11.
[918] FC (1917) pp. 167-168.
[919] CP (1917) pp. 284-285.
[920] Containing numerous references to the Classics, this was obviously written by a well-educated young man.
[921] Friedrich von Bernhardi (1849-1930) was a German militarist, who advocated a policy of ruthless aggression in warfare.
[922] Heinrich Gotthard von Treitschke (1834-1896) was a German nationalist historian, who sought to legitimise the extension of German territory into Poland and the East.
[923] Without a care.
[924] FC (1919) pp. 50-51.
[925] LG (1916) pp. 15-16.
[926] CP (1916) p. 107.
[927] CP (1915) pp. 364-365.
[928] FC (1917) pp. 81-82.
[929] FC (1915) pp. 97-98.
[930] CP (1916) pp. 48-49.
[931] FC (1918) pp. 175-176.
[932] *The Sower* (1918) p. 234.
[933] Revelation 17: 5.
[934] FC (1918) p. 122.
[935] FC (1918) pp. 154-155.
[936] FC (1917) pp. 61-62.
[937] FC (1915) pp. 280-281.
[938] FC (1918) pp. 199-200.
[939] FC (1916) pp. 69-72.
[940] This is probably a reference to the first air raid on Britain during the war, which occurred on 19th January, 1915.

[941] James Muskett was a Strict Baptist minister in Great Yarmouth. See GS (1915) p. 283.
[942] FC (1915) pp. 77-78.
[943] FC (1916) pp. 69-72.
[944] Francis Covell (1808-1879), the much loved pastor of Providence Strict Baptist Chapel, West Street, Croydon for many years. See Ramsbottom, B. A. (Ed.) (1994) *Six Remarkable Ministers*. Gospel Standard Trust Publications. p. 139ff.
[945] FC (1916) pp. 260-261.
[946] FC (1916) pp. 329-331.
[947] FC (1917) pp. 274-275.
[948] FC (1915) pp. 149-150.
[949] FC (1915) pp. 330-332.
[950] FC (1915) pp. 332-333.
[951] FC (1916) pp. 22-23.
[952] FC (1916) pp. 188-189.
[953] FC (1916) pp. 211-212.
[954] FC (1914) pp. 334-335.
[955] FC (1917) pp. 247-248.
[956] Psalm 51: 17.
[957] FC (1915) pp. 12-13.
[958] FC (1917) pp. 151-152.
[959] FC (1917) pp. 267-268.
[960] FC (1914) pp. 331-332.
[961] FC (1918) p. 144.
[962] Originally published as a broadsheet.
[963] FC (1917) pp. 216-217.
[964] CP (1917) pp. 75-76.
[965] FC (1916) pp. 124-125.
[966] FC (1917) pp. 125-126.
[967] FC (1917) pp. 233-234.
[968] CP (1917) p. 111.
[969] CP (1917) p. 42.
[970] CP (1915) pp. 364-365.
[971] CP (1916) p. 238.
[972] A reward.
[973] CP (1916) pp. 337-338.
[974] CP (1916) pp. 364-365.
[975] CP (1916) pp. 238-239.
[976] CP (1916) pp. 300-301.
[977] CP (1918) pp. 224-225.
[978] CP (1919) p. 122.

Appendix – The Muster Rolls

The Muster Rolls were a feature of *The Christian's Pathway* magazine from 1915-1919. To facilitate those who may wish to research further the involvement of individual Strict Baptists in the First World War, the following index to The Muster Roll has been produced. These names do not appear in the index to this book. Because entry on The Muster Roll was subject to payment of a fee, not every Strict Baptist who fought in the First World War is included in this list, and certainly not every Strict Baptist chapel that had men in the congregation who fought in the war are included in this list.

Forename	Surname	Regiment	Chapel	Year	Page
Charles Henry	Abbott	East Lancashire Regiment	Rochdale Road, Manchester	15	290
William	Abbott	East Lancashire Regiment	Rochdale Road, Manchester	15	322
Alfred	Adams	Royal Warwickshire Regiment	Blackheath	19	100
Fred	Adams	Royal Air Force	Blackheath	19	100
G. P.	Adams	Royal Fusiliers	Zion, Leicester	16	36
Samuel	Adams	Royal Warwickshire Regiment	Blackheath	17	128
Walter H.	Adams	Royal Army Medical Corps	Rowley Regis	17	300

Forename	Surname	Regiment	Chapel	Year	Page
Frank	Ainsworth	West Lancashire Division	Preston	16	65
B.	Allen	Royal Engineers	Hove	16	356
J. A.	Allen	Royal Army Medical Corps	Warrington	17	100
A. W. A.	Alsop	NMRET (?)	Rowley Regis	17	297
Horace	Alsop	Worcestershire Regiment (?)	Rowley Regis	17	297
George R.	Ambrose	Canadian Expeditionary Force	Haywards Heath	16	381
William A.	Angrave	Leicestershire Regiment	Zion, Leicester	16	33
William	Appleton	Queen's Regiment	West Street, Croydon	17	65
				18	140
William	Argar	Kent Cyclist's Battalion	Folkestone	17	200
Albert	Astley	Cheshire Regiment	Blackburn	17	152
Arthur	Astley	Army Ordinance Corps	Blackburn	17	152
E. R.	Atha	King's Own Yorkshire Light Infantry	Thornhill	16	320
Harold	Atkinson	Royal Army Medical Corps	West Hartlepool	16	260
Alfred	Bagley	Royal Navy	Rowley Regis	17	297
T.	Bailey	Middlesex Regiment	Station Road, Redhill	17	36
A. E.	Baines	South Lancashire Regiment	Haydock	18	26
James	Baines	Royal Army Medical Corps	Haydock	18	28
W. H.	Baines	Royal Field Artillery	Haydock	18	28
H. J.	Baker	Army Service Corps	Cranbrook	17	99
Joseph	Baker	Wiltshire Regiment	Manningford	17	32
				17	56
Sidney	Balcombe	East Kent Regiment (The Buffs)	Cranbrook	17	99
J.	Ball	Leicestershire Regiment	Zion, Leicester	16	33
Sydney	Bamford	Suffolk Regiment	Rochdale	16	258
Jack	Barber	King's Royal Rifles	Siddal	17	178
Henry	Barker	Royal Field Artillery	Rochdale	16	258
Maurice Thompson	Barker	Red Cross	Hitchin	17	65
Widmer	Barnes	Loyal North Lancashire Regiment	Bolton	16	129
Samuel	Barstow	Royal Field Artillery	Siddal	17	179
William	Barstow	Royal Field Artillery	Siddal	17	179
				17	228
W. J.	Bate	South Lancashire Regiment	Warrington	17	100
Thomas	Batley	East Lancashire Regiment	Rochdale Road, Manchester	15	290
William	Batley	Royal Army Medical Corps	Rochdale Road, Manchester	15	381
William A.	Baughan	King's Liverpool Regiment	Southport	15	383
C. L.	Beall	Yorkshire Hussars	Newcastle	18	140

Forename	Surname	Regiment	Chapel	Year	Page
J. L.	Beall	Northumberland Fusiliers	Newcastle	18	140
Harold Owen Alfred	Bear	Royal Navy	Ramsgate	18	156
John Victor	Bear	Royal Navy	Ramsgate	18	156
Richard Charles Clifford	Bear	Queen's Royal West Sussex	Ramsgate	18	156
John	Beardsall		Blackburn	17	152
F.	Beardsworth	Army Service Corps	Blackburn	17	249
Victor	Beaumont	Duke of Lancaster's Yeomanry	Rochdale Road, Manchester	15	382
David	Beazley	Rifle Brigade	Unknown	17	36
F. T.	Beazley	Royal Flying Corps	Station Road, Redhill	17	36
William Samuel	Beeken	Royal Army Medical Corps	Cranbrook	17	99
C. T.	Belton	Royal Garrison Artillery	Station Road, Redhill	16	291
P. S.	Bennett	King's Own Yorkshire Light Infantry	Thornhill	19	84
W.	Bennett	South Lancashire Regiment	Hindley	16	132
Walter	Bentley	Royal Irish Fusiliers	Ebenezer, Warrington	15	324
Frederick A.	Bevis	Rifle Brigade	Swanwick Shore	17	225
Ebenezer F.	Bewers	Royal Engineers	Crawley	17	228
Clifford G.	Binns	Royal Field Artillery	Siddal	17	178
Abraham	Bird	Motor Transport Company	Blackburn	17	152
David	Bird	Royal Engineers	Blackburn	17	151
T.	Blackler	Royal Garrison Artillery	Thornhill	19	83
Ernest F.	Board	Royal Field Artillery	Chard	15	355
Walter	Board	Seaforth Highlanders	Chard	15	355
Albert J.	Boorman	Army Veterinary Corps	Walkern	16	97
Arthur	Boorman	Motor Machine Gun Regiment	Walkern	16	97
Charles Harold	Boorman	Hertfordshire Regiment	Walkern	16	97
Frank	Boorman	Army Service Corps	Maidstone	16	324
Fred. G.	Boorman	Hertfordshire Regiment	Walkern	16	97
John	Boorman	Hertfordshire Regiment	Walkern	16	100
Thomas	Boorman	Hertfordshire Regiment	Walkern	16	97
Walter	Boorman	Army Service Corps	Walkern	16	97
William E.	Boorman	Wiltshire Regiment	Walkern	16	97
Frank	Booth		Bradford	16	381
Granville	Booth	Duke of Cornwall's Light Infantry	Bradford	16	381
W.	Bowden	Royal Navy	Bradford	16	384
D. B.	Bray	Mechanical Transport	Station Road, Redhill	16	291
P. W.	Bray	London Rifle Brigade	Station Road, Redhill	17	33
David	Bree	Leicestershire Yeomanry	Ebenezer, Leicester	16	324

Forename	Surname	Regiment	Chapel	Year	Page
William H.	Bree	Northern Fusiliers	West Hartlepool	16	292
Roland	Bretton	Territorial Reserve	Siddal	17	179
Edgar Durling	Briant	East Surrey Regiment	Knapp Hill	18	232
Leonard	Britten	Manchester Regiment	Rochdale Road, Manchester	15	292
Albert	Britton	Suffolk Yeomanry	Rehoboth, Sible Hedingham	15	382
William	Broadbridge	Royal Engineers	Haywards Heath	16	380
Joseph	Brooks	King's Royal Rifles	Bexley	18	43
H. J.	Brown	Royal Fusiliers	Ilford	17	152
W.	Bryan	Motor Transport Company	Zion, Leicester	16	36
John	Buckland	Coldstream Guards	Handcross	16	260
Reginald	Buller	Royal Army Medical Corps	Chard	15	355
A. R.	Bullock	Royal Engineers	King's Langley	16	225
Ebenezer Samuel	Burfoot	Royal Field Artillery	Newick, Sussex	18	95
Ebenezer	Burrows	Royal Engineers	Haydock	18	26
Augustus	Butler	Durham Light Infantry	Haywards Heath	17	68
Albert Henry	Card	Royal Field Artillery	Ramsgate	18	174
Thomas	Carpenter	Royal Air Force Cadet	Coventry	19	52
Harry	Carter	East Lancashire Regiment	Providence, Bacup	16	68
Albert Victor	Castle	Royal Field Artillery	Ramsgate	18	174
Paul	Catterall	Army Service Corps	Kirkland (Garstang)	17	224
Tom	Catterall	Royal Field Artillery	Accrington	16	196
Horace	Chamber	Patrol Boat	Ramsgate	18	204
C. F.	Chaplin	Royal Field Artillery	Blackburn	17	249
Jack	Chaplin	Manchester Regiment	Rochdale Road, Manchester	15	322
Aked	Chapman	Army Service Corps	Siddal	17	175
J.	Chapman	Yorkshire Regiment	West Hartlepool	16	260
Julius	Chapman	Royal Flying Corps	Walkern	16	100
Lemuel A.	Chapman	Royal Flying Corps	Siddal	17	178
Harvey	Charlwood	Veterinary Field Hospital	West Street, Croydon	15	353
Alfred G.	Charman	Royal Field Artillery	Charlwood	17	99
Ralph	Charnley	Loyal North Lancashire Regiment	Blackburn	17	152
E.	Choice	Royal Engineers	Zion, Leicester	16	33
A. R.	Clapson	Army Service Corps	Station Road, Redhill	17	33
J. J.	Clark	Royal Field Artillery	Kirkland (Garstang)	17	224
J. J.	Clark	Dragoon Guards	Kirkland (Garstang)	17	225
Joseph H.	Clark	Royal Field Artillery	Kirkland (Garstang)	17	224
Stephen	Clark	Royal Garrison Artillery	Newick, Sussex	18	100

Forename	Surname	Regiment	Chapel	Year	Page
William	Clark	East Surrey Regiment	Kirkland (Garstang)	17	225
A.	Clarke	Machine Gun Corps	Coventry	18	75
J.	Clarke	Leicestershire Regiment	Zion, Leicester	16	36
Moses	Clarke	Royal Field Artillery	Blackburn	17	152
Thomas	Clarke	Royal Navy, H.M.S. St. Vincent	Blackburn	17	152
G. E. P.	Clifton	Royal Engineers	Guildford	17	317
	Cockram	Queen's Regiment	West Street, Croydon	17	65
Ebby	Cole	Royal Navy	Blackheath	17	276
Eddie	Cole	Royal Field Artillery	Blackheath	17	128
Eli	Cole	Royal Garrison Artillery	Blackheath	17	128
Joseph	Cole	Royal Flying Corps	Blackheath	17	128
Marshall	Cole	Royal Naval Volunteer Reserve	Blackheath	19	100
Percy	Cole	Training Reserve Battalion	Blackheath	17	276
Percy	Cole		Blackheath	18	220
Frank	Collins	Army Flying Corps	Cranbrook	17	99
Arthur	Common	Royal Field Artillery	Siddal	17	179
Joseph	Compton	Manchester Regiment	Hindley	16	132
Eli	Cook	Machine Gun Corps	Haydock	18	26
Frederick	Cook	South Wales Borders	Haydock	18	26
Percy	Cook	Queen's Regiment	Charlwood	17	99
Percy	Cook	Queen's Regiment (West Surrey)	Holmwood	17	201
Thomas William	Cook	Queen's Regiment	Charlwood	17	99
Benjamin	Cooper	Royal Horse Artillery	Grittleton	16	356
Harry	Corbitt	East Lancashire Regiment	Rochdale Road, Manchester	15	292
Cecil	Cordell	Hertfordshire Regiment	Walkern	16	100
Stuart	Cordell	Hertfordshire Regiment	Walkern	16	100
Percy	Cornwell	Norfolk Regiment	Brixton	17	228
Percy	Cornwell		Brixton	17	228
Armstrong	Cowsill	Manchester Regiment	Rochdale Road, Manchester	15	322
George	Cox	Army Service Corps	Blackheath	17	276
John	Croasdale	East Lancashire Regiment	Accrington	18	124
Jesse	Croucher	Army Service Corps	Cranbrook	17	99
James	Cuncliffe	Royal Field Artillery	Haydock	18	26
W.	Currington	South Lancashire Regiment	Warrington	17	100
F.	Cutmore	Royal Field Artillery	Ilford	17	152
E. J.	Dacombe	Hampshire Regiment	Farnborough	16	324
James	Davis	Royal Garrison Artillery	Kirkland (Garstang)	17	224

Forename	Surname	Regiment	Chapel	Year	Page
Thomas	Davis	Anti-Aircraft Section	Kirkland (Garstang)	17	224
Samuel	Dawson	East Lancashire Regiment	Rochdale Road, Manchester	15	290
Ed.	Dean	Royal Engineers	Jireh, Pemberton	15	259
E.	Dickinson	Hampshire Yeomanry	Jireh, Pemberton	15	259
John H.	Dickinson	Royal Army Medical Corps	Bolton	16	131
Thomas	Dodd	King's Own Royal Lancaster Regiment	Kirkland (Garstang)	17	224
Bert	Downing	Army	Blackheath	19	98
N.	Downing	Royal Field Artillery	Blackheath	17	273
Samuel	Downing	Royal Warwickshire Regiment	Rowley Regis	16	164
Stanley	Downing	North Staffordshire Regiment	Blackheath	19	100
George	Dransfield	Brant Battalion	Ontario, Canada	17	156
Cyril	Draper	Army Service Corps	Thornhill	16	321
W.	Draper		Thornhill	18	52
Clement	Drury	Army Service Corps	Marden	16	353
Joseph	Drury	Royal Berkshire Regiment	Marden	16	353
Owen John	Drury	Royal Naval Air Service	Southampton	16	353
Percy	Drury	Royal Field Artillery	Marden	16	353
C.	Dunton	Royal Garrison Artillery	Coventry	17	32
George	Durrant	Royal Garrison Artillery	Folkestone	17	200
Jack	Durrant	Royal Field Artillery	Folkestone	17	200
William Henry	Durrant	Royal Navy, H.M.S. Goshawk	Folkestone	17	200
Alfred Muskett	Dye	Royal Engineers	Rowley Regis	17	297
William	Eades	Royal Warwickshire Regiment	Blackheath	17	273
William G.	Eades	Army Service Corps	Blackheath	17	276
E.	Edwards	Royal Garrison Artillery	Holmwood	17	201
Richard C.	Edwards	Royal Engineers	Swanwick Shore	17	225
H.	Elliott	South Lancashire Regiment	Blackburn	17	249
Alfred James	Ellis	Royal Garrison Artillery	Heathfield	17	179
				17	180
E.	Entwistle	Army Service Corps	Blackburn	17	249
J.	Entwistle	Royal Engineers	Fairhaven	16	258
T.	Entwistle	Coldstream Guards	Blackburn	17	249
				17	252
Tom	Errington	Royal Sussex Regiment	Station Road, Redhill	16	289
Fred	Fawcett	Royal Canadian Dragoons	Blackburn	17	151
Jesse	Fay		Coventry	18	75
Fred	Fenton	Royal Army Medical Corps	Preston	18	50

Forename	Surname	Regiment	Chapel	Year	Page
A.	Field	Electrical Engineer	West Street, Croydon	17	65
Thomas	Field	Brant Battalion	Ontario, Canada	17	156
James	Fitton	Royal Fusiliers	Rochdale	16	258
Sam	Fitton	Lancashire Fusiliers	Rochdale	16	258
George A. E.	Forbes	East Kent Regiment (The Buffs)	Folkestone	17	200
John	Forbes	Machine Gun Corps	Folkestone	17	200
David	Foulkes	Royal Horse Artillery	Rowley Regis	17	297
Frederick	Fowler	Royal Field Artillery	Chard	15	355
J. B.	Francis	Cheshire Regiment	Blackburn	17	249
H. C.	Franklin	Honourable Artillery Company	Coventry	18	75
				18	76
G.	Freeman	Royal Army Medical Corps	King's Langley	16	225
Walter M.	Gadd	Royal Navy	Blackheath	17	276
E. S.	Gandy	East Kent Regiment (The Buffs)	Cranbrook	17	99
H. H.	Gandy	East Kent Regiment (The Buffs)	Cranbrook	17	99
Richard	George	Royal Flying Corps	Accrington	18	124
Tom B.	George	Royal Scotch Fusiliers	Accrington	16	195
Albert	Gerraty	Home Service Corps	Preston	18	50
C.	Godfrey	Royal Warwickshire Regiment	Coventry	17	32
A. E.	Golding	Royal Fusiliers	West Street, Croydon	15	353
G.	Goldsmith	Royal Field Artillery	Station Road, Redhill	17	33
G.	Goodinson	York and Lancaster Regiment	Masborough	16	225
George	Goodwin	Army Service Corps	Rowley Regis	17	297
Frank L.	Gosden	Royal Sussex Regiment	Brighton	16	353
Harold	Grace	Durham Light Infantry	Thornhill	18	52
				18	156
Harry	Grace	Royal Army Medical Corps	Thornhill	16	321
L.	Grace		Thornhill	16	321
B. F.	Grant	Imperial Yeomanry	Hitchin	17	65
E. A.	Grant	Imperial Yeomanry	Hitchin	17	65
L. P.	Grant	Royal Engineers	Hitchin	17	65
Walter	Grant	Royal Engineers	Hitchin	17	65
Albert	Gray	East Kent Regiment (The Buffs)	Cranbrook	17	99
Harold	Green	Royal Army Medical Corps	Rochdale Road, Manchester	15	382
Reginald J. H.	Green	Hertfordshire Regiment	Walkern	16	100
Stanley	Green	Royal Naval Volunteer Reserve	Blackheath	19	100
C.	Greengrass	Army Service Corps	Epsom	16	227

Forename	Surname	Regiment	Chapel	Year	Page
Thomas	Gregson	Motor Transport Company	Blackburn	17	152
H.	Grieve	Connaught Rangers	Masborough	16	225
James	Grieve	Connaught Rangers	Masborough	16	225
Samuel	Groves	Worcestershire Yeomanry	Rowley Regis	16	164
				17	300
James	Guest	Royal Field Artillery	Bolton	16	129
John H.	Guest	Lancashire Fusiliers	Bolton	16	129
Arthur Owen	Hadley	Royal Engineers	Rowley Regis	17	300
E.	Hadley	Royal Warwickshire Regiment	Blackheath	17	131
Enoch	Hadley	Oxfordshire and Buckinghamshire Light	Blackheath	17	128
Richard Stanley	Haffenden		Ramsgate	18	52
Lewis	Halstead	Royal Field Artillery	Siddal	17	178
Edward James	Hammond	Royal Flying Corps	Farnborough	16	324
H.	Hardy	East Lancashire Regiment	Bolton	16	131
Frank	Hare	Royal Engineers	Hitchin	17	65
John	Hareldean	Army Service Corps	West Street, Croydon	17	64
Edgar	Hargreaves	Royal Navy	Siddal	17	179
A.	Harris	Army	Coventry	19	52
J	Harris	Royal Warwickshire Regiment	Blackheath	17	131
Joseph	Harris	Royal Army Medical Corps	Blackheath	17	131
Wilfred	Harris	Army Service Corps	Blackheath	17	128
Frank	Harrold	RAD (?)	Rowley Regis	17	297
Albert	Hawkins	Signal Company	Portsmouth	17	319
Thorp	Haworth	Loyal North Lancashire Regiment	Preston	17	317
George	Haydock	East Lancashire Regiment	Blackburn	17	249
G.	Hazlerigg	Rifle Brigade	Zion, Leicester	16	33
T. M.	Hazlerigg	North Midland Division	Zion, Leicester	16	33
Frank	Heaton	Royal Scots Regiment	Rochdale Road, Manchester	15	382
J.	Heaton	King's Own Yorkshire Light Infantry	Thornhill	16	321
John	Heaton	Royal Army Medical Corps	Preston	16	65
W.	Heaton	Loyal North Lancashire Regiment	Preston	16	65
William	Heaton		Preston	17	132
Stanley	Hedges	Royal Engineers	Ramsgate	18	174
J. E.	Hemmings	South Staffordshire Regiment	Jews Lane, Gornal	16	100
William	Herring	East Lancashire Regiment	Rochdale Road, Manchester	15	290
Harold R.	Hesketh	Royal Field Artillery	Kirkland (Garstang)	17	225
T. J.	Hesketh	Dragoon Guards	Kirkland (Garstang)	17	224

Forename	Surname	Regiment	Chapel	Year	Page
Albert	Hill	Royal Army Medical Corps	Accrington	16	196
Edwin	Hill	Royal Engineers	Aldershot	16	356
George	Hills	East Kent Regiment (The Buffs)	Folkestone	17	200
Harry	Hills	East Kent Regiment (The Buffs)	Folkestone	17	200
				17	204
James	Hills	London Regiment	Folkestone	17	200
Arnold	Hinchliffe	Yorkshire Regiment	Thornhill	19	84
James	Hinchliffe	South Lancashire Regiment	Warrington	16	356
Walter	Hinchliffe	Royal defence Corps	Thornhill	18	52
Thomas	Hindle	Royal Army Medical Corps	Blackburn	17	152
W. A.	Hipkiss	Training Reserve Battalion	Rowley Regis	17	300
A. E.	Hitchens	Royal Field Artillery	Portsmouth	17	152
John Owen	Hitchins	Training Reserve Battalion	Portsmouth	17	317
Benjamin	Hodgetts	Royal Fusiliers	Rowley Regis	16	164
George	Holmes	Royal Canadian Dragoons	Ontario, Canada	17	156
Percival J.	Holmes	Royal Naval Air Service	Cranbrook	17	99
C. S.	Holt	King's Liverpool Regiment	Bolton	16	131
H.	Homewood	Royal Army Medical Corps	Station Road, Redhill	16	289
Percy	Houghton	Royal Field Artillery	Jireh, Pemberton	15	260
Sidney	House	Royal Army Medical Corps	Bolton	16	132
Alfred	Howarth	Welsh Regiment	Rochdale Road, Manchester	15	322
Charles	Howarth	East Lancashire Regiment	Rochdale Road, Manchester	15	322
Charles	Hubbard	Wiltshire Regiment	Rowley Regis	16	161
Joseph	Illingworth	West Riding Regiment	Bradford	16	381
Percy	Instone	Army Service Corps	Farnborough	16	324
C.	Isherwood	Royal Army Medical Corps	Oldham	16	356
Percy	Isherwood	Royal Engineers	Preston	18	50
F.	Jackson	Army Ordinance Corps	Blackburn	17	249
Henry	Jackson	Army Service Corps	Rochdale Road, Manchester	15	290
James	Jackson	East Lancashire Regiment	Rochdale Road, Manchester	15	322
Robert	Jackson	Royal Engineers	Kirkland (Garstang)	17	224
Albert	Jarvis	King's Liverpool Regiment	Preston	19	36
Jonathan	Jarvis	Westmoreland and Cumberland Yeomanry	Preston	17	319
John Ernest	Jay	Royal Army Medical Corps	Rehoboth, Sible Hedingham	15	382
Joseph Frank	Jay	Army	Rehoboth, Sible Hedingham	19	36
R.	Jennings	East Lancashire Regiment	Blackburn	17	249
Percy W. H.	Jobson	Royal Naval Air Service	Station Road, Redhill	16	291

Forename	Surname	Regiment	Chapel	Year	Page
Joseph	Johnson	Royal Marine Light Infantry	Zion, Leicester	16	36
Thomas	Johnson	Royal Marine Light Infantry	Zion, Leicester	16	36
Garnett	Jones	Royal Warwickshire Regiment	Blackheath	17	273
Daniel	Keevil	Loyal North Lancashire Regiment	Preston	16	65
				17	132
T.	Keevil	Royal Army Medical Corps	Preston	16	65
W.	Kemp	Royal Sussex Regiment	Shovers Green, Wadhurst	16	353
John	Kenyon	Royal Field Artillery	Jireh, Pemberton	15	260
W.	Kerridge	Royal Field Artillery	Colnbrook	17	317
Robert William	Kilminster	Duke of Wellington's Regiment	Haworth	15	384
				17	100
William Thomas	Kilminster	Duke of Wellington's Regiment	Haworth	15	384
				17	100
Alan J.	King	Royal Engineers	Upavon	17	95
Arthur G.	King	Royal Wiltshire Yeomanry	Upavon	17	95
Hedley J.	King	Army Service Corps	Upavon	17	95
John	King	East Kent Regiment (The Buffs)	Cranbrook	17	99
Isaac	Kitchen	Queen's Own Yorkshire Dragoons	Siddal	17	179
A.	Knight	Royal Grenadiers	Blackheath	17	131
Fred	Knight	Army Veterinary Corps	Blackheath	19	100
John	Knight	Royal Engineers	Ramsgate	18	171
Roland	Knight	Training Reserve Battalion	Blackheath	17	276
Stanley	Knight	Duke of Cornwall's Light Infantry	Blackheath	17	276
C. F.	Lacey	Royal Navy	Haywards Heath	16	381
H. J.	Langley	Army Service Corps	Mayfield	16	353
J. E.	Langton	Royal Flying Corps	Zion, Leicester	16	36
Frederick	Law	Mechanical Transport	Rowley Regis	16	164
John	Law	Worcestershire Regiment	Rowley Regis	16	161
Alfred William	Lawbuary	Royal Army Medical Corps	Ramsgate	18	188
Charles Henry	Lawbuary	West Kent Cycle Corps	Ramsgate	18	188
Ezra	Leach	East Lancashire Regiment	Accrington	19	192
T.	Lee	King's Own Lancaster's	Preston	16	65
W.	Lee	King's Own Lancaster's	Preston	16	65
H.	Lenton	Leicestershire Regiment	Zion, Leicester	16	33
Thomas H.	Levey	Hertfordshire Regiment	Hertford	16	324
John	Liddle	King's Rifles	Ramsgate	18	232
Thomas P.	Lindfield	Army Service Corps	Haywards Heath	17	68

Forename	Surname	Regiment	Chapel	Year	Page
G.	Lines	Leicestershire Regiment	Zion, Leicester	16	196
R.	Litherland	South Lancashire Regiment	Haydock	18	28
W.	Litherland	King's Liverpool Regiment	Haydock	18	28
Frank	Littlewood	Manchester Regiment	Rochdale Road, Manchester	15	322
Fred	Littlewood	Manchester Regiment	Rochdale Road, Manchester	15	322
P.	Lowe	Black Watch	Blackheath	17	131
Albert	Lyles	Royal Army Medical Corps	Bradford	16	384
George	Macklin	Royal Garrison Artillery	Enford	17	319
Alfred George	Maller	Royal Sussex Regiment	Haywards Heath	16	380
Samuel	Malpas	South Staffordshire Regiment	Jews Lane, Gornal	16	100
Peter	Martin	New Zealand Army	Battle	17	64
Wilfred	Martin	Royal Sussex Regiment	Battle	17	64
Harry	Mason	Borders Regiment	Hindley	16	132
James	Mather	Loyal North Lancashire Regiment	Bolton	16	129
Walter	Matthews	Leicester Yeomanry	Zion, Leicester	16	36
					196
Albert	Maxim	Royal Field Artillery	Rochdale	16	258
Robert J.	Metcalf	Lancashire Fusiliers	Rochdale	16	258
Clement	Micklethwaite	King's Own Yorkshire Light Infantry	Thornhill	16	321
				17	320
John	Micklethwaite	King's Own Yorkshire Light Infantry	Thornhill	16	321
L. C.	Miles	West Lancashire Division	Southport	15	383
G. S.	Miller	Manchester Regiment	Blackburn	17	249
James T.	Miller	East Lancashire Regiment	Blackburn	17	152
Russel E.	Miller	Royal Navy	Newcastle	18	140
Thomas B.	Miller	Naval Brigade	Newcastle	18	140
William	Miller	Duke of Cornwall's Light Infantry	Blackburn	17	249
Alfred	Millward	York and Lancaster Regiment	Masborough	16	225
Lewis	Milnes	Royal Garrison Artillery	Siddal	17	179
Samuel	Mitton	Manchester Regiment	Rochdale Road, Manchester	15	290
Richard	Moat	Royal Army Medical Corps	Folkestone	17	200
Gilbert	Mockford	Royal Naval Air Service	Heathfield	17	180
John	Moore	Royal Field Artillery	Ramsgate	16	348
				16	356
Arthur Cornelius	Morley	Northumberland Fusiliers	Nottingham	19	100
R.	Morley	Anti Aircraft Section	Preston	16	65
C. W.	Morriss	Royal Army Medical Corps	Hitchin	17	65

Forename	Surname	Regiment	Chapel	Year	Page
F.	Mortlock	Middlesex Regiment	Coventry	17	33
Arthur	Moulden		Highworth	17	225
F.	Mucklow	Royal Army Medical Corps	Blackheath	17	131
Frank	Mucklow	Field Ambulance	Rowley Regis	16	163
Benjamin	Mullett	East Kent Regiment (The Buffs)	Folkestone	17	201
Albert	Murray	Navy	Warrington	17	100
Albert	Murrell	Army Service Corps	West Street, Croydon	15	353
Ernest	Murrell	Army Service Corps	West Street, Croydon	15	353
Lewis	Myers	Connaught Rangers	Masborough	16	225
Percy	Myers	Royal Navy	Masborough	16	225
S.	Neeves	Middlesex Regiment	Battle	17	64
J. S.	Negus	Royal Field Artillery	Coventry	17	32
Arthur	Neve	Royal Army Medical Corps	Maidenhead	16	292
Rupert Ernest	Neve	Royal Flying Corps	Maidenhead	16	292
				18	124
Clifford	Nevison	Royal Field Artillery	Siddal	17	179
F.	Newington	Royal Sussex Regiment	Shovers Green, Wadhurst	17	252
P.	Newington	Royal Sussex Regiment	Shovers Green, Wadhurst	17	252
Richard	Nock	Devonshire Regiment	Smethwick, Birmingham	18	123
Samuel	Nock	Royal Warwickshire Regiment	Blackheath	19	100
James Herbert	Norton	Royal Sussex Regiment	Haywards Heath	16	381
Harry S.	Nutter	Royal Garrison Artillery	Blackburn	17	152
Alfred	Ofield	Leicestershire Regiment	Zion, Leicester	16	33
Herbert	Ofield	Leicestershire Regiment	Zion, Leicester	16	33
Harold	Oldham	Army Service Corps	Zion, Leicester	18	172
Frank	Omeron	Lincolnshire Regiment	Bradford	16	384
A. G.	Ord	Durham Light Infantry	West Hartlepool	16	258
John T.	Owen	Royal Navy, H.M.S. Latona	Chard	15	356
Sydney G.	Oxendale	Royal Garrison Artillery	Preston	17	319
Douglas	Pankhurst	Coldstream Guards	Handcross	16	260
F. L.	Pankhurst	Royal Field Artillery	Handcross	17	320
G. W.	Papworth	Royal Engineers	Masborough	16	225
John E.	Parish	East Lancashire Regiment	Rochdale Road, Manchester	15	290
Harry	Parker	Duke of Wellington's Regiment	Thornhill	16	321
T.	Parker	Leicestershire Regiment	Zion, Leicester	16	36
W. E.	Parkes	Royal Warwickshire Regiment	Blackheath	17	128
				17	132

Forename	Surname	Regiment	Chapel	Year	Page
Sidney	Parks	East Kent Regiment (The Buffs)	Cranbrook	17	100
William	Parks	Royal Army Medical Corps	Cranbrook	17	100
Reginald	Parris	Royal Flying Corps	Tamworth Road, Croydon	17	217
A. E.	Parrish	Royal Fusiliers	Station Road, Redhill	17	33
E. J.	Parrish	Bedfordshire Regiment	Station Road, Redhill	17	33
John Restorick	Parsons	Field Ambulance	Chard	15	356
J. S.	Partridge	Red Cross	Wellingborough	15	383
James	Pearson	Royal Flying Corps	Kirkland (Garstang)	17	224
L.	Pearson	Grenadier Guards	Blackheath	17	131
E.	Perkins	Army	Coventry	17	33
H. R. S.	Perrott	Army Service Corps	Coventry	18	75
Samuel Frederick	Philip	Royal Berkshire Regiment	Leicester	17	180
E. J.	Phillips	Army Service Corps	Station Road, Redhill	17	36
Leonard	Philpott	Royal Sussex Regiment	West Street, Croydon	15	353
Walter	Pickering	East Lancashire Regiment	Blackburn	17	152
William J.	Pickering	East Lancashire Regiment	Blackburn	17	151
				17	156
Moses	Pickett	East Kent Volunteers	Ramsgate	18	204
Julian	Pickles	Duke of Wellington's Regiment	Haworth	15	384
R. S.	Pickles	Training Reserve Battalion	Thornhill	18	50
W. L.	Pilbeam	London Regiment	Station Road, Redhill	17	33
William Alan	Pilkington	Training Reserve Battalion	Preston	17	319
				17	320
Clive	Pilling	Royal Irish Fusiliers	Accrington	18	122
Ernest	Pilling	Army Service Corps	Accrington	16	196
Tom	Pilling	Royal Army Medical Corps	Accrington	16	195
Tom	Pilling	Royal Field Artillery	Accrington	18	124
Wilson	Pilling	Borders Regiment	Accrington	19	192
Arnold	Pinder	East Lancashire Regiment	Blackburn	17	152
Alexander Walter	Piper	East Kent Regiment (The Buffs)	Ramsgate	18	171
Douglas Graham	Piper	Motor Transport Company	Ramsgate	18	171
E. A.	Pitts	Leicestershire Regiment	Zion, Leicester	16	33
Charles	Pollard	Rifle Brigade	Bexley	18	42
Arthur	Polwin	Ordinance Corps	Oldham	16	356
C. W.	Poole	Military Police	Hove	16	356
Percy	Port	Army Service Corps	Holmwood	17	201
William	Port	Canadian Battalion	Holmwood	17	201

Forename	Surname	Regiment	Chapel	Year	Page
S.	Powell	Army Service Corps	Haydock	18	28
John	Presswood	Canadian Regiment	Siddal	17	179
				17	180
H. W.	Radley	Royal Canadian Army Service Corps	Folkestone	17	201
Clarence	Reddihough	Royal Army Medical Corps	Accrington	16	193
John	Reddihough	Royal Army Medical Corps	Accrington	16	193
E.	Redfern	Royal Field Artillery	Coventry	17	32
S. J.	Redfern	Yeomen of Signals	Coventry	17	33
W. G.	Redfern	Flying Squadron School of Observers	Coventry	19	52
A. H.	Reed	Canadian Engineers	Winnipeg, Canada	17	320
John	Richards	Royal Army Medical Corps	Accrington	16	195
William	Roberts		Blackburn	17	152
Albert Edward	Rogerson	Royal Field Artillery	Providence, Bacup	16	68
Albert	Rose	Royal Air Force	Blackheath	19	98
J. O.	Rose	Royal Warwickshire Regiment	Blackheath	17	128
Joseph	Round	Royal Warwickshire Regiment	Rowley Regis	17	297
Edmund	Rowson	South Lancashire Regiment	Rochdale Road, Manchester	15	382
S.	Rowson	Lancashire Fusiliers	Fairhaven	16	258
J. A.	Rumsey	Royal Army Medical Corps	Folkestone	17	201
R.	Ryall	Royal Engineers	Station Road, Redhill	17	36
J. L.	Saunders	Northamptonshire Regiment	Epsom	16	227
Thomas	Saunders	Duke of Wellington's Regiment	Barton-Le-Clay	16	321
				18	76
Harry	Sayers	Territorials	Ramsgate	18	171
C. W.	See	Army Pay Corps	Newcastle	18	140
Bernard	Sells	Royal Engineers	Hitchin	17	65
C.	Sells	Royal Engineers	Hitchin	17	65
H. W.	Sells	Royal Engineers	Hitchin	17	65
John	Share	Royal Field Artillery	Jews Lane, Gornal	16	100
Frank Paffard	Sharples	Royal Fusiliers	Kirkland (Garstang)	17	224
				17	228
George	Shaw	Loyal North Lancashire Regiment	Kirkland (Garstang)	17	224
H. D.	Shaw	West Lancashire Division	Southport	15	383
R.	Shaw		Station Road, Redhill	17	36
Wallace	Sheppard	East Kent Volunteers	Ramsgate	18	204
G.	Sherrington	Field Ambulance	Jireh, Pemberton	15	259
Ernest	Shields	Machine Gun Corps	Accrington	18	124

Forename	Surname	Regiment	Chapel	Year	Page
William	Shields	Army Service Corps	Accrington	18	122
Charles	Shires	Manchester Regiment	Rochdale Road, Manchester	15	322
Samuel	Sidebottom	Royal Field Artillery	Bradford	16	384
Alfred	Simm	Manchester Regiment	Haydock	18	16
				18	26
John	Simmonds	Yorkshire Regiment	Thornhill	16	321
				18	76
Harry	Slim	Coldstream Guards	Rowley Regis	16	161
Herbert	Slim	Grenadier Guards	Rowley Regis	16	161
A. G.	Smith	Royal Army Medical Corps	Dorking	16	324
Albert	Smith	Royal Army Medical Corps	Accrington	16	196
David	Smith	Royal Warwickshire Regiment	Rowley Regis	16	164
				17	300
Edwin	Smith	Royal Fusiliers	Haydock	18	16
					26
Enoch	Smith	Royal Irish Regiment	Blackheath	17	273
Ernest U.	Smith	Army Service Corps	Siddal	17	178
Fred	Smith	Lancashire Fusiliers	Accrington	16	196
Henry	Smith		Haydock	18	26
				19	55
John Charles	Smith	Royal Marine Light Infantry	Accrington	19	192
John W.	Smith	Borders Regiment	Blackburn	17	152
Leslie H.	Smith	Artist's Rifles	Haywards Heath	17	68
M.	Smith	West Lancashire Division	Preston	16	65
Sydney	Smith	Canadian Dental Corps	Folkestone	17	201
Walter	Smith	Lancashire Fusiliers	Accrington	16	196
O.	Snow	Army Service Corps	Blackburn	17	249
J. E.	Snow	Machine Gun Corps	Blackburn	17	249
George	Snowden	West Riding Regiment	Siddal	17	179
J.	Sowerbutts	East Lancashire Regiment	Blackburn	17	249
T.	Sowerbutts	Army Service Corps	Blackburn	17	249
W.	Sowerbutts	Machine Gun Corps	Blackburn	17	249
Arthur	Spain	Royal Navy	Ramsgate	18	156
Arthur	Spain	East Kent Regiment (The Buffs)	Ramsgate	18	156
Owen	Spain	Army Ordinance Corps	Ramsgate	18	155
Samuel	Spain	Royal Garrison Artillery	Ramsgate	18	155
J.	Stanley	Rifle Brigade	Jireh, Pemberton	15	382

Forename	Surname	Regiment	Chapel	Year	Page
H. W.	Stansfield		Blackburn	17	152
L. I.	Stapleton	Royal Field Artillery	Hitchin	17	65
W. E.	Stevens	Royal Sussex Regiment	Station Road, Redhill	16	289
E.	Stimpson	Royal Army Medical Corps	Zion, Leicester	16	36
William	Stockton	East Yorkshire Regiment	West Hartlepool	16	260
F.	Stone	Royal Field Artillery	Coventry	17	32
W.	Stone	Royal Garrison Artillery	Coventry	17	33
J.	Strickland	King's Own Lancaster's	Preston	16	65
Henry Job	Stubbs	Leicestershire Regiment	Oakham	17	201
				17	204
Frederick	Sturman	Labour Company	Rowley Regis	17	300
P. H.	Surridge	Royal Field Artillery	King's Langley	16	225
T. H.	Sutton	West Lancashire Regiment	Haydock	18	26
David	Taylor	Royal Garrison Artillery	Whitchurch	17	320
Herbert	Taylor	King's Liverpool Regiment	Accrington	16	196
Thomas	Taylor	Lancashire Fusiliers	Haydock	18	26
Norman	Teal	Royal Army Medical Corps	Siddal	17	178
J. T.	Terrett	London Regiment (Queen's)	Folkestone	17	201
Hugh	Thorpe	158th Brigade	Accrington	16	195
Wilf.	Tibbetts	Yorkshire Regiment	Blackheath	17	276
Benjamin	Tingley	Royal Field Artillery	Scaynes Hill	17	155
Thomas	Tingley	Royal Field Artillery	Scaynes Hill	17	155
Cyril Paxman	Tiptaft	Connaught Rangers	Masborough	16	225
William Rutherford	Tiptaft	Duke of Wellington's Regiment	Masborough	16	225
Jesse	Troman	Royal Engineers	Rowley Regis	17	297
John	Troman	7th Dragoons	Rowley Regis	16	164
Sidney	Tucker	Royal Army Medical Corps	Chippenham	16	321
Frank	Turner	King's Royal Rifles	Oldham	16	356
Frederick William	Turner	Royal Berkshire Regiment	Ramsgate	18	171
G.	Turner	London Regiment	Preston	16	65
H.	Turner	London Regiment	Preston	16	68
Colin	Turton	Loyal North Lancashire Regiment	Jireh, Pemberton	15	259
George	Turton	Royal Army Medical Corps	Ebenezer, Warrington	15	324
Percy	Tweedale	Royal Field Artillery	Rochdale	16	258
E.	Upfold	Hampshire Regiment	Station Road, Redhill	16	289
Samuel	Upfold		Station Road, Redhill	17	33
Alfred Henry	Upton	Royal Sussex Regiment	Haywards Heath	16	381

Forename	Surname	Regiment	Chapel	Year	Page
Benjamin	Upton	Royal Navy	Haywards Heath	16	381
Frederick George	Upton	Queen's Royal West Surrey	Haywards Heath	16	380
Hubert S. C.	Vaughan	Royal Flying Corps	Bradford	16	384
O. B.	Vaughan	Royal Army Medical Corps	Bradford	16	384
W. B. G.	Vaughan	Grenadier Guards	Bradford	16	384
F. H.	Vigar	Royal Army Medical Corps	Station Road, Redhill	16	289
H. E.	Vigar	Red Cross	Station Road, Redhill	16	289
James Willie	Waddington	Lowland Division	Providence, Bacup	16	68
Elihu	Wadey	Royal Engineers	West Street, Croydon	15	353
Thomas	Wadey	Royal Engineers	West Street, Croydon	15	353
Wilfred	Wadey	Queen's Royal West Surrey	Station Road, Redhill	16	289
Charles	Walker	Royal Marines	Blackheath	17	128
I.	Walker	Essex Regiment	Blackheath	17	273
James	Walker	Royal Engineers	Blackheath	17	128
Joseph	Walker	L (?)	Blackheath	17	128
Charles	Walsh		Fairhaven	18	100
S.	Walter	Royal Marine Light Infantry	Rehoboth, Tunbridge Wells	18	52
John L.	Walton	West Yorkshire Regiment	Siddal	17	175
				17	180
F. L.	Wapling	East Surrey Regiment	Epsom	16	227
Irwin	Ward	Welsh Regiment	Accrington	19	192
J.	Wardle	Royal Army Medical Corps	Zion, Leicester	16	100
Frank	Washer	Army Service Corps	Station Road, Redhill	16	289
James Philip	Washer	Queen's Royal West Surrey	Station Road, Redhill	16	289
Harold	Waterhouse	Army Service Corps	Rowley Regis	17	300
E.	Webster	Royal Engineers	Hitchin	17	65
J. P.	Webster	Leicestershire Regiment	Zion, Leicester	16	36
Richard	Webster	Middlesex Regiment	Bradford	16	381
Ernest	Weller	King's Liverpool Regiment	Southport	15	383
A. J.	Welton	Royal Army Medical Corps	Coventry	17	32
John	Westwood	Army Service Corps	Blackheath	17	276
				19	100
W.	Whent	Labour Company	Blackheath	17	276
Clarence	Whitaker	Duke of Wellington's Regiment	Haworth	15	384
Hubert	Whitaker	West Riding Regiment	Bradford	16	381
Thomas	Whitaker	Reserved Section	Haworth	16	68
Frank	Whitall	Army Service Corps	Blackheath	17	128

Forename	Surname	Regiment	Chapel	Year	Page
Arthur	Whittall	Army Service Corps	Blackheath	17	128
R.	Whittle	Loyal North Lancashire Regiment	Preston	16	65
William	Whittle	King's Liverpool Regiment	Preston	19	36
R. Leslie	Wickenden	Royal Field Artillery	Folkestone	17	201
W. Frank	Wickenden	Royal Field Artillery	Folkestone	17	201
S.	Wickins	Royal Flying Corps	Jarvis Brook	16	356
James	Wilde	West Yorkshire Regiment	Bradford	16	384
Harold	Wilding	Royal Navy, H.M.S. Gibraltar	Ebenezer, Warrington	15	324
E. J.	Wilkins		Station Road, Redhill	17	33
H.	Wilkins	Royal Army Medical Corps	Station Road, Redhill	17	33
J. H.	Wilkinson	Royal Garrison Artillery	Kirkland (Garstang)	17	224
T. P.	Wilkinson	Manchester Regiment	Rochdale Road, Manchester	15	381
W. O.	Wilkinson	Royal Fusiliers	Rochdale Road, Manchester	15	381
L.	Williams	Royal Army Medical Corps	Jews Lane, Gornal	16	100
L. J.	Williams	Royal Army Medical Corps	Jews Lane, Gornal	16	100
James Alfred	Withington	Stoker on H.M.S. Egmont	Hindley	16	132
W.	Wolstenholm	Royal Scots Fusiliers	Blackburn	17	249
Horace	Wood	East Kent Regiment (The Buffs)	Folkestone	17	201
Newton	Wood	Royal Army Medical Corps	West Street, Croydon	17	65
Charles King	Woodford	Royal Engineers	Upavon	17	95
Frank	Woodford	Army Veterinary Corps	Upavon	17	95
Fred T.	Woodford	Royal Wiltshire Yeomanry	Upavon	17	95
Eric P.	Woodhams	Royal Fusiliers	West Street, Croydon	15	353
William Silas	Woodhams	Royal Fusiliers	West Street, Croydon	15	353
E. L.	Woodier	Leicestershire Yeomanry	Zion, Leicester	16	36
Albert	Woodward	Life Guards	Blackheath	17	128
Joseph	Woodward	Royal Warwickshire Regiment	Blackheath	17	276
F.	Worsley	East Kent Regiment (The Buffs)	Cranbrook	17	100
J.	Worthington	Field Ambulance	Jireh, Pemberton	15	260
George William	Wyatt	Army Service Corps	Aldershot	16	353
Fred	Wylde	Royal Marine Light Infantry	Bolton	16	129
William	Wylde	Loyal North Lancashire Regiment	Bolton	16	129
Samuel	Wyle	AOE	Rowley Regis	17	297
J.	Yates	Royal Navy	Blackheath	17	131
P. O.	Yates	Royal Navy	Blackheath	17	131

384 THE CHRISTIAN'S PATHWAY [Dec., 1915

HAWORTH.

(1)

(2)

(3)

(4)

(1) PRIVATE ROBERT WM. KILMISTER, 2nd Duke of Wellington's Regiment. Has been missing since May 5th, 1915, when he was gassed at Hill 60, having then been in France just three weeks. The family received an unsigned card from the front acquainting them with the fact that he was gassed three weeks previously, and had just spoken for the first time, and it was hoped his sight would be restored. Since then no news of any kind has been received. He was a member of the Church at Haworth.

(2) PRIVATE WILLIAM THOMAS KILMISTER, No. 15315, 3rd Duke of Wellington's Regiment. He is a brother of the above, and likewise a member of the Church. He is now stationed at North Shields. Both the above are sons of Mr. Kilmister, whose name appears as one of the "supplies" amongst the Northern Churches.

(3) PRIVATE JULIAN PICKLES, 10th Battalion Duke of Wellington's Regiment. He is now in France. He was formerly a scholar in the school at Haworth, and has four children now attending there. His mother, Mrs. Pickles, is one of the oldest members in connection with the Chapel at Haworth, being 73 years of age.

(4) PRIVATE CLARENCE WHITAKER, No. 14103, 9th Duke of Wellington's Regiment. Now in France in the trenches. He was a scholar in the Sunday School and a member of the choir. His father and mother attend the Chapel. He is a grandson of the Mrs. Pickles mentioned above. He was quite well when this notice was written, though a few days prior his comrade was shot down by his side and killed instantly.

Left: An example page from The Muster Rolls, taken from *The Christian's Pathway* for 1915. It is the entry for Old Hall Green Chapel, Haworth.

Above: Old Hall Green Strict Baptist Chapel. There is a tune in *The Companion Tune Book* named after this chapel.

Index

Printed by:

Short Run Press Limited
Bittern Road, Sowton Industrial Estate, Exeter, EX2 7LW